CLASSICS *of* PROTESTANTISM

CLASSICS *of* PROTESTANTISM

EDITED BY

Vergilius Ferm

Compton Professor and Head of the Department of Philosophy
in The College of Wooster

PHILOSOPHICAL LIBRARY

New York

CONTENTS

SOURCES

The Sources of the material appearing in this volume are here listed. Grateful appreciation of permission to present copyrighted publications in part or in whole is acknowledged by the publisher and editor.

Theologia Germanica "The Way to a Sinless Life," edited by Thomas S. Kepler. World Publishing Company (Cleveland, 1952). pp. 35-65; 68-81; 89-90; 94-96; 103-106; 109-110; 123-126; 129-131; 157-159.

"A Treatise on Christian Liberty" by Martin Luther. *Three Treatises.* The Muhlenberg Press (Philadelphia, 1943). p. 251 ff.

Institutes of the Christian Religion by John Calvin. Translated from the Latin and Collated with the Author's Last Edition in French, by John Allen, London, 1813, 3 vols. 7th American edition, revised and corrected, with an Introduction by Benjamin B. Warfield. 2 vols. Presbyterian Board of Christian Education (Philadelphia, 1945). Book I Chap. 1, II, III; Chap. 2, I; Chap. 3, I; Chap. 4, I; Chap. 5, I, II, IV; Chap. 6, I; Chap. 7, III, IV, V; Chap. 10, I, II; Chap. 13, I, II, VII; Chap. 15, I. Book II Chap. 1, VIII, IX, X, XI; Chap. 4, I; Chap. 12, I, II; Chap. 14, I, II. Book III Chap. 2, VI, XXVIII; Chap. 6, III, V; Chap. 10, VI; Chap. 11, II, XXI; Chap. 14, XVI, XVII; Chap. 21, V; Chap. 23, XIII, XIV. Book IV Chap. 1, I, II, III, IV; Chap. 17, XXXI, XXXII, XXXVII, XXXVIII, XXXIX; Chap. 18, XIX.

The Scripture Doctrine of the Trinity, by Samuel Clarke. In Three Parts. Wherein All the Texts in the New Testament relating to that Doctrine, and the principal Passages in the Liturgy of the Church of England are collected, compared and explained. (London, 1712). Introduction, pp. i-iv; v-x; xix; xxi-xxiv; xxix-xxxiv. Part II, pp. 209-347.

A Serious Call to a Devout and Holy Life by William Law. J. M. Dent Company (London, 1906) and Dutton. Chap. XI.

"Free Grace" in *Sermons on Several Occasions* by the Rev. John Wesley, A.M. Vol. I, Carlton and Porter (New York, 1856). pp. 482-490.

"Sinners in the Hands of an Angry God" in *Puritan Sage*, Collected Writings of Jonathan Edwards, edited by Vergilius Ferm. Library Publishers (New York, 1953). pp. 365-378.

"A Careful and Strict Enquiry Into The Modern Prevailing Notions of That Freedom of Will, Which Is Supposed To Be Essential To Moral Agency, Vertue and Vice, Reward and Punishment, Praise and Blame" in *Puritan Sage*, Collected Writings of Jonathan Edwards, edited by Vergilius Ferm. Library Publishers (New York, 1953). pp. 480-515.

"Baltimore Sermon." "A Sermon Delivered At The Ordination of the Rev. Jared Sparks To The Pastoral Care of the First Independent Church in Baltimore, May 5, 1819" by William Ellery Channing in *Letters To The Rev. Wm. E. Channing Containing Remarks On His Sermon Recently Preached and Published At Baltimore* by Moses Stuart. 3rd ed. Flaff and Gould (Andover, 1819). 11th ed. Christian Register Office (Boston, 1824). pp. 3-35.

The Christian Faith by Friedrich Schleiermacher. English Translation of the Second German Edition. Edited by H. R. Mackintosh and J. S. Stewart. T. and T. Clark (Edinburgh, 1948). pp. 5-12; 26-29; 49-58; 66-73; 76-85; 95-97; 131-132; 194; 262; 279; 282; 285; 326; 355; 358; 361; 738; 742; 747.

Kierkegaard's Concluding Unscientific Postscript. Translated from the Danish by David F. Swenson and Completed by Walter Lowrie. Princeton University Press (Princeton, 1941). pp. 49; 51-55; 115-116; 164-166; 176-183; 191; 194-195.

Views of Christian Nurture and of Subjects Adjacent Thereto by Horace Bushnell. Edwin Hunt (Hartford, 1847). "Christian Nurture." Discourse I pp. 6-22. Discourse II pp. 33-34; 36-37; 41-46.

Lessons from The World of Matter and The World of Man by Theodore Parker. Selected From Notes of Unpublished

Sermons by Rufus Leighton. Charles H. Kerr and Company (Chicago, 1887) . pp. 15-21; 28-32; 41-44; 66-70; 72-74; 81-100; 137-144; 190-191; 276-287; 315-324.

The Christian Doctrine of Justification and Reconciliation by Albrecht Ritschl. English Translation, edited by H. R. Mackintosh and T. B. Macaulay. T. and T. Clark (Edinburgh, 1900) . pp. 193-214; 219-221; 237; 272-274; 284-285; 385-389; 398-401; 414-415; 451-456; 609-610; 612.

Christian Mysticism by William Ralph Inge. First Published, 1899. Methuen and Company, Ltd. Seventh Edition (London, 1932) . Preface to the Seventh Edition, pp. v-viii. pp. 3-22; 44-53; 60-63; 69-72.

Christianity and the Social Crisis by Walter Rauschenbusch. Hodder and Stoughton. George H. Doran Company. The Macmillan Company (New York, 1907) . pp. xi-xv; 1-4; 9-11; 40-44; 54-58; 85-86; 89-92; 287; 339-352; 354-357; 412-422.

Dogmatics in Outline by Karl Barth. Translated by G. T. Thomson. Philosophical Library (New York, 1949) . pp. 15-17; 18-19; 20-21; 22-26; 28-29; 35-36; 38-40; 43-45; 46; 51-54; 65-69; 72-74; 77-78; 82-85; 90-92; 95-103; 106; 108-122; 124-127; 129-130; 133-135; 137-148; 149-151; 153-155.

CLASSICS *of* PROTESTANTISM

INTRODUCTION

WHAT CONSTITUTES a classic? It is not easy to give to the question a pin-point answer. Estimates of literary works vary considerably. Personal evaluations inevitably are involved. One's own liking of a work may easily evoke the superlative comment "this is a classic"; but such response is too subjective for a definite classification.

Whatever else a classic is, objectively considered, it is a sort of work which is conspicuous in some area. It need not be supremely noteworthy from a literary point of view unless, of course, it is a literary classic in some art form. A classic may be quite an ordinary piece of writing—even dull and somewhat obtuse. Many classics, so called, might well be laid aside by a casual reader in wonder and amazement at its being held by others to merit such distinction. The reason for this is very simple: classics are framed in backgrounds and not to appreciate such frameworks is to stand outside the circle of disciplined evaluation. To justify a work to the rank of a classic would imply basically that it stands on its own as a choice sampling of some conspicuous point of view or of some epoch in the wave of history or as a representative commentary of a phase of thought of some conspicuous leader.

A classic need not be well known except among those disciplined in the field of its expression. Relatively few people, for example, would call *Theologia Germanica* a classic and yet this work could hardly be ignored in any list of writings having to do with sixteenth century Protestantism. The influence of a literary work, or the stature of its author as representative of a conspicuous or major point of view, then, is a criterion of its rank as a classic even though it is not now widely known, appreciated or even read.

In a one volume publication such as this it may seem difficult to make selections from among many classics in Protestant history. One is sensitive to noticeable omissions. And yet, within the limits set, it is reassuring to be conscious of the fact that on any list, of whatever compass, the works or authors here set forth would be included on the most reasonable test. All of them are conspicuous in Protestant history whether we now would acclaim them worthy of our own likes or preferences. Certainly they all play into phases of Christian thought within the course of Protestant channels. In a sense we may say of them that they belong with the elect in any list. They could hardly be left out in the consideration of the sweep of Protestant history.

It is unnecessary here to justify the inclusion of the particular essays or books in this anthology since an editorial summary and evaluation introduces each one in turn. I have had in mind a useful book, the kind which would seem to satisfy the requirements of a first-hand acquaintance in a survey of the history of Protestant thought, with longer selections from fewer authors rather than shorter excerpts from a larger representation. Abbreviated cullings from a wider circle have seemed to me less useful than a generous presentation, the reader being in a more favorable position to apprehend the import of the writing and to appropriate the flair of its total impact. In the case of larger books (here selected) this principle seems quite justified. Since some of the works are now unavailable—except in libraries at inconvenient distance—an anthology in itself is useful to re-circulate them in convenient even though abridged form. For one who has taught a course in the history of Christian thought over a period of many years this type of anthology has seemed to fill a need for students of the subject, especially those who would consult source materials.

The College of Wooster   Vergilius Ferm

THEOLOGIA GERMANICA

AUTHOR UNKNOWN

THIS IS strictly not a Protestant work. It has *become* a Protestant Devotional Classic by reason of its acclaim by Martin Luther ("I have not seen in Latin or in our language a more wholesome and more true-to-the-gospel theology," said Luther) and by reason of its wide circulation and use among Protestants.

Anonymously written about 1350 *Theologia Germanica* was published by the great German reformer first in 1516 (Chapters VI-XXVI) and in complete form in 1518 and given the title by him *Ein Deutsch Theologia.* Seventeen editions appeared during the lifetime of Luther, and some ninety editions thereafter in Germany (not to mention many translations in many languages). In 1851 a more complete manuscript was discovered and published. The Roman Catholic Church in 1621 placed the book on the Index.

It has been called "foremost" in the devotional literature of Protestantism. It consists of "table talk" to young monks, probably by a teacher of the Order of Teutonic Knights (this Order founded in 1118). The ideas suggest those associated with the teachings of The Friends of God—a kind of practical mysticism. These "Friends" were monks, priests and laymen without distinction of rank or sex forming associations in the Rhine valley provinces from Basel to Cologne, in Bavaria and Swabia, in such cities as Nuremburg and Strassburg. Anonymity of authorship is wholly consistent with the practice of self-denial. The "Friends" held that the life eternal is a possible present experience by a complete merging of the self with God in renunciation.

This work teaches that finite man is severed from God. Before he can approach the Infinite man must transcend himself. His transcendence is marked by a complete casting aside of self-will and ownership so that the Divine may enter. Man becomes more aware of his own sinful nature and his estrangement from God. A spiritual ladder from sin to salvation proceeds through three major stages: 1) purification (remorse for sin, confession of sin, reconciliation of life); 2) enlightenment (avoidance of sin, living of virtues and good works, bearing of trial and temptation); and 3) union (pureness and integrity of heart, love, meditation on God). As the goal is reached the consciousness of sin diminishes.

"Next to the Bible and St. Augustine," said Luther, "no book hath ever come into my hands, whence I have learnt, or would wish to learn more of what God, and Christ, and man and all things are."

Editor

THEOLOGIA GERMANICA

I

Of that which is perfect and that which is in part, and how that which is in part is done away, when that which is perfect is come.

ST. PAUL saith, "When that which is perfect is come, then that which is in part shall be done away."[1] Now mark what is "that which is perfect," and "that which is in part."

"That which is perfect" is a Being, who hath comprehended and included all things in Himself and His own Substance, and without whom, and beside whom, there is no true Substance, and in whom all things have their Substance. For he is the Substance of all things, and is in Himself unchangeable and immoveable, and changeth and moveth all things else. But "that which is in part," or the imperfect, is that which hath its source in, or springeth from the Perfect; just as a brightness or a visible appearance floweth out from the sun or a candle, and appeareth to be somewhat this or that. And it is called a creature; and of all these "things which are in part," none is the

1. 1 Cor. xiii. 10.

Perfect. So also the Perfect is none of the things which are in part. The things which are in part can be apprehended, known, and expressed; but the Perfect cannot be apprehended, known, or expressed by any creature as creature. Therefore we do not give a name to the Perfect, for it is none of these. The creature as creature cannot know nor apprehend it, name nor conceive it.

"Now when that which is Perfect is come, then that which is in part shall be done away." But when doth it come? I say, when as much as may be, it is known, felt and tasted of the soul.[1] [For the lack lieth altogether in us, and not in it. In like manner the sun lighteth the whole world, and is as near to one as another, yet a blind man seeth it not; but the fault thereof lieth in the blind man, not in the sun. And like as the sun may not hide its brightness, but must give light unto the earth (for heaven indeed draweth its light and heat from another fountain), so also God, who is the highest Good, willeth not to hide Himself from any, wheresoever He findeth a devout soul, that is thoroughly purified from all creatures. For in what measure we put off the creature, in the same measure are we able to put on the Creator; neither more nor less. For if mine eye is to see anything, it must be single, or else be purified from all other things; and where heat and light enter in, cold and darkness must needs depart; it cannot be otherwise.]

But one might say, "Now since the Perfect cannot be known nor apprehended of any creature, but the soul is a creature, how can it be known by the soul?" Answer: This is why we say, "by the soul *as a creature*." We mean it is impossible to the creature in virtue of its creature-nature and qualities, that by which it saith "I" and "myself." For in whatsoever creature the Perfect shall be known, therein creature-nature, qualities, the I, the Self and the like, must all be lost and done away. This is the meaning of that saying of St. Paul: "When that which is perfect is come," (that is, when it is known,) "then that which is in part" (to wit, creature-nature, qualities, the I, the Self, the Mine) will be despised and counted for nought. So long as we think much of these things, cleave to them with love, joy, pleasure or desire, so long remaineth the Perfect unknown to us.

1. Passages here and elsewhere not found in Luther's edition are enclosed between brackets.

But it might further be said, "Thou sayest, beside the Perfect there is no Substance, yet sayest again that somewhat floweth out from it; now is not that which hath flowed out from it, something beside it?" Answer: This is why we say, beside it, or without it, there is no *true* Substance. That which hath flowed forth from it, is no true Substance, and hath no Substance except in the perfect, but is an accident, or a brightness, or a visible appearance, which is no Substance, and hath no Substance except in the fire whence the brightness flowed forth, such as the sun or a candle.

II

Of what Sin is, and how we must not take unto ourselves any good Thing, seeing that it belongeth unto the true Good alone.

THE SCRIPTURE and the Faith and the Truth say, Sin is nought else, but that the creature turneth away from the unchangeable Good and betaketh itself to the changeable; that is to say, that it turneth away from the Perfect, to "that which is in part" and imperfect, and most often to itself. Now mark: when the creature claimeth for its own anything good, such as Substance, Life, Knowledge, Power, and in short whatever we should call good, as if it were that, or possessed that, or that were itself, or that proceeded from it,—as often as this cometh to pass, the creature goeth astray. What did the devil do else, or what was his going astray and his fall else, but that he claimed for himself to be also somewhat, and would have it that somewhat was his, and somewhat was due to him? This setting up of a claim and his I and Me and Mine, these were his going astray, and his fall. And thus it is to this day.

III

How Man's Fall and going astray must be amended as Adam's Fall was.

WHAT ELSE did Adam do but this same thing? It is said, it was because Adam ate the apple that he was lost, or fell. I say, it was because of his claiming something for his own, and because of his I, Mine, Me, and the like. Had he eaten seven apples, and yet never claimed anything for his own, he would not have fallen: but as soon as he called something his own, he fell, and would have fallen if he had never touched an apple. Behold! I have fallen a hundred times more often and deeply, and gone a hundred times farther astray than Adam; and not all mankind could amend his fall, or bring him back from going astray. But how shall my fall be amended? It must be healed as Adam's fall was healed, and on the self-same wise. By whom, and on what wise was that healing brought to pass? Mark this: man could not without God, and God should not without man. Wherefore God took human nature or manhood upon himself and was made man, and man was made divine. Thus the healing was brought to pass. So also must my fall be healed. I cannot do the work without God, and God may not or will not without me; for if it shall be accomplished, in me, too, God must be made man; in such sort that God must take to himself all that is in me, within and without, so that there may be nothing in me which striveth against God or hindereth his work. Now if God took to himself all men that are in the world, or ever were, and were made man in them, and they were made divine in him, and this work were not fulfilled in me, my fall and my wandering would never be amended except it were fulfilled in me also. And in this bringing back and healing, I can, or may, or shall do nothing of myself, but just simply yield to God, so that He alone may do all things in me and work, and I may suffer him and all his work and his divine will. And because I will not do so, but I count myself to be my own, and say, "I," "mine," "me" and the like, God is hindered, so that he cannot do his work in me alone and without hindrance; for this cause my fall and my going astray remain unhealed. Behold! this all cometh of my claiming somewhat for my own.

IV

How Man, when he claimeth any good Thing for his own, falleth, and toucheth God in his Honour.

GOD SAITH, "I will not give my glory to another."[1] This is as much as to say, that praise and honour and glory belong to none but to God only. But now, if I call any good thing my own, as if I were it, or of myself had power or did or knew anything, or as if anything were mine or of me, or belonged to me, or were due to me or the like, I take unto myself somewhat of honour and glory, and do two evil things: First, I fall and go astray as aforesaid: Secondly, I touch God in his honour and take unto myself what belongeth to God only. For all that must be called good belongeth to none but to the true eternal Goodness which is God only, and whoso taketh it unto himself, committeth unrighteousness and is against God.

V

How we are to take that Saying, that we must come to be without Will, Wisdom, Love, Desire, Knowledge, and the like.

CERTAIN MEN say that we ought to be without will, wisdom, love, desire, knowledge, and the like. Hereby is not to be understood that there is to be no knowledge in man, and that God is not to be loved by him, nor desired and longed for, nor praised and honoured; for that were a great loss, and man were like the beasts [and as the brutes that have no reason]. But it meaneth that man's knowledge should be so clear and perfect that he should acknowledge of a truth [that in himself he neither hath nor can do any good thing, and that none of his knowledge, wisdom and art, his will, love and good works do come from himself, nor are of man, nor of any creature, but] that all these are

1. Isaiah, xlii. 8.

of the eternal God, from whom they all proceed. [As Christ himself saith, "Without me, ye can do nothing."[1] St. Paul saith also, "What hast thou that thou hast not received?"[2] As much as to say—nothing. "Now if thou didst receive it, why dost thou glory as if thou hadst not received it?" Again he saith, "Not that we are sufficient of ourselves to think anything as of ourselves, but our sufficiency is of God."[3]] Now when a man duly perceiveth these things in himself, he and the creature fall behind, and he doth not call anything his own, and the less he taketh this knowledge unto himself, the more perfect doth it become. So also is it with the will, and love and desire, and the like. For the less we call these things our own, the more perfect and noble and godlike do they become, and the more we think them our own, the baser and less pure and perfect do they become.

Behold on this sort must we cast all things from us, and strip ourselves of them; we must refrain from claiming anything for our own. When we do this, we shall have the best, fullest, clearest and noblest knowledge that a man can have, and also the noblest and purest love, will and desire; for then these will be all of God alone. It is much better that they should be God's than the creature's. Now that I ascribe anything good things to myself, as if I were, or had done, or knew, or could perform any good, or that it were mine, this is all of sin and folly. For if the truth were rightly known by me, I should also know that I am not that good thing and that it is not mine, nor of me, and that I do not know it, and cannot do it, and the like. If this came to pass, I should needs cease to call anything my own.

It is better that God, or his works, should be known, as far as it be possible to us, and loved, praised and honoured, and the like, and even that man should but vainly imagine he loveth or praiseth God, than that God should be altogether unpraised, unloved, unhonoured and unknown. For when the vain imagination and ignorance are turned into an understanding and knowledge of the truth, the claiming anything for our own will

1. John xv. 5.
2. 1 Cor. iv. 7.
3. 2 Cor. iii. 5.

cease of itself. Then the man says: "Behold! I, poor fool that I was, imagined it was I, but behold! it is, and was, of a truth, God!"

VI

How that which is best and noblest should also be loved above all Things by us, merely because it is the best.

A MASTER called Boetius saith, "It is of sin that we do not love that which is best." He hath spoken the truth. That which is best should be the dearest of all things to us; and in our love of it, neither helpfulness nor unhelpfulness, advantage nor injury, gain nor loss, honour nor dishonour, praise nor blame, nor anything of the kind should be regarded; but what is in truth the noblest and best of all things, should be also the dearest of all things, and that for no other cause than that it is the noblest and best.

Hereby may a man order his life within and without. His outward life: for among the creatures one is better than another, according as the Eternal Good manifesteth itself and worketh more in one than in another. Now that creature in which the Eternal Good most manifesteth itself, shineth forth, worketh, is most known and loved, is the best, and that wherein the Eternal Good is least manifested is the least Good of all creatures. Therefore when we have to do with the creatures, and hold converse with them, and take note of their diverse qualities, the best creatures must always be the dearest to us, and we must cleave to them, and unite ourselves to them, above all to those which we attribute to God as belonging to him or divine, such as wisdom, truth, kindness, peace, love, justice, and the like. Hereby shall we order our outward man, and all that is contrary to these virtues we must eschew and flee from.

But if our inward man were to make a leap and spring into the Perfect, we should find and taste how that the Perfect is without measure, number or end, better and nobler than all which is imperfect and in part, and the Eternal above the temporal or perishable, and the fountain and source above all that floweth or can ever flow from it. Thus that which is imperfect and in part would become tasteless and be as nothing to us. Be assured of this: All that we have said must come to pass if we are to love that which is noblest, highest and best.

VII

Of the Eyes of the Spirit wherewith Man looketh into Eternity and into Time, and how the one is hindered of the other in its Working.

LET US remember how it is written and said that the soul of Christ had two eyes, a right and a left eye. In the beginning, when the soul of Christ was created, she fixed her right eye upon eternity and the Godhead, and remained in the full intuition and enjoyment of the Divine Essence and Eternal Perfection; and continued thus unmoved and undisturbed by all the accidents and travail, suffering, torment and pain that ever befell the outward man. But with the left eye she beheld the creature and perceived all things therein, and took note of the difference between the creatures, which were better or worse, nobler or meaner; and thereafter was the outward man of Christ ordered.

Thus the inner man of Christ, according to the right eye of his soul, stood in the full exercise of his divine nature, in perfect blessedness, joy and eternal peace. But the outward man and the left eye of Christ's soul, stood with him in perfect suffering, in all tribulation, affliction and travail; and this in such sort that the inward and right eye remained unmoved, unhindered and untouched by all the travail, suffering, grief and anguish that ever befell the outward man. It hath been said that when Christ was bound to the pillar and scourged, and when he hung upon the cross, according to the outward man, yet his inner man, or soul according to the right eye, stood in as full possession of divine joy and blessedness as it did after his ascension, or as it doth now. In like manner his outward man, or soul with the left eye, was never hindered, disturbed or troubled by the inward eye in its contemplation of the outward things that belonged to it.

Now the created soul of man hath also two eyes. The one is the power of seeing into eternity, the other of seeing into time and the creatures, of perceiving how they differ from each other as aforesaid, of giving life and needful things to the body, and ordering and governing it for the best. But these two eyes of the soul of man cannot both perform their work at once; but if the soul shall see with the right eye into eternity, then the left eye must close itself and refrain from working, and be as though it were dead. For if the left eye be fulfilling its office toward outward things; that is, holding converse with time and the creatures; then must the right eye be hindered in its working; that is, in its contemplation. Therefore whosoever will have the one must let the other go; for "no man can serve two masters."

VIII

How the Soul of Man, while it is yet in the Body, may obtain a foretaste of eternal Blessedness.

IT HATH been asked whether it be possible for the soul, while it is yet in the body, to reach so high as to cast a glance into eternity, and receive a foretaste of eternal life and eternal blessedness. This is commonly denied; and truly so in a sense. For it indeed cannot be so long as the soul is taking heed to the body, and the things which minister and appertain thereto, and to time and the creature, and is disturbed and troubled and distracted thereby. For if the soul shall rise to such a state, she must be quite pure, wholly stripped and bare of all images, and be entirely separate from all creatures, and above all from herself. Now many think this is not to be done and is impossible in this present time. But St. Dionysius maintains that it is possible, as we find from his words in his Epistle to Timothy, where he saith: "For the beholding of the hidden things of God, shalt thou forsake sense and the things of the flesh, and all that the senses can apprehend, and that reason of her own powers can bring forth, and all things created and uncreated that reason is able to comprehend and know, and shalt take thy stand upon an utter abandonment of thyself, and as knowing none of the aforesaid things, and enter into union with him who is, and who is above all existence and all knowledge." Now if he did not hold this to be possible in this present time, why should he teach it and enjoin it on us in this present time? But it behoveth you to know that a master hath said on this passage of St. Dionysius, that it is possible, and may happen to a man often, till he become so accustomed to it, as to be able to look into eternity whenever he will. [For when a thing is at first very hard to a man and strange, and seemingly quite impossible, if he put all his strength and energy into it, and persevere therein, that will afterward grow quite light and easy, which he at first thought quite out of reach, seeing that it is of no use to begin any work, unless it may be brought to a good end.]

And a single one of these excellent glances is better, worthier, higher and more pleasing to God, than all that the creature can perform as a creature. [And as soon as a man turneth himself in spirit, and with his whole heart and mind entereth into the mind of God which is above time, all that ever he hath lost is restored in a moment. And if a man were to do thus a thousand times in a day, each time a fresh and real union would take place; and in this sweet and divine work standeth the truest and fullest union that may be in this present time. For he who hath attained thereto, asketh nothing further, for he hath found the Kingdom of Heaven and Eternal Life on earth.]

IX

How it is better and more profitable for a Man that he should perceive what God will do with him, or to what end He will make Use of him, than if he knew all that God had ever wrought, or would ever work through all the Creatures; and how Blessedness lieth alone in God, and not in the Creatures, or in any Works.

WE SHOULD mark and know of a very truth that all manner of virtue and goodness, and even that Eternal Good which is God Himself, can never make a man virtuous, good, or happy, so long as it is outside the soul; [that is, so long as the man is holding converse with outward things through his senses and reason, and doth not withdraw into himself and learn to understand his own life, who and what he is]. The like is true of sin and evil.

[For all manner of sin and wickedness can never make us evil, so long as it is outside of us; that is, so long as we do not commit it, or do not give consent to it.]

Therefore although it be good and profitable that we should ask, and learn and know what good and holy men have wrought and suffered, and how God hath dealt with them, and what he hath wrought in and through them, yet it were a thousand times better that we should in ourselves learn and perceive and understand, who we are, how and what our own life is, what God is and is doing in us, what he will have from us, and to what ends he will or will not make use of us. [For, of a truth, thoroughly to know oneself, is above all art, for it is the highest art. If thou knowest thyself well, thou art better and more praiseworthy before God, than if thou didst not know thyself, but didst understand the course of the heavens and of all the planets and stars, also the virtue of all herbs, and the structure and dispositions of all mankind, also the nature of all beasts, and, in such matters, hadst all the skill of all who are in heaven and on earth. For it is said, there came a voice from heaven, saying, "Man, know thyself."] Thus that proverb is still true, "going out were never so good, but staying at home were much better."

Further, ye should learn that eternal blessedness lieth in one thing alone, and in nought else. And if ever man or the soul is to be made blessed, that one thing alone must be in the soul. Now some might ask, "But what is that one thing?" I answer, it is Goodness, or that which hath been made good, and yet neither this good nor that, which we can name, or perceive or show; but it is all and above all good things.

Moreover, it needeth not to enter into the soul, for it is there already, only it is unperceived. When we say we should come unto it, we mean that we should seek it, feel it, and taste it. And now since it is One, unity and singleness are better than manifoldness. For blessedness lieth not in much and many, but in One and oneness. In one word, blessedness lieth not in any creature, or work of the creatures, but it lieth alone in God and in his works. Therefore I must wait only on God and his work, and leave on one side all creatures with their works, and first of all myself. In like manner all the great works and wonders that God has ever wrought or shall ever work in or through the creatures, or even God himself with all his goodness, so far as these things exist or are done outside of me, can never make me blessed, but only in so far as they exist and are done and loved, known, tasted and felt within me.

X

How the perfect Men have no other Desire than that they may be to the Eternal Goodness what his Hand is to a Man, and how they have lost the Fear of Hell, and Hope of Heaven.

NOW LET us mark: Where men are enlightened with the true light, they perceive that all which they might desire or choose, is nothing to that which all creatures, as creatures, ever desired or chose or knew. Therefore they renounce all desire and choice, and commit and commend themselves and all things to the Eternal Goodness. Nevertheless, there remaineth in them a desire to go forward and get nearer to the Eternal Goodness; that is, to come to a clearer knowledge, and warmer love, and more comfortable assurance, and perfect obedience and subjection; so that every enlightened man could say: "I would fain be to the Eternal Goodness, what his own hand is to a man." And he feareth always that he is not enough so, and longeth for the salvation of all men. And such men do not call this longing their own, nor take it unto themselves, for they know well that this desire is not of man, but of the Eternal Goodness; for whatsoever is good shall no one take unto himself as his own, seeing that it belongeth to the Eternal Goodness only.

Moreover, these men are in a state of freedom, because they have lost the fear of pain or hell, and the hope of reward or heaven, but are living in pure submission to the Eternal Goodness, in the perfect freedom of fervent love. This mind was in Christ in perfection, and is also in his followers, in some more and in some less. But it is a sorrow and shame to think that the Eternal Goodness is ever most graciously guiding and drawing us, and we will not yield to it. What is better and nobler than true poorness in spirit? Yet when that is held up before us, we will have none of it, but are always seeking ourselves, and our own things. [We like to have our mouths always filled with good

things,] that we may have in ourselves a lively taste of pleasure
and sweetness. When this is so, we are well pleased, and think it
standeth not amiss with us. [But we are yet a long way off from
a perfect life. For when God will draw us up to something
higher, that is, to an utter loss and forsaking of our own things,
spiritual and natural, and withdraweth his comfort and sweetness from us, we faint and are troubled, and can in no wise
bring our minds to it; and we forget God and neglect holy exercises, and fancy we are lost for ever.] This is a great error and
a bad sign. For a true lover of God, loveth him or the Eternal
Goodness alike, in having, and in not having, in sweetness and
bitterness, in good or evil report, and the like, for he seeketh
alone the honour of God, and not his own, either in spiritual or
natural things. And therefore he standeth alike unshaken in all
things, at all seasons. [Hereby let every man prove himself, how
he standeth towards God, his Creator and Lord.]

XI

*How a righteous Man in this present time is brought into Hell,
and there cannot be comforted, and how he is taken out of
Hell and carried into Heaven, and there cannot be troubled.*

CHRIST'S SOUL must needs descend into hell, before it ascend into
heaven. So must also the soul of man. But mark ye in what
manner this cometh to pass. When a man truly perceiveth and
considereth himself, who and what he is, and findeth himself
utterly vile and wicked, and unworthy of all the comfort and
kindness that he hath ever received from God, or from the creatures, he falleth into such a deep abasement and despising of
himself, that he thinketh himself unworthy that the earth should
bear him, and it seemeth to him reasonable that all creatures in
heaven and earth should rise up against him and avenge their
Creator on him, and should punish and torment him; and that
he were unworthy even of that. And it seemeth to him that he
shall be eternally lost and damned, and a footstool to all the
devils in hell, and that this is right and just, [and all too little
compared to his sins which he so often and in so many ways
hath committed against God his Creator.] And therefore also

he will not and dare not desire any consolation or release, either from God or from any creature that is in heaven or on earth; but he is willing to be unconsoled and unreleased, and he doth not grieve over his condemnation and sufferings; for they are right and just, and not contrary to God, but according to the will of God. Therefore they are right in his eyes, and he hath nothing to say against them. Nothing grieveth him but his own guilt and wickedness; for that is not right and is contrary to God, and for that cause he is grieved and troubled in spirit.

This is what is meant by true repentance for sin. And he who in this present time entereth into this hell, entereth afterward into the Kingdom of Heaven, and obtaineth a foretaste thereof which excelleth all the delight and joy which he ever hath had or could have in this present time from temporal things. But whilst a man is thus in hell, none may console him, neither God nor the creature, as it is written "In hell there is no redemption."[1] Of this state hath one said, "Let me perish, let me die! I live without hope; from within and from without I am condemned, let no one pray that I may be released."

Now God hath not forsaken a man in this hell, but He is laying His hand upon him, that the man may not desire nor regard anything but the Eternal Good only, and may come to know that that is so noble and passing good, that none can search out or express its bliss, consolation and joy, peace, rest, and satisfaction. And then, when the man neither careth for, nor seeketh nor desireth, anything but the Eternal Good alone, and seeketh not himself, nor his own things, but the honour of God only, he is made a partaker of all manner of joy, bliss, peace, rest and consolation, and so the man is henceforth in the Kingdom of Heaven.

This hell and this heaven are two good, safe ways for a man in this present time, and happy is he who truly findeth them.

> For this hell shall pass away,
> But Heaven shall endure for aye.

Also let a man mark, when he is in this hell, nothing may console him: and he cannot believe that he shall ever be released

1. The writer is probably alluding to Ps. xlix. 8.

or comforted. But when he is in heaven, nothing can trouble him; he believeth also that none will ever be able to offend or trouble him, albeit it is indeed true, that after this hell he may be comforted and released, and after this heaven he may be troubled and left without consolation.

Again: this hell and this heaven come about a man in such sort, that he knoweth not whence they come; and whether they come to him, or depart from him, he can of himself do nothing towards it. Of these things he can neither give nor take away from himself, bring them nor banish them, but as it is written, "The wind bloweth where it listeth, and thou hearest the sound thereof," that is to say, at this time present, "but thou knowest not whence it cometh, nor whither it goeth."[1] And when a man is in one of these two states, all is right with him, and he is as safe in hell as in heaven, and so long as a man is on earth, it is possible for him to pass ofttimes from the one into the other; nay even within the space of a day and night, and all without his own doing. But when the man is in neither of these two states he holdeth converse with the creature, and wavereth hither and thither, and knoweth not what manner of man he is. Therefore he shall never forget either of them, but lay up the remembrance of them in his heart.

XII

Touching that true inward Peace, which Christ left to his Disciples at the last.

MANY SAY they have no peace nor rest, but so many crosses and trials, afflictions and sorrows, that they know not how they shall ever get through them. Now he who in truth will perceive and take note, perceiveth clearly, that true peace and rest lie not in outward things; for if it were so, the Evil Spirit also would have peace when things go according to his will, [which is nowise the case; for the prophet declareth "There is no peace, saith my God, to the wicked."[2]] And therefore we must consider and see what is that peace which Christ left to his disciples at the

1. John iii. 8.
2. Isaiah lvii. 21.

last, when he said: "My peace I leave with you, my peace I give unto you."[1] [We may perceive that in these words Christ did not mean a bodily and outward peace; for his beloved disciples, with all his friends and followers, have ever suffered, from the beginning, great affliction, persecution, nay, often martyrdom, as Christ himself said: "In this world ye shall have tribulation."[2] But Christ meant that true, inward peace of the heart, which beginneth here and endureth for ever hereafter. Therefore he said]: "not as the world giveth," for the world is false, and deceiveth in her gifts; [she promiseth much, and performeth little. Moreover there liveth no man on earth who may always have rest and peace without troubles and crosses, with whom things always go according to his will; there is always something to be suffered here, turn- which way thou wilt. And as soon as thou art quit of one assault, perhaps two come in its place. Wherefore yield thyself willingly to them, and seek only that true peace of the heart, which none can take away from thee, that thou mayest overcome all assaults].

Thus then, Christ meant that inward peace which can break through all assaults and crosses of oppression, suffering, misery, humiliation and what more there may be of the like, so that a man may be joyful and patient therein, like the beloved disciples and followers of Christ. Now he who will in love give his whole diligence and might thereto, will verily come to know that true eternal peace which is God Himself, as far as it is possible to a creature; [insomuch that what was bitter to him before, shall become sweet, and his heart shall remain unmoved under all changes, at all times, and after this life, he shall attain unto everlasting peace.]

*   *   *

1. John xiv. 27.
2. John xvi. 33.

XIV

Of three Stages by which a Man is led upwards till he attaineth true Perfection.

NOW BE assured that no one can be enlightened unless he be first cleansed or purified and stripped. So also, no one can be united with God unless he be first enlightened. Thus there are three stages: first, the purification; secondly, the enlightening; thirdly, the union. [The purification concerneth those who are beginning or repenting, and is brought to pass in a threefold wise; by contrition and sorrow for sin, by full confession, by hearty amendment. The enlightening belongeth to such as are growing, and also taketh place in three ways: to wit, by the eschewal of sin, by the practice of virtue and good works, and by the willing endurance of all manner of temptation and trials. The union belongeth to such as are perfect, and also is brought to pass in three ways: to wit, by pureness and singleness of heart, by love, and by the contemplation of God, the Creator of all things.]

XV

How all Men are dead in Adam and are made alive again in Christ, and of true Obedience and Disobedience.

ALL THAT in Adam fell and died, was raised again and made alive in Christ, and all that rose up and was made alive in Adam, fell and died in Christ. But what was that? I answer, true obedience and disobedience. But what is true obedience? I answer, that a man should so stand free, being quit of himself, that is, of his I, and Me, and Self, and Mine, and the like, that in all things, he should no more seek or regard himself, than if he did not exist, and should take as little account of himself as if he were not, and another had done all his works. Likewise he should count all the creatures for nothing. What is there then, which is, and which we may count for somewhat? I answer, nothing but that which we may call God. Behold! this is very obedience in the truth, and thus it will be in a blessed eternity. There nothing is sought nor thought of, nor loved, but the one thing only.

Hereby we may mark what disobedience is: to wit, that a man maketh some account of himself, and thinketh that he is, and knoweth, and can do somewhat, and seeketh himself and his own ends in the things around him, and hath regard to and loveth himself, and the like. Man is created for true obedience, and is bound of right to render it to God. And this obedience fell and died in Adam, and rose again and lived in Christ. Yea, Christ's human nature was so utterly bereft of Self, and apart from all creatures, as no man's ever was, and was nothing else but "a house and habitation of God." Neither of that in him which belonged to God, nor of that which was a living human nature and a habitation of God, did he, as man, claim any thing for his own. His human nature did not even take unto himself the Godhead, whose dwelling it was, nor any thing that this same Godhead willed, or did or left undone in him, nor yet any thing of all that his human nature did or suffered; but in Christ's human nature there was no claiming of any thing, nor seeking, nor desire, saving that what was due might be rendered to the Godhead, and he did not call this very desire his own. Of this matter no more can be said or written here, for it is unspeakable, and was never yet and never will be fully uttered; for it can neither be spoken nor written but by Him who is and knows its ground; that is, God Himself, who can do all things well.

XVI

Telleth us what is the old Man, and what is the new Man.

AGAIN, WHEN we read of the old man and the new man we must mark what that meaneth. The old man is Adam and disobedience, the Self, the Me, and so forth. But the new man is Christ and true obedience, [a giving up and denying oneself of all temporal things, and seeking the honour of God alone in all things]. And when dying and perishing, and the like are spoken of, it meaneth that the old man should be destroyed, and not seek its own either in spiritual or in natural things. For where this is brought about in a true divine light, there the new man is born again. In like manner, it hath been said that man should die unto himself, [that is, to earthly pleasures, consolations, joys, appetites, the I, the Self, and all that is thereof in man, to which he clingeth and on which he is yet leaning with content, and thinketh much of. Whether it be the man himself, or any other creature, whatever it be, it must depart and die, if the man is to be brought aright to another mind, according to the truth.]

Thereunto doth St. Paul exhort us, saying: "Put off concerning the former conversation the old man, which is corrupt, according to the deceitful lusts: . . . and that ye put on the new man, which after God is created in righteousness and true holiness."[1] Now he who liveth to himself after the old man, is called and is truly a child of Adam; and though he may give diligence to the ordering of his life, he is still the child and brother of the Evil Spirit. But he who liveth in humble obedience and in the new man which is Christ, he is, in like manner, the brother of Christ and the child of God.

Behold! where the old man dieth and the new man is born, there is that second birth of which Christ saith, "Except a man be born again, he cannot enter into the kingdom of God."[2] Likewise St. Paul saith: "As in Adam all die, even so in Christ shall all be made alive."[3] That is to say, all who follow Adam in pride, in lust of the flesh, and in disobedience, are dead in soul, and never will or can be made alive but in Christ. And for this cause, so long as a man is an Adam or his child, he is without God. Christ saith, "he who is not with me is against me."[4] Now he who is against God, is dead before God. Whence it followeth that all Adam's children are dead before God. But he who standeth with Christ in perfect obedience, he is with God and liveth. As it hath been said already, sin lieth in the turning away of the creature from the Creator, which agreeth with what we have now said.

For he who is in disobedience is in sin, and sin can never

1. Ephesians iv. 22. 24.
2. John iii. 3.
3. I Cor. xv. 22.
4. Matt. xxii. 30.

be atoned for or healed but by returning to God, and this is brought to pass by humble obedience. For so long as a man continueth in disobedience, his sin can never be blotted out; let him do what he will, it availeth him nothing. Let us be assured of this. For disobedience is itself sin. But when a man entereth into the obedience of the faith, all is healed, and blotted out and forgiven, and not else. Insomuch that if the Evil Spirit himself could come into true obedience, he would become an angel again, and all his sin and wickedness would be healed and blotted out and forgiven at once. And could an angel fall into disobedience, he would straightway become an evil spirit although he did nothing afresh.

If then it were possible for a man to renounce himself and all things, and to live as wholly and purely in true obedience, as Christ did in his human nature, such a man were quite without sin, and were one thing with Christ, and the same by grace which Christ was by nature. But it is said this cannot be. So also it is said: "there is none without sin." But be that as it may, this much is certain; that the nearer we are to perfect obedience, the less we sin, and the farther from it we are, the more we sin. In brief: whether a man be good, better, or best of all; bad, worse, or worst of all; sinful or saved before God; it all lieth in this matter of obedience. Therefore it hath been said: the more of Self and Me, the more of sin and wickedness. So likewise it hath been said: the more the Self, the I, the Me, the Mine, that is, self-seeking and selfishness abate in a man, the more doth God's I, that is, God Himself, increase in him.

Now, if all mankind abode in true obedience, there would be no grief nor sorrow. For if it were so, all men would be at one, and none would vex or harm another; so also, none would lead a life or do any deed contrary to God's will. Whence then should grief or sorrow arise? But now alas! all men, nay the whole world lieth in disobedience! Now were a man simply and wholly obedient as Christ was, all disobedience were to him a sharp and bitter pain. But though all men were against him, they could neither shake nor trouble him, for while in this obedience a man were one with God, and God Himself were [one with] the man.

Behold now all disobedience is contrary to God, and

nothing else. In truth, no Thing is contrary to God; no creature nor creature's work, nor any thing that we can name or think of is contrary to God or displeasing to Him, but only disobedience and the disobedient man. In short, all that is, is well-pleasing and good in God's eyes, saving only the disobedient man. But he is so displeasing and hateful to God and grieveth him so sore, that if it were possible for human nature to die a hundred deaths, God would willingly suffer them all for one disobedient man, that He might slay disobedience in him, and that obedience might be born again.

Behold! albeit no man may be so single and perfect in this obedience as Christ was, yet it is possible to every man to approach so near thereunto as to be rightly called godlike, and "a partaker of the divine nature."[1] And 'the nearer a man cometh thereunto, and the more godlike and divine he becometh the more he hateth all disobedience, sin, evil and unrighteousness, and the worse they grieve him. Disobedience and sin are the same thing, for there is no sin but disobedience, and what is done of disobedience is all sin. Therefore all we have to do is to keep ourselves from disobedience.

XVII

How we are not to take unto ourselves what we have done well, but only what we have done amiss.

BEHOLD! NOW it is reported there be some who vainly think and say that they are so wholly dead to self and quit of it, as to have reached and abide in a state where they suffer nothing and are moved by nothing, just as if all men were living in obedience, or as if there were no creatures. And thus they profess to continue always in an even temper of mind, so that nothing cometh amiss to them, howsoever things fall out, well or ill. Nay verily! the matter standeth not so, but as we have said. It might be thus, if all men were brought into obedience; but until then, it cannot be.

But it may be asked: Are not we to be separate from all things, and neither to take unto ourselves evil nor good? I

1. 2 Pet. i. 4.

answer, no one shall take goodness unto himself, for that belongeth to God and His goodness only; but thanks be unto the man, and everlasting reward and blessings, who is fit and ready to be a dwelling and tabernacle of the Eternal Goodness and Godhead, wherein God may exert his power, and will and work without hindrance. But if any now will excuse himself for sin, by refusing to take what is evil unto himself, and laying the guilt thereof upon the Evil Spirit, and thus make himself out to be quite pure and innocent (as our first parents Adam and Eve did while they were yet in paradise; when each laid the guilt upon the other,) he hath no right at all to do this; for it is written, "there is none without sin." Therefore I say; reproach, shame, loss, woe, and eternal damnation be to the man who is fit and ready and willing that the Evil Spirit and falsehood, lies and all untruthfulness, wickedness and other evil things should have their will and pleasure, word and work in him, and make him their house and habitation.

XVIII

How that the Life of Christ is the noblest and best Life that ever hath been or can be, and how a careless Life of false Freedom is the worst Life that can be.

OF A TRUTH we ought to know and believe that there is no life so noble and good and well pleasing to God, as the life of Christ, and yet it is to nature and selfishness the bitterest life. A life of carelessness and freedom is to nature and the Self and the Me, the sweetest and the pleasantest life, but it is not the best; and in some men may become the worst. But though Christ's life be the most bitter of all, yet it is to be preferred above all. Hereby shall ye mark this: There is an inward fight which hath power to perceive the One true Good, and that it is neither this nor that, but that of which St. Paul saith; "when that which is perfect is come, then that which is in part shall be done away."[1] By this he meaneth, that the Whole and Perfect excelleth all the fragments, and that all which is in part and imperfect, is as nought compared to the Perfect. Thus likewise all knowledge

1. 1 Cor. xiii. 10.

of the parts is swallowed up when the Whole is known; and where that Good is known, it cannot but be longed for and loved so greatly, that all other love wherewith the man hath loved himself and other things, fadeth away. And that inward sight likewise perceiveth what is best and noblest in all things, and loveth it in the one true Good, and only for the sake of that true Good.

Behold! where there is this inward sight, the man perceiveth of a truth, that Christ's life is the best and noblest life, and therefore the most to be preferred, and he willingly accepteth and endureth it, without a question or a complaint, whether it please or offend nature or other men, whether he like or dislike it, find it sweet or bitter, and the like. And therefore wherever this perfect and true Good is known, there also the life of Christ must be led, until the death of the body. And he who vainly thinketh otherwise is deceived, and he who saith otherwise, lieth, and in what man the life of Christ is not, of him the true Good and eternal Truth will never more be known.

XIX

How we cannot come to the true Light and Christ's Life, by much Questioning or Reading, or by high natural Skill and Reason, but by truly renouncing ourselves and all Things.

LET NO one suppose that we may attain to this true light and perfect knowledge, or life of Christ, by much questioning, or by hearsay, or by reading and study, nor yet by high skill and great learning. Yea so long as a man taketh account of anything which is this or that, whether it be himself, or any other creature; or doeth anything, or frameth a purpose, for the sake of his own likings or desires, or opinions, or ends, he cometh not unto the life of Christ. This hath Christ himself declared, for he saith: "If any man will come after me, let him deny himself, and take up his cross, and follow me."[1] "He that taketh not his cross, and followeth after me, is not worthy of me."[2] And if

1. Matt. xvi. 24.
2. Matt. x. 38.

he "hate not his father and mother, and wife, and children, and brethren and sisters, yea, and his own life also, he cannot be my disciple."[1] He meaneth it thus: "he who doth not forsake and part with every thing, can never know my eternal truth, nor attain unto my life." And though this had never been declared unto us, yet the truth herself sayeth it, for it is so of a truth. But so long as a man clingeth unto the elements and fragments of this world (and above all to himself,) and holdeth converse with them, and maketh great account of them, he is deceived and blinded, and perceiveth what is good no further than as it is most convenient and pleasant to himself and profitable to his own ends. These he holdeth to be the highest good, and loveth above all. [Thus he never cometh to the truth.]

* * *

XXIII

He who will submit himself to God and be obedient to Him, must be ready to bear with all Things; to wit, God, himself, and all Creatures, and must be obedient to them all, whether he hath to suffer or to do.

THERE BE some who talk of other ways and preparations to this end, and say we must lie still under God's hand, and be obedient and resigned and submit to Him. This is true; for all this would be perfected in a man who should attain to the uttermost that can be reached in this present time. But if a man ought and is willing to lie still under God's hand, he must and ought also to be still under all things, whether they come from God, himself, or the creatures, nothing excepted. And he who would be obedient, resigned and submissive to God, must and ought to be also resigned, obedient and submissive to all things, in a spirit of yielding, and not of resistance, and take them in silence, resting on the hidden foundations of his soul, and having a secret inward patience, that enableth him to take all chances or crosses willingly, and whatever befalleth, neither to call for

1. Luke xiv. 26.

nor desire any redress, or deliverance, or resistance, or revenge, but always in a loving, sincere humility to cry, "Father, forgive them, for they know not what they do!"

Behold! this were a good path to that which is Best, and a noble and blessed preparation for the farthest goal which a man may reach in this present time. This is the lovely life of Christ, for he walketh in the aforesaid paths perfectly and wholly unto the end of his bodily life on earth. Therefore there is no other or better way or preparation to the joyful life of Jesus Christ, than this same course, and to exercise oneself therein, as much as may be. And of what belongeth thereunto we have already said somewhat; nay, all that we have here or elsewhere said and written, is but a way or means to that end. But what the end is, knoweth no man to declare. But let him who would know it, follow my counsel and take the right path thereunto, which is the humble life of Jesus Christ; [let him strive after that with unwearied perseverance, and so, without doubt, he shall come to that end which endureth for ever. "For he that endureth to the end shall be saved."][1]

*   *   *

XXV

Of two evil Fruits that do spring up from the Seed of the Evil Spirit, and are two Sisters who love to dwell together. The one is called Spiritual Pride and Highmindedness, the other is false, lawless Freedom.

NOW, AFTER that a man hath walked in all the ways that lead him unto the truth, and exercised himself therein, not sparing his labour; now, as often and as long as he dreameth that his work is altogether finished, and he is by this time quite dead to the world, and come out from Self and given up to God alone, behold! the Devil cometh and soweth his seed in the man's heart. From this seed spring two fruits; the one is spiritual fulness or pride, the other is false, lawless freedom. These are two sisters who love to be together. Now, it beginneth on this

1. Matt. x. 22.

wise: the Devil puffeth up the man, till he thinketh himself to have climbed the topmost pinnacle, and to have come so near to heaven, that he no longer needeth Scripture, nor teaching, nor this nor that, but is altogether raised above any need. Whereupon there ariseth a false peace and satisfaction with himself, and then it followeth that he saith or thinketh: "Yea, now I am above all other men, and know and understand more than any one in the world; therefore it is certainly just and reasonable that I should be the lord and commander of all creatures, and that all creatures, and especially all men, should serve me and be subject unto me." And then he seeketh and desireth the same, and taketh it gladly from all creatures, especially men, and thinketh himself well worthy of all this, and that it is his due, and looketh on men as if they were the beasts of the field, and thinketh himself worthy of all that ministereth to his body and life and nature, in profit, or joy, or pleasure, or even pastime and amusement, and he seeketh and taketh it wherever he findeth opportunity. And whatever is done or can be done for him, seemeth him all too little and too poor, for he thinketh himself worthy of still more and greater honour than can be rendered to him. And of all the men who serve him and are subject to him, even if they be downright thieves and murderers, he saith nevertheless, that they have faithful, noble hearts, and have great love and faithfulness to the truth and to poor men. And such men are praised by him, and he seeketh them and followeth after them wherever they be. But he who doth not order himself according to the will of these high-minded men, nor is subject unto them, is not sought after by them, nay, more likely blamed and spoken ill of, even though he were as holy as St. Peter himself. And seeing that this proud and puffed-up spirit thinketh that she needeth neither Scripture, nor instruction, nor anything of the kind, therefore she giveth no heed to the admonitions, order, laws and precepts of the holy Christian Church, nor to the Sacraments, but mocketh at them and at all men who walk according to these ordinances and hold them in reverence. Hereby we may plainly see that those two sisters dwell together.

Moreover since this sheer pride thinketh to know and understand more than all men besides, therefore she chooseth to prate more than all other men, and would fain have her opinions and speeches to be alone regarded and listened to, and counteth all that others think and say to be wrong, and holdeth it in derision as a folly.

* * *

XXVII

How we are to take Christ's Words when he bade us forsake all Things; and wherein the Union with the Divine Will standeth.

NOW, ACCORDING to what hath been said, ye must observe that when we say, as Christ also saith, that we ought to resign and forsake all things, this is not to be taken in the sense that a man is neither to do nor to purpose any thing; for a man must always have something to do and to order so long as he liveth. But we are to understand by it that the union with God standeth not in any man's powers, in his working or abstaining, perceiving or knowing, nor in that of all the creatures taken together.

Now what is this union? It is that we should be of a truth purely, simply, and wholly at one with the One Eternal Will of God, or altogether without will, so that the created will should flow out into the Eternal Will, and be swallowed up and lost therein, so that the Eternal Will alone should do and leave undone in us. Now mark what may help or further us towards this end. Behold, neither exercises, nor words, nor works, nor any creature nor creature's work, can do this. In this wise therefore must we renounce and forsake all things, that we must not imagine or suppose that any words, works, or exercises, any skill or cunning or any created thing can help or serve us thereto. Therefore we must suffer these things to be what they are, and enter into the union with God. Yet outward things must be, and we must do and refrain so far as is necessary, especially we must sleep and wake, walk and stand still, speak and be silent, and much more of the like. These must go on so long as we live.

XXVIII

How, after a Union with the divine Will, the inward Man standeth immovable, the while the outward Man is moved hither and thither.

NOW, WHEN this union truly cometh to pass and becometh established, the inward man standeth henceforward immovable in this union; and God suffereth the outward man to be moved hither and thither, from this to that, of such things as are necessary and right. So that the outward man saith in sincerity, "I have no will to be or not to be, to live or die, to know or not to know, to do or to leave undone and the like; but I am ready for all that is to be, or ought to be, and obedient thereunto, whether I have to do or to suffer." And thus the outward man hath no Wherefore or purpose, but only to do his part to further the Eternal Will. For it is perceived of a truth, that the inward man shall stand immovable, and that it is needful for the outward man to be moved. And if the inward man have any Wherefore in the actions of the outward man, he saith only that such things must be and ought to be, as are ordained by the Eternal Will. And where God Himself dwelleth in the man, it is thus; as we plainly see in Christ. Moreover, where there is this union, which is the offspring of a Divine light and dwelleth in its beams, there is no spiritual pride, or irreverent spirit, but boundless humility, and a lowly broken heart; also an honest blameless walk, justice, peace, content and all that is of virtue must needs be there. Where they are not, there is no right union, as we have said. For just as neither this thing nor that can bring about or further this union, so there is nothing which hath power to frustrate or hinder it, save the man himself with his self-will, that doeth him this great wrong. Of this be well assured.

*   *   *

XXX

*On what wise we may come to be beyond and above all Custom,
Order, Law, Precepts, and the like.*

SOME SAY further, that we can and ought to get beyond all virtue,
all custom and order, all law, precepts and seemliness, so that
all these should be laid aside, thrown off and set at nought.
Herein there is some truth, and some falsehood. Behold and
mark: Christ was greater than his own life, and above all virtue,
custom, ordinances and the like, and so also is the Evil Spirit
above them, but with a difference. For Christ was and is above
them on this wise, that his words, and works, and ways, his do-
ings and refrainings, his speech and silence, his sufferings, and
whatsoever happened to him, were not forced upon him, neither
did he need them, neither were they of any profit to himself. It
was and is the same with all manner of virtue, order, laws, de-
cency, and the like; for all that may be reached by them is
already in Christ to perfection. In this sense, that saying of St.
Paul is true and receiveth its fulfilment, "As many as are led
by the Spirit of God, they are the sons of God," "and are not
under the law but under grace."[1] That meaneth, man need
not teach them what they are to do or abstain from; for their
Master, that is, the Spirit of God, shall verily teach them what
is needful for them to know. Likewise they do not need that
men should give them precepts, or command them to do right
and not to do wrong, and the like; for the same admirable Master who teacheth them what is good or not good, what is higher
and lower, and in short leadeth them into all truth, He reigneth
also within them, and biddeth them to hold fast that which
is good, and to let the rest go, and to Him they give ear. Behold!
in this sense they need not to wait upon any law, either to teach
or to command them. In another sense also they need no law;
namely, in order to seek or win something thereby, or get any
advantage for themselves. For whatever help toward eternal life,
or furtherance in the way everlasting they might obtain from the

1. Rom. viii. 10, and vi. 14.

aid, or counsel, or words, or works of any creature, they possess
already beforehand. Behold! in this sense also it is true, that
we may rise above all law and virtue, and also above the works
and knowledge and powers of any creature.

*　　　*　　　*

XXXV

How there is deep and true Humility and Poorness of Spirit in
a Man who is "made a Partaker of the Divine Nature."

MOREOVER, IN a man who is "made a partaker of the divine
nature," there is a thorough and deep humility, and where this
is not, the man hath not been "made a partaker of the divine
nature." So Christ taught in words and fulfilled in works. And
this humility springeth up in the man, because in the true Light
he seeth (as it also really is) that Substance, Life, Perceiving,
Knowledge, Power, and what is thereof, do all belong to the
True Good, and not to the creature; but that the creature of
itself is nothing and hath nothing, and that when it turneth itself aside from the True Good in will or in works, nothing is
left to it but pure evil. And therefore it is true to the very
letter, that the creature, as creature, hath no worthiness in itself,
and no right to anything, and no claim over any one, either
over God or over the creature, and that it ought to give itself
up to God and submit to Him because this is just. And this is
the chiefest and most weighty matter.

Now, if we ought to be, and desire to be, obedient and
submit unto God, we must also submit to what we receive at
the hands of any of his creatures, or our submission is all false.
From this latter article floweth true humility, as indeed it doth
also from the former.[1] And unless this verily ought to be, and
were wholly agreeable to God's justice, Christ would not have
taught it in words, and fulfilled it in his life. And herein there
is a veritable manifestation of God; and it is so of a truth, that
of God's truth and justice this creature shall be subject to God
and all creatures, and no thing or person shall be subject or

1. Namely, God's having a right to our obedience.

obedient to her. God and all the creatures have a right over her and to her, but she hath a right to nothing: she is a debtor to all, and nothing is owing to her, so that she shall be ready to bear all things from others, and also if needs be to do all things for others. And out of this groweth that poorness of spirit which Christ said: "Blessed are the poor in spirit" (that is to say, the truly humble) "for theirs is the Kingdom of Heaven." All this hath Christ taught in words and fulfilled with his life.

XXXVI

How nothing is contrary to God but Sin only; and what Sin is in Kind and Act.

FURTHER YE shall mark: when it is said that such a thing, or such a deed is contrary to God, or that such a thing is hateful to God and grieveth His Spirit, ye must know that no creature is contrary to God, or hateful or grievous unto Him, in so far as it is, liveth, knoweth, hath power to do, or produce aught, and so forth, for all this is not contrary to God. That an evil spirit, or a man is, liveth, and the like, is altogether good and of God; for God is the Being of all that are, and the Life of all that live, and the Wisdom of all the wise; for all things have their being more truly in God than in themselves, and also their powers, knowledge, life, and the rest; for if it were not so, God would not be all good. And thus all creatures are good. Now what is good is agreeable to God and He will have it. Therefore it cannot be contrary to Him.

But what then is there which is contrary to God and hateful to Him? Nothing but Sin. But what is Sin? Mark this: Sin is nothing else than that the creature willeth otherwise than God willeth, and contrary to Him. Each of us may see this in himself; for he who willeth otherwise than I, or whose will is contrary to mine, is my foe; but he who willeth the same as I, is my friend, and I love him. It is even so with God: and that is sin, and is contrary to God, and hateful and grievous to Him. And he who willeth, speaketh, or is silent, doeth or leaveth undone, otherwise than as I will, is contrary to me, and an offence unto me. So it is also with God: when a man willeth otherwise than God, or contrary to God, whatever he doeth or leaveth undone, in short all that proceedeth from him, is contrary to God, and is sin. And whatsoever Will willeth otherwise than God, is against God's will. As Christ said: "he who is not with me is against me." Hereby may each man see plainly whether or not he be without sin, and whether or not he be committing sin, and what sin is, and how sin ought to be atoned for, and wherewith it may be healed. And this contradiction to God's will is what we call, and is, disobedience. And therefore Adam, the I, the Self, Self-will, Sin, or the Old Man, the turning aside or departing from God, do all mean one and the same thing.

*   *   *

XXXVIII

How we are to put on the Life of Christ from Love, and not for the sake of Reward, and how we must never grow careless concerning it, or cast it off.

NOW, WHEREVER a man hath been made a partaker of the divine nature, in him is fulfilled the best and noblest life, and the worthiest in God's eyes, that hath been or can be. And of that eternal love which loveth Goodness as Goodness and for the sake of Goodness, a true, noble, Christ-like life is so greatly beloved, that it will never be forsaken or cast off. Where a man hath tasted this life, it is impossible for him ever to part with it, were he to live until the Judgment Day. And though he must die a thousand deaths, and though all the sufferings that ever befell all creatures could be heaped upon him, he would rather undergo them all, than fall away from this excellent life; and if he could exchange it for an angel's life, he would not.

This is our answer to the question, "if a man, by putting on Christ's life, can get nothing more than he hath already, and serve no end, what good will it do him?" This life is not chosen in order to serve any end, or to get anything by it, but for love of its nobleness, and because God loveth and esteemeth it so greatly. And whoever saith that he hath had enough of it, and may now lay it aside, hath never tasted nor known it; for he who hath truly felt or tasted it, can never give it up again. And he who hath put on the life of Christ with the intent to win or deserve aught thereby, hath taken it up as an hireling and not for love, and is altogether without it. For he who doth not take it up for love, hath none of it at all; he may dream indeed that he hath put it on, but he is deceived. Christ did not lead such a life as his for the sake of reward, but out of love; and love maketh such a life light and taketh away all its hardships, so that it becometh sweet and is gladly endured. But to him who hath not put it on from love, but hath done so, as he dreameth, for the sake of reward, it is utterly bitter and a weariness, and he would fain be quit of it. And it is a sure token of an hireling that he wisheth his work were at an end. But he who truly loveth it, is not offended at its toil nor suffering, nor the length of time it lasteth. Therefore it is written, "to serve God and live to Him, is easy to him who doeth it." Truly it is so to him who doth it for love, but it is hard and wearisome to him who doth it for hire. It is the same with all virtue and good works, and likewise with order, laws, obedience to precepts, and the like. But God rejoiceth more over one man who truly loveth, than over a thousand hirelings.

* * *

XLIV

How nothing is contrary to God but Self-will, and how he who seeketh his own Good for his own sake, findeth it not; and how a Man of himself neither knoweth nor can do any good thing.

NOW, IT MAY be asked; is there aught which is contrary to God and the true Good? I say, No. Likewise there is nothing without God, except to will otherwise than is willed by the Eternal Will; that is, contrary to the Eternal Will. Now the Eternal Will willeth that nothing be willed or loved but the Eternal Goodness. And where it is otherwise, there is something contrary to Him, and in this sense it is true that he who is without God is

contrary to God; but in truth there is no Being contrary to God
or the true Good.

We must understand it as though God said: "he who willeth
without Me, or willeth not what I will, or otherwise than as I
will, he willeth contrary to Me, for My will is that no one
should will otherwise than I, and that there should be no will
without Me, and without My will; even as without me, there is
neither Substance, nor Life, nor this, nor that, so also there
should be no Will apart from Me, and without My will." And
even as in truth all beings are one in substance in the Perfect
Being, and all good is one in the One Being, and so forth, and
cannot exist without that One, so shall all wills be one in the
One Perfect Will, and there shall be no will apart from that
One. And whatever is otherwise is wrong, and contrary to God
and His will, and therefore it is sin. Therefore all will apart
from God's will (that is, all self-will,) is sin, and so is all that
is done from self-will. So long as a man seeketh his own will and
his own highest Good, because it is *his,* and for his own sake, he
will never find it; for so long as he doeth this, he is not seeking
his own highest Good, and how then should he find it? For so
long as he doeth this, he seeketh himself, and dreameth that he
is himself the highest Good; and seeing that he is not the highest
Good, he seeketh not the highest Good, so long as he seeketh
himself. But whosoever seeketh, loveth, and pursueth Goodness
as Goodness and for the sake of Goodness, and maketh that
his end, for nothing but the love of Goodness, not for love of
the I, Me, Mine, Self, and the like, he will find the highest
Good, for he seeketh it aright, and they who seek it otherwise
do err. And truly it is on this wise that the true and Perfect
Goodness seeketh and loveth and pursueth itself, and therefore
it findeth itself.

It is a great folly when a man, or any creature dreameth that
he knoweth or can accomplish aught of himself, and above all
when he dreameth that he knoweth or can fulfil any good thing,
whereby he may deserve much at God's hands, and prevail with
Him. If he understood rightly, he would see that this is to put
a great affront upon God. But the True and Perfect Goodness
hath compassion on the foolish simple man who knoweth no

better, and ordereth things for the best for him, and giveth him as much of the good things of God as he is able to receive. But as we have said afore, he findeth and receiveth not the True Good so long as he remaineth unchanged; for unless Self and Me depart, he will never find or receive it.

*　　　*　　　*

A TREATISE ON CHRISTIAN LIBERTY

MARTIN LUTHER

(1483-1546)

LUTHER WAS a person of strong contrasts. He was melancholic and jovial; superstitious and critical; humble and proud; charitable and intolerant; student and organizer; forgiving and spiteful; submissive and self-assertive; non-conformist and conformist; and scores of other conflicts.

In the midst of his tirades against the Mother Church and while still fuming against the strong hand of the ecclesiastical hierarchy he wrote one of his mildest and most irenic treatises called *The Freedom of the Christian Man*. This was in the latter part of the year 1520. Just some months before he had hurled his *The Babylonian Captivity* pamphlet against Catholic teaching, a devastating, radical and undercutting invective. A few weeks before he came out with his *Against the Execrable Bull of Antichrist* when he had heard that the authorities had moved in to crush him. In the *Freedom* pamphlet he addressed the pope with amazing respect and then moved on to pen one of the gentlest expressions of his entire career without any suggestion of rancor over the circumstances of the day and with a mellow exposition of the character of a really Christian person.

In this *Treatise* on Christian Liberty, then, we have Luther at his best, on the broad and constructive side. A Christian, he says, is not somebody who dispenses the wares of good deeds or is ethically correct but one who himself has become like Christ. He is a kind of religious enthusiast who has moved out beyond any rules of conduct, however lofty. He is the freely committed person who suffers in the mistakes of others although he is not responsible for such mistakes: like parents who suffer the punishments of wayward children, like benevolent teachers who suffer through a student's examination, like benefactors who agonize in seeing money wasted on some foolish project, like the physicians who would gladly assume the pains of some helpless young patient. When one has put on the robe of the Christian, one has lost himself in it. This is not ethics. This is mystical religion.

Christian freedom is bi-polar; it sets free and it sets up bondage. One is immune to all rules and at the same time one is burdened in participation of the needs of others. This is the portrait of Christ whose conscience was bound up with himself and yet felt the heavy obligations beyond himself. There are no appropriate rewards here; none are expected. The outgoing personality is under compulsion because his inner experience of freedom has translated him into a new dimension of living.

Editor

A TREATISE ON CHRISTIAN LIBERTY

MANY HAVE thought Christian faith to be an easy thing, and not a few have given it a place among the virtues. This they do because they have had no experience of it, and have never tasted what great virtue there is in faith. For it is impossible that anyone should write well of it or well understand what is correctly written of it, unless he has at some time tasted the courage faith gives a man when trials oppress him. But he who has had even a faint taste of it can never write, speak, meditate, or hear enough concerning it. For it is a living fountain springing up into life everlasting, as Christ calls it in John 4. For my part, although I have no wealth of faith to boast of and know how scant my store is, yet I hope that, driven about by great and various temptations, I have attained to a little faith, and that I can speak of it, if not more elegantly, certainly more to the point, than those literalists and all too subtle disputants have hitherto done, who have not even understood what they have written.

That I may make the way easier for the unlearned—for only

such do I serve—I set down first these two propositions concerning the liberty and the bondage of the spirit:

A Christian man is a perfectly free lord of all, subject to none.

A Christian man is a perfectly dutiful servant of all, subject to all.

Although these two theses seem to contradict each other, yet, if they should be found to fit together they would serve our purpose beautifully. For they are both Paul's own, who says, in 1 Corinthians 9, "Whereas I was free, I made myself the servant of all," and Romans 8, "Owe no man anything, but to love one another." Now love by its very nature is ready to serve and to be subject to him who is loved. So Christ, although Lord of all, was made of a woman, made under the law, and hence was at the same time free and a servant, at the same time in the form of God and in the form of a servant.

Let us start, however, with something more remote from our subject, but more obvious. Man has a twofold nature, a spiritual and a bodily. According to the spiritual nature, which men call the soul, he is called a spiritual, or inner, or new man; according to the bodily nature, which men call the flesh, he is called a carnal, or outward, or old man, of whom the Apostle writes, in 2 Corinthians 4, "Though our outward man is corrupted yet the inward man is renewed day by day." Because of this diversity of nature the Scriptures assert contradictory things of the same man, since these two men in the same man contradict each other, since the flesh lusteth against the spirit and the spirit against the flesh (Galatians 5).

First, let us contemplate the inward man, to see how a righteous, free, and truly Christian man, that is, a new, spiritual, inward man, comes into being. It is evident that no external thing, whatsoever it be, has any influence whatever in producing Christian righteousness or liberty, nor in producing unrighteousness or bondage. A simple argument will furnish the proof. What can it profit the soul if the body fare well, be free and active, eat, drink, and do as it pleases? For in these things even the most godless slaves of all the vices fare well. On the other hand, how will ill health or imprisonment or hunger or thirst or any other external misfortune hurt the soul? With these things even the most godly men are afflicted, and those who because of a clear conscience are most free. None of these things touch either the liberty or the bondage of the soul. The soul receives no benefit if the body is adorned with the sacred robes of the priesthood, or dwells in sacred places, or is occupied with sacred duties, or prays, fasts, abstains from certain kinds of food, or does any work whatsoever that can be done by the body and in the body. The righteousness and the freedom of the soul demand something far different, since the things which have been mentioned could be done by any wicked man, and such works produce nothing but hypocrites. On the other hand, it will not hurt the soul if the body is clothed in secular dress, dwells in unconsecrated places, eats and drinks as others do, does not pray aloud, and neglects to do all the things mentioned above, which hypocrites can do.

Further, to put aside all manner of works, even contemplation, meditation, and all that the soul can do, avail nothing. One thing and one only is necessary for Christian life, righteousness, and liberty. That one thing is the most holy Word of God, the Gospel of Christ, as he says, John 11, "I am the resurrection and the life: he that believeth in me shall not die forever"; and John 8, "If the Son shall make you free, you shall be free indeed"; and Matthew 4, "Not in bread alone doth man live; but in every word that proceedeth from the mouth of God." Let us then consider it certain and conclusively established that the soul can do without all things except the Word of God, and that where this is not there is no help for the soul in anything else whatever. But if it has the Word it is rich and lacks nothing, since this Word is the Word of life, of truth, of light, of peace, of righteousness, of salvation, of joy, of liberty, of wisdom, of power, of grace, of glory, and of every blessing beyond our power to estimate. This is why the prophet in the entire One Hundred and Nineteenth Psalm, and in many other places of Scripture, with so many sighs yearns after the Word of God and applies so many names to it. On the other hand, there is no more terrible plague with which the wrath of God can smite men than a famine of the hearing of His Word, as He says in Amos, just as there is no greater mercy than when He sends forth His Word, as we read in Psalm 107, "He sent His word and healed them, and delivered them from their destructions." Nor was

Christ sent into the world for any other ministry but that of
the Word, and the whole spiritual estate, apostles, bishops and
all the priests, has been called and instituted only for the ministry of the Word.

You ask, "What then is this Word of God, and how shall
it be used, since there are so many words of God?" I answer,
the Apostle explains that in Romans 1. The Word is the
Gospel of God concerning His Son, who was made flesh, suffered,
rose from the dead, and was glorified through the Spirit who
sanctifies. For to preach Christ means to feed the soul, to make
it righteous, to set it free, and to save it, if it believe the preaching. For faith alone is the saving and efficacious use of the
Word of God (Romans 10). "If thou confess with thy mouth
that Jesus is Lord, and believe with thy heart that God hath
raised Him up from the dead, thou shalt be saved"; and again,
"The end of the law is Christ, unto righteousness to everyone
that believeth"; and, in Romans 1, "The just shall live by his
faith." The Word of God cannot be received and cherished by
any works whatever, but only by faith. Hence it is clear that,
as the soul needs only the Word for its life and righteousness, so it is justified by faith alone and not by any works;
for if it could be justified by anything else, it would not need
the Word, and therefore it would not need faith. But this faith
cannot at all exist in connection with works, that is to say, if
you at the same time claim to be justified by works, whatever
their character; for that would be to halt between two sides, to
worship Baal and to kiss the hand, which, as Job says, is a very
great iniquity. Therefore the moment you begin to believe, you
learn that all things in you are altogether blameworthy, sinful,
and damnable, as Romans 3 says, "For all have sinned and lack
the glory of God"; and again, "There is none just, there is none
that doeth good, all have turned out of the way: they are become
unprofitable together." When you have learned this, you will
know that you need Christ, who suffered and rose again for you,
that, believing in Him, you may through this faith become a new
man, in that all your sins are forgiven, and you are justified
by the merits of another, namely, of Christ alone.

Since, therefore, this faith can rule only in the inward man,
as Romans 10 says, "With the heart we believe unto righteous-

ness"; and since faith alone justifies, it is clear that the inward man cannot be justified, made free, and be saved by any outward work or dealing whatsoever, and that works, whatever their character, have nothing to do with this inward man. On the other hand, only ungodliness and unbelief of heart, and no outward work, make him guilty and a damnable servant of sin. Wherefore it ought to be the first concern of every Christian to lay aside all trust in works, and more and more to strengthen faith alone, and through faith to grow in the knowledge, not of works, but of Christ Jesus, who suffered and rose for him, as Peter teaches, in the last chapter of his first Epistle; since no other work makes a Christian. Thus when the Jews asked Christ, John 6, what they should do that they might work the works of God, He brushed aside the multitude of works in which He saw that they abounded, and enjoined upon them a single work, saying, "This is the work of God, that you believe in Him whom He hath sent. For Him hath God the Father sealed."

Hence true faith in Christ is a treasure beyond comparison, which brings with it all salvation and saves from every evil, as Christ says in the last chapter of Mark, "He that believeth and is baptized, shall be saved; but he that believeth not, shall be condemned." This treasure Isaiah beheld and foretold in Chapter 10, "The Lord shall make an abridged and consuming word upon the land, and the consumption abridged shall overflow with righteousness"; as if he said, "Faith, which is a brief and perfect fulfillment of the law, shall fill believers with so great righteousness that they shall need nothing more for their righteousness." So also Paul says, Romans 10, "With the heart we believe unto righteousness."

Should you ask how it comes that faith alone justifies and without works offers us such a treasury of great benefits, when so many works, ceremonies, and laws are prescribed in the Scriptures, I answer: First of all, remember what has been said: faith alone, without works, justifies, makes free and saves, as we shall later make still more clear. Here we must point out that all the Scriptures of God are divided into two parts—commands and promises. The commands indeed teach things that are good, but the things taught are not done as soon as taught; for the commands show us what we ought to do, but do not give us the power to do it; they are intended to teach a man to know himself, that through them he may recognize his inability to do good and may despair of his powers. That is why they are called and are the Old Testament. For example: "Thou shalt not covet" is a command which convicts us all of being sinners, since no one is able to avoid coveting, however much he may struggle against it. Therefore, in order not to covet, and to fulfill the command, a man is compelled to despair of himself, and to seek elsewhere and from someone else the help which he does not find in himself, as is said in Hosea, "Destruction is thy own, O Israel: thy help is only in Me." And as we fare with this one command, so we fare with all; for it is equally impossible for us to keep any of them.

But when a man through the commands has learned to know his weakness, and has become troubled as to how he may satisfy the law, since the law must be fulfilled so that not a jot or tittle shall perish, otherwise man will be condemned without hope; then, being truly humbled and reduced to nothing in his own eyes, he finds in himself no means of justification and salvation. Here the second part of the Scriptures stands ready—the promises of God, which declare the glory of God and say, "If you wish to fulfill the law, and not to covet, as the law demands, come, believe in Christ, in whom grace, righteousness, peace, liberty and all things are promised you; if you believe you shall have all, if you believe not you shall lack all." For what is impossible for you in all the works of the law, many as they are, but all useless, you will accomplish in a short and easy way through faith. For God our Father has made all things depend on faith, so that whoever has faith, shall have all, and whoever has it not, shall have nothing. "For He has concluded all under belief, that He might have mercy on all," Romans 11. Thus the promises of God give what the commands of God ask, and fulfill what the law prescribes, that all things may be of God alone, both the commands and the fulfilling of the commands. He alone commands, He also alone fulfills. Therefore the promises of God belong to the New Testament, nay, they are the New Testament.

And since these promises of God are holy, true, righteous, free and peaceful words, full of all goodness, it comes to pass that the soul which clings to them with a firm faith is so united with them, nay, altogether taken up into them, that it not only shares in all their power, but is saturated and made drunken with it. For if a touch of Christ healed, how much more will this most tender touch in the spirit, rather this absorbing of the Word, communicate to the soul all things that are the Word's. This, then, is how through faith alone without works the soul is justified by the Word of God, sanctified, made true and peaceful and free, filled with every blessing and made truly a child of God, as John 1 says, "To them gave he power to become the sons of God, even to them that believe on his name."

From what has been said it is easily seen whence faith has such great power, and why no good work nor all good works together can equal it: no work can cling to the Word of God nor be in the soul; in the soul faith alone and the Word have sway. As the Word is, so it makes the soul, as heated iron glows like fire because of the union of fire with it. It is clear then that a Christian man has in his faith all that he needs, and needs no works to justify him. And if he has no need of works, neither does he need the law; and if he has no need of the law, surely he is free from the law, and it is true, "the law is not made for a righteous man." And this is that Christian liberty, even our faith, which does not indeed cause us to live in idleness or in wickedness, but makes the law and works unnecessary for any man's righteousness and salvation.

This is the first power of faith. Let us now examine the second also. For it is a further function of faith, that whom it trusts it also honors with the most reverent and high regard, since it considers him truthful and trustworthy. For there is no other honor equal to the estimate of truthfulness and right-eousness with which we honor him whom we trust. Or could we ascribe to a man anything greater than truthfulness, and right-eousness, and perfect goodness? On the other hand, there is no way in which we can show greater contempt for a man than to regard him as false and wicked and to suspect him, as we do when we do not trust him. So when the soul firmly trusts God's promises, it regards Him as truthful and righteous, than which nothing more excellent can be ascribed to God. This is the very highest worship of God, that we ascribe to Him truthfulness, righteousness, and whatever else ought to be ascribed to one who is trusted. Then the soul consents to all His will, then it hallows His name and suffers itself to be dealt with according to God's good pleasure, because, clinging to God's promises, it does not doubt that He, who is true, just and wise, will do, dispose, and provide all things well. And is not such a soul, by this faith, in all things most obedient to God? What commandment is there that such obedience has not abundantly fulfilled? What more complete fulfillment is there than obedience in all things? But this obedience is not rendered by works, but by faith alone. On the other hand, what greater rebellion against God, what greater wickedness, what greater contempt of God is there than not believing His promises? For what is this but to make God a liar or to doubt that He is truthful?—that is, to ascribe truthfulness to one's self, but to God lying and vanity? Does not a man who does this deny God, and in his heart set up himself as his own idol? Then of what avail are works done in such wickedness, even if they were the works of angels and apostles? Rightly, therefore, has God concluded all—not in anger or lust, but in unbelief; so that they who imagine that they are fulfilling the law by doing the works of chastity and mercy required by the law (the civil and human virtues) might not be confident that they will be saved; they are included under the sin of unbelief, and must either seek mercy or be justly condemned.

But when God sees that we count Him to be true, and by the faith of our heart pay Him the great honor which is due Him, He in turn does us the great honor of counting us true and righteous for our faith's sake. For faith works truth and righteousness by giving to God what belongs to Him; therefore, God in turn gives glory to our righteousness. It is true and just that God is truthful and just, and to count Him and confess Him so is to be truthful and just. So in 1 Samuel 2, He says, "Them that honor me, I will honor, and they that despise me shall be lightly esteemed." So Paul says in Romans 4, that Abraham's faith was counted unto him for righteousness, because by it he most perfectly gave glory to God, and that for the same reason our faith shall be counted unto us for righteousness if we believe.

The third incomparable benefit of faith is this, that it unites the soul with Christ as a bride is united with her bridegroom. And by this mystery, as the Apostle teaches Christ and the soul become one flesh. And if they are one flesh and there is between them a true marriage, nay, by far the most perfect of all marriages, since human marriages are but frail types of this one true marriage, it follows that all they have they have in common, the good as well as the evil, so that the believing soul can boast of and glory in whatever Christ has as if it were its own, and whatever the soul has Christ claims as His own. Let us compare these and we shall see things that cannot be estimated. Christ is full of grace, life, and salvation; the soul is full of sins, death, and condemnation. Now let faith come between them, and it shall come to pass that sins, death, and hell are Christ's, and grace, life, and salvation are the soul's. For it behooves Him, if He is a bridegroom, to take upon Himself the things which are His bride's, and to bestow upon her the things that are His. For if He gives her His body and His very self, how shall He not give her all that is His? And if He takes the body of the bride, how shall He not take all that is hers?

*   *   *

Who, then, can fully appreciate what this royal marriage means? Who can understand the riches of the glory of this grace? Here this rich and godly Bridegroom, Christ, marries this poor, wicked harlot, redeems her from all her evil and adorns her with all His good. It is now impossible that her sins should destroy her, since they are laid upon Christ and swallowed up in Him, and she has that righteousness in Christ her husband of which she may boast as of her own, and which she can confidently set against all her sins in the face of death and hell, and say, "If I have sinned, yet my Christ, in Whom I believe, has not sinned, and all His is mine, and all mine is His"—as the bride in the Song of Solomon says, "My beloved is mine, and I am his." This is what Paul means when he says, in 1 Corinthians 15, "Thanks be to God, which giveth us the victory through our Lord Jesus Christ"—that is, the victory over sin and death, as he there says, "The sting of death is sin, and the strength of sin is the law."

From this you see once more why so much is ascribed to faith, that it alone may fulfill the law and justify without works. You see that the First Commandment, which says, "Thou shalt worship one God," is fulfilled by faith alone. For though you were nothing but good works from the sole of your foot to the crown of your head, yet you would not be righteous, nor worship God, nor fulfill the First Commandment, since God cannot be worshiped unless you ascribe to Him the glory of truthfulness and of all goodness, which is due Him. And this cannot be done by works, but only by the faith of the heart. For not by the doing of works, but by believing, do we glorify God and acknowledge that He is truthful. Therefore, faith alone is the righteousness of a Christian man and the fulfilling of all the commandments. For he who fulfills the First, has no difficulty in fulfilling all the rest. But works, being insensate things, cannot glorify God, although they can, if faith be present, be done to the glory of God. At present, however, we are not inquiring what works and what sort of works are done, but who it is that does them, who glorifies God and brings forth the works. This is faith which dwells in the heart, and is the head and substance of all our righteousness. Hence, it is a blind and dangerous doctrine which teaches that the commandments must be fulfilled by works. The commandments must be fulfilled before any works can be done, and the works proceed from the fulfillment of the commandments, as we shall hear.

* * *

Hence we are all priests and kings in Christ, as many as believe on Christ, as 1 Peter 2 says, "Ye are a chosen generation, a peculiar people, a royal priesthood and priestly kingdom, that ye should show forth the virtues of him who hath called you out of darkness into his marvelous light."

This priesthood and kingship we explain as follows: First, as to the kingship, every Christian is by faith so exalted above all things that by a spiritual power he is lord of all things without exception, so that nothing can do him any harm whatever, nay, all things are made subject to him and compelled to serve him to his salvation. Thus Paul says in Romans 8, "All things work together for good to them who are called." And, in 1 Corinthians 3, "All things are yours, whether life or death, or things present or things to come, and ye are Christ's." Not as if every Christian were set over all things, to possess and control them by physical power—a madness with which some churchmen are afflicted—for such power belongs to kings, princes, and men on earth. Our ordinary experiences in life show us that we are subjected to all, suffer many things and even die; nay, the more Christian a man is, the more evils, sufferings, and deaths is he made subject to, as we see in Christ the first-born Prince Himself, and in all His brethren, the saints. The power of which we speak is spiritual; it rules in the midst of enemies, and is mighty in the midst of oppression, which means nothing else than that strength is made perfect in weakness, and that in all things I can find profit unto salvation, so that the cross and death itself are compelled to serve me and to work together with me for my salvation. This is a splendid prerogative and hard to attain, and a true omnipotent power, a spiritual dominion, in which there is nothing so good and nothing so evil, but that it shall work together for good to me, if only I believe. And yet, since faith alone suffices for salvation, I have need of nothing, except that faith exercise the power and dominion of its own liberty. Lo, this is the inestimable power and liberty of Christians.

Not only are we the freest of kings, we are also priests forever, which is far more excellent than being kings, because as priests we are worthy to appear before God to pray for others and to teach one another the things of God. For these are the functions of priests, and cannot be granted to any unbeliever. Thus Christ has obtained for us, if we believe on Him, that we are not only His brethren, co-heirs and fellow-kings with Him, but also fellow-priests with Him, who may boldly come into the presence of God in the spirit of faith and cry, "Abba, Father!" pray for one another and do all things which we see done and prefigured in the outward and visible works of priests. But he who does not believe is not served by anything, nor does anything work for good to him, but he himself is a servant of all, and all things become evils to him, because he wickedly uses them to his own profit and not to the glory of God. And so he is no priest, but a profane man, whose prayer becomes sin and never comes into the presence of God, because God does not hear sinners. Who then can comprehend the lofty dignity of the Christian? Through his kingly power he rules over all things, death, life, and sin, and through his priestly glory is all-powerful with God, because God does the things which he asks and desires, as it is written, "He will fulfill the desire of them that fear Him; He also will hear their cry, and will save them." To this glory a man attains, surely not by any works of his, but by faith alone.

From this anyone can clearly see how a Christian man is free from all things and over all things, so that he needs no works to make him righteous and to save him, since faith alone confers all these things abundantly. But should he grow so foolish as to presume to become righteous, free, saved, and a Christian by means of some good work, he would on the instant lose faith and all its benefits: a foolishness aptly illustrated in the fable of the dog who runs along a stream with a piece of meat in his mouth, and, deceived by the reflection of the meat in the water, opens his mouth to snap at it, and so loses both the meat and the reflection.

You will ask, "If all who are in the Church are priests, how do those whom we now call priests differ from laymen?" I answer: "Injustice is done those words, 'priest,' 'cleric,' 'spiritual,' 'ecclesiastic,' when they are transferred from all other Christians to those few who are now by a mischievous usage called 'ecclesiastics.' For Holy Scripture makes no distinction between them, except that it gives the name 'ministers,' 'servants,' 'stewards,' to those who are now proudly called popes, bishops, and lords, and who should by the ministry of the Word serve others and teach them the faith of Christ and the liberty of believers. For although we are all equally priests, yet we cannot all publicly minister and teach, nor ought we if we could." Thus Paul writes in 1 Corinthians 4, "Let a man so account of us, as of the ministers of Christ, and stewards of the mysteries of God."

But that stewardship has now been developed into so great a pomp of power and so terrible a tyranny, that no heathen empire or earthly power can be compared with it, just as if lay-

men were not also Christians. Through this perversion the
knowledge of Christian grace, faith, liberty, and of Christ Himself has altogether perished, and its place has been taken by an
unbearable bondage of human words and laws, until we have
become, as the Lamentations of Jeremiah say, servants of the
vilest men on earth, who abuse our misfortune to serve only
their base and shameless will.

To return to our purpose, I believe it has now become clear
that it is not enough, nor is it Christian, to preach the works,
life, and words of Christ as historical facts, as if the knowledge
of these would suffice for the conduct of life, although this is
the fashion of those who must today be regarded as our best
preachers; and far less is it enough or Christian to say nothing
at all about Christ and to teach instead the laws of men and
the decrees of the Fathers. And now there are not a few who
preach Christ and read about Him that they may move men's
affections to sympathy with Christ, to anger against the Jews
and such like childish and womanish nonsense. Rather ought
Christ to be preached to the end that faith in Him may be
established, that He may not only be Christ, but be Christ for
thee and for me, and that what is said of Him and what His
Name denotes may be effectual in us. And such faith is produced and preserved in us by preaching why Christ came, what
He brought and bestowed, what benefit it is to us to accept
Him. This is done when that Christian liberty which He bestows
is rightly taught, and we are told in what way we who are
Christians are all kings and priests and so are lords of all, and
may firmly believe that whatever we have done is pleasing and
acceptable in the sight of God, as I have said.

*   *   *

Let this suffice concerning the inward man, his liberty and
its source, the righteousness of faith, which needs neither laws
nor good works, nay, is rather injured by them, if a man trusts
that he is justified by them.

Now let us turn to the second part, to the outward man.
Here we shall answer all those who, misled by the word "faith"
and by all that has been said, now say: "If faith does all things

and is alone sufficient unto righteousness, why then are good works commanded? We will take our ease and do no works, and be content with faith." I answer, Not so, ye wicked men, not so. That would indeed be proper, if we were wholly inward and perfectly spiritual men; but such we shall be only at the last day, the day of the resurrection of the dead. As long as we live in the flesh we only begin and make some progress in that which shall be perfected in the future life. For this reason the Apostle, in Romans 8, calls all that we attain in this life "the first fruits" of the spirit, because, forsooth, we shall receive the greater portion, even the fullness of the spirit, in the future. This is the place for that which was said above, that a Christian man is the servant of all and made subject to all. For in so far as he is free he does no works, but in so far as he is a servant he does all manner of works. How this is possible we shall see.

Although, as I have said, a man is abundantly justified by faith inwardly, in his spirit, and so has all that he ought to have, except in so far as this faith and riches must grow from day to day even unto the future life: yet he remains in this mortal life on earth, and in this life he must needs govern his own body and have dealings with men. Here the works begin; here a man cannot take his ease; here he must, indeed, take care to discipline his body by fastings, watchings, labors, and other reasonable discipline, and to make it subject to the spirit so that it will obey and conform to the inward man and to faith, and not revolt against faith and hinder the inward man, as it is the body's nature to do if it be not held in check. For the inward man, who by faith is created in the likeness of God, is both joyful and happy because of Christ in whom so many benefits are conferred upon him, and therefore it is his one occupation to serve God joyfully and for naught, in love that is not constrained.

While he is doing this, lo, he meets a contrary will in his own flesh, which strives to serve the world and to seek its own advantage. This the spirit of faith cannot tolerate, and with joyful zeal it attempts to put the body under and to hold it in check, as Paul says in Romans 7, "I delight in the law of God after the inward man; but I see another law in my members, warring against the law of my mind, and bringing me into captivity to the law of sin"; and, in another place, "I keep under my body, and bring it into subjection: lest by any means, when I have preached to others, I myself should be a castaway," and in Galatians, "They that are Christ's have crucified the flesh with its lusts."

In doing these works, however, we must not think that a man is justified before God by them: for that erroneous opinion faith, which alone is righteousness before God, cannot endure; but we must think that these works reduce the body to subjection and purify it of its evil lusts, and our whole purpose is to be directed only toward the driving out of lusts. For since by faith the soul is cleansed and made a lover of God, it desires that all things, and especially its own body, shall be as pure as itself, so that all things may join with it in loving and praising God. Hence a man cannot be idle, because the need of his body drives him and he is compelled to do many good works to reduce it to subjection. Nevertheless the works themselves do not justify him before God, but he does the works out of spontaneous love in obedience to God, and considers nothing except the approval of God, whom he would in all things most scrupulously obey.

In this way everyone will easily be able to learn for himself the limit and discretion, as they say, of his bodily castigations: for he will fast, watch and labor as much as he finds sufficient to repress the lasciviousness and lust of his body. But they who presume to be justified by works do not regard the mortifying of the lusts, but only the works themselves, and think that if only they have done as many and as great works as are possible, they have done well, and have become righteousness; at times they even addle their brains and destroy, or at least render useless, their natural strength with their works. This is the height of folly, and utter ignorance of Christian life and faith, that a man should seek to be justified and saved by works and without faith.

*   *   *

These two sayings, therefore, are true: "Good works do not make a good man, but a good man does good works; evil works do not make a wicked man, but a wicked man does evil works"; so that it is always necessary that the "substance" or person itself be good before there can be any good works, and that good works follow and proceed from the good person, as Christ also says, "A corrupt tree does not bring forth good fruit, a good tree does not bring forth evil fruit." It is clear that the fruits do not bear the tree, nor does the tree grow on the fruits, but, on the contrary, the trees bear the fruits and the fruits grow on the trees. As it is necessary, therefore, that the trees must exist before their fruits, and the fruits do not make trees either good or corrupt, but rather as the trees are so are the fruits they bear; so the person of a man must needs first be good or wicked before he does a good or a wicked work, and his works do not make him good or wicked, but he himself makes his works either good or wicked.

Illustrations of the same truth can be seen in all trades. A good or a bad house does not make a good or a bad builder, but a good or a bad builder makes a bad or a good house. And in general, the work never makes the workman like itself, but the workman makes the work like himself. So it is also with the works of man: as the man is, whether believer or unbeliever, so also is his work—good, if it was done in faith; wicked, if it was done in unbelief. But the converse is not true, that the work makes the man either a believer or an unbeliever. For as works do not make a man a believer, so also they do not make him righteous. But as faith makes a man a believer and righteous, so faith also does good works. Since, then, works justify no one, and a man must be righteous before he does a good work, it is very evident that it is faith alone which, because of the pure mercy of God through Christ and in His Word, worthily and sufficiently justifies and saves the person, and a Christian man has no need of any work or of any law in order to be saved, since through faith he is free from every law and does all that he does out of pure liberty and freely, seeking neither benefit nor salvation, since he already abounds in all things and is saved through the grace of God because of his faith, and now seeks only to please God.

Furthermore, no good work helps an unbeliever, so as to justify or save him. And, on the other hand, no evil work makes him wicked or damns him, but the unbelief which makes the person and the tree evil, does the evil and damnable works. Hence when a man is made good or evil, this is effected not by the works, but by faith or unbelief, as the Wise Man says, "This is the beginning of sin, that a man falls away from God," which happens when he does not believe. And Paul, Hebrews 11, says, "He that cometh to God must believe." And Christ says the same: "Either make the tree good and his fruit good; or else make the tree corrupt and his fruit corrupt," as if He would say, "Let him who would have good fruit begin by planting a good tree." So let him who would do good works not begin with the doing of works, but with believing, which makes the person good. For nothing makes a man good except faith, nor evil except unbelief.

It is indeed true that in the sight of men a man is made good or evil by his works, but this being made good or evil is no more than that he who is good or evil is pointed out and known as such; as Christ says, in Matthew 7, "By their fruits ye shall know them." But all this remains on the surface, and very many have been deceived by this outward appearance and have presumed to write and teach concerning good works by which we may be justified, without even mentioning faith; they go their way, always being deceived and deceiving, advancing, indeed, but into a worse state, blind leaders of the blind, wearying themselves with many works, and yet never attaining to true righteousness. Of such Paul says, in 2 Timothy 3, "Having the form of godliness, but denying its power, always learning and never attaining to the knowledge of the truth."

He, therefore, who does not wish to go astray with those blind men, must look beyond works, and laws and doctrines about works; nay, turning his eyes from works, he must look upon the person, and ask how that is justified. For the person is justified and saved not by works nor by laws, but by the Word of God, that is, by the promise of His grace, and by faith, that the glory may remain God's, who saved us not by works of righteousness which we have done, but according to His mercy by the word of His grace, when we believed.

From this it is easy to know in how far good works are to be rejected or not, and by what standard all the teachings of men concerning works are to be interpreted. If works are sought after as a means to righteousness, are burdened with this perverse leviathan and are done under the false impression that through them you are justified, they are made necessary and freedom and faith are destroyed; and this addition to them makes them to be no longer good, but truly damnable works. For they are not free, and they blaspheme the grace of God, since to justify and to save by faith belongs to the grace of God alone. What the works have no power to do, they yet, by a godless presumption, through this folly of ours, pretend to do, and thus violently force themselves into the office and the glory of grace. We do not, therefore, reject good works; on the contrary, we cherish and teach them as much as possible. We do not condemn them for their own sake, but because of this godless addition to them and the perverse idea that righteousness is to be sought through them; for that makes them appear good outwardly, when in truth they are not good; they deceive men and lead men to deceive each other, like ravening wolves in sheep's clothing.

But this leviathan and perverse notion concerning works is insuperable where sincere faith is wanting. Those work-saints cannot get rid of it unless faith, its destroyer, come and rule in their hearts. Nature of itself cannot drive it out, nor even recognize it, but rather regards it as a mark of the most holy will. And if the influence of custom be added and confirm this perverseness of nature, as wicked magisters have caused it to do, it becomes an incurable evil, and leads astray and destroys countless men beyond all hope of restoration. Therefore, although it is good to preach and write about penitence, confession and satisfaction, if we stop with that and do not go on to teach about faith, our teaching is unquestionably deceitful and devilish.

*   *   *

As an example of such a life the Apostle cites Christ, saying, "Let this mind be in you, which was also in Christ Jesus, who, being in the form of God, thought it not robbery to be equal with God: but made himself of no reputation, and took upon him the form of a servant, and was made in the likeness of men: and being found in fashion as a man, he became obedient unto death." This salutary word of the Apostle has been obscured for us by those who have not at all understood the Apostle's words, "form of God," "form of a servant," "fashion," "likeness of men," and have applied them to the divine and the human nature. Paul means this: Although Christ was filled with the form of God and rich in all good things, so that He needed no work and no suffering to make Him righteous and saved (for He had all this always from the beginning), yet He was not puffed up by them, nor did He lift Himself up above us and assume power over us, although He could rightly have done so; but, on the contrary, He so lived, labored, worked, suffered and died, that He might be like other men, and in fashion and in actions be nothing else than a man, just as if He had need of all these things and had nothing of the form of God. But He did all this for our sake, that He might serve us, and that all things He accomplished in this form of a servant might become ours.

So a Christian, like Christ, his Head, is filled and made rich by faith, and should be content with this form of God which he has obtained by faith; only, as I have said, he ought to increase this faith until it be made perfect. For this faith is his life, his righteousness, and his salvation: it saves him and makes him acceptable, and bestows upon him all things that are Christ's, as has been said above, and as Paul asserts in Galatians 2, when he says, "And the life which I now live in the flesh, I live by the faith of the Son of God." Although the Christian is thus free from all works, he ought in this liberty to empty himself, to take upon himself the form of a servant, to be made in the likeness of men, to be found in fashion as a man, and to serve, help and in every way deal with his neighbor as he sees that God through Christ has dealt and still deals with himself. And this he should do freely, having regard to nothing except the divine approval. He ought to think: "Though I am an unworthy and condemned man, my God has given me in Christ all the riches of righteousness and salvation without any merit on my part, out of pure, free mercy, so that henceforth I need nothing whatever except faith which believes that this is true. Why should I not therefore freely, joyfully, with all my heart, and with an eager will, do all things which I know are pleasing and acceptable to such a Father, who has overwhelmed me with His inestimable riches? I will therefore give myself as a Christ to my neighbor, just as Christ offered Himself to me; I will do nothing in this life except what I see is necessary, profitable and salutary to my neighbor, since through faith I have an abundance of all good things in Christ."

Lo, thus from faith flow forth love and joy in the Lord, and from love a joyful, willing and free mind that serves one's neighbor willingly and takes no account of gratitude or ingratitude, of praise or blame, of gain or loss. For a man does not serve that he may put men under obligations, he does not distinguish between friends and enemies, nor does he anticipate their thankfulness or unthankfulness; but most freely and most willingly he spends himself and all that he has, whether he waste all on the thankless or whether he gain a reward. For as his Father does, distributing all things to all men richly and freely, causing His sun to rise upon the good and upon the evil, so also the son does all things and suffers all things with that freely bestowing joy which is his delight when through Christ he sees it in God, the dispenser of such great benefits.

Therefore, if we recognize the great and precious things which are given us, as Paul says, there will be shed abroad in our hearts by the Holy Ghost the love which makes us free, joyful, almighty workers and conquerors over all tribulations, servants of our neighbors and yet lords of all. But for those who do not recognize the gifts bestowed upon them through Christ, Christ has been born in vain; they go their way with their works, and shall never come to taste or to feel those things. Just as our neighbor is in need and lacks that in which we abound, so we also have been in need before God and have lacked His mercy. Hence, as our heavenly Father has in Christ freely come to our help, we also ought freely to help our neighbor through our body and its works, and each should become as it were a Christ to the other, that we may be Christs to one another and Christ may be the same in all; that is, that we may be truly Christians.

Who then can comprehend the riches and the glory of the Christian life? It can do all things, and has all things, and lacks nothing; it is lord over sin, death and hell, and yet at the same time it serves, ministers to, and benefits all men. But, alas, in our day this life is unknown throughout the world; it is neither preached about nor sought after; we are altogether ignorant of our own name and do not know why we are Christians or bear the name of Christians. Surely we are so named after Christ, not because He is absent from us, but because He dwells in us, that is, because we believe on Him and are Christs one to another and do to our neighbors as Christ does to us. But in our day we are taught by the doctrine of men to seek naught but merits, rewards and the things that are ours; of Christ we have made only a taskmaster far more harsh than Moses.

*   *   *

Of the same nature are the precepts which Paul gives, in Romans 13 and Titus 3, that Christians should be subject to the powers that be, and be ready to do every good work, not that they shall in this way be justified, since they already are righteous through faith, but that in the liberty of the Spirit they shall by so doing serve others and the powers themselves, and obey their will freely and out of love. Of this nature should be the works of all colleges, monasteries, and priests. Each one should do the works of his profession and position, not that by them he may strive after righteousness, but that through them he may keep under his body, be an example to others, who also need to keep under their bodies, and finally that by such works he may submit his will to that of others in the freedom of love. But very great care must always be taken that no man in a false confidence imagine that by such works he will be justified, or acquire merit or be saved; for this is the work of faith alone, as I have repeatedly said.

Anyone knowing this could easily and without danger find his way among those numberless mandates and precepts of pope, bishops, monasteries, churches, princes and magistrates, upon which some ignorant pastors insist as if they were necessary to righteousness and salvation, calling them "precepts of the Church," although they are nothing of the kind. For a Christian, as a free man, will say, "I will fast, pray, do this and that as men command, not because it is necessary to my righteousness or salvation; but that I may show due respect to the pope, the bishop, the community, some magistrate, or my neighbor, and give them an example, I will do and suffer all things, just as Christ did and suffered far more for me, although He needed nothing of it all for Himself, and was made under the law for my sake, although He was not under the law." And although tyrants do violence or injustice in making their demands, yet it will do no harm, so long as they demand nothing contrary to God.

From what has been said, everyone can pass a safe judgment on all works and laws and make a trustworthy distinction between them, and know who are the blind and ignorant pastors and who are the good and true. For any work that is not done solely for the purpose of keeping under the body or of serving one's neighbor, so long as he asks nothing contrary to God, is not good nor Christian. And for this reason I mightily fear that few or no colleges, monasteries, altars, and offices of the Church are really Christian in our day: no, nor the special fasts and prayers on certain saints' days either. I fear, I say, that in all these we seek only our own profit, thinking that through them our sins are purged away and that we find salvation in them. In this way Christian liberty perishes altogether. And this comes from our ignorance of Christian faith and of liberty.

This ignorance and suppression of liberty very many blind pastors take pains to encourage: they stir up and urge on their people in these practices by praising such works, puffing them up with their indulgences, and never teaching faith. But I would counsel you, if you wish to pray, fast or establish some foundation in the Church, take heed not to do it in order to obtain some benefit, whether temporal or eternal. For you would do injury to your faith, which alone offers you all things. Your one care should be that faith may increase, whether it be trained by works or by sufferings. Give your gifts freely and for nothing, that others may profit by them and fare well because of you and your goodness. In this way you shall be truly good and Christian. For of what benefit to you are the good works which you do not need for the keeping under of your body? Your faith is sufficient for you, through which God has given you all things.

See, according to this rule the good things we have from God should flow from one to the other and be common to all, so that everyone should "put on" his neighbor, and so conduct himself toward him as if he himself were in the other's place. From Christ they have flowed and are flowing into us: He has so "put on" us and acted for us as if He had been what we are. From us they flow on to those who have need of them, so that I should lay before God my faith and my righteousness that they may cover and intercede for the sins of my neighbor, which I take upon myself and so labor and serve in them as if they were my very own. For that is what Christ did for us. This is true love and the genuine rule of a Christian life. The love is true and genuine where there is true and genuine faith. Hence, the Apostle says of love in 1 Corinthians 13, that it seeketh not its own.

We conclude, therefore, that a Christian man lives not in himself, but in Christ and in his neighbor. Otherwise he is not a Christian. He lives in Christ through faith, in his neighbor through love; by faith he is caught up beyond himself into God, by love he sinks down beneath himself into his neighbor; yet he always remains in God and in His love, as Christ says in John 1, "Verily, I say unto you, Hereafter ye shall see heaven open, and the angels of God ascending and descending upon the Son of man."

*   *   *

Finally, something must be added for the sake of those for whom nothing can be so well said that they will not spoil it by misunderstanding it, though it is a question whether they will understand even what shall here be said. There are very many who, when they hear of this liberty of faith, immediately turn it into an occasion for the flesh, and think that now all things are allowed them. They want to show that they are free men and Christians only by despising and finding fault with ceremonies, traditions, and human laws; as if they were Christians because on stated days they do not fast or eat meat when others fast, or because they do not use the accustomed prayers, and with upturned nose scoff at the precepts of men, although they utterly disregard all else that pertains to the Christian religion. The extreme opposite of these are those who rely for their salvation solely on their reverent observance of ceremonies, as if they would be saved because on certain days they fast or abstain from meats, or pray certain prayers; these make a boast of the precepts of the Church and of the Fathers, and care not a fig for the things which are of the essence of our faith. Plainly, both are in error, because they neglect the weightier things which are necessary to salvation, and quarrel so noisily about those trifling and unnecessary matters.

How much better is the teaching of the Apostle Paul, who bids us take a middle course, and condemns both sides when he says, "Let not him that eateth despise him that eateth not; and let not him which eateth not judge him that eateth." Here you see that they who neglect and disparage ceremonies, not out of piety, but out of mere contempt, are reproved, since the Apostle teaches us not to despise them. Such men are puffed up by knowledge. On the other hand, he teaches those who insist on the ceremonies not to judge the others, for neither party acts toward the other according to the love that edifies. Wherefore, we ought here to listen to the Scriptures, which teach that we should not go aside to the right nor to the left, but follow the statutes of the Lord which are right, rejoicing the heart. For as a man is not righteous because he keeps and clings to the works and forms of the ceremonies, so also will a man not be counted righteous merely because he neglects and despises them.

Our faith in Christ does not free us from works, but from false opinions concerning works, that is, from the foolish presumption that justification is acquired by works. For faith redeems, corrects and preserves our consciences, so that we know that righteousness does not consist in works, although works neither can be nor ought to be wanting; just as we cannot be without food and drink and all the works of this mortal body, yet our righteousness is not in them, but in faith; and yet those works of the body are not to be despised or neglected on that account. In this world we are bound by the needs of our bodily life, but we are not righteous because of them. "My kingdom is not of this world," says Christ, but He does not say, "My kingdom is not here, that is, in this world." And Paul says, "Though we walk in the flesh, we do not war after the flesh," and in Galatians 2, "The life which I now live in the flesh, I live in the faith of the Son of God." Thus what we do, live, and are in works and in ceremonies, we do because of the necessities of this life and of the effort to rule our body; nevertheless we are righteous not in these, but in the faith of the Son of God.

* * *

In brief, as wealth is the test of poverty, business the test of faithfulness, honors the test of humility, feasts the test of temperance, pleasures the test of chastity, so ceremonies are the test of the righteousness of faith. "Can a man," says Solomon, "take fire in his bosom, and his clothes not be burned?" Yet, as a man must live in the midst of wealth, business, honors, pleasures and feasts, so also must he live in the midst of ceremonies, that is, in the midst of dangers. Nay, as infant boys need beyond all else to be cherished in the bosoms and by the hands of maidens to keep them from perishing, and yet when they are grown up their salvation is endangered if they associate with maidens, so the inexperienced and froward youth need to be restrained and trained by the iron bars of ceremonies, lest their unchecked ardor rush headlong into vice after vice. Yet it would be death for them to be always held in bondage to ceremonies, thinking that these justify them. They are rather to be taught that they have been so imprisoned in ceremonies, not that they should be made righteous or gain great merit by them, but that they might thus be kept from doing evil, and might be more easily instructed unto the righteousness of faith. Such instruction they would not endure if the impulsiveness of their youth were not restrained. Hence ceremonies are to be given the same place in the life of a Christian as models and plans have among builders and artisans. They are prepared not as permanent structures, but because without them nothing could be built or made. When the structure is completed they are laid aside. You see, they are not despised, rather, they are greatly sought after; but what we despised is the false estimate of them, since no one holds them to be the real and permanent structure. If any man were so egregiously foolish as to care for nothing all his life long except the most costly, careful, and persistent preparation of plans and models, and never to think of the structure itself, and were satisfied with his work in producing such plans and mere aids to work, and boasted of it, would not all men pity his insanity, and estimate that with what he has wasted something great might have been built? Thus we do not despise ceremonies and works, nay, we set great store by them; but we despise the false estimate placed upon works, in order that no one may think that they are true righteousness, as those hypocrites believe who spend and lose their whole lives in zeal for works, and never reach that for the sake of which he works are to be done; as the Apostle says, "ever learning and never able to come to the knowledge of the truth." For they seem to wish to build, they make their preparations, and yet they never build. Thus they remain caught in the form of godliness and do not attain unto its power. Meanwhile they are pleased with their efforts, and even dare to judge all others whom they do not see shining with a like show of works. Yet with the gifts of God which they have spent and abused in vain they might, if they had been filled with faith, have accomplished great things to the salvation of themselves and of others.

But since human nature and natural reason, as it is called, are by nature superstitious and ready to imagine, when laws and works are prescribed, that righteousness must be obtained through them; and further, since they are trained and confirmed in this opinion by the practice of all earthly lawgivers, it is impossible that they should of themselves escape from the slavery of works and come to a knowledge of the liberty of faith. Therefore there is need of the prayer that the Lord may give us and make us *theodidacti,* that is, taught of God, and Himself, as He has promised, write His law in our hearts; otherwise there is no hope for us. For if He Himself does not teach our hearts this wisdom hidden in a mystery, nature can only condemn it and judge it to be heretical, because nature is offended by it and regards it as foolishness. So we see that it happened in olden times, in the case of the Apostles and prophets, and so godless and blind popes and their flatterers do to me and to those who are like me. May God at last be merciful to them and to us, and cause His face to shine upon us, that we may know His way upon earth, His salvation among all nations, God, who is blessed forever. Amen.

INSTITUTE OF THE CHRISTIAN RELIGION

JOHN CALVIN

(1509-1564)

THE *Institute of the Christian Religion (Institutio Christianae)*, published in 1536, has been regarded in wide circles as the Primer of Protestantism. Institute signifies instruction. It was written as a sort of text-book of the tenets of the Christian religion by the rising Reformation leader, appearing when its author was only twenty-seven years of age. The system of theology and polity which developed from Calvin's Scriptural interpretations became known as Calvinism, a major system in historic Protestant thought.

God is revealed—so said Calvin—in both nature and reason but supremely in the Holy Scriptures. Basic is the commitment to the total sovereignty of God (theocentrism). Since the Fall of Adam all mankind has become impotent to do the will of God and thus stands outside the orbit of the family of God. Man's salvation from this state, however, has been provided for in the holy wisdom and mercy of Deity, by a plan of redemption (ordained by Divine decree of election and reprobation) by means of Christ, God's Son, the Redeemer. The elect (without merit on their part) find it possible to do God's Will by Divine grace, living by faith in union with the Son of God. The church is not a visible organization but consists of those called to redemption (membership known only to God). The sacraments rightly administered and the Word of God rightly preached (together with proper discipline) are marks of a portion of the true visible church.

The *Institute* is divided into four Books, treating of the

knowledge of God the Creator, the knowledge of God the Redeemer, the reception of the grace in Christ, and the Holy
Catholic Church.

University trained (Paris), fugitive for his faith in France
and the Rhine cities, Calvin was persuaded to settle in Geneva
(1536) where he guided the Reformation already begun in
Switzerland. Banished for a period, he returned (1541) to
Geneva to become one of Protestantism's major figures in his
day and through his writings and forceful leadership a major
interpreter of the Reformed faith in the long centuries which
followed—even to our time.

Editor

INSTITUTE OF THE CHRISTIAN RELIGION

BOOK I

ON THE KNOWLEDGE OF GOD THE CREATOR

Chap. I, II, III

TRUE AND substantial wisdom consists principally of two parts:
the knowledge of God and the knowledge of ourselves. But while
these two branches of knowledge are so intimately connected,
which of them precedes and produces the other is not easy to
discover. For, in the first place, no man can take a survey of
himself but he must immediately turn to the contemplation of
God, in whom he "lives and moves,"[1] since it is evident that
the talents which we possess are not from ourselves and that our
very existence is nothing but a subsistence in God alone. These
bounties, distilling to us by drops from heaven, form, as it were,
so many streams conducting us to the fountainhead. Our poverty
conduces to a clearer display of the infinite fullness of God.
Especially, the miserable ruin into which we have been plunged
by the defection of the first man compels us to raise our eyes
toward heaven, not only as hungry and famished to seek thence
a supply for our wants, but, aroused with fear, to learn humility.

1. Acts 17. 2.

For, since man is subject to a world of miseries and has been spoiled of his divine array, this melancholy exposure discovers an immense mass of deformity; every one, therefore, must be so impressed with a consciousness of his own infelicity as to arrive at some knowledge of God. Thus a sense of our ignorance, vanity, poverty, infirmity, depravity, and corruption leads us to perceive and acknowledge that in the Lord alone are to be found true wisdom, solid strength, perfect goodness, and unspotted righteousness; and so by our imperfections we are excited to a consideration of the perfections of God. Nor can we really aspire toward him till we have begun to be displeased with ourselves. For who would not gladly rest satisfied with himself? Where is the man not actually absorbed in self-complacency while he remains unacquainted with his true situation, or content with his own endowments and ignorant or forgetful of his own misery? The knowledge of ourselves, therefore, is not only an incitement to seek after God, but likewise a considerable assistance toward finding him.

On the other hand, it is plain that no man can arrive at the true knowledge of himself without having first contemplated the divine character and then descended to the consideration of his own. For—such is the native pride of us all—we invariably esteem ourselves righteous, innocent, wise, and holy till we are convinced by clear proofs of our unrighteousness, turpitude, folly, and impurity. But we are never thus convinced while we confine our attention to ourselves and regard not the Lord, who is the only standard by which this judgment ought to be formed. Because, from our natural proneness to hypocrisy, any vain appearance of righteousness abundantly contents us instead of the reality; and, everything within and around us being exceedingly defiled, we are delighted with what is least so, as extremely pure, while we confine our reflections within the limits of human corruption. So the eye, accustomed to see nothing but black, judges that to be very white which is but whitish or perhaps brown. Indeed, the senses of our bodies may assist us in discovering how grossly we err in estimating the powers of the soul. For if at noonday we look either on the ground or at any surrounding objects, we conclude our vision to be very strong and piercing; but when we raise our eyes and steadily look at the sun, they are at once dazzled and confounded with such a blaze of brightness, and we are constrained to confess that our sight, so piercing in viewing terrestrial things, when directed to the sun is dimness itself. Thus also it happens in the consideration of our spiritual endowments. For as long as our views are bounded by the earth, perfectly content with our own righteousness, wisdom, and strength, we fondly flatter ourselves and fancy we are little less than demigods. But if we once elevate our thoughts to God and consider his nature and the consummate perfection of his righteousness, wisdom, and strength, to which we ought to be conformed—what before charmed us in ourselves under the false pretext of righteousness will soon be loathed as the greatest iniquity; what strangely deceived us under the title of wisdom will be despised as extreme folly; and what wore the appearance of strength will be proved to be most wretched impotence. So very remote from the divine purity is what seems in us the highest perfection.

Hence that horror and amazement with which the Scripture always represents the saints to have been impressed and disturbed on every discovery of the presence of God. For when we see those who before his appearance stood secure and firm so astonished and affrighted at the manifestation of his glory as to faint and almost expire through fear, we must infer that man is never sufficiently affected with a knowledge of his own meanness till he has compared himself with the divine majesty. Of this consternation we have frequent examples in the Judges and Prophets, so that it was a common expression among the Lord's people: "We shall die, because we have seen God."[1] Therefore the history of Job, to humble men with a consciousness of their pollution, impotence, and folly, derives its principal argument from a description of the divine purity, power, and wisdom. And not without reason. For we see how Abraham, the nearer he approached to behold the glory of the Lord, the more fully acknowledged himself to be but "dust and ashes";[2] and how Elias could not bear his approach without covering his face, his appearance is so formidable.[3] And what can man do, all vile and corrupt, when fear constrains even the cherubim themselves to veil their

1. Judg. 13. 22.
2. Gen. 18. 27.
3. I Kings 19. 13.

faces: This is what the prophet Isaiah speaks of: "The moon shall be confounded, and the sun ashamed, when the Lord of hosts shall reign"[1]—that is, when he shall make a fuller and nearer exhibition of his splendor, it shall eclipse the splendor of the brightest object besides. But though the knowledge of God and the knowledge of ourselves be intimately connected, the proper order of instruction requires us first to treat of the former and then to proceed to the discussion of the latter.

Chap. 2, I

BY THE knowledge of God, I intend not merely a notion that there is such a being, but also an acquaintance with whatever we ought to know concerning him conducing to his glory and our benefit. For we cannot with propriety say there is any knowledge of God where there is no religion or piety. I have no reference here to that species of knowledge by which men, lost and condemned in themselves, apprehend God the Redeemer in Christ the Mediator; but only to that first and simple knowledge to which the genuine order of nature would lead us if Adam had retained his innocence. For though in the present ruined state of human nature no man will ever perceive God to be a father or the author of salvation or in any respect propitious but as pacified by the mediation of Christ, yet it is one thing to understand that God our Maker supports us by his power, governs us by his providence, nourishes us by his goodness, and follows us with blessings of every kind, and another to embrace the grace of reconciliation proposed to us in Christ. Therefore, since God is first manifested, both in the structure of the world and in the general tenor of Scripture, simply as the Creator, and afterward reveals himself in the person of Christ as a Redeemer, hence arises a twofold knowledge of him, of which the former is first to be considered and the other will follow in its proper place. For though our mind cannot conceive of God without ascribing some worship to him, it will not be sufficient merely to apprehend that he is the only proper object of universal worship and adoration unless we are also persuaded that he

1. Isa. 6. 2; 24. 23.

is the fountain of all good and seek for none but in him. This I maintain not only because he sustains the universe, as he once made it, by his infinite power, governs it by his wisdom, preserves it by his goodness, and especially reigns over the human race in righteousness and judgment, exercising a merciful forbearance and defending them by his protection; but because there cannot be found the least particle of wisdom, light, righteousness, power, rectitude, or sincere truth which does not proceed from him and claim him for its author. We should, therefore, learn to expect and supplicate all these things from him and thankfully to acknowledge what he gives us. For this sense of the divine perfections is calculated to teach us piety, which produces religion. By piety I mean a reverence and love of God arising from a knowledge of his benefits. For, till men are sensible that they owe everything to God, that they are supported by his paternal care, that he is the author of all the blessings they enjoy, and that nothing should be sought independently of him, they will never voluntarily submit to his authority; they will never truly and cordially devote themselves to his service unless they rely upon him alone for true felicity.

*   *   *

Chap. 3, I

WE LAY it down as a position not to be controverted that the human mind, even by natural instinct, possesses some sense of a deity. For that no man might shelter himself under the pretext of ignorance, God has given to all some apprehension of his existence,[1] the memory of which he frequently and insensibly renews; so that, as men universally know that there is a God and that he is their Maker, they must be condemned by their own testimony for not having worshiped him and consecrated their lives to his service. If we seek for ignorance of a deity, it is nowhere more likely to be found than among tribes the most stupid and furthest from civilization. But, as the celebrated Cicero observes, there is no nation so barbarous, no race so savage, as not to be firmly persuaded of the being of a

1. Rom. 1. 20.

God.[1] Even those who in other respects appear to differ but little from brutes always retain some sense of religion, so fully are the minds of men possessed with this common principle, which is closely interwoven with their original composition. Now since there has never been a country or family, from the beginning of the world, totally destitute of religion, it is a tacit confession that some sense of the divinity is inscribed on every heart. Of this opinion idolatry itself furnishes ample proof. For we know how reluctantly man would degrade himself to exalt other creatures above him. His preference of worshiping a piece of wood or stone to being thought to have no god evinces the impression of a deity on the human mind to be very strong, the obliteration of which is more difficult than a total change of the natural disposition; and this is certainly changed whenever man leaves his natural pride and voluntarily descends to such meannesses under the notion of worshiping God.

*   *   *

Chap. 4, I

WHILE EXPERIENCE testifies that the seeds of religion are sown by God in every heart, we scarcely find one man in a hundred who cherishes what he has received, and not one in whom they grow to maturity, much less bear fruit in due season. Some perhaps grow vain in their own superstitions, while others revolt from God with intentional wickedness; but all degenerate from the true knowledge of him. The fact is that no genuine piety remains in the world. But in saying that some fall into superstition through error, I would not insinuate that their ignorance excuses them from guilt; because their blindness is always connected with pride, vanity, and contumacy. Pride and vanity are discovered when miserable men, in seeking after God, rise not, as they ought, above their own level, but judge of him according to their carnal stupidity and leave the proper path of investigation in pursuit of speculations as vain as they are curious. Their conceptions of him are formed, not

1. Cicero, *De natura deorum* I; Lactantius, *Divinae institutiones* III. 10.

according to the representations he gives of himself, but by
the inventions of their own presumptuous imaginations. This
gulf being opened, whatever course they take they must be
rushing forward to destruction. None of their subsequent attempts at the worship or service of God can be considered as
rendered to him, because they worship not him but a figment
of their own brains in his stead. This depravity Paul expressly
remarks: "Professing themselves to be wise, they become fools."[1]
He had before said, "They became vain in their imaginations."[2] But lest any should exculpate them, he adds that they
were deservedly blinded because, not content within the bounds
of sobriety, but arrogating to themselves more than was right,
they willfully darkened and even infatuated themselves with
pride, vanity, and perverseness. Whence it follows that their
folly is inexcusable which originates, not only in a vain curiosity,
but in false confidence and an immoderate desire to exceed the
limits of human knowledge.

*   *   *

Chap. 5, I, II

AS THE perfection of a happy life consists in the knowledge of
God, that no man might be precluded from attaining felicity
God has not only sown in the minds of men the seed of religion,
already mentioned, but has manifested himself in the formation
of every part of the world, and daily presents himself to public
view in such a manner that they cannot open their eyes without being constrained to behold him. His essence, indeed, is
incomprehensible, so that his majesty is not to be perceived
by the human senses; but on all his works he has inscribed
his glory in characters so clear, unequivocal, and striking
that the most illiterate and stupid cannot exculpate themselves by the plea of ignorance. The Psalmist, therefore, with
great propriety exclaims, "He covereth himself with light as
with a garment,"[3] as if he had said that his first appearance

1. Rom. 1. 22.
2. Rom. 1. 21.
3. Ps. 104. 2.

in visible apparel was at the creation of the world, when he displayed those glories which are still conspicuous on every side. In the same place, the Psalmist compares the expanded heavens to a royal pavilion; he says that "he layeth the beams of his chambers in the waters; maketh the clouds his chariot; walketh upon the wings of the wind"; and maketh the winds and the lightnings his swift messengers. And because the glory of his power and wisdom is more refulgently displayed above, heaven is generally called his palace. And in the first place, whithersoever you turn your eyes, there is not an atom of the world in which you cannot behold some brilliant sparks at least of his glory. But you cannot at one view take a survey of this most ample and beautiful machine in all its vast extent without being completely overwhelmed with its infinite splendor. Wherefore the author of the Epistle to the Hebrews elegantly represents the world as the manifestations of invisible things,[1] for the exact symmetry of the universe is a mirror in which we may contemplate the otherwise invisible God. For which reason the Psalmist attributes to the celestial bodies a language universally known,[2] for they afford a testimony of the Deity too evident to escape the observation of the most ignorant people in the world. But the Apostle more distinctly asserts this manifestation to men of what was useful to be known concerning God: "for the invisible things of him from the creation of the world are clearly seen, being understood by the things that are made even his eternal power and godhead."[3]

Of his wonderful wisdom, both heaven and earth contain innumerable proofs; not only those more abstruse things, which are the subjects of astronomy, medicine, and the whole science of physics, but those things which force themselves on the view of the most illiterate of mankind so that they cannot open their eyes without being constrained to witness them. Adepts, indeed, in those liberal arts, or persons just initiated into them, are thereby enabled to proceed much further in investigating the secrets of divine wisdom. Yet ignorance of those sciences prevents no man from such a survey of the

1. Heb. 11. 3.
2. Ps. 19. 1, 3.
3. Rom. 1. 20.

workmanship of God as is more than sufficient to excite his admiration of the divine architect. In disquisitions concerning the motions of the stars, in fixing their situations, measuring their distances, and distinguishing their peculiar properties, there is need of skill, exactness, and industry; and the providence of God being more clearly revealed by these discoveries, the mind ought to rise to a sublimer elevation for the contemplation of his glory. But since the meanest and most illiterate of mankind, who are furnished with no other assistance than their own eyes, cannot be ignorant of the excellence of the divine skill exhibiting itself in that endless yet regular variety of the innumerable celestial host, it is evident that the Lord abundantly manifests his wisdom to every individual on earth. Thus it belongs to a man of pre-eminent ingenuity to examine, with the critical exactness of Galen, the connection, the symmetry, the beauty, and the use of the various parts of the human body. But the composition of the human body is universally acknowledged to be so ingenious as to render its Maker the object of deserved admiration.

*   *   *

Chap. 5, IV

BUT HEREIN appears the vile ingratitude of men—that, while they ought to be proclaiming the praises of God for the wonderful skill displayed in their formation and the inestimable bounties he bestows on them, they are only inflated with the greater pride. They perceive how wonderfully God works within them, and experience teaches them what a variety of blessings they receive from his liberality. They are constrained to know, whether willingly or not, that these are proofs of his divinity, yet they suppress this knowledge in their hearts. Indeed, they need not go out of themselves, provided they do not, by arrogating to themselves what is given from heaven, smother the light which illuminates their minds to a clearer discovery of God. Even in the present day there are many men of monstrous dispositions who do not hesitate to pervert all the seeds of divinity sown in the nature of man in order to bury in oblivion the name of God. How detestable is this frenzy, that man, discovering in his body and soul a hundred vestiges of God, should make this very excellence a pretext for the denial of his being! They will not say that they are distinguished from the brutes by chance; but they ascribe it to nature, which they consider as the author of all things, and remove God out of sight. They perceive most exquisite workmanship in all their members, from the head to the feet. Here also they substitute nature in the place of God. . . .

*   *   *

Chap. 6, I

THOUGH THE light which presents itself to all eyes, both in heaven and in earth, is more than sufficient to deprive the ingratitude of men of every excuse—since God, in order to involve all mankind in the same guilt, sets before them all, without exception, an exhibition of his majesty delineated in the creatures—yet we need another and better assistance properly to direct us to the Creator of the world. Therefore he has not unnecessarily added the light of his word to make himself known unto salvation, and has honored with this privilege those whom he intended to unite in a more close and familiar connection with himself. For, seeing the minds of all men to be agitated with unstable dispositions, when he had chosen the Jews as his peculiar flock he enclosed them as in a fold, that they might not wander after the vanities of other nations. And it is not without cause that he preserves us in the pure knowledge of himself by the same means; for otherwise they who seem comparatively to stand firm would soon fall. For, as persons who are old or whose eyes are by any means become dim, if you show them the most beautiful book, though they perceive something written but can scarcely read two words together, yet, by the assistance of spectacles, will begin to read distinctly—so the Scripture, collecting in our minds the otherwise confused notions of deity, dispels the darkness and gives us a clear view of the true God. This, then, is a singular favor, that in the instruction of the Church God not only uses mute teachers, but even opens his own sacred mouth; not only proclaims that some god ought to be worshiped, but at the same time pronounces himself to be the being to whom this worship is due; and not only teaches the elect to raise their view to a deity, but also exhibits himself as the object of their contemplation. This method he has observed toward his Church from the beginning, beside those common lessons of instruction, to afford them also his word; which furnishes a more correct and certain criterion to distinguish him from all fictitious deities. And it was undoubtedly by this assistance that Adam, Noah, Abraham, and the rest of the patriarchs attained to that familiar knowledge which distinguished them from unbelievers. I speak not yet of the peculiar doctrine of faith which illuminated them into the hope of eternal life. For, to pass from death to life, they must have known God not only as the Creator but also as the Redeemer, as they certainly obtained both from his word. For that species of knowledge which related to him as the creator and governor of the world in order preceded the other. To this was afterward added the other internal knowledge, which alone vivifies dead souls and apprehends God not only as the creator of the world and as the sole author and arbiter of all events, but also as the Redeemer in the person of the Mediator. But, being not yet come to the fall of man and the corruption of nature, I also forbear to treat of the remedy. Let the reader remember, therefore, that I am not yet treating of that covenant by which God adopted the children of Abraham, and of that point of doctrine by which believers have always been particularly separated from the profane nations, since that is founded on Christ; but am only showing how we ought to learn from the Scripture that God, who created the world, may be certainly distinguished from the whole multitude of fictitious deities. The series of subjects will, in due time, lead us to redemption. But, though we shall adduce many testimonies from the New Testament, and some also from the Law and the Prophets in which Christ is expressly mentioned, yet they will all tend to prove that the Scripture discovers God to us as the creator of the world, and declares what sentiments we should form of him, that we may not be seeking after a deity in a labyrinth of uncertainty.

* * *

Chap. 7, III, IV, V

I KNOW, indeed, that they commonly cite the opinion of Augustine, where he says "that he would not believe the gospel unless he were influenced by the authority of the Church." But how falsely and unfairly this is cited in support of such a notion it is easy to discover from the context. He was in that contending with the Manichaeans, who wished to be credited without any controversy when they affirmed the truth to be on their side but never proved it. Now, as they made the authority of the gospel a pretext in order to establish the credit of their Manichaeus, he inquires what they would do if they met with a man who did not believe the gospel, with what kind of persuasion they would convert him to their opinion. He afterward adds, "Indeed, I would not give credit to the gospel," etc., intending that he himself, when an alien from the faith, could not be prevailed on to embrace the gospel as the certain truth of God till he was convinced by the authority of the Church. And is it surprising that anyone yet destitute of the knowledge of Christ should pay a respect to men? Augustine, therefore, does not there maintain that the faith of the pious is founded on the authority of the Church, nor does he mean that the certainty of the gospel depends on it, but simply that unbelievers would have no assurance of the truth of the gospel that would win them to Christ unless they were influenced by the consent of the Church. And a little before, he clearly confirms it in these words: "When I shall have commended my own creed and derided yours, what judgment, think you, ought we to form, what conduct ought we to pursue, but to forsake those who invite us to acknowledge things that are certain and afterward command us to believe things that are uncertain; and to follow those who invite us first to believe what we cannot yet clearly see, that, being strengthened by faith, we may acquire an understanding of what we believe, our mind being now internally strengthened and illuminated, not by men, but by God himself?" These are the express words of Augustine; whence the inference is obvious to everyone that this holy man did not design to suspend our faith in the Scriptures on the arbitrary decision of the Church, but only to show (what we all confess to be true) that they who are yet unilluminated by the Spirit of God are, by a reverence for the Church, brought to such a docility as to submit to learn the faith of Christ from the gospel, and that thus the authority of the Church is an introduction to prepare us for the faith of the gospel. For we see that he will have the certainty of the pious to rest on a very different foundation. Otherwise I do not deny his frequently urging on the Manichaeans the universal consent of the Church with a view to prove the truth of the Scripture, which they rejected. Whence his rebuke of Faustus "for not submitting to the truth of the gospel, so founded, so established, so gloriously celebrated, and delivered through certain successions from the apostolic age." But he nowhere insinuates that the authority which we attribute to the Scripture depends on the definitions or decrees of men: he only produces the universal judgment of the Church, which was very useful to his argument and gave him an advantage over his adversaries. If anyone desire a fuller proof of this, let him read his treatise *Of the Advantage of Believing,* where he will find that he recommends no other facility of believing than such as may afford us an introduction and be a proper beginning of inquiry, as he expresses himself; yet that we should not be satisfied with mere opinion, but rest upon certain and solid truth.

It must be maintained, as I have before asserted, that we are not established in the belief of the doctrine till we are indubitably persuaded that God is its author. The principal proof, therefore, of the Scriptures is everywhere derived from the character of the divine speaker. The prophets and apostles boast not of their own genius or any of those talents which conciliate the faith of the hearers; nor do they insist on arguments from reason, but bring forward the sacred name of God to compel the submission of the whole world. We must

now see how it appears, not from probable supposition, but
from clear demonstration, that this use of the divine name is
neither rash nor fallacious. Now, if we wish to consult the true
interest of our consciences that they may not be unstable and
wavering, the subjects of perpetual doubt, that they may not
hesitate at the smallest scruples, this persuasion must be sought
from a higher source than human reasons or judgments or
conjectures—even from the secret testimony of the Spirit. It
is true that, if we were inclined to argue the point, many
things might be adduced which certainly evince, if there be
any God in heaven, that he is the author of the law and the
prophecies and the gospel. Even though men of learning
and deep judgment rise up in opposition, and exert and display all the powers of their minds in this dispute, yet, unless
they are wholly lost to all sense of shame, this confession will
be extorted from them—that the Scripture exhibits the plainest
evidences that it is God who speaks in it, which manifests its
doctrine to be divine. And we shall soon see that all the books
of the sacred Scripture very far excel all other writings. If we
read it with pure eyes and sound minds, we shall immediately
perceive the majesty of God, which will subdue our audacious
contradictions and compel us to obey him. Yet it is acting a
preposterous part to endeavor to produce sound faith in the
Scripture by disputations. Though, indeed, I am far from ex-
celling in peculiar dexterity or eloquence, yet, if I were to
contend with the most subtle despisers of God, who are ambitious to display their wit and their skill in weakening the
authority of Scripture, I trust I should be able, without difficulty, to silence their obstreperous clamor. And, if it were of
any use to attempt a refutation of their cavils, I would easily
demolish the boasts which they mutter in secret corners. But
though anyone vindicates the sacred word of God from the
aspersions of men, yet this will not fix in their hearts that assurance which is essential to true piety. Religion appearing, to
profane men, to consist wholly in opinion, in order that they
may not believe anything on foolish or slight grounds they
wish and expect it to be proved by rational arguments that
Moses and the prophets spoke by divine inspiration. But I
reply that the testimony of the Spirit is superior to all reason.

For as God alone is a sufficient witness of himself in his own word, so also the word will never gain credit in the hearts of men till it be confirmed by the internal testimony of the Spirit. It is necessary, therefore, that the same Spirit who spoke by the mouths of the prophets should penetrate into our hearts to convince us that they faithfully delivered the oracles which were divinely entrusted to them. And this connection is very suitably expressed in these words: "My Spirit that is upon thee, and my word which I have put in thy mouth, shall not depart out of thy mouth, nor out of the mouth of thy seed, nor out of the mouth of thy seed's seed, forever."[1] Some good men are troubled that they are not always prepared with clear proof to oppose the impious when they murmur with impunity against the divine word; as though the Spirit were not therefore denominated a "seal" and "an earnest" for the confirmation of the faith of the pious because, till he illuminate their minds, they are perpetually fluctuating amidst a multitude of doubts.

Let it be considered, then, as an undeniable truth that they who have been inwardly taught by the Spirit feel an entire acquiescence in the Scripture, and that it is self-authenticated, carrying with it its own evidence, and ought not to be made the subject of demonstration and arguments from reason; but it obtains the credit which it deserves with us by the testimony of the Spirit. For though it conciliate our reverence by its internal majesty, it never seriously affects us till it is confirmed by the Spirit in our hearts. Therefore, being illuminated by him, we now believe the divine original of the Scripture not from our own judgment or that of others, but we esteem the certainty that we have received it from God's own mouth by the ministry of men to be superior to that of any human judgment and equal to that of an intuitive perception of God himself in it. We seek not arguments or probabilities to support our judgment, but submit our judgments and understandings as to a thing concerning which it is impossible for us to judge; and that not like some persons who are in the habit of hastily embracing what they do not understand, which displeases them as soon as they examine it, but because we feel

1. Isa. 59. 21.

the firmest conviction that we hold an invincible truth; nor like those unhappy men who surrender their minds captives to superstitions, but because we perceive in it the undoubted energies of the divine power, by which we are attracted and inflamed to an understanding and voluntary obedience but with a vigor and efficacy superior to the power of any human will or knowledge. With the greatest justice, therefore, God exclaims by Isaiah[1] that the prophets and all the people were his witnesses because, being taught by prophecies, they were certain that God had spoken without the least fallacy of ambiguity. It is such a persuasion, therefore, as requires no reasons; such a knowledge as is supported by the highest reason, in which, indeed, the mind rests with greater security and constancy than in any reasons; it is, finally, such a sentiment as cannot be produced but by a revelation from heaven. I speak of nothing but what every believer experiences in his heart, except that my language falls far short of a just explication of the subject. I pass over many things at present, because this subject will present itself for discussion again in another place. Only let it be known here that that alone is true faith which the Spirit of God seals in our hearts. And with this one reason every reader of modesty and docility will be satisfied: Isaiah predicts that "all the children" of the renovated Church "shall be taught of God."[2] Herein God deigns to confer a singular privilege on his elect, whom he distinguishes from the rest of mankind. For what is the beginning of true learning but a prompt alacrity to hear the voice of God? By the mouth of Moses he demands our attention in these terms: "Say not in thine heart, Who shall ascend into heaven? or, Who shall descend into the deep? The word is even in thy mouth."[3] If God has determined that this treasury of wisdom shall be reserved for his children, it is neither surprising nor absurd that we see so much ignorance and stupidity among the vulgar herd of mankind. By this appellation I designate even those of the greatest talents and highest rank till they are incorporated into the Church. Moreover, Isaiah, observing that the prophetical doctrine would be incred-

1. Isa. 43. 10.
2. Isa. 54. 13.
3. Deut. 30; Rom. 10.

ible not only to aliens but also to the Jews who wished to be esteemed members of the family, adds at the same time the reason: because the arm of the Lord will not be revealed to all.[1] Whenever, therefore, we are disturbed at the paucity of believers, let us, on the other hand, remember that none but those to whom it was given have any apprehension of the mysteries of God.

*   *   *

Chap. 10, I, II

BUT SINCE we have shown that the knowledge of God, which is otherwise exhibited without obscurity in the structure of the world and in all the creatures, is yet more familiarly and clearly unfolded in the Word, it will be useful to examine whether the representation which the Lord gives us of himself in the Scripture agrees with the portraiture which he had before been pleased to delineate in his works. This is indeed an extensive subject if we intended to dwell on a particular discussion of it. But I shall content myself with suggesting some hints by which the minds of the pious may learn what ought to be their principal objects of investigation in Scripture concerning God and may be directed to a certain end in that inquiry. I do not yet allude to the peculiar covenant which distinguished the descendants of Abraham from the rest of the nations. For in receiving, by gratuitous adoption, those who were his enemies into the number of his children, God even then manifested himself as a Redeemer; but we are still treating of that knowledge which relates to the creation of the world, without ascending to Christ the Mediator. But though it will be useful soon to cite some passages from the New Testament (since that also demonstrates the power of God in the creation, and his providence in the conservation of the world), yet I wish the reader to be apprised of the point now intended to be discussed, that he may not pass the limits which the subject prescribes. At present, then, let it suffice to

1. Isa. 53. 1.

understand how God, the former of heaven and earth, governs the world which he has made. Both his paternal goodness and the beneficent inclinations of his will are everywhere celebrated; and examples are given of his severity, which discover him to be the righteous punisher of iniquities, especially where his forbearance produces no salutary effects upon the obstinate.

In some places, indeed, we are favored with more explicit descriptions which exhibit to our view an exact representation of his genuine countenance. For Moses, in the description which he gives of it, certainly appears to have intended a brief comprehension of all that it was possible for men to know concerning him: "The Lord, the Lord God, merciful and gracious, long-suffering and abundant in goodness and truth, keeping mercy for thousands, forgiving iniquity and transgression and sin, and that will by no means clear the guilty; visiting the iniquity of the fathers upon the children, and upon the children's children."[1] Where we may observe, first, the assertion of his eternity and self-existence in that magnificent name, which is twice repeated; and secondly, the celebration of his attributes, giving us a description, not of what he is in himself, but of what he is to us, that our knowledge of him may consist rather in a lively perception than in vain and airy speculation. Here we find an enumeration of the same perfections which, as we have remarked, are illustriously displayed both in heaven and on earth: clemency, goodness, mercy, justice, judgment, and truth. For power is comprised in the word *Elohim,* God. The prophets distinguished him by the same epithets when they intend a complete exhibition of his holy name. But, to avoid the necessity of quoting many passages, let us content ourselves at present with referring to one psalm[2] which contains such an accurate summary of all his perfections that nothing seems to be omitted. And yet it contains nothing but what may be known from a contemplation of the creatures. Thus, by the teaching of experience, we perceive God to be just what he declares himself in his word. In Jeremiah, where he announces in what characters he

1. Exod. 34. 6.
2. Ps. 145.

will be known by us, he gives a description, not so full but to the same effect: "Let him that glorieth glory in this, that he understandeth and knoweth me, that I am the Lord, which exercise loving-kindness, judgment, and righteousness in the earth."[1] These three things it is certainly of the highest importance for us to know: mercy, in which alone consists all our salvation; judgment, which is executed on the wicked every day and awaits them in a still heavier degree to eternal destruction; righteousness, by which the faithful are preserved and most graciously supported. When you understand these things, the prophecy declares that you have abundant reason for glorying in God. Nor is this representation chargeable with an omission of his truth, or his power, or his holiness, or his goodness. For how could we have that knowledge, which is here required, of his righteousness, mercy, and judgment unless it were supported by his inflexible veracity? And how could we believe that he governed the world in judgment and justice if we were ignorant of his power? And whence proceeds his mercy but from his goodness? If all his ways, then, are mercy, judgment, and righteousness, holiness also must be conspicuously displayed in them. Moreover, the knowledge of God which is afforded us in the Scriptures is designed for the same end as that which we derive from the creatures: it invites us first to the fear of God and then to confidence in him, that we may learn to honor him with perfect innocence of life and sincere obedience to his will, and to place all our dependence on his goodness.

*　　*　　*

Chap. 13, I, II

WHAT IS taught in the Scriptures concerning the immensity and spirituality of the essence of God should serve not only to overthrow the foolish notions of the vulgar, but also to refute the subtleties of profane philosophy. One of the ancients,[2] in

1. Jer. 9. 24.
2. Seneca, *Quaestiones naturales* I.

his own conception, very shrewdly said that whatever we see, and whatever we do not see, is God. But he imagined that the Deity was diffused through every part of the world. But although God, to keep us within the bounds of sobriety, speaks but rarely of his essence, yet by those two attributes which I have mentioned he supersedes all gross imaginations and represses the presumption of the human mind. For surely his immensity ought to inspire us with awe, that we may not attempt to measure him with our senses; and the spirituality of his nature prohibits us from entertaining any earthly or carnal speculations concerning him. For the same reason, he represents his residence to be "in heaven"; for though, as he is incomprehensible, he fills the earth also, yet, seeing that our minds, from their dullness, are continually dwelling on the earth, in order to shake off our sloth and inactivity he properly raises us above the world. And here is demolished the error of the Manichaeans, who, by maintaining the existence of two original principles, made the devil, as it were, equal to God. This certainly was both dividing the unity of God and limiting his immensity. For their daring to abuse certain testimonies of Scripture betrayed a shameful ignorance, as the error itself evidenced an execrable madness. The Anthropomorphites also, who imagined God to be corporeal because the Scripture frequently ascribes to him a mouth, ears, eyes, hands, and feet, are easily refuted. For who, even of the meanest capacity, does not understand that God lisps, as it were, with us, just as nurses are accustomed to speak to infants? Wherefore such forms of expression do not clearly explain the nature of God, but accommodate the knowledge of him to our narrow capacity; to accomplish which, the Scripture must necessarily descend far below the height of his majesty.

But he also designates himself by another peculiar character, by which he may be yet more clearly distinguished; for while he declares himself to be but One, he proposes himself to be distinctly considered in Three Persons, without apprehending which we have only a bare and empty name of God floating in our brains, without any idea of the true God. Now, that no one may vainly dream of three gods, or suppose that the simple essence of God is divided among the Three Persons, we must seek for a short and easy definition which will preserve us from all error. But since some violently object to the word "person" as of human invention, we must first examine the reasonableness of this objection. When the Apostle denominates the Son the express image of the hypostasis of the Father [Heb. 1, 3], he undoubtedly ascribes to the Father some subsistence in which he differs from the Son. For to understand this word as synonymous with essence (as some interpreters have done, as though Christ, like wax impressed with a seal, represented in himself the substance of the Father) is not only harsh, but also absurd. For the essence of God being simple and indivisible, he who contains all in himself, not in part or by derivation but in complete perfection, could not, without impropriety and even absurdity, be called the express image of it. But since the Father, although distinguished by his own peculiar property, has expressed himself entirely in his Son, it is with the greatest reason asserted that he has made his hypostasis conspicuous in him; with which the other appellation, given him in the same passage, of "the brightness of his glory" exactly corresponds. From the words of the Apostle we certainly conclude that there is in the Father a proper hypostasis which is conspicuous in the Son. And thence also we easily infer the hypostasis of the Son, which distinguishes him from the Father. The same reasoning is applicable to the Holy Spirit; for we shall soon prove him also to be God; and yet he must, of necessity, be considered as distinct from the Father. But this is not a distinction of the essence, which it is unlawful to represent as any other than simple and undivided. It follows, therefore, if the testimony of the Apostle be credited, that there are in God three hypostases. And, as the Latins have expressed the same thing by the word "person," it is too fastidious and obstinate to contend about so clear a matter. If we wish to translate word for word, we may call it "subsistence." Many, in the same sense, have called it "substance." Nor has the word "person" been used by the Latins only; but the Greeks also, for the sake of testifying their consent to this doctrine, taught the existence of three προσωπα (persons) in God. But both Greeks and Latins, notwithstanding any verbal difference, are in perfect harmony respecting the doctrine itself.

* * *

Chap. 13, VII

BUT BEFORE I proceed any further, I must prove the deity of the Son and of the Holy Spirit, after which we shall see how they differ from each other. When the Scripture speaks of "the Word of God," it certainly were very absurd to imagine it to be only a transient and momentary sound, emitted into the air, and coming forth from God himself; of which nature were the oracles given to the fathers and all the prophecies. It is rather to be understood of the eternal wisdom residing in God, whence the oracles and all the prophecies proceeded. For, according to the testimony of Peter,[1] the ancient prophets spoke by the Spirit of Christ no less than the apostles and all the succeeding ministers of the heavenly doctrine. But as Christ had not yet been manifested, we must necessarily understand that the Word was begotten of the Father before the world began. And if the Spirit that inspired the prophets was the Spirit of the Word, we conclude, beyond all doubt, that the Word was truly God. And this is taught by Moses with sufficient perspicuity in the creation of the world, in which he represents the Word as acting such a conspicuous part. For why does he relate that God, in the creation of each of his works, said, "Let this or that be done," but that the unsearchable glory of God may resplendently appear in his image? Captious and loquacious men would readily evade this argument by saying that the Word imports an order or command; but the apostles are better interpreters, who declare that the worlds were created by the Son, and that he "upholds all things by the word of his power."[2] For here we see that the Word intends the nod or mandate of the

1. I Pet. 1. 11.
2. Heb. 1. 2, 3.

Son, who is himself the eternal and essential Son of the Father. Nor, to the wise and sober, is there any obscurity in that passage of Solomon where he introduces Wisdom as begotten of the Father before time began and presiding at the creation of the world and over all the works of God. For to pretend that this denotes some temporary expression of the will of God were foolish and frivolous; whereas God then intended to discover his fixed and eternal counsel, and even something more secret. To the same purpose also is that assertion of Christ, "My Father worketh hitherto, and I work."[1] For, by affirming that from the beginning of the world he had continually cooperated with the Father, he makes a more explicit declaration of what had been briefly glanced at by Moses. We conclude, therefore, that God spoke thus at the creation that the Word might have his part in the work and so that operation be common to both. But John speaks more clearly than all others when he represents the Word, who from the beginning was God with God, as in union with the Father the original cause of all things. For to the Word he both attributes a real and permanent essence and assigns some peculiar property; and plainly shows how God, by speaking, created the world. Therefore, as all divine revelations are justly entitled "the word of God," so we ought chiefly to esteem that substantial Word the source of all revelations, who is liable to no variation, who remains with God perpetually one and the same, and who is God himself.

*   *   *

Chap. 15, I

WE MUST now treat of the creation of man, not only because he exhibits the most noble and remarkable specimen of the divine justice, wisdom, and goodness among all the works of God, but because, as we observed in the beginning, we cannot attain to a clear and solid knowledge of God without a mutual acquaintance with ourselves. But though this is two-

1. John 5. 17.

fold—the knowledge of the condition in which we were originally created and of that into which we entered after the fall
of Adam (for, indeed, we should derive but little advantage
from a knowledge of our creation unless in the lamentable
ruin which has befallen us we discovered the corruption and
deformity of our nature)—yet we shall content ourselves at
present with a description of human nature in its primitive
integrity. And, indeed, before we proceed to the miserable
condition in which man is now involved, it is necessary to
understand the state in which he was first created. For we
must beware lest, in precisely pointing out the natural evils
of man, we seem to refer them to the author of nature, since
impious men suppose that this pretext affords them a sufficient defense—if they can plead that whatever defect or fault
they have proceeds in some measure from God; nor do they
hesitate, if reproved, to litigate with God himself and transfer to him the crime of which they are justly accused. And
those who would be thought to speak with more reverence
concerning the Deity, yet readily endeavor to excuse their
depravity from nature—not considering that they also, though
in a more obscure manner, are guilty of defaming the character of God, to whose dishonor it would redound if nature
could be proved to have had any innate depravity at its formation. Since we see the flesh, therefore, eagerly catching at
every subterfuge by which it supposes that the blame of its
evils may by any means be transferred from itself to any
other, we must diligently oppose this perverseness. The calamity of mankind must be treated in such a manner as
to preclude all tergiversation and to vindicate the divine
justice from every accusation. We shall afterward, in the
proper place, see how far men are fallen from that purity which
was bestowed upon Adam. And first let it be understood that,
by his being made of earth and clay, a restraint was laid upon
pride; since nothing is more absurd than for creatures to
glory in their excellence who not only inhabit a cottage of
clay but who are themselves composed partly of dust and
ashes.[1] But as God not only deigned to animate the earthen
vessel but chose to make it the residence of an immortal spirit,

1. Gen. 2. 7; 3. 19, 23.

Adam might justly glory in so great an instance of the liberality of his Maker.

* * *

BOOK II

ON THE KNOWLEDGE OF GOD THE REDEEMER IN CHRIST WHICH WAS REVEALED FIRST TO THE FATHERS UNDER THE LAW AND SINCE TO US IN THE GOSPEL

* * *

Chap. 1, VIII, IX, X, XI

TO REMOVE all uncertainty and misunderstanding on this subject, let us define original sin. It is not my intention to discuss all the definitions given by writers; I shall only produce one, which I think perfectly consistent with the truth. Original sin, therefore, appears to be a hereditary depravity and corruption of our nature, diffused through all the parts of the soul, rendering us obnoxious to the divine wrath and producing in us those works which the Scripture calls "works of the flesh."[1] And this is indeed what Paul frequently denominates "sin." The works which proceed thence, such as adulteries, fornications, thefts, hatreds, murders, revelings, he calls in the same manner "fruits of sin," although they are also called "sins" in many passages of Scripture and even by himself. These two things, therefore, should be distinctly observed: first, that our nature being so totally vitiated and depraved, we are, on account of this very corruption, considered as convicted and justly condemned in the sight of God, to whom nothing is acceptable but righteousness, innocence, and purity. And this liableness to punishment does not arise from the delinquency of another; for when it is said that the sin of Adam renders us obnoxious to the divine judgment, it is not to be understood as if we, though innocent, were undeservedly loaded with the guilt of his sin, but, because we are all sub-

1. Gal. 5. 19.

ject to a curse in consequence of his transgression, he is therefore said to have involved us in guilt. Nevertheless we derive
from him not only the punishment but also the pollution to
which the punishment is justly due. Wherefore Augustine,
though he frequently calls it the sin of another the more
clearly to indicate its transmission to us by propagation, yet
at the same time also asserts it properly to belong to every
individual. And the Apostle himself expressly declares that
"death has therefore passed upon all men, for that all have
sinned"[1]—that is, have been involved in original sin and defiled with its blemishes. And therefore infants themselves, as
they bring their condemnation into the world with them, are
rendered obnoxious to punishment by their own sinfulness,
not by the sinfulness of another. For though they have not
yet produced the fruits of their iniquity, yet they have the seed
of it within them; even their whole nature is, as it were, a
seed of sin, and therefore cannot but be odious and abominable to God. Whence it follows that it is properly accounted
sin in the sight of God because there could be no guilt without crime. The other thing to be remarked is that this depravity never ceases in us but is perpetually producing new
fruits, those works of the flesh which we have before described, like the emission of flame and sparks from a heated
furnace or like the streams of water from a never-failing
spring. Wherefore those who have defined original sin as a
privation of the original righteousness which we ought to possess, though they comprise the whole of the subject, yet have
not used language sufficiently expressive of its operation and
influence. For our nature is not only destitute of all good,
but is so fertile in all evils that it cannot remain inactive.
Those who have called it "concupiscence" have used an expression not improper, if it were only added, which is far from
being conceded by most persons, that everything in man—the
understanding and will, the soul and body—is polluted and
engrossed by this concupiscence; or, to express it more briefly,
that man is of himself nothing else but concupiscence.

Wherefore I have asserted that sin has possessed all the pow-

1. Rom. 5. 12.

ers of the soul since Adam departed from the fountain of righteousness. For man has not only been ensnared by the inferior appetites, but abominable impiety has seized the very citadel of his mind, and pride has penetrated into the inmost recesses of his heart; so that it is weak and foolish to restrict the corruption which has proceeded thence to what are called the sensual affections, or to call it an incentive which allures, excites, and attracts to sin only what they style the sensual part. In this the grossest ignorance has been discovered by Peter Lombard, who, when investigating the seat of it, says that it is in the flesh, according to the testimony of Paul,[1] not indeed exclusively, but because it principally appears in the flesh; as though Paul designated only a part of the soul and not the whole of our nature, which is opposed to supernatural grace. Now Paul removes every doubt by informing us that the corruption resides not in one part only, but that there is nothing pure and uncontaminated by its mortal infection. For, when arguing respecting corrupt nature, he not only condemns the inordinate motions of the appetites, but principally insists on the blindness of the mind and the depravity of the heart;[2] and the third chapter of his Epistle to the Romans is nothing but a description of original sin. This appears more evident from our renovation. For "the Spirit," which is opposed to "the old man" and "the flesh," not only denotes the grave which corrects the inferior or sensual part of the soul, but comprehends a complete reformation of all its powers. And therefore Paul not only enjoins us to mortify our sensual appetites but exhorts us to be renewed in the spirit of our mind;[3] and in another place he directs us to be transformed by the renewing of our mind.[4] Whence it follows that that part which principally displays the excellence and dignity of the soul is not only wounded but so corrupted that it requires not merely to be healed but to receive a new nature. How far sin occupies both the mind and the heart we shall presently see. My intention here was only to hint, in a brief way, that

1. Rom. 7. 18.
2. Eph. 4. 17, 18.
3. Eph. 4. 23.
4. Rom. 12. 2.

man is so totally overwhelmed, as with a deluge, that no part is free from sin; and therefore that whatever proceeds from him is accounted sin; as Paul says that all the affections or thoughts of the flesh are enmity against God, and therefore death.[1]

Now let us dismiss those who dare to charge God with their corruptions because we say that men are naturally corrupt. They err in seeking for the work of God in their own pollution, whereas they should rather seek it in the nature of Adam while yet innocent and uncorrupted. Our perdition therefore proceeds from the sinfulness of our flesh, not from God, it being only a consequence of our degenerating from our primitive condition. And let no one murmur that God might have made a better provision for our safety by preventing the fall of Adam. For such an objection ought to be abominated, as too presumptuously curious, by all pious minds; and it also belongs to the mystery of predestination, which shall afterwards be treated in its proper place. Wherefore let us remember that our ruin must be imputed to the corruption of our nature that we may not bring an accusation against God himself, the author of nature. That this fatal wound is inherent in our nature is indeed a truth; but it is an important question whether it was in it originally or was derived from any extraneous cause. But it is evident that it was occasioned by sin. We have therefore no reason to complain but of ourselves, which in the Scripture is distinctly remarked. For the Preacher says, "This only have I found, that God hath made man upright; but they have sought out many inventions."[2] It is clear that the misery of man must be ascribed solely to himself, since he was favored with rectitude by the divine goodness but has lapsed into vanity through his own folly.

We say, therefore, that man is corrupted by a natural depravity, but which did not originate from nature. We deny that it proceeded from nature to signify that it is rather an adventitious quality or accident than a substantial property originally innate. Yet we call it natural that no one may suppose it to be contracted by every individual from corrupt

1. Rom. 8. 6, 7.
2. Eccles. 7. 29.

habit whereas it prevails over all by hereditary right. Nor is this representation of ours without authority. For the same reason the Apostle says that we are all by nature the children of wra'th.[1] How could God, who is pleased with all his meanest works, be angry with the noblest of all his creatures? But he is angry rather with the corruption of his work than with his work itself. Therefore, if, on account of the corruption of human nature, man be justly said to be naturally abominable to God, he may also be truly said to be naturally depraved and corrupt; as Augustine, in consequence of the corruption of nature, does not hesitate to call those sins natural which necessarily predominate in our flesh where they are not prevented by the grace of God. Thus vanishes the foolish and nugatory system of the Manichaeans, who, having imagined in man a substantial wickedness, presumed to invent for him a new creator, that they might not appear to assign the cause and origin of evil to a righteous God.

*   *   *

Chap. 4, I

IT HAS now, I apprehend, been sufficiently proved that man is so enslaved by sin as to be of his own nature incapable of an effort, or even an aspiration, toward that which is good. We have also laid down a distinction between coaction and necessity from which it appears that, while he sins necessarily, he nevertheless sins voluntarily. But since, while he is devoted to the servitude of the devil, he seems to be actuated by his will rather than by his own, it remains for us to explain the nature of both kinds of influence. There is also this question to be resolved: whether anything is to be attributed to God in evil actions in which the Scripture intimates that some influence of his is concerned. Augustine somewhere compares the human will to a horse obedient to the direction of his rider, and God and the devil he compares to riders. "If God rides it, he, like a sober and skillful rider, manages it in a graceful manner: stimulates its tardiness, restrains its immoderate celerity,

1. Eph. 2. 3.

represses its wantonness and wildness, tames its perverseness, and conducts it into the right way. But if the devil has taken possession of it, he, like a foolish and wanton rider, forces it through pathless places, hurries it into ditches, drives it down over precipices, and excites it to obstinacy and ferocity." With this similitude, as no better occurs, we will at present be content. When the will of a natural man is said to be subject to the power of the devil so as to be directed by it, the meaning is not that it resists and is compelled to a reluctant submission, as masters compel slaves to an unwilling performance of their commands, but that, being fascinated by the fallacies of Satan, it necessarily submits itself to all his directions. For those whom the Lord does not favor with the government of his Spirit he abandons, in righteous judgment, to the influence of Satan. Wherefore the Apostle says that "the god of this world hath blinded the minds of them which believe not," who are destined to destruction, "lest the light of the gospel should shine unto them."[1] And in another place, that he "worketh in the children of disobedience."[2] The blinding of the wicked, and all those enormities which attend it, are called the works of Satan, the cause of which must nevertheless be sought only in the human will, from which proceeds the root of evil and in which rests the foundation of the kingdom of Satan—that is, sin.

* * *

BOOK III

ON THE MANNER OF RECEIVING THE GRACE OF CHRIST, THE BENEFITS WHICH WE DERIVE FROM IT, AND THE EFFECTS WHICH FOLLOW IT

*　　*　　*

Chap. 2, VI

THIS, THEN, is the true knowledge of Christ: to receive him as he is offered by the Father, that is, invested with his gospel; for, as he is appointed to be the object of our faith, so we cannot advance in the right way to him without the guidance of the gospel. The gospel certainly opens to us those treasures of grace without which Christ would profit us little. Thus Paul connects faith as an inseparable concomitant with doctrine where he says, "Ye have not so learned Christ; if so be that ye have been taught by him, as the truth is in Jesus."[1] Yet I do not so far restrict faith to the gospel but that I admit Moses and the prophets to have delivered what was sufficient for its establishment; but because the gospel exhibits a fuller manifestation of Christ, it is justly styled by Paul "the words of faith and of good doctrine."[2] For the same reason, in another place he represents the law as abolished by the coming of faith,[3] comprehending under this term the new kind of teaching by which Christ, since his appearance as our Master, has given a brighter display of the mercy of the Father and a more explicit testimony concerning our salvation. The more easy and convenient method for us will be to descend regularly from the genus to the species. In the first place, we must be apprised that faith has a perpetual relation to the word, and can no more be separated from it than the rays from the sun whence they proceed. Therefore God proclaims by Isaiah,

1. Eph. 4. 20, 21.
2. I Tim. 4. 6.
3. Gal. 3. 23-25.

CLASSICS OF PROTESTANTISM 99

"Hear, and your souls shall live."[1] And that the word is the fountain of faith is evident from this language of John: "These are written, that ye might believe."[2] The Psalmist also, intending to exhort the people to faith, says, "Today, if ye will hear his voice"[3]—and "to hear" generally means "to believe." Lastly, it is not without reason that in Isaiah God distinguishes the children of the Church from strangers by this character: that they shall all be his disciples and be taught by him;[4] for if this were a benefit common to all, why should he address himself to a few? Correspondent with this is the general use of the words "believers" and "disciples" as synonymous, by the evangelists on all occasions, and by Luke in particular very frequently in the Acts of the Apostles, in the ninth chapter of which he extends the latter epithet even to a woman. Wherefore, if faith decline in the smallest degree from this object, toward which it ought to be directed, it no longer retains its own nature but becomes an uncertain credulity and an erroneous excursion of the mind. The same divine word is the foundation by which faith is sustained and supported, from which it cannot be moved without an immediate downfall. Take away the word, then, and there will be no faith left. We are not here disputing whether the ministry of men be necessary to disseminate the word of God, by which faith is produced, which we shall discuss in another place; but we assert that the word itself, however it may be conveyed to us, is like a mirror in which faith may behold God. Whether, therefore, God in this instance use the agency of men, or whether he operate solely by his own power, he always discovers himself by his word to those whom he designs to draw to himself.[5] Whence Paul defines faith as an obedience rendered to the gospel, and praises the service of faith.[6] For the apprehension of faith is not confined to our knowing that there is a God, but chiefly consists in our understanding what is his disposition toward us. For it is not of so much importance to us

1. Isa. 55. 3.
2. John 20. 31.
3. Ps. 95. 7.
4. Isa. 54. 13.
5. Rom. 1. 5.
6. Phil. 2. 17.

to know what he is in himself as what he is willing to be to us. We find, therefore, that faith is a knowledge of the will of God respecting us, received from his word. And the foundation of this is a previous persuasion of the divine veracity, any doubt of which being entertained in the mind, the authority of the word will be dubious and weak, or rather it will be of no authority at all. Nor is it sufficient to believe that the veracity of God is incapable of deception or falsehood, unless you also admit, as beyond all doubt, that whatever proceeds from him is sacred and inviolable truth.

*   *   *

Chap. 2, XXVIII

NOW IN the divine benevolence, which is affirmed to be the object of faith, we apprehend the possession of salvation and everlasting life to be obtained. For if no good can be wanting when God is propitious, we have a sufficient certainty of salvation when he himself assures us of his love. "O God, cause thy face to shine, and we shall be saved,"[1] says the Psalmist. Hence the Scriptures represent this as the sum of our salvation: that he has "abolished" all "enmity"[2] and received us into his favor. In which they imply that, since God is reconciled to us, there remains no danger, but that all things will prosper with us. Wherefore faith, having apprehended the love of God, has promises for the present life and the life to come, and a solid assurance of all blessings; but it is such an assurance as may be derived from the divine word. For faith certainly promises itself neither longevity nor honor nor wealth in the present state—since the Lord has not been pleased to appoint any of these things for us—but is contented with this assurance: that whatever we may want of the conveniences or necessaries of this life, yet God will never leave us. But its principal security consists in an expectation of the future life, which is placed beyond all doubt by the word of God. For whatever miseries and calamities may on earth await those

1. Ps. 80. 3.
2. Eph. 2. 14, 15.

who are the objects of the love of God, they cannot prevent
the divine benevolence from being a source of complete felicity. Therefore, when we meant to express the perfection of
blessedness, we have mentioned the grace of God as the fountain from which every species of blessings flows down to us.
And we may generally observe in the Scriptures that when
they treat not only of eternal salvation but of any blessing we
enjoy, our attention is recalled to the love of God. For which
reason David says that "the loving-kindness of God," when experienced in a pious heart, "is better" and more desirable
"than life" itself.[1] Finally, if we have an abundance of all
things to the extent of our desires, but are uncertain of the
love or hatred of God, our prosperity will be cursed and therefore miserable. But if the paternal countenance of God shine
on us, even our miseries will be blessed, because they will be
converted into aids of our salvation.[2] Thus Paul, after an
enumeration of all possible adversities, glories that they can
never separate us from the love of God; and in his prayers he
always begins with the grace of God, from which all prosperity
proceeds. David likewise opposes the divine favor alone against
all the errors which disturb us: "Though I walk through the
valley of the shadow of death," says he, "I will fear no evil, for
thou art with me."[3] And we always feel our minds wavering
unless, contented with the grace of God, they seek their peace
in it and are deeply impressed with the sentiment of the Psalmist: "Blessed is the nation whose God is the Lord; and the
people whom he hath chosen for his own inheritance."[4]

* * *

Chap. 6, III

AND AS a further incitement to us, it shows that as God the
Father has reconciled us to himself in Christ, so he has exhibited to us in him a pattern to which it is his will that we

1. Ps. 63. 3.
2. Rom. 8. 39.
3. Ps. 23. 4.
4. Ps. 33. 12.

should be conformed.[1] Now let those who are of opinion that the philosophers have the only just and orderly systems of moral philosophy show me, in any of their works, a more excellent economy than that which I have stated. When they intend to exhort us to the sublimest virtue, they advance no argument but that we ought to live agreeably to nature; but the Scripture deduces its exhortation from the true source when it not only enjoins us to refer our life to God the author of it, to whom it belongs, but, after having taught us that we are degenerated from the original state in which we were created, adds that Christ, by whom we have been reconciled to God, is proposed to us as an example, whose character we should exhibit in our lives. What can be required more efficacious than this one consideration? Indeed, what can be required besides? For if the Lord has adopted us as his sons on this condition— that we exhibit in our life an imitation of Christ, the bond of our adoption—unless we addict and devote ourselves to righteousness, we not only most perfidiously revolt from our Creator but also abjure him as our Saviour. The Scripture derives matter of exhortation from all the blessings of God which it recounts to us, and from all the parts of our salvation. It argues that since God has discovered himself as a Father to us, we must be convicted of the basest ingratitude unless we, on our part, manifest ourselves to be his children; that since Christ has purified us in the laver of his blood, and has communicated this purification by baptism, it does not become us to be defiled with fresh pollution; that since he has united us to his body, we should, as his members, solicitously beware lest we asperse ourselves with any blemish or disgrace; that since he who is our Head has ascended to heaven, we ought to divest ourselves of all terrestrial affection and aspire thither with all our soul; that since the Holy Spirit has dedicated us as temples to God, we should use our utmost exertions that the glory of God may be displayed by us and ought not to allow ourselves to be profaned with the pollution of sin; that since both our soul and our body are destined to heavenly incorruption and a never-fading crown, we ought to exert our most strenuous efforts to preserve them pure and uncorrupt

1. Rom. 6. 4 ff.; 8. 29.

till the day of the Lord. These, I say, are the best foundations for the proper regulation of the life, such as we cannot find in the philosophers, who, in the recommendation of virtue, never rise above the natural dignity of man.

* * *

Chap. 6, V

YET I WOULD not insist upon it as absolutely necessary that the manners of a Christian should breathe nothing but the perfect gospel—which, nevertheless, ought both to be wished and to be aimed at. But I do not so rigorously require evangelical perfection as not to acknowledge as a Christian one who has not yet attained to it; for then all would be excluded from the Church, since no man can be found who is not still at a great distance from it, and many have hitherto made but a very small progress whom it would, nevertheless, be unjust to reject. What then? Let us set before our eyes that mark to which alone our pursuit must be directed. Let that be prescribed as the goal toward which we must earnestly tend. For it is not lawful for you to make such a compromise with God as to undertake a part of the duties prescribed to you in his word and to omit part of them at your own pleasure. For, in the first place, he everywhere recommends integrity as a principal branch of his worship, by which he intends a sincere simplicity of heart, free from all guile and falsehood, the opposite of which is a double heart; as though it had been said that the beginning of a life of uprightness is spiritual, when the internal affection of the mind is unfeignedly devoted to God in the cultivation of holiness and righteousness. But since no man in this terrestrial and corporeal prison has strength sufficient to press forward in his course with a due degree of alacrity, and the majority are oppressed with such great debility that they stagger and halt and even creep on the ground, and so make very inconsiderable advances—let us everyone proceed according to our small ability and prosecute the journey we have begun. No man will be so unhappy but that he may every day make some progress, however small.

Therefore let us not cease to strive, that we may be incessantly advancing in the way of the Lord; nor let us despair on account of the smallness of our success; for however our success may not correspond to our wishes, yet our labor is not lost when this day surpasses the preceding one; provided that, with sincere simplicity, we keep our end in view, and press forward to the goal, not practicing self-adulation nor indulging our own evil propensities, but perpetually exerting our endeavors after increasing degrees of amelioration, till we shall have arrived at a perfection of goodness, which, indeed, we seek and pursue as long as we live, and shall then attain, when, divested of all corporeal infirmity, we shall be admitted by God into complete communion with him.

*   *   *

Chap. 10, VI

LASTLY, IT is to be remarked that the Lord commands every one of us, in all the actions of life, to regard his vocation. For he knows with what great inquietude the human mind is inflamed, with what desultory levity it is hurried hither and thither, and how insatiable is its ambition to grasp different things at once. Therefore, to prevent universal confusion being produced by our folly and temerity, he has appointed to all their particular duties in different spheres of life. And that no one might rashly transgress the limits prescribed, he has styled such spheres of life "vocations," or "callings." Every individual's line of life, therefore, is, as it were, a post assigned him by the Lord, that he may not wander about in uncertainty all his days. And so necessary is this distinction that in his sight all our actions are estimated according to it, and often very differently from the sentence of human reason and philosophy. There is no exploit esteemed more honorable, even among philosophers, than to deliver our country from tyranny; but the voice of the celestial Judge openly condemns the private man who lays violent hands on a tyrant. It is not my design, however, to stay to enumerate examples. It is sufficient if we know that the principle and foundation of right conduct in every case are the vocation of the Lord, and that he who disregards it will never keep the right way in the duties of his station. He may sometimes, perhaps, achieve something apparently laudable; but however it may appear in the eyes of men, it will be rejected at the throne of God; besides which, there will be no consistency between the various parts of his life. Our life, therefore, will then be best regulated when it is directed to this mark, since no one will be impelled by his own temerity to attempt more than is compatible with his calling, because he will know that it is unlawful to transgress the bounds assigned him. He that is in obscurity will lead a private life without discontent so as not to desert the station in which God has placed him. It will also be no small alleviation of his cares, labors, troubles, and other burdens when a man knows that in all these things he has God for his guide. The magistrate will execute his office with greater pleasure, the father of a family will confine himself to his duty with more satisfaction, and all, in their respective spheres of life, will bear and surmount the inconveniences, cares, disappointments, and anxieties which befall them, when they shall be persuaded that every individual has his burden laid upon him by God. Hence also will arise peculiar consolation, since there will be no employment so mean and sordid (provided we follow our vocation) as not to appear truly respectable and be deemed highly important in the sight of God.

* * *

Chap. 11, II

BUT THAT we may not stumble at the threshold (which would be the case were we to enter on a disputation concerning a subject not understood by us), let us first explain the meaning of these expressions: "to be justified in the sight of God," "to be justified by faith" or "by works." He is said to be "justified in the sight of God" who in the divine judgment is reputed righteous and accepted on account of his righteousness; for as iniquity is abominable to God, so no sinner can find favor in his sight, as a sinner or so long as he is considered as such. Wherever sin is, therefore, it is accompanied with the wrath and vengeance of God. He is justified who is considered not as a sinner, but as a righteous person, and on that account stands in safety before the tribunal of God, where all sinners are confounded and ruined. As, if an innocent man be brought under an accusation before the tribunal of a just judge, when judgment is passed according to his innocence, he is said to be justified or acquitted before the judge, so he is justified before God who, not being numbered among sinners, has God for a witness and asserter of his righteousness. Thus he must be said, therefore, to be "justified by works" whose life discovers such purity and holiness as to deserve the character of righteousness before the throne of God, or who, by the integrity of his works, can answer and satisfy the divine judgment. On the other hand, he will be "justified by faith" who, being excluded from the righteousness of works, apprehends by faith the righteousness of Christ, invested in which he appears in the sight of God not as a sinner but as a righteous man. Thus we simply explain justification to be an acceptance, by which God receives us into his favor and esteems us as righteous persons; and we say that it consists in the remission of sins and the imputation of the righteousness of Christ.

* * *

Chap. 11, XXI

NOW LET us examine the truth of what has been asserted in the definition—that the righteousness of faith is a reconciliation with God which consists solely in remission of sins. We must always return to this axiom: that the divine wrath remains on all men as long as they continue to be sinners. This Isaiah has beautifully expressed in the following words: "The Lord's hand is not shortened, that it cannot save; neither is his ear heavy, that it cannot hear; but your iniquities have separated between you and your God, and your sins have hid his face from you, that he will not hear."[1] We are informed that sin makes a division between man and God and turns the

1. Isa. 59. 1, 2.

divine countenance away from the sinner. Nor can it be otherwise, because it is incompatible with his righteousness to have any communion with sin. Hence the Apostle teaches that man is an enemy to God till he be reconciled to him through Christ.[1] Whom, therefore, the Lord receives into fellowship, him he is said to justify, because he cannot receive anyone into favor or into fellowship with himself without making him from a sinner to be a righteous person. This, we add, is accomplished by the remission of sins. For if they whom the Lord has reconciled to himself be judged according to their works, they will still be found actually sinners, who, notwithstanding, must be absolved and free from sin. It appears, then, that those whom God receives are made righteous no otherwise than as they are purified by being cleansed from all their defilements by the remission of their sins, so that such a righteousness may, in one word, be denominated a remission of sins.

* * *

Chap. 14, XVI, XVII

ON THIS subject our minds require to be guarded chiefly against two pernicious principles: that we place no confidence in the righteousness of our works, and that we ascribe no glory to them. The Scriptures everywhere drive us from all confidence when they declare that all our righteousnesses are odious in the divine view unless they are perfumed with the holiness of Christ, and that they can only excite the vengeance of God unless they are supported by his merciful pardon. Thus they leave us nothing to do but to deprecate the wrath of our Judge with the confession of David, "Enter not into judgment with thy servant; for in thy sight shall no man living be justified."[2] And where Job says, "If I be wicked, woe unto me; and if I be righteous, yet will I not lift up my head,"[3] though he refers to that consummate righteousness of God compared to which even the angels are deficient, yet he

1. Rom. 5. 8-10.
2. Ps. 143. 2.
3. Job 10. 15.

at the same time shows that, when God comes to judgment, all men must be dumb. For he not only means that he would rather freely recede than incur the danger of contending with the rigor of God, but signifies that he experiences in himself no other righteousness than what would instantaneously vanish before the divine presence. When confidence is destroyed, all boasting must of necessity be relinquished. For who can give the praise of righteousness to his works, in which he is afraid to confide in the presence of God? We must therefore have recourse to the Lord, in whom we are assured, by Isaiah, that "all the seed of Israel shall be justified, and shall glory";[1] for it is strictly true, as he says in another place, that we are "the planting of the Lord, that he might be glorified."[2] Our minds therefore will then be properly purified when they shall in no degree confide nor glory in our works. But foolish men are led into such a false and delusive confidence by the error of always considering their works as the cause of their salvation.

But if we advert to the four kinds of causes which the philosophers direct us to consider in the production of effects, we shall find none of them consistent with works in the accomplishment of our salvation. For the Scripture everywhere proclaims that the efficient cause of eternal life being procured for us was the mercy of our heavenly Father and his gratuitous love toward us; that the material cause is Christ and his obedience, by which he obtained a righteousness for us; and what shall we denominate the formal and instrumental cause, unless it be faith? These three John comprehends in one sentence when he says that "God so loved the world that he gave his only begotten Son, that whosoever believeth in him should not perish, but have everlasting life."[3] The final cause the Apostle declares to be both the demonstration of the divine righteousness and the praise of the divine goodness, in a passage in which he also expressly mentions the other three causes. For this is his language to the Romans: "All have sinned, and come short of the glory of God, being justified freely by his

1. Isa. 45. 25.
2. Isa. 61. 3.
3. John 3. 16.

grace";[1] here we have the original source of our salvation, which is the gratuitous mercy of God toward us. There follows "through the redemption that is in Christ Jesus": here we have the matter of our justification. "Through faith in his blood": here he points out the instrumental cause by which the righteousness of Christ is revealed to us. Lastly, he subjoins the end of all when he says, "To declare his righteousness; that he might be just, and the justifier of him which believeth in Jesus." And to suggest, by the way, that this righteousness consists in reconciliation or propitiation, he expressly asserts that Christ was "set forth to be a propitiation." So also in the first chapter to the Ephesians he teaches that we are received into the favor of God through his mere mercy; that it is accomplished by the mediation of Christ; that it is apprehended by faith; and that the end of all is that the glory of the divine goodness may be fully displayed.[2] When we see that every part of our salvation is accomplished without us, what reason have we to confide or to glory in our works? Nor can even the most inveterate enemies of divine grace raise any controversy with us concerning the efficient or the final cause, unless they mean altogether to renounce the authority of the Scripture. Over the material and formal causes they superinduce a false coloring; as if our own works were to share the honor of them with faith and the righteousness of Christ. But this also is contradicted by the Scripture, which affirms that Christ is the sole author of our righteousness and life, and that this blessing of righteousness is enjoyed by faith alone.

* * *

Chap. 21, V

PREDESTINATION, BY which God adopts some to the hope of life and adjudges others to eternal death, no one, desirous of the credit of piety, dares absolutely to deny. But it is involved in many cavils, especially by those who make foreknowledge

1. Rom. 3. 23 ff.
2. Eph. 1. 5-7, 13.

the cause of it. We maintain that both belong to God; but it is preposterous to represent one as dependent on the other. When we attribute foreknowledge to God, we mean that all things have ever been, and perpetually remain, before his eyes, so that to his knowledge nothing is future or past, but all things are present; and present in such a manner that he does not merely conceive of them from ideas formed in his mind, as things remembered by us appear present to our minds, but really beholds and sees them as if actually placed before him. And this foreknowledge extends to the whole world and to all the creatures. Predestination we call the eternal decree of God by which he has determined in himself what he would have to become of every individual of mankind. For they are not all created with a similar destiny, but eternal life is foreordained for some and eternal damnation for others. Every man, therefore, being created for one or the other of these ends, we say he is predestined either to life or to death. This God has not only testified in particular persons, but has given a specimen of it in the whole posterity of Abraham, which should evidently show the future condition of every nation to depend upon his decision. "When the Most High divided the nations, when he separated the sons of Adam, the Lord's portion was his people; Jacob was the lot of his inheritance."[1] The separation is before the eyes of all: in the person of Abraham, as in the dry trunk of a tree, one people is peculiarly chosen to the rejection of others; no reason for this appears, except that Moses, to deprive their posterity of all occasion of glorifying, teaches them that their exaltation is wholly from God's gratuitous love. He assigns this reason for their deliverance, that "he loved their fathers, and chose their seed after them."

*   *   *

Chap. 23, XIII, XIV

THIS DOCTRINE is maliciously and impudently calumniated by others as subversive of all exhortations to piety of life. This

1. Deut. 32. 8, 9.

formerly brought great odium upon Augustine, which he removed by his treatise *On Correction and Grace,* addressed to Valentine, the perusal of which will easily satisfy all pious and teachable persons. Yet I will touch on a few things which I hope will convince such as are honest and not contentious. How openly and loudly gratuitous election was preached by Paul we have already seen; was he therefore cold in admonitions and exhortations? Let these good zealots compare his vehemence with theirs; theirs will be found ice itself in comparison with his incredible fervor. And certainly every scruple is removed by this principle, that "God hath not called us to uncleanness, but that everyone should know how to possess his vessel in sanctification and honor";[1] and again, that "we are his workmanship, created in Christ Jesus unto good works, which God hath before ordained, that we should walk in them."[2] Indeed, a slight acquaintance with Paul will enable anyone to understand, without tedious arguments, how easily he reconciles things which they pretend to be repugnant to each other. Christ commands men to believe in him. Yet his limitation is neither false nor contrary to his command when he says, "No man can come unto me, except it were given unto him of my Father."[3] Let preaching therefore have its course to bring men to faith, and by a continual progress to promote their perseverance. Nor let the knowledge of predestination be prevented, that the obedient may not be proud as of anything of their own but may glory in the Lord. Christ had some particular meaning in saying, "Who hath ears to hear, let him hear."[4] Therefore when we exhort and preach, persons endowed with ears readily obey; and those who are destitute of them exhibit an accomplishment of the Scripture, that hearing they hear not.[5] "But why," says Augustine, "should some have ears, and others not? 'Who hath known the mind of the Lord?'[6] Must that which is evident be denied, because that which is concealed cannot be comprehended?" These obser-

1. I Thess. 4. 4, 7.
2. Eph. 2. 10.
3. John 6. 65.
4. Matt. 13. 9.
5. Isa. 6. 9.
6. Rom. 11. 34.

vations I have faithfully borrowed from Augustine; but as his words will perhaps have more authority than mine, I will proceed to an exact quotation of them. "If, on hearing this, some persons become torpid and slothful, and, exchanging labor for lawless desire, pursue the various objects of concupiscence, must what is declared concerning the foreknowledge of God be therefore accounted false? If God foreknew that they would be good, will they not be so, in whatever wickedness they now live? And if he foreknew that they would be wicked, will they not be so, in whatever goodness they now appear? Are these, then, sufficient causes why the truths which are declared concerning the foreknowledge of God should be either denied or passed over in silence, especially when the consequence of silence respecting these would be the adoption of other errors? The reason of concealing the truth," he says, "is one thing, and the necessity of declaring it is another. It would be tedious to inquire after all the reasons for passing the truth over in silence, but this is one of them: lest those who understand it not should become worse, while we wish to make those who understand it better informed—who, indeed, are not made wiser by our declaring any such thing, nor are they rendered worse. But since the truth is of such a nature that, when we speak of it, he becomes worse who cannot understand it, and when we are silent about it, he who can understand it becomes worse, what do we think ought to be done? Should not the truth rather be spoken, that he who is capable may understand it, than buried in silence; the consequence of which would be, not only that neither would know it, but even the more intelligent of the two would become worse, who, if he heard and understood it, would also teach it to many others? And we are unwilling to say what we are authorized to say by the testimony of Scripture. For we are afraid, indeed, lest by speaking we may offend him who cannot understand, but are not afraid lest, in consequence of our silence, he who is capable of understanding the truth may be deceived by falsehood." And condensing this sentiment afterwards into a smaller compass, he places it in a still stronger light. "Wherefore, if the apostles and the succeeding teachers of the Church both piously treated of God's eternal election, and held believers under the discipline of a pious life, what reason have these our opponents, when silenced by the invincible force of truth, to suppose themselves right in maintaining that what is spoken of predestination, although it be true, ought not to be preached to the people? But it must by all means be preached, that he who has ears to hear may hear. But who has them, unless he receives them from him who has promised to bestow them? Certainly he who receives not may reject, provided he who receives takes and drinks, drinks and lives. For as piety must be preached that God may be rightly worshiped, so also must predestination, that he who has ears to hear of the grace of God may glory in God and not in himself."

And yet, being peculiarly desirous of edification, that holy man regulates his mode of teaching the truth so that offense may as far as possible be prudently avoided. For he suggests that whatever is asserted with truth may also be delivered in a suitable manner. If anyone address the people in such a way as this: "If you believe not, it is because you are by a divine decree already destined to destruction"—he not only cherishes slothfulness, but even encourages wickedness. If anyone extend the declaration to the future—that they who hear will never believe because they are reprobated—this would be rather imprecation than instruction. Such persons, therefore, as foolish teachers or inauspicious, ominous prophets Augustine charges to depart from the Church. In another place, indeed, he justly maintains "that a man then profits by correction when he, who causes whom he pleases to profit even without correction, compassionates and assists. But why some in one way and some in another? Far be it from us to ascribe the choice to the clay instead of the potter." Again afterwards: "When men are either introduced or restored into the way of righteousness by correction, who works salvation in their hearts but he who gives the increase, whoever plants and waters, he whose determination to save is not resisted by any free will of man? It is beyond all doubt, therefore, that the will of God, who has done whatever he has pleased in heaven and in earth, and who has done even things that are yet future, cannot possibly be resisted by the will of man so as to prevent the execution of his purposes since he controls the wills of men according to his pleasure." Again: "When he designs to bring men to himself, does he bind them by corporeal bonds? He acts inwardly; he inwardly seizes their hearts; he inwardly moves their hearts and draws them by their wills, which he has wrought in them." But he immediately subjoins, what must by no means be omitted, "that because we know not who belongs, or does not belong, to the number of the predestinated, it becomes us affectionately to desire the salvation of all. The consequence will be that whomsoever we meet we shall endeavor to make him a partaker of peace. But our peace shall rest upon the sons of peace. On our part, therefore, salutary and severe reproof, like a medicine, must be administered to all, that they may neither perish themselves nor destroy others; but it will be the province of God to render it useful to them whom he had foreknown and predestinated."

* * *

BOOK IV

ON THE EXTERNAL MEANS OR AIDS BY WHICH GOD CALLS US INTO COMMUNION WITH CHRIST AND RETAINS US IN IT

Chap. 1, I, II, III, IV

THAT BY the faith of the gospel Christ becomes ours, and we become partakers of the salvation procured by him and of eternal happiness, has been explained in the preceding Book. But as our ignorance and slothfulness—and, I may add, the vanity of our minds—require external aids for the production of faith in our hearts and its increase and progressive advance even to its completion, God has provided such aids in compassion to our infirmity; and that the preaching of the gospel might be maintained, he has deposited this treasure with the Church. He has appointed pastors and teachers, that his people might be taught by their lips; he has invested them with authority; in short, he has omitted nothing that could contribute to a holy unity of faith and to the establishment of good order.[1] First of all, he has instituted sacraments, which we know by experience to be means of the greatest utility for the nourishment and support of our faith. For as, during our confinement in the prison of our flesh, we have not yet attained to the state of angels, God has, in his wonderful providence, accommodated himself to our capacity by prescribing a way in which we might approach him, notwithstanding our immense distance from him. Wherefore the order of instruction requires us now to treat of the Church and its government, orders, and power; secondly, of the sacraments; and lastly, of civil government; and at the same time to call off the pious readers from the abuses of the Papacy, by which Satan has corrupted everything that God had appointed to be instrumental to our salvation. I shall begin with the Church, in whose bosom it is God's will that all his children should be collected, not only to be nourished by her assistance and ministry during their infancy and childhood, but also to be governed by her maternal care till they attain a mature age and at length reach the end of their faith. For it is not lawful to "put asunder" those things "which God hath joined together";[2] that the Church is the mother of all who have him for their Father; and that not only under the law, but since the coming of Christ also, according to the testimony of the Apostle, who declares the new and heavenly Jerusalem to be "the mother of us all."[3]

That article of the Creed in which we profess to believe "the Church" refers not only to the visible Church of which we are now speaking, but likewise to all the elect of God, including the dead as well as the living. The word "believe" is used because it is often impossible to discover any difference between the children of God and the ungodly, between his peculiar flock and wild beasts. The particle "in," interpolated by many, is not supported by any probable reason. I confess that it is generally adopted at present, and is not destitute of the suffrage of antiquity, being found in the Nicene Creed as

1. Eph. 4. 11-16.
2. Mark 10. 9.
3. Gal. 4. 26.

it is transmitted to us in ecclesiastical history. Yet it is evident from the writings of the Fathers that it was anciently admitted without controversy to say "I believe the Church," not *"in* the Church." For not only is this word not used by Augustine and the ancient writer of the work *On the Exposition of the Creed,* which passes under the name of Cyprian, but they particularly remark that there would be an impropriety in the expression if this preposition were inserted, and they confirm their opinion by no trivial reason. For we declare that we believe *in* God because our mind depends upon him as true and our confidence rests in him. But this would not be applicable to the Church, any more than to "the remission of sins" or the "resurrection of the body." Therefore, though I am averse to contentions about words, yet I would rather adopt a proper phraseology adapted to express the subject than affect forms of expression by which the subject would be unnecessarily involved in obscurity. The design of this clause is to teach us that though the devil moves every engine to destroy the grace of Christ, and all the enemies of God exert the most furious violence in the same attempt, yet his grace cannot possibly be extinguished, nor can his blood be rendered barren so as not to produce some fruit. Here we must regard both the secret election of God and his internal vocation, because he alone "knoweth them that are his" and keeps them enclosed under his "seal," to use the expression of Paul,[1] except that they bear his impression, by which they may be distinguished from the reprobate. But because a small and contemptible number is concealed among a vast multitude, and a few grains of wheat are covered with a heap of chaff, we must leave to God alone the knowledge of his Church whose foundation is his secret election. Nor is it sufficient to include in our thoughts and minds the whole multitude of the elect unless we conceive of such a unity of the Church, into which we know ourselves to be truly ingrafted. For unless we are united with all the other members under Christ our Head, we can have no hope of the future inheritance. Therefore the Church is called "catholic," or universal, because there could not be two or three churches without Christ being divided, which is impos-

1. II Tim. 2. 19.

sible. But all the elect of God are so connected with each other
in Christ that, as they depend upon one head, so they grow up
together as into one body, compacted together like members
of the same body—being made truly one, as living by one faith,
hope, and charity, through the same divine Spirit, being called
not only to the same inheritance of eternal life, but also to a
participation of one God and Christ. Therefore, though the
melancholy desolation which surrounds us seems to proclaim
that there is nothing left of the Church, let us remember that
the death of Christ is fruitful, and that God wonderfully preserves his Church as it were in hiding-places, according to
what he said in Elijah: "I have reserved to myself seven thousand men, who have not bowed the knee to Baal."[1]

This article of the Creed, however, relates in some measure
to the external Church, that every one of us may maintain a
brotherly agreement with all the children of God, may pay due
deference to the authority of the Church, and, in a word, may
conduct himself as one of the flock. Therefore we add "the
communion of saints"—a clause which, though generally omitted by the ancients, ought not to be neglected, because it excellently expresses the character of the Church; as though it
had been said that the saints are united in the fellowship of
Christ on this condition, that whatever benefits God confers
upon them they should mutually communicate to each other.
This does not destroy the diversity of grace, for we know that
the gifts of the Spirit are variously distributed; nor does it disturb the order of civil polity, which secures to every individual
the exclusive enjoyment of his property, as it is necessary for
the preservation of the peace of society that men should have
peculiar and distinct possessions. But the community asserted
is such as Luke describes, that "the multitude of them that
believed were of one heart and of one soul";[2] and Paul, when
he exhorts the Ephesians to be "one body, and one spirit, even
as they were called in one hope."[3] Nor is it possible, if they
are truly persuaded that God is a common Father to them all
and Christ their common Head, but that, being united in

1. Rom. 11. 4; Kings 19. 18.
2. Acts 4. 32.
3. Eph. 4. 4.

brotherly affection, they should mutually communicate their advantages to each other. Now it highly concerns us to know what benefit we receive from this. For we believe the Church in order to have a certain assurance that we are members of it. For thus our salvation rests on firm and solid foundations, so that it cannot fall into ruin though the whole fabric of the world should be dissolved. First, it is founded on the election of God, and can be liable to no variation or failure but with the subversion of his eternal providence. In the next place, it is united with the stability of Christ, who will no more suffer his faithful people to be severed from him than his members to be torn in pieces. Besides, we are certain, as long as we continue in the bosom of the Church, that we shall remain in possession of the truth. Lastly, we understand these promises to belong to us: "In mount Zion shall be deliverance";[1] "God is in the midst of her; she shall not be moved."[2] Such is the effect of union with the Church, that it retains us in the fellowship of God. The very word "communion" likewise contains abundant consolation; for while it is certain that whatever the Lord confers upon his members and ours belongs to us, our hope is confirmed by all the benefits which they enjoy. But in order to embrace the unity of the Church in this manner, it is unnecessary, as we have observed, to see the Church with our eyes or feel it with our hands; on the contrary, from its being an object of faith, we are taught that it is no less to be considered as existing when it escapes our observation than if it were evident to our eyes. Nor is our faith the worse because it acknowledges the Church which we do not fully comprehend; for we are not commanded here to distinguish the reprobate from the elect, which is not our province, but that of God alone; we are only required to be assured in our minds that all those who, by the mercy of God the Father, through the efficacious influence of the Holy Spirit, have attained to the participation of Christ are separated as the peculiar possession and portion of God, and that, being numbered among them, we are partakers of such great grace.

But as our present design is to treat of the *visible* Church,

1. Joel 2. 32; Obad. 17.
2. Ps. 46. 5.

we may learn even from the title of "mother" how useful and even necessary it is for us to know her; since there is no other way of entrance into life unless we are conceived by her, born of her, nourished at her breast, and continually preserved under her care and government till we are divested of this mortal flesh and "become like the angels."[1] For our infirmity will not admit of our dismission from her school; we must continue under her instruction and discipline to the end of our lives. It is also to be remarked that out of her bosom there can be no hope of remission of sins or any salvation, according to the testimony of Joel and Isaiah;[2] which is confirmed by Ezekiel[3] when he denounces that those whom God excludes from the heavenly life shall not be enrolled among his people. So, on the contrary, those who devote themselves to the service of God are said to inscribe their names among the citizens of Jerusalem. For which reason the Psalmist says, "Remember me, O Lord, with the favor that thou bearest unto thy people; O visit me with thy salvation that I may see the good of thy chosen, that I may rejoice in the gladness of thy nation, that I may glory with thine inheritance."[4] In these words the paternal favor of God and the peculiar testimony of the spiritual life are restricted to his flock to teach us that it is always fatally dangerous to be separated from the Church.

*   *   *

Chap. 12, I, II

THE DISCIPLINE of the Church, the discussion of which I have deferred to this place, must be despatched in a few words, that we may proceed to the remaining subjects. Now the discipline depends chiefly on the power of the keys, and the spiritual jurisdiction. To make this more easily understood, let us divide the Church into two principal orders—the clergy and the people. I use the word "clergy" as the common, though im-

1. Matt. 22. 30.
2. Isa. 37. 35; Joel 2. 32.
3. Ezek. 13. 9.
4. Ps. 106. 4, 5.

proper, appellation of those who execute the public ministry in the Church. We shall, first, speak of the common discipline to which all ought to be subject; and in the next place we shall proceed to the clergy, who, beside this common discipline, have a discipline peculiar to themselves. But as some have such a hatred of discipline as to abhor the very name, they should attend to the following consideration: that if no society, and even no house, though containing only a small family, can be preserved in a proper state without discipline, this is far more necessary in the Church, the state of which ought to be the most orderly of all. As the saving doctrine of Christ is the soul of the Church, so discipline forms the ligaments which connect the members together and keep each in its proper place. Whoever, therefore, either desires the abolition of all discipline or obstructs its restoration, whether they act from design or inadvertency, they certainly promote the entire dissolution of the Church. For what will be the consequence if every man be at liberty to follow his own inclinations? But such would be the case, unless the preaching of the doctrine were accompanied with private admonitions, reproofs, and other means to enforce the doctrine and prevent it from being altogether ineffectual. Discipline, therefore, serves as a bridle to curb and restrain the refractory, who resist the doctrine of Christ; or as a spur to stimulate the inactive; and sometimes as a father's rod, with which those who have grievously fallen may be chastised in mercy, and with the gentleness of the Spirit of Christ. Now when we see the approach of certain beginnings of a dreadful desolation in the Church, since there is no solicitude or means to keep the people in obedience to our Lord, necessity itself proclaims the want of a remedy; and this is the only remedy which has been commanded by Christ, or which has ever been adopted among believers.

The first foundation of discipline consists in the use of private admonitions; that is to say, that if anyone be guilty of a voluntary omission of duty, or conduct himself in an insolent manner, or discover a want of virtue in his life, or commit any act deserving of reprehension, he should suffer himself to be admonished; and that everyone should study to admonish his brother, whenever occasion shall require; but that pastors and presbyters, beyond all others, should be vigilant in the discharge of this duty, being called by their office, not only to preach to the congregation, but also to admonish and exhort in private houses, if in any instances their public instructions may not have been sufficiently efficacious; as Paul inculcates, when he says that he "taught publicly and from house to house," and protests himself to be "pure from the blood of all men," having "ceased not to warn everyone night and day with tears."[1] For the doctrine then obtains its full authority and produces its due effect when the minister not only declares to all the people together what is their duty to Christ, but has the right and means of enforcing it upon them whom he observes to be inattentive or not obedient to the doctrine. If anyone either obstinately reject such admonitions or manifest his contempt of them by persisting in his misconduct, after he shall have been admonished a second time in the presence of witnesses, Christ directs him to be summoned before the tribunal of the Church—that is, the assembly of the elders —and there to be more severely admonished by the public authority, that if he reverence the Church he may submit and obey; but if this do not overcome him, and he still persevere in his iniquity, our Lord then commands him, as a despiser of the Church, to be excluded from the society of believers.[2]

*   *   *

Chap. 14, I, II

CONNECTED WITH the preaching of the gospel, another assistance and support for our faith is presented to us in the sacraments; on the subject of which it is highly important to lay down some certain doctrine, that we may learn for what end they were instituted and how they ought to be used. In the first place, it is necessary to consider what a sacrament is. Now I think it will be a simple and appropriate definition if we say that it is an outward sign by which the Lord seals in our

1. Acts 20. 20, 26, 31.
2. Matt. 18. 15-17.

consciences the promises of his good will toward us to support the weakness of our faith; and we on our part testify our piety toward him, in his presence and that of angels, as well as before men. It may, however, be more briefly defined, in other words, by calling it a testimony of the grace of God toward us, confirmed by an outward sign, with a reciprocal attestation of our piety toward him. Whichever of these definitions be chosen, it conveys exactly the same meaning as that of Augustine, which states a sacrament to be "a visible sign of a sacred thing," or "a visible form of invisible grace"; but it expresses the thing itself with more clearness and precision, for as his conciseness leaves some obscurity, by which many inexperienced persons may be misled, I have endeavored to render the subject plainer by more words, that no room might be left for any doubt.

The reason why the ancient Fathers used this word in such a sense is very evident. For whenever the author of the old common version of the New Testament wanted to render the Greek word μυστηριον "mystery," into Latin, especially where it related to divine things, he used the word sacramentum, "sacrament." Thus, in the Epistle to the Ephesians, "Having made known unto us the *mystery* of his will."[1] Again: "If ye have heard of the dispensation of the grace of God which is given me to you-ward; how that by revelation he made known unto me the *mystery*."[2] In the Epistle to the Colossians: "The *mystery* which hath been hid from ages and from generations, but now is made manifest to his saints; to whom God would make known what is the riches of the glory of this *mystery*."[3] Again, to Timothy: "Great is the *mystery* of godliness; God was manifest in the flesh."[4] In all these places, where the word "mystery" is used, the author of that version has rendered it "sacrament." He would not say "arcanum," or "secret," lest he should appear to degrade the majesty of the subject. Therefore he has used the word "sacrament" for a sacred or divine secret. In this signification it frequently occurs in the writings

1. Eph. 1. 9.
2. Eph. 3. 2, 3.
3. Col. 1. 26, 27.
4. I Tim. 3. 16.

of the Fathers. And it is well known that baptism and the Lord's Supper, which the Latins denominate "sacraments," are called "mysteries" by the Greeks, a synonymous use of the terms which removes every doubt. And hence the word "sacrament" came to be applied to those signs which contained a representation of sublime and spiritual things; which is also remarked by Augustine, who says, "It would be tedious to dispute respecting the diversity of signs, which, when they pertain to divine things, are called *sacraments*."

*　　*　　*

Chap. 17, XXXI, XXXII

THEY ARE exceedingly deceived who cannot conceive of any presence of the flesh of Christ in the supper except it be attached to the bread. For on this principle they leave nothing to the secret operation of the Spirit, which unites us to Christ. They suppose Christ not to be present unless he descends to us, as though we cannot equally enjoy his presence if he elevates us to himself. The only question between us, therefore, respects the manner of this presence, because they place Christ in the bread and we think it unlawful for us to bring him down from heaven. Let the readers judge on which side the truth lies. Only let us hear no more of that calumny that Christ is excluded from the sacrament unless he be concealed under the bread. For as this is a heavenly mystery, there is no necessity to bring Christ down to the earth in order to be united to us.

If anyone inquire of me respecting the manner, I shall not be ashamed to acknowledge that it is a mystery too sublime for me to be able to express, or even to comprehend; and, to be still more explicit, I rather experience it than understand it. Here, therefore, without any controversy, I embrace the truth of God, on which I can safely rely. He pronounces his flesh to be the food and his blood the drink of my soul. I offer him my soul to be nourished with such aliment. In his sacred supper he commands me, under the symbols of bread and wine, to take and eat and drink his body and blood. I doubt

not that he truly presents and that I receive them. Only I reject the absurdities which appear to be either degrading to
his majesty or inconsistent with the reality of his human nature and are at the same time repugnant to the word of God,
which informs us that Christ has been received into the glory
of the celestial kingdom where he is exalted above every condition of the world, and which is equally careful to attribute
to his human nature the properties of real humanity. Nor
ought this to seem incredible or unreasonable, because, as the
kingdom of Christ is wholly spiritual, so his communications
with his Church are not at all to be regulated by the order of
the present world; or, to use the words of Augustine, "This
mystery, as well as others, is celebrated by man, but in a
divine manner; it is administered on earth, but in a heavenly
manner." The presence of Christ's body, I say, is such as the
nature of the sacrament requires, where we affirm that it appears with so much virtue and efficacy as not only to afford our
minds an undoubted confidence of eternal life, but also to give
us an assurance of the resurrection and immortality of our
bodies. For they are vivified by his immortal flesh, and in
some degree participate his immortality. Those who go beyond this in their hyperbolical representations merely obscure
the simple and obvious truth by such intricacies. If any person
be not yet satisfied, I would request him to consider that we
are now treating of a sacrament, every part of which ought to
be referred to faith. Now we feed our faith by this participation of the body of Christ which we have mentioned as fully
as they do who bring him down from heaven. At the same
time, I candidly confess that I reject that mixture of the flesh
of Christ with our souls, or that transfusion of it into us,
which they teach, because it is sufficient for us that Christ inspires life into our souls from the substance of his flesh, and
even infuses his own life into us, though his flesh never actually enters into us. I may also remark that the analogy of
faith, to which Paul directs us to conform every interpretation of the Scripture, is in this case, beyond all doubt, emi-
nently in our favor. Let the adversaries of so clear a truth
examine by what rule of faith they regulate themselves. "He
that confesseth not that Jesus Christ is come in the flesh, is

not of God."[1] Such persons, though they may conceal it, or may not observe it, do, in effect, deny the reality of his flesh.

* * *

Chap. 17, XXXVII, XXXVIII, XXXIX

NOW AS superstition, when it has once gone beyond the proper limits, proceeds in sinning without end, they have wandered still further; they have invented ceremonies altogether incompatible with the institution of the sacred supper for the sole purpose of giving divine honors to the sign. When we remonstrate with them, they reply that they pay this veneration to Christ. In the first place, if this were done in the supper, I would still say that that is the only legitimate adoration which terminates not in the sign but is directed to Christ enthroned in heaven. Now what pretense have they for alleging that they worship Christ in the bread when they have no promise of such a thing? They consecrate their "host," as they call it, to carry it about in procession, to display it in pomp, and to exhibit it in a box, to be seen, adored, and invoked by the people. I inquire how they consider it to be rightly consecrated. They immediately adduce these words: "This is my body." I object that it was said at the same time, "Take and eat." And I have sufficient reason for this, for when a promise is annexed to a precept, it is so included in the precept that, separated from it, it ceases to be a promise at all. This shall be further elucidated by a similar example. The Lord gave a command when he said, "Call upon me"; he added a promise, "I will deliver thee."[2] If anyone should invoke Peter or Paul, and boast of this promise, will not his conduct be universally condemned? And wherein would this differ from the conduct of those who suppress the command to eat and lay hold of the mutilated promise, "This is my body," in order to misapply it to ceremonies foreign from the institution of Christ? Let us remember, then, that this promise is given to those who observe the commandment connected

1. I John 4. 3.
2. Ps. 50. 15.

with it, but that they are entirely unsupported by the word of God who transfer the sacrament to any other usage. We have already shown how the mystery of the supper promotes our faith before God. But as God here not only recalls to our remembrance the vast exuberance of his goodness, but delivers it, as it were, into our hands, as we have already declared, and excites us to acknowledge it, so he also admonishes us not to be ungrateful for such a profusion of beneficence, but, on the contrary, to magnify it with the praises it deserves and to celebrate it with thanksgivings. Therefore, when he gave the institution of this sacrament to the apostles, he said to them, "This do in remembrance of me,"[1] which Paul explains to be "showing the Lord's death"[2]—that is, publicly and all together, as with one mouth, to confess that all our confidence of life and salvation rests on the death of the Lord, that we may glorify him by our confession and by our example may exhort others to give him the same glory. Here again we see the object to which the sacrament tends, which is to exercise us in a remembrance of the death of Christ. For the command which we have received, to "show the Lord's death till he come" to judgment, is no other than to declare, by the confession of our lips, what our faith has acknowledged in the sacrament, that the death of Christ is our life. This is the second use of the sacrament, which relates to external confession.

In the third place, the Lord intended it to serve us as an exhortation, and no other could be better adapted to animate and influence us in the most powerful manner to purity and sanctity of life, as well as to charity, peace, and concord. For there the Lord communicates his body to us in such a manner that he becomes completely one with us, and we become one with him. Now as he has only one body, of which he makes us all partakers, it follows of necessity that by such participation we also are all made one body; and this union is represented by the bread which is exhibited in the sacrament. For as it is composed of many grains, mixed together in such a manner that one cannot be separated or distinguished from another, in the same manner we ought, likewise, to be connected

1. Luke 22. 10.
2. I Cor. 11. 26.

and united together by such an agreement of minds as to admit of no dissension or division between us. This I prefer expressing in the language of Paul: "The cup of blessing which we bless, is it not the communion of the blood of Christ? The bread which we break, is it not the communion of the body of Christ? For we, being many, are one bread and one body; for we are all partakers of that one bread."[1] We have derived considerable benefit from the sacrament if this thought be impressed and engraved upon our minds: that it is impossible for us to wound, despise, reject, injure, or in any way to offend one of our brethren but we at the same time wound, despise, reject, injure, and offend Christ in him; that we have no discord with our brethren without being, at the same time, at variance with Christ; that we cannot love Christ without loving him in our brethren; that such care as we take of our own body, we ought to exercise the same care of our brethren, who are members of our body; that as no part of our body can be in any pain without every other part feeling correspondent sensations, so we ought not to suffer our brother to be afflicted with any calamity without our sympathizing in the same. Wherefore, it is not without reason that Augustine so frequently calls this sacrament "the bond of charity." For what more powerful stimulus could be employed to excite mutual charity among us than when Christ, giving himself to us, not only invites us by his example mutually to devote ourselves to the promotion of one another's welfare, but also, by making himself common to all, makes us all to be one with himself?

This furnishes the best confirmation of what I have stated before—that there is no true administration of the sacrament without the word. For whatever advantage accrues to us from the sacred supper requires the word; whether we are to be confirmed in faith, exercised in confession, or excited to duty, there is need of preaching. Nothing more preposterous, therefore, can be done with respect to the supper than to convert it into a mute action as we have seen done under the tyranny of the pope. For they have maintained that all the validity of the consecration depends on the intention of the priests, as

1. I Cor. 10. 16, 17.

if it had nothing to do with the people, to whom the mystery ought principally to be explained. They fell into this error for want of observing that those promises on which the consecration rests are not directed to the elements themselves but to the persons who receive them. Christ does not address the bread to command it to become his body, but enjoins his disciples to eat and promises them the communication of his body and blood. Nor does Paul teach any other order than that the promises should be offered to believers together with the bread and the cup. And this is the truth. We are not to imagine any magical incantation, or think it sufficient to have muttered over the words, as if they were heard by the elements, but we are to understand those words by which the elements are consecrated to be a lively preaching, which edifies the hearers, which penetrates their minds, which is deeply impressed upon their hearts, which exerts its efficacy in the accomplishment of that which it promises. These considerations clearly show that the reservation of the sacrament, insisted upon by many persons, for the purpose of extraordinary distribution to the sick, is perfectly useless. For either they will receive it without any recital of the institution of Christ, or the minister will accompany the sign with a true explication of the mystery. If nothing be said, it is an abuse and corruption. If the promises are repeated and the mystery declared, that those who are about to receive it may communicate with advantage, we have no reason to doubt that this is the true consecration. What end will be answered, then, by the former consecration, which, having been pronounced when the sick persons were not present, is of no avail to them? But it will be alleged that those who adopt this practice have the example of the ancient Church in their favor. This I confess; but in a matter of such great importance, and in which any error must be highly dangerous, there is nothing so safe as to follow the truth itself.

*　　*　　*

Chap. 18, XIX

THE READERS may now see, collected into a brief summary, almost everything that I have thought important to be known respecting these two sacraments, the use of which has been enjoined on the Christian Church from the commencement of the New Testament until the end of time—that is to say, baptism, to be a kind of entrance into the Church and an initiatory profession of faith, and the Lord's supper, to be a continual nourishment with which Christ spiritually feeds his family of believers. Wherefore, as there is but "one God, one Christ, one faith," one Church, the body of Christ, so there is only "one baptism" and that is never repeated; but the supper is frequently distributed, that those who have once been admitted into the Church may understand that they are continually nourished by Christ. Besides these two, as no other sacrament has been instituted by God, so no other ought to be acknowledged by the Church of believers. For that it is not left to the will of man to institute new sacraments will be easily understood if we remember what has already been very plainly stated—that sacraments are appointed by God for the purpose of instructing us respecting some promise of his, and assuring us of his good will toward us—and if we also consider that no one has been the counselor of God, capable of affording us any certainty respecting his will[1] or furnishing us any assurance of his disposition toward us, what he chooses to give or to deny us. Hence it follows that no one can institute a sign to be a testimony respecting any determination or promise of his; he alone can furnish us a testimony respecting himself by giving a sign. I will express myself in terms more concise, and perhaps more homely, but more explicit—that there can be no sacrament unaccompanied with a promise of salvation. All mankind, collected in one assembly, can promise us nothing respecting our salvation. Therefore they can never institute or establish a sacrament.

*   *   *

1. Isa. 40. 14; Rom. 11. 34.

THE SCRIPTURE DOCTRINE OF THE TRINITY

SAMUEL CLARKE

(1675-1729)

SAMUEL CLARKE was a theologian of high repute in his day. A friend of Newton and of many of the celebrities of his time he participated as a leader in academic debates, his opinion being sought by those associated with philosophy, classical scholarship, mathematics and theological disciplines.

Born in Norwich, England, he was trained at the University of Cambridge. He became rector of St. James, Piccadilly, London. He achieved the stature of the most outstanding English speculative philosopher following John Locke.

The Scripture Doctrine of the Trinity which he authored and published in 1712 (in three Parts, Part III having to do with the Liturgy of the Anglican Church) led to the accusation that he was an Arian, that is, that he disbelieved in the accepted doctrine of the church that Christ was of the same co-eternal substance as God. Great excitement attended the publication of this work, continuing through several decades and causing divisions among the clergy. Clarke believed in the sufficiency of the Scriptures to elucidate Christian doctrines. In this volume, therefore, he set out to determine if the Trinitarian view, following that of Nicea, was genuinely the view in the New Testament. He cited and examined some 1,250 texts of Scripture (Part I of the volume) and found that the metaphysics implied in the doctrine is unscriptural. In Part II (from which the propositional conclusions are here given) he declared the Scriptural view to be: that the Father is alone Supreme; that the Son is Divine only so far as Divinity is communicable by the Supreme

God; and that the Holy Spirit is inferior to the Father and the Son not in order only but also in dominion and authority.

This work, initiating an important controversy in England, was condemned by a convocation in 1714. A war of pamphlets followed. Although vigorously attacked, Clarke remained in good graces in the Anglican church. The loss of certain preferments did not disturb him, compensated as he was by the security of his own reputation and the satisfaction of his own honest convictions. The Christian faith, he held, is not opposed to right reason. Even morals follow the dictates of logical necessity— a position defended by him which initiated a well-defined school of ethics.

His own so-called Arianism was succeeded by an anti-Trinitarian movement. Subordinationism—the view that Christ is subordinate to God—developed during the first decades of that century (in which his work appeared) and was followed by a more distinctly Unitarian ideology.

The significance of Clarke's treatise on the Trinity lies in the challenge he had so strongly made against the long accepted claim that the Trinitarian formula of ancient days rested upon Scriptural authority. The Scriptures, he sought to show, do not sustain such metaphysical Trinitarianism as demanded by orthodoxy.

Editor

THE SCRIPTURE DOCTRINE OF THE TRINITY

INTRODUCTION

AS, IN Matters of *Speculation* and *Philosophical Inquiry*, the only Judge of what is right or wrong, is *Reason* and *Experience;* so in Matters either of *humane Testimony* or *divine Revelation*, the only certain Rule of Truth is the *Testimony* or the *Revelation itself*.

The *Christian Revelation* is the Doctrine of Christ and his Apostles; that is, the Will of God made known to Mankind by Christ, and by Those whom Christ intrusted with infallible Authority to teach it. For the right apprehending of which

Doctrine, men are (as in other matters of the greatest importance to them) sincerely to make use of their best Understanding; and, in order thereunto, to take in all the Helps they can
find, either from living Instructors or ancient Writers: But this,
only as a Means to assist and clear up their own Understanding, not to over-rule it; As a Means to afford them Light to
see what Christ has taught them, not to prejudice them with
supposing that Christ has taught any thing, which, after the
strictest inquiry and most careful examination, they cannot find
to be delivered in his Doctrine.

If in all things which the Gospel *declares* absolutely necessary to be believed and practiced in order to Salvation, the
Revelation of Christ was not in itself so clear, as that every
sincere person, using the best Helps and Assistances he can
meet with, might sufficiently understand it; it would follow,
that God had not at all made sufficient provision for the Salvation of men. For the Doctrine of Christ and his Apostles
being the only Foundation we have to go upon, and no man
since pretending to have had any new Revelation; 'tis evident
there can never possibly be any Authority upon Earth, sufficient
to oblige any man to receive any thing as of divine Revelation,
which it cannot make appear to that Man's own Understanding
(sincerely studying and inquiring after the Truth,) to be
included in That Revelation. For if any man can by any
external Authority be bound to believe anything to be the
Doctrine of Christ, which at the same time his best Understanding necessitates him to believe is not that Doctrine; he
is unavoidably under the Absurdity of being obliged to obey
Two contrary Masters, and to follow Two inconsistent Rules
at once. The *only Rule of Faith* therefore to every Christian, is
the Doctrine of Christ; and That Doctrine, as applied to him
by his own Understanding. In which matter, to preserve his
Understanding from erring, he is obliged indeed, at his utmost
peril, to lay aside all Vice and all Prejudice, and to make use
of the best Assistances he can procure: But after he has done
all that can be done, he must of necessity at last understand
with his own Understanding, and believe with his own, not
another's, Faith. For (whatever has sometimes been absurdly
pretended to the contrary,) 'tis evidently as impossible in

Nature, that in these things any one Person should submit himself to another, as that one man should *see* or *taste,* should *live* or *breathe* for another.

Wherefore in every Inquiry, Doubt, Question or Controversy concerning Religion, every man that is solicitous to avoid erring, is obliged to have recourse (according to the best of his Capacity) to the Rule itself, to the original Revelation. Using (as is before said) all the Helps and Assistances he can obtain: But still taking care to use them, only as Helps and Assistances; not confounding and blending them with the Rule itself.

Where That Rule is to be found by every sincere Christian, is very evident. Whatever *our Lord himself taught,* (because his Miracles proved his divine Authority,) was infallibly *True,* and to Us (in matters of Religion) the *Rule* of Truth. Whatever *his Apostles preached,* (because they were inspired by the same Spirit, and proved their Commission by the like Testimony of Miracles,) was likewise a Part of the Rule of Truth. Whatever the Apostles *writ,* (because they writ under the Direction of the same Spirit by which they preached) was in like manner a part of the Rule of Truth. Now in *the Books of Scripture* is conveyed down to us the Sum of what our Saviour taught, and of what the Apostles preached and writ. And were there as good evidence, by any certain means of *Tradition* whatsoever, of any *other* things taught by Christ or his Apostles, as there is for those delivered down to us in these Writings; it could not be denied but that such Tradition would be of the *same* Authority, and in every respect as much a part of the Rule of Truth, as the Scripture itself. But since there is no such Tradition (and indeed in the nature of things there can be no such Tradition) at this distance of Time; therefore *the Books of Scripture* are to Us *Now* not only *the Rule,* but *the Whole* and the *Only Rule of Truth* in matters of Religion.

*   *   *

Part II   DISTINCT PROPOSITIONS

NEVERTHELESS, THOUGH the *Whole* Scripture is the Rule of *Truth;* and whatever is there delivered, is infallibly *True;* yet because there is contained in those Writings great Variety of things, and many occasional Doctrines and decisions of controversies, which though all equally true, yet are not all equally *necessary* to be known and understood by all Christians of all capacities; therefore the Church from the Beginning, has out of Scripture selected those plain *fundamental* Doctrines, which were there delivered as the *Terms* or *Conditions* of Salvation, of necessity to be known and understood by all Christians whatsoever. And These, all persons were taught in their *Baptismal Creed:* Which was therefore universally called, *the Rule of Faith.* Not that itself was of any Authority, any otherwise than as it expressed the Sense of Scripture; but that it was agreed to be such an *Extract* of the *Rule of Truth,* as contained all the things immediately, *fundamentally,* and universally necessary to be understood and believed distinctly by every Christian.

The *Baptismal Creed,* I say, must of necessity contain explicitly in it at least all the *Fundamentals* of *Faith.* Because whatever is *Fundamental,* is necessary to Salvation; And 'tis a manifest Absurdity, that any thing should be necessary to the Salvation of a Christian, and yet not be expresly required to be explicitly believed by him at his *Baptism,* [or *Confirmation,*] when he is Admitted into the Christian Church. For, to admit any Person to be a Member upon *certain Terms* or *Conditions,* and afterwards to alter or add to those Terms, is what in other Cases men never allow.

But in Process of Time, as men grew *less pious,* and *more contentious;* so in the several Churches they *inlarged* their Creeds and Confessions of Faith; and grew more minute, in determining unnecessary Controversies; and made more and more things explicitly necessary to be understood; and (under pretence of explaining authoritatively,) imposed things much harder to be understood than the Scripture itself; and became more uncharitable in their Censures; and the farther they departed from the Fountain of Catholick Unity, the Apostolical

Form of sound words, the more uncertain and unintelligible their Definitions grew; and good men found no where to rest the Sole of their Foot, but in having recourse to the original words of Christ himself and of the Spirit of Truth, in which the Wisdom of God had thought fit to express itself.

For, Matters of *Speculation* indeed, of *Philosophy,* or *Art;* things of *human invention, experience,* or *Disquisition;* improve generally from small beginnings, to greater and greater Certainty, and arrive at Perfection by degrees: But matters of *Revelation and divine Testimony,* are on the contrary complete at first; and Christian Religion, was most perfect at the Beginning; and the words of God, are the most proper significations of his Will, and adequate expressions of his own Intention; and the Forms of Worship set down in Scripture, by way either of Precept or Example, are the best and most unexceptionable Manner of serving him.

In the days of the Apostles therefore, Christianity was perfect; and continued for some Ages in a tolerable Simplicity and Purity of Faith and Manners; supported by singular Holiness of Life, by Charity in matters of Form and Opinions, and by the extraordinary Guidance of the Spirit of God, the Spirit of Peace, Holiness and Love. But needless Contentions, soon began to arise; and Faith became more intricate; and Charity diminished; and Humane Authority and Temporal Power increased; and the Regards of *This Life* grew greater, and of the *Next Life* less; and Religion decayed continually more and more, till at last (according to the Predictions of the Apostles) it was swallowed up in the *great Apostasy.* Out of which, it began to recover in good measure at the Reformation; when the Doctrine of Christ and his Apostles was again declared to be the Only Rule of Truth, in which were clearly contained all things necessary to Faith and Manners. And had That Declaration constantly been adhered to, and Human Authority in Matters of Faith been disclaimed in *Deeds* as well as in *Words;* there had been, possibly, no more Schisms in the Church of God; nor Divisions, of any considerable moment, among Protestants.

But though Contentions and Uncharitableness have prevailed in Practice, yet (thanks be to God) the Root of Unity has continued amongst us; and the Scripture hath universally been declared to be the only Rule of Truth, a sufficient Guide both in Faith and Practice; And Those who differ in opinion, have done so only because each party has thought their own opinion founded in Scripture; And men are required to receive things for no other cause and upon no other authority, than because they are found (and consequently *in no other sense than* wherein they are found) in the Holy Scriptures. Wherefore in any Question of Controversy concerning a Matter of *Faith,* Protestants are obliged (for the deciding of it) to have recourse to no other Authority whatsoever, but to that of Scripture only.

*   *   *

To apply this *general Doctrine* (which is the great *Foundation* of the Protestant and of the Christian Religion,) to the Controversies which have been raised *in particular,* with too much Animosity and Uncharitableness, concerning the manner of explaining the *Scripture-Doctrine of the Trinity;* I have in the *First Part* of the following Treatise, (that it might appear what was, not the Sound of single Texts which may be easily mistaken, but the whole Tenour of Scripture,) collected EVERY *Text in the New Testament* relating to that matter, (which I am not sensible has been done before,) and set them before the Reader in One View, with such References and Observations, as may ('tis hoped) be of considerable Use towards the Understanding of their true Meaning.

*   *   *

It is a thing very destructive of Religion, and the Cause of almost all Divisions among Christians; when young persons at their first entring upon the Study of Divinity, look upon *Humane* and perhaps *Modern* Forms of speaking, as the *Rule* of their Faith; understanding These also according to the accidental Sound of the Words, or according to the Notions which happen *at any particular Time* to prevail in the World; and then picking out (as Proofs) some few single Texts of Scripture, which to minds already strongly prejudiced must needs seem to sound, or may easily be accommodated the same way; while they attend, not impartially to the whole Scope and general Tenour of Scripture. Whereas on the contrary, were the Whole Scriptures first thoroughly studied, and seriously considered, as the Rule and Only Rule of Truth in matters of Religion; and the Sense of all humane Forms and Expressions, deduced from thence; the greatest part of Errors, at least the greatest part of the uncharitable Divisions that have happen'd among Christians, might in all probability have been prevented. The different States which the Controversies concerning *Predestination, Original Sin, Infant-Baptism, Justification, Free-will, Faith and good Works,* and the doctrine of *the ever-blessed Trinity,* have at different Times gone through; are a sufficient Evidence of this Truth.

The Church of *Rome* indeed, (That Great *Human* Authority *sitting in the Seat of God,*) requires Men to receive her particular Doctrines (or Explications of Doctrines) and Traditions, not as humane and fallible Determinations, to be perpetually compared with, and examined by the infallible Rule; but as being part of the Rule itself of their Faith. But the *Protestant* Churches, utterly and solemnly disclaim all such authority; and require Men to comply with their respective Forms, upon no other Ground but that of their being agreeable to Scripture; and consequently *in such Sense only, wherein* they are agreeable to Scripture.

The first Reformers, when they had laid aside what to Them seemed intolerable in the Doctrines of the Church of *Rome,* in other matters chose to retain the Words which they found in Use in That Church; yet declaring that they meant thereby to express only the Sense of Scripture, and not that of Tradition, or of the Schools. If Tradition or Custom, if Carelessness or Mistake, either in the *Compiler* or *Receiver,* happen at any time to put a Sense upon any humane Forms, different from that of the Scripture, which those very Forms were intended to explain, and which is at the same time declared to be the only Rule of Truth; 'tis evident no Man can be bound to understand those Forms in such Sense; nay, on the contrary, he is indispensably bound not to understand or receive them in such Sense. For (as the learned Mr. *Thorndike* rightly observes,) *That which once was not Matter of Faith, can never by process of Time, or any Act the Church can do,* [or by any Interpretation of Words, that Custom or Carelessness or Contentiousness may have introduced,] *become Matter of Faith.* Epilog. Part II. pag. 155.

As, in reading a Comment upon any Book whatsoever, he that would thence understand the true meaning of the Text, must not barely consider what the words of the Comment may possibly of themselves happen most obviously to signify; but how they may be so understood, as to be a consistent Interpretation of the Text they are to explain: *So* in considering all Forms of Humane Composition in matters of Religion, it is not of importance what the words may in themselves possibly most naturally signify, or what they may vulgarly and carelessly be understood to mean; (for there is in almost all words, some Ambiguity;) but in what Sense they can be consistent Expositions of those Texts of Scripture, which they were intended and are professed to interpret. Otherwise it may easily (nay it will frequently) happen, that a Comment shall in effect come into the place of the Text, and another Interpretation afterwards into the place of That Comment; till in process of time, men by insensible degrees depart entirely from the meaning of the Text, and Human Doctrines swallow up those which are Divine. Which Evil can no otherwise be prevented, than by having recourse perpetually to the Original it self; and allowing no Authority to any Interpretation, any further than 'tis evidently agreeable to the Text itself.

*   *   *

I am well aware, it may to Many seem *Needless,* to enter at all into Questions of This Nature; and that, in matters of such Nicety and Difficulty as the Doctrine of the *Trinity* is generally supposed to be, it were better (in their opinion) to let every man frame to himself such obscure Notions as he can, and not to perplex him with subtle Speculations. And indeed, with regard to *Scholastick and Philosophical Inquiries* concerning *metaphysical Natures and Substances,* this manner of judging is so right and true, that had *These* things Never been meddled with, and had men contented themselves with what is plainly revealed in Scripture, (more than which, they can never certainly know;) the Peace of the Catholick Church, and the Simplicity of Christian Faith and Worship, had possibly never been disturbed. But That which is properly *Theological* in this matter; *viz.* the distinct POWERS *and* OFFICES of the *Father,* the *Son,* and the *Holy Spirit,* in the *Creation, Government, Redemption, Sanctification,* and *Salvation* of man; and the *proper* RESPECTIVE HONOUR due consequently from Us to each of Them distinctly, (that we may not *worship we know not How* nor *What:*) This is the great Foundation, and the main Oeconomy of the Christian Religion; the Doctrine, into which we were baptized; and which every sincere Christian ought, according to the best of his Ability and the Means he has of informing himself, to endeavour thoroughly to understand. The *absolute and incommunicable Supremacy* of *God the Father* over all, and our *Reconciliation* and *Subjection* to *him* as such our *Supreme Governour;* the *Redemption* purchased by the *Son;* and the *Sanctification* worked in us by the *Holy Spirit;* are the Three great Articles of our Creed. And in maintaining these rightly, so as seriously to affect men's Understandings, and influence their Lives accordingly; is the Honour of God, and the Interest of True Religion greatly concerned. *Tritheism, Sabellianism, Arianism, Socinianism,* and the like, have, to the great disparagement of Christianity, puzzled the plain and practical Doctrine of Scripture, with endless speculative Disputes. And it has been no small Injury to Religion, in the midst of those Disputes; that as on the one hand, men by guarding unwarily against *Tritheism,* have often in the other extreme run into *Socinianism,* to the diminution of the Honour of the *Son* of God, and to the taking away the very Being of the *Holy Spirit;* so on the contrary, incautious Writers, in their Zeal against *Socinianism* and *Arianism,* have no less frequently laid themselves open to *Sabellianism* or *Tritheism,* and to the *greatest Confusion and most unintelligible Obscurity in the* WORSHIP *of God,* by neglecting to maintain the Honour and *Supremacy of the Father.* The Design of the following Papers, is to show how This Evil may be prevented, and in what manner Both Extremes may rationally be avoided. Nor can the avoiding *One* of these Extremes, be esteemed by considerate Persons, of less Importance than the *Other.* For, the same *pious Disposition* of mind, which makes serious Persons careful not to diminish the Honour of the *Son of God,* and of *his Holy Spirit;* ought certainly to render them at least as sollicitous, not to diminish the *singular* and *supreme* Honour of *God the Father himself;* of whose alone Grace and Mercy it is, that his *Son* was given for their *Redemption,* and his *Spirit* for their *Sanctification.*

There are Others who have thought, that we *ought not at all to* treat concerning any of these matters, because they are *Mysterious.* By which if they meant, that so far as *the Words of* GOD are mysterious, we ought to acquiesce in *them* implicitly, and not presume to be *wise beyond what is written;* no man could say that herein they judged amiss. But if they mean, that *the Words of* MEN are mysterious; and that we must not reason concerning *Them,* nor inquire *whether or no,* and *in what Sense,* they are agreeable to *the words of God:* What is This, but substituting *another mystery* in the stead of the *true one;* and paying deference to the *mystery* of MAN's making, instead of *the mystery of* GOD? The True *Veneration of Mysteries* consists, not in *Making them* our selves, and in receiving blindly *the words of Men* without understanding them; but it consists, either in taking care *There* to *stop,* where the Scripture it self has *stopped,* without presuming to go further at all; or else, in taking care to understand all words of humane institution in Such a sense, as that they be sure to signify neither more nor less than the words of Scripture necessarily and indisputably do. Whosoever puts any Meaning upon words of humane institution, which does not appear to Another (upon his sincerest and most careful Examination) to be the same with the Sense of the words of Scripture; must not complain that the Other opposes his own Reason to the Authority of God, when indeed he opposes it only to Those who would make *Humane Authority* the same with *Divine.* Affecting to speak unintelligibly, where the Scripture it self has not done so; is indeed promoting *Scepticism* only, not *True Religion.* Nor can there be any other so effectual a way of confuting all *Heresies,* as it would be to *restrain* men within the bounds of the *uncontested* Doctrine of Scripture; and give them as few Advantages as possible, of raising Objections against humane and fallible Forms of speaking.

Lastly; as to Those, who, in the Whole, are of Opinion that

every man ought to study and consider these things according to his Ability; and yet, in the Particulars of the Explication, have quite different Notions from those which I have thought reasonable and necessary to set forth in the following Papers; I have, with regard to such Persons as These, endeavoured to express my self with all Modesty and due Submission. And if any Learned Person, who thinks me in an Error, shall in the Spirit of Meekness and Christianity, propose a different Interpretation of *All the Texts* I have produced, and deduce Consequences therefrom, different from those which seem to Me unavoidably to follow; I shall think my self obliged, either to return him a clear and distinct Answer in the same Spirit of Meekness and Candour, or else fairly and publickly to retract whatsoever is not capable of being so defended. But if, on the contrary, any nameless and careless Writer shall, in the Spirit of *Popery,* contend only that men must never use *their own* Understandings, that is, must have *no Religion* of *their own;* but, without regarding what is right or wrong, must always plead for what Notions happen at any time to prevail; I shall have no reason, in such case, to think my self under the same Obligation of answering him. It is the *Great,* and indeed of all others the most *Fatal* Calamity in the Church of *Rome,* that while the People think they cannot but be very safe in following the unanimous *Opinion* of such *Numbers* of very *Learned* Men; those Learned Men are not, in Truth, at Liberty to have Any *Opinion* at all; but are obliged to employ all their Learning, merely in defending what the most *Ignorant* men in former Ages have determined for them beforehand.

* * *

Part II

BEING THE foregoing DOCTRINE [of the Trinity] set forth at large, and explained in more particular and distinct Propositions.

I. There is *One* Supreme Cause and Original of Things; *One* simple, uncompounded, undivided, *intelligent Agent,* or

Person; who is the Author of all Being, and the Fountain of all Power.

This is the *Great Foundation* of all Piety; the *First Principle* of *Natural Religion,* and every where supposed in the *Scripture-Revelation.* And the Acknowledgment of This Truth in one Faith and Worship, is the *First and Great Commandment,* both in the Old Testament and in the New . . . .

For, *Intelligent Agent,* is the proper and adequate Definition of the word, *Person;* neither can it otherwise be understood, with any Sense or Meaning at all . . . . .

II. *With* This *First* and Supreme Cause or *Father* of all Things, there has existed from the Beginning, a *Second* divine Person, which is his *Word* or *Son* . . . .

III. *With* the Father and the Son, there has existed from the Beginning, a *Third* divine Person, which is *the Spirit* of the Father and of the Son . . . .

IV. What the proper Metaphysical *Nature, Essence,* or *Substance* of any of these divine Persons is, the Scripture has no where at all declared; but describes and distinguishes them always, by their PERSONAL *Characters, Offices, Powers,* and *Attributes* . . . .

All Reasonings therefore, (beyond what is *strictly demonstrable* by the most evident and undeniable Light of Nature) deduced from their *supposed metaphysical Nature, Essence,* or *Substance;* instead of their PERSONAL *Characters, Offices, Powers* and *Attributes* delivered in *Scripture;* are uncertain and at best but probable Hypotheses.

V. The Father *Alone,* is *Self-existent, Underived, Unoriginated, Independent; made of None, begotten of None, Proceeding from None* . . . .

VI. The *Father* is the *Sole Origin* of all *Power and Authority,* and is the *Author* and *Principle* of whatsoever is done by *the Son* or by *the Spirit* . . . .

VII. The *Father Alone,* is, in the highest, strict, and proper Sense, absolutely *Supreme over All.* . . . .

VIII. The *Father Alone,* is absolutely speaking, the *God of the Universe;* the *God of Abraham, Isaac and Jacob;* the *God of Israel;* of *Moses,* of *the Prophets* and *Apostles;* and the *God and Father of our Lord Jesus Christ* . . . .

IX. The Scripture, when it mentions the *One God,* or the

Only God, always means the Supreme *Person of the Father* . .

The Reason is: because the Words, *One* and *Only,* are used, by way of *Eminence,* to signify Him who is *absolutely Supreme, Self-existent, and Independent;* which Attributes are *Personal,* and evidently *impossible to be communicated* from one Person to another . . . .

X. When the Word, *God,* is mentioned in Scripture, with any High *Epithet, Title,* or *Attribute* annex'd to it; it generally (I think, *always*) means the *Person* of *the Father* . . . .

XII. The *Son* is *not Self-existent;* but derives his *Being,* and All his *Attributes,* from the *Father,* as from the *Supreme Cause.* . . . .

XIII. In *what particular metaphysical Manner,* the Son derives his Being from the Father, the Scripture has no where distinctly declared; and therefore men ought not to presume to be able to define . . . .

For *Generation,* when applied to God, is but a *figurative* Word, signifying only in general, *immediate derivation of Being and Life from God himself.* And *Only-begotten,* signifies, *being so derived from the Father in a singular and inconceivable manner, as thereby to be distinguished from all other Beings.* Among *Men,* a *Son* does not, *properly* speaking, *derive* his *Being* from his *Father; Father,* in *This* Sense, signifying *merely* an *Instrumental,* not an *Efficient* Cause. But *God,* when *He* is stiled *Father,* must Always be understood to be . . . a *True* and *Proper* Cause, *really* and *efficiently* giving Life. Which Consideration, clearly removes the *Argument* usually drawn from the *Equality* between a *Father and Son* upon Earth.

'Tis observable that St. *John,* in That passage, where he not only speaks of *the Word* before his Incarnation, but carries his Account of him further back, than any other place in the whole New Testament; gives not the least Hint of the *Metaphysical Manner, how* he derived his Being from the Father; does not say He was *created,* or *emitted,* or *begotten,* or was *an emanation* from him; but only that he *WAS,* that he *WAS in the Beginning,* that he *WAS with God,* and that he was . . . . Partaker of *Divine* Power and *Glory with* and *from* the Father, not only before he was *made flesh* or *became man,* but also *before the World Was* . . . .

XIV. They are *Both* therefore worthy of Censure; both They

who on the one hand presume to affirm, that the *Son* was *made
. . . . out of Nothing;* and They who, on the other hand, affirm
that He is the *Self-existent Substance . . . .*

XV. The Scripture, in declaring the *Son's Derivation* [Mat.
vii, 21; x, 40; xi, 25, 26, 27; xii, 50; xvi, 27; xix, 17; xx, 23; xxvi, 39,
42, 53; xxvii, 46; Mar. ix, 37; xiii, 32; Luke 11, 49; iv, 18; xxii,
29; xxiii, 35; John, iii, 16, 17, 34; iv, 34; v, 19, 20, 21, 22, 23;
v, 26, 27, 30, 31, 36, 37, 43; vi, 44; vii, 16, 17; x, 29, 37; xi, 22;
xii, 44, 49, 50; xiii, 3; xiv, 10, 16, 24, 28. etc. etc.] from the
Father, never makes mention of any Limitation of *Time* but
always supposes and affirms him to have existed with the Father
from the Beginning, and *before All Worlds. . . .*

XVI. They therefore have also justly been censured, who
taking upon them to be wise above what is written, and intrud-
ing into things which they have not seen; have presumed to
affirm . . . . . *that there was a time when the Son was not . . .*

XVII. The Son (according to the Reasoning of the Primitive
Writers) derives his Being from the Father, (whatever the
particular Manner of That Derivation be,) not by *mere Necessity of Nature,* (which would be in reality *Self-existence,* not
Filiation;) but by an *Act of the Father's incomprehensible Power
and Will . . . .*

XVIII. The . . . . *Word* or *Son* of the Father, sent into the
World to assume our Flesh, to become Man, and die for the
Sins of Mankind; was not the . . . . *internal Reason* or *Wisdom*
of God, an *Attribute* or *Power* of the Father; but a *real* Person,
the same who from the Beginning had been the *Word,* or
Revealer of the Will, of the Father to the World . . . .

XIX. The *Holy Spirit* is not *Self-existent,* but derives his
Being from the *Father,* (by the Son) as from the *Supreme Cause.*

XX. The Scripture, speaking of the *Spirit of God,* never
mentions any Limitation of *Time,* when he derived his Being
from the Father; but supposes him to have existed with the
Father from the Beginning . . . .

XXI. In *what particular metaphysical Manner* the Holy
Spirit derives his Being from the Father, the Scripture hath no
where at all defined, and therefore men ought not to presume
to be able to explain . . . .

XXII. The *Holy Spirit of God* does not in Scripture *gener-*

ally signify a mere *Power* or *Operation* of the Father, but more usually a *real Person*. . . .

XXIV. The Person of the *Son,* is, in the New Testament, sometimes stiled, *God* . . . .

XXV. The *reason* why the *Son* in the New Testament is sometimes stiled *God,* is not so much upon Account of his *metaphysical Substance,* how Divine soever; as of his *relative Attributes* and divine *Authority* (communicated to him from the Father) over *Us* . . . .

So far indeed as the Argument holds good from *Authority* to *Substance,* so far the Inferences are just, which in the School Divinity are drawn concerning the *Substance* of the Son. But the Scripture itself, being written as a Rule of Life; neither in This, nor in any other matter, ever professedly mentions any *metaphysical Notions,* but only *Moral Doctrines;* and *metaphysical or physical Truths* accidentally only, and so far as they happen to be connected with *Moral.*

The word, *God,* when spoken of the *Father himself,* is never intended in Scripture to express Philosophically his *abstract metaphysical* Attributes; but to raise in us a Notion of his Attributes *relative to Us,* his *Supreme Dominion, Authority, Power, Justice, Goodness,* etc. . . . And hence (I suppose) it is, that the *Holy Ghost* in the New Testament is never expressly stiled *God;* because whatever be his real *metaphysical Substance,* yet, in the divine Oeconomy, he is no where represented as *sitting upon a Throne,* or *exercising Supreme Dominion,* or *judging the World;* but always as executing the Will of the Father and the Son, in the Administration of the Government of the Church of God . . . .

XXVII. Concerning *the Son,* there are Other the *greatest Things* spoken in Scripture, and the *Highest Titles* ascribed to him; even such as include *All divine Powers,* excepting only *Supremacy and Independency,* which to suppose *Communicable* is an express Contradiction in Terms . . . .

XXVIII. The *Holy Spirit* is described in the New Testament, as the immediate *Author* and *Worker* of *All Miracles,* even of those done by our Lord *himself,* and as the *Conducter* of Christ in all the Actions of his Life, during his State of *Humiliation* here upon Earth . . . .

XXIX. The *Holy Spirit* is declared in Scripture to be the *Inspirer* of the *Prophets and Apostles,* and the Great *Teacher and Director* of the *Apostles* in the whole Work of their Ministry . . .

XXX. The *Holy Spirit* is represented in the New Testament, as the *Sanctifier* of all Hearts, and the *Supporter and Comforter* of good Christians under all their Difficulties . . . .

XXXI. Concerning the *Holy Spirit* there are Other *Greater things* spoken in Scripture, and *Higher Titles* ascribed to him, than to any *Angel,* or *any other Being whatsoever,* except the *only-begotten Son of God* . . . .

XXXII. The Person of the *Holy Ghost,* is no where in Scripture expressly stiled, *God* . . .

XXXIII. The Word, *God,* in Scripture, never signifies a complex Notion of *more persons* [or *Intelligent Agents*] *than One;* but always means *One person only, viz.* either the person of the *Father* singly, or the person of the *Son* singly . . . .

XXXIV. The *Son,* whatever his metaphysical Essence or Substance be, and Whatever divine Greatness and Dignity is ascribed to him in Scripture; yet in This He is evidently *Subordinate* to the *Father,* that *He derives* his *Being* and Attributes from the *Father,* the *Father* Nothing from *Him* . . . .

Among *Men,* (as I have observed above,) a *Son* does not, *properly* speaking, *derive* his *Being* from his *Father; Father,* in *This* Sense, signifying *merely* an *Instrumental,* not an *Efficient* Cause. But *God,* when *He* is stiled *Father,* must Always be understood to be . . . . a *True* and *Proper* cause, *really* and *efficiently* giving Life. Which Consideration, clearly removes the *Argument* usually drawn from the *Equality* between a *Father and Son* upon Earth.

Concerning this *Supremacy* of the Father, as being alone . . . . *God of himself, Underived, Perfect in himself, Independent;* the *Cause,* the *Principle,* the *Root,* the *Fountain;* the *Original,* where of *the Son is the Image* . . . .

XXXV. Every *Action* of the *Son,* both in *making the World,* and in all other his *Operations;* is only the Exercise of the *Father's Power,* communicated to him after an ineffable manner . . . .

XXXVI. The *Son,* whatever his metaphysical Nature or

Essence be; yet, in this whole Dispensation, in the Creation and Redemption of the World, acts in all things according to the *Will,* and by the *Mission* or *Authority* of *the Father* . . . .

XXXVII. The *Son,* how great soever the metaphysical Dignity of his Nature was, yet in the whole Dispensation entirely directed all his Actions *to the Glory of the Father* . . . .

XXXVIII. Our Saviour, Jesus Christ, as, before his Incarnation, he was sent forth by the Will and good Pleasure, and with the Authority of the Father; so in the Flesh, both before and after his Exaltation, He [*not a Part* of him, but *Himself,* his whole *Person,*] in acknowledgment of the Supremacy of the Person of the Father, always *Prayed* to Him, and returned him *Thanks,* stiling Him *his* God, etc. . . . .

XXXIX. The reason why the Scripture, though it stiles the *Father* God, and also stiles the *Son* God, yet at the same time always declares there is but *One God;* is because, there being in the *Monarchy* of the Universe but *One Authority,* original in the *Father,* derivative in the *Son;* therefore the *One* God (absolutely speaking) always signifies *Him* in whom the Power or Authority is *original and underived* . . . . .

XL. The *Holy Spirit,* whatever his Metaphysical Nature, Essence or Substance be; and whatever divine Power or Dignity is ascribed to him in Scripture, yet in This he is evidently *Subordinate* to the Father, that He derives his Being and Powers from the Father, the Father nothing from Him . . . .

XLIII. Upon these Grounds, *absolutely Supreme Honour* is due to the Person of the *Father* singly, as being Alone the *Supreme* and *Original* Author of all Being and Power . . . .

XLIV. For the same Reason, All *Prayers* and *Praise* ought *primarily* or *ultimately* to be directed to the Person of the *Father,* as the *Original and Primary Author* of all Good . . . .

XLV. And upon the same Account, whatever *Honour* is paid to the *Son* who redeemed, or to the *Holy Spirit,* who sanctifies us, must always be understood as tending finally to the *Honour and Glory* of the *Father,* by whose good pleasure the *Son* redeemed, and the *Holy Spirit* sanctifies us . . . .

XLVI. For, the *Great Oeconomy,* or the Whole *Dispensation* of *God* towards Mankind in Christ, consists and terminates in This; that as all *Authority and Power* is originally in the *Father,* and from him derived to the *Son,* and exercised according to the *Will of the Father* by the *Operation of the Son* and by the *Influence of the Holy Spirit;* and all *Communications* from God to the *Creature,* are conveyed through the *Intercession of the Son,* and by the *Inspiration and Sanctification of the Holy Spirit;* so on the contrary, *All Returns* from the *Creature,* of *Prayers and Praises,* of *Reconciliation and Obedience,* of *Honour and Duty* to *God;* are made in and by the *Guidance* and *Assistance of the Holy Spirit,* through the *Mediation of the Son* to the *Supreme Father* and *Author of All things . . .*

LII. The *Honour paid . . . .* to the *Son,* must (as before) always be understood as redounding ultimately to the Glory of *God the Father . . . .*

LIV. For putting up *Prayers and Doxologies* directly and expressly to the *Person of the Holy Spirit* it must be acknowledged there is no clear *Precept* or *Example* in Scripture . . . .

A SERIOUS CALL TO A DEVOUT AND HOLY LIFE

WILLIAM LAW

(1686-1761)

RELIGIOUS LIFE in England was at low ebb when William Law issued his famous affirmation of Christian piety, *A Serious Call To a Devout and Holy Life,* in 1728. Law defended Christian theism, promoted a spiritual awakening and espoused the belief in miracles. He came later to develop mystical tendencies (influenced by Jakob Boehme, German Protestant mystic), defending the experience of the inward light as the real verification of the Christian life.

A Serious Call had an influence far and wide. Dr. Samuel Johnson by it was first aroused "to thinking in earnest about religion." John Wesley as a young man read this book and was moved by it. It confirmed his own direction to a more austere religious commitment. The young Holy Club of "Methodists" at Oxford under Wesley's leadership sought to realize Law's ideal of the consecrated life. John Henry Newman, as a young man, too, had been touched by Law's earnest *Call.* Williston Walker, Yale's eminent ecclesiastical historian of a generation ago, estimated this work as "one of the monuments of English hortatory literature, though it is to be feared now seldom read."

Law received his training at Emmanuel College, Cambridge. Ordained in the Anglican Church he early became involved in a dispute (along with others) over the swearing allegiance to new sovereigns, and as a member of the non-juror party lost the possibility of preferments within the established church. Contentedly, he devoted himself to a life of simplicity, of dedication both to study and consecrated living. He stood for what has been called "Christian perfectionism."

Editor

A SERIOUS CALL TO A DEVOUT AND HOLY LIFE

Some people will perhaps object, that all these rules of holy living unto God in all that we do, are too great a restraint upon human life; that it will be made too anxious a state, by thus introducing a regard to God in all our actions; and that by depriving ourselves of so many seemingly innocent pleasures, we shall render our lives dull, uneasy, and melancholy.

To which it may be answered,

First, That these rules are prescribed for, and will certainly procure a quite contrary end. That instead of making our lives dull and melancholy, they will render them full of content and strong satisfactions. That by these rules, we only change the childish satisfactions of our vain and sickly passions, for the solid enjoyment and real happiness of a sound mind.

Secondly, That as there is no foundation for comfort in the enjoyments of this life, but in the assurance that a wise and good God governeth the world, so the more we find out God in every thing, the more we apply to Him in every place, the more we look up to Him in all our actions, the more we conform to His will, the more we act according to His wisdom, and imitate His goodness, by so much the more do we enjoy God, partake of the Divine nature, and heighten and increase all that is happy and comfortable in human life.

Thirdly, He that is endeavouring to subdue, and root out of his mind all those passions of pride, envy, and ambition, which religion opposes, is doing more to make himself happy, even in this life, than he that is contriving means to indulge them. For these passions are the causes of all the disquiets and vexations of human life: they are the dropsies and fevers of our minds, vexing them with false appetites, and restless cravings after such things as we do not want, and spoiling our taste for those things which are our proper good.

Do but imagine that you somewhere or other saw a man that

proposed reason as the rule of all his actions; that had no desires but after such things as nature wants, and religion approves; that was as pure from all the motions of pride, envy, and covetousness, as from thoughts of murder; that, in this freedom from worldly passions, he had a soul full of Divine love, wishing and praying that all men may have what they want of worldly things, and be partakers of eternal glory in the life to come. Do but fancy a man living in this manner, and your own conscience will immediately tell you, that he is the happiest man in the world, and that it is not in the power of the richest fancy to invent any higher happiness in the present state of life.

And, on the other hand, if you suppose him to be in any degree less perfect; if you suppose him but subject to one foolish fondness or vain passion, your own conscience will again tell you that he so far lessens his own happiness, and robs himself of the true enjoyment of his other virtues. So true is it, that the more we live by the rules of religion, the more peaceful and happy do we render our lives.

Again; as it thus appears that real happiness is only to be had from the greatest degrees of piety, the greatest denials of our passions, and the strictest rules of religion; so the same truth will appear from a consideration of human misery. If we look into the world, and view the disquiets and troubles of human life, we shall find that they are all owing to our violent and irreligious passions.

Now all trouble and uneasiness are founded in the want of something or other: would we, therefore, know the true cause of our troubles and disquiets, we must find out the cause of our wants; because that which creates and increaseth our wants, does, in the same degree, create and increase our troubles and disquiets.

God Almighty has sent us into the world with very few wants; meat, and drink, and clothing, are the only things necessary in life; and as these are only our present needs, so the present world is well furnished to supply these needs.

If a man had half the world in his power, he can make no more of it than this; as he wants it only to support an animal life, so is it unable to do any thing else for him, or to afford him any other happiness.

This is the state of man,—born with few wants, and into a large world very capable of supplying them. So that one would reasonably suppose that men should pass their lives in content and thankfulness to God; at least, that they should be free from violent disquiets and vexations, as being placed in a world that has more than enough to relieve all their wants.

But if to all this we add, that this short life, thus furnished with all that we want in it, is only a short passage to eternal glory, where we shall be clothed with the brightness of Angels, and enter into the joys of God, we might still more reasonably expect that human life should be a state of peace, and joy, and delight in God. Thus it would certainly be, if reason had its full power over us.

But, alas! though God, and nature, and reason, make human life thus free from wants and so full of happiness; yet our passions, in rebellion against God, against nature and reason, create a new world of evils, and fill human life with imaginary wants, and vain disquiets.

The man of pride has a thousand wants, which only his own pride has created; and these render him as full of trouble as if God had created him with a thousand appetites, without creating any thing that was proper to satisfy them. Envy and ambition have also their endless wants, which disquiet the souls of men, and by their contradictory motions, render them as foolishly miserable, as those that want to fly and creep at the same time.

Let but any complaining, disquieted man tell you the ground of his uneasiness, and you will plainly see that he is the author of his own torment; that he is vexing himself at some imaginary evil, which will cease to torment him as soon as he is content to be that which God, and nature, and reason, require him to be.

If you should see a man passing his days in disquiet, because he could not walk upon the water, or catch birds as they fly by him, you would readily confess that such a one might thank himself for such uneasiness. But now if you look into all the most tormenting disquiets of life, you will find them all thus absurd; where people are only tormented by their own folly, and vexing themselves at such things as no more concern them, nor are any more their proper good, than walking upon the water or catching birds.

What can you conceive more silly and extravagant, than to suppose a man racking his brains, and studying night and day how to fly?—wandering from his own house and home, wearying himself with climbing upon every ascent, cringing and courting everybody he meets to lift him up from the ground, bruising himself with continual falls, and at last breaking his neck?—and all this from an imagination that it would be glorious to have the eyes of people gazing up at him, and mighty happy to eat, and drink, and sleep, at the top of the highest trees in the kingdom: would you not readily own that such a one was only disquieted by his own folly?

If you ask, what it signifies to suppose such silly creatures as these, as are nowhere to be found in human life?

It may be answered, that wherever you see an ambitious man, there you see this vain and senseless flyer.

Again: if you should see a man that had a large pond of water, yet living in continual thirst, not suffering himself to drink half a draught, for fear of lessening his pond; if you should see him wasting his time and strength, in fetching more water to his pond; always thirsty, yet always carrying a bucket of water in his hand, watching early and late to catch the drops of rain, gaping after every cloud, and running greedily into every mire and mud, in hopes of water, and always studying how to make every ditch empty itself into his pond: if you should see him grow grey and old in these anxious labours, and at last end a careful, thirsty life, by falling into his own pond; would you not say that such a one was not only the author of all his own disquiets, but was foolish enough to be reckoned amongst idiots and madmen? But yet foolish and absurd as this character is, it does not represent half the follies, and absurd disquiet, of the covetous man.

I could now easily proceed to show the same effects of all our other passions, and make it plainly appear that all our miseries, vexations, and complaints, are entirely of our own making, and that, in the same absurd manner, as in these instances of the covetous and ambitious man. Look where you will, you will see all worldly vexations, but like the vexation of him that was always in mire and mud in search of water to drink, when he had more at home than was sufficient for a hundred horses.

Caelia is always telling you how provoked she is, what intolerable, shocking things happen to her, what monstrous usage she suffers, and what vexations she meets with everywhere. She tells you that her patience is quite worn out, and there is no bearing the behaviour of people. Every assembly that she is at, sends her home provoked; something or other has been said, or done, that no reasonable, well-bred person ought to bear. Poor people that want her charity are sent away with hasty answers, not because she has not a heart to part with any money, but because she is too full of some trouble of her own to attend to the complaints of others. Caelia has no business upon her hands but to receive the income of a plentiful fortune; but yet, by the doleful turn of her mind, you would be apt to think that she had neither food nor lodging. If you see her look more pale than ordinary, if her lips tremble when she speaks to you, it is because she is just come from a visit, where Lupus took no notice at all of her, but talked all the time to Lucinda, who has not half her fortune. When cross accidents have so disordered her spirits, that she is forced to send for the doctor, to make her able to eat, she tells him in great anger at Providence, that she never was well since she was born, and that she envies every beggar that she sees in health.

This is the disquiet life of Caelia, who has nothing to torment her but her own spirit.

If you could inspire her with Christian humility, you need do no more to make her as happy as any person in the world. This virtue would make her thankful to God for half so much health as she has had, and help her to enjoy more for the time to come. This virtue would keep off tremblings of the spirits, and loss of appetite, and her blood would need nothing else to sweeten it.

I have touched upon these absurd characters, for no other end but to convince you, in the plainest manner, that the strictest rules of religion are so far from rendering a life dull, anxious, and uncomfortable (as is above objected), that, on the contrary, all the miseries, vexations, and complaints, that are in the world, are owing to the want of religion; being directly caused by those absurd passions which religion teaches us to deny.

For all the wants which disturb human life, which make us uneasy to ourselves, quarrelsome with others, and unthankful to God; which weary us in vain labours and foolish anxieties; which carry us from project to project, from place to place, in a poor pursuit of we know not what, are the wants which neither God, nor nature, nor reason, hath subjected us to, but are solely infused into us by pride, envy, ambition, and covetousness.

So far, therefore, as you reduce your desires to such things as nature and reason require; so far as you regulate all the motions of your heart by the strict rules of religion, so far you remove yourself from that infinity of wants and vexations, which torment every heart that is left to itself.

Most people, indeed, confess that religion preserves us from a great many evils, and helps us in many respects to a more happy enjoyment of ourselves; but then they imagine that this is only true of such a moderate share of religion, as only gently restrains us from the excesses of our passions. They suppose that the strict rules and restraints of an exalted piety are such contradictions to our nature, as much needs make our lives dull and uncomfortable.

Although the weakness of this objection sufficiently appears from what hath been already said, yet I shall add one word more to it.

This objection supposes that religion, moderately practised, adds much to the happiness of life; but that such heights of piety as the perfection of religion requireth, have a contrary effect.

It supposes, therefore, that it is happy to be kept from the excesses of envy, but unhappy to be kept from other degrees of envy. That it is happy to be delivered from a boundless ambition, but unhappy to be without a more moderate ambition. It supposes, also, that the happiness of life consists in a mixture of virtue and vice, a mixture of ambition and humility, charity and envy, heavenly affection and covetousness. All which is as absurd as to suppose that it is happy to be free from excessive pains, but unhappy to be without more moderate pains; or that the happiness of health consisted in being partly sick and partly well.

For if humility be the peace and rest of the soul, then no one has so much happiness from humility, as he that is the most humble. If excessive envy is a torment of the soul, he most perfectly delivers himself from torment, that most perfectly extinguishes every spark of envy. If there is any peace and joy in doing any action according to the will of God, he that brings the most of his actions to this rule, does most of all increase the peace and joy of his life.

And thus it is in every virtue; if you act up to every degree of it, the more happiness you have from it. And so of every vice; if you only abate its excesses, you do but little for yourself; but if you reject it in all degrees, then you feel the true ease and joy of a reformed mind.

As for example: If religion only restrains the excesses of revenge, but lets the spirit still live within you in lesser instances, your religion may have made your life a little more outwardly decent, but not made you at all happier, or easier in yourself. But if you have once sacrificed all thoughts of revenge, in obedience to God, and are resolved to return good for evil at all times, that you may render yourself more like to God, and fitter for His mercy in the kingdom of love and glory; this is a height of virtue that will make you feel its happiness.

Secondly, As to those satisfactions and enjoyments, which an exalted piety requireth us to deny ourselves, this deprives us of no real comfort of life.

For, 1st, Piety requires us to renounce no ways of life, where we can act reasonably, and offer what we do to the glory of God. All ways of life, all satisfactions and enjoyments, that are within these bounds, are no way denied us by the strictest rules of piety. Whatever you can do, or enjoy, as in the presence of God, as His servant, as His rational creature that has received reason and knowledge from Him; all that you can perform conformably to a rational nature, and the will of God, all this is allowed by the laws of piety. And will you think that your life will be uncomfortable unless you may displease God, be a fool, and mad, and act contrary to that reason and wisdom which He has implanted in you?

And as for those satisfactions which we dare not offer to a holy God, which are only invented by the folly and corruption of the world, which inflame our passions, and sink our souls into grossness and sensuality, and render us incapable of the Divine favour, either here or hereafter; surely it can be no uncomfortable state of life to be rescued by religion from such self-murder, and to be rendered capable of eternal happiness.

Let us suppose a person destitute of that knowledge which we have from our senses, placed somewhere alone by himself, in the midst of a variety of things which he did not know how to use; that he has by him bread, wine, water, golden dust, iron chains, gravel, garments, fire, etc. Let it be supposed that he has no knowledge of the right use of these things, nor any direction from his senses how to quench his thirst, or satisfy his hunger, or make any use of the things about him. Let it be supposed, that in his drought he puts golden dust into his eyes; when his eyes smart, he puts wine into his ears; that in his hunger, he puts gravel into his mouth; that in pain, he loads himself with the iron chains; that feeling cold, he puts his feet in the water; that being frighted at the fire, he runs away from it; and that being weary, he makes a seat of his bread. Let it be supposed, that through his ignorance of the right use of the things that are about him, he will vainly torment himself whilst he lives, and at last die, blinded with dust, choked with gravel, and loaded with irons. Let it be supposed that some good being came to him, and showed him the nature and use of all the things that were about him, and gave him such strict rules of using them, as would certainly, if observed, make him the happier for all that he had, and deliver him from the pains of hunger, and thirst, and cold.

Now could you with any reason affirm, that those strict rules of using those things that were about him, had rendered that poor man's life dull and uncomfortable?

Now this is in some measure a representation of the strict rules of religion; they only relieve our ignorance, save us from tormenting ourselves, and teach us to use everything about us to our proper advantage.

Man is placed in a world full of variety of things; his ignorance makes him use many of them as absurdly as the man that put dust in his eyes to relieve his thirst, or put on chains to remove pain.

Religion, therefore, here comes in to his relief, and gives him strict rules of using everything that is about him; that by so using them suitably to his own nature, and the nature of the things, he may have always the pleasure of receiving a right benefit from them. It shows him what is strictly right in meat, and drink, and clothes; and that he has nothing else to expect from the things of this world, but to satisfy such wants of his own; and then to extend his assistance to all his brethren, that, as far as he is able, he may help all his fellow-creatures to the same benefit from the world that he hath.

It tells him that this world is incapable of giving him any other happiness; and that all endeavours to be happy in heaps of money, or acres of land, in fine clothes, rich beds, stately equipage, and show and splendour, are only vain endeavours, ignorant attempts after impossibilities, these things being no more able to give the least degree of happiness, than dust in the eyes can cure thirst, or gravel in the mouth satisfy hunger; but, like dust and gravel misapplied, will only serve to render him more unhappy by such an ignorant misuse of them.

It tells him that although this world can do no more for him than satisfy these wants of the body, yet that there is a much greater good prepared for man than eating, drinking, and dressing; that it is yet invisible to his eyes, being too glorious for the apprehension of flesh and blood; but reserved for him to enter upon, as soon as this short life is over; where, in a new body formed to an angelic likeness, he shall dwell in the light and glory of God to all eternity.

It tells him that this state of glory will be given to all those that make a right use of the things of this present world, who do not blind themselves with golden dust, or eat gravel, or groan under loads of iron of their own putting on; but use bread, water, wine, and garments, for such ends as are according to nature and reason; and who, with faith and thankfulness, worship the kind Giver of all that they enjoy here, and hope for hereafter.

Now can any one say that the strictest rules of such a religion as this debar us of any of the comforts of life? Might it not as justly be said of those rules that only hinder a man from choking himself with gravel? For the strictness of these rules only consists in the exactness of their rectitude.

Who would complain of the severe strictness of a law that, without any exception, forbade the putting of dust into our eyes? Who could think it too rigid, that there were no abatements? Now this is the strictness of religion; it requires nothing of us strictly, or without abatements, but where every degree of the thing is wrong, where every indulgence does us some hurt.

If religion forbids all instances of revenge, without any exception, it is because all revenge is of the nature of poison; and though we do not take so much as to put an end to life, yet if we take any at all, it corrupts the whole mass of blood, and makes it difficult to be restored to our former health.

If religion commands an universal charity, to love our neighbor as ourselves, to forgive and pray for all our enemies without any reserve; it is because all degrees of love are degrees of happiness, that strengthen and support the Divine life of the soul, and are as necessary to its health and happiness, as proper food is necessary to the health and happiness of the body.

If religion has laws against laying up treasures upon earth, and commands us to be content with food and raiment, it is because every other use of the world is abusing it to our own vexation, and turning all its conveniences into snares and traps to destroy us. It is because this plainness and simplicity of life secures us from the care and pains of restless pride and envy, and makes it easier to keep that straight road that will carry us to eternal life.

If religion saith, "Sell that thou hast, and give to the poor," it is because there is no other natural or reasonable use of our riches, no other way of making ourselves happier for them; it is because it is as strictly right to give others that which we do not want ourselves, as it is right to use so much as our own wants require. For if a man has more food than his own nature requires, how base and unreasonable is it to invent foolish ways of wasting it, and make sport for his own full belly, rather than let his fellow-creatures have the same comfort from food which he hath had. It is so far, therefore, from being a hard law or religion, to make this use of our riches, that a reasonable man would rejoice in that religion which teaches him to be happier in that which he gives away, than in that which he keeps for himself; which teaches him to make spare food and raiment be greater blessings to him, than that which feeds and clothes his own body.

If religion requires us sometimes to fast, and deny our natural appetites, it is to lessen that struggle and war that is in our nature, it is to render our bodies fitter instruments of purity, and more obedient to the good motions of Divine grace; it is to dry up the springs of our passions that war against the soul, to cool the flame of our blood, and render the mind more capable of Divine meditations. So that although these abstinences give some pain to the body, yet they so lessen the power of bodily appetites and passions, and so increase our taste of spiritual joys, that even these severities of religion, when practised with discretion, add much to the comfortable enjoyment of our lives.

If religion calleth us to a life of watching and prayer it is because we live amongst a crowd of enemies, and are always in need of the assistance of God. If we are to confess and bewail our sins, it is because such confessions relieve the mind, and restore it to ease; as burdens and weights taken off the shoulders, relieve the body, and make it easier to itself. If we are to be frequent and fervent in holy petitions, it is to keep us steady in the sight of our true God, and that we may never want the happiness of a lively faith, a joyful hope, and well-grounded trust in God. If we are to pray often, it is that we may be often happy in such secret joys as only prayer can give; in such communications of the Divine Presence, as will fill our minds with all the happiness that beings not in Heaven are capable of.

Was there anything in the world more worth our care, was there any exercise of the mind, or any conversation with men, that turned more to our advantage than this intercourse with God, we should not be called to such a continuance in prayer. But if a man considers what it is that he leaves when he retires to devotion, he will find it no small happiness to be so often relieved from doing nothing, or nothing to the purpose; from dull idleness, unprofitable labour, or vain conversation. If he considers that all that is in the world, and all that is doing in it, is only for the body, and bodily enjoyments, he will have reason to rejoice at those hours of prayer, which carry him to higher consolations, which raise him above these poor concerns, which open to his mind a scene of greater things, and accustom his soul to the hope and expectation of them.

If religion commands us to live wholly unto God, and to do all to His glory, it is because every other way is living wholly against ourselves, and will end in our own shame and confusion of face.

As everything is dark, that God does not enlighten; as everything is senseless, that has not its share of knowledge from Him; as nothing lives, but by partaking of life from Him; as nothing exists, but because He commands it to be; so there is no glory or greatness, but what is of the glory and greatness of God.

We indeed may talk of human glory as we may talk of human life, or human knowledge: but as we are sure that human life implies nothing of our own but a dependent living in God, or enjoying so much life in God; so human glory, whenever we find it, must be only so much glory as we enjoy in the glory of God.

This is the state of all creatures, whether men or Angels; as they make not themselves, so they enjoy nothing from themselves: if they are great, it must be only as great receivers of the gifts of God; their power can only be so much of the Divine power acting in them; their wisdom can be only so much of the Divine wisdom shining within them; and their light and glory, only so much of the light and glory of God shining upon them.

As they are not men or Angels, because they had a mind to be so themselves, but because the will of God formed them to be what they are; so they cannot enjoy this or that happiness of men or Angels, because they have a mind to it, but because it is the will of God that such things be the happiness of men, and such things the happiness of Angels. But now if God be thus all in all; if His will is thus the measure of all things, and all natures; if nothing can be done, but by His power; if nothing can be seen, but by a light from Him; if we have nothing to fear, but from His justice; if we have nothing to hope for, but from His goodness; if this is the nature of man, thus helpless in himself; if this is the state of all creatures, as well those in Heaven as those on earth; if they are nothing, can do nothing, can suffer no pain, nor feel any happiness, but so far, and in such degrees, as the power of God does all this; if this be the state of things, then how can we have the least glimpse of joy or comfort, how can we have any peaceful enjoyment of ourselves, but by living wholly unto that God, using and doing everything conformably to His will? A life thus devoted unto God, looking wholly unto Him in all our actions, and doing all things suitable to His glory, is so far from being dull and uncomfortable, that it creates new comforts in everything that we do.

On the contrary, would you see how happy they are who live according to their own wills, who cannot submit to the dull and melancholy business of a life devoted unto God; look at the man in the parable, to whom his Lord had given one talent.

He could not bear the thoughts of using his talent according to the will of Him from whom he had it, and therefore he chose to make himself happier in a way of his own. "Lord," says he, "I knew thee, that thou art an hard man, reaping where thou hadst not sown, and gathering where thou hadst not strawed: and I was afraid, and went and hid thy talent in the earth! lo, there thou hast that is thine."

His Lord, having convicted him out of his own mouth, despatches him with this sentence, "Cast the unprofitable servant into outer darkness: there shall be weeping and gnashing of teeth." (Matt. xxv. 24, 25, 30)

Here you see how happy this man made himself, by not acting wholly according to his Lord's will. It was, according to his own account, a happiness of murmuring and discontent; I knew thee, says he, that thou wast an hard man: it was a happiness of fears and apprehensions; I was, says he, afraid: it was a happiness of vain labours and fruitless travels; I went, says he, and hid thy talent; and after having been awhile the sport of foolish passions, tormenting fears, and fruitless labour, he is rewarded with darkness, eternal weeping, and gnashing of teeth.

Now this is the ·happiness of all those who look upon a strict and exalted piety, that is, a right use of their talent, to be a dull and melancholy state of life.

They may live a while free from the restraints and directions of religion; but, instead thereof, they must be under the absurd government of their passions: they must, like the man in the parable, live in murmurings and discontents, in fears and apprehensions. They may avoid the labour of doing good, of spending their time devoutly, of laying up treasures in Heaven, of clothing the naked, of visiting the sick; but then they must, like this man, have labours and pains in vain, that tend to no use or advantage, that do no good either to themselves or others; they must travel, and labour, and work, and dig, to hide their talent in the earth. They must, like him, at their Lord's coming, be convicted out of their own mouths, be accused by their own hearts, and have everything that they have said and thought of religion, be made to show the justice of their condemnation to eternal darkness, weeping, and gnashing of teeth.

This is the purchase that they make, who avoid the strictness and perfection of religion, in order to live happily.

On the other hand, would you see a short description of the happiness of a life rightly employed, wholly devoted to God, you must look at the man in the parable to whom his Lord had given five talents. "Lord," says he, "thou deliveredst unto me five talents; behold, I have gained beside them five talents more. His Lord said unto him, Well done, thou good and faithful servant; thou hast been faithful over a few things, I will make thee ruler over many things: enter thou into the joy of thy Lord."

Here you see a life that is wholly intent upon the improvement of the talents, that is devoted wholly unto God, is a state of happiness, prosperous labours, and glorious success. Here are not, as in the former case, any uneasy passions, murmurings, vain fears, and fruitless labours. The man is not toiling and digging in the earth for no end or advantage; but his pious labours prosper in his hands, his happiness increases upon him; the blessing of five becomes the blessing of ten talents; and he is received with a "Well done, good and faithful servant: enter thou into the joy of thy Lord."

Now as the case of these men in the parable left nothing else to their choice, but either to be happy in using their gifts to the glory of the Lord, or miserable by using them according to their own humours and fancies; so the state of Christianity leaves us no other choice.

All that we have, all that we are, all that we enjoy, are only so many talents from God: if we use them to the ends of a pious and holy life, our five talents will become ten, and our labours will carry us into the joy of our Lord; but if we abuse them to the gratifications of our own passions, sacrificing the gifts of God to our own pride and vanity, we shall live here in vain labours and foolish anxieties, shunning religion as a melancholy thing, accusing our Lord as a hard master, and then fall into everlasting misery.

We may for a while amuse ourselves with names and sounds, and shadows of happiness; we may talk of this or that greatness and dignity; but if we desire real happiness, we have no other possible way to it but by improving our talents, by so holily and piously using the powers and faculties of men in this present state, that we may be happy and glorious in the powers and faculties of Angels in the world to come.

How ignorant, therefore, are they of the nature of religion, of the nature of man, and the nature of God, who think a life of strict piety and devotion to God to be a dull uncomfortable state; when it is so plain and certain that there is neither comfort nor joy to be found in anything else!

FREE GRACE

JOHN WESLEY

(1703-1791)

JOHN WESLEY's sermon on "Free Grace" (here presented) was a
stirring discourse for the times. Preached at Bristol in 1739 this
was an explicit denial of "the horrible decree of predestination"
and a repudiation of those who would revive the old Calvinistic
determinism. George Whitefield, Wesley's friend and co-worker
in the evangelical movement, felt the sting of this sermon, im-
ploring Wesley not to print it. His Calvinism and Wesley's
Arminianism severed their relationship, spotted with hot controversy in 1740 and 1741 (to be reconciled personally years later).

Calvinistic Methodism developed into a school. But Arminian
Methodism carried on the Wesleyan tradition. (Arminius [1560-
1609] held the view that man has freedom as opposed to unconditional election to salvation.) God, said Wesley, has elected to
salvation those who repent, believe and persevere. A person is
said to suffer reprobation only if such a person remains aloof
from the proffered salvation. Thus man is responsible in part
for his ultimate destiny.

Methodism has no rigid theology. In 1788 John Wesley, its
original key figure, declared "There is no other religious Society
under Heaven which requires nothing of man in order to their
admission into it but a desire to save their souls. . . . The Methodists alone do not insist on your holding this or that opinion;
but they think and let think. Neither do they impose any particular mode of worship. . . . Now I do not know any other
religious society, either ancient or modern, wherein such liberty
of conscience is now allowed, since the age of the Apostles."

The only decisive concern of Wesley's, qualifying the above declaration—and it was deeply set in him—was to turn his followers away from predestinarian Calvinism and to the acceptance of the free grace doctrine in which there is universal redemption for all men who accept and persevere in such acceptance.

Editor

FREE GRACE

"HE THAT spareth not his own Son, but delivered him up for us all, how shall he not with him also freely give us all things?" Rom. viii, 32.

1. How freely does God love the world! While we were yet sinners, "Christ died for the ungodly." While we were "dead in sin," God "spared not his own Son, but delivered him up for us all." And how freely with him does he "give us all things!" Verily, FREE GRACE is all in all!

2. The grace or love of God, whence cometh our salvation, is FREE IN ALL, and FREE FOR ALL.

3. First: It is free IN ALL to whom it is given. It does not depend on any power or merit in man; no, not in any degree, neither in whole, nor in part. It does not in any wise depend either on the good works or righteousness of the receiver; not on any thing he has done, or any thing he is. It does not depend on his endeavours. It does not depend on his good tempers, or good desires, or good purposes and intentions; for all these flow from the free grace of God; they are the streams only, not the fountain. They are the fruits of free grace, and not the root. They are not the cause, but the effects of it. Whatsoever good is in man, or is done by man, God is the author and doer of it. Thus is his grace free in all; that is, no way depending on any power or merit in man, but on God alone, who freely gave us his own Son, and "with him freely giveth us all things."

4. But is it free FOR ALL, as well as IN ALL? To this some have answered, "No: it is free only for those whom God hath ordained to life; and they are but a little flock. The greater part

of mankind God hath ordained to death; and it is not free for them. Them God hateth; and therefore, before they were born, decreed they should die eternally. And this he absolutely decreed; because so was his good pleasure; because it was his sovereign will. Accordingly they are born for this, to be destroyed body and soul in hell. And they grow up under the irrevocable curse of God, without any possibility of redemption; for what grace God gives, he gives only for this, to increase, not prevent, their damnation."

5. This is that decree of predestination. But methinks I hear one say, "This is not the predestination which I hold: I hold only, the election of grace. What I believe is no more than this: that God, before the foundation of the world, did elect a certain number of men to be justified, sanctified, and glorified. Now all these will be saved, and none else: for the rest of mankind God leaves to themselves; so they follow the imaginations of their own hearts, which are only evil continually, and, waxing worse and worse, are at length justly punished with everlasting destruction."

6. Is this all the predestination which you hold? Consider: perhaps this is not all. Do not you believe, God ordained them to this very thing? If so, you believe the whole decree; you hold predestination in the full sense, which has been above described. But it may be, you think you do not. Do not you then believe, God hardens the hearts of them that perish? Do not you believe, he (literally) hardened Pharaoh's heart, and that for this end he raised him up, or created him? Why this amounts to just the same thing. If you believe Pharaoh, or any one man upon earth, was created for this end, to be damned, you hold all that has been said of predestination. And there is no need you should add, that God seconds his decree, which is supposed unchangeable and irresistible, by hardening the hearts of those vessels of wrath, whom that decree had before fitted for destruction.

7. Well; but it may be you do not believe even this: you do not hold any decree of reprobation: you do not think God decrees any man to be damned, nor hardens, irresistibly fits him for damnation: you only say, "God eternally decreed, that all being dead in sin, he would say to some of the dry bones, Live, and to others he would not; that, consequently, these

should be made alive, and those abide in death,—these should glorify God by their salvation, and those by their destruction."

8. Is not this what you mean by the election of grace? If it be, I would ask one or two questions: Are any who are not thus elected, saved? Or, were any, from the foundation of the world? Is it possible any man should be saved, unless he be thus elected? If you say, No; you are but where you was: you are not got one hair's breadth farther: you still believe, that in consequence of an unchangeable, irresistible decree of God, the greater part of mankind abide in death, without any possibility of redemption; inasmuch as none can save them but God, and he will not save them. You believe he hath absolutely decreed not to save them; and what is this, but decreeing to damn them? It is, in effect, neither more nor less: it comes to the same thing: for if you are dead, and altogether unable to make yourself alive; then, if God has absolutely decreed he will make only others alive, and not you, he hath absolutely decreed your everlasting death; you are absolutely consigned to damnation. So then, though you use softer words than some, you mean the self same thing; and God's decree concerning the election of grace, according to your own account of it, amounts to neither more nor less than what others call, "God's decree of reprobation."

9. Call it therefore by whatever name you please, election, preterition, predestination, or reprobation, it comes in the end to the same thing. The sense of all is plainly this: by virtue of an eternal, unchangeable, irresistible decree of God, one part of mankind are infallibly saved, and the rest infallibly damned; it being impossible that any of the former should be damned, or that any of the latter should be saved.

10. But if this be so, then is all preaching vain. It is needless to them that are elected; for they, whether with preaching or without, will infallibly be saved. Therefore the end of preaching, to save souls, is void with regard to them. And it is useless to them that are not elected, for they cannot possibly be saved. They, whether with preaching or without, will infallibly be damned. The end of preaching is therefore void with regard to them likewise; so that in either case, our preaching is vain, as your hearing is also vain.

11. This, then, is a plain proof that the doctrine of pre-destination is not a doctrine of God, because it makes void the ordinance of God: and God is not divided against himself. A second is, that it directly tends to destroy that holiness, which is the end of all the ordinances of God. I do not say, none who hold it are holy; (for God is of tender mercy to those who are unavoidably entangled in errors of any kind;) but that the doc-trine itself,—That every man is either elected or not elected from eternity, and that the one must inevitably be saved, and the other inevitably damned,—has a manifest tendency to destroy holiness in general. For it wholly takes away those first motives to follow after it. [sic] so frequently proposed in Scripture, the hope of future reward and fear of punishment, the hope of heaven and fear of hell. That these shall go away into everlasting punishment, and those into life eternal, is no motive to him to struggle for life, who believes his lot is cast already: it is not rea-sonable for him so to do, if he thinks he is unalterably adjudged either to life or death. You will say, "But he knows not whether it is life or death." What then?—this helps not the matter: for if a sick man knows that he must unavoidably die, or unavoidably recover, though he knows not which, it is unreasonable for him to take any physic at all. He might justly say, (and so I have heard some speak, both in bodily sickness and in spiritual,) "If I am ordained to life, I shall live; if to death, I shall die: so I need not trouble myself about it." So directly does this doc-trine tend to shut the very gate of holiness in general, to hinder unholy men from ever approaching thereto, or striving to enter in thereat.

12. As directly does this doctrine tend to destroy several par-ticular branches of holiness. Such as meekness and love: love, I mean, of our enemies; of the evil and unthankful. I say not, that none who hold it have meekness and love; (for as is the power of God, so is his mercy;) but that it naturally tends to inspire, or increase, a sharpness or eagerness of temper, which is quite contrary to the meekness of Christ; as then especially appears, when they are opposed on this head. And it as naturally inspires contempt or coldness towards those whom we suppose outcasts from God. "Oh but," you say, "I suppose no particular man a reprobate." You mean, you would not if you could help it.

But you cannot help sometimes applying your general doctrine to particular persons: the enemy of souls will apply it for you. You know how often he has done so. But you rejected the thought with abhorrence. True: as soon as you could: but how did it sour and sharpen your spirit in the mean time? You well know it was not the spirit of love which you then felt towards that poor sinner, whom you supposed or suspected, whether you would or no, to have been hated of God from eternity.

13. Thirdly, This doctrine tends to destroy the comfort of religion, the happiness of Christianity. This is evident as to all those who believe themselves to be reprobated; or who only suspect or fear it. All the great and precious promises are lost to them; they afford them no ray of comfort: for they are not the elect of God; therefore they have neither lot nor portion in them. This is an effectual bar to their finding any comfort or happiness, even in that religion whose ways are designed to be "ways of pleasantness, and all her paths peace."

14. And as to you who believe yourselves the elect of God, what is your happiness? I hope not a notion; a speculative belief; a bare opinion of any kind; but a feeling possession of God in your heart, wrought in you by the Holy Ghost, or the witness of God's Spirit with your spirit that you are a child of God. This, otherwise termed "the full assurance of faith," is the true ground of a Christian's happiness. And it does indeed imply a full assurance that all your past sins are forgiven, and that you are *now* a child of God. But it does not necessarily imply a full assurance of our future perseverance. I do not say this is never joined to it, but that it is not necessarily implied therein; for many have the one, who have not the other.

15. Now this witness of the Spirit, experience shows to be much obstructed by this doctrine; and not only in those who, believing themselves reprobated, by this belief thrust it far from them, but even in them that have tasted of that good gift, who yet have soon lost it again, and fallen back into doubts, and fears, and darkness,—horrible darkness, that might be felt! And I appeal to any of you who hold this doctrine, to say, between God and your own hearts, whether you have not often a return of doubts and fears concerning your election or perseverance? If you ask, who has not? I answer, very few of those

that hold this doctrine,—but many, very many of those that hold it not, in all parts of the earth, many of those who know and feel they are in Christ to day, and "take no thought for the morrow," who "abide in him" by faith from hour to hour, or rather from moment to moment,—many of these have enjoyed the uninterrupted witness of his Spirit, the continual light of his countenance, from the moment wherein they first believed, for many months or years, to this day.

16. That assurance of faith, which these enjoy, excludes all doubt and fear. It excludes all kinds of doubt and fear concerning their future perseverance; though it is not properly, as was said before, an assurance of what is future, but only of what *now* is. And this needs not for its support a speculative belief that whoever is once ordained to life must live; for it is wrought, from hour to hour, by the mighty power of God, "by the Holy Ghost which is given unto them." And therefore that doctrine is not of God, because it tends to obstruct, if not destroy, this great work of the Holy Ghost, whence flows the chief comfort of religion, the happiness of Christianity.

17. Again: how uncomfortable a thought is this, that thousands and millions of men, without any preceding offence or fault of theirs, were unchangeably doomed to everlasting burnings! How peculiarly uncomfortable must it be to those who have put on Christ! To those who, being filled with bowels of mercy, tenderness, and compassion, could even "wish themselves accursed for their brethren's sake!"

18. Fourthly: This uncomfortable doctrine directly tends to destroy our zeal for good works. And this it does, first, as it naturally tends (according to what was observed before) to destroy our love to the greater part of mankind, namely, the evil and unthankful. For whatever lessens our love, must so far lessen our desire to do them good. This it does, secondly, as it cuts off one of the strongest motives to all acts of bodily mercy, such as feeding the hungry, clothing the naked, and the like; viz. the hope of saving their souls from death. For what avails it to relieve their temporal wants, who are just dropping into eternal fire? "Well: but run and snatch them as brands out of the fire."—Nay, this you suppose impossible. They were appointed thereunto, you say, from eternity, before they had done

either good or evil. You believe it is the will of God they should die. And "who hath resisted his will?" But you say, you do not know whether these are elected or not. What then? If you know they are the one or the other, that they are either elected, or not elected, all your labour is void and vain. In either case, your advice, reproof, or exhortation, is as needless and useless as our preaching. It is needless to them that are elected; for they will infallibly be saved without it. It is useless to them that are not elected; for with or without it they will infallibly be damned: therefore you cannot, consistently with your principles, take any pains about their salvation. Consequently those principles directly tend to destroy your zeal for good works; for all good works; but particularly for the greatest of all, the saving of souls from death.

19. But, fifthly, This doctrine not only tends to destroy Christian holiness, happiness, and good works, but hath also a direct and manifest tendency to overthrow the whole Christian revelation. The point which the wisest of the modern unbelievers most industriously labour to prove, is that the Christian revelation is not necessary. They well know, could they once show this, the conclusion would be too plain to be denied, "If it be not necessary, it is not true." Now this fundamental point you give up. For supposing that eternal, unchangeable decree, one part of mankind must be saved though the Christian revelation were not in being, and the other part of mankind must be damned, notwithstanding that revelation. And what would an infidel desire more? You allow him all he asks. In making the gospel thus unnecessary to all sorts of men, you give up the whole Christian cause. "Oh tell it not in Gath! Publish it not in the streets of Askelon! lest the daughters of the uncircumcised rejoice;" lest the sons of unbelief triumph!

20. And as this doctrine manifestly and directly tends to overthrow the whole Christian revelation, so it does the same thing, by plain consequence, in making that revelation contradict itself. For it is grounded on such an interpretation of some texts (more or fewer it matters not) as flatly contradicts all the other texts, and indeed the whole scope and tenor of Scripture. For instance: the assertors of this doctrine interpret that text of Scripture, "Jacob have I loved, but Esau have I hated," as

implying, that God in a literal sense hated Esau, and all the reprobated, from eternity. Now what can possibly be a more flat contradiction than this, not only to the whole scope and tenor of Scripture, but also to all those particular texts which expressly declare, "God is love?" Again: they infer from that text, "I will have mercy on whom I will have mercy," Rom. ix, 15, that God is love only to some men, viz. the elect, and that he hath mercy for those only; flatly contrary to which is the whole tenor of Scripture, as is that express declaration in particular, "The Lord is loving unto every man, and his mercy is over all his works," Psalm cxlv, 9. Again: they infer from that and the like texts, "It is not of him that willeth, nor of him that runneth, but of God that showeth mercy," that he showeth mercy only to those to whom he had respect from all eternity. Nay, but who replieth against God now? You now contradict the whole oracles of God, which declare throughout, "God is no respecter of persons," Acts x, 34; "There is no respect of persons with him," Rom. ii, 11. Again: from that text,—"The children being not yet born, neither having done any good or evil, that the purpose of God according to election might stand, not of works, but of him that calleth; it was said unto her, [unto Rebecca,] the elder shall serve the younger;"—you infer, that our being predestinated, or elect, no way depends on the foreknowledge of God: flatly contrary to this are all the Scriptures; and those in particular, "Elect according to the foreknowledge of God," 1 Pet. i, 2; "Whom he did foreknow, he also did predestinate," Rom. viii, 29.

21. And, "the same Lord over all is rich in mercy to all that call upon him," Rom. x, 12: But you say, no; he is such only to those for whom Christ died. And those are not all, but only a few, whom God hath chosen out of the world; for he died not for all, but only for those who were "chosen in him before the foundation of the world," Eph. i, 4. Flatly contrary to your interpretation of these Scriptures, also, is the whole tenor of the New Testament; as are in particular those texts;—"Destroy not him with thy meat, for whom Christ died," Rom. xiv, 15: [a clear proof that Christ died, not only for those that are saved, but also for them that perish;] he is "The Saviour of the world," John iv, 42; he is "The Lamb of God that taketh away the

sins of the world," John i, 29; "He is the propitiation, not for our sins only, but also for the sins of the whole world," 1 John ii, 2; "He [the living God] is the Saviour of all men," 1 Tim. iv, 10; "He gave himself a ransom for all," 1 Tim. ii, 6; "He tasted death for every man," Heb. ii, 9.

22. If you ask, why then are not all men saved? The whole law and the testimony answer, first, not because of any decree of God; not because it is his pleasure they should die; for, "as I live, saith the Lord God," "I have no pleasure in the death of him that dieth," Ezek. xviii, 32. Whatever be the cause of their perishing, it cannot be his will if the oracles of God are true; for they declare, "He is not willing that any should perish, but that all should come to repentance," 2 Pet. iii, 9; "He willeth that all men should be saved." And they, secondly, declare what is the cause why all men are not saved, namely, that they will not be saved: so our Lord expressly; "Ye will not come unto me that ye may have life," John v, 40. "The power of the Lord is present to heal" them, but they will not be healed. "They reject the counsel," the merciful counsel of God "against themselves," as did their stiff necked forefathers. And therefore are they without excuse; because God would save them, but they will not be saved: this is the condemnation, "How often would I have gathered you together, and ye would not," Matt. xxiii, 37.

23. Thus manifestly does this doctrine tend to overthrow the whole Christian revelation, by making it contradict itself; by giving such an interpretation of some texts, as flatly contradicts all the other texts, and indeed the whole scope and tenor of Scripture;—an abundant proof that it is not of God. But neither is this all: for, seventhly, it is a doctrine full of blasphemy; of such blasphemy as I should dread to mention, but that the honour of our gracious God, and the cause of his truth, will not suffer me to be silent. In the cause of God, then, and from a sincere concern for the glory of his great name, I will mention a few of the horrible blasphemies, contained in this horrible doctrine. But first, I must warn every one of you that hears, as ye will answer it at the great day, not to charge me (as some have done) with blaspheming, because I mention the blasphemy of others. And the more you are grieved with them that do thus blaspheme, see that ye "confirm your love towards

them" the more, and that your hearts' desire, and continual prayer to God, be, "Father, forgive them, for they know not what they do."

24. This premised, let it be observed, that this doctrine represents our blessed Lord, "Jesus Christ, the righteous," "the only begotten Son of the Father, full of grace and truth," as a hypocrite, a deceiver of the people, a man void of common sincerity. For it cannot be denied, that he every where speaks as if he was willing that all men should be saved. Therefore, to say he was not willing that all men should be saved, is to represent him as a mere hypocrite and dissembler. It cannot be denied that the gracious words which came out of his mouth, are full of invitations to all sinners. To say then, he did not intend to save all sinners, is to represent him as a gross deceiver of the people. You cannot deny that he says, "Come unto me, all ye that are weary and heavy laden." If, then, you say he calls those that cannot come; those whom he knows to be unable to come; those whom he can make able to come, but will not; how is it possible to describe greater insincerity? You represent him as mocking his helpless creatures, by offering what he never intends to give. You describe him as saying one thing, and meaning another; as pretending the love which he had not. Him, in "whose mouth was no guile," you make full of deceit, void of common sincerity;—then especially, when, drawing nigh the city, he wept over it, and said, "Oh Jerusalem, Jerusalem, thou that killest the prophets, and stonest them that are sent unto thee, how often *would I* have gathered thy children together,—and *ye would not;*" ηθελησα—και ουχ πθελησατε. Now if you say, *would,* but *he would not,* you represent him (which who could hear?) as weeping crocodile's tears; weeping over the prey which himself had doomed to destruction!

25. Such blasphemy this, as one would think might make the ears of a Christian to tingle! But there is yet more behind; for just as it honours the Son, so doth this doctrine honour the Father. It destroys all his attributes at once: it overturns both his justice, mercy, and truth: yea, it represents the most holy God as worse than the devil, as both more false, more cruel, and more unjust. More *false;* because the devil, liar as he is, hath never said, "He willeth all men to be saved:" more *unjust;*

because the devil cannot, if he would, be guilty of such injustice as you ascribe to God, when you say, that God condemned millions of souls to everlasting fire, prepared for the devil and his angels, for continuing in sin, which, for want of that grace *he will not* give them, they cannot avoid: and more *cruel;* because that unhappy spirit "seeketh rest and findeth none;" so that his own restless misery is a kind of temptation to him to tempt others. But God resteth in his high and holy place; so that to suppose him, of his own mere motion, of his pure will and pleasure, happy as he is, to doom his creatures, whether they will or no, to endless misery, is to impute such cruelty to him, as we cannot impute even to the great enemy of God and man. It is to represent the Most High God (he that hath ears to hear, let him hear!) as more cruel, false, and unjust than the devil!

26. This is the blasphemy clearly contained in *the horrible decree* of predestination! And here I fix my foot. On this I join issue with every asserter of it. You represent God as worse than the devil; more false, more cruel, more unjust. But you say, you will prove it by Scripture Hold! What will you prove by Scripture? That God is worse than the devil? It cannot be. Whatever that Scripture proves, it never can prove this; whatever its true meaning be, this cannot be its true meaning. Do you ask, What is its true meaning then? If I say, I know not, you have gained nothing; for there are many scriptures, the true sense whereof neither you nor I shall know, till death is swallowed up in victory. But this I know, better it were to say it had no sense at all, than to say it had such a sense as this. It cannot mean, whatever it mean besides, that the God of truth is a liar. Let it mean what it will, it cannot mean that the Judge of all the world is unjust. No scripture can mean that God is not love, or that his mercy is not over all his works: that is, whatever it prove besides, no scripture can prove predestination.

27. This is the blasphemy for which (however I love the persons who assert it) I abhor the doctrine of predestination; a doctrine, upon the supposition of which, if one could possibly suppose it for a moment, (call it election, reprobation, or what you please, for all comes to the same thing,) one might say to our adversary the devil, "Thou fool, why dost thou roar about

any longer? Thy lying in wait for souls is as needless and use-less as our preaching. Hearest thou not, that God hath taken thy work out of thy hands; and that he doeth it much more effectually? Thou, with all thy principalities and powers, canst only so assault that we may resist thee; but he can irresistibly destroy both body and soul in hell! Thou canst only entice; but his unchangeable decree, to leave thousands of souls in death, compels them to continue in sin, till they drop into ever-lasting burnings. Thou temptest; he forceth us to be damned: for we cannot resist his will. Thou fool, why goest thou about any longer, seeking whom thou mayest devour? Hearest thou not that God is the devouring lion, the destroyer of souls, the murderer of men? Moloch caused only children to pass through the fire; and that fire was soon quenched; or, the corruptible body being consumed, its torment was at an end: but God, thou art told, by his eternal decree, fixed before they had done good or evil, causes not only children of a span long, but the parents also, to pass through the fire of hell, the 'fire which never shall be quenched:' and the body which is cast thereinto, being incor-ruptible and immortal, will be ever consuming and never con-sumed, but 'the smoke of their torment,' because it is God's good pleasure, 'ascendeth up for ever and ever.' "

28. Oh how would the enemy of God and man rejoice to hear these things were so! How would he cry aloud and spare not! How would he lift up his voice and say, "To your tents, oh Israel! Flee from the face of this God, or ye shall utterly perish! But whither will ye flee? Into heaven? He is there. Down to hell? He is there also. Ye cannot flee from an omnipresent, almighty tyrant. And whether ye flee or stay, I call heaven his throne, and earth his footstool, to witness against you, ye shall perish, ye shall die eternally. Sing, oh hell, and rejoice, ye that are under the earth! for God, even the mighty God, hath spoken, and devoted to death thousands of souls, from the rising of the sun, unto the going down thereof! Here, oh death, is thy sting! They shall not, cannot escape, for the mouth of the Lord hath spoken it. Here, oh grave, is thy victory! Nations yet unborn, or ever they have done good or evil, are doomed never to see the light of life, but thou shalt gnaw upon them for ever and ever: Let all those morning stars sing together, who fell

with Lucifer, son of the morning! Let all the sons of hell shout
for joy! For the decree is past, and who can disannul it?"

29. Yea, the decree is past: and so it was before the foundation of the world. But what decree? Even this: "I will set before
the sons of men, 'life and death, blessing and cursing.' And
the soul that chooseth life shall live, as the soul that chooseth
death shall die." This decree, whereby "whom God did foreknow, he did predestinate," was indeed from everlasting: this,
whereby all who suffer Christ to make them alive are "elect,
according to the foreknowledge of God," now standeth fast, even
as the moon, and as the faithful witnesses in heaven; and when
heaven and earth shall pass away, yet this shall not pass away,
for it is as unchangeable and eternal, as is the being of God
that gave it. This decree yields the strongest encouragement to
abound in all good works, and in all holiness; and it is a well
spring of joy, of happiness also, to our great and endless comfort. This is worthy of God: it is every way consistent with all
the perfections of his nature. It gives us the noblest view both
of his justice, mercy, and truth. To this agrees the whole scope
of the Christian revelation, as well as all the parts thereof. To
this Moses and all the prophets bear witness, and our blessed
Lord and all his apostles. Thus Moses, in the name of his
Lord, "I call heaven and earth to record against you this day,
that I have set before you life and death, blessing and cursing;
therefore choose life, that thou and thy seed may live." Thus
Ezekiel: (to cite one prophet for all:) "The soul that sinneth,
it shall die: the son shall not bear [eternally] the iniquity of
the father. The righteousness of the righteous shall be upon
him, and the wickedness of the wicked shall be upon him," chap.
xviii, 20. Thus our blessed Lord: "If any man thirst, let him
come unto me and drink," John vii, 37. Thus his great apostle,
St. Paul, Acts xvii, 30, "God commandeth all men every where
to repent;"—"all men, every where;" every man in every place,
without any exception, either of place or person. Thus St. James:
"If any of you lack wisdom, let him ask of God, who giveth to
all men liberally, and upbraideth not, and it shall be given him,"
James i, 5. Thus St. Peter: 2 Pet. iii, 9, "The Lord is not willing
that any should perish, but that all should come to repentance."
And thus St. John: "If any man sin, we have an advocate with

the Father: and he is the propitiation for our sins: and not for ours only, but for the sins of the whole world," 1 John ii, 1, 2.

30. Oh hear ye this, ye that forget God! Ye cannot charge your death upon him! "Have I any pleasure at all, that the wicked should die, saith the Lord God? Ezek. xviii, 23, &c. Repent, and turn from all your transgressions: so iniquity shall not be your ruin. Cast away from you all your transgressions whereby ye have transgressed,—for why will ye die, oh house of Israel? For I have no pleasure in the death of him that dieth, saith the Lord God. Wherefore turn yourselves, and live ye." "As I live, saith the Lord God, I have no pleasure in the death of the wicked.—Turn ye, turn ye, from your evil ways: for why will ye die, oh house of Israel?" Ezek. xxxiii. 11.

SINNERS IN THE HANDS OF AN ANGRY GOD

FREEDOM OF WILL

JONATHAN EDWARDS

(1703-1758)

OF THE many published literary works of Jonathan Edwards two are the best known.

The one is the famous Enfield Sermon preached in 1741 (July 8th) entitled "Sinners in the Hands of an Angry God." Edwards, at this stage of his life, was at the height of power and popularity as a preacher. It is a hell-fire appeal to repentance, a warning to those who play fast and loose with the disfavor of God; it is the proclamation of the fleeting chance of salvation. To this sermon sinners responded with moans and cries and shrieks. The Christian religion is a serious business.

The other, the "Freedom of Will," his *magnum opus,* published in 1754, is a philosophical defense of Edwards' own Calvinism. God is free but bound in His Will by His own wisdom. Man is a total person not subject to arbitrary and causeless will within his own personality. Choices are tied in with dispositions and drives. The Will of God is bound up with God's own Nature and is sovereign. No one can do what he pleases. Our volitions are bound up with and determined by our motives and inclinations—expressing the prevailing nature of ourselves. There is no freedom apart from our natures. Moral necessity is not incompatible with moral judgments of praise or blame, reward or punishment.

A graduate of Yale College in 1720, Edwards became in 1727 a colleague minister with his celebrated grandfather, Solomon

Stoddard of Northampton, Massachusetts, and then his successor until 1750.

Calvinism became for him a live scriptural option, the sovereignty of God a basic doctrine "exceeding pleasant, bright and sweet." The revivals in New England (he felt certain) were visitations of God demanding a purified church of regenerate members. Arminianism with its notion of limitations to God's sovereignty was the beast to be slain.

Editor

SINNERS IN THE HANDS OF AN ANGRY GOD

DEUT. xxxii. 35.

Their foot shall slide in due time.

IN THIS verse is threatened the vengeance of God on the wicked unbelieving Israelites, who were God's visible people, and who lived under the means of grace; but who, notwithstanding all God's wonderful works towards them, remained (as ver. 28.) void of counsel, having no understanding in them. Under all the cultivations of heaven, they brought forth bitter and poisonous fruit; as in the two verses next preceding the text.—The expression I have chosen for my text, *Their foot shall slide in due time,* seems to imply the following things, relating to the punishment and destruction to which these wicked Israelites were exposed.

1. That they were always exposed to *destruction;* as one that stands or walks in slippery places is always exposed to fall. This is implied in the manner of their destruction coming upon them, being represented by their foot sliding. The same is expressed, Psalm lxxiii. 18. "Surely thou didst set them in slippery places; thou castedst them down into destruction."

2. It implies, that they were always exposed to sudden unexpected destruction. As he that walks in slippery places is every moment liable to fall, he cannot foresee one moment whether he shall stand or fall the next; and when he does fall, he falls at once without warning: Which is also expressed in Psalm lxxiii.

18, 19. "Surely thou didst set them in slippery places; thou castedst them down into destruction: How are they brought into desolation as in a moment!"

3. Another thing implied is, that they are liable to fall *of themselves*, without being thrown down by the hand of another; as he that stands or walks on slippery ground needs nothing but his own weight to throw him down.

4. That the reason why they are not fallen already, and do not fall now, is only that God's appointed time is not come. For it is said, that when that due time, or appointed time comes *their foot shall slide*. Then they shall be left to fall, as they are inclined by their own weight. God will not hold them up in these slippery places any longer, but will let them go; and then, at that very instant, they shall fall into destruction; as he that stands on such slippery declining ground, on the edge of a pit, he cannot stand alone, when he is let go he immediately falls and is lost.

The observation from the words that I would now insist upon is this.—"There is nothing that keeps wicked men at any one moment out of hell, but the mere pleasure of God"—By the *mere* pleasure of God, I mean his *sovereign* pleasure, his arbitrary will, restrained by no obligation, hindered by no manner of difficulty, any more than if nothing else but God's mere will had in the least degree, or in any respect whatsoever, any hand in the preservation of wicked men one moment.—The truth of this observation may appear by the following considerations.

1. There is no want of *power* in God to cast wicked men into hell at any moment. Men's hands cannot be strong when God rises up. The strongest have no power to resist him, nor can any deliver out of his hands.—He is not only able to cast wicked men into hell, but he can most easily do it. Sometimes an earthly prince meets with a great deal of difficulty to subdue a rebel, who has found means to fortify himself, and has made himself strong by the numbers of his followers. But it is not so with God. There is no fortress that is any defence from the power of God. Though hand join in hand, and vast multitudes of God's enemies combine and associate themselves, they are easily broken in pieces. They are as great heaps of light chaff before the whirlwind; or large quantities of dry stubble before devouring flames.

We find it easy to tread on and crush a worm that we see crawling on the earth; so it is easy for us to cut or singe a slender thread that any thing hangs by: thus easy is it for God, when he pleases, to cast his enemies down to hell. What are we, that we should think to stand before him, at whose rebuke the earth trembles, and before whom the rocks are thrown down?

2. They *deserve* to be cast into hell; so that divine justice never stands in the way, it makes no objection against God's using his power at any moment to destroy them. Yea, on the contrary, justice calls aloud for an infinite punishment of their sins. Divine justice says of the tree that brings forth such grapes of Sodom, "Cut it down, why cumbereth it the ground?" Luke xiii. 7. The sword of divine justice is every moment brandished over their heads, and it is nothing but the hand of arbitrary mercy, and God's mere will, that holds it back.

3. They are already under a sentence of *condemnation* to hell. They do not only justly deserve to be cast down thither, but the sentence of the law of God, that eternal and immutable rule of righteousness that God has fixed between him and mankind, is gone out against them, and stands against them; so that they are bound over already to hell. John iii. 18. "He that believeth not is condemned already." So that every unconverted man properly belongs to hell; that is his place; from thence he is, John viii. 23. "Ye are from beneath:" and thither he is bound; it is the place that justice, and God's word, and the sentence of his unchangeable law assign to him.

4. They are now the objects of that very same *anger* and wrath of God, that is expressed in the torments of hell. And the reason why they do not go down to hell at each moment, is not because God, in whose power they are, is not then very angry with them; as he is with many miserable creatures now tormented in hell, who there feel and bear the fierceness of his wrath. Yea, God is a great deal more angry with great numbers that are now on earth; yea, doubtless, with many that are now in this congregation, who it may be are at ease, than he is with many of those who are now in the flames of hell.

So that it is not because God is unmindful of their wickedness, and does not resent it, that he does not let loose his hand and cut them off. God is not altogether such an one as themselves, though they may imagine him to be so. The wrath of God burns against them, their damnation does not slumber; the pit is prepared, the fire is made ready, the furnace is now hot, ready to receive them; the flames do now rage and glow. The glittering sword is whet, and held over them, and the pit hath opened its mouth under them.

5. The *devil* stands ready to fall upon them, and seize them as his own, at what moment God shall permit him. They belong to him; he has their souls in his possession, and under his dominion. The scripture represents them as his goods, Luke xi. 12. The devils watch them; they are ever by them at their right hand; they stand waiting for them, like greedy hungry lions that see their prey, and expect to have it, but are for the present kept back. If God should withdraw his hand, by which they are restrained, they would in one moment fly upon their poor souls. The old serpent is gaping for them; hell opens its mouth wide to receive them; and if God should permit it, they would be hastily swallowed up and lost.

6. There are in the souls of wicked men those hellish *principles* reigning, that would presently kindle and flame out into hell fire, if it were not for God's restraints. There is laid in the very nature of carnal men, a foundation for the torments of hell. There are those corrupt principles, in reigning power in them, and in full possession of them, that are seeds of hell fire. These principles are active and powerful, exceeding violent in their nature, and if it were not for the restraining hand of God upon them, they would soon break out, they would flame out after the same manner as the same corruptions, the same enmity does in the hearts of damned souls, and would beget the same torments as they do in them. The souls of the wicked are in scripture compared to the troubled sea. Isa. lvii. 20. For the present, God restrains their wickedness by his mighty power, as he does the raging waves of the troubled sea, saying, "Hitherto shalt thou come, but no further;" but if God should withdraw that restraining power, it would soon carry all before it. Sin is the ruin and misery of the soul; it is destructive in its nature; and if God should leave it without restraint, there would need nothing else to make the soul perfectly miserable. The corruption

of the heart of man is immoderate and boundless in its fury; and while wicked men live here, it is like fire pent up by God's restraints, whereas if it were let loose, it would set on fire the course of nature; and as the heart is now a sink of sin, so if sin was not restrained, it would immediately turn the soul into a fiery oven, or a furnace of fire and brimstone.

7. It is no security to wicked men for one moment, that there are no visible means of death at hand. It is no security to a natural man, that he is now in health, and that he does not see which way he should now immediately go out of the world by any accident, and that there is no visible danger in any respect in his circumstances. The manifold and continual experience of the world in all ages, shows this is no evidence, that a man is not on the very brink of eternity, and that the next step will not be into another world. The unseen, unthought-of ways and means of persons going suddenly out of the world are innumerable and inconceivable. Unconverted men walk over the pit of hell on a rotten covering, and there are innumerable places in this covering so weak that they will not bear their weight, and these places are not seen. The arrows of death fly unseen at noonday; the sharpest sight cannot discern them. God has so many different unsearchable ways of taking wicked men out of the world and sending them to hell, that there is nothing to make it appear, that God had need to be at the expence of a miracle, or go out of the ordinary course of his providence, to destroy any wicked man, at any moment. All the means that there are of sinners going out of the world, are so in God's hands, and so universally and absolutely subject to his power and determination, that it does not depend at all the less on the mere will of God, whether sinners shall at any moment go to hell, than if means were never made use of, or at all concerned in the case.

8. Natural men's prudence and care to preserve their own lives, or the care of others to preserve them, do not secure them a moment. To this, divine providence and universal experience do also bear testimony. There is this clear evidence that men's own wisdom is no security to them from death; that if it were otherwise we should see some difference between the wise and

politic men of the world, and others, with regard to their liableness to early and unexpected death: but how is it in fact? Eccles. ii. 16. "How dieth the wise man? even as the fool."

9. All wicked men's pains and *contrivance* which they use to escape hell, while they continue to reject Christ, and so remain wicked men, do not secure them from hell one moment. Almost every natural man that hears of hell, flatters himself that he shall escape it; he depends upon himself for his own security; he flatters himself in what he has done, in what he is now doing, or what he intends to do. Every one lays out matters in his own mind how he shall avoid damnation, and flatters himself that he contrives well for himself, and that his schemes will not fail. They hear indeed that there are but few saved, and that the greater part of men that have died heretofore are gone to hell; but each one imagines that he lays out matters better for his own escape than others have done. He does not intend to come to that place of torment; he says within himself, that he intends to take effectual care, and to order matters so for himself as not to fail.

But the foolish children of men miserably delude themselves in their own schemes, and in confidence in their own strength and wisdom; they trust to nothing but a shadow. The greater part of those who heretofore have lived under the same means of grace, and are now dead, are undoubtedly gone to hell; and it was not because they were not as wise as those who are now alive: it was not because they did not lay out matters as well for themselves to secure their own escape. If we could speak with them, and inquire of them, one by one, whether they expected, when alive, and when they used to hear about hell, ever to be the subjects of that misery: we doubtless, should hear one and another reply, "No, I never intended to come here: I had laid out matters otherwise in my mind; I thought I should contrive well for myself: I thought my scheme good. I intended to take effectual care; but it came upon me unexpected; I did not look for it at that time, and in that manner; it came as a thief: Death outwitted me: God's wrath was too quick for me. Oh, my cursed foolishness! I was flattering myself, and pleasing myself with vain dreams of what I would do hereafter; and when I was saying, Peace and safety, then suddenly destruction came upon me."

10. God has laid himself under *no obligation,* by any promise to keep any natural man out of hell one moment. God certainly has made no promises either of eternal life, or of any deliverance or preservation from eternal death, but what are contained in the covenant of grace, the promises that are given in Christ, in whom all the promises are yea and amen. But surely they have no interest in the promises of the covenant of grace who are not the children of the covenant, who do not believe in any of the promises, and have no interest in the Mediator of the covenant.

So that, whatever some have imagined and pretended about promises made to natural men's earnest seeking and knocking, it is plain and manifest, that whatever pains a natural man takes in religion, whatever prayers he makes, till he believes in Christ, God is under no manner of obligation to keep him a moment from eternal destruction.

So that, thus it is that natural men are held in the hand of God, over the pit of hell; they have deserved the fiery pit, and are already sentenced to it; and God is dreadfully provoked, his anger is as great towards them as to those that are actually suffering the executions of the fierceness of his wrath in hell, and they have done nothing in the least to appease or abate that anger, neither is God in the least bound by any promise to hold them up one moment; the devil is waiting for them, hell is gaping for them, the flames gather and flash about them, and would fain lay hold on them, and swallow them up; the fire bent up in their own hearts is struggling to break out: and they have no interest in any Mediator, there are no means within reach that can be any security to them. In short, they have no refuge, nothing to take hold of; all that preserves them every moment is the mere arbitrary will, and uncovenanted, unobliged forbearance of an incensed God.

APPLICATION.

The use of this awful subject may be for awakening unconverted persons in this congregation. This that you have heard is the case of every one of you that are out of Christ.—That world of misery, that lake of burning brimstone, is extended abroad under you. There is the dreadful pit of the glowing flames of the wrath of God; there is hell's wide gaping mouth open; and you have nothing to stand upon, nor any thing to take hold of; there is nothing between you and hell but the air; it is only the power and mere pleasure of God that holds you up.

You probably are not sensible of this; you find you are kept out of hell, but do not see the hand of God in it; but look at other things, as the good state of your bodily constitution, your care of your own life, and the means you use for your own preservation. But indeed these things are nothing; if God should withdraw his hand, they would avail no more to keep you from falling, than the thin air to hold up a person that is suspended in it.

Your wickedness makes you as it were heavy as lead, and to tend downwards with great weight and pressure towards hell; and if God should let you go, you would immediately sink and swiftly descend and plunge into the bottomless gulf, and your healthy constitution, and your own care and prudence, and best contrivance, and all your righteousness, would have no more influence to uphold you and keep you out of hell, than a spider's web would have to stop a fallen rock. Were it not for the sovereign pleasure of God, the earth would not bear you one moment; for you are a burden to it; the creation groans with you; the creature is made subject to the bondage of your corruption, not willingly; the sun does not willingly shine upon you to give you light to serve sin and Satan; the earth does not willingly yield her increase to satisfy your lusts; nor is it willingly a stage for your wickedness to be acted upon; the air does not willingly serve you for breath to maintain the flame of life in your vitals, while you spend your life in the service of God's enemies. God's creatures are good, and were made for men to serve God with, and do not willingly subserve to any other purpose, and groan when they are abused to purposes so directly contrary to their nature and end. And the world would spew you out, were it not for the sovereign hand of him who hath subjected it in hope. There are black clouds of God's wrath now hanging directly over your heads, full of the dreadful storm, and big with thunder; and were it not for the restraining hand of God, it would immediately burst forth upon you. The sovereign pleasure of God, for the present, stays his rough wind; otherwise it would come with fury, and your destruction would come like a whirlwind, and you would be like the chaff of the summer threshing floor.

The wrath of God is like great waters that are dammed for the present; they increase more and more, and rise higher and higher, till an outlet is given; and the longer the stream is stopped, the more rapid and mighty is its course, when once it is let loose. It is true, that judgment against your evil works has not been executed hitherto; the floods of God's vengeance have been withheld; but your guilt in the mean time is constantly increasing, and you are every day treasuring up more wrath; the waters are constantly rising, and waxing more and more mighty; and there is nothing but the mere pleasure of God, that holds the waters back, that are unwilling to be stopped, and press hard to go forward. If God should only withdraw his hand from the flood-gate, it would immediately fly open, and the fiery floods of the fierceness and wrath of God, would rush forth with inconceivable fury, and would come upon you with omnipotent power; and if your strength were ten thousand times greater than it is, yea, ten thousand times greater than the strength of the stoutest, sturdiest devil in hell, it would be nothing to withstand or endure it.

The bow of God's wrath is bent, and the arrow made ready on the string, and justice bends the arrow at your heart, and strains the bow, and it is nothing but the mere pleasure of God, and that of an angry God, without any promise or obligation at all, that keeps the arrow one moment from being made drunk with your blood. Thus all you that never passed under a great change of heart, by the mighty power of the Spirit of God upon your souls; all you that were never born again, and made new creatures, and raised from being dead in sin, to a state of new, and before altogether unexperienced light and life, are in the hands of an angry God. However you may have reformed your life in many things, and may have had religious affections, and may keep up a form of religion in your families and closets, and in the house of God, it is nothing but his mere pleasure that keeps you from being this moment swallowed up in everlasting destruction. However unconvinced you may now be of the truth of what you hear, by and by you will be fully convinced of it. Those that are gone from being in the like circumstances with you, see that it was so with them; for destruction came suddenly upon most of them; when they expected nothing of it, and while they were saying, Peace and safety: now they see, that those things on which they depended for peace and safety, were nothing but thin air and empty shadows.

The God that holds you over the pit of hell, much as one holds a spider, or some loathsome insect over the fire, abhors you, and is dreadfully provoked: his wrath towards you burns like fire; he looks upon you as worthy of nothing else, but to be cast into the fire; he is of purer eyes than to bear to have you in his sight; you are ten thousand times more abominable in his eyes, than the most hateful venomous serpent is in ours. You have offended him infinitely more than ever a stubborn rebel did his prince; and yet it is nothing but his hand that holds you from falling into the fire every moment. It is to be ascribed to nothing else, that you did not go to hell the last night; that you was suffered to awake again in this world, after you closed your eyes to sleep. And there is no other reason to be given, why you have not dropped into hell since you arose in the morning, but that God's hand has held you up. There is no other reason to be given why you have not gone to hell, since you have sat here in the house of God, provoking his pure eyes by your sinful wicked manner of attending his solemn worship. Yea, there is nothing else that is to be given as a reason why you do not this very moment drop down into hell.

O sinner! Consider the fearful danger you are in: it is a great furnace of wrath, a wide and bottomless pit, full of the fire of wrath, that you are held over in the hand of that God, whose wrath is provoked and incensed as much against you, as against many of the damned in hell. You hang by a slender thread, with the flames of divine wrath flashing about it, and ready every moment to singe it, and burn it asunder; and you have no interest in any Mediator, and nothing to lay hold of to

CLASSICS OF PROTESTANTISM

save yourself, nothing to keep off the flames of wrath, nothing of your own, nothing that you ever have done, nothing that you can do, to induce God to spare you one moment.—And consider here more particularly.

1. *Whose* wrath it is: it is the wrath of the infinite God. If it were only the wrath of man, though it were of the most potent prince, it would be comparatively little to be regarded. The wrath of kings is very much dreaded, especially of absolute monarchs, who have the possessions and lives of their subjects wholly in their power, to be disposed of at their mere will. Prov. xx. 2. "The fear of a king is as the roaring of a lion: Whoso provoketh him to anger, sinneth against his own soul." The subject that very much enrages an arbitrary prince, is liable to suffer the most extreme torments that human art can invent, or human power can inflict. But the greatest earthly potentates in their greatest majesty and strength, and when clothed in their greatest terrors, are but feeble, despicable worms of the dust, in comparison of the great and almighty Creator and King of heaven and earth. It is but little that they can do, when most enraged, and when they have exerted the utmost of their fury. All the kings of the earth, before God, are as grasshoppers; they are nothing, and less than nothing: both their love and their hatred are to be despised. The wrath of the great King of kings, is as much more terrible than theirs, as his majesty is greater. Luke xii. 4, 5. "And I say unto you, my friends, Be not afraid of them that kill the body, and after that, have no more that they can do. But I will forewarn you whom you shall fear: fear him, which after he hath killed, hath power to cast into hell; yea, I say unto you, Fear him."

2. It is the *fierceness* of his wrath that you are exposed to. We often read of the fury of God; as in Isaiah lix. 18. "According to their deeds, accordingly he will repay fury to his adversaries." So Isaiah lxvi. 15. "For behold, the Lord will come with fire, and with his chariots like a whirlwind, to render his anger with fury, and his rebuke with flames of fire." And in many other places. So, Rev. xix. 15. we read of "the wine press of the fierceness and wrath of Almighty God." The words are exceeding terrible. If it had only been said, "the wrath of God," the words would have implied that which is infinitely dreadful: but it is

"the fierceness and wrath of God." The fury of God! the fierceness of Jehovah! Oh, how dreadful must that be! Who can utter what such expressions carry in them! But it is also "the fierceness and wrath of *Almighty* God." As though there would be a very great manifestation of his almighty power in what the fierceness of his wrath should inflict, as though omnipotence should be as it were enraged, and exerted, as men are wont to exert their strength in the fierceness of their wrath. Oh! then, what will be the consequence! What will become of the poor worms that shall suffer it! Whose hands can be strong? And whose heart can endure? To what a dreadful, inexpressible, inconceivable depth of misery must the poor creature be sunk who shall be the subject of this!

Consider this, you that are here present, that yet remain in an unregenerate state. That God will execute the fierceness of his anger, implies, that he will inflict wrath without any pity. When God beholds the ineffable extremity of your case, and sees your torment to be so vastly disproportioned to your strength, and sees how your poor soul is crushed, and sinks down, as it were, into an infinite gloom; he will have no compassion upon you, he will not forbear the executions of his wrath, or in the least lighten his hand; there shall be no moderation or mercy, nor will God then at all stay his rough wind; he will have no regard to your welfare, nor be at all careful lest you should suffer too much in any other sense, than only that you shall *not suffer beyond what strict justice requires*. Nothing shall be withheld, because it is so hard for you to bear. Ezek. viii. 18. "Therefore will I also deal in fury: mine eye shall not spare, neither will I have pity; and though they cry in mine ears with a loud voice, yet I will not hear them." Now God stands ready to pity you; this is a day of mercy; you may cry now with some encouragement of obtaining mercy. But when once the day of mercy is past, your most lamentable and dolorous cries and shrieks will be in vain; you will be wholly lost and thrown away of God, as to any regard to your welfare. God will have no other use to put you to, but to suffer misery; you shall be continued in being to no other end; for you will be a vessel of wrath fitted to destruction; and there will be no other use of this vessel, but to be filled full of wrath. God will be so far from pitying you when you cry to him, that it is said he will only "laugh and mock," Prov. i. 25, 26 &c.

How awful are those words, Isa. lxiii. 3, which are the words of the great God. "I will tread them in mine anger, and will trample them in my fury, and their blood shall be sprinkled upon my garments, and I will stain all my raiment." It is perhaps impossible to conceive of words that carry in them greater manifestations of these three things, *viz.* contempt, and hatred, and fierceness of indignation. If you cry to God to pity you, he will be so far from pitying you in your doleful case, or showing you the least regard or favour, that instead of that, he will only tread you under foot. And though he will know that you cannot bear the weight of omnipotence treading upon you, yet he will not regard that, but he will crush you under his feet without mercy; he will crush out your blood, and make it fly, and it shall be sprinkled on his garments, so as to stain all his raiment. He will not only hate you, but he will have you in the utmost contempt: no place shall be thought fit for you, but under his feet to be trodden down as the mire of the streets.

3. The *misery* you are exposed to is that which God will inflict to that end, that he might show what that wrath of Jehovah is. God hath had it on his heart to show to angels and men, both how excellent his love is, and also how terrible his wrath is. Sometimes earthly kings have a mind to show how terrible their wrath is, by the extreme punishments they would execute on those that would provoke them. Nebuchadnezzar, that mighty and haughty monarch of the Chaldean empire, was willing to show his wrath when enraged with Shadrach, Meshech, and Abednego; and accordingly gave orders that the burning fiery furnace should be heated seven times hotter than it was before; doubtless, it was raised to the utmost degree of fierceness that human art could raise it. But the great God is also willing to show his wrath, and magnify his awful majesty and mighty power in the extreme sufferings of his enemies. Rom. ix. 22. "What if God, willing to show his wrath, and to make his power known, endure with much long-suffering the vessels of wrath fitted to destruction?" And seeing this is his design, and what he has determined, even to show how terrible the unrestrained wrath, the fury and fierceness of Jehovah is, he will do

it to effect. There will be something accomplished and brought to pass that will be dreadful with a witness. When the great and angry God hath risen up and executed his awful vengeance on the poor sinner, and the wretch is actually suffering the infinite weight and power of his indignation, then will God call upon the whole universe to behold that awful majesty and mighty power that is to be seen in it. Isa. xxxiii. 12-14. "And the people shall be as the burnings of lime, as thorns cut up shall they be burnt in the fire. Hear ye that are far off, what I have done; and ye that are near, acknowledge my might. The sinners in Zion are afraid; fearfulness hath surprised the hypocrites," &c.

Thus it will be with you that are in an unconverted state, if you continue in it; the infinite might, and majesty, and terribleness of the omnipotent God shall be magnified upon you, in the ineffable strength of your torments. You shall be tormented in the presence of the holy angels, and in the presence of the Lamb; and when you shall be in this state of suffering, the glorious inhabitants of heaven shall go forth and look on the awful spectacle, that they may see what the wrath and fierceness of the Almighty is; and when they have seen it, they will fall down and adore that great power and majesty. Isa. lxvi. 23, 24. "And it shall come to pass, that from one new moon to another, and from one sabbath to another, shall all flesh come to worship before me, saith the Lord. And they shall go forth and look upon the carcasses of the men that have transgressed against me; for their worm shall not die, neither shall their fire be quenched, and they shall be an abhorring unto all flesh."

4. It is *everlasting* wrath. It would be dreadful to suffer this fierceness and wrath of Almighty God one moment; but you must suffer it to all eternity. There will be no end to this exquisite horrible misery. When you look forward, you shall see a long for ever, a boundless duration before you, which will swallow up your thoughts, and amaze your soul; and you will absolutely despair of ever having any deliverance, any end, any mitigation, any rest at all. You will know certainly that you must wear out long ages, millions of millions of ages, in wrestling and conflicting with this almighty merciless vengeance; and then when you have so done, when so many ages have actually

been spent by you in this manner, you will know that all is but a point to what remains. So that your punishment will indeed be infinite. Oh, who can express what the state of a soul in such circumstances is! All that we can possibly say about it, gives but a very feeble, faint representation of it; it is inexpressible and inconceivable: For "who knows the power of God's anger?"

How dreadful is the state of those that are daily and hourly in the danger of this great wrath and infinite misery! But this is the dismal case of every soul in this congregation that has not been born again, however moral and strict, sober and religious, they may otherwise be. Oh that you would consider it, whether you be young or old! There is reason to think, that there are many in this congregation now hearing this discourse, that will actually be the subjects of this very misery to all eternity. We know not who they are, or in what seats they sit, or what thoughts they now have. It may be they are now at ease, and hear all these things without much disturbance, and are now flattering themselves that they are not the persons, promising themselves that they shall escape. If we knew that there was one person, and but one, in the whole congregation, that was to be the subject of this misery, what an awful thing would it be to think of! If we knew who it was, what an awful sight would it be to see such a person! How might all the rest of the congregation lift up a lamentable and bitter cry over him! But, alas! instead of one, how many is it likely will remember this discourse in hell? And it would be a wonder, if some that are now present should not be in hell in a very short time, even before this year is out. And it would be no wonder if some persons, that now sit here, in some seats of this meeting-house, in health, quiet and secure, should be there before to-morrow morning. Those of you that finally continue in a natural condition, that shall keep out of hell longest will be there in a little time! your damnation does not slumber; it will come swiftly, and, in all probability, very suddenly upon many of you. You have reason to wonder that you are not already in hell. It is doubtless the case of some whom you have seen and known, that never deserved hell more than you, and that heretofore appeared as likely to have been now alive as you. Their case is past all hope; they are crying in extreme misery and perfect despair; but here you are in the land of the living and in the house of God, and have an opportunity to obtain salvation. What would not those poor damned hopeless souls give for one day's opportunity such as you now enjoy!

And now you have an extraordinary opportunity, a day wherein Christ has thrown the door of mercy wide open, and stands in calling and crying with a loud voice to poor sinners; a day wherein many are flocking to him, and pressing into the kingdom of God. Many are daily coming from the east, west, north and south; many that were very lately in the same miserable condition that you are in, are now in a happy state, with their hearts filled with love to him who has loved them, and washed them from their sins in his own blood, and rejoicing in hope of the glory of God. How awful is it to be left behind at such a day! To see so many others feasting, while you are pining and perishing! To see so many rejoicing and singing for joy of heart, while you have cause to mourn for sorrow of heart, and howl for vexation of spirit! How can you rest one moment in such a condition? Are not your souls as precious as the souls of the people at Suffield,* where they are flocking from day to day to Christ?

Are there not many here who have lived long in the world, and are not to this day born again? and so are aliens from the commonwealth of Israel, and have done nothing ever since they have lived, but treasure up wrath against the day of wrath? Oh, sirs, your case, in an especial manner, is extremely dangerous. Your guilt and hardness of heart is extremely great. Do you not see how generally persons of your years are passed over and left, in the present remarkable and wonderful dispensation of God's mercy? You had need to consider yourselves, and awake thoroughly out of sleep. You cannot bear the fierceness and wrath of the infinite God.—And you, young men, and young women, will you neglect this precious season which you now enjoy, when so many others of your age are renouncing all youthful vanities, and flocking to Christ? You especially have now an extraordinary opportunity; but if you neglect it, it will soon be with you as with those persons who spent all the precious days of youth in sin, and are now come to such a dreadful pass in blindness

* A town in the neighbourhood.

and hardness.—And you, children, who are unconverted, do not you know that you are going down to hell, to bear the dreadful wrath of that God, who is now angry with you every day and every night? Will you be content to be the children of the devil when so many other children in the land are converted, and are become the holy and happy children of the King of kings?

And let every one that is yet of Christ, and hanging over the pit of hell, whether they be old men and women, or middle aged, or young people, or little children, now hearken to the loud calls of God's word and providence. This acceptable year of the Lord, a day of such great favours to some, will doubtless be a day of as remarkable vengeance to others. Men's hearts harden, and their guilt increases apace at such a day as this, if they neglect their souls; and never was there so great danger of such persons being given up to hardness of heart and blindness of mind. God seems now to be hastily gathering in his elect in all parts of the land; and probably the greater part of adult persons that ever shall be saved, will be brought in now in a little time, and that it will be as it was on the great out-pouring of the Spirit upon the Jews in the apostles' days; the election will obtain, and the rest will be blinded. If this should be the case with you, you will eternally curse this day, and will curse the day that ever you was born, to see such a season of the pouring out of God's Spirit, and will wish that you had died and gone to hell before you had seen it. Now undoubtedly it is, as it was in the days of John the Baptist, the axe is in an extraordinary manner laid at the root of the trees, that every tree which brings not forth good fruit, may be hewn down and cast into the fire.

Therefore, let every one that is out of Christ, now awake and fly from the wrath to come. The wrath of Almighty God is now undoubtedly hanging over a great part of this congregation: Let every one fly out of Sodom: "Haste and escape for your lives, look not behind you, escape to the mountain, lest you be consumed."

A

CAREFUL AND STRICT
ENQUIRY

INTO THE

MODERN PREVAILING NOTIONS

OF

THAT FREEDOM OF WILL,

WHICH IS SUPPOSED TO BE ESSENTIAL

TO

MORAL AGENCY,

VERTUE AND VICE, REWARD AND PUNISHMENT,

PRAISE AND BLAME.

PART I.

WHEREIN ARE EXPLAINED AND STATED VARIOUS TERMS AND THINGS
BELONGING TO THE SUBJECT OF THE ENSUING DISCOURSE.

SECT. I.

Concerning the Nature of the Will.

IT MAY possibly be thought, that there is no great need of going
about to define or describe the *Will;* this word being generally
as well understood as any other words we can use to explain
it: and so perhaps it would be, had not philosophers, metaphysicians and polemic divines brought the matter into obscurity

by the things they have said of it. But since it is so, I think it may be some use, and will tend to greater clearness in the following discourse, to say a few things concerning it.

And therefore I observe, that the *Will* (without any metaphysical refining) is, *That by which the mind chooses any thing.* The faculty of the *Will,* is that power, or principle of mind, by which it is capable of *choosing*: an act of the *Will* is the same as an act of *choosing* or *choice.*

If any think it is a more perfect definition of the Will, to say, that it is that by which the soul either *chooses* or *refuses;* I am content with it: though I think it enough to say, It is that by which the soul chooses; for in every act of Will whatsoever, the mind chooses one thing rather than another; it chooses something rather than the contrary, or rather than the want or non-existence of that thing. So in every act of refusal, the mind chooses the absence of the thing refused; the positive and the negative are set before the mind for its choice, and it chooses the negative; and the mind's making its choice in that case is properly the act of the Will: the Will's determining between the two, is a voluntary determination; but that is the same thing as making a choice. So that by whatever names we call the act of the Will, choosing, refusing, approving, disapproving, liking, disliking, embracing, rejecting, determining, directing, commanding, forbidding, inclining or *being* averse, *being* pleased or displeased *with;* all may be reduced to this of *choosing.* For the soul to act *voluntarily,* is evermore to act *electively.*

Mr. Locke* says, "The Will signifies nothing but a power or ability to *prefer* or *choose.*" And, in the foregoing page, he says, "The word *preferring* seems best to express and in the act of volition;" but adds, that "it does it not precisely; for, though a man would *prefer* flying to walking, yet who can say he ever *wills* it?" But the instance he mentions, does not prove that there is any thing else in *willing,* but merely *preferring*: for it should be considered what is the immediate object of the Will, with respect to a man's walking, or any other external action; which is not being removed from one place to another; on the earth, or through the air, these are remoter objects of preference; but such or such an immediate *exertion* of himself. The thing next

* *Human Understanding.* Edit. 7. vol. i. p. 197.

chosen, or preferred, when a man wills to walk, is not his being removed to such a place where he would be, but such an exertion and motion of his legs and feet, &c. in order to it. And his willing such an alteration in his body in the present moment, is nothing else but his choosing or preferring such an alteration in his body at such a moment, or his liking it better than the forbearance of it. And God has so made and established the human nature, the soul being united to a body in proper state, that the soul preferring or choosing such an immediate exertion or alteration of the body, such an alteration instantaneously follows. There is nothing else in the actions of my mind, that I am conscious of while I walk, but only my preferring or choosing, through successive moments, that there should be such alterations of my external sensations and motions; together with a concurring habitual expectation that it will be so; having ever found by experience, that on such an immediate preference, such sensations and motions do actually, instantaneously, and constantly arise. But it is not so in the case of flying: though a man may be said *remotely* to choose or prefer flying: yet he does not prefer, or desire, under circumstances in view, any *immediate exertion* of the members of his body in order to it; because he has no expectation that he should obtain the desired end by any such exertion; and he does not prefer, or incline to, any bodily exertion, under this apprehended circumstance, of its being wholly in vain. So that if we carefully distinguish the *proper objects* of the several acts of the Will, it will not appear by this, and such like instances, that there is any difference between *volition* and *preference;* or that a man's choosing, liking best, or being best pleased with a thing, are not the same with his *willing* that thing. Thus an act of the Will is commonly expressed *by its pleasing a man* to do thus or thus; and a man doing as he *wills,* and doing as he *pleases,* are in common speech the same thing.

Mr. Locke* says, "The Will is perfectly distinguished from Desire; which in the very same action may have a quite contrary tendency from that which our Wills set us upon. A man, says he, whom I cannot deny, may oblige me to use persuasions to another, which, at the same time I am speaking, I may wish

* *Hum. Und.* vol. i. p. 203, 204.

may not prevail on him. In this case, it is plain the Will and Desire run counter." I do not suppose, that *Will* and *Desire* are words of precisely the same signification: Will seems to be a word of a more general signification, extending to things present and absent. *Desire* respects something absent. I may prefer my present situation and posture, suppose sitting still, or having my eyes open, and so may *will* it. But yet I cannot think they are so entirely distinct, that they can ever be properly said to run counter. A man never, in any instance, wills any thing contrary to his desires, or desires any thing contrary to his Will. The forementioned instance, which Mr. Locke produces, is no proof that he ever does. He may, on some consideration or other *will* to utter speeches which have a tendency to persuade another, and still may *desire* that they may not persuade him; but yet his Will and Desire do not run counter at all: the thing which he wills, the very same he desires; and he does not will a thing, and desire the *contrary*, in any particular. In this instance, it is not carefully observed, what is the thing willed, and what is the thing desired: if it were, it would be found, that Will and Desire do not clash in the least. The thing willed on some consideration, is to utter such words; and certainly, the same consideration so influences him, that he does not desire the contrary; all things considered, he chooses to utter such words, and does not desire not to utter them. And so as to the thing which Mr. Locke speaks of as *desired,* viz. That the words, though they tend to persuade, should not be effectual to that end, his Will is not contrary to this; he does not will that they should be effectual, but rather wills that they should not, as he desires. In order to prove that the Will and Desire may run counter, it should be shown that they may be contrary one to the other in the same thing, or with respect to the *very same object* of Will or desire; but here the objects are two; and in each, taken by themselves, the Will and Desire agree. And it is no wonder that they should not agree in *different* things, though but little distinguished in their nature. The Will may not agree with the Will, nor Desire agree with Desire, in different things. As in this very instance which Mr. Locke mentions, a person may, on *some* consideration, desire to use persuasions, and at the same time may desire they may not prevail; but yet no body will say, that *Desire* runs counter to *Desire;* or that this proves that *Desire* is perfectly a distinct thing from *Desire.*—The like might be observed of the other instance Mr. Locke produces, of a man's desiring to be eased of pain, &c.

But, not to dwell any longer on this, whether *Desire* and *Will,* and whether *Preference* and *Volition* be precisely the same things, I trust it will be allowed by all, that in every act of *will* there is an act of *choice;* that in every *volition* there is a *preference,* or a prevailing inclination of the soul, whereby, at that instant, it is out of a state of perfect indifference, with respect to the direct object of the volition. So that in every act, or going forth of the Will, there is some preponderation of the mind, one way rather than another; and the soul had rather *have* or *do* one thing, than another, or than *not* to have or do that thing; and that where there is absolutely no preferring or choosing, but a perfect, continuing equilibrium, there is no volition.

SECT. II.

Concerning the Determination of the Will.

By *determining* the Will, if the phrase be used with any meaning, must be intended, *causing* that the act of the Will or Choice should be thus, and not otherwise: and the Will is said to be determined, when, in consequence of some action, or influence, its choice is directed to, and fixed upon a particular object. As when we speak of the determination of motion, we mean causing the motion of the body to be in such a direction, rather than another.

The Determination of the Will, supposes an effect, which must have a cause. If the Will be determined, there is a Determiner. This must be supposed to be intended even by them that say the Will determines itself. If it be so, the Will is both Determiner and determined; it is a cause that acts and produces effects upon itself, and is the object of its own influence and action.

With respect to that grand enquiry, "What determines the Will?" it would be very tedious and unnecessary, at present, to examine all the various opinions, which have been advanced concerning this matter; nor is it needful that I should enter into a particular discussion of all points debated in disputes on that other question, "Whether the Will always follows the last dictate of the understanding?" It is sufficient to my present purpose to say, *It is that motive, which, as it stands in the view of the mind, is the strongest, that determines, the Will.* But it may be necessary that I should a little explain my meaning.

By *motive,* I mean the whole of that which moves, excites, or invites the mind to volition, whether that be one thing singly, or many things conjunctly. Many particular things may concur, and unite their strength, to induce the mind; and when it is so, all together are as one complex motive. And when I speak of the *strongest* motive, I have respect to the strength of the whole that operates to induce a particular act of volition, whether that be the strength of one thing alone, or of many together.

Whatever is objectively a motive, in this sense, must be something that is *extant in the view or apprehension of the understanding,* or perceiving faculty. Nothing can induce or invite the mind to will or act any thing, any further than it is perceived, or is some way or other in the mind's view; for what is wholly unperceived and perfectly out of the mind's view, cannot affect the mind at all. It is most evident, that nothing is in the mind, or reaches it, or takes any hold of it, any otherwise than as it is perceived or thought of.

And I think it must also be allowed by all, that every thing that is properly called a motive, excitement, or inducement to a perceiving, willing agent, has some sort and degree of *tendency,* or *advantage* to move or excite the Will, previous to the effect, or to the act of the Will excited. This previous tendency of the motive is what I call the *strength* of the motive. That motive which has a less degree of previous advantage, or tendency to move the will, or which appears less inviting, as it stands in the view of the mind, is what I call a *weaker* motive. On the contrary, that which appears most inviting, and has, by what appears concerning it to the understanding or apprehension, the greatest degree of previous tendency to excite and induce the choice, is what I call the *strongest* motive. And in this sense, I suppose the Will is always determined by the strongest motive.

Things that exist in the view of the mind have their strength, tendency, or advantage to move, or excite its Will, from many things appertaining to the nature and circumstances of the *thing viewed,* the nature and circumstances of the *mind that views,* and the degree and manner of its *view;* of which it would perhaps be hard to make a perfect enumeration. But so much I think may be determined in general, without room for controversy, that whatever is perceived or apprehended by an intelligent and voluntary agent, which has the nature and influence of a motive to volition or choice, is considered or viewed *as good,* nor has it any tendency to engage the election of the soul in any further degree than it appears such. For to say otherwise, would be to say, that things that appear, have a tendency, by the appearance they make, to engage the mind to elect them, some other way than by their appearing eligible to it; which is absurd. And therefore it must be true, in some sense, that *the Will always is, as the greatest apparent good is.* But only, for the right understanding of this, two things must be well and distinctly observed.

It appears from these things, that in some sense, *the Will always follows the last dictate of the understanding.* But then the *understanding* must be taken in a large sense, as including the whole faculty of perception or apprehension, and not merely what is called *reason* or *judgment.* If by the dictate of the understanding is meant what reason declares to be best, or most for the person's happiness, taking in the whole of its duration, it is not true, that the Will always follows the last dictate of the understanding. Such a dictate of reason is quite a different matter from things appearing now most *agreeable,* all things being put together which pertain to the mind's present preceptions in any respect: although that dictate of reason, when it takes place, has concern in the compound influence which moves the Will; and should be considered in estimating the degree of that appearance of good which the Will always follows; either as having its influence added to other things, or subdued from them. When such dictate of reason concurs with other things, then its weight is added to them, as put into the same scale; but when it is against them, it is as a weight in the opposite scale, resisting the influence of other things: yet its resistance is often overcome by their greater weight, and so the act of the Will is determined in opposition to it.

These things may serve, I hope, in some measure, to illustrate and confirm the position laid down in the beginning of this section, viz. "That the Will is always determined by the strongest motive," or by that view of the mind which has the greatest degree of *previous* tendency to excite volition. But whether I have been so happy as rightly to explain the thing wherein consists the strength of motives, or not, yet my failing in this will not overthrow the position itself; which carries much of its own evidence with it, and is a point of chief importance to the purpose of the ensuing discourse: And the truth of it, I hope, will appear with great clearness, before I have finished what I have to say on the subject of human liberty.

SECT. III.

Concerning the Meaning of the Terms Necessity, Impossibility, Inability, &c. and of Contingence.

The words *necessary, impossible,* &c. are abundantly used in controversies about Free-Will and Moral Agency; and therefore the sense in which they are used, should be clearly understood.

Here I might say, that a thing is then said to be *necessary,* when it *must* be, and cannot be otherwise. But this would not properly be a definition of Necessity, any more than if I explained the word *must* by the phrase, there being a Necessity. The words *must, can,* and *cannot,* need explanation as much as the words *necessary* and *impossible;* excepting that the former are words that in earliest life we more commonly use.

The word *necessary,* as used in common *speech,* is a relative term; and relates to some supposed opposition made to the existence of a thing, which opposition is overcome, or proves sufficient to hinder or alter it. That is necessary, in the original and proper sense of the word, which is, or will be, notwithstanding all supposable opposition. To say, that a thing is necessary, is the same thing as to say, that it is impossible, it should not be. But the word *impossible* is manifestly a relative term, and has reference to supposed power exerted to bring a thing to pass, which is insufficient for the effect; as the word *unable* is relative, and has relation to ability or endeavour, which is insufficient. Also the word *irresistible* is relative, and has always reference to resistance which is made, or may be made, to some force or power tending to an effect, and is insufficient to withstand the power, or hinder the effect. The common notion of Necessity and Impossibility implies something that frustrates endeavour or desire.

Here several things are to be noted.

1. Things are said to be necessary in *general*, which are or will be notwithstanding any supposable opposition from whatever quarter. But things are said to be necessary *to us*, which are or will be notwithstanding all opposition supposable in the case *from us*. The same may be observed of the word *impossible*, and other such like terms.

2. These terms *necessary, impossible, irresistible*, &c. more especially belong to controversies about liberty and moral agency, as used in the latter of the two senses now mentioned, *viz.* as necessary or impossible *to us*, and with relation to any supposable opposition or endeavour of *ours*.

3. As the word *Necessity*, in its vulgar and common use, is relative, and has always reference to some supposable insufficient opposition; so when we speak of any thing as necessary *to us*, it is with relation to some supposable opposition of *our Wills*, or some voluntary exertion or effect of ours to the contrary. For we do not properly make opposition to an event, any otherwise than as we *voluntarily* oppose it. Things are said to be what must be, or *necessarily* are, *as to us*, when they are, or will be, though we desire or endeavour the contrary, or try to prevent or remove their existence: but such opposition of ours always either consists in, or implies opposition of our wills.

It is manifest that all such like words and phrases, as vulgarly used, are understood in this manner. A thing is said to be *necessary*, when we cannot help it, let us do what we will. So any thing is said to be *impossible* to us, when we would do it, or would have it brought to pass, and endeavour it; or at least may be supposed to desire and seek it; but all our desires and endeavours are, or would be vain. And that is said to be *irresistible*, which overcomes all our opposition, resistance, and endeavour to the contrary. And we are said to be *unable* to do a thing, when our supposable desires and endeavours are insufficient.

We are accustomed, in the common use of language, thus to apply and understand these phrases: we grow up with such a habit; which, by the daily use of these terms from our childhood, becomes fixed and settled; so that the idea of a relation to a supposed will, desire, and endeavour of ours, is strongly connected with these terms, whenever we hear the words used. Such ideas, and these words, are so associated, that they unavoidably go together; one suggests the other, and never can be easily separated as long as we live. And though we use the words, as terms of art, in another sense, yet, unless we are exceedingly circumspect, we shall insensibly slide into the vulgar use of them, and so apply the words in a very inconsistent manner, which will deceive and confound us in our reasonings and discourses, even when we pretend to use them as terms of art.

4. It follows from what has been observed, that when these terms *necessary, impossible, irresistible, unable,* &c. are used in cases wherein no insufficient will is supposed, or can be supposed, but the very nature of the supposed case itself excludes any opposition, will or endeavour, they are then not used in their proper signification. The reason is manifest; in such cases we cannot use the words with reference to a supposable opposition, will or endeavour. And therefore if any man uses these terms in such cases, he either uses them nonsensically, or in some new sense, diverse from their original and proper meaning. As for instance; if any one should affirm after this manner, That it is *necessary* for a man, or what *must* be, that he should choose virtue rather than vice, during the time that he prefers virtue to vice; and that it is a thing impossible and irresistible, that it should be otherwise than that he should have this choice, so long as this choice continues; such a one would use the terms *must, irresistible,* &c. with either perfect insignification, or in some new sense, diverse from their common use; which is with reference, as has been observed, to supposable opposition, unwillingness and resistance; whereas, here, the very supposition excludes and denies any such thing: for the case supposed is that of being willing, and choosing.

5. It appears from what has been said, that these terms *necessary, impossible,* &c. are often used by philosophers and metaphysicians in a sense quite diverse from their common and original signification; for they apply them to many cases in which no opposition is supposable. Thus they use them with respect to God's existence before the creation of the world, when there was no other being; with regard to many of the dispositions and acts of the divine Being, such as his loving himself, his loving righteousness, hating sin, &c. So they apply them to many cases of the inclinations and actions of created intelligent beings, wherein all opposition of the Will is excluded in the very supposition of the case.

Metaphysical or *Philosophical* Necessity is nothing different from their certainty. I speak not now of the certainty of knowledge, but the certainty that is in things themselves, which is the foundation of the certainty of the knowledge, or that wherein lies the ground of the infallibility of the proposition which affirms them.

What is sometimes given as the definition of philosophical Necessity, namely, *"That by which a thing cannot but be,"* or *"whereby it cannot be otherwise,"* fails of being a proper explanation of it, on two accounts: *First,* the words *can,* or *cannot,* need explanation as much as the word *Necessity;* and the former may as well be explained by the latter, as the latter by the former. Thus, if any one asked us what we mean, when we say, a thing *cannot but be,* we might explain ourselves by saying, it must necessarily be so; as well as explain Necessity, by saying, it is that by which a thing cannot but be. And *Secondly,* this definition is liable to the forementioned great inconvenience; the words *cannot,* or *unable,* are properly relative, and have relation to power exerted, or that may be exerted, in order to the thing spoken of; to which as I have now observed, the word *Necessity,* as used by philosophers, has no reference.

Philosophical Necessity is really nothing else than the full and fixed connection between the things signified by the subject and predicate of a proposition, which affirms something to be true. When there is such a connection, then the thing affirmed in the proposition is necessary, in a philosophical sense; whether any opposition, or contrary effort be supposed, or no. When the subject and predicate of the proposition, which affirms the existence of any thing, either substance, quality, act, or circumstance, have a full and certain connection, then the existence or being of that thing is said to be *necessary* in a metaphysical sense. And in this sense I use the word *Necessity,* in the following discourse, when I endeavour to prove *that Necessity is not inconsistent with Liberty.*

SECT. IV.

Of the Distinction of natural and moral Necessity, and Inability.

That Necessity which has been explained, consisting in an infallible connection of the things signified by the subject and predicate of a proposition, as intelligent beings are the subjects of it, is distinguished into *moral* and *natural* Necessity.

I shall not now stand to enquire whether this distinction be a proper and perfect distinction; but shall only explain how these two sorts of Necessity are understood, as the terms are sometimes used, and as they are used in the following discourse.

The phrase, *moral Necessity,* is used variously; sometimes it is used for a necessity of moral obligation. So we say, a man is under Necessity, when he is under bonds of *duty* and conscience, from which he cannot be discharged. Again, the word *Necessity* is often used for great obligation in point of *interest.* Sometimes by moral Necessity is meant that apparent connection of things, which is the ground of *moral evidence;* and so is distinguished from *absolute Necessity,* or that sure connection of things, that is a foundation for *infallible certainty.* In this sense, moral Necessity signifies much the same as that high degree of *probability,* which is ordinarily sufficient to satisfy mankind, in their conduct and behaviour in the world, as they would consult their own safety and interest, and treat others properly as members of society. And sometimes by moral Necessity is meant that Necessity of connection and *consequence,* which arises from such *moral causes,* as the strength of inclination, or motives, and the connection which there is in many cases between these, and such certain volitions and actions. And it is in *this* sense, that I use the phrase, *moral Necessity,* in the following discourse.

By *natural Necessity,* as applied to men, I mean such Necessity as men are under through the force of natural causes; as distinguished from what are called moral causes, such as habits and dispositions of the heart, and moral motives and inducements. Thus men placed in certain circumstances, are the subjects of particular sensations by Necessity: they feel pain when their bodies are wounded; they see the objects presented before them in a clear light, when their eyes are opened: so they assent to the truth of certain propositions, as soon as the terms are understood; as that two and two make four, that black is not white, that two parallel lines can never cross one another; so by a natural Necessity men's bodies move downwards, when there is nothing to support them.

But here several things may be noted concerning these two kinds of Necessity.

1. Moral Necessity may be as *absolute,* as natural Necessity. That is, the effect may be as perfectly connected with its moral cause, as a natural necessary effect is with its natural cause. Whether the Will in every case is necessarily determined by the strongest motive, or whether the Will ever makes any resistance to such a motive, or can ever oppose the strongest present inclination, or not; if that matter should be controverted, yet I suppose none will deny, but that, in some cases, a previous bias and inclination, or the motive presented, may be so powerful, that the act of the Will may be certainly and indissolubly connected therewith. When motives or previous bias are very strong, all will allow that there is some *difficulty* in going against them. And if they were yet stronger, the difficulty would be still greater. And therefore, if more were still added to their strength, to a certain degree, it would make the difficulty so great, that it would be wholly *impossible* to surmount it; for this plain reason, because whatever power men may be supposed to have to surmount difficulties, yet that power is not infinite; and so goes not beyond certain limits. If a man can surmount ten degrees of difficulty of this kind with twenty degrees of strength, because the degrees of strength are beyond the degrees of difficulty; yet if the difficulty be increased to thirty, or an hundred, or a thousand degrees, and his strength not also increased, his

strength will be wholly insufficient to surmount the difficulty. As therefore it must be allowed, that there may be such a thing as a *sure* and *perfect* connection between moral causes and effects; so this only is what I call by the name of *moral Necessity.*

2. When I use this distinction of *moral* and *natural Necessity,* I would not be understood to suppose, that if any thing come to pass by the former kind of Necessity, the *nature* of things is not concerned in it, as well as in the latter. I do not mean to determine, that when a *moral* habit or motive is so strong, that the act of the Will infallibly follows, this is not owing to the *nature of things.* But *natural* and *moral* are the terms by which these two kinds of Necessity have usually been called; and they must be distinguished by some names, for there is a difference between them, that is very important in its consequences. This difference, however, does not lie so much in the nature of the *connection,* as in the two terms *connected.* The cause with which the effect is connected, is of a particular kind; viz. that which is of a moral nature; either some previous habitual disposition, or some motive exhibited to the understanding. And the effect is also of a particular kind; being likewise of a moral nature; consisting in some inclination or volition of the soul, or voluntary action.

I suppose, that Necessity which is called *natural* in distinction from *moral* necessity, is so called, because *mere nature* as the word is vulgarly used, is concerned, without any thing of *choice.* The word *nature* is often used in opposition to *choice;* not because nature has indeed never any hand in our choice; but, probably, because we first get our notion of nature from that obvious course of events, which we observe in many things where our choice has no concern; and especially in the material world; which, in very many parts of it, we easily perceive to be in a settled course; the stated order, and manner of succession, being very apparent. But where we do not readily discern the rule and connection, (though there be a connection, according to an established law, truly taking place) we signify the manner of event by some other name. Even in many things which are seen in the material and inanimate world, which do not obviously come to pass according to any settled course, men do not call the manner of the event by the name of *nature,* but by such names as *accident, chance, contingence,* &c. So men make a distinction between nature and choice; as if they were completely and universally distinct. Whereas, I suppose none will deny but that choice, *in many cases,* arises from nature, as truly as other events. But the connection between acts of choice, and their causes, according to established laws, is not so obvious. And we observe that choice is, as it were, a new principle of motion and action, different from that established order of things which is most obvious, and seen especially in corporeal things. The choice also often interposes, interrupts, and alters the chain of events in these external objects, and causes them to proceed otherwise than they would do, if let alone. Hence it is spoken of as if it were a principle of motion entirely distinct from nature, and properly set in opposition to it. Names being commonly given to things, according to what is most obvious, and is suggested by what appears to the senses without reflection and research.

3. It must be observed, that in what has been explained, as signified by the name of *moral Necessity,* the word *Necessity* is not used according to the original design and meaning of the word: for, as was observed before, such terms, *necessary, impossible, irresistible,* &c. in common speech, and their most proper sense, are always relative; having reference to some supposable voluntary opposition or endeavour, that is insufficient. But no such opposition, or contrary will and endeavour, is supposable in the case of moral Necessity; which is a certainty of the inclination and will itself; which does not admit of the supposition of a will to oppose and resist it. For it is absurd, to suppose the same individual will to oppose itself, in its present act; or the present choice to be opposite to, and resisting present choice: as absurd as it is to talk of two contrary motions, in the same moving body, at the same time.—And therefore the very case supposed never admits of any trial, whether an opposing or resisting will can overcome this Necessity.

What has been said of natural and moral Necessity, may serve to explain what is intended by natural and moral *Inability.* We are said to be *naturally* unable to do a thing, when we cannot do it if we will, because what is most commonly called *nature* does not allow of it, or because of some impending defect or obstacle that is extrinsic to the will; either in the faculty of understanding, constitution of body, or external objects. *Moral Inability* consists not in any of these things; but either in the want of inclination; or the strength of a contrary inclination; or the want of sufficient motives in view, to induce and excite the act of the will, or the strength of apparent motives to the contrary. Or both these may be resolved into one; and it may be said in one word, that moral Inability consists in the opposition or want of inclination. For when a person is unable to will or choose such a thing, through a defect of motives, or prevalence of contrary motives, it is the same thing as his being unable through the want of an inclination, or the prevalence of a contrary inclination, in such circumstances, and under the influence of such views.

To give some instances of this *moral Inability.*—A woman of great honour and chastity may have a moral Inability to prostitute herself to her slave. A child of great love and duty to his parents, may be thus unable to kill his father. A very lascivious man, in case of certain opportunities and temptations, and in the absence of such and such restraints, may be unable to forbear gratifying his lust. A drunkard, under such and such circumstances, may be unable to forbear taking strong drink. A very malicious man may be unable to exert benevolent acts to an enemy, or to desire his prosperity; yea, some may be so under the power of a vile disposition, that they may be unable to love those who are most worthy of their esteem and affection. A strong habit of virtue, and a great degree of holiness, may cause a moral Inability to love wickedness in general, and may render a man unable to take complacence in wicked persons or things; or to choose a wicked, in preference to a virtuous life. And on the other hand, a great degree of habitual wickedness may lay a man under an Inability to love and choose holiness; and render him utterly unable to love an infinitely holy Being, or to choose and cleave to him as his chief good.

SECT. V.

Concerning the Notion of Liberty, and of Moral Agency.

THE PLAIN and obvious meaning of the words *Freedom* and *Liberty,* in common speech, is *The power, opportunity, or advantage that any one has, to do as he pleases.* Or in other words, his being free from hinderance or impediment in the way of doing, or conducting in any respect as he wills.* And the contrary to Liberty, whatever name we call that by, is a person's being hindered or unable to conduct as he will, or being necessitated to do otherwise.

If this which I have mentioned be the meaning of the word Liberty, in the ordinary use of language; as I trust that none that has ever learned to talk, and is unprejudiced, will deny; then it will follow, that in propriety of speech, neither Liberty, nor its contrary, can properly be ascribed to any being or thing, but that which has such a faculty, power, or property, as is called will. For that which is possessed of no *will,* cannot have any *power* or *opportunity* of doing *according to its will,* nor be necessitated to act *contrary to its will,* nor be restrained from acting agreeably to it. And therefore to talk of Liberty, or the contrary, as belonging to the *very will itself,* is not to speak good sense; if we judge of sense, and nonsense, by the original and proper signification of words.—For the *will itself* is not an Agent that *has a will*: the power of choosing, itself, has not a power of choosing. That which has the power of volition is the man, or the soul, and not the power of volition itself. And he that has the Liberty of doing according to his will, is the Agent who is possessed of the will; and not the will which he is possessed of. We say with propriety, that a bird let loose has power and liberty to fly; but not that the bird's power of flying has a power and Liberty of flying. To be free is the property of an agent, who is possessed of powers and faculties, as much as to

---

* I say not only *doing,* but *conducting;* because a voluntary forbearing to do, sitting still, keeping silence, &c. are instances of persons' *conduct,* about which Liberty is exercised; though they are not so properly called *doing.*

be cunning, valiant, bountiful, or zealous. But these qualities are the properties of persons; and not the properties of properties.

There are two things contrary to what is called Liberty in common speech. One is *constraint;* otherwise called *force, compulsion,* and *coaction;* which is a person's being necessitated to do a thing *contrary* to his will. The other is *restraint;* which is, his being hindered, and not having power to do *according* to his will. But that which has no will cannot be the subject of these things.—I need say the less on this head, Mr. Locke having set the same thing forth, with so great clearness, in his *Essay on the Human Understanding.*

But one thing more I would observe concerning what is vulgarly called *Liberty;* namely, that power and opportunity for one to do and conduct as he will, or according to his choice, is all that is meant by it; without taking into the meaning of the word, any thing of the *cause* of that choice; or at all considering how the person came to have such a volition; whether it was caused by some external motive, or internal habitual bias; whether it was determined by some internal antecedent volition, or whether it happened without a cause; whether it was necessarily connected with something foregoing, or not connected. Let the person come by his choice any how, if he is able, and there is nothing in the way to hinder his pursuing and executing his will, the man is perfectly free, according to the primary and common notion of freedom.

What has been said may be sufficient to shew what is meant by *Liberty,* according to the common notions of mankind, and in the usual and primary acceptation of the word: but the word, as used by *Arminians, Pelagians* and others, who oppose the *Calvinists,* has an entirely different signification.—These several things belong to their notion of Liberty. 1. That it consists in a *self-determining power* in the will, or a certain sovereignty the will has over itself, and its own acts, whereby it determines its own volitions; so as not to be dependent in its determinations, on any cause without itself, nor determined by any thing prior to its own acts. 2. *Indifference* belongs to Liberty in their notion of it, or that the mind, previous to the act of volition, be *in equilibrio.* 3. *Contingence* is another thing that belongs and is essential to it; not in the common acceptation of the word, as that has been already explained, but as opposed to all *necessity,* or any fixed and certain connection with some previous ground or reason of its existence. They suppose the essence of Liberty so much to consist in these things, that unless the will of man be free in this sense, he has no real freedom, how much soever he may be at Liberty to act according to his will.

A *moral Agent* is a being that is capable of those actions that have a *moral* quality, and which can properly be denominated good or evil in a moral sense, virtuous or vicious, commendable or faulty. To moral Agency belongs a *moral faculty,* or sense of moral good and evil, or of such a thing as desert or worthiness, of praise or blame, reward or punishment; and a capacity which an Agent has of being influenced in his actions by moral induce-ments or motives, exhibited to the view of understanding and reason, to engage to a conduct agreeable to the moral faculty.

The sun is very excellent and beneficial in its actions and influence on the earth, in warming and causing it to bring forth its fruits; but it is not a moral Agent: its action, though good, is not virtuous or meritorious. Fire that breaks out in a city, and consumes great part of it, is very mischievous in its operation; but is not a moral Agent: what it does is not faulty or sinful, or deserving of any punishment. The brute creatures are not moral Agents: the actions of some of them are very profitable and pleasant; others are very hurtful: yet seeing they have no moral faculty, or sense of desert, and do not act from choice guided by understanding, or with a capacity of reasoning and reflecting, but only from instinct, and are not capable of being influenced by moral inducements, their actions are not properly sinful or virtuous; nor are they properly the subjects of any such moral treatment for what they do, as moral Agents are for their faults or good deeds.

PART II.

WHEREIN IT IS CONSIDERED WHETHER THERE IS OR CAN 'BE ANY SUCH
SORT OF FREEDOM OF WILL, AS THAT WHEREIN ARMINIANS PLACE
THE ESSENCE OF THE LIBERTY OF ALL MORAL AGENTS; AND
WHETHER ANY SUCH THING EVER WAS OR CAN BE CONCEIVED OF.

SECT. I.

*Shewing the manifest Inconsistence of the Arminian Notion of
Liberty of Will, consisting in the Will's self-determining Power.*

HAVING TAKEN notice of those things which may be necessary to
be observed, concerning the meaning of the principal terms and
phrases made use of in controversies concerning human Liberty,
and particularly observed what *Liberty* is according to the common language and general apprehension of mankind, and what
it is as understood and maintained by *Arminians;* I proceed to
consider the *Arminian* notion of the *Freedom of the Will,* and
the supposed necessity of it in order to moral agency, or in order
to any one's being capable of virtue or vice, and properly the
subject of command or counsel, praise or blame, promises or
threatenings, rewards or punishments; or whether that which
has been described, as the thing meant by Liberty in common
speech, be not sufficient, and the only Liberty, which makes, or
can make any one a moral agent, and so properly the subject
of these things. In *this Part,* I shall consider whether any such
thing be possible or conceivable, as that Freedom of Will which
Arminians insist on; and shall enquire, whether any such sort
of Liberty be necessary to moral agency, &c. in the *next* Part.

And first of all, I shall consider the notion of a *self-determining Power* in the will: wherein, according to the *Arminians,*
does most essentially consist the Will's Freedom; and shall particularly enquire, whether it be not plainly absurd, and a manifest inconsistence, to suppose that *the will itself determines all
the free acts of the will.*

Here I shall not insist on the great impropriety of such
ways of speaking, as *the Will determining itself;* because actions

are to be ascribed to agents, and not properly to the powers of agents; which improper way of speaking leads to many mistakes, and much confusion, as Mr. Locke observes. But I shall suppose that the *Arminians,* when they speak of the Will's determining itself, do by the *Will* mean the *soul willing.* I shall take it for granted, that when they speak of the Will, as the determiner, they mean *the soul in the exercise of a power of willing,* or acting voluntarily. I shall suppose this to be their meaning, because nothing else can be meant, without the grossest and plainest absurdity. In all cases when we speak of the powers or principles of acting, or doing such things, we mean that the agents which have these Powers of acting, do them, in the exercise of those Powers. So when we say, valour fights courageously, we mean the man, who is under the influence of valour fights courageously. When we say, love seeks the object loved, we mean, the person loving seeks that object. When we say the understanding discerns, we mean the soul in the exercise of that faculty. So when it is said, the will decides or determines, the meaning must be, that the person in the exercise of a Power of willing and choosing, or the soul acting voluntarily, determines.

Therefore, if the Will determines all its own free acts, the *soul* determines them in the exercise of a Power of willing and choosing; or, which is the same thing, it determines them of choice; it *determines* its own acts, by *choosing* its own acts. If the Will determines the Will, then choice orders and determines the choice: and acts of choice are subject to the decision, and follow the conduct of *other* acts of choice. And therefore if the Will determines all its own free acts, then every free act of choice is determined by a preceding act of choice, choosing that act. And if that preceding act of the Will be also a free act, then by these principles, in this act too, the Will is self-determined: that is, this, in like manner, is an act that the soul voluntarily chooses; or, which is the same thing, it is an act determined still by a preceding act of the Will, choosing that. Which brings us directly to a contradiction: for it supposes an act of the Will preceding the first act in the whole train, directing and determining the rest; or a free act of the Will, before the first free act of the Will. Or else we must come at last to an act of the Will, determining the consequent acts, wherein the Will is not self-determined, and so is not a free act, in this notion of freedom: but if the first act in the train, determining and fixing the rest, be not free, none of them all can be free; as is manifest at first view, but shall be demonstrated presently.

If the Will, which we find governs the members of the body, and determines their motions, does also govern itself, and determines its own actions, it doubtless determines them the same way, even by antecedent volitions. The Will determines which way the hands and feet shall move, by an act of choice: and there is no other way of the Will's determining, directing or commanding any thing at all. Whatsoever the Will commands, it commands by an act of the Will. And if it has itself under its command, and determines itself in its own actions, it doubtless does it the same way that it determines other things which are under its command. So that if the freedom of the Will consists in this, that it has itself and its own actions under its command and direction, and its own volitions are determined by itself, it will follow, that every free volition arises from another antecedent volition, directing and commanding that: and if that *directing* volition be also free, in that also the Will is determined; that is to say, that directing volition is determined by another going before that; and so on, till we come to the first volition in the whole series: and if that first volition be free, and the Will self-determined in it, then that is determined by another volition preceding that. Which is a contradiction; because by the supposition it can have none before it, to direct or determine it, being the first in the train. But if that first volition is not determined by any preceding act of the Will, then that act is not determined by the Will, and so is not free in the *Arminian* notion of freedom, which consists in the Will's self-determination. And if that first act of the Will which determines and fixes the subsequent acts, be not free, none of the following acts, which are determined by it can be free.—If we suppose there are five acts in the train, the fifth and last determined by the fourth, and the fourth by the third, the third by the second, and the second by the first; if the first is not determined by the Will, and so not free, then none of them are truly determined by the Will: that is, that each of them are as they are, and not otherwise, is not first owing to the Will, but to the determination of the first in the series, which is not dependent on the Will, and is that which the Will has no hand in determining. And this being that which decides what the rest shall be, and determines their existence; therefore the first determination of their existence is not from the Will. The case is just the same, if instead of a chain of five acts of the Will we should suppose a succession of ten, or an hundred, or ten thousand. If the first act be not free, being determined by something out of the Will, and this determines the next to be agreeable to itself, and that the next, and so on; none of them are free, but all originally depend on, and are determined by some cause out of the Will: and so all freedom in the case is excluded, and no act of the Will can be free, according to this notion of freedom. If we should suppose a long chain of ten thousand links, so connected, that if the first link moves, it will move the next, and that the next; and so the whole chain must be determined to motion, and in the direction of its motion, by the motion of the first link; and that is moved by something else; in this case, though all the links, but one, are moved by other parts of the same chain; yet it appears that the motion of no one, nor the direction of its motion, is from any self-moving or self-determining Power in the chain, any more than if every link were immediately moved by something that did not belong to the chain.—If the will be not free in the first act, which causes the next, then neither is it free in the next, which is caused by that first act: for though indeed the will caused it, yet it did not cause it freely; because the preceding act, by which it was caused, was not free. And again, if the will be not free in the second act, so neither can it be in the third, which is caused by that; because, in like manner, that third was determined by an act of the will that was not free. And so we may go on to the next act, and from that to the next; and how long soever the succession of acts is, it is all one; if the first on which the whole chain depends, and which determines all the rest, be not a free act, the will is not free in causing or determining any one of those acts; because the act by which it determines them all is not a free act; and therefore the will is no more free in determining them, than if it did not cause them at all.—Thus, this *Arminian* notion of Liberty of the Will, consisting in the

Will's *Self-determination,* is repugnant to itself, and shuts itself wholly out of the world.

* * *

SECT. III.

Whether any Event whatsoever, and Volition in particular, can come to pass without a Cause of its existence.

BEFORE I enter on any argument on this subject, I would explain how I would be understood, when I use the word *Cause* in this discourse; since, for want of a better word, I shall have occasion to use it in a sense which is more extensive, than that in which it is sometimes used. The word is often used in so restrained a sense as to signify only that which has a *positive efficiency* or influence to *produce* a thing, or bring it to pass. But there are many things which have no such positive productive influence: which yet are Causes in this respect, that they have truly the nature of a reason why some things are, rather than others; or why they are thus, rather than otherwise. Thus, the absence of the sun in the night, is not the Cause of the fall of dew at that time, in the same manner as its beams are the Cause of the ascent of vapours in the day-time; and its withdrawment in the winter, is not in the same manner the Cause of the freezing of the waters, as its approach in the spring is the cause of their thawing. But yet the withdrawment or absence of the sun is an antecedent, with which these effects in the night and winter are connected, and on which they depend; and is one thing that belongs to the ground and reason why they come to pass at that time, rather than at other times, though the absence of the sun is nothing positive, nor has any positive influence.

It may be further observed, that when I speak of *connection of Causes and Effects,* I have respect to *moral* Causes, as well as those which are called *natural* in distinction from them. Moral Causes may be Causes in as proper a sense, as any Causes whatsoever; may have as real an influence, and may as truly be the ground and reason of an Event's coming to pass.

Therefore I sometimes use the word *Cause,* in this enquiry, to signify any *antecedent,* either natural or moral, positive or negative, on which an Event, either a thing, or the manner and circumstance of a thing, so depends, that it is the ground and reason, either in whole, or in part, why it is, rather than not; or why it is as it is, rather than otherwise: or, in other words, any antecedent with which a consequent Event is so connected, that it truly belongs to the reason why the proposition which affirms that Event, is true; whether it has any positive influence, or not. And agreeably to this, I sometimes use the word effect for the consequence of another thing, which is perhaps rather an occasion than a Cause, most properly speaking.

I am the more careful thus to explain my meaning, that I may cut off occasion, from any that might seek occasion to cavil and object against some things which I may say concerning the dependence of all things which come to pass, on some Cause, and their connection with their Cause.

Having thus explained what I mean by *Cause,* I assert that nothing ever comes to pass without a Cause. What is self-existent must be from eternity, and must be unchangeable: but as to all things that *begin to be,* they are not self-existent, and therefore must have some foundation of their existence without them-selves. That whatsoever begins to be, which before was not, must have a Cause why it then begins to exist, seems to be the first dictate of the common and natural sense which God hath im-planted in the minds of all mankind, and the main foundation of all our reasonings about the existence of things, past, present, or to come.

And this dictate of common sense equally respects substances and modes, or things, and the manner and circumstances of things. Thus, if we see a body which has hitherto been at rest, start out of a state of rest, and begin to move, we do as naturally and necessarily suppose there is some Cause, or reason of this new mode of existence, as of the existence of a body itself which had hitherto not existed. And so if a body, which had hitherto moved in a certain direction, should suddenly change the direction of its motion; or if it should put off its old figure, and take a new one; or change its colour: the beginning of these new modes is a new Event, and the human mind necessarily supposes that there is some Cause or reason of them.

If this grand principle of common sense be taken away, all arguing from Effects to Causes ceaseth, and so all knowledge of any existence, besides what we have by the most direct and immediate intuition, particularly all our proof of the being of God ceases: we argue His being from our own being, and the being of other things, which we are sensible once were not, but have begun to be; and from the being of the world, with all its constituent parts, and the manner of their existence; all which we see plainly are not necessary in their own nature, and so not self-existent, and therefore must have a Cause. But if things, not in themselves necessary, may begin to be without a Cause, all this arguing is vain.

Indeed, I will not affirm, that there is in the nature of things no foundation for the knowledge of the Being of God without any evidence of it from his works. I do suppose there is a great absurdity in denying Being in general, and imagining an eternal, absolute, universal nothing: and therefore that there would be, in the nature of things, a foundation of intuitive evidence, that there must be an eternal, infinite, most perfect Being; if we had strength and comprehension of mind sufficient, to have a clear idea of general and universal Being. But then we should not properly come to the knowledge of the Being of God by arguing; our evidence would be intuitive: we should see it, as we see other things that are necessary in themselves, the contraries of which are in their own nature absurd and contradictory; as we see that twice two is four; and as we see that a circle has no angles. If we had as clear an idea of universal, infinite entity, as we have of these other things, I suppose we should most intuitively see the absurdity of supposing such Being not to be; should immediately see there is no room for the question, whether it is possible that Being, in the most general, abstracted notion of it, should not be. But we have not that strength and extent of mind, to know this certainly in this intuitive, independent manner: but the way that mankind come to the knowledge of the Being of God, is that which the apostle speaks of, Rom. i. 20. *The invisible things of him, from the creation of the world, are clearly seen; being understood by the things that are made; even his eternal power and Godhead.* We *first ascend,* and prove *a posteriori,* or from effects, that there must be an eternal Cause; and then *secondly,* prove by argumentation, not intuition, that this Being must be necessarily existent; and then *thirdly,* from the proved necessity of his existence, we may *descend,* and prove many of his perfections *a priori.*

But if once this grand principle of common sense be given up, that *what is not necessary in itself, must have a Cause;* and we begin to maintain, that things which heretofore have not been, may come into existence, and begin to be of themselves, without any cause; all our means of ascending in our arguing from the creature to the Creator, and all our evidence of the Being of God, is cut off at one blow. In this case, we cannot prove that there is a God, either from the Being of the world, and the creatures in it, or from the manner of their being, their order, beauty and use. For if things may come into existence without any Cause at all, then they doubtless may without any Cause answerable to the effect. Our minds do alike naturally suppose and determine both these things; namely, that what begins to be has a Cause, and also that it has a cause proportionable to the effect. The same principle which leads us to determine, that there cannot be any thing coming to pass without a Cause, leads us to determine that there cannot be more in the effect than in the cause.

Yea, if once it should be allowed, that things may come to pass without a Cause, we should not only have no proof of the Being of God, but we should be without evidence of the existence of any thing whatsoever, but our own immediately present ideas and consciousness. For we have no way to prove any thing else, but by arguing from effects to Causes; from the ideas now immediately in view, we argue other things not immediately in view; from sensations now excited in us, we infer the existence of things without us, as the Causes of these sensations; and from the existence of these things, we argue other things, on which they depend, as effects on Causes. We infer the past existence of ourselves, or any thing else, by memory; only as we argue, that the ideas, which are now in our minds, are the consequences of past ideas and sensations. We immediately perceive nothing else but the ideas which are this moment extant in our minds. We perceive or know other things only *by means* of these, as necessarily connected with others, and dependent on them. But if things may be without Causes, all this necessary connection and dependence is dissolved, and so all means of our knowl-

edge is gone. If there be no absurdity or difficulty in supposing
one thing to start out of non-existence into being, of itself without a Cause; then there is no absurdity or difficulty in supposing
the same of millions of millions. For nothing, or no difficulty
multiplied, still is nothing, or no difficulty: nothing multiplied
by nothing, does not increase the sum.

If any should imagine, there is something in the sort of
Event that renders it possible for it to come into existence without a cause, and should say, that the free acts of the will are
existences of an exceeding *different nature* from other things: by
reason of which they may come into existence without any previous ground or reason of it, though other things cannot: if they
make this objection in good earnest, it would be an evidence of
their strangely forgetting themselves; for they would be giving
an account of some ground of the existence of a thing, when at
the same time they would maintain there is no ground of
its existence. Therefore I would observe, that the particular
nature of existence, be it never so diverse from others, can lay
no foundation for that thing coming into existence without a
cause: being to suppose this, would be to suppose the *particular
nature* of existence to be a thing prior to the existence, and so
a thing which makes way for existence, without a cause or reason
of existence. But that which in any respect makes way for a
thing coming into being, or for any manner of circumstance of
its first existence, must be prior to the existence. The distinguished nature of the effect, which is something belonging to
the effect, cannot have influence backward, to act before it is.
The peculiar nature of that thing called volition, can do
nothing, can have no influence, while it is not. And afterwards
it is too late for its influence: for then the thing has made sure
of existence already, without its help.

So that it is indeed as repugnant to reason, to suppose that
an act of the will should come into existence without a cause,
as to suppose the human soul, or an angel, or the globe of the
earth, or the whole universe, should come into existence without a cause. And if once we allow, that such a sort of effect as
a Volition may come to pass without a Cause, how do we know
but that many other sorts of effects may do so too? It is not the
particular *kind* of effect that makes the absurdity of supposing it

has being without a Cause, but something which is common to all things that ever begin to be, *viz.* That they are not self-existent, or necessary in the nature of things.

PART III.

WHEREIN IS ENQUIRED, WHETHER ANY SUCH LIBERTY OF WILL AS ARMINIANS HOLD, BE NECESSARY TO MORAL AGENCY, VIRTUE AND VICE, PRAISE AND DISPRAISE, &c.

SECT. I.

God's moral Excellency necessary, yet virtuous and praiseworthy.

HAVING CONSIDERED the *first* thing proposed, relating to that freedom of will which *Arminians* maintain; namely, Whether any such thing does, ever did, or ever can exist, I come now to the *second* thing proposed to be the subject of enquiry, *viz.* Whether any such kind of liberty be requisite to moral agency, virtue and vice, praise and blame, reward and punishment, &c.

I shall begin with some consideration of the virtue and agency of the Supreme moral Agent, and Fountain of all Agency and Virtue.

Dr. Whitby in his Discourse on the five Points, (p. 14.) says, "If all human actions are necessary, virtue and vice must be empty names; we being capable of nothing that is blameworthy, or deserveth praise; for who can blame a person for doing only what he could not help, or judge that he deserveth praise only for what he could not avoid?" To the like purpose he speaks in places innumerable; especially in his Discourse on the *Freedom of the Will;* constantly maintaining, that a *freedom not only from coaction, but necessity,* is absolutely requisite, in order to actions being either worthy of blame, or deserving of praise. And to this agrees, as is well known, the current doctrine of *Arminian* writers, who, in general, hold that there is no virtue or vice, reward or punishment, nothing to be commended or blamed, without this freedom. And yet Dr. Whitby, (p. 300,) allows, that God is without this freedom; and *Arminians,* so far as I have had opportunity to observe, generally acknowledge, that God is necessarily holy, and his will necessarily determined to that which is good.

So that, putting these things together, the infinitely holy God—who always used to be esteemed by God's people not only virtuous, but a Being in whom is all possible virtue, in the most absolute purity and perfection, brightness and amiableness; the most perfect pattern of virtue, and from whom all the virtue of others is but as beams from the sun; and who has been supposed to be, (being thus every where represented in Scripture,) on the account of his virtue and holiness, infinitely more worthy to be esteemed, loved, honoured, admired, commended, extolled, and praised, than any creature—this Being, according to this notion of Dr. Whitby, and other *Arminians,* has no virtue at all; virtue, when ascribed to Him, is but *an empty name;* and he is deserving of no commendation or praise; because he is under necessity. He cannot avoid being holy and good as he is; therefore no thanks to him for it. It seems the holiness, justice, faithfulness, &c. of the Most High, must not be accounted to be of the nature of that which is virtuous and praiseworthy. They will not deny, that these things in God are good; but then we must understand them, that they are no more virtuous, or of the nature of any thing commendable, than the good that is in any other being that is not a moral agent; as the brightness of the sun, and the fertility of the earth, are good, but not virtuous, because these properties are necessary to these bodies, and not the fruit of self-determining power.

There needs no other confutation of this notion, to Christians acquainted with the Bible, but only stating and particularly representing it. To bring texts of Scripture, wherein God is represented as in every respect in the highest manner virtuous, and supremely praiseworthy, would be endless, and is altogether needless to such as have been brought up in the light of the Gospel.

*   *   *

PART IV.

WHEREIN THE CHIEF GROUNDS OF THE REASONINGS OF ARMINIANS, IN SUPPORT AND DEFENCE OF THE FOREMENTIONED NOTIONS OF LIBERTY, MORAL AGENCY, &C. AND AGAINST THE OPPOSITE DOCTRINE, ARE CONSIDERED.

SECT. I.

The Essence of the Virtue and Vice of Dispositions of the Heart, and Acts of the Will, lies not in their Cause, but their Nature.

* * *

SECT. II.

The Falseness and Inconsistence of that metaphysical Notion of Action, and Agency, which seems to be generally entertained by the Defenders of the Arminian Doctrine concerning Liberty, moral Agency, &c.

ONE THING that is made very much a ground of argument and supposed demonstration by *Arminians,* in defence of the forementioned principles, concerning moral Agency, Virtue, Vice, &c. is their metaphysical notion of *Agency* and *Action.* They say, unless the soul has a self-determining power, it has no power of *Action;* if its volitions be not caused by itself, but are excited and determined by some extrinsic cause, they cannot be the soul's own *acts;* and that the soul cannot be *active,* but must be wholly *passive,* in those effects of which it is the subject necessarily, and not from its own free determination.

Mr. Chubb lays the foundation of his scheme of liberty and of his arguments to support it, very much in this position, that *man is an Agent and capable of Action.* Which doubtless is true: but *self-determination* belongs to his notion of *Action,* and is the very essence of it. Whence he infers, that it is impossible for a man to act and be acted upon, in the same thing, at the same time; and that no Action can be the effect of the Action of another: and he insists, that a *necessary Agent,* or an Agent that is necessarily determined to act, is a *plain contradiction.*

But those are a precarious sort of demonstrations, which men build on the meaning that they arbitrarily affix to a word; especially when that meaning is abstruse, inconsistent, and entirely diverse from the original sense of the word in common speech.

That the meaning of the word *Action,* as Mr. Chubb and many others use it, is utterly unintelligible and inconsistent, is manifest, because it belongs to their notion of an Action, that it is something wherein is no passion or passiveness; that is (according to their sense of passiveness) it is under the power, influence, or Action of no cause. And this implies that Action has no cause, and is no effect; for to be an effect implies *passiveness,* or the being subject to the power and Action of its cause. And yet they hold that the mind's *Action* is the effect of its own determination, yea, the mind's free and voluntary determination; which is the same with free choice. So that Action is the effect of something preceding, even a preceding act of choice: and consequently, in this effect the mind is passive, subject to the power and Action of the preceding cause, which is the foregoing choice, and therefore cannot be active. So that here we have this contradiction, that Action is always the effect of foregoing choice; and therefore cannot be action; because it is *passive* to the power of that preceding causal choice; and the mind cannot be active and passive in the same thing, at the same time. Again they say, necessity is utterly inconsistent with Action, and a necessary Action is a contradiction; and so their notion of Action implies contingence, and excludes all necessity. And therefore, their notion of Action implies, that it has no necessary dependence on, or connection with, any thing foregoing; for such a dependence or connection excludes contingence, and implies necessity. And yet their notion of Action implies necessity, and supposes that it is necessary, and cannot be contingent. For they suppose, that whatever is properly called Action, must be determined by the will and free choice; and this is as much as to say, that it must be necessary, being dependent upon, and determined by something foregoing; namely, a foregoing act of choice. Again, it belongs to their notion of Action, that it is the beginning of motion, or of exertion of power; but yet it is implied in their notion of Action, that it is not the beginning of motion or exertion of power, but is consequent and dependent on a preceding exertion of power, *viz.* the power of will and choice: for they say there is no proper Action but what is freely *chosen,* or, which is the same thing, determined by a foregoing act of free choice. But if any of them shall see cause to deny this, and say they hold no such thing as that every Action is chosen or determined by a foregoing choice; but that the very first exertion of will only, undetermined by any preceding act, is properly called Action; then I say, such a man's notion of Action implies necessity; for what the mind is the subject of, without the determination of its own previous choice, it is the subject of necessarily, as to any hand that free choice has in the affair; and without any ability the mind has to prevent it, by any will or election of its own; because by the supposition it precludes all previous acts of the will or choice in the case, which might prevent it. So that it is again, in this other way, implied in their notion of act, that it is both necessary and not necessary. Again, it belongs to their notion of an *act,* that it is no effect of a predetermining bias or preponderation, but springs immediately out of indifference; and this implies, that it cannot be from foregoing choice, which is foregoing preponderation; if it be not habitual, but occasional, yet if it causes the act, it is truly previous, efficacious and determining. And yet, at the same time, it is essential to their notion of the act, that it is what the Agent is the Author of freely and voluntarily, and that is, by previous choice and design.

So that, according to their notion of the act, considered with regard to its consequences, these following things are all essential to it; *viz.* That it should be necessary, and not necessary; that it should be from a cause, and no cause; that it should be the fruit of choice and design, and not the fruit of choice and design; that it should be the beginning of motion or exertion, and yet consequent on previous exertion; that it should be before it is; that it should spring immediately out of indifference and equilibrium, and yet be the effect of preponderation; that it should be self-originated, and also have its original from something else; that it is what the mind causes itself, of its own will, and can produce or prevent according to its choice or pleasure, and yet what the mind has no power to prevent, precluding all previous choice in the affair.

So that an act, according to their metaphysical notion of it, is something of which there is no idea; it is nothing but a confusion of the mind, excited by words without any distinct meaning, and is an absolute nonentity; and that in two respects: (1.) There is nothing in the world that ever was, is, or can be, to answer the things which must belong to its description, according to what they suppose to be essential to it. And (2.) There neither is, nor ever was, nor can be, any notion or idea to answer the word, as they use and explain it. For if we should suppose any such notion, it would many ways destroy itself. But it is impossible any idea or notion should subsist in the mind, whose very nature and essence, which constitutes it, destroys it.— If some learned philosopher, who had been abroad, in giving an account of the curious observations he had made in his travels, should say, "He had been in *Terra del Fuego*, and there had seen an animal, which he calls by a certain name, that begat and brought forth itself, and yet had a sire and dam distinct from itself; that it had an appetite, and was hungry before it had a being; that his master, who led him, and governed him at his pleasure, was always governed by him, and driven by him where he pleased; that when he moved, he always took a step before the first step: that he went with his head first, and yet always went tail foremost; and this, though he had neither head nor tail;" it would be no impudence at all, to tell such a traveller, though a learned man, that he himself had no idea of such an animal as he gave an account of, and never had, nor ever would have.

*   *   *

SECT. IV.

It is agreeable to common Sense, and the natural Notions of Mankind, to suppose moral Necessity to be consistent with Praise and Blame, Reward and Punishment.

WHETHER THE reasons that have been given, why it appears difficult to some persons to reconcile with common Sense the praising or blaming, rewarding or punishing those things which are morally necessary, are thought satisfactory or not; yet it most evidently appears by the following things, that if this matter be rightly understood, setting aside all delusion arising from the impropriety and ambiguity of terms, this is not at all inconsistent with the natural apprehensions of mankind, and that sense of things which is found every where in the common people; who are furthest from having their thoughts perverted from their natural channel by metaphysical and philosophical subtilties; but, on the contrary, altogether agreeable *to,* and the very voice and dictate *of* this natural and vulgar Sense.

I. This will appear, if we consider what the vulgar Notion of *blameworthiness* is. The idea which the common people through all ages and nations, have of faultiness, I suppose to be plainly this; *a person being or doing wrong, with his own will and pleasure;* containing these two things; 1. *His doing wrong, when he does as he pleases.* 2. *His pleasure being wrong.* Or, in other words, perhaps more intelligibly expressing their Notion; *a person having his heart wrong, and doing wrong from his heart.* And this is the sum total of the matter.

The common people do not ascend up in their reflections and abstractions to the metaphysical sources, relations and dependencies of things, in order to form their Notion of faultiness or blameworthiness. They do not wait till they have decided by their refinings what first determines the will, whether it be determined by something extrinsic or intrinsic; whether volition determines volition, or whether the understanding determines the will; whether there be any such thing as metaphysicians mean by contingence (if they have any meaning;) whether there be a sort of a strange unaccountable sovereignty in the will, in the exercise of which, by its own sovereign acts, it brings to pass all its own sovereign acts. They do not take any part of their Notion of fault or blame from the resolution of any such questions. If this were the case, there are multitudes, yea the far greater part of mankind, nine hundred and ninety-nine out of a thousand, would live and die without having any such Notion as that of fault ever entering into their heads, or without so much as once having any conception that any body was to be either blamed or commended for any thing. If this were the case, it would be a long time before men came to have such Notions. Whereas it is manifest, they are in fact some of the first Notions that appear in children; who discover, as soon as they can think, or speak, or act at all as rational creatures, a Sense of desert. And certainly, in forming their Notion of it, they make no use of metaphysics. All the ground they go upon consists in these two things; *experience,* and a *natural sensation* of a certain fitness or agreeableness which there is in uniting such moral evil as is above described, *viz. a being or doing wrong with the will,* and resentment in others, and pain inflicted on the person in whom this moral evil is. Which *natural Sense* is what we call by the name of *conscience.*

It is true, the common people and children, in their Notion of any faulty act or deed of any person, do suppose that it is the person's *own act and deed.* But this is all that belongs to what they understand by a thing being a person's *own deed or action;* even that it is something done by him of *choice.* That some exercise or motion should begin of itself, does not belong to their Notion of *an action or doing.* If so, it would belong to their Notion of it that it is the cause of its own beginning: and that is as much as to say, that it is before it begins to be. Nor is their Notion of *an action* some motion or exercise, that begins accidentally without any cause or reason; for that is contrary to one of the prime dictates of common Sense, namely, that every thing that begins to be, has some cause or reason why it is.

The common people, in their Notion of a faulty or praiseworthy work done by any one, do suppose, that the man does it in the exercise of *liberty.* But then their Notion of liberty is only a person having an opportunity of doing as he pleases. They have no Notion of liberty consisting in the will first acting, and so causing its own acts; determining, and so causing its own determinations; or choosing, and so causing its own choice. Such a Notion of liberty is what none have, but those that have darkened their own minds with confused metaphysical speculation, and abstruse and ambiguous terms. If a man is not restrained from acting as his will determines, or constrained to act otherwise; then he has liberty, according to common Notions of liberty, without taking into the idea that grand contradiction of all, the determinations of a man's free will being the effects of the determinations of his free will.—Nor have men commonly any Notion of freedom consisting in indifference. For if so, then it would be agreeable to their Notion, that the greater indifference men act with, the more freedom they act with; whereas, the reverse is true. He that in acting proceeds with the fullest inclination, does what he does with the greater freedom, according to common Sense. And so far it is from being agreeable to common Sense that such liberty as consists in indifference is requisite to praise or blame, that, on the contrary, the dictate of every man's natural sense through the world is, that the further he is from being indifferent in his acting good or evil, and the more he does either with full and strong inclination, the more is he esteemed or abhorred, commended or condemned.

II. If it were inconsistent with the common Sense of mankind, that men should be either blamed or condemned in any volitions, in case of moral necessity or impossibility; then it would surely also be agreeable to the same Sense and reason of mankind, that the nearer the case approaches to such a moral necessary or impossibility—either through a strong antecedent moral propensity, on the one hand,* or a great antecedent opposition and difficulty, on the other—the nearer does it approach to a person being neither blameable nor commendable; so that acts exerted with such preceding propensity, would be worthy of proportionably less praise; and when omitted, the act being attended with such difficulty, the omission would be worthy of the less blame. It is so, as was observed before, with natural necessity and impossibility, propensity and difficulty: as it is a

---

* It is here argued, on supposition that not all propensity implies moral necessity, but only some very high degree; which none will deny.

plain dictate of the sense of all mankind, that natural necessity and impossibility take away *all* blame and praise; and therefore, that the nearer the approach is to these, through previous propensity or difficulty, so praise and blame are proportionably *diminished*. And if it were as much a dictate of common Sense that moral necessity of doing, or impossibility of avoiding, takes away *all* praise and blame, as that natural necessity or impossibility does; then by a perfect parity of reason, it would be as much the dictate of common Sense, that an *approach* of moral necessity of doing, or impossibility of avoiding, *diminishes* praise and blame, as that an approach to natural necessity and impossibility does so. It is equally the voice of common Sense, that persons are *excusable in part,* in neglecting things *difficult* against their wills, as that they are *excusable wholly* in neglecting things *impossible* against their wills. And if it made no difference, whether the impossibility were natural and against the will, or moral, lying in the will, with regard to excusableness; so neither would it make any difference, whether the difficulty, or approach to necessity be natural against the will, or moral, lying in the propensity of the will.

But it is apparent that the reverse of these things is true. If there be an approach to a moral necessity in a man's exertion of good acts of will, they being the exercise of a strong propensity to good and a very powerful love to virtue; it is so far from being the dictate of common Sense that he is less virtuous, and the less to be esteemed, loved and praised, that it is agreeable to the natural Notions of all mankind, that he is so much the better man, worthy of greater respect, and higher commendation. And the stronger the inclination is, and the nearer it approaches to necessity in that respect; or to impossibility of neglecting the virtuous act, or of doing a vicious one; still the more virtuous, and worthy of higher commendation. And, on the other hand, if a man exerts evil acts of mind; as, for instance, acts of pride or malice from a rooted and strong habit or principle of haughtiness and maliciousness, and a violent propensity of heart to such acts; according to the natural Sense of men he is so far from being the less hateful and blameable on that account, that he is so much the more worthy to be detested and condemned by all that observe him.

Moreover, it is manifest that it is no part of the Notion which mankind commonly have of a blameable or praiseworthy act of the will, that it is an act which is not determined by an antecedent bias or motive, but by the sovereign power of the will itself; because, if so, the greater hand such causes have in determining any acts of the will, so much the less virtuous or vicious would they be accounted; and the less hand, the more virtuous or vicious. Whereas, the reverse is true: men do not think a good act to be the less praiseworthy for the agent being much determined in it by a good inclination or a good motive, but the more. And if good inclination, or motive, has but little influence in determining the agent, they do not think his act so much the more virtuous, but the less. And so concerning evil acts, which are determined by evil motives or inclinations.

Yea, if it be supposed that good or evil dispositions are implanted in the hearts of men by nature itself (which, it is certain, is vulgarly supposed in innumerable cases) yet it is not commonly supposed that men are worthy of no praise or dispraise for such dispositions; although what is natural is undoubtedly necessary, nature being prior to all acts of the will whatsoever. Thus, for instance, if a man appears to be of a very haughty or malicious disposition, and is supposed to be so by his natural temper, it is no vulgar Notion, no dictate of the common Sense and apprehension of men, that such dispositions are no vices or moral evils, or that such persons are not worthy of disesteem, or odium and dishonour; or that the proud or malicious acts which flow from such natural dispositions are worthy of no resentment. Yea, such vile natural dispositions, and the strength of them, will commonly be mentioned rather as an *aggravation* of the wicked acts that come from such a fountain, than an extenuation of them. It being natural for men to act thus, is often observed by men in the height of their indignation: they will say, "It is his very nature: he is of a vile natural temper; it is as natural to him to act so, as it is to breathe; he cannot help serving the devil, &c." But it is not thus with regard to hurtful mischievous things, that any are the subjects or occasions of, by *natural necessity,* against their inclinations. In such a case, the necessity, by the common voice of mankind, will be spoken of as a full excuse.—Thus it is very plain, that common Sense makes a vast difference between these two kinds of necessity, as to the judgment it makes of their influence on the moral quality and desert of men's actions.

Upon the whole, I presume there is no person of good understanding who impartially considers these things, but will allow, that it is not evident, from the dictates of common sense or natural notions, that moral necessity is inconsistent with praise and blame. And, therefore, if the *Arminians* would prove any such inconsistency, it must be by some philosophical and metaphysical arguments, and not common sense.

*   *   *

SECT. XIV.

The Conclusion.

WHETHER THE things which have been alleged, are liable to any tolerable answer in the way of calm, intelligible and strict reasoning, I must leave others to judge: but I am sensible they are liable to one sort of answer. It is not unlikely that some, who value themselves on the supposed rational and generous principles of the modern fashionable divinity, will have their indignation and disdain raised at the sight of this discourse, and on perceiving what things are pretended to be proved in it. And if they think it worthy of being read, or of so much notice as to say much about it, they may probably renew the usual exclamations, with additional vehemence and contempt, about the *fate of the heathen,* Hobbes *Necessity,* and *making men mere machines;* accumulating the terrible epithet is of *fatal, unfrustrable, inevitable, irresistible,* &c. and it may be, with addition of *horrid* and *blasphemous;* and perhaps much skill may be used to set forth things which have been said, in colours which shall be shocking to the imaginations, and moving to the passions of those, who have either too little capacity or too much confidence of the opinions they have imbibed, and contempt of the contrary, to try the matter by any serious and circumspect examination.* Or difficulties may be stated and insisted on, which do not belong to the controversy; because, let them be more or less real, and hard to be resolved, they are not what are owing to any thing distinguishing of this scheme from that of the *Arminians,* and would not be removed nor diminished by renouncing the former, and adhering to the latter. Or some particular things may be picked out which they may think will sound harshest in the ears of the generality; and these may be glossed and descanted on with tart and contemptuous words; and from thence, the whole discourse may be treated with triumph and insult.

It is easy to see how the decision of most of the points in controversy between *Calvinists* and *Arminians,* depends on the determination of this grand article concerning *the Freedom of the Will requisite to moral agency;* and that by clearing and establishing the *Calvinistic* doctrine in this point, the chief arguments are obviated by which *Arminian* doctrines in general are supported, and the contrary doctrines demonstratively confirmed. Hereby it becomes manifest, that God's moral government over mankind, his treating them as moral agents, making them the objects of his commands, counsels, calls, warnings, expostulations, promises, threatenings, rewards and punishments, is not inconsistent with a *determining disposal* of all events, of every kind, throughout the universe, *in his Providence;* either by positive efficiency or permission. Indeed such an *universal determining Providence,* infers some kind of necessity of all

* A writer of the present age, whom I have several times had occasion to mention, speaks once and again of those who hold the doctrine of *Necessity* as scarcely worthy of the name of *philosophers.* I do not know whether he has respect to any particular notion of necessity that some may have maintained; and, if so, what doctrine of necessity it is that he means. Whether I am worthy of the name of a philosopher or not would be a question little to the present purpose. If any, and ever so many, should deny it, I should not think it worth while to enter into a dispute on that question: though, at the same time, I might expect some better answer should be given to the arguments brought for the truth of the doctrine I maintain; and I might further reasonably desire, that it might be considered whether it does not become those who are *truly worthy* of the name of philosophers to be sensible that there is a difference between *argument* and *contempt;* yea, and a difference between the contemptibleness of the *person* that argues and the inconclusiveness of the *arguments* he offers.

events, such a necessity as implies an infallible previous fixedness of the futurity of the event: but no other necessity of moral events, or volitions of intelligent agents, is needful in order to this, than *moral necessity;* which does as much ascertain the futurity of the event, as any other necessity. But, as has been demonstrated, such a necessity is not at all repugnant to moral agency, and a reasonable use of commands, calls, rewards, punishments, &c. Yea, not only are objections of this kind against the doctrine of an universal *determining Providence,* removed by what has been said, but the truth of such a doctrine is demonstrated. As it has been demonstrated, that the futurity of all future events is established by previous necessity, either natural or moral; so it is manifest, that the sovereign Creator and Disposer of the world has ordered this necessity, by ordering his own conduct, either in designedly acting, or forbearing to act. For, as the being of the world is from God, so the circumstances in which it had its being at first, both negative and positive, must be ordered by him, in one of these ways; and all the necessary consequences of these circumstances, must be ordered by him. And God's active and positive interpositions, after the world was created, and the consequences of these interpositions; also every instance of his forbearing to interpose, and the sure consequences of this forbearance, must all be determined according to his pleasure. And therefore every event, which is the consequence of any thing whatsoever, or that is connected with any foregoing thing or circumstances, either positive or negative, as the ground or reason of its existence, must be ordered of God; either by a designing efficiency and interposition, or a designed forbearing to operate or interpose. But, as has been proved, all events whatsoever are necessarily connected with something foregoing, either positive or negative, which is the ground of its existence. It follows, therefore, that the whole series of events is thus connected with something in the state of things either positive or negative, which is *original* in the series, *i.e.* something which is connected with nothing preceding that, but God's own immediate conduct, either his acting or forbearing to act. From whence it follows, that as God designedly orders his own conduct, and its connected consequences, it must necessarily be, that he designedly orders all things.

But I must leave all these things to the consideration of the impartial reader; and when he has maturely weighed them, I would propose it to his consideration, whether many of the first reformers, and others that succeeded them, whom God in their day made the chief pillars of his church, and the greatest instruments of their deliverance from error and darkness, and of the support of the cause of piety among them, have not been injured, in the contempt with which they have been treated by many late writers, for their teaching and maintaining such doctrines as are commonly called *Calvinistic*. Indeed, some of these new writers, at the same time that they have represented the doctrines of these ancient and eminent divines as in the highest degree ridiculous, and contrary to common sense, in an ostentation of a very generous charity, have allowed that they were honest well-meaning men; yea, it may be some of them, as though it were in great condescension and compassion to them, have allowed, that they did pretty well for the day in which they lived, and considering the great disadvantages they laboured under; when, at the same time, their manner of speaking has naturally and plainly suggested to the minds of their readers, that they were persons, who—through the lowness of their genius, and the greatness of the bigotry with which their minds were shackled, and their thoughts confined, living in the gloomy caves of superstition—fondly embraced, and demurely and zealously taught the most absurd, silly, and monstrous opinions, worthy of the greatest contempt of gentlemen possessed of that noble and generous freedom of thought, which happily prevails in this age of light and enquiry. When, indeed, such is the case that we might, if so disposed, speak as big words as they, and on far better grounds. And really all the *Arminians* on earth might be challenged without arrogance or vanity, to make these principles of theirs, wherein they mainly differ from their fathers, whom they so much despise, consistent with common sense; yea, and perhaps to produce any doctrine ever embraced by the blindest bigot of the church of *Rome,* or the most ignorant *Mussulman,* or extravagant enthusiast, that might be reduced to more demonstrable inconsistencies, and repugnancies to common sense, and to themselves; though their inconsistencies indeed may not lie so deep, or be so artfully veiled by a deceitful ambiguity of words, and an indeterminate signification of phrases. I will not deny, that these gentlemen, many of them, are men of great abilities, and have been helped to higher attainments in philosophy, than those ancient divines, and have done great service to the Church of God in some respects: but I humbly conceive, that their differing from their fathers, with such magisterial assurance, in these points in divinity, must be owing to some other cause than superior wisdom.

It may also be worthy of consideration, whether the great alteration which has been made in the state of things in our nation, and some other parts of the Protestant world, in this and the past age, by exploding so generally *Calvinistic* doctrines —an alteration so often spoken of as worthy to be greatly rejoiced in by the friends of truth, learning, and virtue, as an instance of the great increase of light in the Christian Church— be indeed a happy change, owing to any such cause as an increase of true knowledge and understanding in the things of religion; or whether there is not reason to fear, that it may be owing to some worse cause.

And I desire it may be considered, whether the boldness of some writers may not deserve to be reflected on, who have not scrupled to say, that if these and those things are true (which yet appear to be the demonstrable dictates of reason, as well as the certain dictates of the mouth of the Most High) then God is unjust, and cruel, and guilty of manifest deceit and double dealing, and the like. Yea, some have gone so far as confidently to assert, that if any book which pretends to be Scripture, teaches such doctrines, that alone is sufficient warrant for mankind to reject it, as what cannot be the word of God. Some, who have not gone so far, have said, that if the Scripture seems to teach any such doctrines, so contrary to reason, we are obliged to find out some other interpretation of those texts, where such doctrines seem to be exhibited. Others express themselves yet more modestly: they express a tenderness and religious fear, lest they should receive and teach any thing that should seem to reflect on God's moral character, or be a disparagement to his methods of administration, in his moral government; and therefore express themselves as not daring to embrace some doctrines, though they seem to be delivered in Scripture, according to the more obvious and natural construction of the words. But indeed it would shew a truer modesty and humility, if they would more entirely rely on God's wisdom and discernment, who knows infinitely better than we what is agreeable to his own perfections, and never intended to leave these matters to the decision of the wisdom and discernment of men; but by his own unerring instruction, to determine for us what the truth is; knowing how little our judgment is to be depended on, and how extremely prone vain and blind men are to err in such matters.

The truth of the case is, that if the Scripture plainly taught the opposite doctrines to those that are so much stumbled at, *viz.* the *Arminian* doctrine of free will, and others depending thereon, it would be the greatest of all difficulties that attend the Scriptures, incomparably greater than its containing any, even the most mysterious of those doctrines of the first reformers, which our late freethinkers have so superciliously exploded. Indeed, it is a glorious argument of the divinity of the holy Scriptures, that they teach such doctrines, which in one age and another, through the blindness of men's minds, and strong prejudices of their hearts are rejected, as most absurd and unreasonable, by the wise and great men of the world; which yet, when they are most carefully and strictly examined, appear to be exactly agreeable to the most demonstrable, certain, and natural dictates of reason. By such things it appears, that "the foolishness of God is wiser than men." (I. Cor. i. 19, 20.) "For it is written, I will destroy the wisdom of the wise; I will bring to nothing the understanding of the prudent. Where is the wise! Where is the scribe! Where is the disputer of this world! Hath not God made foolish the wisdom of this world?" And as it was in time past, so probably it will be in time to come, as it is also written, (ver. 27-29.) "But God hath chosen the foolish things of the world, to confound the wise: and God hath chosen the weak things of the world, to confound the things that are mighty: and base things of the world, and things which are despised, hath God chosen: yea, and things which are not, to bring to nought things that are; that no flesh should glory in his presence." Amen.

"BALTIMORE SERMON"

WILLIAM ELLERY CHANNING

(1780-1842)

IN HIS famous "Baltimore Sermon" preached in 1819 (here presented) Channing launched the Unitarian controversy. In this
sermon he asserted that Christ is "a being distinct from the one
God" and thus not in 'the same status as God. (The traditional
orthodox view held that Christ, as the Son of God, was of the
same substance as God and thus fully of equal worship as God,
the Father.)

The sermon was a call to arms to battle against entrenched
Calvinism and particularly against Trinitarianism.

In 1825 the American Unitarian Association was organized,
precipitated by Channing, after a long period of incubation of
Unitarian views.

This Baltimore ordination service at which this carefully
prepared sermon was preached was not an ordinary occasion.
Present were liberal leaders from Boston and points north,
among whom was Henry Ware, Sr., pivotal controversial figure
at Harvard, target for the traditionalists. Jared Sparks, a protégé
of Channing's, was to be ordained as minister of the First Independent Church in Baltimore and Channing was to make clear
and precise the views of Unitarian Protestant Christianity, and
particularly to show the unreasonableness of the dogma of the
Trinity and of the view that Christ had a double nature (human
and divine).

Channing took this occasion to denounce the traditional
views that man is depraved and his salvation dependent on a
Divine election—both doctrines unworthy of the moral perfec-

tion of God. Christ's life of suffering, he affirmed, was not a price paid for man's sins and thus an exhibition of God's mercy as a purchase-price; rather it was a manifestation of God's mercy to reorientate the mind of man to His own excellence. Man, he suggested, is quite capable of attaining the knowledge of God's nature, man and God being qualitatively different only in degree, in purity and extent of operation; he possesses the potentiality or the capacity of perfectibility. The whole of traditional theology, in a word, must be morally reconstructed.

Channing was Harvard trained and a member of the Harvard corporation. Non-controversial as a person, his preaching touched controversial subjects not only in theology but on questions of social reform (such as slavery, temperance, penal practices). His voice reached far beyond his parish pulpit in the Federal Street Society of Boston in the spirit of a *protesting* Protestant ready to champion new ideas amidst the frozen patterns of orthodoxy.

Editor

"BALTIMORE SERMON"

1. THESS. v. 21.—*"Prove all things; hold fast that which is good."*

THE PECULIAR circumstances of this occasion not only justify, but seem to demand, a departure from the course generally followed by preachers at the introduction of a brother into the sacred office. It is usual to speak of the nature, design, duties and advantages of the Christian ministry; and on those topics I should now be happy to insist, did I not remember that a minister is to be given this day to a religious society, whose peculiarities of opinion have drawn upon them much remark, and may I not add, much reproach. Many good minds, many sincere Christians, I am aware, are apprehensive that the solemnities of this day are to give a degree of influence to principles which they deem false and injurious. The fears and anxieties of such men I respect; and, believing that they are grounded in part on mistake, I have thought it my duty to lay before you, as clearly as I can, some of the distinguishing opinions of that class of

Christians in our country, who are known to sympathize with this religious society. I must ask your patience, for such a subject is not to be despatched in a narrow compass. I must also ask you to remember, that it is impossible to exhibit, in a single discourse, our views of every doctrine of revelation, much less the differences of opinion which are known to subsist among ourselves. I shall confine myself to topics on which our sentiments have been misrepresented, or which distinguish us most widely from others. May I not hope to be heard with candour. God deliver us from prejudice and unkindness, and fill us with the love of truth and virtue.

There are two natural divisions under which my thoughts will be arranged. I shall endeavour to unfold, 1st, the principles which we adopt in interpreting the Scriptures. And 2dly, some of the doctrines which the Scriptures, so interpreted, seem to us clearly to express.

I. We regard the Scriptures as the records of God's successive revelations to mankind, and particularly of the last and most perfect revelation of his will by Jesus Christ. Whatever doctrines seem to us to be clearly taught in the Scriptures, we receive without reserve or exception. We do not, however, attach equal importance to all the books in this collection. Our religion, we believe, lies chiefly in the New Testament. The dispensation of Moses, compared with that of Jesus, we consider as imperfect, earthly, obscure, adapted to the childhood of the human race, a preparation for a nobler system, and chiefly useful now as serving to confirm and illustrate the Christian Scriptures. Jesus Christ is the only master of Christians, and whatever he taught, either during his personal ministry, or by his inspired apostles, we regard as of divine authority, and profess to make the rule of our lives.

This authority, which we give to the Scriptures, is a reason, we conceive, for studying them with peculiar care, and for inquiring anxiously into the principles of interpretation, by which their true meaning may be ascertained. The principles adopted by the class of Christians, in whose name I speak, need to be explained, because they are often misunderstood. We are particularly accused of making an unwarrantable use of reason in the interpretation of Scripture. We are said to exalt reason above revelation, to prefer our own wisdom to God's. Loose and undefined charges of this kind are circulated so freely, and with such injurious intentions, that we think it due to ourselves, and to the cause of truth, to express our views with some particularity.

Our leading principle in interpreting Scripture is this,—that the Bible is a book written for men, in the language of men, and that its meaning is to be sought in the same manner, as that of other books. We believe that God, when he condescends to speak and write, submits, if we may so say, to the established rules of speaking and writing. How else would the Scriptures avail us more than if communicated in an unknown tongue?

Now all books and all conversation require in the reader or hearer the constant exercise of reason; or their true import is only to be obtained by continual comparison and inference. Human language, you well know, admits various interpretations, and every word and every sentence must be modified and explained according to the subject which is discussed, according to the purposes, feelings, circumstances, and principles of the writer, and according to the genius and idioms of the language which he uses. These are acknowledged principles in the interpretation of human writings; and a man, whose words we should explain without reference to these principles, would reproach us justly with a criminal want of candour, and an intention of obscuring or distorting his meaning.

Were the Bible written in a language and style of its own, did it consist of words which admit but a single sense, and of sentences wholly detached from each other, there would be no place for the principles now laid down. We could not reason about it, as about other writings. But such a book would be of little worth; and perhaps of all books, the Scriptures correspond least to this description. The word of God bears the stamp of the same hand, which we see in his works. It has infinite connexions and dependences, Every proposition is linked with others, and is to be compared with others, that its full and precise import may be understood. Nothing stands alone. The New Testament is built on the Old. The Christian dispensation is a continuation of the Jewish, the completion of a vast scheme of providence, requiring great extent of view in the reader. Still more, the Bible treats of subjects on which we receive ideas from other sources besides itself; such subjects as the nature, passions, relations, and duties of man; and it expects us to restrain and modify its language, by the known truths which observation and experience furnish on these topics.

We profess not to know a book which demands a more frequent exercise of reason than the Bible. In addition to the remarks now made on its infinite connexions, we may observe, that its style no where affects the precision of science, or the accuracy of definition. Its language is singularly glowing, bold, and figurative, demanding more frequent departures from the literal sense, than that of our own age and country, and consequently demanding more continual exercise of judgment.—We find too, that the different portions of this book, instead of being confined to general truths, refer perpetually to the times when they were written, to states of society, to modes of thinking, to controversies in the church, to feelings and usages, which have passed away, and without the knowledge of which we are constantly in danger of extending to all times and places, what was of temporary and local application. We find, too, that some of these books are strongly marked by the genius and character of their respective writers, that the Holy Spirit did not so guide the apostles as to suspend the peculiarities of their minds, and that a knowledge of their feelings, and of the influences under which they were placed, is one of the preparations for understanding their writings. With these views of the Bible, we feel it our bounden duty to exercise our reason upon it perpetually, to compare, to infer, to look beyond the letter to the spirit, to seek in the nature of the subject, and the aim of the writer, his true meaning; and, in general, to make use of what is known, for explaining what is difficult, and for discovering new truths.

Need I descend to particulars, to prove that the Scriptures demand the exercise of reason? Take, for example, the style in which they generally speak of God, and observe how habitually they apply to him human passions and organs. Recollect the declarations of Christ, that he came not to send peace, but a sword; that unless we eat his flesh, and drink his blood, we have no life in us; that we must hate father and mother; pluck out the right eye; and a vast number of passages equally bold and unlimited. Recollect the unqualified manner in which it is said of Christians, that they possess all things, know all things, and can do all things. Recollect the verbal contradiction between Paul and James, and the apparent clashing of some parts of Paul's writings, with the general doctrines and end of Christianity. I might extend the enumeration indefinitely, and who does not see that we must limit all these passages by the known attributes of God, of Jesus Christ, and of human nature, and by the circumstances under which they were written, so as to give the language a quite different import from what it would require, had it been applied to different beings, or used in different connexions?

Enough has been said to shew in what sense we make use of reason in interpreting Scripture. From a variety of possible interpretations, we select that which accords with the nature of the subject and the state of the writer, with the connexion of the passage, with the general strain of Scripture, with the known character and will of God, and with the obvious and acknowledged laws of nature. In other words, we believe that God never contradicts, in one part of Scripture, what he teaches in another; and never contradicts in revelation, what he teaches in his works and providence. And we, therefore, distrust every interpretation, which, after deliberate attention, seems repugnant to any established truth. We reason about the Bible precisely as civilians do about the constitution under which we live, who, you know, are accustomed to limit one provision of that venerable instrument by others, and to fix the precise import of its parts by inquiring into its general spirit, into the intentions of its authors, and into the prevalent feelings, impressions, and circumstances of the time when it was framed. Without these principles of interpretation, we frankly acknowledge that we cannot defend the divine authority of the Scriptures. Deny us this latitude, and we must abandon this book to its enemies.

We do not announce these principles as original or peculiar to ourselves. All Christians occasionally adopt them, not excepting those who most vehemently decry them, when they happen to menace some favourite article of their creed. All Christians are compelled to use them in their controversies with infidels.

All sects employ them in their warfare with one another. All willingly avail themselves of reason, when it can be pressed into the service of their own party, and only complain of it when its weapons wound themselves. None reason more frequently than our adversaries. It is astonishing what a fabric they rear from a few slight hints about the fall of our first parents; and how ingeniously they extract from detached passages, mysterious doctrines about the divine nature. We do not blame them for reasoning so abundantly, but for violating the fundamental rules of reasoning, for sacrificing the plain to the obscure, and the general strain of Scripture, to a scanty number of insulated texts.

We object strongly to the contemptuous manner in which human reason is often spoken of by our adversaries, because it leads, we believe, to universal scepticism. If reason be so dreadfully darkened by the fall, that its most decisive judgments on religion are unworthy of trust, then Christianity, and even natural theology, must be abandoned; for the existence and veracity of God, and the divine original of Christianity, are conclusions of reason, and must stand or fall with it. If revelation be at war with this faculty, it subverts itself, for the great question of its truth is left by God to be decided at the bar of reason. It is worthy of remark, how nearly the bigot and the sceptic approach. Both would annihilate our confidence in our faculties, and both throw doubt and confusion over every truth. We honour revelation too highly to make it the antagonist of reason, or to believe, that it calls us to renounce our highest powers.

We indeed grant, that the use of reason in religion is accompanied with danger. But we ask any honest man to look back on the history of the church and say, whether the renunciation of it be not still more dangerous. Besides, it is a plain fact, that men reason as erroneously on all subjects as on religion. Who does not know the wild and groundless theories, which have been framed in physical and political science? But who ever supposed, that we must cease to exercise reason on nature and society, because men have erred for ages in explaining them? We grant, that the passions continually and sometimes fatally, disturb the rational faculty in its inquiries into revelation. The ambitious contrive to find doctrines in the Bible, which favour their love of dominion. The timid and dejected discover there a gloomy system; and the mystical and fanatical, a visionary theology. The vicious can find examples or assertions on which to build the hope of a late repentance, as of acceptance on easy terms; whilst the falsely refined contrive to light on doctrines which have not been soiled by vulgar handling. But the passions do not distract the reason in religious, any more than in other inquiries, which excite strong and general interest; and this faculty, of consequence, is not to be renounced in religion, unless we are prepared to discard it universally. The true inference from the almost endless errors, which have darkened theology, is, not that we are to neglect and disparage our powers, but to exert them more patiently, circumspectly, uprightly. The worst errors, after all, have sprung up in that church which proscribes reason, and demands from its members implicit faith. The most pernicious doctrines have been the growth of the darkest times, when the general credulity encouraged bad men and enthusiasts to broach their dreams and inventions, and to stifle the faint remonstrances of reason by the menaces of everlasting perdition. Say what we may, God has given us a rational nature, and will call us to account for it. We may let it sleep, but we do so at our peril. Revelation is addressed to us as rational beings. We may wish, in our sloth, that God had given us a system, demanding no labour of comparing, limiting and inferring. But such a system would be at variance with the whole character of our present existence; and it is the part of wisdom to take revelation, as it is given to us, and to interpret it by the help of the faculties, which it every where supposes, and on which it is founded.

To the views now given, an objection is commonly urged from the character of God. We are told, that God being infinitely wiser than men, his discoveries will surpass human reason. In a revelation from such a teacher, we ought to expect propositions, which we cannot reconcile with one another, and which may seem to contradict established truths; and it becomes us not to question or explain them away, but to believe, and adore, and to submit our weak and carnal reason to the divine word. To this objection, we have two short answers. We say, first, that it is impossible that a teacher of infinite wisdom, should expose those, whom he would teach, to infinite error. But if once we admit, that propositions, which in their literal sense appear plainly repugnant to one another, or to any known truth, are still to be literally understood and received, what possible limit can we set to the belief of contradictions? What shelter have we from the wildest fanaticism, which can always quote passages, that in their literal and obvious sense, give support to its extravagances? How can the Protestant escape from transubstantiation, a doctrine most clearly taught us, if the submission of reason, now contended for, be a duty? How can we even hold fast the truth of revelation, for if one apparent contradiction may be true, so may another, and the proposition, that Christianity is false, though involving inconsistency, may still be a verity?

We answer again, that, if God be infinitely wise, he cannot sport with the understandings of his creatures. A wise teacher discovers his wisdom in adapting himself to the capacities of his pupils, not in perplexing them with what is unintelligible, not in distressing them with apparent contradictions, not in filling them with a sceptical distrust of their own powers. An infinitely wise teacher, who knows the precise extent of our minds, and the best method of enlightening them, will surpass all other instructors in bringing down truth to our apprehension, and in showing its loveliness and harmony. We ought, indeed, to expect occasional obscurity in such a book as the Bible, which was written for past and future ages, as well as for the present. But God's wisdom is a pledge, that whatever is necessary for *us*, and necessary for salvation, is revealed too plainly to be mistaken, and too consistently to be questioned, by a sound and upright mind. It is not the mark of wisdom, to use an unintelligible phraseology, to communicate what is above our capacities, to confuse and unsettle the intellect by appearances of contradiction. We honor our heavenly Teacher too much to ascribe to him such a revelation. A revelation is a gift of light. It cannot thicken our darkness, and multiply our perplexities.

II. Having thus stated the principles according to which we interpret Scripture, I now proceed to the second great head of this discourse, which is, to state some of the views, which we derive from that sacred book, particularly those which distinguish us from other Christians.

First. We believe in the doctrine of God's UNITY, or that there is one God, and one only. To this truth we give infinite importance, and we feel ourselves bound to take heed, lest any man spoil us of it by vain philosophy. The proposition, *that there is one God,* seems to us exceedingly plain. We understand by it, that there is one being, one mind, one person, one intelligent agent, and one only, to whom underived and infinite perfection and dominion belong. We conceive, that these words could have conveyed no other meaning to the simple and uncultivated people, who were set apart to be the depositaries of this great truth, and who were utterly incapable of understanding those hair-breadth distinctions between *being* and *person,* which the sagacity of latter ages has discovered. We find no intimation, that this language was to be taken in an unusual sense, or that God's unity was a quite different thing from the oneness of other intelligent beings.

We object to the doctrine of the Trinity, that it subverts the unity of God. According to this doctrine, there are three infinite and equal persons, possessing supreme divinity, called the Father, Son, and Holy Ghost. Each of these persons as described by theologians, has his own particular consciousness, will, and perceptions. They love each other, converse with each other, and delight in each other's society. They perform different parts in man's redemption, each having his appropriate office, and neither doing the work of the other. The Son is mediator and not the Father. The Father sends the Son, and is not himself sent; nor is he conscious, like the Son, of taking flesh. Here then, we have three intelligent agents, possessed of different consciousness, different wills, and different perceptions, performing different acts, and sustaining different relations; and if these things do not imply and constitute three minds or beings, we are utterly at a loss to know how three minds or beings are to be formed. It is difference of properties, and acts, and consciousness, which leads us to the belief of different intelligent beings, and if this mark fails us, our whole knowledge falls; we have no proof, that all the agents and persons in the universe are not one and the same mind. When we attempt to conceive of three

Gods, we can do nothing more, than represent to ourselves three agents, distinguished from each other by similar marks and peculiarities to those, which separate the persons of the Trinity; and when common Christians hear these persons spoken of as conversing with each other, loving each other, and performing different acts, how can they help regarding them as different beings, different minds?

We do then, with all earnestness, though without reproaching our brethren, protest against the irrational and unscriptural doctrine of the Trinity. "To us," as to the apostle and the primitive christians, "there is one God, even the Father." With Jesus, we worship the Father, as the only living and true God. We are astonished, that any man can read the New Testament, and avoid the conviction, that the Father alone is God. We hear our Saviour continually appropriating this character to the Father. We find the Father continually distinguished from Jesus by this title. "God sent his Son." "God anointed Jesus." Now, how singular and inexplicable is this phraseology, which *fills* the New Testament, if this title belong equally to Jesus, and if a principal object of this book is to reveal him as God, as partaking equally with the Father in supreme divinity! We challenge our opponents to adduce one passage in the New Testament, where the word God means three persons, where it is not limited to one person, and where, unless turned from its usual sense by the connexion, it does not mean the Father. Can stronger proof be given, that the doctrine of three persons in the Godhead is not a fundamental doctrine of Christianity?

This doctrine, were it true, must, from its difficulty singularity, and importance, have been laid down with great clearness, guarded with great care, and stated with all possible precision. But where does this statement appear? From the many passages which treat of God, we ask for one, one only, in which we are told, that he is a threefold being, or, that he is three persons, or that he is Father, Son, and Holy Ghost. On the contrary, in the New Testament, where, at least, we might expect many express assertions of this nature, God is declared to be one, without the least attempt to prevent the acceptation of the words in their common sense; and he is always spoken of and addressed in the singular number, that is, in language which was universally understood to intend a single person, and to which no other idea could have been attached, without an express admonition. So entirely do the Scriptures abstain from stating the Trinity, that when our opponents would insert it into their creeds and doxologies, they are compelled to leave the bible, and to invent forms of words altogether unsanctioned by scriptural phraseology. That a doctrine so strange, so liable to misapprehension, so fundamental as this is said to be, and requiring such careful exposition, should be left so undefined and unprotected, to be made out by inference, and to be hunted through distant and detached parts of scripture, this is a difficulty, which, we think, no ingenuity can explain.

We have another difficulty. Christianity, it must be remembered, was planted and grew up amidst sharp-sighted enemies, who overlooked no objectionable part of the system, and who must have fastened with great earnestness on a doctrine involving such apparent contradictions as the Trinity. We cannot conceive an opinion, against which the Jews, who prided themselves on an adherence to God's unity, would have raised an equal clamour. Now, how happens it, that in the apostolic writings, which relate so much to objections against Christianity, and to the controversies which grew out of this religion, not *one word* is said, implying that objections were brought against the gospel from the doctrine of the Trinity, not one word is uttered in its defence and explanation, not a word to rescue it from reproach and mistake? This argument has almost the force of demonstration. We are persuaded, that had three divine persons been announced by the first preachers of Christianity, all equal, and all infinite, one of whom was the very Jesus, who had lately died on a cross, this peculiarity of Christianity would have almost absorbed every other, and the great labour of the apostles would have been to repel the continual assaults, which it would have awakened. But the fact is, that not a whisper of objection to Christianity, on that account, reaches our ears from the apostolic age. In the epistles we see not a trace of controversy called forth by the Trinity.

We have further objections to this doctrine, drawn from its practical influence. We regard it as unfavourable to devotion, by dividing and distracting the mind in its communion with

God. It is a great excellence of the doctrine of God's unity, that it offers to us ONE OBJECT of supreme homage, adoration and love, one infinite Father, one Being of Beings, one original and fountain, to whom we may refer all good, on whom all our powers and affections may be concentrated, and whose lovely and venerable nature may pervade all our thoughts. True piety, when directed to an undivided Deity, has a chasteness, a singleness, most favourable to religious awe and love. Now the Trinity sets before us three distinct objects of supreme adoration; three infinite persons, having equal claims on our hearts; three divine agents, performing different offices, and to be acknowledged and worshipped in different relations. And is it possible, we ask, that the weak and limited mind of man can attach itself to these with the same power and joy, as to one *infinite Father,* the only First Cause, in whom all the blessings of nature and redemption meet as their centre and source? Must not devotion be distracted by the equal and rival claims of three equal persons, and must not the worship of the conscientious, consistent Christian be disturbed by an apprehension, lest he withhold from one or another of these, his due proportion of homage?

We also think, that the doctrine of the Trinity injures devotion, not only by joining to the Father other objects of worship, but by taking from the Father the supreme affection, which is his due, and transferring it to the Son. This is a most important view. That Jesus Christ, if exalted into the infinite Divinity, should be more interesting than the Father, is precisely what might be expected from history, and from the principles of human nature. Men want an object of worship like themselves, and the great secret of idolatry lies in this propensity. A God, clothed in our form, and feeling our wants and sorrows, speaks to our weak nature more strongly, than a Father in heaven, a pure spirit, invisible, and unapproachable, save by the reflecting and purified mind.—We think too, that the peculiar offices ascribed to Jesus by the popular theology, make him the most attractive person in the Godhead. The Father is the depositary of the justice, the vindicator of the rights, the avenger of the laws of the Divinity. On the other hand, the Son, the brightness of the divine mercy, stands between the incensed

Deity and guilty humanity, exposes his meek head to the storms, and his compassionate breast to the sword of the divine justice, bears our whole load of punishment, and purchases with his blood every blessing which descends from heaven. Need we state the effect of these representations, especially on common minds, for whom Christianity was chiefly designed, and whom it seeks to bring to the Father as the loveliest being? We do believe, that the worship of a bleeding, suffering God, tends strongly to absorb the mind, and to draw it from other objects, just as the human tenderness of the Virgin Mary has given her so conspicuous a place in the devotions of the church of Rome. We believe too, that this worship, though attractive, is not most fitted to spiritualize the mind, that it awakens human transport, rather than that deep veneration of the moral perfections of God, which is the essence of piety.

Secondly. Having thus given views of the unity of God, I proceed to observe, that we believe in the *unity of Jesus Christ*. We believe that Jesus is one mind, one soul, one being, as truly one as we are, and equally distinct from the one God. We complain of the doctrine of the Trinity, that not satisfied with making God three beings, it makes Jesus Christ two beings, and thus introduces infinite confusion into our conceptions of his character. This corruption of Christianity, alike repugnant to common sense, and to the general strain of Scripture, is a remarkable proof of the power of a false philosophy in disfiguring the simple truth of Jesus.

According to this doctrine, Jesus Christ instead of being one mind, one conscious intelligent principle, whom we can understand, consists of two souls, two minds; the one divine, the other human; the one weak, the other almighty; the one ignorant, the one omniscient. Now we maintain, that this is to make Christ two beings. To denominate him one person, one being, and yet to suppose him made up of two minds, infinitely different from each other, is to abuse and confound language, and to throw darkness over all our conceptions of intelligent natures.—According to the common doctrine, each of these two minds in Christ has its own consciousness, its own will, its own perceptions. They have in fact no common properties. The divine mind feels none of the wants and sorrows of the human, and the human is infinitely removed from the perfection and happiness of the divine. Can you conceive of two beings in the universe more distinct? We have always thought that one person was constituted and distinguished by one consciousness. The doctrine, that one and the same person should have two consciousnesses, two wills, two souls, infinitely different from each other, this we think an enormous tax on human credulity.

We say, that if a doctrine, so strange, so difficult, so remote from all the previous conceptions of men, be indeed a part and an essential part of revelation, it must be taught with great distinctness, and we ask our brethren to point to some plain, direct passage, where Christ is said to be composed of two minds infinitely different, yet constituting one person. We find none. Our opponents, indeed, tell us, that this doctrine is necessary to the harmony of the Scriptures, that some texts ascribe to Jesus Christ human, and others divine properties, and that to reconcile these, we must suppose two minds, to which these properties may be referred. In other words, for the purpose of reconciling certain difficult passages, which a just criticism can in a great degree, if not wholly, explain, we must invent an hypothesis vastly more difficult, and involving gross absurdity. We are to find our way out of a labyrinth, by a clue, which conducts us into mazes infinitely more inextricable.

Surely if Jesus Christ felt that he consisted, of two minds and that this was a leading feature of his religion, his phraseology respecting himself would have been coloured by this peculiarity. The universal language of men is framed upon the idea, that one person is one mind, and one soul; and when the multitude heard this language from the lips of Jesus, they must have taken it in its usual sense, and must have referred to a single soul all which he spoke, unless expressly instructed to interpret it differently. But where do we find this instruction? Where do you meet, in the New Testament, the phraseology which abounds in Trinitarian books, and which necessarily grew from the doctrine of two natures in Jesus? Where does this divine teacher say, "This I speak as God, and this as man; this is true only of my human mind, this only of my divine?"

Where do we find in the epistles a trace of this strange phraseology? Nowhere. It was not needed in that day. It was demanded by the errors of a later age.

We believe, then, that Christ is one mind, one being, and, I add, a being distinct from the one God. That Christ is not the one God, not the same being with the Father, is a necessary inference from our former head, in which we saw that the doctrine of three persons in God is a fiction. But on so important a subject, I would add a few remarks. We wish, that our opponents would weigh one striking fact. Jesus, in his preaching, continually spoke of God. The word was always in his mouth. We ask, does he, by this word, ever mean himself? We say, *never*. On the contrary, he most plainly distinguishes between God and himself, and so do his disciples. How this is to be reconciled with the idea, that the manifestation of Christ, as God, was a primary object of Christianity, our adversaries must determine.

If we examine the passages in which Jesus is distinguished from God, we shall see, that they not only speak of him as another being, but seem to labour to express his inferiority. He is continually spoken of as the Son of God, sent of God, receiving all his powers from God, working miracles because God was with him, judging justly because God taught him, having claims on our belief, because he was anointed and sealed by God, and as able of himself to do nothing. The New Testament is *filled* with this language. Now we ask, what impression this language was fitted and intended to make? Could any, who heard it, have imagined, that Jesus was the *very God,* to whom he was so industriously declared to be inferior, the *very being,* by whom he was sent, and from whom he professed to have received his message, and power? Let it here be remembered, that the human birth, and bodily form, and humble circumstances, and mortal sufferings of Jesus, must all have prepared men to interpret, in the most unqualified manner, the language in which his inferiority to God was declared. Why then was this language used so continually, and without limitation, if Jesus were the Supreme Deity, and if this truth were an essential part of his religion? I repeat it, the human condition and sufferings of Christ, tended strongly to exclude from men's minds the idea of his proper Godhead; and of course, we should expect to find in the New Testament perpetual care and effort to counteract this tendency, to hold him forth as the same being with his Father, if this doctrine were, as is pretended, the soul and centre of his religion. We should expect to find the phraseology of Scripture cast into the mould of this doctrine, to hear familiarly of God the Son, of our Lord God Jesus, and to be told, that to us there is one God, even Jesus. But instead of this, the inferiority of Christ pervades the New Testament. It is not only implied in the general phraseology, but repeatedly and decidedly expressed, and unaccompanied with any admonition to prevent its application to his whole nature. Could it then have been the great design of the sacred writers, to exhibit Jesus as the Supreme God?

I am aware that these remarks will be met by two or three texts, in which Christ is called God, and by a class of passages, not very numerous, in which divine properties are said to be ascribed to him. To these we offer one plain answer. We say that it is one of the most established and obvious principles of criticism, that language is to be explained according to the known properties of the subject to which it is applied. Every man knows, that the same words convey very different ideas, when used in relation to different beings. Thus Solomon *built* the temple in a different manner from the architect whom he employed; and God *repents* differently from man. Now, we maintain, that the known properties and circumstances of Christ, his birth, sufferings, and death, his constant habit of speaking of God as a distinct being from himself, his praying to God, his ascribing to God all his power and offices, these acknowledged properties of Christ, we say, oblige us to interpret the comparatively few passages, which are thought to make him the supreme God, in a manner consistent with his distinct and inferior nature. It is our duty to explain such texts, by the rule which we apply to other texts, in which human beings are called Gods, and are said to be partakers of the divine nature, to know and possess all things, and to be filled with all God's fulness. These latter passages we do not hesitate to modify, and restrain, and turn from the most obvious sense, because this sense is opposed to the known properties of the beings to whom they relate; and we maintain, that we adhere to the same principle, and use no greater latitude, in explaining, as we do, the passages which are thought to support the Godhead of Christ.

Trinitarians profess to derive some important advantages from their mode of viewing Christ. It furnishes them, they tell us, with an infinite atonement, for it shows them an infinite being, suffering for their sins. The confidence with which this fallacy is repeated astonishes us. When pressed with the question, whether they really believe, that the infinite and unchangeable God suffered and died on the cross, they acknowledge that this is not true, but that Christ's human mind alone sustained the pains of death.—How have we then an infinite sufferer? This language seems to us an imposition on common minds, and very derogatory to God's justice, as if this attribute could be satisfied by a sophism and a fiction.

We are also told, that Christ is a more interesting object, that his love and mercy are more felt, when he is viewed as the Supreme God, who left his glory to take humanity and to suffer for men. That Trinitarians are strongly moved by this representation, we do not mean to deny; but we think their emotions altogether founded on a misapprehension of their own doctrines. They talk of the second person of the Trinity's leaving his glory and his Father's bosom, to visit and save the world. But this second person, being the unchangeable and infinite God, was evidently incapable of parting with the least degree of his perfection and felicity. At the moment of his taking flesh, he was as intimately present with his Father as before, and equally with his Father filled heaven, and earth, and immensity. This Trinitarians acknowledge; and still they profess to be touched and overwhelmed by the amazing humiliation of this immutable being!!—But not only does their doctrine, when fully explained, reduce Christ's humiliation to a fiction, it almost wholly destroys the impressions with which his cross ought to be viewed. According to their doctrine, Christ was, comparatively, no sufferer at all. It is true, his human mind suffered; but this, they tell us, was an infinitely small part of Jesus, bearing no more proportion to his whole nature, than a single hair of our heads to the whole body; or, than a drop to the ocean. The divine mind of Christ, that which was most

properly himself, was infinitely happy, at the very moment of
the suffering of his humanity. Whilst hanging on the cross, he
was the happiest being in the universe, as happy as the infinite
Father; so that, his pains, compared with his felicity, were
nothing. This Trinitarians do, and must acknowledge. It follows necessarily, from the immutableness of the divine nature,
which they ascribe to Christ; so that their system, justly viewed,
robs his death of interest, weakens our sympathy with his sufferings, and is, of all others, most unfavourable to a love of
Christ, founded on a sense of his sacrifices for mankind. We
esteem our own views to be vastly more affecting, especially those
of us, who believe in Christ's pre-existence. It is our belief, that
Christ's humiliation was real and entire, that the whole Saviour,
and not a part of him, suffered, that his crucifixion was a scene
of deep and unmixed agony. As we stand round his cross, our
minds are not distracted, or our sensibility weakened, by contemplating him as composed of incongruous and infinitely differing minds, and as having a balance of infinite felicity. We
recognise in the dying Jesus but one mind. This, we think,
renders his sufferings, and his patience and love in bearing
them, incomparably more impressive and affecting, than the
system we oppose.

Thirdly. Having thus given our belief on two great points,
namely, that there is one God, and that Jesus Christ is a being
distinct from, and inferior to God, I now proceed to another
point on which we lay still greater stress. We believe in the
moral perfection of God. We consider no part of theology so
important as that which treats of God's moral character; and
we value our views of Christianity chiefly, as they assert his
amiable and venerable attributes.

It may be said, that in regard to this subject, all Christians
agree, that all ascribe to the Supreme Being, infinite justice,
goodness, and holiness. We reply, that it is very possible to
speak of God magnificently, and to think of him meanly; to
apply to his person high-sounding epithets, and to his government, principles which make him odious. The heathens called
Jupiter the Greatest and the Best; but his history was black
with cruelty and lust. We cannot judge of men's real ideas of
God by their general language, for in all ages, they have hoped

to sooth the Deity by adulation. We must inquire into their particular views of his purposes, of the principles of his administration, and of his disposition towards his creatures.

We conceive that Christians have generally leaned towards a very injurious view of the Supreme Being. They have too often felt, as if he were raised by his greatness and sovereignty above the principles of morality, above those eternal laws of equity and rectitude, to which all other beings are subjected. *We* believe, that in no being, is the sense of right so strong, so omnipotent, as in God. We believe that his almighty power is entirely submitted to his perception of rectitude; and this is the ground of our piety. It is not because he is our creator merely, but because he created us for good and holy purposes; it is not because his will is irresistible, but because his will is the perfection of virtue, that we pay him allegiance. We cannot bow before a being, however great and powerful, who governs tyrannically. We respect nothing but excellence, whether on earth, or in heaven. We venerate not the loftiness of God's throne, but the equity of goodness in which it is established.

We believe that God is infinitely good, kind, benevolent, in the proper sense of these words; good in disposition, as well as in act; good not to a few, but to all; good to every individual, as well as to the general system.

We believe too, that God is just; but we never forget, that his justice is the justice of a good being, dwelling in the same mind, and acting in harmony with perfect benevolence. By this attribute we understand God's infinite regard to virtue or moral worth, expressed in a moral government: that is, in giving excellent and equitable laws, and in conferring such rewards, and inflicting such punishments as are most fitted to secure their observance. God's justice has for its end the highest virtue of the creation, and it punishes for this end alone, and thus it coincides with benevolence; for virtue and happiness, though not the same, are inseparably conjoined.

God's justice, thus viewed, appears to us to be in perfect harmony with his mercy. According to the prevalent systems of theology, these attributes are so discordant and jarring, that to reconcile them is the hardest task, and the most wonderful achievement of infinite wisdom. To *us*, they seem to be intimate friends, always at peace, breathing the same spirit, and seeking the same end. By God's mercy, we understand not a blind, instinctive compassion, which forgives without reflection, and without regard to the interests of virtue. This, we acknowledge, would be incompatible with justice, and also with enlightened benevolence. God's mercy, as we understand it, desires strongly the happiness of the guilty, but only through their penitence. It has a regard to character as truly as his justice. It defers punishment, and suffers long, that the sinner may return to his duty; but leaves the impenitent and unyielding to the fearful retribution threatened in God's word.

To give our views of God in one word, we believe in his *parental character*. We ascribe to him, not only the name but the dispositions and principles of a father. We believe that he has a father's concern for his creatures, a father's desire for their improvement, a father's equity in proportioning his commands to their powers, a father's joy in their progress, a father's readiness to receive the penitent, and a father's justice for the incorrigible. We look upon this world as a place of education, in which he is training men by mercies and sufferings, by aids and temptations, by means and opportunities of various virtues, by trials of principle, by the conflicts of reason and passion, by a discipline suited to free and moral beings, for union with himself, and for a sublime and ever growing virtue in heaven.

Now we object to the systems of religion, which prevail among us, that they are adverse, in a greater or less degree, to these purifying, comforting, and honourable views of God, that they take from us our father in heaven, and substitute for him a being, whom we cannot love if we would, and whom we ought not to love if we could. We object, particularly on this ground, to that system, which arrogates to itself the name of orthodoxy, and which is now most industriously propagated through our country.—This system teaches, that God brings us into existence wholly depraved, so that under the innocent features of our childhood is hidden a nature averse to all good, and propense to all evil; and it teaches that God regards us with displeasure before we have acquired power to understand our duties, or reflect upon our actions. Now if there be one plain principle of morality, it is this, that we are accountable beings, only because we have conscience, a power of knowing and performing our duty, and in as far as we want this power, we are incapable of sin, guilt, or blame. We should call a parent a monster, who should judge and treat his children in opposition to this principle, and yet this enormous immorality is charged on our Father in heaven.

This system also teaches, that God selects from the corrupt mass of men a number to be saved, and that they are plucked, by an irresistible agency, from the common ruin, whilst the rest are commanded, under penalty of aggravated woe, to make a change in their characters, which their natural corruption places beyond their power, and are also promised pardon on conditions, which necessarily avail them nothing, unless they are favoured with a special operation of God's grace, which he is predetermined to withhold. This mockery of mercy, this insult offered to the misery of the non-elect, by hollow proffers of forgiveness, completes the dreadful system which is continually obtruded upon us as the gospel, and which strives to monopolize the reputation of sanctity.

That this religious system does not produce all the effects on character, which might be anticipated, we most joyfully admit. It is often, very often, counteracted by nature, conscience, common sense, by the general strain of Scripture, by the mild example and precepts of Christ, and by the many positive declarations of God's universal kindness, and perfect equity. But still we think that we see occasionally its unhappy influence. It discourages the timid, gives excuses to the bad, feeds the vanity of the fanatical, and offers shelter to the bad feelings of the malignant. By shocking, as it does, the fundamental principles of morality, and by exhibiting a severe and partial Deity, it tends strongly to pervert the moral faculty, to form a gloomy, forbidding, and servile religion, and to lead men to substitute censoriousness, bitterness, and persecution, for a tender and impartial charity. We think too, that this system, which begins with degrading human nature, may be expected to end in pride; for pride grows out of a consciousness of high distinctions, however obtained, and no distinction is so great as that, which subsists between the elected and abandoned of God.

The false and dishonourable views of God which have now been stated, we feel ourselves bound to resist unceasingly. Other errors we can pass over with comparative indifference. But we ask our opponents to leave to us a GOD, worthy of our love and trust, in whom our moral sentiments may delight, in whom our weakness and sorrows may find refuge. We cling to the divine perfections. We meet them everywhere in creation, we read them in the Scriptures, we see a lovely image of them in Jesus Christ; and gratitude, love and veneration call on us to assert them. Reproached as we often are, by men, it is our consolation and happiness, that one of our chief offences is the zeal with which we vindicate the dishonoured goodness and rectitude of God.

Fourthly. Having thus spoken of the unity of God; of the unity of Jesus, and his inferiority to God; and of the perfections of the divine character; I now proceed to give our views of the *mediation of Christ* and *of the purposes of his mission.* With regard to the great object, which Jesus came to accomplish, there seems to be no possibility of mistake. We believe, that he was sent by the Father to effect a moral or spiritual deliverance of mankind; that is, to rescue men from sin and its consequences, and to bring them to a state of everlasting purity and happiness. We believe, too, that he accomplishes this sublime purpose by a variety of methods; by his instructions respecting God's unity, parental character, and moral government, which are admirably fitted to reclaim the world from idolatry and impiety, to the knowledge, love, and obedience of the Creator; by his promises of pardon to the penitent, and of divine assistance to those, who labour for progress in moral excellence; by the light which he has thrown on the path of duty; by his own spotless example, in which the loveliness and sublimity of virtue shine forth to warm and quicken as well as guide us to perfection; by his threatenings against incorrigible guilt; by his glorious discoveries of immortality; by his sufferings and death; by that signal event, the resurrection, which powerfully bore witness to his divine mission, and brought down to men's senses a future life; by his continual intercession, which obtains for us spiritual aid and blessings; and by the power with which he is invested of raising the dead, judging the world, and conferring the everlasting rewards, promised to the faithful.

We have no desire to conceal the fact, that a difference of opinion exists among us, in regard to an interesting part of Christ's mediation; I mean, in regard to the precise influence of his death on our forgiveness. Some suppose, that this event contributes to our pardon, as it was a principal means of confirming his religion, and of giving it a power over the mind; in other words, that it procures forgiveness by leading to that repentance and virtue, which is the great and only condition on which forgiveness is believed. Many of us are dissatisfied with this explanation, and think that the Scriptures ascribe the remission of sins to Christ's death, with an emphasis so peculiar, that we ought to consider this event as having a special influence in removing punishment, as a condition or method of pardon, without which repentance would not avail us, at least to that extent, which is now promised by the gospel.

Whilst, however, we differ in explaining the connexion between Christ's death and human forgiveness, a connexion which we all gratefully acknowledge, we agree in rejecting many sentiments which prevail in regard to his mediation. The idea which is conveyed to common minds by the popular system, that Christ's death has an influence in making God placable or merciful, in quenching his wrath, in awakening his kindness towards men, we reject with horror. We believe, that Jesus, instead of making the Father merciful, is sent by the Father's mercy to be our Saviour; that he is nothing to the human race, but what he is by God's appointment; that he communicates nothing but what God empowers him to bestow; that our Father in heaven is originally, essentially, and eternally placable, and disposed to forgive; and that his unborrowed, underived, and unchangeable love, is the only fountain of what flows to us through his Son. We conceive, that Jesus is dishonoured, not glorified, by ascribing to him an influence which clouds the splendour of divine benevolence.

We farther agree in rejecting, as unscriptural and absurd, the explanation given by the popular system, of the manner in which Christ's death procures forgiveness for men. This system teaches, that man, having sinned against an infinite being, is infinitely guilty, and some even say that a single transgression, though committed in our early and inconsiderate years, merits the eternal pains of hell. Thus an infinite penalty is due from every human being; and God's justice insists, that it shall be borne either by the offender, or a substitute. Now, from the nature of the case, no substitute is adequate to the work of sustaining the full punishment of a guilty world, save the infinite God himself; and accordingly, God took on him human nature, that he might pay to his own justice the debt of punishment incurred by men, and might enable himself to exercise mercy. Such is the prevalent system. Now, to us, this doctrine seems to carry on its front strong marks of absurdity; and we maintain that Christianity ought not to be encumbered with it, unless it be laid down in the New Testament fully and expressly. We ask our adversaries, then, to point to some plain passages where it is taught. We ask for one text in which we are told that God took human nature, that he might appease his own anger towards men, or make an infinite satisfaction to his own justice;—for one text, which tells us, that human guilt is infinite, and requires a correspondent substitute; that Christ's sufferings owe their efficacy to their being borne by an infinite being; or that his divine nature gives infinite value to the sufferings of the human. Not one word of this description can we find in the Scriptures; not a text which even hints at these strange doctrines.—They are altogether, we believe, the fictions of theologians. Christianity is in no degree responsible for them. We are astonished at their prevalence. What can be plainer, than that God cannot, in any sense, be a sufferer, or bear a penalty in the room of his creatures? How dishonourable to him is the supposition, that his justice is now so severe as to exact infinite punishment for the sins of frail and feeble men, and now so easy and yielding as to accept the limited pains of Christ's human soul, as a full equivalent for the infinite and endless woes due from the world? How plain is it also, according to this doctrine, that God instead of being plenteous in forgiveness, never forgives; for it is absurd to speak of men as forgiven, when their whole punishment is borne by a substitute. A scheme more fitted to bring Christianity into contempt, and less suited to give comfort to a guilty and troubled mind, could not, we think, be easily invented.

We believe too, that this system is unfavourable to the character. It naturally leads men to think, that Christ came to change God's mind, rather than their own; that the highest object of his mission, was to avert punishment, rather than to communicate holiness; and that a large part of religion consists in disparaging good works and human virtue, for the purpose of magnifying the value of Christ's vicarious sufferings. In this way, a sense of the infinite importance, and indispensable necessity of personal improvement is weakened, and high sounding praises of Christ's cross seem often to be substituted for obedience to his precepts. For ourselves, we have not so learned Jesus. Whilst we gratefully acknowledge, that he came to rescue us from punishment, we believe, that he was sent on a still nobler errand, namely, to deliver us from sin itself, and to form us to a sublime and heavenly virtue. We regard him as a Saviour, chiefly as he is the light, physician, and guide of the dark, diseased, and wandering mind.—No influence in the universe seems to us so glorious, as that over the character; and no redemption so worthy of thankfulness, as the restoration of the soul to purity. Without this, pardon, were it possible, would be of little value. Why pluck the sinner from hell, if a hell be left to burn in his own breast? Why raise him to heaven, if he remain a stranger to its sanctity and love? With these impressions, we are accustomed to value the gospel, chiefly, as it abounds in effectual aids, motives, excitements to a generous and divine virtue. In this virtue, as in a common centre, we see all its doctrines, precepts, promises meet, and we believe, that faith in this religion is of no worth, and contributes nothing to salvation, any farther than as it uses these doctrines, precepts, promises, and the whole life, character, sufferings, and triumphs of Jesus, as the means of purifying the mind, of changing it into the likeness of his celestial excellence.

Fifthly. Having thus stated our views of the highest object of Christ's mission, that it is the recovery of men to virtue, or holiness, I shall now, in the last place, give our views of the *nature of Chistian virtue* or *true holiness.* We believe that all virtue has its foundation in the moral nature of man, that is, in conscience, or his sense of duty, and in the power of forming his temper and life according to conscience. We believe that these moral faculties are the grounds of responsibility, and the highest distinctions of human nature, and that no act is praise-worthy, any farther than it springs from their exertion. We believe, that no dispositions, infused into us without our own moral activity, are of the nature of virtue, and therefore, we reject the doctrine of irresistible divine influence on the human mind, moulding it into goodness, as marble is hewn into a statue. Such goodness, if this word may be used, would not be the object of moral approbation, any more than the instinctive affections of inferior animals, or the constitutional amiableness of human beings.

By these remarks, we do not mean to deny the importance of God's aid or Spirit; but by his Spirit we mean a moral, illu-minating, and persuasive influence, not physical, not compulsory, not involving a necessity of virtue. We object strongly to the idea of many Christians respecting man's impotence and God's irresistible agency on the heart, believing that they subvert our responsibility and the laws of our moral nature, that they make men machines, that they cast on God the blame of all evil deeds, that they discourage good minds, and inflate the fanatical with wild conceits of immediate and sensible inspiration.

Among the virtues, we give the first place to the *love of God*. We believe, that this principle is the true end and happiness of our being, that we were made for union with our Creator, that his infinite perfection is the only sufficient object and true resting place for the insatiable desires and unlimited capacities of the human mind, and that without him, our noblest senti-ments, admiration, veneration, hope, and love, would wither and decay. We believe too, that the love of God is not only essen-tial to happiness, but to the strength and perfection of all the virtues; that conscience, without the sanction of God's authority and retributive justice, would be a weak directer; that benevo-lence, unless nourished by communion with his goodness, and encouraged by his smile, could not thrive amidst the selfishness and thanklessness of the world; and that self government, without a sense of the divine inspection, would hardly extend beyond an outward and partial purity. God, as he is essentially goodness, holiness, justice, and virtue, so is he the life, motive, and sustainer of virtue in the human soul.

But whilst we earnestly inculcate the love of God, we believe that great care is necessary to distinguish it from counterfeits. We think that much, which is called piety, is worthless. Many have fallen into the error, that there can be no excess in feelings, which have God for their object; and, distrusting as coldness, that self-possession, without which virtue and devotion lose all their dignity, they have abandoned themselves to extravagances, which have brought contempt on piety. Most certainly, if the love of God be that, which often bears its name, the less we have of it, the better. If religion be the shipwreck of the understanding, we cannot keep too far from it. On this subject, we always speak plainly. We cannot sacrifice our reason to the reputation of zeal. We owe it to truth and religion, to maintain, that fanaticism, partial insanity, sudden impressions, and ungovernable transports, are any thing, rather than piety.

We conceive, that the true love of God is a moral sentiment, founded on a clear perception, and consisting in a high esteem and veneration of his moral perfections. Thus, it perfectly coincides, and is in fact the same thing, with the love of virtue, rectitude, and goodness. You will easily judge, then, what we esteem the surest and only decisive signs of piety. We lay no stress on strong excitements. We esteem *him,* and *him only,* a pious man, who practically conforms to God's moral perfections and government; who shows his delight in God's benevolence, by loving and serving his neighbour; his delight in God's justice, by being resolutely upright; his sense of God's purity, by regulating his thoughts, imagination, and desires; and whose conversation, business, and domestic life are swayed by a regard to God's presence and authority. In all things else men may deceive themselves. Disordered nerves may give them strange sights, and sounds, and impressions.—Texts of Scripture may come to them, as from heaven.—Their whole souls may be moved, and their confidence in God's favour be undoubting. But in all this there is no religion. The question is, do they love God's commands, in which his character is fully displayed, and give up to these their habits and passions. Without this, ecstasy is a mockery. One surrender of desire to God's will is worth a thousand transports. We do not judge of the bent of men's minds by their raptures, any more than we judge of the direction of a tree during a storm. We rather suspect loud profession, for we have observed, that deep feeling is generally noiseless, and least seeks display.

We would not, by these remarks, be understood as wishing to exclude from religion warmth, and even transport. We honour, and highly value true religious sensibility.—We believe, that Christianity is intended to act powerfully on our whole nature, on the heart, as well as the understanding and the conscience. We conceive of heaven as a state where the love of God will be exalted into an unbounded fervour and joy; and we desire, in our pilgrimage here, to drink into the spirit of that better world. But we think, that religious warmth is only to be valued, when it springs naturally from an improved character, when it comes unforced, when it is the recompense of obedience, when it is the warmth of a mind which understands God by being like him, and when, instead of disordering, it exalts the understanding, invigorates conscience, gives a pleasure to common duties, and is seen to exist in connexion with cheerfulness, judiciousness, and a reasonable frame of mind. When we observe a fervour, called religious, in men whose general character expresses little refinement and elevation, and whose piety seems at war with reason, we pay it little respect. We honour religion too much to give its sacred name to a feverish, forced, fluctuating zeal, which has little power over the life.

Another important branch of virtue we believe to be love to Christ. The greatness of the work of Jesus, the spirit with which he executed it, and the sufferings which he bore for our salvation, we feel to be strong claims on our gratitude and veneration. We see in nature no beauty to be compared with the loveliness of his character, nor do we find on earth a benefactor, to whom we owe an equal debt. We read his history with delight, and learn from it the perfection of our nature. We are particularly touched by his death, which was endured for our redemption, and by that strength of charity which triumphed over his pains. His resurrection is the foundation of our hope of immortality. His intercession gives us boldness to draw nigh to the throne of grace, and we look up to heaven with new desire, when we think, that if we follow him here, we shall there see his benignant countenance, and enjoy his friendship for ever.

I need not express to you our views on the subject of the *benevolent virtues*. We attach such importance to these, that we are sometimes reproached with exalting them above piety. We regard the spirit of love, charity, meekness, forgiveness, liberality, and beneficence, as the badge and distinction of Christians, as the brightest image we can bear of God, as the best proof of piety. On this subject I need not, and cannot enlarge; but there is one branch of benevolence, which I ought not to pass over in silence, because we think that we conceive of it more highly and justly, than many of our brethren. I refer to the duty of candour, charitable judgment, especially towards those who differ in religious opinion. We think, that in nothing have Christians so widely departed from their religion, as in this particular. We read with astonishment and horror, the history of the church, and sometimes when we look back on the fires of persecution, and the zeal of Christians in building up walls of separation, and in giving up one another to perdition, we feel as if we were reading the records of an infernal, rather than a heavenly kingdom. An enemy to our religion, if asked to describe a Christian, would, with some show of reason, depict him as an idolator of his own distinguishing opinions; covered with badges of party; shutting his eyes on the virtues, and his ears on the arguments of his opponents; arrogating all excellence to his own sect, and all saving power to his own creed; sheltering under the name of pious zeal, the love of domination, the conceit of infallibility and the spirit of intolerance; and trampling on men's rights under the pretence of saving their souls.

We can hardly conceive of a plainer obligation on beings of our frail and fallible nature, who are instructed in the duty of candid judgment, than to abstain from condemning men of apparent conscientiousness and sincerity, who are chargeable with no crime but that of differing from us in the interpretation of the Scriptures, and differing too on topics of great and acknowledged obscurity. We are astonished at the hardihood of those, who, with Christ's warnings sounding in their ears, take on them the responsibility of making creeds for his church, and cast out professors of virtuous lives for imagined errors, for the guilt of thinking for themselves. We know that zeal for truth is the cover for this usurpation of Christ's prerogative; but we think that zeal for truth, as it is called, is very suspicious, except in men, whose capacities and advantages, whose patient deliberations, and whose improvements in humility, mildness, and candour, give them a right to hope that their views are more just, than those of their neighbours. Much of what passes for a zeal for truth, we look upon with little respect, for it often appears to thrive most luxuriantly, where other virtues shoot up thinly and feebly; and we have no gratitude for those reformers, who would force upon us a doctrine, which has not sweetened their own tempers, or made them better men than their neighbours.

We are accustomed to think much of the difficulties attending religious inquiries; difficulties springing from the slow development of our minds, from the power of early impressions, from the state of society, from human authority, from the general neglect of the reasoning powers, from the want of just principles of criticism, and of important helps in interpreting Scripture, and from various other causes. We find, that on no subject have men, and even good men, engrafted so many strange conceits, wild theories, and fictions of fancy, as on religion; and remembering, as we do, that we ourselves are sharers of the common frailty, we dare not assume infallibility in the treatment of our fellow Christians, or encourage in common Christians, who have little time for investigation, the habit of denouncing and contemning other denominations, perhaps more enlightened and virtuous than their own. Charity, forbearance, a delight in the virtues of different sects, a backwardness to censure and condemn, these are virtues, which, however poorly practised by us, we admire and recommend, and we would rather join ourselves to the church in which they abound than to any other communion, however elated with the belief of its own orthodoxy, however strict in guarding its creed, however burning with zeal against imagined error.

I have thus given the distinguishing views of those Christians in whose names I have spoken. We have embraced this system, not hastily or lightly, but after much deliberation; and we hold it fast, not merely because we believe it to be true, but because we regard it as purifying truth, as "a doctrine according to godliness," as able to "work mightily" and to "bring forth fruit" in them who believe. That we wish to spread it, we have no desire to conceal; but we think, that we wish its diffusion, because we regard it as more friendly to practical piety and pure morals, than the opposite doctrines, because it gives clearer and nobler views of duty, and stronger motives to its perform-ance, because it recommends religion at once to the understand-ing and the heart, because it asserts the lovely and venerable attributes of God, because it tends to restore the benevolent spirit of Jesus to his divided and afflicted church, and because it cuts off every hope of God's favour, except that which springs from practical conformity to the life and precepts of Christ. We see nothing in our views to give offence, save their purity, and it is their purity, which makes us seek and hope their exten-sion through the world.

I now turn to the usual addresses of the day.

My friend and brother;—You are this day to take upon you important duties; to be clothed with an office, which the Son of God did not disdain; to devote yourself to that religion, which the most hallowed lips have preached, and the most pre-cious blood sealed. We trust that you will bring to this work a willing mind, a firm purpose, a martyr's spirit, a readiness to toil and suffer for the truth, a devotion of your best powers to the interests of piety and virtue. I have spoken of the doc-trines which you will probably preach; but I do not mean, that you are to give yourself to controversy. You will remember, that good practice is the end of preaching, and will labour to make your people holy livers, rather than skilful disputants. Be careful, lest the desire of defending what you deem truth, and of repelling reproach and misrepresentation, turn you aside from your great business, which is to fix in men's minds a living conviction of the obligation, sublimity and happiness of Chris-tian virtue. The best way to vindicate your sentiments, is to show in your preaching and life, their intimate connexion with Christian morals, with a high and delicate sense of duty, with candour towards your opposers, with inflexible integrity, and with an habitual reverence for God. If any light can pierce and scatter the clouds of prejudice, it is that of pure example. You are to preach a system which has nothing to recommend it, but its fitness to make men better; which has no unintelligible doctrine for the mystical, no extravagances for the fanatical, no dreams for the visionary, no contradictions for the credulous, which asks no sacrifice of men's understandings, but only of their passions and vices; and the best and only way to recommend such a system is, to show forth its power in purifying and exalting the character.—My brother, may your life preach more loudly than your lips. Be to this people a pattern of all good works, and may your instructions derive authority from a well grounded belief in your hearers, that you speak from the heart, that you preach from experience, that the truth which you dispense has wrought powerfully in your own breast, that God, and Jesus, and heaven are not merely words on your lips, but most affecting realities to your mind, and springs of hope and consolation, and strength in all your trials. Thus labouring may you reap abundantly, and have a testimony of your faithfulness, not only in your own conscience, but in the esteem, love, virtues, and improvements of your people.

Brethren of this church and society;—We rejoice with you in the prospects of this day. We rejoice in the zeal, unanimity and liberality, with which you have secured to yourselves the administration of God's word and ordinances, according to your own understanding of the Scriptures. We thank God that he has disposed you to form an association on the true principles of Christianity and of protestantism; that you have solemnly resolved to call no man master in religion, to take your faith from no human creed, to submit your consciences to no human authority, but to repair to the gospel, to read it with your own eyes, to exercise upon it your own understanding, to search it, as if not a sect existed around you, and to follow it wherever it may lead you. Brethren, hold fast your Christian and Protestant liberty. We wish you continued peace, and growing prosperity. We pray God, that your good works may glorify your Christian profession, that your candour and serious attention may encourage your young brother in the arduous work to which you have called him, and that your union with him, beginning in hope, may continue in joy, and may issue in the friendship and union of heaven.

To all who hear me, I would say, with the apostle, *Prove all things, hold fast that which is good.* Do not, brethren, shrink from the duty of searching God's word for yourselves, through fear of human censure and denunciation. Do not think that you may innocently follow the opinions, which prevail around you, without investigation, cn the ground that Christianity is now so purified from errors, as to need no laborious research. There is much reason to believe, that Christianity is at this moment dishonoured by gross and cherished corruptions. If you remember the darkness, which hung over the gospel for ages; if you consider the impure union, which still subsists in almost every Christian country between the church and the state, and which enlists men's selfishness, and ambition, on the side of established error; if you recollect in what degree the spirit of intolerance has checked free inquiry, not only before, but since the reformation; you will see that Christianity cannot have freed itself from all the human inventions which disfigured it under the papal tyranny. No. Much stubble is yet to be burnt; much rubbish to be removed; many gaudy decorations, which a false taste has hung around Christianity, must be swept away; and the earth-born fogs, which have long shrouded it, must be scattered, before this divine fabric will rise before us in its native and awful majesty, in its harmonious proportions, in its mild and celestial splendours. This glorious reformation in the church, we hope, under God's blessing, from the demolition of human authority in matters of religion, from the fall of those hierarchies, huge establishments, general convocations or assemblies, and other human institutions, by which the minds of individuals are oppressed under the weight of numbers, and a papal dominion is perpetuated in the protestant church. Our earnest prayer to God is, that he will "overturn and overturn and overturn" the strong holds of spiritual usurpation, "until

He shall come, whose right it is" to rule the minds of men; that the conspiracy of ages against the liberty of Christians may be brought to an end; that the servile assent, so long yielded to human creeds, may give place to honest and fearless inquiry into the Scriptures; and that Christianity thus purified from error, may put forth its almighty energy, and prove itself, by its ennobling influence on the mind, to be indeed "the power of God unto salvation."

THE CHRISTIAN FAITH

FRIEDRICH DANIEL ERNST SCHLEIERMACHER

(1768-1834)

THEOLOGY, SCHLEIERMACHER maintained, is grounded in religious feeling. Religion is not built out of theology but, like art, out of an inner experience. Morality, similarly, is a flowering of the inner life, not a system of imposed rules. Christian doctrines have their base and worth in significant human experiences.

This whole point of view, known as "religious empiricism," opened up a new era in Protestant theology and in the scientific study of religion. Schleiermacher initially directed himself to the "cultural despisers" of religion, courting their approval by pointing out that religion is a natural phenomenon of mental outlook, open to all and universally accessible in the feeling of absolute dependence.

In his *Addresses,* published in 1799, the subject of the nature of religion was subjected to analysis. In *The Christian Faith* (from which selections are here given), first published in 1821, he addressed himself to the further consideration of the question "What is Christianity?"

For three generations this latter work became a sort of textbook for students of theology. In it Schleiermacher departed completely from traditional orthodoxy with its emphasis on objective claims and from sheer rationalism with its reliance on deductive method. Man's own experience, his immediate self-consciousness, is the new base of operation for a Christian theology. In the feeling of dependence man finds the locus of Christian piety—ideas being secondary effects. Christianity is to be distinguished from other religions not by the feeling of dependence but by this same feeling in relation to Jesus Christ as Redeemer. What this means to the individual is for the individual to ascertain; certainly it is not a system of doctrines merely to be assented to. Christ is the heart of the Christian religion and redemption is Christ's chief characteristic. Jesus' own feeling for or consciousness of God provides the power of communication to others, creating a community (or church) of followers.

The doctrine of the Trinity serves to point out the Divinity of Christ who is also a part of the unifying Divine Spirit in the Christian Church—not a doctrine *per se* but a symbol of a Christian experience of God and the unity of those whose experience follows the same channel. Other traditional doctrines are reinterpreted in the light of experience: original sin manifests the awful reality of social interrelationships in which evil deeds unwittingly pass through; the redemptive work of Christ moves beyond that of propitiation of God to a transformation of man; petitional prayers are submerged by the higher attitude of resignation and gratitude; revelation becomes appropriated in religious discovery; justification becomes the regenerative change in experience; faith becomes the feeling of satisfaction which Christ offers to man's spiritual needs. And so on.

From 1804 to 1806 Schleiermacher was professor of theology and preacher at the University of Halle; later he filled the pulpit of Trinity Church in Berlin and helped to establish the University of Berlin, where he also became professor of theology (1810-1834). He wrote and lectured on many subjects besides theology and religion, including those which concerned the affairs of state.

Editor

THE CHRISTIAN FAITH

1. That a Church is nothing but a communion or association relating to religion or piety, is beyond all doubt for us Evangelical (Protestant) Christians, since we regard it as equivalent to degeneration in a Church when it begins to occupy itself with other matters as well, whether the affairs of science or of out-

ward organization; just as we also oppose any attempt on the part of the leaders of State or of science, as such, to order the affairs of religion. But, at the same time, we have no desire to keep the leaders of science from scrutinizing and passing judgment from their own point of view upon both piety itself and the communion relating to it, and determining their proper place in the total field of human life; since piety and Church, like other things, are material for scientific knowledge. Indeed, we ourselves are here entering upon such a scrutiny. And, similarly, we would not keep the leaders of State from fixing the outward relations of the religious communions according to the principles of civil organization—which, however, by no means implies that the religious communion is a product of the State or a component part of it.

However, not only we, but even those Churches which are not so clear about keeping apart Church and State, or ecclesiastical and scientific association, must assent to what we have laid down. For they cannot assign to the Church more than an indirect influence upon these other associations; and it is only the maintenance, regulation, and advancement of piety which they can regard as the essential business of the Church.

2. When Feeling and Self-consciousness are here put side by side as equivalent, it is by no means intended to introduce generally a manner of speech in which the two expressions would be simply synonymous. The term 'feeling' has in the language of common life been long current in this religious connexion; but for scientific usage it needs to be more precisely defined; and it is to do this that the other word is added. So that if anyone takes the word 'feeling' in a sense so wide as to include unconscious states, he will by the other word be reminded that such is not the usage we are here maintaining. Again, to the term 'self-consciousness' is added the determining epithet 'immediate', lest anyone should think of a kind of self-consciousness which is not feeling at all; as e.g., when the name of self-consciousness is given to that consciousness of self which is more like an objective consciousness, being a representation of oneself, and thus mediated by self-contemplation. Even when such a representation of ourselves, as we exist in a given portion of time, in thinking, e.g., or in willing, moves quite close to, or even

interpenetrates, the individual moments of the mental state, this kind of self-consciousness does appear simply as an *accompaniment* of the state itself. But the real immediate self-consciousness, which is not representation but in the proper sense feeling, is by no means always simply an accompaniment. It may rather be presumed that in this respect everyone has a twofold experience. In the first place, it is everybody's experience that there are moments in which all thinking and willing retreat behind a self-consciousness of one form or another; but, in the second place, that at times this same form of self-consciousness persists unaltered during a series of diverse acts of thinking and willing, taking up no relation to these, and thus not being in the proper sense even an accompaniment of them. Thus joy and sorrow—those mental phases which are always so important in the realm of religion—are genuine states of feeling, in the proper sense explained above; whereas self-approval and self-approach, apart from their subsequently passing into joy and sorrow, belong in themselves rather to the objective consciousness of self, as results of an analytic contemplation. Nowhere, perhaps, do the two forms stand nearer to each other than here, but just for that reason this comparison puts the difference in the clearest light.

*   *   *

3. Our proposition seems to assume that in addition to Knowing, Doing, and Feeling, there is no fourth. This is not done, however, in the sense which would be required for an apagogic proof; but those other two are placed alongside of Feeling simply in order that, with the exposition of our own view, we may at the same time take up and discuss those divergent views which are actually in existence. So that we might leave the question entirely aside whether there is a fourth such element in the soul, but for two reasons: namely, in the first place, that it is our duty to convince ourselves as to whether there is still another region to which piety might be assigned; and, in the second place, that we must set ourselves to grasp clearly the relation which subsists between Christian piety in itself, on the one hand, and both Christian belief (so far as it

can be brought into the form of knowledge) and Christian action, on the other. Now, if the relation of the three elements above-mentioned were anywhere set forth in a universally recognized way, we could simply appeal to that. But, as things are, we must in this place say what is necessary on the subject; though this is to be regarded as simply borrowed from Psychology, and it should be well noted that the truth of the matter (namely, that piety is feeling) remains entirely independent of the correctness of the following discussion. Life, then, is to be conceived as an alternation between an abiding-in-self (*Insichbleiben*) and a passing-beyond-self (*Aussichheraustreten*) on the part of the subject. The two forms of consciousness (Knowing and Feeling) constitute the abiding-in-self, while Doing proper is the passing-beyond-self. Thus far, then, Knowing and Feeling stand together in antithesis to Doing. But while Knowing, in the sense of possessing knowledge, is an abiding-in-self on the part of the subject, nevertheless as the act of knowing, it only becomes real by a passing-beyond-self of the subject, and in this sense it is a Doing. As regards Feeling, on the other hand, it is not only in its duration as a result of stimulation that it is an abiding-in-self: even as the process of being stimulated, it is not effected by the subject, but simply takes place in the subject, and thus, since it belongs altogether to the realm of receptivity, it is entirely an abiding-in-self; and in this sense it stands alone in antithesis to the other two—Knowing and Doing.

As regards the question whether there is a fourth to these three, Feeling, Knowing, and Doing; or a third to these two, abiding-in-self and passing-beyond-self: the unity of these is indeed not one of the two or the three themselves; but no one can place this unity alongside of these others as a co-ordinate third or fourth entity. The unity rather is the essence of the subject itself, which manifests itself in those severally distinct forms, and is thus, to give it a name which in this particular connexion is permissible, their common foundation. Similarly, on the other hand, every actual moment of life is, in its total content, a complex of these two or these three, though two of them may be present only in vestige or in germ. But a third to those two (one of which is again divided into two) will scarcely be found.

4. But now (these three, Feeling, Knowing, and Doing being granted) while we here set forth once more the oft-asserted view that, of the three, Feeling is the one to which piety belongs, it is not in any wise meant, as indeed the above discussion shows, that piety is excluded from all connexion with Knowing and Doing. For, indeed, it is the case in general that the immediate self-consciousness is always the mediating link in the transition between moments in which Knowing predominates and those in which Doing predominates, so that a different Doing may proceed from the same Knowing in different people according as a different determination of self-consciousness enters in. And thus it will fall to piety to stimulate Knowing and Doing, and every moment in which piety has a predominant place will contain within itself one or both of these in germ. But just this is the very truth represented by our proposition, and is in no wise an objection to it; for were it otherwise the religious moments could not combine with the others to form a single life, but piety would be something isolated and without any influence upon the other mental functions of our lives. However, in representing this truth, and thus securing to piety its own peculiar province in its connexion with all other provinces, our proposition is opposing the assertions from other quarters that piety is a Knowing, or a Doing, or both, or a state made up of Feeling, Knowing, and Doing; and in this polemical connexion our proposition must now be still more closely considered.

If, then, piety did consist in Knowing, it would have to be, above all, that knowledge, in its entirety or in its essence, which is here set up as the content of Dogmatics (*Glaubenslehre*) : otherwise it must be a complete mistake for us here to investigate the nature of piety in the interests of our study of Dogmatics. But if piety *is* that knowledge, then the amount of such knowledge in a man must be the measure of his piety. For anything which, in its rise and fall, is not the measure of the perfection of a given object cannot constitute the essence of that object. Accordingly, on the hypothesis in question, the most perfect master of Christian Dogmatics would always be likewise the most pious Christian. And no one will admit this to be the case, even if we premise that the most perfect master is only he who keeps most to what is essential and does not forget it in accessories and side-issues; but all will agree rather that the same degree of perfection in that knowledge may be accompanied by very different degrees of piety, and the same degree of piety by very different degrees of knowledge. It may, however, be objected that the assertion that piety is a matter of Knowing refers not so much to the content of that knowledge as to the certainty which characterizes its representations; so that the knowledge of doctrines is piety only in virtue of the certainty attached to them, and thus only in virtue of the strength of the conviction, while a possession of the doctrines without conviction is not piety at all. Then the strength of the conviction would be the measure of the piety; and this is undoubtedly what those people have chiefly in mind who so love to paraphrase the word *Faith* as 'fidelity to one's convictions.' But in all other more typical fields of knowledge the only measure of conviction is the clearness and completeness of the thinking itself. Now if it is to be the same with *this* conviction, then we should simply be back at our old point, that he who thinks the religious propositions most clearly and completely, individually and in their connexions, must likewise be the most pious man. If, then, this conclusion is still to be rejected, but the hypothesis is to be retained (namely, that conviction is the measure of piety), the conviction in this case must be of a different kind and must have a different measure. However closely, then, piety may be connected with this conviction, it does not follow that it is connected in the same way with that knowledge. And if, nevertheless, the knowledge which forms Dogmatics has to relate itself to piety, the explanation of this is that while piety is, of course, the object of this knowledge, the knowledge can only be explicated in virtue of a certainty which inheres in the determination of self-consciousness.

If, on the other hand, piety consists in Doing, it is manifest that the Doing which constitutes it cannot be defined by its content; for experience teaches that not only the most admirable but also the most abominable, not only the most useful but also the most inane and meaningless things, are done as pious and out of piety. Thus we are thrown back simply upon the form, upon the method and manner in which the thing comes to be done. But this can only be understood from the two *termini,* the underlying motive as the starting-point, and the intended result as the goal. Now no one will pronounce an action more or less pious because of the greater or less degree of completeness with which the intended result is achieved. Suppose we then are thrown back upon the motive. It is manifest that underlying every motive there is a certain determination of self-consciousness, be it pleasure or pain, and that it is by these that one motive can most clearly be distinguished from another. Accordingly an action (a Doing) will be pious in so far as the determination of self-consciousness, the feeling which had become affective and had passed into a motive impulse, is a pious one.

Thus both hypotheses lead to the same point: that there are both a Knowing and a Doing which pertain to piety, but neither of these constitutes the essence of piety: they only pertain to it inasmuch as the stirred-up Feeling sometimes comes to rest in a thinking which fixes it, sometimes discharges itself in an action which expresses it.

Finally, no one will deny that there are states of Feeling, such as penitence, contrition, confidence, and joy in God, which we pronounce pious in themselves, without regard to any Knowing or Doing that proceeds from them, though, of course, we expect both that they will work themselves out in actions which are otherwise obligatory, and that the reflective impulse will turn its attention to them.

5. From what we have now said it is already clear how we must judge the assertion that piety is a state in which Knowing, Feeling, and Doing are combined. Of course we reject it if it means that the Feeling is derived from the Knowing and the Doing from the Feeling. But if no subordination is intended, then the assertion might just as well be the description of any other quite clear and living moment as of a religious one. For though the idea of the goal of an action precedes the action itself, at the same time it continues to accompany the action, and the relation between the two expresses itself simultaneously in the self-consciousness through a greater or less degree of satisfaction and assurance; so that even here all three elements are combined in the total content of the state. A similar situation exists in the case of Knowing. For the thinking activity, as a

successfully accomplished operation, expresses itself in the self-consciousness as a confident certainty. But simultaneously it becomes also an endeavour to connect the apprehended truth with other truths or to seek out cases for its application, and thus there is always present simultaneously the commencement of a Doing, which develops fully when the opportunity offers; and so here also we find Knowing, Feeling, and Doing all together in the total state. But now, just as the first-described state remains, notwithstanding, essentially a Doing, and the second a Knowing, so piety in its diverse expressions remains essentially a state of Feeling. This state is subsequently caught up into the region of thinking, but only in so far as each religious man is at the same time inclined towards thinking and exercised therein; and only in the same way and according to the same measure does this inner piety emerge in living movement and representative action. It also follows from this account of the matter that Feeling is not to be thought of as something either confused or inactive; since, on the one hand, it is strongest in our most vivid moments, and either directly or indirectly lies at the root of every expression of our wills, and, on the other hand, it can be grasped by thought and conceived of in its own nature.

But suppose there are other people who would exclude Feeling altogether from our field, and therefore describe piety simply as a Knowledge which begets actions or as a Doing which proceeds from a Knowing: these people not only would have to settle first among themselves whether piety is a Knowing or a Doing, but would also have to show us how a Doing can arise from a Knowing except as mediated by a determination of self-consciousness. And if they have eventually to admit this point, then they will also be convinced by the above discussion that if such a complex does bear the character of piety, nevertheless the element of Knowing in it has not in itself got the length of being piety, and the element of Doing is in itself no longer piety, but the piety is just the determination of self-consciousness which comes in between the two. But that relationship can always hold in the reverse order also: the Doing has not got the length of being piety in those cases in which a determinate self-consciousness only results from an accomplished action; and the Knowing is in itself no longer piety when it has no other content than that determination of self-consciousness caught up into thought.

*   *   *

1. If the feeling of absolute dependence, expressing itself as consciousness of God, is the highest grade of immediate self-consciousness, it is also an essential element of human nature. This cannot be controverted on the ground that there is for every individual man a time when that consciousness does not yet exist. For this is the period when life is incomplete, as may be seen both from the fact that the animal confusion of consciousness has not yet been overcome, and from the fact that other vital functions too are only developing themselves gradually. Nor can it be objected that there are always communities of men in which this feeling has not yet been awakened; for these likewise only exhibit on a large scale that undeveloped state of human nature which betrays itself also in other functions of their lives. Similarly it cannot be argued that the feeling is accidental (non-essential), because even in a highly developed religious environment individuals may be found who do not share it. For these people cannot but testify that the whole matter is not so alien to them but that they have at particular moments been gripped by such a feeling, though they may call it by some name that is not very honouring to themselves. But if anyone can show, either that this feeling has not a higher value than the sensible, or that there is besides it another of equal value—only then can anyone be entitled to regard it as a merely accidental form, which, while it may perhaps exist for some people in every age, is nevertheless not to be reckoned as part of a complete human nature for everybody.

2. The truth that every essential element of human nature becomes the basis of a fellowship or communion, can only be fully explicated in the context of a scientific theory of morals. Here we can only allude to the essential points of this process, and then ask everybody to accept it as a fact. Fellowship, then, is demanded by the *consciousness of kind* which dwells in every man, and which finds its satisfaction only when he steps forth

beyond the limits of his own personality and takes up the facts of other personalities into his own. It is accomplished through the fact that everything inward becomes, at a certain point of its strength or maturity, an outward too, and, as such, perceptible to others. Thus feeling, as a self-contained determination of the mind (which on the other side passes into thought and action, but with that we are not here concerned), will, even *qua* feeling, and purely in virtue of the consciousness of kind, not exist exclusively for itself, but becomes an outward, originally and without any definite aim or pertinence, by means of facial expression, gesture, tones, and (indirectly) words; and so becomes to other people a revelation of the inward. This bare expression of feeling, which is entirely caused by the inward agitation, and which can be very definitely distinguished from any further and more separate action into which it passes, does indeed at first arouse in other people only an idea of the person's state of mind. But, by reason of the consciousness of kind, this passes into living imitation; and the more able the percipient is (either for general reasons, or because of the greater liveliness of the expression, or because of closer affinity) to pass into the same state, the more easily will that state be produced by imitation. Everybody must in his own experience be conscious of this process from both its sides, the expressing and the perceiving, and must thus confess that he always finds himself, with the concurrence of his conscience, involved in a multifarious communion of feeling, as a condition quite in conformity with his nature, and therefore that he would have co-operated in the founding of such a communion if it had not been there already.

As regards the feeling of absolute dependence in particular, everyone will know that it was first awakened in him in the same way, by the communicative and stimulative power of expression or utterance.

3. Our assertion that this communion is at first variable and fluid follows from what we have just been saying. For as individuals in general resemble each other in variable degrees, both as regards the strength of their religious emotions and as regards the particular region of sensible self-consciousness with which their God-consciousness most easily unites, each person's religious emotions have more affinity with those of one of his fellows than

with those of another, and thus communion of religious feeling comes to him more easily with the former than with the latter. If the difference is great, he feels himself attracted by the one and repelled by the others; yet not repelled directly or absolutely, so that he could not enter into any communion of feeling with them at all; but only in the sense that he is more powerfully attracted to others; and thus he could have communion even with these, in default of the others, or in circumstances which specially drew them together. For there can hardly exist a man in whom another would recognize no religious affection whatever as being in any degree similar to his own, or whom another would know to be quite incapable of either moving or being moved by him. It remains true, however, that the more uninterrupted the communion is to be, *i.e.* the more closely the kindred emotions are to follow each other, and the more easily the emotions are to communicate themselves, so much the smaller must be the number of people who can participate. We may conceive as great an interval as we like between the two extremes, that of the closest and that of the feeblest communion; so that the man who experiences the fewest and feeblest religious emotions can have the closest kind of communion only with those who are equally little susceptible to these emotions, and is not in a position to imitate the utterances of those who derive religious emotions from moments where he himself never finds it. A similar relation holds between the man whose piety is purer, in the sense that in every moment of it he clearly distinguishes the religious content of his self-consciousness from the sensible to which it is related, and the man whose piety is less pure, *i.e.* more confused with the sensible. However, we may conceive the interval between these extremes as being, for each person, filled up with as many intermediate stages as we like; and this is just what constitutes the fluidity of the communion.

4. This is how the interchange of religious consciousness appears when we think of the relation of individual men to each other. But if we look at the actual condition of men, we also find well-established relationships in this fluid, and therefore (strictly speaking) undefined communion or fellowship. In the first place, as soon as human development has advanced to the

point of a domestic life, even if not a completely regulated one, every family will establish within itself such a communion of the religious self-consciousness—a communion which, however, has quite definite limits as regards the outside world. For the members of the family are bound together in a peculiar manner by definite congruity and kinship, and, moreover, their religious emotions are associated with the same occasions, so that strangers can only have an accidental and transitory, and therefore a very unequal share in them.

But we also find families not isolated but standing collectively in distinctly defined combinations, with common language and customs, and with some knowledge or inkling of a closer common origin. And then religious communion becomes marked off among them, partly in the form of predominating similarity in the individual families, and partly by one family, which is particularly open to religious emotions, coming to predominate as the paramountly active one, while the others, being as it were scarcely out of their nonage, display only receptivity (a state of affairs which exists wherever there is a hereditary priesthood). Every such relatively closed religious communion, which forms an ever self-renewing circulation of the religious self-consciousness within certain definite limits, and a propagation of the religious emotions arranged and organized within the same limits, so that there can be some kind of definite understanding as to which individuals belong to it and which do not—this we designate a *Church*.

*   *   *

The words *'reveal,' 'revealed,' 'revelation,'* present still further difficulties, since even originally they sometimes signify the illumination of what was obscure, confused, unobserved, and sometimes rather the disclosing and unveiling of what was hitherto concealed and kept secret, and still further confusion has been introduced by the distinction between mediate and immediate (direct and indirect) revelation. To begin with, all will at once agree that the word 'revealed' is never applied either to what is discovered in the realm of experience by one man and handed on to others, or to what is excogitated in thought by one man and so learned by others; and further, that the word presupposes a divine communication and declaration. And in this sense we find the word very generally applied to the origin of religious communions. For of what religious mysteries and varieties of worship, either among the Greeks or among the Egyptians and Indians, would it not be asserted that they originally came from heaven or were proclaimed by Deity in some way which fell outside the human and natural order? Not seldom, indeed, we find even the beginning of civic communities (just as from the beginning we often find the moral and the religious unseparated) traced to a divine sending of the man who first gathered the tribe together into a civic union, and so the new organization of life is based on a revelation. Accordingly we might say that the idea of revelation signifies the *originality* of the fact which lies at the foundation of a religious communion, in the sense that this fact, as conditioning the individual content of the religious emotions which are found in the communion, cannot itself in turn be explained by the historical chain which precedes it.

Now the fact that in this original element there is a divine causality requires no further discussion; nor does the fact that it is an activity which aims at and furthers the salvation of man. But I am unwilling to accept the further definition that it operates upon man as a cognitive being. For that would make the revelation to be originally and essentially *doctrine;* and I do not believe that we can adopt that position, whether we consider the whole field covered by the idea, or seek to define it in advance with special reference to Christianity. If a system of propositions can be understood from their connexion with others, then nothing supernatural was required for their production. But if they cannot, then they can, in the first instance, only be apprehended (we need only appeal for confirmation to the first principles of Hermeneutics) as parts of another whole, as a moment of the life of a thinking being who works upon us directly as a distinctive existence by means of his total impression on us; and this working is always a working upon the self-consciousness. Thus the original fact will always be the appearing of such a being, and the original working will always be upon the self-consciousness of those into whose circle he enters.

That this does not exclude doctrine, but implies it, is obvious. For the rest, it always remains very difficult, indeed almost impossible, to give definite limits to this idea, and, if it is thus definitely grasped, to explain its rise wherever it appears. For everywhere in the realm of mythology, Greek as well as Oriental and Norse, these divine communications and declarations border so closely on the higher states of heroic and poetic inspiration that it is difficult to distinguish them from each other. And thus it becomes difficult to avoid a widened application of the idea, to the effect that every original ideal which arises in the soul, whether for an action or for a work of art, and which can neither be understood as an imitation nor be satisfactorily explained by means of external stimuli and preceding mental states, may be regarded as revelation. For the fact that the one is greater and the other less cannot here make a dividing line. And, indeed, the inward generation of a new and peculiar idea of God in a moment of inspiration has often been one and the same thing with the rise of a distinctive worship. Indeed, it would be difficult to draw any clear dividing line at all between what is revealed and what comes to light through inspiration in a natural way, unless we are prepared to fall back on the position that revelation is only to be assumed when not a single moment but a whole existence is determined by such a divine communication, and that what is then proclaimed by such an existence is to be regarded as revealed. This, in the polytheistic religions, would include not only the divine declarations and oracles attached to certain holy places which the divinity has made known to be his specially chosen habitations, but also those persons who, because they are descended from the divinity, make known the divine archetype in a human life in an original way which cannot be explained by the historical context. In this same sense Paul calls even the world the original revelation of God (Rom. 1, 20). But this may again lead us to the conclusion that no particular thing, since it always belongs to the world, can in itself be regarded as divine revelation. For just as the dawning of an archetypal idea in an individual soul, even if it cannot be explained by the previous states of that very soul, can certainly be explained by the total state of the society to which the individual belongs: so even the men who are credited with divine descent always appear as determined by the character of their people, and thus it is from the total energy of the people that their existence is to be explained or comprehended. Hence even if we do venture to establish, in the way we have done above, the relation of the idea of 'revelation' and 'revealed' to the idea of the 'positive' for the whole realm of historically actual religious communions, we shall nevertheless naturally and inevitably find that the application of the idea to the fact which forms the basis of any particular religious communion will be contested by all other communions, while each will claim it for its own basal fact.

Finally, this must be added: that if one faith wishes to establish the validity of its own application of the idea as against the others, it cannot at all accomplish this by the assertion that its own divine communication is pure and entire truth, while the others contain falsehood. For complete truth would mean that God made Himself known as He is in and for Himself. But such a truth could not proceed outwardly from any fact, and even if it did in some incomprehensible way come to a human soul, it could not be apprehended by that soul, and retained as a thought; and if it could not be in any way perceived and retained, it could not become operative. Any proclamation of God which is to be operative upon and within us can only express God in His relation to us; and this is not an infra-human ignorance concerning God, but the essence of human limitedness in relation to Him. On the other hand, there is the connected fact that a consciousness of God which arose in a realm of complete barbarity and degradation might be really a revelation, and might nevertheless, through the fault of the mind in which it arose, become, in the form in which it was apprehended and retained, an imperfect one. And therefore it may truly be said even of the imperfect forms of religion, so far as they can be traced, in whole or in part, to a particular starting-point and their content cannot be explained by anything previous to that point, that they rest upon revelation, however much error may be mingled in them with the truth.

*   *   *

1. The only pertinent way of discovering the peculiar essence of any particular faith and reducing it as far as possible to a

formula is by showing the element which remains constant throughout the most diverse religious affections within this same communion, while it is absent from analogous affections within other communions. Now since we have little reason to expect that this peculiarity is equally strongly marked in all the different varieties of emotions, there is all the greater possibility of our missing the mark in this attempt, and so coming in the end to the opinion that there is no hard-and-fast inward difference at all, but only the outward difference as determined by time and place. However, we may with some certainty conclude from what has been said above, that we shall be least likely to miss the peculiarity if we keep principally to what is most closely connected with the basal fact, and this is the procedure which underlies the formula of our proposition. But Christianity presents special difficulties, even in this fact alone, that it takes a greater variety of forms than other faiths and is split up into a multiplicity of smaller communions or churches; and thus there arises a twofold task, first, to find the peculiar essence, common to all these communions, of Christianity as such, and secondly, to find the peculiar essence of the particular communion whose right is to be authenticated or whose system of doctrine is to be established. But still further difficulty lies in the fact that even in each particular ecclesiastical communion almost every doctrine appears with the most multifarious variations at different times and places; and this implies as its basis, not indeed, perhaps, an equally great diversity in the religious affections themselves, but always at least a great diversity in the manner of understanding and appraising them. Indeed, the worst of all is that, owing to this variation, the bounds of the Christian realm become a matter of dispute even among Christians themselves, one asserting of this form of teaching, and another of that form, that though it was indeed engendered within Christianity it is nevertheless really un-Christian in content. Now, if he who wishes to solve our problem belongs himself to one of these parties, and assumes at the outset that only what is found within the realm of that one view ought to be taken into account in ascertaining what is distinctive of Christianity, he is at the outset taking controversies as settled, for the settlement of which he professes to be only discovering the conditions. For only when the peculiar essence of Christianity has been ascertained can it be decided how far this or that is compatible with it. But if the investigator succeeds in freeing himself from all partiality, and therefore takes into account everything, however opposed, so long as it professes to be Christian, then on the other hand he is in danger of reaching a result far scantier and more colourless in its content, and consequently less suitable to the aims of our present task. That is the present state of affairs, and it cannot be concealed. Now since each man, the more religious he is, usually brings his individual religion the more into this investigation, there is a large majority of the people who form their idea of the peculiar essence of Christianity according to the interests of their party. But for the interests of Apologetics as well as of Dogmatics it seems advisable rather to be content with a scanty result at the beginning and to hope for its completion in the course of further procedure, than to begin with a narrow and exclusive formula, which is of necessity confronted by one or more opposing formulae, with which there must be a conflict sooner or later. And it is in this sense that the formula of our proposition is set up.

2. It is indisputable that all Christians trace back to Christ the communion to which they belong. But here we are also presupposing that the term *Redemption* is one to which they all confess: not only that they all *use* the word, with perhaps different meanings, but that there is some common element of meaning which they all have in mind, even if they differ when they come to a more exact description of it. The term itself is in this realm merely figurative, and signifies in general a passage from an evil condition, which is represented as a state of captivity or constraint,[1] into a better condition—this is the passive side of it. But it also signifies the help given in that process by some other person, and this is the active side of it. Further, the usage of the word does not essentially imply that the worse condition must have been preceded by a better condition, so that the better one which followed would really be only a restoration: that point may at the outset be left quite open. But

1. [This does not apply as precisely to the English word *redemption* as to the German word *Erlösung*, which primarily means release or deliverance. —Transl.]

now apply the word to the realm of religion, and suppose we are dealing with the teleological type of religion. Then the evil condition can only consist in an obstruction or arrest of the vitality of the higher self-consciousness, so that there comes to be little or no union of it with the various determinations of the sensible self-consciousness, and thus little or no religious life. We may give to this condition, in its most extreme form, the name of *God-lessness,* or, better, *God-forgetfulness.* But we must not think this means a state in which it is quite impossible for the God-consciousness to be kindled. For if that were so, then, in the first place, the lack of a thing which lay outside of one's nature could not be felt to be an evil condition; and in the second place, a re-creating in the strict sense would then be needed in order to make good this lack, and that is not included in the idea of redemption. The possibility, then, of kindling the God-consciousness remains in reserve even where the evil condition of that consciousness is painted in the darkest colours. (Rom. 1, 18ff.) Hence we can only designate it as an absence of facility for introducing the God-consciousness into the course of our actual lives and retaining it there. . . . . .

3. The recognition of such a condition undeniably finds a place in all religious communions. For the aim of all penances and purifications is to put an end to the consciousness of this condition or to the condition itself. But our proposition establishes two points which in this connexion distinguish Christianity from all other religious communions. In the first place, in Christianity the incapacity and the redemption, and their connexion with each other, do not constitute simply one particular religious element among others, but all other religious emotions are related to this, and this accompanies all others, as the principal thing which makes them distinctively Christian. And secondly, redemption is posited as a thing which has been universally and completely accomplished by Jesus of Nazareth. And these two points, again, must not be separated from each other, but are essentially interconnected. Thus it could not by any means be said that Christian piety is attributable to every man who in all his religious moment is conscious of being in process of redemption, even if he stood in no relation to the person of Jesus or even knew nothing of Him—a case which,

of course, will never arise. And no more could it be said that a man's religion is Christian if he traces it to Jesus, even supposing that therein he is not at all conscious of being in process of redemption—a case which also, of course, will never arise. The reference to redemption is in every Christian consciousness simply because the originator of the Christian communion is the Redeemer; and Jesus is Founder of a religious communion simply in the sense that its members become conscious of redemption through Him. Our previous exposition ensures that this will not be understood to mean that the whole religious consciousness of a Christian can have no other content than simply Jesus and redemption, but only that all religious moments, so far as they are free expressions of the feeling of absolute dependence, are set down as having come into existence through that redemption, and, so far as the feeling appears still unliberated, are set down as being in need of that redemption. It likewise goes without saying that, while this element is always present, different religious moments may and will possess it in varying degrees of strength or weakness, without thereby losing their Christian character. But it *would*, of course, follow from what has been said, that if we conceive of religious moments in which all reference to redemption is absent, and the image of the Redeemer is not introduced at all, these moments must be judged to belong no more intimately to Christianity than to any other monotheistic faith.

4. The more detailed elaboration of our proposition, as to how the redemption is effected by Christ and comes to consciousness within the Christian communion, falls to the share of the dogmatic system itself. Here, however, we have still to discuss, with reference to the general remarks we made above, the relation of Christianity to the other principal monotheistic communions. These also are traced back each to an individual founder. Now if the difference of founder were the only difference, this would be a merely external difference, and the same thing would be true if these others likewise set up their founder as a redeemer and thus related everything to redemption. For that would mean that in all these religions the religious moments were of like content, only that the personality of the founder was different. But such is not the case: rather must

we say that only through Jesus, and thus only in Christianity, has redemption become the central point of religion. For inasmuch as these other religions have instituted particular penances and purifications for particular things, and these are only particular parts of their doctrine and organization, the effecting of redemption does not appear as their main business. It appears rather as a derivative element. Their main business is the founding of the communion upon definite doctrine and in definite form. If, however, there are within the communion considerable differences in the free development of the God-consciousness, then some people, in whom it is most cramped, are more in need of redemption, and others, in whom it works more freely, are more capable of redemption; and thus through the influence of the latter there arises in the former an approximation to redemption; but only up to the point at which the difference between the two is more or less balanced, simply owing to the fact that there exists a communion or fellowship. In Christianity, on the other hand, the redeeming influence of the Founder is the primary element, and the communion exists only on this presupposition, and as a communication and propagation of that redeeming activity. Hence within Christianity these two tendencies always rise and fall together: the tendency to give pre-eminence to the redeeming work of Christ, and the tendency to ascribe great value to the distinctive and peculiar element in Christian piety. And the same is true of the two opposite tendencies: the tendency to regard Christianity simply as a means of advancing and propagating religion in general (its own distinctive nature being merely accidental and secondary), and the tendency to regard Christ principally as a teacher and the organizer of a communion, while putting the redeeming activity in the background.

Accordingly, in Christianity the relation of the Founder to the members of the communion is quite different from what it is in the other religions. For those other founders are represented as having been, as it were, arbitrarily elevated from the mass of similar or not very different men, and as receiving just as much for themselves as for other people whatever they do receive in the way of divine doctrine and precept. Thus even an adherent of those faiths will hardly deny that God could just as well have given the law through another as through Moses, and the revelation could just as well have been given through another as through Mohammed. But Christ is distinguished from all others as Redeemer alone and for all, and is in no wise regarded as having been at any time in need of redemption Himself; and is therefore separated from the beginning from all other men, and endowed with redeeming power from His birth.

*　　*　　*

Postscript.—According to the view of religion which we have taken as our basis, the peculiar being of the Redeemer and of the redeemed in their connexion with Him is the original point at which this question of the supernatural and the supra-rational in Christianity emerges; so that there is no ground whatever for admitting anything supernatural or supra-rational which is not connected with the appearing of the Redeemer but would in itself form another original element. The question is usually handled, partly with reference to the individual facts for which a super-natural quality is especially claimed (we cannot yet speak of them here), and partly with reference to the Christian doctrines, which are for us nothing but the expressions given to the Christian self-consciousness and its connexions. But if the supernatural in the Christian self-consciousness consists in the fact that it cannot, in the form in which it actually exists, be produced by the activity of reason, it by no means follows from this that the expressions given to this self-consciousness must also be supra-rational. For in the same sense in which the Christian self-consciousness is supra-rational, the whole of Nature is supra-rational too, and yet we do not apply that epithet to the things we say *about* Nature, but call them purely rational. But the whole process of formulating our expressions concerning the religious self-consciousness is just as much a rational process as in the case of Nature; and the difference is merely that this objective consciousness is given at first hand only to him who is affected by Nature, while that (Christian) self-consciousness is given only to him who is affected by the Redeemer in the manner which is peculiar to His followers.

Now this itself makes plain what we are to think of the prevalent view that Christian doctrine consists partly of rational and partly of supra-rational dogmas. It is, indeed, of itself obvious that this can be no more than a juxtaposition, and that these two kinds of dogmas cannot form one whole. Between the rational and the supra-rational there can be no connexion. This further becomes pretty clearly evident in all treatises upon Christian doctrine which divide themselves into a natural theology, purely rational and thus valid not only within, but also outside of Christianity, and a positive supra-rational theology, valid only within the compass of Christianity. For then the two are and remain separate from each other. The apparent practicability of a union of the two arises from the fact that there are, of course, Christian dogmas in which the peculiarly Christian element retreats considerably into the background, so that they may be taken to be purely rational in those respects in which the others are recognized as supra-rational. But if that peculiarly Christian element were not in them at all, they would, of course, not be Christian dogmas. Hence the truth of the matter is as follows: In one respect all Christian dogmas are supra-rational, in another they are all rational. They are supra-rational in the respect in which everything experimental is supra-rational. For there is an inner experience to which they may all be traced: they rest upon a *given;* and apart from this they could not have arisen, by deduction or synthesis, from universally recognized and communicable propositions. If the reverse were true, it would mean that you could instruct and demonstrate any man into being a Christian, without his happening to have had any experience. Therefore this supra-rationality implies that a true appropriation of Christian dogmas cannot be brought about by scientific means, and thus lies outside the realm of reason: it can only be brought about through each man willing to have the experience for himself, as indeed it is true of everything individual and characteristic, that it can only be apprehended by the love which wills to perceive. In this sense the whole of Christian doctrine is supra-rational. It may, however, be further asked whether the dogmas which give expression to the religious affections of the Christian and their connexions are not subject to the same laws of conception and synthesis as regulate all speech, so that the more perfectly these laws are satisfied in such a presentation, the more will each individual be constrained to apprehend correctly what is thought and intended, even if he cannot, for lack of the fundamental inward experience, convince himself of the truth of the matter. It must be answered that in this sense everything in Christian doctrine is entirely according to reason. Accordingly, the supra-rationality of all particular Christian dogmas is the measure by which it can be judged whether they succeed in expressing the peculiarly Christian element; and again, their rationality is the test of how far the attempt to translate the inward emotions into thoughts has succeeded. But to assert that it cannot be demanded that what goes beyond reason should be rationally presented, appears to be only a subterfuge designed to cover up some imperfection in the procedure; just as the opposite view that in Christian doctrine everything must be, in every sense, based on reason, is simply meant to cover up the lack of a fundamental experience of one's own.

The usual formula, that the supra-rational in Christianity must not be contrary to reason, seems intended to say the same thing as our proposition. For it implies, on the one hand, the recognition of the supra-rational, and, on the other hand, the task of showing that it is not contrary to reason, and this can only be achieved by means of a rational presentation.

*　　*　　*

1. To participate in the Christian communion means to seek in Christ's institution an approximation to the above-described state of absolute facility and constancy of religious emotions. No one can wish to belong to the Christian Church on any other ground. But since each can only enter through a free resolve of his own, this must be preceded by the certainty that the influence of Christ puts an end to the state of being in need of redemption, and produces that other state; and this certainty is just faith in Christ. That is to say, this term always signifies, in our present province, the certainty which accompanies a state of the higher self-consciousness, and which is therefore different from, but not for that reason less than, the

certainty which accompanies the objective consciousness. In the same sense we spoke above of faith in God, which was nothing but the certainty concerning the feeling of absolute dependence, as such, *i.e.* as conditioned by a Being placed outside of us, and as expressing our relation to that Being. The faith of which we are now speaking, however, is a purely factual certainty, but a certainty of a fact which is entirely inward. That is to say, it cannot exist in an individual until, through an impression which he has received from Christ, there is found in him a beginning— perhaps quite infinitesimal, but yet a real premonition—of the process which will put an end to the state of needing redemption. But the term 'faith in Christ' here (as the term 'faith in God' formerly) relates the state of redemption, as effect, to Christ as cause. That is how John describes it. And so from the beginning only those people have attached themselves to Christ in His new community whose religious self-consciousness had taken the form of a need of redemption, and who now became assured in themselves of Christ's redeeming power (John I:45, 46; 6:68, 69, Matt. 16:15-18). So that the more strongly those two phases appeared in any individual, the more able was he, by representation of the fact (which includes description of Christ and His work) to elicit this inward experience in others. Those in whom this took place became believers, and the rest did not. (Acts 2:37, 41). This, moreover, is what has ever since constituted the essence of all direct Christian preaching. Such preaching must always take the form of testimony; testimony as to one's own experience, which shall arouse in others the desire to have the same experience. But the impression which all later believers received in this way from the influence of Christ, *i.e.* from the common Spirit communicated by Him and from the whole communion of Christians, supported by the historical representation of His life and character, was just the same impression which His contemporaries received from Him directly. Hence those who remained unbelieving were not blamed because they had not let themselves be persuaded by reasons, but simply because of their lack of self-knowledge, which must always be the explanation when the Redeemer is truly and correctly presented and people show themselves unable to recognize Him as such. But even Christ

Himself represented this lack of self-knowledge, *i.e.* of the consciousness of needing redemption, as the limit to His activity. And so the ground of unbelief is the same in all ages, as is also the ground of belief or faith.

2. The attempt has often been made to demonstrate the necessity of redemption, but always in vain. We need not, however, appeal to these cases, for it is clear in itself that the thing is impossible. Any man who is capable of being satisfied with himself as he is will always manage to find a way out of the argument. And no more can it be demonstrated, once the consciousness of this need has been awakened, that Christ is the only One who can work redemption. In His own time there were many who did believe that redemption was near, and yet did not accept Him. And even when we have a more correct idea of the end to be sought, it is not easy to see how it could be proved that any particular individual is in a position to achieve the desired effect. For in this matter we are concerned with amount of spiritual power, which we have no means of calculating; and even if we had, we should also require some fixed datum against which the calculation could be set. It cannot even be proved in a general way that such a redemption is bound to come, even if we presuppose a general knowledge not only of what men are like but also of what God is like. There would still be plenty of room for different sophistical arguments to draw opposite conclusions from the same data, according as God's purpose for man was conceived in one way or in another.

Agreed, then, that we must adhere to the kind of certainty which we have just described, and that faith is nothing other than the incipient experience of the satisfaction of that spiritual need by Christ: there can still be very diverse ways of experiencing the need and the succour; and yet they will all be faith. Moreover, the consciousness of need may be present for a long time in advance, or it may, as is often the case, be fully awakened only by the contrast which the perfection of Christ forms with our own condition, so that the two things come into existence simultaneously, the supreme consciousness of need and the beginning of its satisfaction.

3. It is true that in the Scriptures themselves proofs are often

mentioned, which the witnesses of the Gospel employed. (Acts 6:9, 10; 9:20, 22, also 18:27, 28.) Yet it never asserted that faith sprang from the proof, but from the preaching. Those proofs were only applied among the Jews, with reference to their current ideas of the coming Messiah, in order to repulse the opposition presented by these ideas to the witness of the Gospel, or to anticipate any such opposition. This was an indispensable line of defence for witnesses of Christ who were Jews and who were dealing with Jews. If they wished to assert that they themselves had never expected any other kind of redemption than this, or that their expectations had been transformed by the appearing and the influence of Christ, they must either break with the whole Jewish religion, which they had no warrant for doing, or show that the prophetic representations were applicable to this Jesus as Redeemer. If we took the other view of the matter, it would mean that the faith of the Gentile Christians was not the same as that of the Jewish Christians; and then it would not have been possible for these two to become really one, but the Gentiles would have had to become Jews first, in order then to be brought to Christ by the authority of the prophets.

Postscript.—Our proposition says nothing of any intermediate link between faith and participation in the Christian communion, and is accordingly to be taken as directly combining the two, so that faith of itself carries with it that participation; and not only as depending on the spontaneous activity of the man who has become a believer, but also as depending on the spontaneous activity of the communion (Church), as the source from which the testimony proceeded for the awakening of faith. At the same time, in shutting up the whole process between these two points, the witness or testimony and its effect, our proposition is intended to make an end of everything which, in the form of demonstration, is usually brought to the aid of the proper witness or even substituted for it. This refers principally to the attempts to bring about a recognition of Christ by means of the miracles which He performs, or the prophecies which predicted Him, or the special character of the testimonies originally borne to Him, regarded as the work of divine inspiration. In all this there seems to be more or less illusion on the following point:

that the efficacy of these things somehow always presupposes faith, and therefore cannot produce it.

First consider *Miracle,* taking the word in its narrower sense, so that prophecy and inspiration are not included, but simply phenomena in the realm of physical nature which are supposed not to have been caused in a natural manner. Whether we confine ourselves to those performed by Jesus Himself, or include those which took place in connexion with Him, these miracles cannot bring about a recognition of Him at all. In the first place, we know of these miracles only from those same Holy Scriptures (for the miracles related in less pure sources are never adduced along with them) which relate similar miracles of people who did not adhere to Christianity at all, but are rather to be reckoned among its enemies; and Scripture gives us no marks for distinguishing evidential miracles from non-evidential. But further, Scripture itself bears witness that faith has been produced without miracles, and also that miracles have failed to produce it; from which it may be concluded that even when it has existed along with miracles it was not produced by miracles but in its own original way. Hence if the purpose of miracles had been to produce faith, we should have to conclude that God's breaking into the order of Nature proved ineffectual. Accordingly, many find the purpose of miracles simply in the fact that they turn the attention to Christ. But this, again, is at least so far contradicted by Christ's oft-repeated command not to make the miracles more widely known, that we should have to limit their efficacy to the immediate eye-witnesses, and thus this efficacy would no longer exist to-day. But, finally, the following question cannot be avoided. In any other context than that of such faith and its realm, we may encounter any number of facts which we cannot explain naturally, and yet we never think of miracle, but simply regard the explanation as deferred until we have a more exact knowledge both of the fact in question and of the laws of Nature. But when such a fact occurs in connexion with some faith-realm which has to be established, we think at once of miracle; only, each man claims miracle as real for the realm of his own faith alone, and sets down the others as false. On what is this distinction based? The question can hardly be answered except as follows. In general we do, perhaps, assume so exclusive a connexion between miracles and the formation of a new faith-realm, that we only admit miracle for this kind of case; but the state of each individual's faith determines his judgment of the alleged miracle, and so the miracle does not produce the faith. As regards that universal connexion, however, the state of the case seems to be as follows. Where a new point in the development of the spiritual life, and indeed primarily of the self-consciousness, is assumed to exist, new phenomena in physical Nature, mediated by the spiritual power which is manifested, are also expected, because both the contemplative and the outwardly active spiritual states all proceed from the self-consciousness, and are determined by its movements. Thus, once Christ is recognized as Redeemer, and consequently as the beginning of the supreme development of human nature in the realm of the self-consciousness, it is a natural assumption that, just because at the point where such an existence communicates itself most strongly, spiritual states appear which cannot be explained from what went before, He who exercises such a peculiar influence upon human nature around Him will be able, in virtue of the universal connexion of things, to manifest also a peculiar power of working upon the physical side of human nature and upon external Nature. That is to say, it is natural to expect miracles from Him who is the supreme divine revelation; and yet they can be called miracles only in a relative sense, since our ideas of the susceptibility of physical Nature to the influence of the spirit and of the causality of the will acting upon physical Nature are as far from being finally settled and as capable of being perpetually widened by new experiences as are our ideas of the forces of physical Nature themselves. Now, since, in connexion with the divine revelation in Christ, phenomena presented themselves which could be brought under this concept of miracle, it was natural that they should actually come to be regarded from this point of view, and adduced as confirmation of the fact that this was a new point of development. But this confirmation will be effectual only where there is already present a beginning of faith; failing that, the miracle would either be declared false or be reserved, as regards the understanding of it, for some natural explanation which the future would reveal. Still less could it be proved from the miracles which accompanied it that Christianity is the supreme revelation, since similar phenomena are on the same grounds to be expected in the lower faiths too, and miracles themselves cannot, as such, be divided into higher and lower. Indeed, the possibility cannot be excluded that similar phenomena might occur even apart from all connexion with the realm of religion, whether as accompanying other kinds of development or as signalizing deeper movements in physical Nature itself.

* * *

1. All religious emotions, to whatever type and level of religion they belong, have this in common with all other modifications of the affective self-consciousness, that as soon as they have reached a certain stage and a certain definiteness they manifest themselves outwardly by mimicry in the most direct and spontaneous way, by means of facial features and movements of voice and gesture, which we regard as their expression. Thus we definitely distinguish the expression of devoutness, from that of a sensuous gladness or sadness, by the analogy of each man's knowledge of himself. Indeed, we can even conceive that, for the purpose of maintaining the religious affections and securing their repetition and propagation (especially if they were common to a number of people), the elements of that natural expression of them might be put together into sacred signs and symbolical acts, without the thought having perceptibly come in between at all. But we can scarcely conceive such a low development of the human spirit, such a defective culture, and such a meagre use of speech, that each person would not, according to the level of reflection on which he stands, become in his various mental states likewise an object to himself, in order to comprehend them in idea and retain them in the form of thought. Now this endeavour has always directed itself particularly to the religious emotions; and this, considered in its own inward meaning, is what our proposition means by an account of the religious affections. But while thought cannot proceed even inwardly without the use of speech, nevertheless there are, so long as it remains merely inward, fugitive elements in this procedure, which do indeed in some measure indicate the object, but not in such a

way that either the formation of the synthesis of concepts (in
however wide a sense we take the word 'concept') is sufficiently
definite for communication. It is only when this procedure has
reached such a point of cultivation as to be able to represent
itself outwardly in definite speech, that it produces a real doctrine (*Glaubenssatz*), by means of which the utterances of the
religious consciousness come into circulation more surely and
with a wider range than is possible through the direct expression. But no matter whether the expression is natural or figurative, whether it indicates its objects directly or only by comparison and delimitation, it is still a doctrine.

2. Now Christianity everywhere presupposes that consciousness has reached this stage of development. The whole work of
the Redeemer Himself was conditioned by the communicability
of His self-consciousness by means of speech, and similarly Christianity has always and everywhere spread itself solely by preaching. Every proposition which can be an element of the Christian
preaching (κήρυγμα) is also a doctrine, because it bears witness
to the determination of the religious self-consciousness as inward
certainty. And every Christian doctrine is also a part of the
Christian preaching, because every such doctrine expresses as a
certainty the approximation to the state of blessedness which is
to be effected through the means ordained .by Christ. But this
preaching very soon split up into three different types of speech,
which provide as many different forms of doctrine: the poetic,
the rhetorical (which is directed partly outwards, as combative
and commendatory, and partly inwards, as rather disciplinary
and challenging) , and finally the descriptively didactic. But the
relation of communication through speech to communication
through symbolic action varies very much according to time and
place, the former having always retreated into the background in
the Eastern Church (for when the letter of doctrine has become
fixed and unalterable, it is in its effect much nearer to symbolic
action than to free speech) , and having become ever more prom-
inent in the Western Church. And in the realm of speech it is
just the same with these three modes of communication. The
relation in which they stand to each other, the general degree of
richness, and the amount of living intercourse in which they unfold themselves, as they nourish themselves on one another and

pass over into one another—these things testify not so much to the degree or level of piety as rather to the character of the communion or fellowship and its ripeness for reflection and contemplation. Thus this communication is, on the one hand, something different from the piety itself, though the latter cannot, any more than anything else which is human, be conceived entirely separated from all communication. But, on the other hand, the doctrines in all their forms have their ultimate ground so exclusively in the emotions of the religious self-consciousness, that where these do not exist the doctrines cannot arise.

* * *

1. The poetic expression is always based originally upon a moment of exaltation which has come purely from within, a moment of enthusiasm or inspiration; the rhetorical upon a moment whose exaltation has come from without, a moment of stimulated interest which issues in a particular definite result. The former is purely descriptive (*darstellend*), and sets up in general outlines images and forms which each hearer completes for himself in his own peculiar way. The rhetorical is purely stimulative, and has, in its nature, to do for the most part with such elements of speech as, admitting of degrees of signification, can be taken in a wider or narrower sense, content if at the decisive moment they can accomplish the highest, even though they should exhaust themselves thereby and subsequently appear to lose somewhat of their force. Thus both of these forms possess a different perfection from the logical or dialectical perfection described in our proposition. But, nevertheless, we can think of both as being primary and original in every religious communion, and thus in the Christian Church, in so far as we ascribe to everyone in it a share in the vocation of preaching. For when anyone finds himself in a state of unusually exalted religious self-consciousness, he will feel himself called to poetic description, as that which proceeds from this state most directly. And, on the other hand, when anyone finds himself particularly challenged by insistent or favourable outward circumstances to attempt an act of preaching, the rhetorical form of expression will be the most natural to him for obtaining from the given circumstances the greatest

possible advantage. But let us conceive of the comprehension and appropriation of what is given in a direct way in these two forms, as being now also wedded to language and thereby made communicable: then this cannot again take the poetic form, nor yet the rhetorical; but, being independent of that which was the important element in those two forms, and expressing as it does a consciousness which remains self-identical, it becomes, less as preaching than as confession (ὁμολογία), precisely that third form—the didactic—which, with its descriptive instruction, remains distinct from the two others, and is made up of the two put together, as a derivative and secondary form.

2. But let us confine ourselves to Christianity, and think of its distinctive beginning, namely, the self-proclamation of Christ, Who, as subject of the divine revelation, could not contain in Himself any distinction of stronger and weaker emotion, but could only partake in such a diversity through His common life with others. Then we shall not be able to take either the poetic or the rhetorical form of expression as the predominating, or even as the really primary and original, force of His self-proclamation. These have only a subordinate place in parabolic and prophetic discourses. The essential thing in His self-proclamation was that He had to bear witness regarding His ever unvarying self-consciousness out of the depths of its repose, and conequently not in poetic but in strictly reflective form; and thus had to set Himself forth, while at the same time communicating His alone true objective consciousness of the condition and constitution of men in general, thus instructing by description or representation, the instruction being sometimes subordinate to the description, and sometimes *vice versa*. But this descriptively didactic mode of expression used by Christ is not included in our proposition, and such utterances of the Redeemer will hardly be set up anywhere as dogmatic propositions; they will only, as it were, provide the text for them. For in such essential parts of the self-proclamation of Christ the definiteness was absolute, and it is only the perfection of the apprehension and appropriation which reproduces these, that can be characterized by the endeavour after the greatest possible definiteness. Subordinate to these, however, there do appear genuinely dogmatic propositions in the discourses of Christ, namely, at those points at which He had to

start from the partly erroneous and partly confused ideas current among His contemporaries.

3. As regards the poetic and rhetorical forms of expression, it follows directly from what we have said, that they may fall into apparent contradiction both with themselves and with each other, even when the self-consciousness which is indicated by different forms of expression is in itself one and the same. And a solution will only be possible, in the first place, when it is possible in interpreting propositions that are apparently contradictory to take one's bearings from the original utterances of Christ (a thing which can in very few cases be done directly), and, in the second place, when the descriptively didactic expression, which has grown out of those three original forms put together, is entirely or largely free from those apparent contradictions. This, however, will not be possible of achievement so long as the descriptively didactic expression itself keeps vacillating between the emotional and the didactic, in its presentation to the catechumens or the community, and approaches sometimes more to the rhetorical and sometimes more to the figurative. It will only be possible in proportion as the aim indicated in our proposition underlies the further development of the expression and its more definite separation from the rhetorical and the poetic, both of which processes are essentially bound up with the need of settling the conflict. Now, of course, this demand, that the figurative expression be either exchanged for a literal one or transformed into such by being explained, and that definite limits be imposed on the corresponding element in the rhetorical expressions, is unmistakably the interest which science has in the formation of language; and it is mainly with the formation of religious language that we are here concerned. Hence dogmatic propositions develop to any considerable extent and gain recognition only in such religious communions as have reached a degree of culture in which science is organized as something distinct both from art and from business, and only in proportion as friends of science are found and have influence within the communion itself, so that the dialectical function is brought to bear on the utterances of the religious self-consciousness, and guides the expression of them. Such a union with organized knowledge has had a place in Christianity ever since the earliest

ages of the Church, and therefore in no other religious communion has the form of the dogmatic proposition evolved in such strict separation from the other forms, or developed in such fulness.

Postscript.—This account of the origin of dogmatic propositions, as having arisen solely out of logically ordered reflection upon the immediate utterances of the religious self-consciousness, finds its confirmation in the whole of history. The earliest specimens of preaching preserved for us in the New Testament Scriptures already contain such propositions; and on closer consideration we can see in all of them, in the first place, their deviation from the original self-proclamation of Christ, and, in the second place, their affinity to figurative and rhetorical elements which, for permanent circulation, had to approximate more to the strictness of a formula. Similarly in later periods it is clear that the figurative language, which is always poetic in its nature, had the most decided influence upon the dogmatic language, and always preceded its development, and also that the majority of the dogmatic definitions were called forth by contradictions to which the rhetorical expressions had led.

But when the transformation of the original expressions into dogmatic propositions is ascribed to the logical or dialectical interest, this is to be understood as applying only to the form. A proposition which had originally proceeded from the speculative activity, however akin it might be to our propositions in content, would not be a dogmatic proposition. The purely scientific activity, whose task is the contemplation of existence, must, if it is to come to anything, either begin or end with the Supreme Being; and so there may be forms of philosophy containing propositions of speculative import about the Supreme Being which, in spite of the fact that they arose out of the purely scientific interest, are, when taken individually, difficult to distinguish from the corresponding propositions which arose purely out of reflection upon the religious emotions, but have been worked out dialectically. But when they are considered in their connexions, these two indubitably show differences of the most definite kind. For dogmatic propositions never make their original appearance except in trains of thought which have received their impulse from religious moods of mind; whereas, not only do speculative propositions about the Supreme Being appear for the most part in purely logical or natural-scientific trains of thought, but even when they come in as ethical presuppositions or corollaries, they show an unmistakable leaning towards one or other of those two directions. Moreover, in the dogmatic developments of the earliest centuries, if we discount the quite unecclesiastical Gnostic schools, the influence of speculation upon the content of dogmatic propositions may be placed at zero. At a later time, certainly, when the classical organization of knowledge had fallen into ruins, and the conglomerate-philosophy of the Middle Ages took shape within the Christian Church, and at the same time came to exercise its influence upon the formation of dogmatic language, a confusion of the speculative with the dogmatic, and consequently a mingling of the two, was almost inevitable. But this was for both an imperfect condition, from which philosophy freed itself by means of the avowal, growing ever gradually louder, that at that time it had stood under the tutelage of ecclesiastical faith, and therefore under an alien law. Having, however, since then made so many fresh starts in its own proper development, it was able to escape from the wearisome task of inquiring exactly as to what kind of speculative propositions were at that time taken to be dogmatic, and *vice versa*. For the Christian Church, however, which is not in a position ever and anon to begin the development of its doctrine over again from the start, this separation is of the greatest importance, in order to secure that speculative matter (by which neither the poetic and rhetorical nor the popular expression can consent to be guided) may not continue to be offered to it as dogmatic. The Evangelical (Protestant) Church in particular is unanimous in feeling that the distinctive form of its dogmatic propositions does not depend on any form or school of philosophy, and has not proceeded at all from a speculative interest, but simply from the interest of satisfying the immediate self-consciousness solely through the means ordained by Christ, in their genuine and uncorrupted form. Thus it can consistently adopt as dogmatic propositions of its own no propositions except such as can show this derivation. Our dogmatic theology will not, however, stand on its proper ground and soil with the same assurance with which philosophy has so long stood upon its own, until the separation of the two types of proposition is so complete that, *e.g.*, so extraordinary a question as whether the same proposition can be true in philosophy and false in Christian theology, and *vice versa,* will no longer be asked, for the simple reason that a proposition cannot appear in the one context precisely as it appears in the other: however similar it sounds, a difference must always be assumed. But we are still very far from this goal, so long as people take pains to base or deduce dogmatic propositions in the speculative manner, or even set themselves to work up the products of speculative activity and the results of the study of religious affections into a single whole.

* * *

1. The ecclesiastical value of a dogmatic proposition consists in its reference to the religious emotions themselves. Every such emotion, regarded singly, is indeed for description an infinite, and all dogmatic concepts, as well as all concepts of psychology, would have to be used to describe one moment of life. But just as in such a moment the religious strain may be the dominant one, so again in every such strain some one relation of the higher self-consciousness stands out as determinative; and it is to this strain, uniformly for all analogous moments of religious emotion, that the dogmatic propositions refer. Thus, in all completely expressed dogmatic propositions, the reference to Christ as Redeemer must appear with the same measure of prominence which it has in the religious consciousness itself. Naturally, however, this is not equally strongly the case in all religious moments, any more than in the life of any civic state the distinctive character of its constitution can appear equally strongly in all moments. Accordingly, the less strongly the reference to Christ is expressed in a dogmatic proposition, as, *e.g.*, in the religious emotions mediated by our relation to the external world, the more easily may it resemble a doctrinal proposition of another religious communion, in cases where the distinctive character of that communion too remains for the most part in the background. Now this occurs even within the Christian Church itself, in respect to the various modifications of the Christian consciousness which separate into larger or smaller groups. Now, if a dog-

matic proposition is so formed that it satisfies the Christian consciousness for all alike, then it actually holds good in a larger circle, but it is not calculated to show up differences, which are thus indirectly marked as unimportant or in process of disappearing. If, on the other hand, it has respect only to one of these different modifications, then it holds good only within this smaller compass. Sometimes the former kind of dogma may seem colourless, and the latter be the right kind; at other times the latter may be factious or sectarian, and the former be the right kind. But such differences in dogmatic propositions dealing with the same subject, which do not represent any differences at all in the immediate religious self-consciousness, are of no significance for their ecclesiastical value.

2. The scientific value of a dogmatic proposition depends in the first place upon the definiteness of the concepts which appear in it, and of their connexion with each other. For the more definite these become, the more does the proposition pass out of the indefinite realm of the poetic and rhetorical, and the more certain will it be that the proposition cannot enter into apparent contradiction with other dogmatic propositions belonging to the same form of religious consciousness. But in forming its concepts Dogmatics has not succeeded—indeed, one might say that from the nature of the subject it cannot succeed—in everywhere substituting the exact expression for the figurative; and thus the scientific value of dogmatic propositions depends, from this side, for the most part simply upon the highest possible degree of precision and definiteness in explaining the figurative expressions which occur. And we can the more readily leave it at that, since, even if the exact expression could throughout be substituted for the figurative, the latter is the original, and therefore the identity of the two would have to be shown, which would come to the same thing in the end. In the second place, the scientific value of a dogmatic proposition consists in its fruitfulness, that is to say, its many-sidedness in pointing us towards other kindred ones; and not so much in a heuristic way (since no dogmatic proposition is based on another, and each one can only be discovered from contemplation of the Christian self-consciousness) as in a critical way, because then it can be the more easily tested how well one dogmatic expression harmonizes with others. For

it is undeniable that, of a number of dogmatic expressions which are supposed to refer to the same fact of the Christian consciousness, that one will deserve the preference which opens up and enters into combination with the largest range of other expressions referring to kindred facts. And when we find a realm or system of dogmatic language which is closely bound together and forms a self-contained whole, that is an account of the facts which we may presume to be correct.

A proposition which lacks the first of these two properties, and which thus belongs entirely to the poetic or the rhetorical realm of language, has not got the length of being a dogmatic proposition. A proposition which, as regards the second of the two properties, goes beyond the principle we have set up, and seeks to establish anything objectively without going back to the higher self-consciousness, would not be a religious doctrine (*Glaubenssatz*) at all, and would simply not belong to our field.

3. Now since every doctrine of the faith has, as such, an ecclesiastical value, and since these doctrines become dogmatic when they acquire a scientific value, dogmatic propositions are the more perfect the more their scientific character gives them an outstanding ecclesiastical value, and also the more their scientific content bears traces of having proceeded from the ecclesiastical interest.

*   *   *

1. If we think of the Christian Church as being what we call a moral Person, *i.e.*, as being, though of course made up of many personalities, nevertheless a genuine individual life, then it must at once be admitted that in every such life, just as in individual lives in the narrower sense, there is a distinction between healthy and diseased conditions. The latter are always conditions which do not arise from the inward foundation of the life and in its clear course, but are to be explained only by foreign influences. So when among any race of people individuals arise who exhibit a quite alien physiological type, so that they do not take very kindly to the majority and their mode of life, or when in a republican state citizens arise with monarchist sentiments, or *vice versa*, we regard this as a disease of the whole, and also assume

that it can only be explained by foreign influences. Now, even if this last point might not be admitted by everybody, yet everybody will reserve the name of 'heretical' in the realm of Christian doctrine for that which he cannot explain from his idea of the distinctive essence of Christianity, and cannot conceive as accordant therewith, but which nevertheless gives itself out as Christian and seeks to be regarded as such by others. Now, it is a matter of fact that during the period of the actual development of Christian doctrine a multitude of such elements appeared which the majority persistently rejected as of alien type, while they recognized the remainder, as self-consistent and as forming a coherent continuum, under the name of Catholic, *i.e.* common to the whole Church. In this connexion it may, of course, sometimes be the case that the religious emotions set forth in the doctrine are themselves at variance with the true essence of Christian piety; but sometimes it is only in the working out of the doctrine that this variance arises, so that the religious affections themselves are not diseased, and only misunderstanding or false method produces an appearance of heresy. Now these two cases are of course seldom properly distinguished, and therefore many things have been too hastily declared heretical. But, nevertheless, real heresy has not been lacking; and in its case foreign influences will readily be admitted, when one reflects that the Christian Church originally sprang solely from people who belonged before to other faiths, so that alien matter could easily creep in unawares.

2. It is undeniable that this makes the determination of what is heretical, and must therefore be excluded from the system of doctrine, appear a very uncertain thing, and people will all fix it differently who start from different formulae of the distinctive essence of Christianity. But that cannot be otherwise, as the whole course of events in the Christian Church proves. For new heresies no longer arise, now that the Church recruits itself out of its own resources; and the influence of alien faiths on the frontier and in the mission-field of the Church must be reckoned at zero so far as regards the formation of doctrine, though there may long remain in the piety of the new converts a great deal which has crept in from their religious affections of former times, and which, if it came to clear consciousness and were expressed

as doctrine, would be recognized as heretical. But concerning the earlier heresies, on the other hand, there are the most diverse judgments, just as there are different ways and modes of conceiving the essence of Christianity. Hence anyone who aims at setting up a system of doctrine can only follow the rule of our proposition in the sense that he will not adopt anything which, according to the fundamental type of Christian doctrine which he has established, can only be traced to a foreign source. If, however, we are not to proceed by haphazard but with due certainty, we cannot hold by the antithesis of Catholic and heretical as it presented itself in history down to a certain point, especially as subsequent revindications of this or that heresy have not been unheard-of. We must rather start from the essence of Christianity, and seek to construe the heretical in its manifold forms by asking in how many different ways essence of Christianity can be contradicted and the appearance of Christianity yet remain. Conducted in this way, the inquiry into the heretical serves to supplement the inquiry into the essence of Christianity, and the two confirm each other. The more it turns out that what is thus set up problematically as heretical is also actually given in history, the more ground have we to regard the formula upon which the construction is based as a correct expression of the essence of Christianity. And the more naturally there develops out of this same formula the form of doctrine which Christianity has constantly professed, the more ground have we to regard as really diseased and worthy of rejection whatever conflicts on any side with that formula.

*   *   *

1. The fact that the whole Christian religious consciousness is here presupposed is entirely legitimate, for here we abstract entirely from the specific content of the particular Christian experiences, and what we have stated is in no way affected by these differences. Hence nothing can be deduced from the above proposition [*the immediate feeling of absolute dependence is presupposed and actually contained in every religious and Christian self-consciousness as the only way in which, in general, our own being and the infinite Being of God can be one in self-conscious-*

ness] either for or against any dogmatic formulation of such specific content. But if anyone should maintain that there might be Christian religious experiences in which the Being of God was not involved in such a manner, *i.e.* experiènces which contained absolutely no consciousness of God, our proposition would certainly exclude him from the domain of that Christian belief which we are going to describe. Our proposition appeals, therefore, against such a person to the religious self-consciousness as it appears and is recognized everywhere in the Evangelical (Protestant) Church: that is, we assert that in every religious affection, however much its special contents may predominate, the God-consciousness must be present and cannot be neutralized by anything else, so that there can be no relation to Christ which does not contain also a relation to God. At the same time, we also assert that this God-consciousness, as it is here described, does not constitute by itself alone an actual moment in religious experience, but always in connexion with other particular determinations; so that this God-consciousness maintains its identity through its particular moments in all manifestations of Christian piety, just as in life generally the self-consciousness of an individual does in the different moments of his existence. Hence the view that in every Christian affection there must be a relation to Christ does not in the least contradict our proposition. Much more is this the case when the pious feeling comes to expression as an actual moment in the form of pleasure or pain. For the Christian faith, however, the incapacity implied in religious pain must be ascribed to lack of fellowship with the Redeemer, while, on the other hand, the ease of evoking pious feeling which goes along with religious pleasure is regarded as a possession which comes to us from this fellowship. Thus it is evident that, within the Christian communion, there can be no religious experience which does not involve a relation to Christ.

2. It is possible to give a non-religious explanation of this sense of absolute dependence; it might be said that it only means the dependence of finite particulars on the whole and on the system of all finite things, and that what is implied and made the centre of reference is not God but the world. But we can only regard this explanation as a misunderstanding. For we recognize in our self-consciousness an awareness of the world, but it

is different from the awareness of God in the same self-consciousness. For the world, if we assume it to be a unity, is nevertheless in itself a divided and disjointed unity which is at the same time the totality of all contrasts and differences and of all the resulting manifold determinations, of which every man is one, partaking in all the contrasts. To be one with the world in self-consciousness is nothing else than being conscious that we are a living part of this whole; and this cannot possibly be a consciousness of absolute dependence; the more so that all living parts stand in reciprocal interaction with each other. This oneness with the whole in each several part is essentially twofold: a feeling of dependence, indeed, so far as the other parts act spontaneously upon it, but also a feeling of freedom in so far as it likewise reacts spontaneously on the other parts. The one is not to be separated from the other.

The feeling of absolute dependence, accordingly, is not to be explained as an awareness of the world's existence, but only as an awareness of the existence of God, as the absolute undivided unity.

* * *

50. *All attributes which we ascribe to God are to be taken as denoting not something special in God, but only something special in the manner in which the feeling of absolute dependence is to be related to Him.*

* * *

63. *While in general the manner in which the God-consciousness takes shape in and with the stimulated self-consciousness can be traced only to the action of the individual, the distinctive feature of Christian piety lies in the fact that whatever alienation from God there is in the phases of our experience, we are conscious of it as an action originating in ourselves, which we call Sin; but whatever fellowship with God there is, we are conscious of it as resting upon a communication from the Redeemer, which we call Grace.*

* * *

69. *We are conscious of sin partly as having its source in ourselves, partly as having its source outside our own being.*

*   *   *

70. *The sinfulness that is present in an individual prior to any action of his own, and has its ground outside his own being, is in every case a complete incapacity for good, which can be removed only by the influence of Redemption.*

*   *   *

71. *Original sin, however, is at the same time so really the personal guilt of every individual who shares in it that it is best represented as the corporate act and the corporate guilt of the human race, and that the recognition of it as such is likewise recognition of the universal need of redemption.*

*   *   *

80. *As in our self-consciousness sin and grace are opposed to each other, God cannot be thought of as the Author of sin in the same sense as that in which He is the Author of redemption. But as we never have a consciousness of grace without a consciousness of sin, we must also assert that the existence of sin alongside of grace is ordained for us by God.*

*   *   *

86. *The more distinctly conscious we become that the misery involved in our natural state cannot be removed either by the recognition that sin is inevitable, or by the assumption that it is decreasing of itself, the higher becomes the value we place upon Redemption.*

*   *   *

87. *We are conscious of all approximations to the state of blessedness which occur in the Christian life as being grounded*

in a new divinely-effected corporate life, which works in opposition to the corporate life of sin and the misery which develops in it.

* * *

88. *In this corporate life which goes back to the influence of Jesus, redemption is effected by Him through the communication of His sinless perfection.*

* * *

170. [*The Divine Trinity*] . . . *this doctrine itself, as ecclesiastically framed, is not an immediate utterance concerning the Christian self-consciousness, but only a combination of several such utterances.*

* * *

171. *The ecclesiastical doctrine of the Trinity demands that we think of each of the three Persons as equal to the Divine Essence, and* vice versa, *and each of the three Persons as equal to the others. Yet we cannot do either the one or the other, but can only represent the Persons in a gradation, and thus either represent the unity of the Essence as less real than the Three Persons, or* vice versa.

* * *

172. *We have the less reason to regard this doctrine as finally settled since it did not receive any fresh treatment when the Evangelical (Protestant) Church was set up; and so there must still be in store for it a transformation which will go back to its very beginnings.*

* * *

CONCLUDING UNSCIENTIFIC POSTSCRIPT

Søren Kierkegaard

(1813-1855)

During his lifetime Kierkegaard was hardly known outside of his native Denmark. His recognition came later among German and French thinkers and only after two decades had passed of the present century in a wider surge of interest. With the renaissance of Reformation theology of our time and with the translation of his works into English his name has acquired the stature of a star of first magnitude to those of this school of conservative thought.

A melancholic temperament mingled with an incisive analytic mind, undergirded by a strong ambition to create a viewpoint fresh and different from traditional philosophy (particularly Hegelianism) coupled with a strong aversion to the ecclesiasticism of his day, plus an imagination of unique fertility, Kierkegaard set up a viewpoint in which Christianity is held to be beyond speculation, beyond ethical codes and meanings and beyond contemplation. The Christian is a subjective, inward existent (meaning for him a coming-into-being of a unique living) confronted with a transcendental Existence in contrast to it, achieving that living by realizing its isolation, its despair and inadequacy in a commitment (a launching of faith) to It without regard for cost or any earned achievement.

His is an "existential" view and he is one of the fathers of the existential philosophy now currently popular. It is a philosophy of paradoxes of thought, a theology of the Absolute and a psychology of human inadequacy except by the realization that comes with utter Christian commitment. A sick-soul like Augustine, his life was short (he died at the age of forty-two), solitary, introspective, conscious of physical handicaps and full of remembrance of a weird love-affair. His pessimistic view of human nature was offset by an optimism gained by a complete submission to a supernatural order and to a religion supernaturally grounded.

In the *Concluding Unscientific Postscript* (his book titles are awkward and their authorship carried pseudonyms) we find his exposition of the subjectivity of truth, the subjective nature of Christianity and a fundamental tenet of existentialism: the subjectivity of a (passionate) experience. Published in 1846 it is only one of many of his works, obtuse to cursory reading yet full of illustrative metaphors. "Unscientific" in its title suggests his own view: that the ethical-religious sphere is quite apart from scientific objectivity ("dangerous and pernicious when it would encroach also upon the sphere of spirit"). "Concluding Postscript" in the title signified the author's intention to terminate his literary work—a resolution not consummated.

Of this long work (from which excerpts are presented) Kierkegaard said that it "constitutes the turning point in my whole work as an author. It presents the 'problem,' that of becoming a Christian."

Editor

CONCLUDING UNSCIENTIFIC POSTSCRIPT

* * *

From the speculative standpoint, Christianity is viewed as an historical phenomenon. The problem of its truth therefore becomes the problem of so interpenetrating it with thought, that Christianity at last reveals itself as the eternal truth.

The speculative approach to the problem is characterized by one excellent trait: it has no presuppositions. It proceeds from nothing, it assumes nothing as given, it begs no postulates. Here then we may be sure of avoiding such presuppositions as were met with in the preceding.

And yet, something is after all assumed: Christianity is assumed as given. Alas and alack! philosophy is altogether too polite. How strange is the way of the world! Once it was at the risk of his life that a man dared to profess himself a Christian; now it is to make oneself suspect to venture to doubt that one is a Christian. Especially when this doubt does not mean that the individual launches a violent attack against Christianity with a view to abolishing it; for in that case it would perhaps be admitted that there was something in it. But if a man were to say quite simply and unassumingly, that he was concerned for himself, lest perhaps he had no right to call himself a Christian, he would indeed not suffer persecution or be put to death, but he would be smothered in angry glances, and people would say: "How tiresome to make such a fuss about nothing at all; why can't he behave like the rest of us, who are all Christians? It is just as it is with F. F., who refuses to wear a hat on his head like others, but insists on dressing differently." And if he happened to be married, his wife would say to him: "Dear husband of mine, how can you get such notions into your head? How can you doubt that you are a Christian? Are you not a Dane, and does not the geography say that the Lutheran form of the Christian religion is the ruling religion in Denmark? For you are surely not a Jew, nor are you a Mohammedan; what then can you be if not a Christian? It is a thousand years since paganism was driven out of Denmark, so I know you are not a pagan. Do you not perform your duties at the office like a conscientious civil servant; are you not a good citizen of a Christian nation, a Lutheran Christian state? So then of course you must be a Christian."

*   *   *

The speculative philosopher, unless he is as objective as the wife of our civil servant, proposes to contemplate Christianity from the philosophical standpoint. It is a matter of indifference to him whether anyone accepts it or not; such anxieties are left to theologues and laymen—and also surely to those who really are Christians, and who are by no means indifferent as to whether they are Christians or not. The philosopher contemplates Christianity for the sake of interpenetrating it with his speculative thought; aye, with his genuinely speculative thought. But suppose this whole proceeding were a chimera, a sheer impossibility;

suppose that Christianity is subjectivity, an inner transformation, an actualization of inwardness, and that only two kinds of people can know anything about it: those who with an infinite passionate interest in an eternal happiness base this their happiness upon their believing relationship to Christianity, and those who with an opposite passion, but in passion, reject it—the happy and the unhappy lovers. Suppose that an objective indifference can therefore learn nothing at all. Only the like is understood by the like, and the old principle: *quidquid cognoscitur, per modum cognoscentis cognoscitur,* must be so expanded as to make room for a mode of knowing in which the knower fails to know anything at all, or has all his knowledge reduced to an illusion. In the case of a kind of observation where it is requisite that the observer should be in a specific condition, it naturally follows that if he is not in this condition, he will observe nothing. He may, of course, attempt to deceive by saying that he is in this condition without being so; but when fortunately he himself avers that he is not in this condition, he deceives nobody.

Now if Christianity is essentially something objective, it is necessary for the observer to be objective. But if Christianity is essentially subjectivity, it is a mistake for the observer to be objective. In every case where the object of knowledge is the very inwardness of the subjectivity of the individual, it is necessary for the knower to be in a corresponding condition. But the utmost tension of human subjectivity finds its expression in the infinite passionate interest in an eternal happiness. Even in the case of earthly love it is a necessary requirement for a would-be observer, that he should know the inwardness of love. But here the interest is not so great as it is in the case of an eternal happiness, because all love is affected by illusion, and hence has a quasi-objective aspect, which makes it possible to speak of something like an experience at second-hand. But when love is interpenetrated with a God-relationship, this imperfection of illusion disappears, together with the remaining semblance of objectivity; and now it holds true that one not in this condition can gain nothing by all his efforts to observe. In the infinite passionate interest for his eternal happiness, the subject is in a state of the utmost tension, in the very extremity of subjectivity, not indeed where there is no object, which is the imperfect and undialectical distinction, but where God is negatively present in the subject; whose mode of subjectivity becomes, by virtue of this interest, the form for an eternal happiness.

The speculative philosopher views Christianity as an historical phenomenon. But suppose Christianity is nothing of the kind. "How stupid," I think I hear someone say, "what an extraordinary hankering after originality to say such a thing, especially now, when philosophy has arrived at an understanding of the necessity of the historical." Aye, indeed, what is it not given philosophy to understand! But if a philosopher were to assert that he had understood the necessity of an historical phenomenon, I would ask him to give a moment's attention to the critical considerations that were quite simply presented in the *Fragments,* in the "Interlude" between Chapters IV and V. To this little essay I must for the present refer; I shall always be willing to make it the point of departure for further dialectical developments, whenever I am so fortunate as to have a philosopher before me, a human being, for I dare not argue with speculative philosophy.

And now this extraordinary hankering after originality! Let us consider an analogy. Take husband and wife: their marriage expresses itself clearly in terms of external fact, and constitutes a phenomenon in existence, just as Christianity has stamped its impress upon life on the larger stage of the world's history. But their wedded love is no historical phenomenon. The phenomenal is here in itself the insignificant, and it receives significance for husband and wife only through their love; but otherwise considered, i.e. objectively, the phenomenal is a deception. And so also with Christianity. Is this then so original? To be sure, over against the Hegelian principle, that the external is the internal and the internal the external, it is highly original. But it would be a case of still greater originality if the Hegelian axiom were not only admired by contemporaries, but also had retroactive power to abolish, in historical retrospect, the distinction between the visible and the invisible Church. The invisible Church is no historical phenomenon; it cannot be observed objectively at all, since it exists only in the subjectivity of the individuals. Alas, my originality does not seem to be so very great after all; in spite of all my hankering, of which however

I am not conscious, I say only what every schoolboy knows, though he may not be able to express himself quite so clearly. And this is a trait which the schoolboy shares with great philosophers, only that the schoolboy is still too immature, the great philosopher over-mature.

That the speculative point of view is objective I do not deny. On the contrary, and in order to give a further demonstration of this fact, I shall here again repeat the experiment of placing a subject who is in passion infinitely concerned for his eternal happiness, in relation to speculative philosophy; when it will become evident that the speculative point of view is objective, from the fact that the so interested subject becomes comical. He does not become comical because he is infinitely interested; on the other hand, everyone who is not infinitely and passionately interested, but tries nevertheless to make people believe that he has an interest in his eternal happiness, is a comic figure. No, the comical inheres precisely in the incommensurability between his interest and the speculative objectivity.

If the speculative philosopher is at the same time a believer, as is also affirmed, he must long ago have perceived that philosophy can never acquire the same significance for him as faith. It is precisely as a believer that he is infinitely interested in his eternal happiness, and it is in faith that he is assured of it. (It should be noted that the assurance is the sort of assurance that can be had in faith, i.e. not an assurance once for all, but a daily acquisition of the sure spirit of faith through the infinite personal passionate interest.) And he does not base his eternal happiness upon his philosophical speculations. Rather, he associates circumspectly with philosophy, lest it lure him away from the certainty of faith (which has in every moment the infinite dialectic of uncertainty present with it) so as to rest in an indifferent objective knowledge. This is the simple dialectical analysis of the situation. If, therefore, he says that he bases his eternal happiness on his speculation, he contradicts himself and becomes comical, because philosophy in its objectivity is wholly indifferent to his and my and your eternal happiness. An eternal happiness inheres precisely in the recessive self-feeling of the subject, acquired through his utmost exertion. And besides contradicting himself, such a philosopher lies, with respect to his pretensions to be a believer.

Or the speculative philosopher is not a believer. In this case, he is of course not comical, since he does not raise the question of his eternal happiness at all. The comical appears only when the subject with an infinite passionate interest tries to attach his eternal happiness to philosophical speculation. But the speculative philosopher does not pose the problem of which we speak; for precisely as a speculative philosopher he becomes too objective to concern himself about an eternal happiness.

Let me here say merely a word, in case any one misunderstands many of my expressions, to make it clear that it is he who wishes to misunderstand me, and that I am without responsibility. All honor to philosophy, all praise to everyone who brings a genuine devotion to its service. To deny the value of speculation (though one might wish that the money-changers in the forecourts of the temple could be banished as profane) would be, in my opinion, to prostitute oneself. It would be particularly stupid in one whose own energies are for the most part, and in proportion to aptitude and opportunity, consecrated to its service; especially stupid in one who admires the Greeks. For he must know that Aristotle, in treating of what happiness is, identifies the highest happiness with the joys of thought, recalling in this connection the blessed pastime of the eternal gods in speculation. And he must furthermore have some conception of, and respect for, the fearless enthusiasm of the philosophical scholar, his persistent devotion to the service of the Idea. But for the speculating philosopher the question of his personal eternal happiness cannot arise; precisely because his task consists in getting more and more away from himself so as to become objective, thus vanishing from himself and becoming what might be called the contemplative energy of philosophy itself. This sort of thing I am quite conversant with myself. But the blessed gods, those great prototypes for the speculative philosopher, were not concerned for their eternal happiness; and so the problem did not at all arise in paganism. But to treat Christianity in the same manner is simply to invite confusion. Since man is a synthesis of the temporal and the eternal, the happiness that the speculative philosopher may enjoy will be an illusion, in that he desires in time to be merely eternal. Herein lies the error of the speculative philosopher. Higher than this speculative happiness, therefore, is the infinite passionate interest in a personal eternal happiness. It is higher because it is truer, because it definitely expresses the synthesis.

So understood (and in a certain sense it would not need to be shown that the infinite interest in one's eternal happiness is higher, since the point is merely that it is what we here inquire about), the comical will readily become apparent in the emergence of the contradiction. The subject is in passion infinitely interested in his eternal happiness, and is now supposed to receive assistance from speculation, i.e. by himself philosophizing. But in order to philosophize he must proceed in precisely the opposite direction, giving himself up and losing himself in objectivity, thus vanishing from himself. The incommensurability thus confronting him will wholly prevent him from beginning, and will throw a comic illumination upon every assurance that he has gained anything in this manner. This is, from the opposite side, quite the same as what was said in the preceding about an observer's relationship to Christianity. Christianity does not lend itself to objective observation, precisely because it proposes to intensify subjectivity to the utmost; and when the subject has thus put himself in the right attitude, he cannot attach his eternal happiness to speculative philosophy.

This contradiction between the subject who is in passion infinitely interested, and philosophical speculation viewed as something that might assist him, I shall permit myself to illustrate by means of an image from the sensible world. In sawing wood it is important not to press down too hard on the saw; the lighter the pressure exerted by the sawyer, the better the saw operates. If a man were to press down with all his strength, he would no longer be able to saw at all. In the same way it is necessary for the philosopher to make himself objectively light; but everyone who is in passion infinitely interested in his eternal happiness makes himself subjectively as heavy as possible. Precisely for this reason he prevents himself from speculating. Now if Christianity requires this interest in the individual subject (which is the assumption, since this is the point on which the problem turns), it is easy to see that he cannot find what he seeks in speculation. This can also be expressed by saying that speculative philosophy does not permit the problem to arise at all; and it follows that all its pretense of answering the problem constitutes only a mystification.

* * *

Objectively we consider only the matter at issue, subjectively we have regard to the subject and his subjectivity; and behold, precisely this subjectivity is the matter at issue. This must constantly be borne in mind, namely, that the subjective problem is not something about an objective issue, but is the subjectivity itself. For since the problem in question poses a decision, and since all decisiveness, as shown above, inheres in subjectivity, it is essential that every trace of an objective issue should be eliminated. If any such trace remains, it is at once a sign that the subject seeks to shirk something of the pain and crisis of the decision; that is, he seeks to make the problem to some degree objective. If the Introduction still awaits the appearance of another work before bringing the matter up for judgment, if the System still lacks a paragraph, if the speaker has still another argument up his sleeve, it follows that the decision is postponed. Hence we do not here raise the question of the truth of Christianity in the sense that when this has been determined, the subject is assumed ready and willing to accept it. No, the question is as to the mode of the subject's acceptance; and it must be regarded as an illusion rooted in the demoralization which remains ignorant of the subjective nature of the decision, or as an evasion springing from the disingenuousness which seeks to shirk the decision by an objective mode of approach, wherein there can in all eternity be no decision, to assume that the transition from something objective to the subjective acceptance is a direct transition, following upon the objective deliberation as a matter of course. On the contrary, the subjective acceptance is precisely the decisive factor; and an objective acceptance of Christianity (*sit venia verbo*) is paganism or thoughtlessness.

Christianity proposes to endow the individual with an eternal happiness, a good which is not distributed wholesale, but only to one individual at a time. Though Christianity assumes that there inheres in the subjectivity of the individual, as being the potentiality of the appropriation of this good, the possibility for its acceptance, it does not assume that the subjectivity is immediately ready for such acceptance, or even has, without further ado, a real conception of the significance of such a good. The development or transformation of the individual's subjectivity, its infinite concentration in itself over against the conception of an eternal happiness, that highest good of the infinite—this constitutes the developed potentiality of the primary potentiality which subjectivity as such presents. In this way Christianity protests every form of objectivity; it desires that the subject should be infinitely concerned about himself. It is subjectivity that Christianity is concerned with, and it is only in subjectivity that its truth exists, if it exists at all; objectively, Christianity has absolutely no existence. If its truth happens to be in only a single subject, it exists in him alone; and there is greater Christian joy in heaven over this one individual than over universal history and the System, which as objective entities are incommensurable for that which is Christian.

*   *   *

It is now about four years ago that I got the notion of wanting to try my luck as an author. I remember it quite clearly; it was on a Sunday, yes, that's it, a Sunday afternoon. I was seated as usual, out-of-doors at the café in the Frederiksberg Garden, that wonderful garden which for the child was fairyland, where the King dwelt with his Queen, that delightful garden which for the youth was his happy diversion in the joyful merriment of the people, where now for the man of riper years there is such a homely feeling of sad exaltation above the world and all that is of the world, where even the envied glory of the royal dignity has faded to what it is indeed out there, a queen's remembrance of her deceased lord. There I sat as usual and smoked my cigar. Unfortunately, the only resemblance I have been able to discover between the beginning of my bit of philosophic effort and the miraculous beginning of that poetical hero is the fact that it was in a public resort. For the rest there is no resemblance whatever, and notwithstanding I am the author of the *Fragments,* I am so insignificant that I stand outside of literature, have not even contributed to increase literature on the subscription plan, nor can with truth affirm that I occupy an important place in it.

I had been a student for half a score of years. Although never lazy, all my activity nevertheless was like a glittering inactivity, a kind of occupation for which I still have a great partiality, and for which perhaps I even have a little genius. I read much, spent the remainder of the day idling and thinking, or thinking and idling, but that was all it came to; the earliest sproutings, of my productivity barely sufficed for my daily use and were consumed in their first greening. An inexplicable persuasive power constantly held me back, by strength as well as by artifice. This power was my indolence. It is not like the impetuous inspiration of love, nor like the strong prompting of enthusiasm, it is rather like a housekeeper who holds one back, with whom one is very well off, so well off that it never occurs to one to get married. So much at least is certain, that although I am not unacquainted with the comforts and conveniences of life, of all conveniences indolence is the most comfortable.

So there I sat and smoked my cigar until I lapsed into thought. Among other thoughts I remember these: "You are going on," I said to myself, "to become an old man, without being anything, and without really undertaking to do anything. On the other hand, wherever you look about you, in literature and in life, you see the celebrated names and figures, the precious and much heralded men who are coming into prominence and are much talked about, the many benefactors of the age who know how to benefit mankind by making life easier and easier, some by railways, others by omnibuses and steamboats, others by the telegraph, others by easily apprehended compendiums and short recitals of everything worth knowing, and finally the true benefactors of the age who make spiritual existence in virtue of thought easier and easier, yet more and more significant. And what are you doing?" Here my soliloquy was interrupted, for my cigar was smoked out and a new one had to be lit. So I smoked again, and then suddenly this thought flashed through my mind: "You must do something, but inasmuch as with your limited capacities it will be impossible to make anything easier than it has become, you must, with the same humanitarian enthusiasm as the others, undertake to make something harder." This notion pleased me immensely, and at the same time it flattered me to think that I, like the rest of them, would be loved and esteemed by the whole community. For when all combine in every way to make everything easier, there remains only one possible danger, namely, that the ease becomes so great that it becomes altogether too great; then there is only one want left, though it is not yet a felt want, when people will want difficulty. Out of love for mankind, and out of despair at my embarrassing situation, seeing that I had accomplished nothing and was unable to make anything easier than it had already been made, and moved by a genuine interest in those who make everything easy, I conceived it as my task to create difficulties everywhere. I was struck also with the strange reflection, whether it was not really my indolence I had to thank for the fact that this task became mine. For far from having found it, as Aladdin did the lamp, I must rather suppose that my indolence, by hindering me from intervening at an opportune time to make things easy, has forced upon me the only task that was left over.

* * *

If an existing individual were really able to transcend himself, the truth would be for him something final and complete; but where is the point at which he is outside himself? The I-am-I is a mathematical point which does not exist, and in so far there is nothing to prevent everyone from occupying this standpoint; the one will not be in the way of the other. It is only momentarily that the particular individual is able to realize existentially a unity of the infinite and the finite which transcends existence. This unity is realized in the moment of passion. Modern philosophy has tried anything and everything in the effort to help the individual to transcend himself objectively, which is a wholly impossible feat; existence exercises its restraining influence, and if philosophers nowadays had not become mere scribblers in the service of a fantastic thinking and its preoccupation, they would long ago have perceived that suicide was the only tolerable practical interpretation of its striving. But the scribbling modern philosophy holds passion in contempt; and yet passion is the culmination of existence for an existing individual—and we are all of us existing individuals. In passion the existing subject is rendered infinite in the eternity of the imaginative representation, and yet he is at the same time most definitely himself. The fantastic I-am-I is not an identity of the infinite and the finite, since neither the one nor the other is real; it is a fantastic rendezvous in the clouds, an unfruitful embrace, and the relationship of the individual self to this mirage is never indicated.

All essential knowledge relates to existence, or only such knowledge as has an essential relationship to existence is essential knowledge. All knowledge which does not inwardly relate itself to existence, in the reflection of inwardness, is essentially viewed, accidental knowledge; its degree and scope is essentially indifferent. That essential knowledge is essentially related to existence does not mean the above-mentioned identity which abstract thought postulates between thought and being; nor does it signify, objectively, that knowledge corresponds to something existent as its object. But it means that knowledge has a relationship to the knower, who is essentially an existing individual, and that for this reason all essential knowledge is essentially related to existence. Only ethical and ethico-religious knowledge has an essential relationship to the existence of the knower.

* * *

In an attempt to make clear the difference of way that exists between an objective and a subjective reflection, I shall now proceed to show how a subjective reflection makes its way inwardly in inwardness. Inwardness in an existing subject culminates in passion; corresponding to passion in the subject the truth becomes a paradox; and the fact that the truth becomes a paradox is rooted precisely in its having a relationship to an existing subject. Thus the one corresponds to the other. By forgetting that one is an existing subject, passion goes by the board and the truth is no longer a paradox; the knowing subject becomes a fantastic entity rather than a human being, and the truth becomes a fantastic object for the knowledge of this fantastic entity.

When the question of truth is raised in an objective manner, reflection is directed objectively to the truth, as an object to which the knower is related. Reflection is not focused upon the relationship, however, but upon the question of whether it is the truth to which the knower is related. If only the object to which he is related is the truth, the subject is accounted to be in the truth. When the question of the truth is raised subjectively, reflection is directed subjectively to the nature of the individual's relationship; if only the mode of this relationship is in the truth, the individual is in the truth even if he should happen to be thus related to what is not true. Let us take as an example the knowledge of God. Objectively, reflection is directed to the problem of whether this object is the true God; subjectively, reflection is directed to the question whether the individual is related to a something *in such a manner* that his relationship is in truth a God-relationship. On which side is the truth now to be found? Ah, may we not here resort to a mediation, and say: It is on neither side, but in the mediation of both? Excellently well said, provided we might have it explained how an existing individual manages to be in a state of mediation. For to be in a state of mediation is to be finished, while to exist is to become. Nor can an existing individual be in two places at the same time—he cannot be an identity of subject and object. When he is nearest to being in two places at the same time he is in passion; but passion is momentary, and passion is also the highest expression of subjectivity.

The existing individual who chooses to pursue the objective way enters upon the entire approximation-process by which it is proposed to bring God to light objectively. But this is in all eternity impossible, because God is a subject, and therefore exists only for subjectivity in inwardness. The existing individual who chooses the subjective way apprehends instantly the entire dialectical difficulty involved in having to use some time, perhaps a long time, in finding God objectively; and he feels this dialectical difficulty in all its painfulness, because every moment is wasted in which he does not have God.* That very instant he has God, not by virtue of any objective deliberation, but by virtue of the infinite passion of inwardness. The objective inquirer, on the other hand, is not embarrassed by such dialectical difficulties as are involved in devoting an entire period of investigation to finding God—since it is possible that the inquirer may die tomorrow; and if he lives he can scarcely regard God as something to be taken along if convenient, since God is precisely that which one takes *a tout prix,* which in the understanding of passion constitutes the true inward relationship to God.

It is at this point, so difficult dialectically, that the way swings off for everyone who knows what it means to think, and to think existentially; which is something very different from sitting at a desk and writing about what one has never done, something very different from writing *de omnibus dubitandum* and at the same time being as credulous existentially as the most sensuous of men. Here is where the way swings off, and the change is marked by the fact that while objective knowledge rambles comfortably on by way of the long road of approximation without being impelled by the urge of passion, subjective knowledge counts every delay a deadly peril, and the decision so infinitely important and so instantly pressing that it is as if the opportunity had already passed.

Now when the problem is to reckon up on which side there is most truth, whether on the side of one who seeks the true God objectively, and pursues the approximate truth of the God-idea; or on the side of one who, driven by the infinite passion of his need of God, feels an infinite concern for his own relationship to God in truth (and to be at one and the same time on both sides equally, is as we have noted not possible for an

* In this manner God certainly becomes a postulate, but not in the otiose manner in which this word is commonly understood. It becomes clear rather that the only way in which an existing individual comes into relation with God, is when the dialectical contradiction brings his passion to the point of despair, and helps him to embrace God with the "category of despair" (faith). Then the postulate is so far from being arbitrary that it is precisely a life-necessity. It is then not so much that God is a postulate, as that the existing individual's postulation of God is a necessity.

existing individual, but is merely the happy delusion of an imaginary I-am-I) : the answer cannot be in doubt for anyone who has not been demoralized with the aid of science. If one who lives in the midst of Christendom goes up to the house of God, the house of the true God, with the true conception of God in his knowledge, and prays, but prays in a false spirit; and one who lives in an idolatrous community prays with the entire passion of the infinite, although his eyes rest upon the image of an idol: where is there most truth? The one prays in truth to God though he worships an idol; the other prays falsely to the true God, and hence worships in fact an idol.

When one man investigates objectively the problem of immortality, and another embraces an uncertainty with the passion of the infinite: where is there most truth, and who has the greater certainty? The one has entered upon a never-ending approximation, for the certainty of immortality lies precisely in the subjectivity of the individual; the other is immortal, and fights for his immortality by struggling with the uncertainty. Let us consider Socrates. Nowadays everyone dabbles in a few proofs; some have several such proofs, others fewer. But Socrates! He puts the question objectively in a problematic manner: *if* there is an immortality. He must therefore be accounted a doubter in comparison with one of our modern thinkers with the three proofs? By no means. On this "if" he risks his entire life, he has the courage to meet death, and he has with the passion of the infinite so determined the pattern of his life that it must be found acceptable—*if* there is an immortality. Is any better proof capable of being given for the immortality of the soul? But those who have the three proofs do not at all determine their lives in conformity therewith; if there is an immortality it must feel disgust over their manner of life: can any better refutation be given of the three proofs? The bit of uncertainty that Socrates had, helped him because he himself contributed the passion of the infinite; the three proofs that the others have do not profit them at all, because they are dead to spirit and enthusiasm, and their three proofs, in lieu of proving anything else, prove just this. A young girl may enjoy all the sweetness of love on the basis of what is merely a weak hope that she is beloved, because she rests everything on this weak hope;

but many a wedded matron more than once subjected to the strongest expressions of love, has in so far indeed had proofs, but strangely enough has not enjoyed *quod erat demonstrandum.* The Socratic ignorance, which Socrates held fast with the entire passion of his inwardness, was thus an expression for the principle that the eternal truth is related to an existing individual, and that this truth must therefore be a paradox for him as long as he exists; and yet it is possible that there was more truth in the Socratic ignorance as it was in him, than in the entire objective truth of the System, which flirts with what the times demand and accommodates itself to *Privatdocents.*

* * *

When subjectivity is the truth, the conceptual determination of the truth must include an expression for the antithesis to objectivity, a memento of the fork in the road where the way swings off; this expression will at the same time serve as an indication of the tension of the subjective inwardness. Here is such a definition of truth: *An objective uncertainty held fast in an appropriation-process of the most passionate inwardness is the truth,* the highest truth attainable for an *existing* individual. At the point where the way swings off (and where this is cannot be specified objectively, since it is a matter of subjectivity), there objective knowledge is placed in abeyance. Thus the subject merely has, objectively, the uncertainty; but it is this which precisely increases the tension of that infinite passion which constitutes his inwardness. The truth is precisely the venture which chooses an objective uncertainty with the passion of the infinite. I contemplate the order of nature in the hope of finding God, and I see omnipotence and wisdom; but I also see much else that disturbs my mind and excites anxiety. The sum of all this is an objective uncertainty. But it is for this very reason that the inwardness becomes as intense as it is, for it embraces this objective uncertainty with the entire passion of the infinite. In the case of a mathematical proposition the objectivity is given, but for this reason the truth of such a proposition is also an indifferent truth.

But the above definition of truth is an equivalent expression of faith. Without risk there is no faith. Faith is precisely the contradiction between the infinite passion of the individual's inwardness and the objective uncertainty. If I am capable of grasping God objectively, I do not believe, but precisely because I cannot do this I must believe. If I wish to preserve myself in faith I must constantly be intent upon holding fast the objective uncertainty, so as to remain out upon the deep, over seventy thousand fathoms of water, still preserving my faith.

In the principle that subjectivity, inwardness, is the truth, there is comprehended the Socratic wisdom, whose everlasting merit it was to have become aware of the essential significance of existence, of the fact that the knower is an existing individual. For this reason Socrates was in the truth by virtue of his ignorance, in the highest sense in which this was possible within paganism.

* * *

Christianity has declared itself to be the eternal essential truth which has come into being in time. It has proclaimed itself as the *Paradox,* and it has required of the individual the inwardness of faith in relation to that which stamps itself as an offense to the Jews and a folly to the Greeks—and an absurdity to the understanding. It is impossible more strongly to express the fact that subjectivity is truth, and that the objectivity is repellent, repellent even by virtue of its absurdity. And indeed it would seem very strange that Christianity should have come into the world merely to receive an explanation; as if it had been somewhat bewildered about itself, and hence entered the world to consult that wise man, the speculative philosopher, who can come to its assistance by furnishing the explanation.

* * *

That God has existed in human form, has been born, grown up, and so forth, is surely the paradox *sensu strictissimo,* the absolute paradox. As such it cannot relate itself to a relative difference between men. A relative paradox relates itself to the relative difference between more or less cleverness and brains;

but the absolute paradox, just because it is absolute, can be relevant only to the absolute difference that distinguishes man from God, and has nothing to do with the relative wrangling between man and man with respect to the fact that one man has a little more brains than another. But the absolute difference between God and man consists precisely in this, that man is a particular existing being (which is just as much true of the most gifted human being as it is of the most stupid), whose essential task cannot be to think *sub specie aeterni,* since as long as he exists he is, though eternal, essentially an existing individual, whose essential task it is to concentrate upon inwardness in existing; while God is infinite and eternal. As soon as I make the understanding of the paradox commensurable for the difference between more or less of intellectual talent (a difference which cannot take us beyond being human, unless a man were to become so gifted that he was not merely a man but also God), my words show *eo ipso* that what I have understood is not the absolute paradox but a relative one, for in connection with the absolute paradox the only understanding possible is that it cannot be understood. "But if such is the case, speculative philosophy cannot get hold of it at all." "Quite right, this is precisely what the paradox says; it merely thrusts the understanding away in the interests of inwardness in existing." This may possibly have its ground in the circumstance that there is objectively no truth for existing beings, but only approximations; while subjectively the truth exists for them in inwardness, because the decisiveness of the truth is rooted in the subjectivity of the individual.

* * *

CHRISTIAN NURTURE

HORACE BUSHNELL

(1802-1876)

Christian Nurture, published in 1847, some ten years in preparation, was Horace Bushnell's most important literary work. Its thesis rested on the proposition "that the child is to grow up a Christian, and never know himself as being otherwise." This simple affirmation was a bomb-shell which set off an explosion that rocked the very foundation stones of the New England theology of his day.

Bushnell appealed to the ordinary laws of social relations as over against the prevailing view that Christian experience was something non-natural. Revivalism and an orthodox conversion-experience were attacked. Current views held that a Christian individual must pass through a narrow gate: a feeling of personal sin and the corruptness of human nature, a racial as well as an individual guilt. He must feel this burden by himself, experience a theology whether or not it was natural to him.

A child, Bushnell held, need not grow up to a climax of sin-guilt but to natural renewals of spirit under the environmental osmosis of parental cultivation. All society is organic and the child is included. The nurture of the soul begins with the nurture of the body and the very earliest years constitute the time of deepest impressions.

The book met with strong and bitter resistance. Nevertheless, its influence continued in a steady, quiet and increasing growth, crowding out the harsh features of the inherited New England theology.

Connecticut born, Horace Bushnell grew up in a home where

religion was real but unobtrusive. His *Christian Nurture* was undergirded by the life he knew in his formative years—a life of good sense. Yale educated, both in law and theology, he became a tutor at his alma mater and then minister and celebrated preacher in North Church in Hartford.

Coleridge's *Aids to Reflection* cast a spell upon the core of his thinking and remained, next to the Scriptures, the strongest influence on the pattern of his theological outlook. In Protestant theology he was an emancipator, pointing to new directions of interpretation. In doctrinal matters he touched critically upon such sensitive topics as the Trinity, atonement and miracles. Experience and nature were for him the foundation for realistic religious beliefs, more trustworthy than the niceties of formulae so many of which had become for him senile and sterile.

Editor

CHRISTIAN NURTURE

*   *   *

WHAT IS the true idea of Christian education?—I answer in the following proposition, which it will be the aim of my argument to establish, viz:

THAT THE CHILD IS TO GROW UP A CHRISTIAN. In other words, the aim, effort and expectation should be, not, as is commonly assumed, that the child is to grow up in sin, to be converted after he comes to a mature age; but that he is to open on the world as one that is spiritually renewed, not remembering the time when he went through a technical experience, but seeming rather to have loved what is good from his earliest years. I do not affirm that every child may, in fact and without exception, be so trained that he certainly will grow up a Christian. The qualifications it may be necessary to add, will be given in another place, where they can be stated more intelligibly.

This doctrine is not a novelty, now rashly and for the first time propounded, as some of you may be tempted to suppose. I shall show you, before I have done with the argument, that it is as old as the Christian church, and prevails extensively at the present day, in other parts of the world. Neither let your own experience raise a prejudice against it. If you have endeavored to realize the very truth I here affirm, but find that your children do not exhibit the character you have looked for; if they seem to be intractable to religious influences, and sometimes to display an apparent aversion to the very subject of religion itself, you are not, of course, to conclude that the doctrine I here maintain is untrue or impracticable. You may be unreasonable in your expectations of your children. Possibly, there may be seeds of holy principle in them, which you do not discover. A child acts out his present feelings, the feelings of the moment, without qualification or disguise. And how, many times, would all you appear, if you were to do the same? Will you expect of them to be better and more constant and consistent than yourselves; or will you rather expect them to be children, human children still, living a mixed life, trying out the good and evil of the world, and preparing, as older Christians do, when they have taken a lesson of sorrow and emptiness, to turn again to the true good? Perhaps they will go through a rough mental struggle, at some future day, and seem, to others and to themselves, there to have entered on a Christian life. And yet it may be true that there was still some root of right principle established in their childhood, which is here only quickened and developed, as when Christians of a mature age are revived in their piety, after a period of spiritual lethargy; for it is conceivable that regenerate character may exist, long before it is fully and formally developed. But suppose there is really no trace or seed of holy principle in your children, has there been no fault of piety and constancy in your church, no want of Christian sensibility and love to God, no carnal spirit visible to them and to all, and imparting its noxious and poisonous quality to the Christian atmosphere in which they have had their nurture? For it is not for you alone to realize all that is included in the idea of Christian education. It belongs to the church of God, according to the degree of its social power over you and in you and around your children, to bear a part of the responsibility with you. Then, again, have you nothing to blame in yourselves, no lack of faithfulness, no indiscretion of manner, or of temper, no mistake of duty, which, with a better and more cultivated piety, you would have been able to avoid? Have you been so nearly even with your privilege and duty, that you can find no relief but to lay some charge upon God, or comfort yourselves in the conviction that he has appointed the failure you deplore? When God marks out a plan of education, or sets up an aim to direct its efforts, you will see, at once, that he could not base it on a want of piety in you, or on any imperfections that flow from a want of piety. It must be a plan measured by Himself and the fullness of his own gracious intentions. Besides, you must not assume that we, in this age, are the best Christians that ever lived, or most likely to produce all the fruits of piety. An assumption so pleasing to our vanity is more easily made than verified, but vanity is the weakest as it is the cheapest of all arguments. We have some good points, in which we compare favorably with other Christians, and Christians of other times, but our style of piety is sadly deficient, in many respects, and that to such a degree that we have little cause for self-congratulation. With all our activity and boldness of movement, there is a certain hardness and rudeness, a want of sensibility to things that do not lie in action, which cannot be too much deplored, or too soon rectified. We hold a piety of conquest rather than of love. A kind of public piety that is strenuous and fiery on great occasions, but wants the beauty of holiness, wants constancy, singleness of aim, loveliness, purity, richness, flamelessness, and—if I may add another term not so immediately religious, but one that carries, by association, a thousand religious qualities—wants domesticity of character; wants them, I mean, not as compared with the perfect standard of Christ, but as compared with other examples of piety that have been given in former times, and others that are given now.

For some reason, we do not make a Christian atmosphere about us,—do not produce the conviction that we are living unto God. There is a marvelous want of savor in our piety. It is a flower of autumn, colored as highly as it need be to the eye, but destitute of fragrance. It is too much to hope that, with such an instrument, we can fulfill the true idea of Christian education. Any such hope were even presumptuous. At the same time, there is no so ready way of removing the deficiencies just described, as to recall our churches to their duties in domestic life; those humble, daily, hourly duties, where the spirit we breathe shall be a perpetual element of power and love bathing the life of childhood.

*   *   *

There is then, as the subject appears to us—

1. No absurdity in supposing that children are to grow up in Christ. On the other hand, if there is no absurdity, there is a very clear moral incongruity in setting up a contrary supposition, to be the aim of a system of Christian education. There could not be a worse or more baleful implication given to a child, than that he is to reject God and all holy principle, till he has come to a mature age. What authority have you from the Scriptures to tell your child, or, by any sign, to show him that you do not expect him truly to love and obey God, till after he has spent whole years in hatred and wrong? What authority to make him feel that he is the most unprivileged of all human beings, capable of sin, but incapable of repentance; old enough to resist all good, but too young to receive any good whatever? It is reasonable to suppose that you have some express authority for a lesson so manifestly cruel and hurtful, else you would shudder to give it. I ask you for the chapter and verse, out of which it is derived. Meantime, wherein would it be less incongruous for you to teach your child that he is to lie and steal, and go the whole round of the vices and then, after he comes to mature age, reform his conduct by the rules of virtue? Perhaps you do not give your child to expect that he is to grow up in sin, you only expect that he will yourself. That is scarcely better, for that which is your expectation, will assuredly be his; and what is more, any attempt to maintain a discipline at war with your own secret expectations, will only make a hollow and worthless figment of that which should be an open earnest reality. You will never practically aim at what you practically despair of, and if you do not practically aim to unite your child to God, you will aim at something less, that is, something unchristian, wrong, sinful.

But my child is a sinner, you will say, and how can I expect him to begin a right life, until God gives him a new heart? This is the common way of speaking, and I state the objection in its own phraseology, that it may recognize itself. Who then has told you that a child cannot have the new heart of which you speak? Whence do you learn that if you live the life of Christ, before him and with him, the law of the Spirit of Life may not be such as to include and quicken him also? And why should it be thought incredible that there should be some really good principle awakened in the mind of the child? For this is all that is implied in a Christian state. The Christian is one who has simply *begun* to love what is good for its own sake, and why should it be thought impossible for a child to have this love begotten in him? Take any scheme of depravity you please, there is yet nothing in it to forbid the possibility that a child should be led, in his first moral act, to cleave unto what is good and right, any more than in the first of his twentieth year. He is, in that case, only a child converted to good, leading a mixed life as all Christians do. The good in him goes into combat with the evil, and holds a qualified sovereignty. And why may not this internal conflict of goodness cover the whole life from its dawn, as well as any part of it? And what more appropriate to the doctrine of spiritual influence itself, than to believe that as the Spirit of Jehovah fills all the worlds of matter, and holds a presence of power and government in all objects, so all human souls, the infantile as well as the adult, have a nurture of the Spirit appropriate to their age and their wants? What opinion is more essentially monstrous, in fact, than that which regards the Holy Spirit as having no agency in the immature souls of children, who are growing up helpless and unconscious into the perils of time?

2. It is to be expected that Christian education will radically differ from that which is not Christian. Now it is the very character and mark of all unchristian education, that it brings up the child for future conversion. No effort is made, save to form a habit of outward virtue, and, if God please to convert the family to something higher and better, after they come to the age of maturity, it is well. Is then Christian education, or the nurture of the Lord, no way different from this? Or is it rather to be supposed that it will have a higher aim and a more sacred character?

And, since it is the distinction of Christian parents, that they are themselves in the nurture of the Lord, since Christ and the Divine Love, communicated through him, are become the food of their life, what will they so naturally seek as to have their children partakers with them, heirs together with them in the grace of life? I am well aware of the common impression that Christian education is sufficiently distinguished by the endeavor of Christian parents to teach their children the lessons of scripture history, and the doctrines or dogmas of scripture theology. But if they are given to understand, at the same time, that these lessons can be expected to produce no fruit till they are come to a mature age, that they are to grow up still in the same character as other children do, who have no such instruction, what is this but to enforce the practical rejection of all the lessons taught them? And which, in truth, is better for them, to grow up in sin under scripture light, with a heart hardened by so many religious lessons; or to grow up in sin unvexed and unannoyed, by the wearisome drill of lectures that only discourage all practical benefit? Which is better, to be piously brought up to sin, or to be allowed quietly to vegetate in it? These are questions that I know not how to decide, but the doubt in which they leave us, will at least suffice to show that Christian education has, in this view, no such eminent advantages over that which is unchristian, as to raise any broad and dignified distinction between them. We certainly know that much of what is called Christian nurture, only serves to make the subject of religion odious, and that, as nearly as we can discover, in exact proportion to the amount of religious teaching received. And no small share of the difficulty to be overcome afterwards, in the struggle of conversion, is created in just this way. On the other hand, you will hear, for example, of cases like the following. A young man, correctly but not religiously brought up, light and gay in his manners and thoughtless hitherto in regard to anything of a serious nature, happens accidentally one Sunday, while his friends are gone to ride, to take down a book on the evidences of Christianity. His eye, floating over one of the pages, becomes fixed, and he is surprised to find his feelings flowing out strangely into its holy truths. He is conscious of no struggle of hostility, but a new joy dawns in his being. Henceforth, to the end of a long and useful life, he is a Christian man. The love into which he was surprised continues to flow, and he is remarkable, in the churches, all his life long, as one of the most beautiful, healthful and dignified examples of Christian piety. Now a very little mis-education, called Christian, discouraging the piety it teaches, and making enmity itself a necessary ingredient in the struggle of conversion, conversion no reality without a struggle, might have sufficed to close the mind of this man against every thought of religion to the end of life. Such facts (for the case above given is a fact and not a fancy) compel us to suspect the value of much that is called Christian education. They suggest the possibility also that Christian piety should begin in other and milder forms of exercise, than those which commonly distinguish the conversion of adults —that Christ himself, by that renewing Spirit who can sanctify from the womb, should be practically infused into the childish mind; in other words, that the house, having a domestic Spirit of grace dwelling in it, should become the church of childhood, the table and hearth a holy rite, and life an element of saving power. Something is wanted that is better than teaching, something that transcends mere effort and will-work—the loveliness of a good life, the repose of faith, the confidence of righteous expectation, the sacred and cheerful liberty of the Spirit—all glowing about the young soul, as a warm and genial nurture, and forming in it, by methods that are silent and imperceptible, a spirit of duty and religious obedience to God. This only is Christian nurture, the nurture of the Lord.

3. It is a fact that all Christian parents would like to see their children grow up in piety; and, the better Christians they are, the more earnestly they desire it; and, the more lovely and constant the Christian spirit they manifest, the more likely is it, in general, that their children will early display the Christian character. This is current opinion. But why should a Christian parent, the deeper his piety and the more closely he is drawn to God, be led to desire, the more earnestly, what, in God's view, is even absurd or impossible? And, if it be generally seen that the children of such are the more likely to become Christians early, what forbids the hope that, if they were better Christians still, living a more single and Christ-like life, and more cultivated in their views of family nurture, they might not see their

children grow up in piety towards God. Or if they may not always see it as clearly as they desire, might they not still be able to implant some holy principle, which shall be the seed of a Christian character in their children, though not developed fully and visibly till a later period in life?

4. Assuming the corruption of human nature, when should we think it wisest to undertake or expect a remedy? When evil is young and pliant to good, or when it is confirmed by years of sinful habit? And when, in fact, is the human heart found to be so ductile to the motives of religion, as in the simple, ingenuous age of childhood? How easy it is then, as compared with the stubbornness of adult years, to make all wrong seem odious, all good lovely and desirable. If not discouraged by some ill-temper, which bruises all the gentle sensibilities, or repelled by some technical view of religious character, which puts it beyond his age, how ready is the child to be taken by good, as it were, beforehand, and yield his ductile nature to the truth and Spirit of God, and to a fixed prejudice against all that God forbids. He cannot understand, of course, in the earliest stage of childhood, the philosophy of religion as a renovated experience, and that is not the form of the first lessons he is to receive. He is not to be told that he must have a new heart and exercise faith in Christ's atonement. We are to understand, that a right spirit may be virtually exercised in children, when, as yet, it is not intellectually received, or as a form of doctrine. Thus if they are put upon an effort to be good, connecting the fact that God desires it and will help them in the endeavor, that is all which, in a very early age, they can receive, and that includes everything—repentance, love, duty, dependence, faith. Nay, the operative truth necessary to a new life, may possibly be communicated through and from the parent, being revealed in his looks, manners and ways of life, before they are of an age to understand the teaching of words; for the Christian scheme, the gospel, is really wrapped up in the life of every Christian parent and beams out from him as a living epistle, before it escapes from the lips, or is taught in words. And the Spirit of truth may as well make this living truth effectual, as the preaching of the gospel itself. Never is it too early for good to be communicated.

Infancy and childhood are the ages most pliant to good. And who can think it necessary that the plastic nature of childhood must first be hardened into stone, and stiffened into enmity towards God and all duty, before it can become a candidate for Christian character! There could not be a more unnecessary mistake, and it is as unnatural and pernicious, I fear, as it is unnecessary.

There are many who assume the radical goodness of human nature, and the work of Christian education is, in their view, only to educate, or educe the good that is in us. Let no one be disturbed by the suspicion of a coincidence between what I have here said and such a theory. The natural pravity of man is plainly asserted in the scriptures, and, if it were not, the familiar laws of physiology would require us to believe, what amounts to the same thing. And if neither scripture nor physiology taught us the doctrine, if the child was born as clear of natural prejudice or damage, as Adam before his sin, spiritual education, or, what is the same, probation, that which trains a being for a stable, intelligent virtue hereafter, would still involve an experiment of evil, therefore a fall and bondage under the laws of evil; so that, view the matter as we will, there is no unreasonable assumption, none so wide of all just philosophy, as that which proposes to form a child to virtue, by simply educing or drawing out what is in him. The growth of Christian virtue is no vegetable process, no mere onward development. It involves a struggle with evil, a fall and rescue. The soul becomes established in holy virtue, as a free exercise, only as it is passed round the corner of fall and redemption, ascending thus unto God through a double experience, in which it learns the bitterness of evil and the worth of good, fighting its way out of one and achieving the other as a victory. The child, therefore, may as well begin life under a law of hereditary damage, as to plunge himself into evil by his own experiment, which he will as naturally do from the simple impulse of curiosity, or the instinct of knowledge, as from any noxious quality in his mold derived by descent. For it is not sin which he derives from his parents; at least not sin in any sense which imports blame, but only some prejudice to the perfect harmony of his mold, some kind of pravity or obliquity which inclines him to evil. These suggestions are offered, not as necessary to be received in every particular, but simply to show that the scheme of education proposed, is not to be identified with another, which assumes the radical goodness of human nature, and according to which, if it be true, Christian education is insignificant.

5. It is implied in all our religious philosophy, that if a child ever does any thing in a right spirit, ever loves any thing because it is good and right, it involves the dawn of a new life. This we cannot deny or doubt, without bringing in question our whole scheme of doctrine. Is it then incredible that some really good feeling should be called into exercise in a child? In all the discipline of the house, quickened as it should be by the Spirit of God, is it true that he can never once be brought to submit to parental authority lovingly and because it is right? Must we even hold the absurdity of the scripture counsel— "Children, obey your parents in the Lord, for this is right"? When we speak thus of a love to what is right and good, we must of course discriminate between the mere excitement of a natural sensibility to pleasure in the contemplation of what is good, (of which the worst minds are more or less capable) and a practical subordination of the soul to its power, a practical embrace of its law. The child must not only be touched with some gentle emotions towards what is right, but he must love it with a fixed love, love it for the sake of its principle, receive it as a vital and formative power. Nor is there any age, which offers itself to God's truth and love, and to that quickening spirit whence all good proceeds, with so much of ductile feeling and susceptibilities so tender. The child is under parental authority too for the very purpose, it would seem, of having the otherwise abstract principle of all duty impersonated in his parents and thus brought home to his practical embrace; so that, learning to obey his parents in the Lord because it is right, he may thus receive, before he can receive it intellectually, the principle of all piety and holy obedience. And when he is brought to exercise a spirit of true and loving submission to the good law of his parents, what will you see, many times, but

a look of childish joy and a happy sweetness of manner and a ready delight in authority, as like to all the demonstrations of Christian experience, as any thing childish can be to what is mature?

6. Children have been so trained as never to remember the time when they began to be religious. Baxter was, at one time, greatly troubled concerning himself, because he could recollect no time, when there was a gracious change in his character. But he discovered, at length, that "education is as properly a means of grace as preaching," and thus found a sweeter comfort in his love to God, that he learned to love him so early. The European churches, generally, regard Christian piety more as a habit of life, formed under the training of childhood, and less as a marked spiritual change in experience. In Germany, for example, the church includes all the people, and it is remarkable that, under a scheme so loose, and with so much of pernicious error taught in the pulpit, there is yet so much of deep religious feeling, so much of lovely and simple character, and a savor of Christian piety so generally prevalent in the community. So true is this, that the German people are every day spoken of as a people religious by nature; no other way being observed of accounting for the strong religious bent they manifest. Whereas it is due, beyond any reasonable question, to the fact that children are placed under a form of treatment which expects them to be religious, and are not discouraged by the demand of an experience above their years. Again, the Moravian Brethren, it is agreed by all, give as ripe and graceful an exhibition of piety, as any body of Christians living on the earth, and it is the radical distinction of their system that it rests its power on Christian education. They make their churches schools of holy nurture to childhood, and expect their children to grow up there, as plants in the house of the Lord. Accordingly it is affirmed that not one in ten of the members of that church, recollects any time, when he began to be religious. Is it then incredible that what has been can be? Would it not be wiser and more modest, when facts are against us, to admit that there is certainly some bad error, either in our life, or in our doctrine, or in both, which it becomes us to amend?

Once more, if we narrowly examine the relation of parent and child, we shall not fail to discover something like a law of organic connection,[1] as regards character, subsisting between them. Such a connection as makes it easy to believe, and natural to expect that the faith of the one will be propagated in the other. Perhaps I should rather say, such a connection as induces the conviction that the character of one is actually included in that of the other, as a seed is formed in the capsule; and being there matured, by a nutriment derived from the stem, is gradually separated from it. It is a singular fact, that many believe substantially the same thing, in regard to evil character, but have no thought of any such possibility in regard to good. There has been much speculation, of late, as to whether a child is born in depravity, or whether the depraved character is superinduced afterwards. But, like many other great questions, it determines much less than is commonly supposed; for, according to the most proper view of the subject, a child is really not born till he emerges from the infantile state, and never before that time can be said to receive a separate and properly individual nature. The declaration of scripture, and the laws of physiology, I have already intimated, compel the belief that a child's nature is somehow depravated by descent from parents, who are under the corrupting effects of sin. But this, taken as a question relating to the mere *punctum temporis,* or precise point of birth, is not a question of any so grave import, as is generally supposed; for the child, after birth, is still within the matrix of the parental life, and will be more or less, for many years. And the parental life will be flowing into him all that time, just as naturally, and by a law as truly organic, as when the sap of the trunk flows into a limb. We must not govern our thoughts, in

1. Some persons have blamed the use here made of the term "organic," as a singularity of mine. So far from that, it is a term in common philosophic use in connection with all the great questions of government and society. The days of the "social compact" theory, for example, are gone by, and it is now held by almost all the late writers, that we naturally exist as organic bodies, just as we do as individuals, and that civil government is born with us, in virtue of our organic unity in bodies or States—that the State must legislate for itself in some way, just as the conscience legislates for the individual. Government is, in this view, the organic conscience of the State—no matter what may be the form, or who presides.

such a matter, by our eyes; and because the physical separation has taken place, conclude that no organic relation remains. Even the physical being of the child is dependent still for nutrition on organic processes not in itself. Meantime, the mental being and character have scarcely begun to have a proper individual life. Will, in connection with conscience, is the basis of personality, or individuality, and these exist as yet only in their rudimental type, as when the form of a seed is beginning to be unfolded at the root of a flower. At first, the child is held as a mere passive lump in the arms, and he opens into conscious life under the soul of the parent streaming into his eyes and ears, through the manners and tones of the nursery. The kind and degree of passivity are gradually changed as life advances. A little farther on it is observed that a smile wakens a smile—any kind of sentiment or passion, playing in the face of the parent, wakens a responsive sentiment or passion. Irritation irritates, a frown withers, love expands a look congenial to itself, and why not holy love? Next the ear is opened to the understanding of words, but what words the child shall hear, he cannot choose, and has as little capacity to select the sentiments that are poured into his soul. Farther on, the parents begin to govern him by appeals to will, expressed in commands, and whatever their requirement may be, he can as little withstand it, as the violet can cool the scorching sun, or the tattered leaf can tame the hurricane. Next they appoint his school, choose his books, regulate his company, decide what form of religion, and what religious opinions he shall be taught, by taking him to a church of their own selection. In all this, they infringe upon no right of the child, they only fulfill an office which belongs to them. Their will and character are designed to be the matrix of the child's will and character. Meantime he approaches more and more closely, and by a gradual process, to the proper rank and responsibility of an individual creature, during all which process of separation, he is having their exercises and ways translated into him. Then, at last, he comes forth to act his part in such color of evil, (and why not of good?) as he has derived from them. The tendency of all our modern speculations is to an extreme individualism, and we carry our doctrines of free will so far as to make little or nothing of organic laws; not observing that character may be, to a great extent, only the free development of exercises previously wrought in us, or extended to us, when other wills had us within their sphere. All the Baptist theories of religion are based in this error. They assume as a first truth, that no such thing is possible as an organic connection of character, an assumption which is plainly refuted by what we see with our eyes, and, as I shall by and by show, by the declarations of scripture. We have much to say also, in common with the Baptists, about the beginning of moral agency, and we seem to fancy that there is some definite moment when a child becomes a moral agent, passing out of a condition where he is a moral nullity, and where no moral agency touches his being. Whereas he is rather to be regarded at the first, as lying within the moral agency of the parent and passing out by degrees through a course of mixed agency, to a proper independency and self-possession. The supposition that he becomes, at some certain moment, a complete moral agent, which a moment before he was not, is clumsy and has no agreement with observation. The separation is gradual. He is never, at any moment after birth, to be regarded as perfectly beyond the sphere of good and bad exercises; for the parent exercises himself in the child, playing his emotions and sentiments, and working a character in him, by virtue of an organic power. And this is the very idea of Christian education, that it begins with nurture or cultivation. And the intention is that the Christian life and spirit of the parents shall flow into the mind of the child, to blend with his incipient and half-formed exercises; that they shall thus beget their own good within him, their thoughts, opinions, faith and love, which are to become a little more, and yet a little more, his own separate exercise, but still the same in character. The contrary assumption, that virtue must be the product of separate and absolutely independent choice, is pure assumption. As regards the measure of personal merit and demerit, it is doubtless true that every subject of God is to be responsible only for what is his own. But virtue still is rather a *state* of being than an act or series of acts; and if we look at the causes which induce or prepare such a state, the will of the person himself may have a part among those causes more or less important and it works no absurdity to suppose that one may be even prepared to such a state, by causes prior to his own will; so that, when he sets off to act for himself, his struggle and duty may be rather to sustain and perfect the state begun, than to produce a new one. Certain it is that we are never, at any age, so independent as to be wholly out of the reach of organic laws which affect our character. All society is organic—the church, the state, the school, the family,—and there is a spirit in each of these organisms, peculiar to itself, and more or less hostile, more or less favorable to religious character, and to some extent, at least, sovereign over the individual man. A very great share of the power in what is called a revival of religion, is organic power; nor is it any the less divine on that account. The child is only more within the power of organic laws than we all are. We possess only a mixed individuality all our life long. A pure, separate, individual man, living *wholly* within, and from himself, is a mere fiction. No such person ever existed, or ever can. I need not say that this view of an organic connection of character subsisting between parent and child, lays a basis for notions of Christian education, far different from those which now prevail, under the cover of a merely fictitious and mischievous individualism.

Perhaps it may be necessary to add, that, in the strong language I have used concerning the organic connection of character between the parent and the child, it is not designed to assert a power in the parent to renew the child, or that the child can be renewed by any agency of the Spirit less immediate, than that which renews the parent himself. When a germ is formed on the stem of any plant, the formative instinct of the plant may be said in one view to produce it; but the same solar heat which quickens the plant, must quicken also the germ and sustain the internal action of growth, by a common presence in both. So if there be an organic power of character in the parent, such as that of which I have spoken, it is not a complete power in itself, but only such a power as demands the realizing presence of the Spirit of God, both in the parent and the child, to give it effect. As Paul said, "I have begotten you through the gospel," so may we say of the parent, who having a living gospel enveloped in his life, brings it into organic connection with the soul of childhood. But the declaration excludes the necessity of a divine influence, not more in one case than in the other.

Such are some of the considerations that offer themselves, viewing our subject on the human side, or as it appears in the light of human evidence—all concurring to produce the conviction, that it is the only true idea of Christian education, that the child is to grow up in the life of the parent, and be a Christian, in principle, from his earliest years.

*　　*　　*

We have much to say of baptismal regeneration as a great error, which undoubtedly it is, in the form in which it is held; but it is only a less hurtful error that some of us hold in denying it. The distinction between our doctrine of baptismal regeneration, and the ancient scripture view, is too broad and palpable to be mistaken. According to the modern church dogma, no faith, in the parents, is necessary to the effect of the rite. Sponsors too are brought in between all parents and their duty, to assume the very office which belongs only to them. And, what is worse, the child is said to be actually regenerated by the act of the priest. According to the more ancient view, or that of the scriptures, nothing depends upon the priest or minister, save that he execute the rite in due form. The regeneration is not actual, but only presumptive, and everything depends upon the organic law of character pertaining between the parent and the child, the church and the child, thus upon duty and holy living and gracious example. The child is too young to choose the rite for himself, but the parent, having him as it were in his own life, is allowed the confidence that his own faith and character will be reproduced in the child, and grow up in his growth, and that thus the propriety of the rite as a seal of faith will not be violated. In giving us this rite, on the grounds stated, God promises, in fact, on his part, to dispense that spiritual grace which is necessary to the fulfillment of its import. In this way too is it seen that the Christian economy has a place for all ages; for it would be singular, if after all we say of the universality of God's mercy as a gift to the human race, it could yet not limber itself to man, so as to adapt a place for the age of childhood, but must leave a full fourth part of the race, the part least hardened in evil and tenderest to good unrecognized and unprovided for,—gathering a flock without lambs, or, I should rather say, gathering a flock away from the lambs. Such is not the spirit of Him who said, "forbid them not, for of such is the kingdom of heaven." Therefore we bring them into the school of Christ, and the pale of his mercy with us, there to be trained up in the holy nurture of the Lord. And then the result is to be tested afterwards, or at an advanced period in life, by trying their character in the same way as the characer of all Christians is tried; for many are baptized in adult age, who truly do not believe, as is afterwards discovered.

*　　*　　*

Simply to tell a child, as he just begins to make acquaintance with words, that he "must have a new heart, before he can be good," is to inflict a double discouragement. First, he cannot guess what this technical phraseology means, and thus he takes up the impression that he can do, or think nothing right, till he is able to comprehend what is above his age—why then should he make the endeavor? Secondly, he is told that he must have a new heart *before* he can be good, not that he may hope to exercise a renewed spirit, *in* the endeavor to be good—why then attempt what must be worthless, till something *previous* befalls him? Discouraged thus on every side, his tender soul turns hither and thither, in hopeless despair, and finally he consents to be what he must—a sinner against God and that only. Well is it, under such a process, wearing down his childish soul into soreness and despair of good, sealing up his nature in silence and cessation as regards all right endeavors, and compelling him to turn his feelings into other channels, where he shall find his good in evil—well is it, I say, if he has not contracted a dislike to the very subject of religion, as inveterate as the subject is impossible. Many teach in this way, no doubt, with the best intentions imaginable, their design is only to be faithful, and sometimes they appear even to think that the more they discourage their children the better and more faithful they are. But the mistake, if not cruelly meant, is certainly most cruel in the experience, and it is just this mistake, I am confident, which accounts for a large share of the unhappy failures made by Christian parents, in the training of their children. Rather should they begin with a kind of teaching suited to the age of the child. First of all, they should rather seek to teach a feeling than a doctrine, to bathe the child in their own feeling of love to God, and dependence on him, and contrition for wrong before him, bearing up their child's heart in their own, not fearing to encourage every good motion they can call into exercise; to make what is good, happy and attractive; what is wrong, odious and hateful. Then as the understanding advances, give it food suited to its capacity, opening upon it, gradually, the more difficult views of Christian doctrine and experience.

Sometimes Christian parents fail of success in the religious training of their children, because the church counteracts their effort and example. The church makes a bad atmosphere about the house and the poison comes in at the doors and windows. It is rent by divisions, burnt up by fanaticism, frozen by the chill of a worldly spirit, petrified in a rigid and dead orthodoxy. It makes no element of genial warmth and love about the child, according to the intention of Christ in its appointment, but gives to religion, rather, a forbidding aspect, and thus, instead of assisting the parent, becomes one of the worst impediments to his success.

* * *

. . . . . What motives are laid upon all Christian parents, by the doctrine I have established, to make the first article of family discipline a constant and careful discipline of themselves? I would not undervalue a strong and decided government in families. No family can be rightly trained without it. But there is a kind of virtue, my brethren, which is not in the rod, the virtue, I mean, of a truly good and sanctified life. And a reign of brute force is much more easily maintained, than a reign whose power is righteousness and love. There are too, I must warn you, many who talk much of the rod as the orthodox symbol of parental duty, but who might really as well be heathens as Christians; who only storm about their house with heathenish ferocity, who lecture, and threaten, and castigate, and bruise, and call this family government. They even dare to speak of this as the nurture of the Lord. So much easier is it to be violent than to be holy, that they substitute force for goodness and grace, and are wholly unconscious of the imposture. It is frightful to think how they batter and bruise the delicate, tender souls of their children, extinguishing in them what they ought to cultivate, crushing that sensibility which is the hope of their being, and all in the sacred name of Christ Jesus. By no such summary process can you dispatch your duties to your children. You are not to be a savage to them, but a father, and a Christian. Your real aim and study must be to infuse into them a new life, and, to this end, the Life of God must perpetually reign in you. Gathered round you as a family, they are all to be so many motives, strong as the love you bear them, to make you Christlike in your spirit. It must be seen and felt with them that religion is a first thing with you. And it must be first, not in words and talk, but visibly first in your love—that which fixes your aims, feeds your enjoyments, sanctifies your pleasures, supports your trials, satisfies your wants, contents your ambition, beautifies and blesses your character. No mock piety, no sanctimony of phrase, or longitude of face on Sundays will suffice. You must live in the light of God and hold such a spirit of exercise, as you wish to see translated into your children. You must take them into your feelings, as a loving and joyous element, and beget, if by the grace of God you may, the spirit of your own heart in theirs. This is Christian education, the nurture of the Lord. Ah, how dismal is the contrast of a half-worldly, carnal piety, proposing money as the good thing of life, stimulating ambition for place and show, provoking ill-nature by petulance and falsehood, praying to save the rule of family worship, having now and then a religious fit, and, when it is on, weeping and exhorting the family to undo all that the life has taught them to do, and then, when the passions have burnt out their fire, dropping down again to sleep in the cinders, only hoping still that the family will sometime be converted! When shall we discover that families ought to be ruined by such training as this? When shall we turn ourselves wholly to God, and looking on our children as one with us and drawing their character from us, make them arguments to duty and constancy—duty and constancy not as a burden, but, since they are enforced by motives so dear, our pleasure and delight. For these ties and duties exist not for the religious good of our children only, but quite as much for our own. And God, who understands us well, has appointed them to keep us in a perpetual frame of love; for so ready is our bad nature to kindle with our good, and burn with it, that what we call our piety is, otherwise, in constant danger of degenerating into a fiery, censorious, unmerciful and intolerant spirit. Hence it is that monks have been so prone to persecution. Not dwelling with children as the objects of affection, having their hearts softened by no family love, their life identified with no objects that excite gentleness, their nature hardens into a Christian abstraction, and blood and doctrine go together.

*   *   *

. . . . . It is to be deeply considered, in connection with this view of family nurture, whether it does not meet many of the deficiencies we deplore in the Christian character of our times, and the present state of our churches. We have been expecting to thrive too much by conquest, and too little by growth. I desire to speak with all caution of what are very unfortunately called revivals of religion; for, apart from the name, which is modern, and from certain crudities and excesses that go with it, which name, crudities and excesses are wholly adventitious as regards the substantial merits of such scenes,—apart from these, I say, there is abundant reason to believe that God's spiritual economy includes varieties of exercise, answering, in all important respects, to these visitations of mercy, so much coveted in our churches. They are needed. A perfectly uniform demonstration in religion is not possible or desirable. Nothing is thus uniform but death. Our exercise varies every year and day from childhood onward. Society is going through new modes of exercise in the same manner, excited by new subjects, running into new types of feeling, and struggling with new combinations of thought. Quite as necessary is it that all holy principle should have a

varied exercise, now in one duty, now in another; now in public
aims and efforts, now in bosom struggles; now in social methods, now in those which are solitary and private; now in high
emotion, now in deliberative thought and study. Accordingly
the Christian church began with a scene of extraordinary social
demonstration, and the like, in one form or another, may be
traced in every period of its history since that day. But the
difficulty is with us that we idolize such scenes and make them
the whole of our religion. We assume that nothing good is
doing, or can be done at any other time. And what is even
worse, we often look upon these scenes, and desire them, rather
as scenes of victory, than of piety. They are the harvest times of
conversion, and conversion is too nearly every thing with us. In
particular, we see no way to gather in disciples, save by means
of certain marked experiences, developed in such scenes, in adult
years. Our very children can possibly come to no good, save
in this way. Instrumentalities are invented to compass our object, that are only mechanical, and the hope of mere present
effect is supposed to justify them. Present effect, in the view of
many, justifies any thing and every thing. We strain every nerve
of motion, exhaust every capacity of endurance, and push on
till nature sinks in exhaustion. We preach too much, and live
Christ too little. We do many things, which, in a cooler mood,
are seen to hurt the dignity of religion, and which somewhat
shame and sicken ourselves. Hence the present state of religion
in our country. We have worked a vein till it has run out. The
churches are exhausted. There is little to attract them, when
they look upon the renewal of scenes through which many of
them have passed. They look about them, with a sigh, to ask
if possibly there is no better way, and some are ready to find
that better way, in a change of their religion. Nothing different
from this ought to have been expected. No nation can long
thrive by a spirit of conquest; no more can a church. There
must be an internal growth, that is made by holy industry, in
the common walks of life and duty. Let us turn now, not away
from revivals of religion, certainly not away from the conviction that God will bring upon the churches tides of spiritual
exercise, and vary his divine culture by times and seasons suited

to their advancement; but let us turn to inquire whether there is not a fund of increase in the very bosom of the church itself. Let us try if we may not train up our children in the way that they should go. Simply this, if we can do it, will make the church multiply her numbers many fold more rapidly than now, with the advantage that many more will be gained from without than now. For she will cease to hold a mere piety of occasions, a piety whose chief use is to get up occasions; she will follow a gentler and more constant method, as her duty is more constant and blends with the very life of her natural affections. Her piety will be of a more even and genial quality, and will be more respected. She will not strive and cry, but she will live. The school of John the Baptist will be succeeded by the school of Christ, as a dew comes after a fire. Families will not be a temptation to you, half the time hurrying you on to get money, and prepare a show, and the other half, a motive to repentance and shame, and profitless exhortation; but, all the time, an argument for Christian love and holy living. Then also the piety of the coming age will be deeper and more akin to habit than yours, because it begun earlier. It will have more of an air of naturalness and will be less a work of will. A generation will come forward, who will have been educated to all good undertakings and enterprises, ardent without fanaticism, powerful without machinery. Not born so generally, in a storm, and brought to Christ by an abrupt transition, the latter portion of life will not have an unequal war to maintain with the beginning, but life will be more nearly one, and in harmony with itself. Is not this a result to be desired? Could we tell our American churches at this moment, what they want, should we not tell them this? Neither, if God, as many fear, is about to bring upon his church a day of wrath and stormy conflict, let any one suspect that such a kind of piety will want vigor and nerve, to withstand the fiery assaults anticipated. See what turn the mind of our apostle took, when he was arming his disciples for the great conflict of their age. Children obey your parents,— Fathers provoke not your children,—Servants be obedient to your masters,—Masters forbear threatening,—Finally, to include all, put on the whole armor of God. As if the first thought, in arming the church for great trials and stout victories, was to fill common life and the relations of the house with a Christian spirit. There is no truer truth, or more sublime. Religion never thoroughly penetrates life, till it becomes domestic. Like that patriotic fire, which makes a nation invincible, it never burns with inextinguishable devotion, till it burns at the hearth.

*　　*　　*

LESSONS FROM THE WORLD OF MATTER AND THE

WORLD OF MAN

THEODORE PARKER

(1810-1860)

THEODORE PARKER is a typical *philosophical* theologian. Theology for him must respect reason and be grounded in assumptions open to critical reflection. No authority, be it Biblical, ecclesiastical or accepted custom, standing alone, can ever satisfy the philosophical mind. Christianity as a religion for some people may be grounded in an intuitional and emotional appeal or, for others, it may be contained in dogmas set in the framework of an alleged revelation—but such unphilosophical substructures and claims do not satisfy the critically inquisitive mind. A philosopher of the genuine order looks to human experience itself and to the best in critical and comprehensive knowledge for the charting of his course.

Although he remained a Congregationalist in some of his theological thinking, Theodore Parker launched out freely in ideas daring for his time, greatly influencing Unitarian thought for more than a generation. He introduced into his public utterances the suggestions of German Biblical criticism and interpreted Christianity in the light of philosophical idealism. He was described by his conservative critics as an "infidel" and hailed by his admirers as a vibrant and helpful preacher, drawing thousands to hear his eloquence in the Boston Music Hall.

Victor Cousin, the eclectic philosopher, the harmonizer of viewpoints, was the inspirer of the Transcendentalists with whom Parker is to be identified. This school taught the doctrine of "spontaneous reason" as the immediate apprehension of Divine matters and the immanent work of Divinity Itself. Along with Emerson and others, Protestant liberalism found in Parker a strong voice and a spokesman unashamed. "The world," he said, "is a perpetual miracle" without the need for the miracles of unreason as taught in conventional Christian theology. His great humanitarianism and optimism were set in the conviction that God is love. Such a God knows no favorites and is continuously self-disclosing, certainly no party to a closed circuit (or canon) of revelation.

The selections here presented are taken from contemporary notes of unpublished sermons during a period of ten years, from 1849 to 1859.

Here we find "familiar lessons with which his sermons abound," and a "happy faculty" of presenting highest themes in an attractive manner. Here we see Protestantism interpreted not in terms of the "popular theology" (Parker's term) of orthodoxy and conventionalism but in terms of the "absolute religion" of "love to God and love to man," with piety and morality brought to focus "in their numberless modes of manifestation."

Editor

LESSONS FROM THE WORLD OF MATTER

AND THE WORLD OF MAN

THE NATURAL world which a man lives on and lives by—I mean the material world of nature all about us—is the same thing to all who live in the same latitude and place. And what a grand world it is! I do not wonder that our old German heathen fathers, and so many other heathens, worshipped it. The ground under our feet is so firm-set and solid, the heavens over our head are so magnificent, the air about us is so bland when it is still, so powerful when it is stirred into stormy motion,— what a world it is! All day long there are the light, the clouds, the trees, the waters,

"Never weary of flowing
Under the Sun,"

the winds,

"Never weary of fleeting,
Since Time has begun."

All night long the good God shepherds the stars in the wide pasture of heaven; He goeth before them, leadeth them out, calleth every star by name, and they know his voice, the motherly voice of the good Shepherd of the universe, to whom each star is a little lamb, fed and folded by the infinite presence of Him

"Who doth preserve the stars from wrong."

This natural world is a glory and a delight,
"A thing of beauty, and a joy forever."

Men hard entreated with toil, or chasing after pleasure, after honor, after riches, after power, catch glimpses of it by stealth, as it were, as the ox at the plough reaches out from the yoke, and, hard-breathing, licks up a morsel of grass. So, many men see the world of nature, and get, now and then, a mouthful of beauty. We all get something of its use, for we not only live on it, as a foundation, but by it, as food and shelter.

This natural world is "a cupboard of food and a cabinet of pleasure," as an old poet quaintly puts it. All sorts of things are therein stored up for present or future use. On the lower shelves, which the savage man can reach to, there are the rudest things,—acorns, roots, nuts, berries, wild apples, fish, and flesh. Higher up there are corn, salt, wool, cotton, stones with fire to be beaten out of them by striking them together; then live animals of various sorts; next, metals, iron, copper, silver, gold, and the like,—all ready to spring into man's hand, and serve him, when he can reach up to them and take them down. A little further up there are things to adorn the body—ochre to paint the cheeks, feathers to trim the head, rubies and diamonds, and many a twisted shell, still further to ornament and set off the world; all sorts of finery for the Nootka Sound female and the Parisian woman. Still higher up are laid the winds to grind man's corn, waters to sift his meal; and above these are coals waiting to become fire, and to be made the force of oxen, winds, rivers, and men. Yet higher up lie the gases which are to light a city, or take away the grief of a wound, and make a man invulnerable and invincible to pain. Higher still are things which no man has climbed up to and looked on as yet. There they lie, shelf rising above shelf, gallery above gallery, and the ceiling is far out of the telescopic sight of the farthest-sighted man. A short savage, like King Philip of Pokanoket, looks on the lower shelves and takes what he wants,—a club, a chip of stone, a handful of sea-shells, a deer-skin, a bit of flesh, a few ears of corn,—and is content with them, and thanks God for the world he lives in. But the civilized man who has grown as tall as Captain Ericsson reaches higher, and takes down cattle power, wind power, water power, steam power, lightning power, and hands them to the smaller boys, to us who have not yet grown up to reach so high. Some of the tallest-minded of the human tribe stand on tip-toe and look up as high as they can see, and then report to us the great machinery and astronomical wheel work which keeps the sun and moon in their place; or report of the smaller machinery, the nice chemical and electrical gearing which holds the atoms of a pebble together, and whereby the great world grows grass for oxen and corn for men. This is as high as any mortal man has got as yet; and it is a great way to climb from the acorn on the bottom shelf up to the celestial mechanics on the upper shelf, which Newton and La Place are only tall enough to look over and handle.

Such is the natural world that we live on and by. It is the home of us all, and the dear God is the great housekeeper and the ever-present mother therein. He lights the fires every morning, and puts them out every night; yea, hangs up the lamps, and makes it all snug for the family to sleep in, beneath his motherly watchfulness, all night long, till the morning fire awakes again, and, glittering along the east, shines into his children's brightening eyes.

This world of nature is meant for all. The sun shines on

the evil and the good, and the rain rains on the just and the unjust. The same ground is under General Pierce and his pig, and the same heavens are over the astronomer and his dog; and dog and astronomer, pig and president, all live on, live under, live in the same natural world, and the All-Bountiful is father and mother to them all, not over-honoring the astronomer, not undervaluing the dog or the swine. And yet what a very different world it is to pig and president, to dog and astronomer! To such as look only at the lower shelves it is a dull, hard, prosy world. To those who reach up to fashion and finery, to the nicknacks of nature, it is a dainty show of pretty things, a sort of great Vanity Fair, where Mrs. Jezebel and Mr. Absalom are to adorn and make themselves comely. To others—who see the great uses in the power of things, the great loveliness in the beauty of things, the great wisdom in the meaning of things—it is a serious world, very serious; but a lovely world, very lovely; and a divine world, very divine; full of God's power, God's wisdom, God's justice, God's beauty, and God's love, running out into the blossoms of the ground and the blossoms of the sky; the whole universe a great manifold flower of God, who holds it in his own right hand.

It always seemed to me that this material world prophesied something a great many times greater and grander than the highest man had yet seen or told of. I do not believe that God made this grand world of nature as the background to a little dwarfish picture of spirit. The great power of nature, the great beauty of nature, and its great sense, are all prophetic of a power, beauty, and sense which matter knows not of, which it will take great men and great generations of great men to fulfil and accomplish. But it will one day be. It will take place in the golden ages, which are not behind us, but before us, and which are to be reached by your toil, and your prayer, and your thought, and sweat, and watching. I love to read the prophecy which God himself has writ in the world of nature. Every piece of coal, every bit of iron,—why, it was a prophecy of steam-engines and steam-ships, if men had only the wit to read the oracle! And so this natural world, with its powers, its beauty, its meaning,—why, it is a prophecy of a great human world that is to come, whereof the Isaiahs, the Socrateses, the Jesuses, and the Newtons, were only the prophets who foretold the beginning of the golden ages that are to come.

* * *

In the universe, all is done according to law, by the regular and orderly action of the forces thereof; there is a constant mode of operation, which never changes. Nothing is done by human magic, nothing by divine miracle. Religious poets tell us that God said in Hebrew speech, "Let the earth be!" and it was forthwith. "Let the waters bring forth fish, the air fowls, and the earth cattle!"—and it was done. But when you consult the record of the earth itself, you find that the six days' miracle of the poet are millions of years' work of divine forces of the universe. These forces are always adequate to achieve their divine purpose, with no miraculous help, no intervention, no new creation of forces; and in that immense book of space, whose leaves date back through such vast periods of time, there is not a single miracle recorded; not once does it appear that God intervened and changed the normal action of any single thing.

* * *

The law of the world of matter is knowable by man, and when his thought comprehends that, the world of matter is manageable by his toil, and he can use its forces to serve his end. This power of science depends not only on the mind itself, but on the nice relation between that and the world of matter outside. What if this world of matter were—as the ministers oftentimes tell us it is—a bundle of incoherent things, no constant law in force therein, God intervening by capricious miracle, to turn a stick into a snake, water to blood, dust to flies and creeping things, mud to frogs, and ashes to a plague on beasts and men; what if he sent miraculous darkness which could be felt, to revenge him on some handful of wicked men; what if by miracle he opened the sea and let a nation through, and then poured the waters back on the advancing foe; what if the rocks became water, and the heavens rained bread for forty years; what if the sun and moon stood still and let a filibustering troop destroy their foe; what if iron swam at some man's command; what if a whale engulfed a disobedient prophet who fled from God's higher law, and kept him three days shut up, till he made a great poetic psalm; what if a son were born with no human father, and could by miracle walk on the waves as on dry land, feed five thousand men with five little barley loaves, and have in reserve twelve baskets-full of broken bread; what if he could still the winds and the waters with a word, rebuke disease, restore the lame and the blind at a touch, and wake the dead with "Lazarus, come forth!" Why! science would not be possible; there would be nothing but stupid wonder and amazement, and instead of the grand spectacle of a universe, with law everywhere, thought waking reason everywhere, and stirring Newton to write the Principia of Natural Science, Linnaeus to describe the systems of plants, La Place to cipher out the mechanics of the sky, Kant to unfold the metaphysics of man and the philosophy of human history, and the masterly intellect of Cuvier to classify the animal kingdom,—mankind thereby growing wiser, and still more powerful,—we should have a priest's world of capricious chaos, some prophet going up to heaven on his own garment, some witch careering on a broom, and man vulgarly staring, as in a farmer's yard a calf stands gaping at some new barn-door. What is the world of monkish legend, the world of the Arabian Nights' Entertainments, the world of the Catholic Church, the world of the Calvinistic Church, or of the popular theology of our times, compared with the grand world which God has made it,—stars millions of millions of miles away looking down on these flowers at my side, and all the way between, law, order, never once a miracle, and all this so wondrously and tenderly related to man's mind!

* * *

Everywhere in the world there is an exhibition of power, force active to-day. Everywhere, likewise, there is a reserve of power, force waiting for to-morrow. Force is potent everywhere, but latent as well. All men see the active power, all do not see the power which waits till it comes of age to do its work.

In order to get the general analogy of the universe to bear

upon this particular matter in hand, the power of progressive development in the human race, look at the plainest examples of this reserved power in nature. All around us the fields lie sleeping under their coverlet of frost. Only the mosses, the lichens, and other cryptogamy have any green and growing life. Every hide-bound tree has taken in sail, and sent down its top-mast, housed the rigging, and lies stripped there in bay, waiting for navigation to open in March and April. Even the well-clad bear has coiled himself up for his hibernating sleep all winter long; the frogs and snakes and toads have hid their heads; the swarms of insects are all still. Nature has put her little ones to bed.

> "Hush, my babe! lie still and slumber!
> Holy angels guard thy bed,
> Heavenly blessings without number
> Rest upon thy infant head!"

This is the evening cradle-song wherewith Nature lulls the reptile, insect, bear, and tree, to their winter sleep.

Look at the scene next June. What life in the ground, in the trees spreading their sails to every wind, in the reptiles, in the insects! Nature wakens her little ones in the new morning, and sends them out to the world's great vineyard to bear the burthen in the heat of the day, sure of their penny at its end.

What a reserve of power lies in the ground under our feet, in the silent throat of every bird, in the scale-clad buds on oak and apple-tree! What energy sleeps in that hibernating bear, who in spring will come out from his hole in the Green Mountains, and woo his shaggy mate, and ere long rejoice in the parental joys of home,

> "His wee bit ingle blinkin' bonnily,
> His clean hearth-stane, his thriftie wifie's smile."

A few years ago men brought from Egypt to Tuscany some grains of wheat which a farmer had laid up thirty-five or forty hundred years ago. They put it in the ground in Italy, and the power which those little grains had kept so long waked up bright, and grew wheat there, just as if nothing had happened since Sesostris marched his Egyptians, and set up pillars and temples from Asia Minor to the Indus, which Herodotus saw two-and-twenty hundred years ago. All the coffee plants in America, it is said, have come from two little trees which a Dominican priest brought here from Spain; and when the ship was on short allowance for water, he divided his pint a day, taking a half-pint for himself, and sparing a gill for each of his trees; and so they lasted, and were planted in Saint Domingo, and now they are spread all over the tropic continent.

Three hundred years ago New-England was a wilderness, with wild beasts howling in the forests, and thirty thousand lazy, half-naked Indians howling wilder than the beasts. Idle rivers ran idly to an idle sea, flapping to the moon's attraction, as restless and as lazy as a summer cloud. Then New-England was shaggy with awful woods, the only garment of the savage land. In April the windflower came out, and the next month the maple saw his red beauties reflected in the Connecticut and the Merrimac. In June the water-lily opened her fragrant bosom. Who saw it? Only here and there some young squaw, thinking of her dusky lover, turned to look at its beauty, or the long-lipped moose came down in the morning and licked up its fragrance from the river's breast; and otherwise the maple bloomed and blushed unseen, and the lily wasted its sweetness on the desert air.

Now civil-suited New-England has gardens, orchards, fields, is nicely girded with earthen and iron roads, and jewelled all over with cities and fair towns. The shaggy wood has been trimmed away, and is only

"A scarf about her decent shoulders thrown."

Three millions of men are snugly cradled in New-England's lap. The winds have been put to work. The ground, so lazy once, has no Sunday but the winter now. The rivers have been put out to apprentice, and become blacksmiths, paper-makers, spinners, and weavers. The ocean is a constant ferryman, always at work, fetching and carrying between the corners of the world. Even the lightning has been called in from his play-ground, and set to work; he must keep the side-walk now when he travels, for we regulate the police of the sky; Dr. Franklin began that work. The lightning must no longer burn up meeting-houses,— a favorite errand which the devil used to send him on of old time, as Cotton Mather said,—he must keep the peace now; swift-footed, he must run of errands for the family. We say "Go!" and the lightning has gone; "Come!" and the lightning is at our hand; "Do this!" and the lightning sets about it.

Now the difference between the New-England of three hundred years ago and the New-England of to-day, was all a reserved power once. The Merrimac was the same river to the Indian that it is now to the American; the ground and sky were the same; the earth does not secrete a different form of lightning from that which of old crinkled through the sky, uttering its thunder as it went.

The change in the human race from the beginning till now is immensely greater than the change from the Massachusetts of red Governor Massasoit to the Massachusetts of pale Governor Clifford. All the difference between the first generation of men on earth—without house or garment, without wife or speech, without consciousness of God or consciousness of self—and the most cultivated society of religious men of England and America, was once a power of progress which lay there in human nature. The savage bore within him the germ of Michael Angelo, of La Place, and Moses, and Jesus. The capability of the nineteenth century lay in the first generation of men, as the New-England of to-day lay in the New-England of three hundred years ago, or as the wheat of the Tuscan harvest lay in those few Egyptian grains; it lay there in the human faculties, asleep, unseen, and unfelt, with the instinct of progressive development belonging thereto. All the mighty growth of the Pagan civilization, of the Hebrew, the Buddhistic, the Mahometan, and the Christian, lay there unseen in man. A thousand years ago, who would have dared to prophesy the industrial civilization of New-England today? When Sir Francis Drake scoured the seas, capturing every vessel that he could overmaster, great pirate that he was, murdering the crews of Spanish galleons, and burning them at sea after he had taken the silver, when he landed on the coast of Peru and Chili, and violated the women, and butchered the men, and burned the towns, leaving blackness and desolation behind him, and doing it for sport's sake,—who would have dared to prophesy the peaceful commerce which, under the two-fold Anglo-Saxon flag of England and America, now covers the ocean with the white blossom of the peace of the nineteenth century? Nobody would have dared to prophesy this in the days of Sir Francis Drake.

But, is this progress to stop here? Have the average nations reached the capacity of mankind? Have the most enlightened nations exhausted the capacity for human improvement? Has the foremost man of all the world drank dry the cup of humanity? Newton, Humboldt, Moses, Jesus,—they have only scooped out and drank a handful of water from the well which opens into that vast ocean of faculties which God created, the mighty deep of human nature.

How has the civilization of the world thus far been achieved? By the great men coming together, a thousand years ago, and saying, "Let us advance mankind"? The great men were not great enough for that. It has taken place in the providence of God, who, from perfect motives, of perfect material, for a perfect purpose, as perfect means, created this human nature, put into it this reserve of power, put about it this reserve of material elements, wherewith to make a Jacob's ladder to clamber continually upwards toward God, our prayer being the hand which reaches up, while our practice is the foot which sustains the weight which the prayer steadies. There is no end to this power of progressive development in man, at least none that you and I can discover.

*   *   *

Man feels the force of circumstances, and longs for power over the world. First he asks it by miracle, of God, and tells how Moses crossed the Red Sea; then by magic, of the devil, and tells how witches ride a broom from Salem to Marblehead. But this power of man comes of a different kind. The Golden Age is no temptation of a devil, offering bread instead of a stone; no miraculous gift outright from God. This power over matter and human instinct, this power to create new circumstances, comes by work,—work of the body, work of the mind. Eden is not behind us; Paradise is not a land of idleness which Adam lost by his first free step. It is before us. It is the result of toil; and that toil brings with it opportunity for the use, development, and enjoyment of every faculty of the body, every power of the mind. A poetic Hebrew said that Moses led Israel through the Red Sea by miracle. Suppose it were true; it were nothing in comparison with the English Transportation Company, with a line of steamers sailing each week, which carry Egyptians, Israelites, men of all nations, and will insure any man's property for a penny in the pound. The New-England puritan told how, by magic, a witch rode from Salem to Boston, the devil before, and she behind, on the crupper of a broom; and he looked up and trembled, and wished he had the power. What was that in comparison with what we see every day, when, not a witch, but lightning, rides, not the crupper of a broom, but a permanent wire, from Boston to New York, or where you will, and when it is not the devil, but a scientific man who postilions the thought across the air? What, I say, is miracle, what is magic, what are the dreams of miracle, the superstitions of magic, in comparison with the results of plain work which God puts in our power? Ask a miracle of God,—and there is no answer. The world is the answer, and it lies before us. Ask magic of the devil,—there is none that moves the wind. Ask the result by thought and work, and the result comes.

Man wants a farm, and he asks for it,—"Lord, give me a farm," in his prayer. Says the Father, "There is land and water; make your farm just as you like it. Is not the soil rich enough? There is sea-weed on the shore, lime at Thomaston, guano at the Lobos Islands; make it as rich as you like." Man wants summer roses in the winter hour; and the Lord says, "Rear them just as you will." He wants ships, and the Lord sends him to the mountain and mine, and under his plastic hand the mast grows in the valley, and the hemp-field blossoms with sail-cloth. He wants a factory, and the Merrimac is ready to turn his wheels; wants schools, colleges, lyceums, libraries, and the Infinite God says to him, "My little child, for these there are the material means under your hand; there are the human means over your shoulders. Use them, make what you like." If the man learns, Joy plucks a rose by every path-way, and puts it in his bosom. If he learns not, Want cuts a birch in every hedge-row, and the idle fool is whipped *to* school.

At this day the men of foremost religious development are the idealizing power of the human race, that family of prophets which never dies out. They have the ideal of a better state of things, a family of equals, a community without want, without ignorance, without crime, a church of righteousness, and a state where the intuitions of conscience have been codified into statutes. These things are all possible, just as possible as the farm, the shop, the factory, and the school. Desire only points to the reserve of power that one day shall satisfy it.

There are two little birds fluttering about the human family. One is *I have;* the other is *Oh, had I.* One is the bird in the hand; the other the bird in the bush, which is worth two of the bird in the hand. The highest function of *I have* is to lay the egg, whence comes forth the fairer and lovelier bird *Oh, had I.* She flies off to the bush, and we journey thither, finding new treasures at every step. We see the ideal good. The child cries for it; the child-boy cries to his mother, the child-man cries to his God, both clamoring for the result. But the wise God does not give it outright. He says to the child-man, "Pay for it, and take it. Earn your breakfast before you eat it, and then take what you like. Desire the end, do you, my little man? Desire the means to it, and then you shall have it. There is a reserved power in matter, another in man. Build your family, church, and state, just as beautiful as you like. All things are possible to him that believeth. Build and be blessed. Lo, I am with you to the end of the world!"

* * *

Of all the wonderful things of God, man the wonderer is himself the most wonderful. He is so well-born, so variously and richly gifted with personal faculties, which are so numerous for action, and which aspire so high; so amply furnished with material means to exercise his faculties and achieve his aspiration, with all eternity for his work-day, and all immensity to grow in, —it is amazing how much is shut up within how little; within a creature a few feet high, living on earth some threescore years! Man is the jewel of God, who has created this material universe as a casket to keep his treasure in. All the material world is made to minister to man's development,—a cupboard of food or a cabinet of pleasure. The ox bears his burdens; the arctic whale feeds the scholar's or the housewife's lamp; the lightnings take their master's thought on their wings, and bear it over land or underneath the sea. The amaranthine gems which blossom slowly in the caverns of the ground,—these are the rose-buds for his bosom. The human Elias goes up in his chariot of flame; he has his sky-chariot, and his sea-chariot, and his chariots for land, drawn by steeds of fire which himself has made.

You admire the height of the mountains. But man's mind is higher than the tallest of them. You wonder at the "great and wide sea, wherein are things creeping innumerable, both small and great beasts," as the Psalmist says. But man's mind is wider than the sea, comprehends the deep, learns its laws, makes the tide serve him, and the ocean becomes a constant ferryman and common carrier of the world. Nay, in the stone which was once the ocean's rim, man reads the most private history of the sea itself, what fishes swam in its deeps a million years ago, what rushes grew on its border, what thundershowers, from what direction, left their mark on its sandy beach, what oyster sucked its ooze. For him the waters chronicle "the ocean wave's immeasurable laugh," and record the smile which rippled round the ocean's face a million years ago, and there man reads it to-day.

In all the wonders of God, nought is so admirable as the admiring man! Other things in comparison seem only as the sparks which flew when God's arm beat the anvil, and fashioned man. The material splendors of the world, grand and gorgeous as they are, to me seem very little when measured by the spiritual glories of the meanest man. The Andes fill me with less amazement than the mountain-minded Humboldt, who ascends and measures them. To the Christian pilgrim, the mountains about compact Jerusalem are as nothing to the vast soul of Moses, Esaias, Samuel, Jesus, who made the whole land sanctified in our remembrance. Yonder unexpected comet, whose coming science had not heralded, who brought no introduction from

Arago or Leverrier, and presented himself with no letter of recommendation, save the best of all, his comely face, is far less
glorious than the rustic lover, who thinks of those dear eyes
which are watching those two stars that every evening so sweetly
herald the night. Nay, this hairy stranger is far inferior to the
mind that shall calculate its orbit, and foretell its next arrival
to our sight. High and glorious are the stars! What a flood of
loveliness do they pour through the darkness every night,—a
beauty and a mystery! But the civilized man who walks under
them, nay, the savage who looks up at them only as the wolf he
slays regards them, has a fairer and a deeper beauty, is a more
mysterious mystery; and when the youngest of that family has
grown old and hollow-eyed, and its light has gone out from
its household hearth, the savage man, no longer savage, shall
still flame in his career, which has no end, passing from glory
to glory, and pouring a fairer light across the darkness of the
material world. The orbit of the mind is wider than creation's
utmost rim; nor ever did centripetal and centrifugal forces describe in their sweep a comet's track so fair-proportioned as the
sweep of human life round these two foci, the mortal here, and
the immortal in the world not seen.

*   *   *

Certainly we do find in human nature some things which are
revolting. Many things of that character come out in human
history. I suppose there is not a grown person in this audience
who has not often been disgusted with himself, finding meannesses, littlenesses, basenesses in his own character. The amount
of selfishness and consequent cruelty now in the world, and the
still greater amount in times past, has a very dark and ugly look.
Sometimes it does seem as if it would have been better if mankind could have started on a little higher plane of existence,
and been more developed before they were created, so to say.
Attend a thieves' ball, of small thieves, with their appropriate
partners, in a dancing garret in Boston, or a thieves' ball in the
President's House at Washington, of great political thieves, who
steal territories and islands,—watch their motions, study their
character, and you do not think very highly of human nature,—

at the first thought and sight, I mean. But—not to pause now, and look a little deeper, in a ball of little thieves in a garret, or of great thieves in the President's saloon—it is rather idle to grumble against human nature, for, after all, this human nature is the best nature we have got, and we are not likely either to get rid of the old or to get hold of a new; and besides, it is exactly the nature which the Infinite God has given us, and it is probable, not to look deeper at this moment, that he made it just as he meant to make it, neither better, neither worse, and made it for a good end, an end, too, which the dancing of little thieves with their partners or of great thieves with theirs will not frustrate nor ultimately pervert.

* * *

The idea which we form of man, like the idea which we form of God, is a powerful element in our civilization, either for good or ill. This idea will strongly affect the condition and character of every one. "Call a man a thief, and he will pick a pocket," is already a proverb. Convince him that he is the noblest creation of the great God, that his beauty shames these flowers at my side, and outblazons the stars of heaven,—then he begins to aspire to have a history, to be a man; and this aspiration corresponds to the great nature in him. Soon as you convince him of this nature he takes a step forward, and puts out wings to fly upwards.

I look with anguish on the two schemes of thought which degrade the nature of man, hostile in many other respects,—the materialism of the last or the present century, and the popular theology of all Christendom, both of which put a low estimate on man. The one makes him a selfish and mortal animal, only body and bones and brains, and his soul but a function of the brute matter he is made of. The other makes him a selfish and immortal devil, powerful only to sin, and immortal only to be eternally tormented. The popular theology of Christendom, one of the many errors which man has cast out of him, as incidents of his development, has much to answer for. It debases God, and it degrades man. It makes us think meanly of ourselves, and dreadfully of our Creator. What makes it more dangerous and more difficult is that both of these errors are taught as a miraculous revelation from God himself, and accordingly not amenable to human correction.

Now self-esteem is commonly large enough in the individual man; it is but rarely that one thinks of himself less and less highly than he ought to think; for the great function to be accomplished by self-esteem is so very important that it is always, or almost always, abundantly provided for. But it is one of the commonest errors in the world to think meanly of human nature itself. It is also one of the most fatal of mistakes. Nay, individual self-esteem is often elated by the thought that general human nature is rather contemptible, and the special excellence that I have does not come from my human nature, which I have in common with every beggar in the street and every culprit that was ever hanged, but from my personal nature, and is singular to me; not the possibility of the meanest man, but the peculiar possession of myself. A man thus gratifies his self-esteem at the expense of his real self-advancement and bliss.

Then, too, it is thought an acceptable and beautiful mode of honoring God to think meanly of his chief work, that it is good for nothing; for then, it is said, we do not exalt the creature above the Creator, but give God the glory. That is, in reality, we give God the glory of making a work that is good for nothing, and not worth the making. I could never think that I honored an artist by thinking as meanly as it was possible on trial to think of the best work which that artist had brought to pass.

*   *   *

A great man is never an accident. He comes as the end of a long series of causes, which get summed up in him. There is nothing miraculous in the origin of such a man; least of all should we say, that a man of genius was born of no human father, for none is so obviously connected with the present condition and past history of mankind. There is a special preparation made for him in the nation whence he comes; the seed of that crop was put into the ground ages before, and he sums up and represents the particular character of his nation. Men like Christopher Columbus are born only of maritime people; their mothers smell of the sea. Mathematicians like Archimedes and

Leverrier do not spring up among the Sacs and Foxes, but in the most thoughtful nations only. I take it that Socrates could have come only out of the Greeks. He was Athenian all through. The special character of Rome re-appears in Julius Caesar, her greatest man; her ambition, her taste for war and politics, her immense power to organize men, and her utter indifference to human life, all come out in him. The two Bacons, the Monk and the Chancellor, Shakespeare, Newton, Cromwell, the five greatest Englishmen, are not only human, but they are marked with British peculiarities all through. Franklin, the greatest man who ever touched our soil, is most intensely national; our good and ill are condensed in him. This bright consummate flower of New England, this Universal Yankee, could have been born and bred in no other land; that human gold was minted into American coin. God makes the family of mankind, but he divides it out into special peoples, and each man is born with his nationality in him, and the Ethiopian cannot change his skin. Von Humboldt is possible only in Germany, and though he has lived in all the world, and talks and writes in many a tongue, yet the great features of his nationality are as plain in every book and letter he writes as his parents' likeness in his face. How quickly we distinguish between black, red, and white men; how readily separate those of our own color into English, American, German, French, Irish! So the inner man is colored and shaped by the stock we come of. All that we do is stamped with nationality.

This imperious condition of nationality would seem terrible if it came from accident or from blind fate. As the result of that divine Providence which knows all things beforehand, and makes all work together for good, it looks beautiful, and I take it for a blessing. God makes us one human nature, but diverse in nationality, that we may help each other. So the hand is one, but it is separated into five fingers, to make it pliant and manifold useful. Climate, natural scenery, the business, institutions, and history of the nation,—each makes its special mark on you and me. The mantle of destiny girdeth us all.

The credentials of the great man of genius are writ in a larger and stronger hand, because he is to represent his nation in the great court of posterity. Great men are the highest product of any people, and they have never come out of mean nations, more than great trees out of a thin and ill-adapted soil. So every great man has the marks, I think, of his special family. Therefore a particular prepaartion is long making, the ancestral ground for several generations sloping upwards towards the great mountainous man. If you study the family history of such a one, I think you always find finger-posts, one or two hundred years off, pointing to him, on the maternal or paternal side,—some aunt or uncle, or great-great-grandfather, who looks like him. So when he comes it is not by a *coup de famille,* not like a thunder-stroke out of the clear sky, but like the growth of an apple out of an apple-tree, a regular development out of the ancestral stock, and no more surprising than that a lily root bears a lily flower. Each tree, material or human, bears after its kind. If any one of us could trace our ancestral stock back two hundred years, we should find the proximate cause of the disposition born in us. Every farmer knows that is the rule of animals. So when he buys a cow, he wants to know not only the father and mother, but the creature's grandparents also. We all thus depend on our special parentage, and it is only more apparent in a great man. None of us stands alone, but we all lean on our fathers and mothers, and they on such as came behind them; only as a great man is taller than the rest of us, we see how he leans, because it is on a larger scale.

Now I take it that Jesus of Nazareth could have been born of no other nation than the Hebrew. That people comes out in his character, both its good and ill. The story that he had the Holy Ghost for his father is a fiction. The noble man is colored Hebrew all through. He is a Jew all over, and did not take that from one parent alone. He is as intensely national as Benjamin Franklin or Robert Burns. Men say that divine inspiration controlled the human disposition in him; but you see how the literature of his people colored his mind, and gave a hue to his every thought and word. He is so full of the Old Testament that it runs over in all his speech. The history of his people comes out with his religious doctrines and expectations. The national idea of a Messiah affected him very strongly, turning his human genius into a special channel. He was not the less human because he was also a Jew.

When a great man comes, he affects men deeply and widely.

Every Columbus leaves a new world for mankind, some continent of art, science, literature, morals, religion, philanthropy. But just in proportion as such a man is great and original, and so capable to influence mankind for centuries, so does he at first waken opposition, and fail to be appreciated, and that by whole multitudes of men. In his lifetime, nobody thought much of William Shakespeare as a poet. Bacon, a man of the world, the most original and cultivated thinker in the British Islands, must often have heard his plays. Cudworth, a man of the university, the most learned man in all England, truly great, with a mighty range of comprehension, and familiar with all literature, quoting the plays of other ages and other nations, never refers to Shakespeare. Neither of these great comprehensive men took any notice of the greatest genius Great Britain ever saw. That poetical sun rose and went up into the heavens, while these scholars sat in their corners and read by their rushlights, but knew nothing of that great luminary which was making a new day all round the world.

Colleges confer their degrees on the vulgarest of ministers, and none others, save in exceptional cases. I doubt that Saint Paul ever got a D.D. put after his name in large letters; possibly it was put before it in small ones. No Academy of Science bestows honor on the inventors of science. Men grumble at this; even men of genius are sorry, and whine at such a fate, and complain to their wives and daughters that it is an ungrateful world, and a man of genius has a hard time of it;—for he wants not only his genius to ride on through the sky, but a coach and six to trundle him along the street. Poor man! When God sends genius, the philosophic of Socrates, the poetic of Shakespeare, or the religious of Jesus, there is no need that academies bestow their honors on him; he gets his degree at first-hand, not from delegated officials. Such good wine needs no academic nor ecclesiastical bush. His college honors are conferred by the university of the people; not until after he has ceased to be mortal, and gone home, where he sighs not for approbation, ecclesiastic or academic.

The great man of genius is the immediate result of all the people's work. It comes not of himself. With much toil the Egyptians build up their pyramid, the work of a whole nation, its most lasting monument. But Jesus of Nazareth is not less the work of the Hebrew people, the last result of all their life, by far the greatest of the Hebrew pyramids, Palestine's noblest monument; and the beginning of Jesus was when Moses led Israel up out of Egypt.

The great man affects his people and their thought for a time proportionate to his power, and the direction he gives it. When he dies, his character lives for him; his ideas, his spirit, have passed into the consciousness of the people, and continue there, a new force to create men like him. Shakespeare, Bacon, Newton, have been gathered to their fathers long since; but how much is there which is Shakespearian, Baconian, Newtonian; certainly a thousand times as much as when their great genius was condensed into the poet, the philosopher, and the mathematician. Benjamin Franklin is dead, and his body sleeps in the little Quaker churchyard at Philadelphia. But how much is there of the Franklin kind of man in America; more than there ever was before, a thousand times as much as when he had it all. One or two hundred places in the United States are called after him, and his mind has gone into our mind more than his name into the continent's geography. The great man's character is not kept in the line of a single family. The ancestral tree roots underground a great while, grows in its modest way for centuries, and in due time bears the great aloe blossom of genius, and then the tree dies. I think no family on earth ever bears two first-rate men. There is one Shakespeare, one Burns, and if there were two Bacons, they were not otherwise known to be related than that both were Englishmen. There is one Franklin, one Cuvier, one Leibnitz, one Kant. These men may have a thousand children, but the aloe flower of genius does not appear again on the tree that has borne it once. Perhaps every family is destined to bear a great man in the ages; only some put out that blossom early, and others it may take a thousand years to mature it. But if the flower breaks down the tree, the fruit scatters its seed across the continent. Mankind inherits the personal estate of genius, which does not descend in the family. To-day there is no Jesus, but how much more that is Jesus-like; not in Judaea alone, but in all the world. All that he was now vests in the human race. This millionaire of religion left his estate in trust to mankind. God is the guardian who manages it for the advantage of all ages. It

"Spreads undivided, operates unspent:"

nay, it thickens as it spreads, and is enlarged when it is spent.

How pliant is human nature before the plastic power of a great genius! When you and I hear some man of great mind and great rhetorical art utter his humanest thoughts, we swing to and fro as he also vibrates. His thought is in our thoughts, and if his cheek but blanch, ours also turns pale; and we flush as his blood reddens in his face. So the great man affects mankind, not for a minute but for ages long.

* * *

At first sight, the most attractive and popular quality in woman is always beauty, the completeness of the whole frame, and the perfection of its several parts,—for it is this which like morning light earliest strikes the eye, the most salient sense, which travels quickest and farthest too. At a distance the eye comprehends and appreciates this genius of the flesh,—the most spiritual organ of the body doing homage to the least material part of matter. But by and by, some faculty nobler than sight looks for what corresponds to itself, and finding it not, turns off sadly from the pretty face and dainty shape; or discerning therein lofty powers of mind and conscience and heart and soul, things too fair for the corporeal eye to touch, is rejoiced thereat, and then values physical handsomeness as the alabaster-box which holds the precious spikenard and frankincense, with whose odor the whole house is filled.

So the most popular and attractive quality in the public man, —lecturer, politician, lawyer, reformer, minister,—at first is doubtless eloquence, the power of handsome speech, for that is to larger and nobler qualities what physical beauty is to loveliness of the whole spirit. It is quickly discerned, felt as we feel lightning, it flashes in the hand, runs through our bones, and along the nerves, this music of argument. But the flash, the dazzle, the electric thrill, pass by, we recover ourselves, and look for something more than words fitly spoken. So in the long-run, the quality men value most in all public persons is integrity. Webster, Everett, and Choate, we value for their eloquence, their masterly power of speech; but the three Adamses, Washington, and Franklin, the nation values for their integrity. This is to eloquence what a wise, good, religious mother is to the painted girl at the opera, decked out, poor thing, to please the audience for a single hour, and win their cheap applause. Integrity is a marble statue which survives the sacking of cities and the downfall of an empire, and comes to us from the age of Augustus or the time of Pericles, all the more beautiful for its travel through space and time; while eloquence is like forms of chalk painted on a rich man's floor for one feast-night, the next morning to be scrubbed off and cast into the street.

Integrity is to a man what impenetrability is to matter. It is the cohesive force which binds the personal particles of my nature into a person. It is that quality of stableness which enables me to occupy my place, which makes me my own master, and keeps me from getting lost in the person of other men, or in the tumultuous crowd of my own passional or calculating desires. It is the centripetal force which holds me together, and keeps me from flattening out and thinning off until I am all gone into something else. It is domination over myself, not servility to another. It is self-rule by my own highest qualities. By the primal instinct of the body we fend off every thing that would destroy the individuality of our corporeal frame, and thereby keep our flesh safe, whole, and sound. Everybody repels another who would wrench from him a farthing. By a similar instinct of spirit we keep off all that would impair the inner man and disturb its wholeness, and put another man's mind and conscience and heart and soul in place of our own, or which would make any evil passion to rule in place of what is highest and dearest in us. Thereby we keep our spirit safe and whole and sound. Integrity is made up of these two forces: it is justice and firmness. It is the mingling of moral emotions and ideas with a strong will, which controls and commands them.

Now the first duty which God demands of men is that they be faithful, each man to his own nature, and each woman to hers, to respect it, to discipline it to its proper manner, and to use it in well-proportioned life. If I fail in that, I fail of every thing besides; I lose my individual self-hood. Gain what else I may, the gain is of small consequence; I have lost my own soul, and to get any thing without this and hope to keep it, is like keeping money in a purse which has no bottom. Personal fidelity is the first of all duties. I am responsible for what gifts God has given me, not at all for your gifts. You may be great, and I very little; still I must use my little faithfully, nor ever let it be swallowed up in the stream of a great powerful man, nor in the grand ocean of mankind. Though I may be the feeblest and smallest of mortal men, my individuality is just as precious to me as nationality is to the largest nation, or humanity to mankind. This impenetrability and toughness of character is indispensable to all nobleness, to all sturdy manhood. It is the most masculine of virtues, the most feminine at the same time. It is fortitude of the flesh, chastity of the soul. But while I keep the mastery of myself in my own hands, I must use the help of the great men and the little men by my side, and of humanity. I must touch everybody, not mingle and lose myself in any one. I must be helped and helpful, and not mastered and overcome. So I can be taught by all teachers, advised by all history, past and present, and yet keep my flag on its own staff, and never strike my colors to any man, however venerable, or any multitude, however great. Self-reliant independence, discreet faithfulness to the gifts God has given me, is the primal duty, is the Adam and Eve in the Paradise of duties; and if this fails, others are not at all.

Now there are two forces which disturb and often prevent this absolute personal integrity. The first is subjective, from within; the other is objective, from without. First, the instinctive passions, by their rapid, spontaneous, and energetic activity, and the ambitious desires, love of money, respect, and official power, get easily the mastery over a man, and his noble faculties are nipped in the bud. He has no blossom of manhood, and of course bears no manly fruit. The higher faculties of his intellect are stifled, the conscience dries up in the man, the affections fade out and perish, and in place of that womanly religion which his soul longed for as its fitting mate, a foreign superstition, a horrible darkness, sits in his gate, making night hideous. In this case, the man fails of his personal integrity by allowing his meaner appetites to rule him. I am a free, self-mastered man only when all my faculties have each their proper place; I am a slave if any one of them domineers, and treads me down. I may be the slave of passion or of calculation, and in either case my personal integrity is gone more completely than if a master from without had welded his collar about my neck and his chain on my feet. I am more disgracefully conquered, for a man may be overcome from without by superior force, and while he suffers loss incurs no reproach, and his dignity is not harmed. But if I am overmastered by my own flesh, how base is my defeat?

The other disturbing force is objective, from without. Here other men fool me away from myself, and divulse me from my soul. Public opinion takes my free mind out of me, and I dare not think and speak till some one has told me what to say. Sometimes public law runs off with all individual morality. The man never asks what is right and manly, and squares with his conscience, but, "How far can I go and not be caught up by the sheriff?" How mean it is to silence the voice of God within you, and instead thereof have only the harsh formula of the crier of the court. Sometimes the popular theology turns off the man's soul from him, and sits there mumbling over those words which once flamed out of the religious consciousness of saints and martyrs, prophets and apostles; but to him they are nothing but cold, hard cinders from another's hearth, once warm to some one, now good for nothing. How contemptible seems the man who commits high treason against himself, levies war on his own noblest faculties, and betrays himself, and goes over to his own enemies. Of what avail then is money got by indirect means? Justice makes us pay for it all; it takes it out of our hide, if not out of our purse. How base is a man's respectability, the praise of men which falls on him, when he has lost that foundation which alone can hold up any praise, his own self-respect, and faithfulness to himself! How ridiculous is official power when the personal power of self-trust has gone! How mean looks that man who has turned his soul out of doors to bring in the whole world! I see him in his wine-cups, the victim of appetites and passions that war against the soul. I see him amid his riches, the slave of covetousness. I look at him when the applause of a convention of similar men repays his falseness to himself, the

mere tool of the hand that feeds him. Is it worth while to take
the opinion of the pavement instead of your own opinion, your
own manly or womanly sense? Shame on us that we are such
cowards and betray ourselves!

But how grand, and not less than magnificent, appears

> "The man who still suspects and still reveres
> Himself, in nobleness and lowliness
> Of soul, whom no temptations from within
> Force to deformity of life; whom no
> Seductions from without corrupt and turn
> Astray."

Look at such a man in his pleasures,—temperate, full of open,
daily blessedness, with no silent meanness of concealed joy! See
him in his business,—erect as a palm-tree, no lies on his tongue,
no fraud of tricky mind, no bad money running into his purse,
but the New Testament's Golden Rule lying on his counter, his
desk, his bench, as a meet one by which to buy and sell! See him
in the public meeting,—faithful to himself, though he stands all
alone; public opinion, public law, public theology, may be
against him, but a man on the side of his own soul has the
Infinite God for his ally. Think not of his ever lacking friends.
This is the foundation of all the rest. It is the first quality you
ask of every man and of every woman. This you can build into
any thing that you will; but as the granite must be solid in the
block before it is solid in the building, so you must have this
integral personal impenetrability in the individual man or
woman, before they are worth much in any relation of life
where they are placed.

Alas! There is not much pains taken just now to promote
this personal integrity. How men laugh at it continually and hiss
it down. The husband asks this young woman, whom he weds,
to surrender her personal integrity, and she ceases to be an individual woman, and becomes only his wife. The magistrate asks
the people to give up their personal integrity; they have only to
do just as they are bid and it will all come out right, he tells
them, whether their souls be trod under the government hoofs
or not; and so the man who accepts that doctrine turns into a

fraction of the state, and is not a person of the state. The little silken virtues, perfumed with rosemary, current in what is called the world of fashion, fit its inhabitants to be beaux and belles, not men and women, with great manly and womanly character, thoughts, feelings, prayers, aspirations, life. Some one said to me the other day, To be respectable in Boston and welcomed into the best society, a man must sacrifice his soul; individuality must go down before sociality. Jesus of Nazareth had a personal integrity as hard as the British cannon-balls which beat down Sebastopol; but nine ministers in every ten, in his name, tell men they must cast away all integral consciousness, and be only a branch of Christ. Not so! I also am a tree, not a branch of any man. My individuality, though it is but the smallest shrub of humanity, roots into that great field of the world where Jesus and Moses and Plato and Aristotle and Leibnitz and Newton also stood and rooted and grew. God loves me as well as he loved those great and gorgeous souls, and if he gave them ten talents, and me only two mites, which joined together make but the fourth part of a penny, he demands the same faithful use of me as of him who has the ten talents. This personal integrity is the oldest of virtues. To the spirit it is what bravery is to the body. It is the father of all the rest.

What honors do we pay to saints and martyrs who kept their spirit clean amid the fire, and laid down their body's life rather than stain the integrity of their spirit! At the head of American statesmen stand Washington and Franklin. Neither of them had a brilliant quality, but each had such faithfulness to his idea of official duty that their influence is ploughed into the consciousness of the land they lived in.

Integrity is a virtue which costs much. In the period of passion, it takes self-denial to keep down the appetites of the flesh; in the time of ambition, with us far more dangerous, it requires very much earnestness of character to keep covetousness within its proper bounds, not to be swerved by love of the praise of men, or official power over them. But what a magnificent recompense does it bring to any and every man! Any pleasure which costs conscience a single pang is really a pain, and not a pleasure. All gain which robs you of your integrity is a gain which profits not; it is a loss. Honor is infamy if won by the sale of your own soul. But what womanly and manly delights does this costly virtue bring into our consciousness, here and hereafter!

*   *   *

When you see old Mr. Goodness, an unpretending man, honest, industrious, open-hearted, pure in his life, full of justice and mercy and kind deeds, you say, "That man is a Christian, if anybody is." You do not ask what he thinks about Jonah and the whale, about the beast with seven heads and ten horns, the plagues of Egypt, the inspiration of the Bible, the nature of Christ, or the miraculous atonement. You see that man's religion in the form of manly life; you ask no further proof, and no other proof is possible. When you say you wish Christianity could get preached and practised all round the world, thereby you do not mean the Christianity of Dr. Beecher, of Dr. Wayland, of Calvin or Luther; you mean that religion which is natural to the heart of man, the ideal piety and morality which mankind aims at. But when the Rev. Dr. Banbaby speaks of Brother Zerubbabel Zealous as a great Christian, he means no such thing. He means that Zerubbabel has been baptized,—sprinkled or dipped,—that he believes in the Trinity, in the infallible inspiration of every word in the Bible, in the miracles, no matter how ridiculous or unattested; that he believes in the total depravity of human nature, in the atonement, in the omnipresence of a personal devil, going about as a roaring lion, seeking whom he may devour, and eternally champing in his insatiate maw nine hundred and ninety-nine out of every thousand, while God, and Christ, and the Holy Ghost, can only succeed in saving one out of a thousand—perhaps one out of a million. Banbaby reckons him a Christian because he has been "born again," "put off the natural man,"—that is, made away with his common sense and common humanity so far as to believe these absurd things,—draws down the corners of his mouth, attends theological meetings, makes long prayers in words, reads the books of his sect, gives money for ecclesiastical objects, and pays attention to ecclesiastical forms. He does not think old Mr. Goodness's life of industry, temperance, charity, patriotism, justice, brotherly love, profits him at all. He is only an unregenerate, impenitent man, who trusts in his own righteousness, leans on an arm of flesh, has been born but once, and will certainly perish everlastingly. It is of no sort of consequence that Zerubbabel is a sharper, has ships in the coolie-trade, and is building swift clippers down in Maine to engage in the African slave-trade, as soon as the American Government closes that little corner of its left eye which it still keeps open to look after that. Old Mr. Goodness's "righteousness" is regarded "as filthy rags," while Zerubbabel's long face and long prayers are held to be a ticket entitling him to the very highest seat in the kingdom of heaven. At the Monthly Concert for Foreign Missions the Rev. Dr. leads in prayer, and Brother Zerubbabel follows. Both ask the same thing,—the Christianization of heathen lands. But they do not mean that form of the Christian religion which is piety in the heart and morality in the outer life. They mean compliance with the popular theology, not the Christian religion proclaimed in those grand words, "Thou shalt love the Lord thy God with all thy heart, and with all thy soul, and with all thy strength, and with all thy mind, and thy neighbor as thyself," and illustrated by a life as grand as the words. They mean the Christian formality, as set forth in the little creed, and illustrated by the lesser conduct, of a very mean, bigoted, and yet earnest and self-denying sect.

*   *   *

As I look over a year of time, I am astonished at the amount of goodness which I have seen, more than I am at anything besides. The evil lies atop, it is in sight of all men who open their eyes, while deeper down there is laid the solid goodness of mankind, which is not always visible, and never at a glance.

What we name goodness is made up of four elements. The topmost and chiefly obvious thing is benevolence, general good willing, what we call kindness, a feeling of relationship toward all mankind, or toward those special members of the human family who stand nearest to us. This benevolence is colored into various complexions by the circumstances of the individual, and is turned to various specialties of human action, directed now to one form of humanity, and then another, but it is always marked by good temper, good humor, or good nature.

Benevolence being the most conspicuous element in goodness, we think it is all. But as you look a little deeper, you find the next most obvious element is sincerity. The benevolent man is what he seems. He does not wax himself over with a fair outside, to hide his mean substance by a surface show of splendid and costly qualities. His wood is solid; it is not a plank of deal, veneered over with a thin coating of rosewood, but as he seems outside he is inside. His virtuous complexion is not painted on him, but runs through all his substance.

Thirdly, there comes justice, that fairness which aims to give every man his due. But with our good man, it is commonly justice which is more anxious to do duty for others than to claim right for himself; more anxious to pay an obligation than to collect a debt. It is justice mixed with that sweet leaven of mercy which makes it a lighter but more attractive bread, a good deal different from that sour unleavened bread of justice merely. In those that we call good men, the affections are a little stronger than conscience; so the good man's justice is sometimes not quite plumb, it bends a little from his personal interest. But that is a failing which leans to virtue's side. The good man has more justice than other men, but designs to be a little more than just towards others, and is a little less than just to himself. Such a man is like those generous traders who always make a liberal scalage in selling, and then make some little deduction also when they come to settle. His conscience makes him just, and his affections go further and make him generous also, for generosity is justice *plus* kindness.

At the bottom of all there lies piety,—the universal love of the first good, first perfect, and first fair, the love of God, "who is of all Creator and defence." The good man may not be always conscious of this piety; there have been cases where such have called themselves atheists, that ugliest of all names. But, depend upon it, piety is always there at the bottom of all goodness; for piety is not that merely technical and special thing which it is sometimes mistaken for, but it is that general steadfastness and integrity, that faithfulness, which is to a man what perpendicularity is to a wall or a column, what solidity and impenetrability are to matter in general. If a pyramid stands six thousand years, and never cracks in a single stone, you will be pretty sure that it rests on a good bottom, even if the pyramid does not know it, not know what it stands on.

If I were to express the proportions of goodness by figures, I would call the complete goodness ten; and piety would be four parts, justice two, sincerity one, and benevolence three.

I suppose many of us are a little disappointed with mankind. The world of the girl's dream is not the world of the young woman's actual sight and touch, and still less is it so of the woman no longer young. In the moonlight of dreamy youth, as we look out of the windows, and rejoice in the blooming apple-trees, how different does the world seem from what we find it the next day, when, in the heat of a May sun, we go about and remove the caterpillars from the scrubby trees. A boy bred in a wealthy family in a little village, secluded from the eyes of men, filling his consciousness with nature and the reflection of human life which deep poems and this great magnificent Bible and other religious books mirror down into his own soul, goes out into the world, and finds things very different from what they appeared when seen through the windows of the home which his father's and mother's affection colored with the rose and violet of their own nature. A young minister bred in a frugal, literary, and religious home, living a quiet life, has rather a hard experience when he comes to his actual work,—the world seems so different from what he dreamed it was, and he encounters so much covetousness, hypocrisy, selfishness in its many forms. "It is a very bad world," says he, looking at it with eyes too pure for iniquity, across the New Testament. "If it appears so to me, how damnable it must look to God, in whose sight the very heavens are not clean, and who charges the angels with folly." So some night, after preaching, as he walks home through the darkness, discouraged and despairing, and looks up to the stars, so old and so young, so heavenly bright, so distant, yet looking so large and near and familiar,—he says, "What is man that thou art mindful of him, and the Son of man that thou regardest him?" And his womanly wife, who walks close at his side, whose "meddling intellect" does not "misshape the form of things," but, like a star itself, lets God shine through her and sparkle out of her, answers him, saying, "He made him a little lower than the angels." But after our man has learned to orient himself in the universe, knowing which way the east is, after the moonlight has gone, and he has removed the caterpillars from the apple-trees, and has felt the summer, and draws towards the appointed weeks of harvest, and sees the same branches which the caterpillars eat in the spring now bending down with great rosy apples,—things look more hopeful, and he finds a great deal of goodness which he did not expect.

We find that much of the wickedness we see is only a chance-shot the gun went off before the man was ready. In human action there is always more virtue of every kind than vice, more industry than idleness, more thrift than spendthrift, more temperance than intemperance, more wisdom than folly. Even the American politician does not tell so many lies as he tells truths. Sincerity is more common than hypocrisy; no nation is ever affected; the mass of men are in real earnest. All the natural trees grow solid all the way through; they have bark on them, but it is a real bark, there is no veneering of mahogany on any northern pine. Even the hypocrisy which a man varnishes himself withal is only the homage which he pays to the virtue he imitates. It is a gilt jewel; he does not like to pay the price of the gold one; the gilt jewel is a testimonial that he would like to have the gold one if it did not cost too much. There is more conscious justice than conscious injustice in the world, more trust than jealousy, more peace than war, more men who help the good time coming than men who stave it off, more piety than impiety, more goodness than badness. In all the world, mankind never put up a single gravestone to evil, as such. There are many temples, no doubt, which are made dens of thieves, but they were all built as houses for the Father, not one of them ever dedicated to the devil. The Christian year, as put down in the calendar of the Catholics and Episcopalians, is full of saints; but nobody ever publishes the Devil's Calendar, full of wicked men. No man will ever write on his father's tomb, "He was an eminent slave-trader." Mr. Mason's sons will not write on his tombstone, "Author of the Fugitive-slave Bill." No miserable minister who, for the meanest fee, shall stand in some pulpit, and preach funeral eulogies on such wicked men, will praise them for deeds of this kind; he will try to varnish them over, and say they were mistakes.

All these things show how constantly the good preponderates in mankind. Do you doubt this? Sometimes it does not seem so, but it all becomes plain from this great fact, that mankind continually improves; for nothing is clearer than this, that the human race is perpetually advancing in all sorts of virtue. Those Adams and Eves whom God sent into the world, naked and rough and savage as a wild ass's colt, have grown up to a quiet, respectable civilization, and dotted the world over with monuments of human excellence. Soon as a scholar studies history, his common sense sees this great fact, that the human tree grows up out of the ground, not down into it, and at each recurring White Sunday it is more beautiful with blossoms, and heavier laden with apples at each harvest. It would be a sorry impeachment of the great God to charge upon him that the world was made so badly that the wheels could never overcome their friction. Take the world, and you see no great improvement from month to month, or perhaps year to year. Look at a star for ten minutes, and it does not seem to have moved at all; look at it at six o'clock and then again at twelve, and you will see that it has changed immensely. So look at mankind from one hundred years to another, and you see what progress Christendom has made.

But not to look over so wide a field, what does any man see in his little sphere of observation? Truth prevailing over error, right over wrong, piety over impiety, goodness over wickedness. The seed of goodness does not come up very quick, but it never rots in the soil; it comes up at last. It does not grow very swiftly at first, but it does grow stout and stocky, as the farmers say of good substantial corn. When I see a young man with any truth that others have not, any justice, any kindly charity, any higher degree of piety, I am sure that he will prevail, just as certainly as that the best corn will ultimately be planted by the farmer, bought by the miller, and eaten by the rest of mankind. Let a little modest minister to the smallest audience utter some new truth, propose some better form of religion, and though the timid man clutches the pulpit cushion, and does not dare look the church members in the face, while his cheek turns pale, and his eye flashes with unwonted light, though all the ministerial associations shall cry, "Away with such a fellow!"—I go up to him and say, "Fear not! Humanity is on your side, and

if the swine trample your pearls under their feet, do not mind
it; it is because they know no better; one day the human race
will sift the ground under your feet, and gather even the dust
of the pearls and fashion it into beauty to wear about humanity's
neck as an ornament." The team of elements carries you swiftly
over iron roads, where oxen once slowly dragged you along; and
just so it is with all goodness. It is certain to come up when it
is planted, sure to grow and to live forever. All this shows the
superiority of the good in the human race over the evil therein.
The swine that is washed may return to his wallowing in the
mire; it is his element; but the man, when the devil has been
cast out, haunts the tombs no longer, crying, and cutting himself
with stones. Perfection is the pole-star of humanity, and our
little needle has its dip, and its variation, and sometimes de-
clines from the pole, now at this angle, then at that,

> "But, though it trembles as it lowly lies,
> Points to that light which changes not in heaven."

These are very encouraging things. But without looking so
far as that, I am often struck with the amount of goodness all
around me. Sometimes in a railroad car by night I love to
people the hours by counting up the good men and women I
know in all walks of life, and in all denominations of Christians,
and some not Christian, and not Hebrew even, who have no
religious name whatsoever, but who have so much religion in
them that they have not counted it yet. After all there is only
one religion, just as there is but one ocean, and though you
call it North Ocean, South Ocean, Atlantic, Pacific, it is still only
one water. In some places it is deep, in others shallow; here it is
cold, there warm; it is troubled here, smooth there; still it is
always the same ocean, and the chemical qualities of the water
are still the same. When I run over the moral inventory of the
persons I know, I am astonished to find how many good men
and women there are, and what a little dear kingdom of heaven
is about us all the time, though we take small account of it.

I love to look for some excellence amongst bad men, and
almost always find it. There is no dead sea of humanity anywhere. Though you toil all night and catch nothing, in some

lucky moment you throw over on the right side of the ship, and presently your net breaks with the draught of fishes, only not miraculous. Those Boston men who in Congress voted for the Fugitive-slave Bill, do no such thing in private, but both of them contributed honest money to hide the outcast, and carry him where the stripes of America shall never keep him from the stars of freedom. There are many depraved things done without any conscious depravity.

See how many good things are continually coming to pass. Not long since this circumstance came to my knowledge. A Maryland woman lost her husband, a "fast man," who spent more readily than he earned. He had the reputation of wealth, but when his estate came to be settled, there was no property remaining but sixteen slaves. His widow, a kind-hearted woman, hired these persons out, and lived very comfortably on their earnings. One day it occurred to her that it was a little hard for her to be living on the earnings of these persons, to whom she contributed nothing. She asked one of the most sensible of them what she thought of it, saying, "Would you like to be free? Why don't you run away?" "We had thought of it," was the answer, "and some of us came together and talked it over, but we said you had no property excepting us, and we did not like to bring you upon the town." The good woman was so much struck with this that that day she set them free. Some offered to bring back their wages to her. She is now supporting herself with her needle. This shows an amount of self-denial that very few men would be willing to come to. One of our own countrywomen, who has travelled the United States over, making exploring expeditions of loving-kindness and tender mercy, passing through wildernesses and deserts that burned with vice, in order to establish hospitals for the insane and lift up the poor, was once robbed of her purse by a highwayman in Georgia, who gave it back to her when he found it was Miss Dix, scorning to rob such a woman. Need I mention again that woman whose humanity seems sweetest in the wintry darkness of Crimean war, that Nightingale of mercy who makes perpetual spring and summer in the desolate camp of the soldier? No star shines so beautifully as a good deed in a naughty world, and there is not a street in Boston, however short, not a lane, however dirty, but some window thereof burns with that light which shines in the darkness, though the darkness comprehendeth it not. If a wrong is done to anybody, somebody by and by finds it out. Men scourge the apostle of humanity in the market-place, but there is always some good woman, some kind man, to wash the apostle's stripes and bind up his bruises, and lay healing herbs of grace on the tortured flesh, and carry a soothing balm to the soul that smarts, but will not forbear from its work; and when the martyr dies, somebody gathers up his ashes and sows them as seeds of goodness, one day to blossom all round the religious world. How many good men you find, always taking offices of charitable trust which bring no money or honor, but who will not be forgotten in the recompense of the just men whose hearts grow white and blossom with benevolence as they grow old. How many good Samaritans there are in the world, always happening to pass where somebody lies fallen among thieves.

I love to walk through a library full of old books, the works of mighty men who once shook the ground under them; yet all forgotten now; and I think how rich-minded the human race is when it can afford to let such intellect lie, and never miss that wealth. But goodness is hid much oftener than great intellect. I do not mean that it is hid in its action, but from men's sight. But for each man of this stamp, there are several women. There is no town but has many sisters to every Lazarus, generous mothers, kindly aunts, faithful friends, whose footsteps are like those of spring, flowery to-day, in some weeks fruitful,—those who leave tracks of benevolence all through the cold and drifted snow of selfishness which piles the streets of a great metropolis. It is these persons, women and men, who carry on the great movements of mankind. They clear and till the fields where some Moses, Jesus, Paul, or Luther gathers an abundant harvest, brought home amid the shouting of the people, "Hosanna! Hosanna!" The topstone of yonder monument is only the highest because it rests on every block underneath, and the lowest and smallest helps to hold it up; only the foundation was laid with sweat and sore toil, while the capstone was hoisted to its

place amid the shouting of multitudes. It is in this way that all
the great humanities are carried forward. They advance most
rapidly in New England, because we have more men and women
of this stamp amongst us than elsewhere are to be found in the
world. Nobody knows the power of a good woman, in the quiet
duties of her home, where she is wife, mother, sister, aunt; and
in the neighborly charities of the street and village she sets
afoot powers of excellence which run and are not weary, or
walk and never faint.

You and I may not have much intellectual power; perhaps
our thought will never fill the world's soul, nor guide the
world's helm; we may not have reason enough to dig down to
the roots of things, not imagination enough to reach up to the
fruits and flowers, nor memory to reach back to the causes, not
prophetic power to reach forward to their consequences. But all
the little space within our reach we can occupy with goodness,
and then the whole house will be filled with the fragrant beauty
of our incense, which we offer towards man, and which steals
up as a welcome sacrifice towards God. In a wintry day, I have
sometimes found a geranium in some poor woman's kitchen,
and it filled the whole house with its sweet fragrance. So it is
with this goodness. Piety is the root of all manly excellence, and
it branches out into a great many things. How you and I can
increase this goodness in ourselves, and then in the world; for,
though the bodily power is capable of great increase and development, and you see the odds between the thrifty hand of the
mechanic and the clumsy hand of the Irish clown; though the
intellectual power is capable of wondrous culture, as you see
how the use which the well-bred scholar makes of his intellect
differs from the clumsy attainment which the poor ignorant man
can only reach,—yet neither the cunning hand nor the cunning
brain of man is capable of such immense development as those
moral, affectional, and religious faculties whose fairest, sweetest blossom is what we call goodness. And what you and I set
foot for ourselves, ere long belongs to the whole world. This
is the precious privilege which God gives us, that when we
attain it for ourselves, we win it for the whole human race, and
though when we go thitherward we carry the fragrance of our

flower along with us, its seeds drop into the ground, and live forever on the earth to bless mankind.

* * *

It is plain that Jesus was a man of large intellectual character. He had an uncommon understanding, was clear in his sight, shrewd in his judgment, extraordinarily subtle in his arguments, coming to the point with the quickness of lightning. What an eye he had for the beauty of nature,—the little things under his feet, the great things all about him; for cities set on a hill, and for the heavens over his head! What an eye for the beauty of the relations of things! He saw a meaning in the salt without savor, with which men were mending the streets, not fit even for the dunghill,—and what a lesson he drew from it! He saw the beauty of relation in the lilies, clad by God in more beauty than kingly Solomon; in the ravens, who gather not into storehouses and barns, and yet the Great Father feeds and shelters them under his own godly wings. He had reason also which saw intuitively the great universal law of man's nature. And as the result of this three-fold intellect, he had an eloquence which held crowds of men about him till they forgot hunger, thirst, and weariness, even the drawing-on of night. He had a power of reasoning which sent away the scholarly Pharisee, who had journeyed all the way from Jerusalem to confute this peasant. His eloquence was quite peculiar. His mind full of great ideas, his heart aflame with noble sentiments,—he knew how to put these into the homeliest words, and yet give them the most lovely and attractive shape. In that common speech, Religion was the text, his commentary was the salt without savor, the raven flying over his head, the lilies of the valley, the grass, dried in the sun yesterday, to-day heating the earthen vessel whereon a poor woman clapped her unbaked bread; it was the tower of Siloam, which fell on men not worse than the survivors; it was the temple, the great idol of the nation, of which should be left not one stone upon another: all these were his commentaries. It was no vulgar mind that could weave such things into common speech in a moment, and make the heavens come down, and the earth come up,—with marvellous rapidity and instinctive skill, seizing and using every implement that might serve as a medium between his heavenly thought and the understandings of common men. When he spoke, some said it thundered; some said that an angel spoke; and some said it was the eloquence of genius. Studying in the schools makes nothing like it.

Then there is this peculiarity about his intellect. In reading the first three Gospels, you find in him a mind which does not so much generalize by a copious induction from a great many facts; but it sees the law, as a woman sees it, from a very few principles. And so there is less of philosophical talent than of philosophical genius. You are surprised more at the nice quality of this intellect, than at its great quantity. On this account he anticipated experience. There is not a single word in the three Gospels which betrays the youth of Jesus. You would all say,— Behold a full-grown man, long familiar with the ways of men. You would never think he was a young man, scarce thirty years old. But I do not say you find in Jesus at thirty the immense philosophical reason which marks Socrates, Aristotle, and Bacon at sixty or seventy, in the maturity of their wisdom; nor would I say that you find such monuments of imagination as you meet at every step in Milton, Shakespeare, or Dante; nor that you find such a vast and comprehensive understanding as you meet in the practical managers of states and empires. The thing would not be possible. In the Old Testament you find the writings of some men of distinguished ability,—the author of the Book of Job, of various parts of the Book of Proverbs, of Ecclesiasticus, of Ecclesiastes, of the Wisdom of Solomon, of the Prophecy of Isaiah. They were men of very large intellect, old, familiar with men, had seen peace and instituted war, knew the ways of the market-house and of kings' courts. In comparison, the words of Jesus, a Nazarene peasant, only thirty years old, are fully up to the highest level of their writings. You never feel that he was inferior to them in intellectual grasp.

Now the common idea that Jesus received this intellectual power from miraculous inspiration destroys all the individuality of his character,—for it makes him God, or else a mere pipe on which God plays. In either case there is nothing human about it, and it is of no use to us.

But his greater greatness came not from the intellect, but from a higher source. It is eminence of conscience, heart and soul; in one word, it is religious eminence. Here are the proofs of it: He makes religion consist in piety and morality, not in belief in forms, not in outside devotion. He knew it is a very easy thing to be devout after the common fashion, as easy to make prayers as to fill your hand with dust from the street. Was it a little thing in Jesus to declare that religion consisted in piety and morality? All the world over, the priests made religion to consist in forms, rituals, mutilating the body and spirit, in attending to artificial ordinances. Jesus summed up all the law and the prophets in love to God and love to man. Men worshipped the Sabbath; he religiously broke it. They thought God loved only the Jew, and above all some Jewish priest, with bells on his garments; but he set up a travelling Samaritan as the religious man. What a gnashing of teeth there was in the Jerusalem Association when he said the Samaritan was a great man! Doubtless it was a story founded on fact,—some good-natured Samaritan, jogging on his donkey from Jerusalem to Jericho, seeing the poor man, and giving him his sympathy and aid. It took a man of great religious genius to say that two thousand years ago; it is a rare thing to comprehend it to-day. See the same thing in his love of the wicked. He went to cure the sick; not to cure the righteous, and save the well. His sympathy was with the oppressed and trodden down, and very practical sympathy it was too. The finest picture of an ideal gentleman which antiquity has left is contained in the Book of Job. But Job's ideal gentleman is very proud, over-bearing to men beneath him. "Their fathers," said he, "I would have disdained to set with the dogs of my flock." The Book of Job is one of the best in the Old Testament,—full of poetry, which is a small thing; and full of piety and morality which is a great thing. This is the limitation of that ideal gentleman. Now Jesus goes out to that despised class of men, and says he came to seek and save them. Was that a small thing? Even to-day, in democratic Boston, to be a minister to the poor is a reproach. He is esteemed the most fortunate minister who is ministered unto, and not who ministers. The man who in Boston gathers crowds of men from the common walks of life,—what is he called? "A preacher to the rabble,"—that is the ecclesiastical title. What was it in the old civilization two thousand years ago,—a civilization controlled by priests and soldiers, who had a sword to offer to the beggar and the slave, and who looked with haughty scorn, like Aristotle and Cicero, on men who got their bread by the work of their hand?

The third thing was his trust in God. The Hebrews were and are more remarkable for their faith in God than any other nation that ever lived. In this, Jesus was a Hebrew of Hebrews, the most eminent of his tribe in this vast quality. But witness that his faith was in a God who loved all men, in the God who went out to meet the prodigal, and met him a great way off, and fell on his neck and kissed him, and was more joyous over one sinner that repented than over ninety-nine that needed no repentance. The first Gospel does not understand this, and therefore denies the width of Jesus' faith in God, and makes him limit his ministry to his own nation; but the second and third Gospels put it beyond a doubt.

Now the impression that he has made on the world, the character of his influence, the opinion which the human race has formed of him,—all confirm this judgment, derived from the historical record of his words and works. It seems to me that his actual character was higher than the character assigned to Jehovah in the Old Testament, to Zeus in Greece, or Jupiter in Rome. He made a revolution in the idea of God, and himself went up and took the throne of the world. That was a step in progress; and if called upon to worship the Jehovah of the Old Testament, or Jesus of Nazareth, a plain man, as he is painted in the first three Gospels, I should not hesitate, I should worship my brother; for in the highest qualities this actual man is superior to men's conception of God. He loves men of all nations, is not angry with the wicked every day; hating sin, he has the most womanly charity for the sinner. Jesus turned the heathen gods out of the heathen heaven, because he was more God than they; and he ascended the throne of Jehovah, because in his life he gave more proofs of justice and love than

Jehovah, as he is represented in the Old Testament. Let us not be harsh; let us not blame men for worshipping the creature more than the Creator. They saw the Son higher than the Father, and they did right. The popular adoration of Jesus to-day is to me the best thing in the popular ecclesiastical religion.

But I do not believe in the perfection of Jesus, that he had no faults of character, was never mistaken, never angry, never out of humor, never dejected, never despairing. I do not believe that from his cradle to his cross he never did, nor said, nor felt, nor thought, a wrong thing. To say that was his character, I think would be as absurd as to say that he learned to walk without stumbling, or to talk without stammering, or could see as well at three hours old as at twelve years, and could reason as well at thirty days as at thirty years. God does not create monsters, he creates men. I cannot say that in his popular teachings there are no errors. It seems to me very plain that he taught the existence of a devil; that he ascribed evil qualities to God, wrath that would not sleep at the Day of Judgment; that he believed in eternal torment. His prediction that the world would soon be destroyed, and that the Son of Man would come back in the clouds of heaven, and that this should take place during the life of men then living, was obviously a mistake. So with the promise of temporal power to the twelve apostles. All this shows the limitations of the man. Men claim that Jesus had no error in his creed or his life, no defect in his character. Then of course he is not a man, but God himself, or a bare pipe on which God plays; and in either case there was no virtue, no warning, no example in the man. And I think that Jesus would be the last man in the world ever to have claimed the exemption that is claimed for him by the clergy in all Christian lands. I know that what I say is a great heresy.

The coming of such a man was of the greatest importance to mankind. He showed a higher type of manliness than the world had ever seen before, or men deemed possible. There was manly intellect joined with womanly conscience and affection and soul; there was manhood and womanhood united into one great humanhood of character. Men were shut up in nationalities. He looked at humanity; all men were as brothers.

Men looked out at some old conception of a God, who once spoke on Sinai, and who said his last word years ago. He told them there was a living God, numbering the hairs of their head, loving the eighteen men whom the tower of Siloam slew, and just as ready to inspire the humblest fisherman by the Galilean lake as Moses. He found men undertaking to serve God by artificial rites and ceremonies, sacrifices, fast days, feast days; and he bade them serve him by daily piety and morality; and, if they could not find the way, he walked before and showed them,—and this was the greatest thing that could be done.

I think that Jesus of Nazareth was greater than the Evangelists supposed him to be. They valued him for his miraculous birth and works, because he was the Hebrew Messiah. I do not believe his miraculous birth and works, I am sure he was not the Hebrew Messiah. I should not think him any better for being miraculously born; the common birth is good enough for mankind. I think the Christian churches greatly underrate Jesus. They make his death his great merit. To be willing to spend a few hours in dying for mankind,—what is that? We must all meet death; if not to-day, some other day, and to spend a few hours in dying is a trifle any day; for a few dollars a month, and a bit of bunting with stripes on it, you may hire men any day for that. But to be a man with such a character as that, possessed of such a masculine quantity of intellect, and of such a womanly quality, with such a feminine affection and soul,— I would rather be that than be a dozen Hebrew Messiahs wrought into one. To teach men that religion was piety and morality, and what belonged to them; to tell them that religion was not for Saturday only, but for Sunday, Monday and every day; for the fireside and the wayside; to live that religion, merciful to the merciless, hating sin with all his character, but loving the sinner with all his heart; able as the ablest-minded, but shedding his sunlight on the dark places of the earth,—I would rather be such a man than a hundred incarnations of the Olympian Jove. Men vastly underrate the character of Jesus in looking to make him a God. They have forgotten the mighty manhood which burned in that Galilean breast.

This was the cause of his success: He was a great man, and of the highest kind of greatness; not without faults, but the manliest of men; not without errors in his doctrine, as it has been reported. He called men off from a dead Deity to a living God, from artificial sacraments to natural piety and morality. He preached natural religion, gave men a new sight of humanity. It was too great for them. The first generation said he was a devil, and slew him; the next said he was a God, and worshipped him. He was not a God, but a man showing us the way to God; not saving us by his death, but leading us by his life; crucified between two *other* malefactors, as the Scripture tells, buried secretly at night, and now worshipped as God.

Though almost two thousand years have passed by, Christendom has not yet got high enough to reverence the Galilean peasant who was our brother. We honor his death, but not his life; look to him to save us *in* our sins, not to save us *from* them. Men call him "Master," and scorn his lesson; "Lord," and reject the religion which he taught,—to visit the fatherless and widows in their affliction, and to keep a life unspotted from the world.

I look on Jesus as the highest product of the human race. I honor intellectual greatness; I bend my neck to Socrates, and Newton, and La Place, and Hegel, and Kant, and the vast minds of our own day. But what are they all, compared with this greatness of justice, greatness of philanthropy, greatness of religion? Why, they are as nothing! I look on Jesus not only as a historical prophet, but as a prophetic foretelling. He shows what is in you and me, and only comes as the earliest flower of the spring comes, to tell us that summer is near at hand. Amid the Caesars, the Maximuses, the Herculeses, the Vishnus, the Buddhas, and the Jehovahs, who have been successively the objects of the earthly or heavenly worship of men, Jesus comes out as these fair flowers come in the wintry hour, tokens of a summer yet to come of tropic realms, where all this beauty blossoms all the year. I thank God for the history which Jesus is! I thank him more for the prophecy which he is!

*   *   *

THE CHRISTIAN DOCTRINE OF JUSTIFICATION

AND RECONCILIATION

Albrecht Ritschl

(1822-1889)

RITSCHL INAUGURATED the most celebrated school of Protestant theology of the nineteenth century. Rich in suggestive thought he provoked much controversy.

Ritschl took a stand against metaphysics and mysticism and even against the sciences for their encroachment in the area of religion, particularly the Christian point of view. Religion, he held, has to do with man's practical solution to the questions of the meaning of reality. Man feels dominated by a world of nature and yet he, as a spiritual being, has the strong impulse to assert his independence of nature. Independent of theories and obstacles man asserts his own worth and needs and makes independent judgments of value (his religious nature).

Value judgments are of two kinds: concomitant and independent. The first operate in the realm of fact and reason; the second reach out and make judgments of worth beyond the sphere of fact and reason. The religious spirit moves in this second realm. It is akin to moral judgments. As such, whatever metaphysics or the sciences may say, man expresses his own superiority and higher dependence, his commitment to a superhuman spiritual power and his own independent worth and victory over every obstacle. There is nothing mystical or romantic about this. It is a judgment of worth, existing in its own dimension, asserting God and man's deliverance.

It is from this independent value-judgment that Christianity as a religion is to be asserted, measured and possessed.

Christianity contains its own metaphysics and theology and pattern. It is a revealed religion, indeed historical but more than history. There is a witness in it which focuses upon a transcendent order. There is a freedom in it which sets free. There is an ethic in it which is absolute. There is a redemption in it which is a vocation. There is a righteousness in it which is offered and shared by Christ and mediated by his church to his disciples. All such ideas are not the end-result of speculation or mystical awareness but the particulars of a general pattern appropriated by man's will (not intellect) when his religious value-judgment confronts the Christian religion.

Man as a moral being lays down the law to his faith and the Christian religion responds to this demand of his nature.

Ritschl was born in Berlin, his father a celebrated Lutheran preacher. After an excellent university education he became lecturer (1846) and later professor in the University of Bonn. In 1864 he moved to Göttingen where as professor he remained until his death. *The Christian Doctrine of Justification and Reconciliation,* his chief theological work, was published in 1870-1874. He believed himself to be in true succession to Reformation theology and close to Luther. Did not Luther, while appealing to the New Testament and the Scriptures, particularly to Christ, assert an independent judgment of value which lifted him above philosophical frameworks and was not his approach fundamentally that of the moral problem within himself and did he not hold that the historical church, in its essentially redemptive character, mediated the gospel of justification and reconciliation? This is the Ritschlianism of Ritschl out of which a great variety of interpretations developed among his spiritual disciples.

Editor

THE CHRISTIAN DOCTRINE OF JUSTIFICATION

AND RECONCILIATION

THE DOCTRINE OF GOD

. . . . THE ENDEAVOUR to construct *theology* in the Gentile-Christion Church arose from the belief that the positive conception of God as the Father of Christ, and of Christ as the Son of God, must be demonstrated as a universal truth of reason, in relation to the knowledge of the world which men had then attained. This belief has been, not confirmed, but rather shaken to the very foundation, by the manifold turns which the history of theology and philosophy has taken. For one thing, we can no longer conceal from ourselves the fact that the Greek Fathers carried the thought of God and Christ out into notions of the ultimate and the mediate ground of the world, which are peculiar to the later eclectic philosophy of Greece, and neither cover nor exhaust the original sense of the former conceptions. On the other hand, Gentile-Christian theology always insists on the reservation that the Christian religion presents an element which transcends all merely secular knowledge, namely, the end and the means of the blessedness of man. Whatever content may have been ascribed to this word *blessedness,* it expressly denotes a goal, the knowledge of which is unattainable by philosophy, and the realisation of which cannot be secured by the natural means at the command of men, but depends upon the positive character of Christianity. Consequently, the theology of the Greek Fathers is not merely cosmology, but, above all, a doctrine of redemption; the cosmology upon which the doctrine of redemption is built, however, is developed by means of ideas borrowed from Plato and the Stoics. The Scholastics carry on this method, and Thomas Aquinas makes a statement on the point which harmonises with the foregoing criticism of Greek theology. For, in the assurance of blessedness given by Christianity, he sees a destiny for men which was not provided for in their creation by God, nor included in their natural constitution, and which cannot be understood merely by the use of their reason. But he does not make this special feature of Christianity the key to his view of the world as a whole; rather, it is underpropped by a thoroughly rational theology, the material of which has no relation to Christianity, and which is unmistakably derived from Greek Philosophy. The same procedure is still adhered to by the traditional theology among ourselves. Nevertheless the division of the material of theology into propositions given by reason and propositions given by revelation is a method whose validity can no longer be maintained. In opposition thereto there has gradually come into force the contrary principle, that religion and theoretical knowledge are different functions of spirit, which, when they deal with the same objects, are not even partially coincident, but wholly diverge. This heterogeneity must be accurately established ere it can be decided what use is to be made of general theoretical knowledge in the scientific exposition of Christianity.

If religion in every case is an interpretation of man's relation to God and the world, guided by the thought of the sublime power of God to realise the end of this blessedness of man, advancing insight into the history of religions has forced on us the task of formulating a universal *conception of religion,* under which all the particular species of religion might find their peculiar features determined. But this task involves no slight difficulties, and contributes less to the understanding of Christianity than is often expected. The formula by which this very thing, religion in general, has just been described, makes no claim to be a definition proper of the generic conception of religion. It is too definite for that. The ideas which it employs—God, world, blessedness—have so directly Christian a stamp, that they apply to other religions only in a comparative degree, *i.e.* in order to indicate the general idea of religion, we should have to specify at the same time the different modifications which they undergo in different religions. For, besides belief in the One God, there falls to be considered the ascription to the Godhead of multiplicity, or duplicity, or difference in sex, and there is, further, the recognition of superhuman power in the spirits of the dead. Again, the relation of the Godhead to the world undergoes modification according as the world is conceived as a unity, or this point is left obscure, or the immediate surroundings of a particular wild tribe are taken as its world. It is modified, further, according as the Divine beings are identified with the forces and phenomena of nature, or distinguished from nature and creation, or, in the latter case, occupy a more negative or more positive relation to the world. Lastly, as regards blessedness, we have to consider the different cases in which what is sought through adoration or adjuration of the superhuman powers is merely some chance benefit, or the idea of a supreme good is formed, and this again is sought in the world, or apart from the world, or in a combination of both forms. As, therefore, the historical religions offer, under each of these heads, a rich supply of specific and sub-specific characteristics, which have no place in the general conception of religion, language can furnish no terms sufficiently neutral and indeterminate to express the general conception of religion desired. But, besides, it would be impossible to state in their proper place the above-discussed modifications of the several parts of the definition, without making obscure the very point which is professedly of importance.

If, however, we have once arrived at a general conception of religion more or less distinct in outline, it serves, as do all general ideas, as a clue by which to determine the chief characteristics of the various species of religion. Now we have no difficulty in ascertaining by an examination of all other religions, that the secular knowledge which they involve is not disinterestedly theoretical, but guided by practical ends. The circumstance, therefore, when given a place provisionally in the general conception, suggests, first, that objection may justly be taken to the exactly contrary use of secular knowledge which has made its way into the Christian Church; and next, that the later should be expelled, as something accidental, from the idea of the Christian religion. In the investigation of Christianity the general conception of religion should be used *regulatively*. I desire to distinguish myself very precisely in this respect from those who, in interpreting Christianity, make a *constitutive* use of the general conception. For when this method is employed, no longer as Scholasticism employs it, but in such a way that the influence of the general conception of religion makes one even for a moment neutral towards the Christian religion itself, in order to be able to deduce its meaning from the conditions of the general conception, then the only effect of this is to undermine Christian conviction. Christian conviction, however, is necessarily left intact when, as a theologian, one forms a general conception of religion, whatever the nature of that conception may be, for regulative use. For the observation and comparison of the various historical religions from which the general conception is abstracted, likewise shows that they stand to one another not merely in the relation of species, but also in the relation of stages. They exhibit an ever more rich and determinate manifestation of the chief features of religion; their connection is always more close, their aims more worthy of man. Such a way of looking at them opens up more fruitful vistas than are offered by the abstraction of a general conception of religion, followed by the comparison of the historical religions as species of this genus. For in this case the various religions are treated merely as natural phenomena; in the other case they are viewed as elements in the spiritual history of humanity. To prove that religions are related to one another as stages, is a scientific problem which still awaits an impartial and unprejudiced solution. Consequently we have to consider that several religions, such as Christianity and Islam, claim to occupy the highest stage above all others; and that Buddhists and Hindus who have become acquainted with Christianity put forward reasons which are meant to demonstrate the superiority of their faiths over the Christian. When, therefore, as Christians, in reviewing the series of stages presented by the religions of the world, we judge them by the principle that Christianity transcends them all, and that in Christianity the tendency of all the others finds its perfect consummation, the claim of the science of religion to universal validity may seem to be sacrificed to the prejudice arising from our own personal convictions. But it is aimless and impracticable to attempt to prove the universal validity of the view that religions can be arranged in an ascending series. Do people expect to discover thus a way of demonstrating scientifically to a Mohammedan or a Buddhist that the Christian religion, and not theirs, occupies the highest rank? In carrying out the task we have indicated, we have no such aim. It were indeed a desirable result, in the case of people who have been born Christians, and now, *e.g.,* declare the verdict of their scientific knowledge to be the inferiority of Christianity to Buddhism, if we could detach them from their error. But it is impossible for us, when arranging religions in a series of stages, to shut our eyes to the claim of Christianity to occupy the highest place. For those qualities in other religions by which they *are* religions are intelligible to us chiefly as measured by the perfection which they assume in Christianity, and by the clearness which distinguishes the perfect religion from the imperfect. The arrangement of religions in stages, consequently, amounts to no more than a scientific attempt to promote mutual understanding among Christians; and assent to the statement that Christianity is the highest and most perfect religion is therefore no obstacle to the scientific character of the theory.

Here, therefore, our task is not to elaborate the serial arrangement of religions, but to seek a solution of the question how Christianity, as a religion, is related to general philosophical knowledge. Consequently, it is desirable that the qualities by which *Christianity reveals its religious character* should be brought out with that distinctness which they claim to possess at the level of Christianity. If in doing so we glance at other religions, our business will just be to point out the modifications for the worse which they exhibit when compared with Christianity. The various historical religions are always of a social character, belonging to a multitude of persons. Thence it follows that to assign to religion a merely psychological complexion, in particular to refer it to feeling, is not a solution, but only an abridgement of the problem. In a community the influence of the individual is conditioned by two factors, inasmuch as he is both like and unlike the others, alternately dependent on them and affecting them actively. Consequently a psychological explanation of religion is inadequate, for it deals only with those phenomena of spirit in which all men are alike, and one is the type for all. The above-mentioned dissimilarity of men within the common life of a religion falls under the scope of ethics. Now the multiplicity pertaining to a religion is one of distribution, partly in space and partly in time. An illustration of the latter is presented by the successive stages of life. Thence it follows that every social religion implies a doctrinal tradition.

The dispersion in space of the members of the same religion is a direct obstacle to their fellowship, but it is compensated for when the religion takes real shape in the gathering for worship. Feeling, as pleasure or pain, as blessedness or suffering, is the personal gain or the personal presupposition which impels individuals to participate in religious fellowship. Nor in all religions does this aspect stand out so clearly and distinctly from the other functions as it is customary to suppose. In orgiastic faiths, contending emotions of feeling are the very material of worship; in the Roman, religious feeling assumes the form of painful attention to the correctness of ceremonial actions; in the Greek, the same factor appears in the serenity and the seriousness which affect, and are affected by, the worship. Hence it follows that for different reasons the historical religions claim service from all the functions of spirit—knowledge, for the doctrinal tradition, *i.e.* for a particular view of the world; will, for the common worship; feeling, for the alternation of satisfaction and dissatisfaction, moods by which religious life is removed from the ordinary level of existence. No religion is correctly or completely conceived when one element of this succession is regarded as more important or more fundamental than the others. At the same time the question is reserved whether our scientific explanation of the total fact of religion shall give the preference to one or other of the functions of spirit.

In every religion what is sought, with the help of the superhuman spiritual power reverenced by man, is a solution of the contradiction in which man finds himself, as both a part of the world of nature and a spiritual personality claiming to dominate nature. For in the former *rôle* he is a part of nature, dependent upon her, subject to and confined by other things; but as spirit he is moved by the impulse to maintain his independence against them. In this juncture, religion springs up as faith in superhuman spiritual powers, by whose help the power which man possesses of himself is in some way supplemented, and elevated into a unity of its own kind which is a match for the pressure of the natural world. The idea of gods, or Divine powers, everywhere includes belief in their spiritual personality, for the support to be received from above can only be reckoned on in virtue of an affinity between God and man. Even where merely invisible natural powers are regarded as Divine, they are conceived in a way analogous to that in which man distinguishes himself from nature. For the rest, the ease with which definite stupendous natural phenomena, whether beneficent or destructive, are personified, proves that it is in the spiritual personality of the gods that man finds the foothold which he seeks for in every religion. The assertion that the religious view of the world is founded upon the idea of a whole[1] certainly holds true of Christianity: as regards the other religions it must be modified thus far, that in them what is sought is a supplementary addition to human self-feeling or to human independence over against and above the restrictions of the world. For in order to know the world as a totality, and in order himself to become a totality in or over it by the help of God, man needs the idea of the oneness of God, and of the consummation of the world in an end which is for man both knowable and realisable. But this condition is fulfilled in Christianity alone. For in the religion of the Old Testament the presuppositions, indeed, are given, but the world-end aimed at is merely the perfecting of the one chosen people in moral, political, and economical independence; the human perfecting of the individual Israelite, each in his own personal character, is not kept in view, as it is in the Christian conception of life and blessedness. Nevertheless, in heathen and even in polytheistic religions there is always a tendency at work towards belief in the unity of the Divine power, and in the measure in which this is the case the supplement to his own resources which man seeks in religion becomes more clear and more worthy. When, as in Brahminism, the world which has sprung from the original Being is so constituted that it returns to the distinctionless unity of real existence, what takes the place of the maintenance of selfhood is its absorption in the Divine Being. In its own way, this too is a kind of unity, for it is viewed as the consummation of asceticism and quietistic piety.

Christianity, by its completely rounded view of the world, guarantees to believers that they shall be preserved unto eternal life in the Kingdom of God, which is God's revealed end in the world—and that, too, in the full sense that man is thus in the

1. Lotze, *Mikrokosmus*, III. p. 331.

Kingdom of God set over the world as a whole in his own order. Not only the Christian's tone of feeling, but also his estimate of self is determined by this highest and all-inclusive good. For this religion offers no passionate impulse, no vacillation between changing tones of feeling arising from confused ideas, no voluptuous alternation of aesthetic pleasure and pain; on the contrary, such emotions must be viewed in the light of the antitheses of sin and grace, of bondage as to what is good, and liberty to give God thanks and to act aright. The temper produced by these conclusions, therefore, normally issues in the reverence for God proper to the level reached by Christianity. This combination is the rule in other religions also. Those religious affections of feeling which are called forth by the effort to secure blessings obtainable from the gods, and which have a complexion of their own, universally manifest themselves solely in correlative acts of worship. At this point, however, in the sacrifice of acquired property, and in religious and moral self-abnegation, there comes into view a universal characteristic of all religions. In this way the domain of religious action is marked off from secular life as a sacred domain; at the same time, however, the value of the blessings bestowed by the gods is gauged by pleasurable feelings of another class than those which accrue to man naturally or as a result of work. Religious feeling, with or without the accompaniment of a clear estimate of self, will always be found to be the material of worship; but the form which such feeling assumes witnesses at the same time to a decision of the will, which gives reality to the acknowledgment of God and the personal satisfaction this entails. The idea of God is the ideal bond between a definite view of the world and the idea of man as constituted for the attainment of goods or the highest good. Worship is the realisation of the blessing sought by the practical acknowledgment of the power that bestows it. In Christianity, thanksgiving for God's grace, prayer for its continuance, and service of God in His Kingdom, have attached to them eternal life and that blessedness which corresponds to the highest good, the Kingdom of God.

Common worship has a still closer relation to the revelation which forms the organic center of every connected religious view of the world. The factor, too, appears with various modifications at the various stages of religion. In the religion of sorcery, acts of worship are employed to elicit revelations from mysterious superhuman powers. In Christianity, revelation through God's Son is the *punctum stans* of all knowledge and religious conduct. In the developed natural religions, success in obtaining Divine revelations is bound up with their being regularly acknowledged in worship. No idea of a religion complete after its own order can be formed if the characteristic of revelation which belongs to it is either denied or even merely set aside as indifferent. True, this very method has long been customary. People think themselves justified in abstracting from the characteristic of revelation found in every religion, inasmuch as they regard the myths of natural religions, and the doctrines of the religions of the Bible, as veiled or undeveloped philosophy. But the original purpose of myths is to explain why particular acts of worship, intended to do honour to Divine self-manifestations, are performed at some definite spot and at regularly recurrent intervals. What we may regard as the doctrinal material of the religion of the Old Testament—the free creation of the world by God, and His intention that man, who, as spirit, is the image of God, should bear rule over it—denotes the presuppositions of the belief that the Israelites are called by God in an especial covenant, under which they have to achieve their historical destiny in the world under the government of their Divine King. The speciality of the spot at which a god has ordained that he shall be adored, the speciality of the times at which the gods move through the land and summon their worshippers to celebrate their festivals, the speciality of the choice of Israel by the Lord of all nations—in short, *specialty* is the element which impels men to grasp the different aspects of religion, and to combine them practically in worship. The significance which revelation thus has for common worship also indicates an indispensable precondition of our understanding Christianity. The Person of its Founder is not only the key to the Christian view of the world, and the standard of Christians' self-judgment and moral effort, but also the standard which shows how prayer must be composed, for in prayer both individual and united adoration of God consists. At the same time the acknowledgment of the revelation of God in Christ yields this preeminent excellence of Christianity, namely, that its view of the world is a rounded whole, and that the goal it sets to life is this, that in Christianity man becomes a whole, a spiritual character supreme over the world. For speciality is ever the condition under which a universal end is realised through the combination of individual things and relations.

. . . . . How, then, is *religious knowledge* related to theoretical or philosophical knowledge? This question, indeed, has already been raised by the very fact of Greek Philosophy; still, much more tangible and comprehensive reasons for raising it are to be found in the mutual relations of Christianity and philosophy. Accordingly, it is best that we should limit the question to Christianity in so far as it is a religion, intelligible as such from the characteristics noted above. The possibility of both kinds of knowledge mingling, or, again, colliding, lies in this, that they deal with the same object, namely, the world. Now we cannot rest content with the amiable conclusion that Christian knowledge comprehends the world as a whole, while philosophy fixes the special and universal laws of nature and spirit. For with this task every philosophy likewise combines the ambition to comprehend the universe under one supreme law. And for Christian knowledge also one supreme law is the form under which the world is comprehensible as a whole under God. Even the thought of God, which belongs to religion, is employed in some shape or other by every non-materialistic philosophy. Thus no principle of discrimination between the two kinds of knowledge is, at least provisionally, to be found in the object with which they deal.

Now, in order to elicit the distinction between the two from the realm of the subject, I recall the twofold manner in which the mind (*Geist*) further appropriates the sensations aroused in it. They are determined, according to their value for the Ego, by the feeling of pleasure or pain. Feeling is the basal function of mind, inasmuch as in it the Ego is originally present to itself. In the feeling of pleasure or pain, the Ego decides whether a sensation, which touches the feeling of self, serves to heighten or depress it. On the other hand, through an idea the sensation is judged in respect of its cause, the nature of the latter, and its connection with other causes: and by means of observation, etc., the knowledge of things thus gained is extended until it becomes scientific. The two functions of spirit mentioned are always in operation simultaneously, and always also in some degree mutually related, even though it be in the inverse ration of prominence. In particular, it must not be forgotten that all continuous cognition of the things which excite sensation is not only accompanied, but likewise guided, by feeling. For in so far as attention is necessary to attain the end of knowledge, will, as representing the desire for accurate cognition, comes in between; the proximate cause of will, however, is feeling as expressing the consciousness that a thing or an activity is worth desiring, or that something ought to be put away. Value-judgments therefore are determinative in the case of all connected knowledge of the world, even when carried out in the most objective fashion. Attention during scientific observation, always denote that such knowledge has a value for him who employs it. This fact makes its presence all the more distinctly felt when knowledge is guided through a richly diversified field by attention of a technical or practical kind.

But even if we have made up our mind that religious knowledge in general, and therefore Christian knowledge too, consists of value-judgments, such a definition is as lacking in precision as it would be to describe philosophical knowledge contrariwise as disinterested. For without interest we do not trouble ourselves about anything. We have therefore to distinguish between *concomitant* and *independent* value-judgments. The former are operative and necessary in all theoretical cognition, as in all technical observation and combination. But *independent* value-judgments are all perceptions of moral ends or moral hindrances, in so far as they excite moral pleasure or pain, or, it may be, set in motion the will to appropriate what is good or repel the opposite. If the other kinds of knowledge are called "disinterested," this only means that they are without these moral effects. But even in them pleasure or pain must be present, according as they succeed or fail. Religious knowledge forms another class of independent value-judgments. That is, it cannot be traced back to the conditions which mark the knowledge belonging to moral will, for there exists religion which goes on without any relation whatever to the moral conduct of life.

Besides, in many religions religious pleasure is of a purely natural kind, and is independent of those conditions which lift religious above natural pleasure. For only at the higher stages do we find religion combined with the ethical conduct of life. Religious knowledge moves in independent value-judgments, which relate to man's attitude to the world, and call forth feelings of pleasure or pain, in which man either enjoys the dominion over the world vouchsafed him by God, or feels grievously the lack of God's help to that end. This theory is almost more easily intelligible if it be tested by religions which possess no moral character. Orgiastic worships represent contending natural feelings with extraordinary intensity and with abrupt changes, in virtue of their recognition of the value which the identity of the Godhead with the vegetation as it decays and again revives, has for the man who modifies his attitude towards the world of nature in sympathy with the Godhead which he adores. The peculiar nature of religious value-judgments is less clear in the case of religions of an explicitly ethical character. Nevertheless, in Christianity we can distinguish between the religious functions which relate to our attitude towards God and the world, and the moral functions which point directly to men, and only indirectly to God, Whose end in the world we fulfill by moral service in the Kingdom of God. In Christianity, the religious motive of ethical action lies here, that the Kingdom of God, which it is our task to realise, represents also the highest good which God destines for us as our supramundane goal. For here there emerges the value-judgment that our blessedness consists in that elevation above the world in the Kingdom of God which accords with our true destiny. This is a religious judgment, inasmuch as it indicates the value of this attitude taken up by believers towards the world, just as those judgments are religious in which we set our trust in God, even when He condemns us to suffering.

In its day the Hegelian philosophy represented theoretical knowledge as not merely the most valuable function of spirit, but likewise the function which has to take up the problem of religion and solve it. To this Feuerbach opposed the observation that in religion the chief stress falls upon the wishes and needs of the human heart. But as the latter philosopher also continued to regard professedly pure and distinterested knowledge as the highest achievement of man, religion, and especially the Christian religion—which he held to be the expression of a purely individual and therefore egoistic interest, and a self-delusion in respect of its object, God—was by him declared to be worthless, as compared not merely with the knowledge of philosophic truth, but also with purely moral conduct. But an interest in salvation in the Christian sense, when rightly understood, is incompatible with egoism. Egoism is a revolt against the common tasks of action. Now, people might say that faith in God for our salvation, and a dutiful public spirit towards our fellows, have nothing to do with one another, and that therefore there is no conceivable reason why religion, as a rule, should not be egoistic. But in Christianity precisely faith in God and moral duty within the Kingdom of God *are* related to one another. As a rule, therefore, it is impossible that Christian faith in God should be egoistic. On the other hand, theoretical knowledge in itself, as has been shown, is not disinterested; but moral conduct is still less so. For in the latter domain the vital point is that one realises as one's own interest the interest of others to whom the service is rendered. The moral disposition can nowhere strike root save in such motives. It is true that, contrary to the rule, faith in God may be combined with egoistic arrogance towards others. But the same danger attaches to both of the other kinds of activity which have been compared. It is possible for one occupied with theoretical knowledge to be vain and haughty, and for one devoted to the moral service of others to be tyrannical or sycophantic.

Scientific knowledge is accompanied or guided by a judgment affirming the worth of impartial knowledge gained by observation. In Christianity, religious knowledge consists in independent value-judgments, inasmuch as it deals with the relation between the blessedness which is assured by God and sought by man, and the whole of the world which God has created and rules in harmony with His final end. Scientific knowledge seeks to discover the laws of nature and spirit through observation, and is based on the presupposition that both the observations and their arrangement are carried out in accordance with the ascertained laws of human cognition. Now the desire for scientific knowledge carries with it no guarantee that, through the medium of observation and the combination of observations according to known laws, it will discover the supreme universal law of the world, from which, as a starting-point, the differentiated orders of nature and spiritual life, each in its kind, might be explained, and understood as forming one whole. On the contrary, the intermingling and collision of religion and philosophy always arises from the fact that the latter claims to produce in its own fashion a unified view of the world. This, however, betrays rather an impulse religious in its nature, which philosophers ought to have distinguished from the cognitive methods they follow. For in all philosophical systems the affirmation of a supreme law of existence, from which they undertake to deduce the world as a whole, is a departure from the strict application of the philosophic method, and betrays itself as being quite as much an object of the intuitive imagination, as God and the world are for religious thought. This is the case at all stages and in all forms of Greek philosophy, especially in those forms in which the ultimate universal grounds of existence, through which the universe is interpreted, are identified with the idea of God. In these cases the combination of heterogeneous kinds of knowledge—the religious and the scientific—is beyond all doubt; and it is to be explained by the fact that philosophers who, through their scientific observation of nature, had destroyed the foundations of the popular faith, sought to obtain satisfaction for their religious instincts by another path. In a certain respect, too, they were able to follow this tendency with especial confidence, so far as they succeeded in making out the unity of the Divine Being to be the ground of the universe. But in another respect they failed to satisfy the essential conditions of the religious view of the world, partly in so far as they surrendered the personality of the Godhead thus identified with the ground of the world, partly because they had to give up the active influence of a personal God upon the world. Nor, under these circumstances, could any worship be deduced from the idea of God. Thus the collision of Greek philosophy with the popular faith was twofold, and in both respects inevitable. For one thing, the actual observation of nature and her laws is incompatible with the religious combination of popular views of nature and the idea of God. Further, the rigidly unified view of the world held by philosophers is incompatible with the religious view of the world which is only loosely developed in polytheism. But the real force of the latter incompatibility is to be found in the fact that, under the guise of philosophic knowledge, what was really only the religious imagination has been operative in designing the general philosophic view of the world, the supreme principle of which is never proved as such, but always merely anticipatively assumed.

The opposition to Christianity which has been raised by Pantheism in its various modifications and by materialism, arises likewise from the fact that the law of a particular realm of being is set up as the supreme law of all being, though the other forms of existence neither would nor could be explained by its means. It may be admitted that natural science is right and consistent in explaining the mechanical regularity of all sensible things by the manifold movement of simple limited forces or atoms. But within this whole realm of existence, which is interpretable by the category of causality, observation reveals to us the narrower realm of organisms, which cannot be exhaustively explained by the laws of mechanism, but demand, besides, the application of the idea of end. But among organic beings, again, one section, differentiated in manifold ways, is animate, that is, endowed with the capacity of free movement. Finally, a still smaller section of animate beings is so constituted as to act freely from the conception of ends, to discover the laws of things, to conceive things as a whole, and themselves as in ordered interaction with them, further to identify all these activities with their own Ego by means of the manifold affections of feeling, and to exchange their spiritual possessions with others through speech and action. Now the claim of materialism to invalidate the Christian view of the world rests on the belief that it must succeed in deducing the organic from what is mechanical, and similarly the more complex orders of being from those immediately below. The materialistic interpretation of the world busies itself with the pursuit of these empty possibilities. Its scientific character is limited, however, by the fact that it can only suggest chance as the moving force of the ultimate causes of the world, and of the evolution of special realms of being out of those which are more general; for this is really to confess that science cannot penetrate to the supreme law of things. In all the combinations exhibited by the materialistic theory of the genesis of the world, there is manifest an expenditure of the power of imagination which finds its closest parallel in the cosmogonies of heathenism—which is of itself a proof that what rules in this school is not scientific method, but an aberrant and confused religious impulse. Thus the opposition which professedly exists between natural science and Christianity, really exists between an impulse derived from natural religion blended with the scientific investigation of nature, and the validity of the Christian view of the world, which assures to spirit its pre-eminence over the entire world of nature.

The same holds true of the various forms of Pantheism which have alternately assumed the guise of the Christian view of the world, and entered the lists against it. The deceptive power of the imagination has to be called in to deduce all the diversified orders of reality from the laws either of spatial construction, or of vegetable life, or of lyrico-musical sensation, or of logical thought. None of these laws is the key to an adequate view of the world as a whole; none has been elevated by the use of properly scientific method, *i.e.* by means of observation and orderly inferences, into the supreme principle of interpretation; but philosophers have been surprised into accepting one or other by the religious desire for a complete view of things which they did not distinguish from their scientific cognition. The claims, adverse to the Christian view of the world, which have been made as a consequence of this self-deception, are further supported by the assumption, by which philosophical idealism is dominated, that the laws of theoretical knowledge are the laws of the human spirit in all its functions. From the standpoint of such a principle many aspects of the Christian view of the world and of the Christian estimate of self appear contradictory, and consequently untrue. But as certainly as feeling and will cannot be reduced to ideational knowledge, the last-named is not justified in imposing its laws upon the former. Feeling is admittedly not susceptible to what are called the "reasons of the understanding," and the verdict of logic upon a contradiction, that it denotes something which is impossible and therefore unreal, is incommensurate with the moral verdict we pass on a bad will. It is true, the responsibility for the pretensions addressed by philosophy to the Christian religion often lies in part with the champions of Christianity themselves. It is so when they represent as the Christian faith some imperfect form of theology, that is, some system of the ideas of God and humanity which is as far away as possible from expressing the whole view of the world implied by the religious estimate of self which Christians are known to exercise, and by the character of their worship of God. Under these circumstances, philosophy often enough regards it as sufficient to demonstrate that the law of faith outlined in theology collides with laws of experience, and then declares religion untenable as an illegitimate trespass of the fancy upon the field of rigorous science. But the fact is, Pantheism is very far from rising to that estimate of the destiny and worth of human personality which is determinative in Christianity. Whenever the boundary-line between the Divine nature and the world is erased, whenever the universe in any one of its aspects is defined as the Absolute, there is nothing for man but to regard himself as a transient emanation of the World-Soul, or as an element in the spiritual development of humanity, whose progress leaves him behind and degrades him to a position of dependence. Nor is this result of the pantheistic view of the world sufficiently compensated for by the permission it accords us to cherish aesthetic sympathy with the universe, or to exercise ethical resignation in presence of the ceaseless advance of intellectual culture. These sentiments have already appeared on the soil of heathenism, and they indicate no reason why we should interest ourselves in free-thought. He who thinks that this view of the world is to be preferred to the Christian, ignores the principle of the Christian estimate of self—that the individual is worth more than the whole world, and that each soul can test and prove this truth through faith in God as His Father, and by service to Him in His Kingdom. For the Christian view of the world, disclosing as it does the all-inclusive moral and spiritual end of the world, which is also the proper end of God Himself, evidences itself as the perfect religion.

. . . . That religious knowledge consists of value-judgments is brought out in a felicitous way by Luther in his *Larger Cate-chism,* in the explanation of the First Commandment: "Deus est et vocatur, de cuius bonitate et potentia omnia bona certo tibi pollicearis, et ad quem quibuslibet adversis rebus ac peri-culis ingruentibus confugias, ut deum habere, nihil aliud sit, quam illi ex toto corde fidere et credere. . . . Haec duo, fides et deus, una copula coniungenda sunt." In these sentences are expressed various truths of which the theology of the schools both earlier and later has taken no account, and which its mod-ern successors combat even yet. Knowledge of God can be demon-strated as religious knowledge only when He is conceived as securing to the believer such a position in the world as more than counterbalances its restrictions. Apart from this value-judg-ment of faith, there exists no knowledge of God worthy of this content. So that we ought not to strive after a purely theoretical and "disinterested" knowledge of God, as an indispensable pre-liminary to the knowledge of faith. To be sure, people say that we must first know the nature of God and Christ ere we can ascertain their worth for us. But Luther's insight perceived the incorrectness of such a view. The truth rather is that we know the nature of God and Christ only in their worth for us. For God and faith are inseparable conceptions; faith, however, con-fessedly does not consist in abstract knowledge, or knowledge which deals with merely historical facts. On the contrary, it cannot be conceived save as possessed of those qualities which Luther vindicates for it. But, finally, his explanation of the First Commandment is bound up with the revelation of God in Christ, and is unintelligible apart from it. For the "goodness and power" of God, on which faith casts itself, is in Luther's view revealed in the work of Christ alone. Apart from Christ, apart from the reflection of God in Him, Luther finds the idea of God to be accompanied by terrors and annihilating effects. This dilemma absolutely excludes the possibility of "disinter-ested" knowledge of God, as in some way correlative to the idea of the world.

While I am explaining that I maintain the religious concep-tion of God as conditioned in the way Luther describes, I should also like to adduce these further remarks of his: "Quemadmodum saepenumero a me dictum est, quod sola cordis fiducia deum pariter atque idolum faciat et constituat. Quodsi fides et fiducia recta et sincera est, deum rectum habebis, contra si falsa fuerit et mendax fiducia, etiam deum tuum falsum et mendacem esse necesse est. . . . Iam in quacunque re animi tui fiduciam et cor fixum habueris, haec haud dubie deus tuus est." For here the religious character of the knowledge of God seems to be reduced to the arbitrary feeling of the subject, and we seem to be furnished with a corroboration of the maxim that a man's God varies as his faith. But this interpretation of Luther's words cannot be the true one, for this reason, that he distinguished between two kinds of faith, that which is sincere, and that which is infected with illusion. If he reduced everything to arbitrary caprice, he would not make this distinction, which depends on whether one takes or does not take the right way to knowledge of God, namely, through Christ. For faith which is genuine and sincere can be exercised only in response to the true revelation of God. This is as far as possible from the case referred to in Luther's last sentence above, when it is said that everything on which a man sets his heart, be it sensual pleasure, or honour, or power, has the value of an idol. Between the two stands the case of trust infected with self-deception, with which an illusory idea of God is so combined as to show clearly that the person concerned will only consent to believe in a God Whose nature he can first determine in general by disinterested knowledge through analysis of his experience of the world. Not only is such an idea of God false, but it is contrary to truth to separate, in relation to Him, between knowledge and trust. Now theology is not devotion; as a science, rather, it is "disinterested" cognition. But as such it must be accompanied and guided by a sense of the worth of the Christian religion. The theologian, in his scientific work, must so far keep this degree of "interest" in sight as to conserve all those characteristics of the conception of God which render possible the trust described above. All other theological ideas—*e.g.* the idea we have to form of Christ and His Divinity—must be treated either in quite the same way, or with the most careful reference to the nature of these supreme ideas.

*   *   *

In religious cognition the idea of God is dependent on the presupposition that man opposes himself to the world of nature, and secures his position, in or over it, by faith in God. Consequently no proof of God's existence starts properly save that which accepts as given man's self-distinction from nature, and his endeavours to maintain himself against it or over it. This condition is satisfied in the case of the so-called moral argument, stated by Kant in his *Critique of Judgment*. It is true that Kant directly attaches to this theistic argument the cautious limitation, that *it is necessary to think God* in order strictly to explain the existence in the world of rational beings under moral laws, who view their own action, when worthy of their nature, as the final end of the world. For this involves likewise, as its precondition, the hope of felicity: the supreme good, therefore, which shall express the final end of rational beings under moral laws, is the combination of virtue and felicity, of moral and physical good (vol. i. p. 439). Both orders of existence, which follow laws quite different in kind, are conceived as meeting in this goal. The supreme good, thus determined, depends neither on our use of freedom nor on natural causes; consequently, in order to set the final end before us as the moral law directs, we must assume a moral Creator of the world. That is, it is necessary to think God as vouching for the satisfaction of the moral necessity we are under of conceiving the supreme good as a combination of virtue and felicity or lordship over nature (*Critique of Judgment,* §87). To begin with, there can be no doubt that Kant is in agreement with the Christian idea of God in his description of the Moral Creator and Ruler of the world. For everywhere in this connection God denotes the ethical Power Who assures to man the position above the world befitting his ethical worth, and this, too, as the final end of the world. Moreover, the argument is not merely the outcome of the reflection of religious knowledge upon the connection of its own elements. For its starting-point—the estimate of moral action as springing from freedom, and the hope of the union of felicity and virtue —is conceived independently of the authority of God. But, lastly, it appears from Kant's further explanations that he himself puts considerable limitations upon the necessary validity of this conception of God as the explanatory ground of the supreme good above described. He insists that the necessity of the thought of God can be adequately demonstrated solely for the practical Reason, for the idea of final end itself is rooted solely in the use of freedom according to moral laws, and does not arise out of the investigation of nature, and thus possesses only subjectivo-practical reality. He asserts that the argument in question does not comply with any form of theoretical proof, not even with that of an hypothesis set up to explain the possibility of a given fact. For we lack the material for the idea of a supersensuous being; and therefore it is impossible to determine such an idea specifically, and employ it as a basis of explanation. He maintains, accordingly, that the idea of God is only a conviction of personal faith, *i.e.* necessarily to be conceived as standing in relation to the dutiful use of the practical Reason. So also the idea of the final end of the world, by which we judge the use of freedom, can claim reality for us solely in a practical sense, and is therefore a matter of faith (*Critique of Judgment*, §88). These explanations of Kant are for one thing in accord with the dualism which in general he maintains between the theoretical and the practical Reason, and at the same time obey the principle that the reflective judgment attains merely to subjective truth.

Under these circumstances Kant's line of thought implies that, as his philosophy is incapable of combining into one whole the two heterogeneous theories of practical reason and of nature, he hands over the task of solving the problem to the Christian religion.

* * *

Personality is the form in which the idea of God is given through Revelation. As theology has to do with the God revealed in Christ, this is justified scientifically as the only practicable form of the conception of God. The content of the Divine will is to be deduced from the revealed reciprocal relations between Christ and God, and from no other principle.

* * *

Theology, in delineating the moral order of the world, must take as its starting-point that conception of God in which the relation of God to His Son our Lord is expressed, a relation which, by Christ's mediation, is extended likewise to His community. For when the Apostles, in the Epistles of the New Testament, describe God as our Father, that is an abbreviated expression for the Christian name for God, which when fully stated runs, "the God and Father of our Lord Jesus Christ" (2 Cor. i. 3, xi. 31; Rom. xv. 6; Col. i. 3; 1 Pet. i. 3; Eph. i. 3). As the name of God is always used in Scripture as a compendious description of His revelation, it is clear that, when God reveals Himself as Father through His Son Jesus Christ, the process is only completed when the community accepts the revelation by acknowledging the Mediator who brings it as its Lord. Any attempt, therefore, to construct a scientific doctrine of God must be wrong which fails to keep in view all the aspects of this name. The name God has the same sense when used of Father, Son, and Holy Spirit (Matt. xxviii. 19). For the name denotes God in so far as He reveals Himself, while the Holy Spirit is the power of God which enables the community to appropriate His self-revelation as Father through His Son (1 Cor. ii. 12). That the revelation of God through His Son, however, embraces the community which acknowledges His Son as her Lord, and how it does so, is explained by saying that God manifests Himself to the Son and to the community as *loving Will* (vol. ii. p. 96 ff.). As this conception of God is recognised as coming from the source of knowledge which is authoritative for the Christian community, it likewise follows that the goodness of God to all men, in bestowing on them the good things of nature (Matt. v. 45; Acts xiv. 17), is an inference which Christ drew from the knowledge He possessed of the love of God to Him and to His community. Thus the goodness of God, as the general presupposition of everything, is embraced in the specific attribute of the Divine Fatherhood; or, in other words, the truth that He has revealed Himself to the Christian community as love. There is no other conception of equal worth beside this which need be taken into account. This is especially true of the conception of the Divine holiness, which, in its Old Testament sense, is for various reasons not valid in Christianity, while its use in the New Testament is obscure (vol. ii. pp. 89, 101). Even the recognition of the personality of God does not imply independent knowledge apart from our defining Him as loving Will. It only decides the form to be given to this content, for without this content of loving Will the conception of spiritual personality is not sufficient to explain the world as a connected whole. The step, therefore, which we take now in bringing forward the truly Christian view of God ought not to be understood as though in His contrast to the world God were conceived, first of all, in general, as personality, and secondly, in particular, as loving Will;—and this in such a way that while consistent knowledge of the world might be drawn from the first conception, the second would yield simply more knowledge of the same sort. What I mean is rather this, that the conception of love is the only adequate conception of God, for it enables us, both to understand the revelation which comes through Christ to His community, and at the same time to solve the problem of the world. For this purpose the merely formal conception of personality is insufficient: for it leaves us free to ascribe all possible kinds of content to the Divine Will.

*   *   *

The Christian idea of the Kingdom of God, which has been proved the correlate of the conception of God as love, denotes the association of mankind—an association both extensively and intensively the most comprehensive possible—through the reciprocal moral action of its members, action which transcends all merely natural and particular considerations. Now it has been shown that this, the ruling idea of Jesus, failed to maintain itself as central in the practical interest of the apostles, and came to possess only the limited sense of the redemptive consummation expected in the future. Cares about the formation of congregations came so much to the front, that the entire moral interest was concentrated on their internal consolidation. In order to preserve the true articulation of the Christian view of the world, it is necessary clearly to distinguish between viewing

the followers of Christ, first, under the conception of the Kingdom of God, and secondly, under the conception of the *worshipping community,* or the Church. This distinction depends on
the difference which exists between moral and devotional action,
despite the fact that in Christianity moral action likewise can
claim the value of service to God. Now every devotional act, in
the technical sense of the word, is an end in itself to this extent,
that it never can be at the same time a means to an act of the
same kind. One may intend sacrifice and prayer to be the means
of winning Divine favour and Divine gifts; but, among all the
various possible devotional rites, it is neither conceivable nor
justifiable to subordinate any one of them to another as a means
to an end. Each devotional act, rather, just like artistic action,
possesses in itself its end and its power to satisfy the human
heart. On the other hand, every moral act, whatever its range,
has this peculiarity, that it must be conceived at once as an
end and as a means to all other possible moral acts. This is true
even when the agent's original intention does not include the
thought of morality as a means to itself, but the fact is brought
out only subsequently that those moral goods, which are produced by action, always stimulate action afresh. Those who believe in Christ, therefore, constitute a Church in so far as they
express in prayer their faith in God the Father, or present themselves to God as men who through Christ are well-pleasing to
Him. The same believers in Christ constitute the Kingdom of
God in so far as, forgetting distinctions of sex, rank, or nationality, they act reciprocally from love, and thus call into existence
that fellowship of moral disposition and moral blessings which
extends, through all possible gradations, to the limits of the
human race. The fellowship of Christians for the purpose of
religious worship manifests itself in the sphere of sense, and
therefore betrays its peculiar nature to every observer. On the
other hand, the moral Kingdom of God, even while it manifests
itself sensibly in action, as a whole reveals its peculiar nature
to Christian faith alone. Moreover, the fellowship of Christians
for worship gives rise to legal ordinances which it requires for
its own sake; but the Kingdom of God, while not injuriously
affected by the fact that moral action under certain circum-

stances assumes the garb of legal forms, does not in the least depend on them for its continued existence.

*   *   *

THE DOCTRINE OF CHRIST'S PERSON AND

LIFE-WORK

. . . THE NATURE of Christianity as a universal religion is such that *in the Christian view of the world a definite place is assigned to its historical founder.* In the two ethnic religions which come nearest to Christianity (though in different degrees), and which have preserved some recollection of their historical founders, namely in the Persian religion and in the religion of Israel, Zoroaster and Moses are indeed acknowledged as the founders and lawgivers of the faith; but there is no need of a personal confession either of the one or of the other, because for the religions which they founded the religious community is the nation, and the nation is the community. In the universal religions, on the other hand, it is through express recognition of the founder of the religion that membership in the religious community is described and attained. At the same time, in these religions a certain gradation presents itself in the worth and significance of personal adherence to the founder. In Islam it is enough to name the Prophet alongside of God, because for this religion of law he is merely the lawgiver. Nearer to the religious estimate of Jesus Christ in the Christian religion comes the significance which in Buddhism is attached to Sakyamuni Buddha as an incarnation of Deity. But in this case there is the difference that, whereas what Buddha aimed at was not by any means what his followers believe themselves to have received from him, Jesus, on the other hand, had in view for His own Person essentially that significance which is claimed for it in His religious community. In other words, Buddha had no intention of founding a religion; he did not so much as set forth any conception of God, or any explanation of the world in its relation to God; he did not explain how man is to reach a definite attitude towards the world or a definite position in the world:

he merely indicated the direction along which man is to achieve his own redemption from the misery of actual existence, namely, by the ascetic annihilation of personal life. A philosophy or ethic such as this, which addresses itself to human freedom, may be the basis of a school, but not of religious fellowship; therefore, the significance it secures for its author is that of the founder of a school. That it was afterwards associated with the Indian idea of God, and that the corresponding idea of Divine incarnation was applied to Buddha and to his successors, was a result utterly foreign to the view of the antagonist of Brahmanism. It is true that within the Christian community there are those who hold exactly the same view with regard to the purpose of Jesus, and the fate which has befallen the doctrine of His Person in the Christian Church. According to their reading of the Gospels, Jesus taught a lofty morality, but in the exercise of this vocation never transgressed the limits of a purely human estimate of Himself; only through influences that are wholly external have His followers been led to regard Him as an incarnation of the Deity. But this view is historically inaccurate. For beyond all doubt Jesus was conscious of a new and hitherto unknown relation to God, and said so to His disciples; and His aim was to bring His disciples into the same attitude toward the world as His own, and to the same estimate of themselves, that under these conditions He might enlist them in the worldwide mission of the Kingdom of God, which He knew to be not only His own business, but theirs. But this involves the assumption that He Himself means more for His disciples than the passing occasion of their religion or a lawgiver for their conduct, who would be of no more account when once the law which He proclaimed was thoroughly learned. In the case of Buddhism, on the other hand, the system as a system does not secure for its founder any abiding significance. For if Buddha himself has attained to that personal annihilation to which he showed his followers the way, he can be remembered by them only as a pattern of past days, because each one becomes himself a Buddha, an enlightened one, that is, he too recognises the worthlessness of existence, and acts accordingly, with a view to his own annihilation.

In Christianity the case is otherwise. The aim of the Christian is conceived as the attainment of eternal life. This means the consistent realisation of the personal self-end, of which the test is that the whole world does not compare in worth with the personal life, and that by the acquisition of spiritual lord-ship over the world, this, the true worth of life, is vindicated. Now this religious vocation of the members of the Christian community is prefigured in the person of its Founder, and rests upon His person as its abiding source of strength for all imita-tion of Him, because He Himself made God's supreme purpose of the union of men in the Kingdom of God the aim of His own personal life; and thereby realised in His own experience that independence toward the world which through Him has become the experience of the members of His community. This ideal, the true development of the spiritual personality, cannot be rightly or fully conceived apart from contemplation of Him Who is the prototype of man's vocation. Thus what in the historically complete figure of Christ we recognise to be the real worth of His existence, gains for ourselves, through the unique-ness of the phenomenon and its normative bearing upon our own religious and ethical destiny, the worth of an abiding rule, since we at the same time discover that only through the im-pulse and direction we receive from Him, is it possible for us to enter into His relation to God and to the world.[1] On the other hand, this specific estimate of their founders, even when known, is quite alien to the ethnic religions, because in these there is not posited as ideal aim the independent development of the personal character to the worth of a whole, as against the natural and particular impulses of life. The genius of an ethnic religion is satisfied if there be participation in the fixed tradition and custom of the nation; and such participation, when regarded as the supreme standard of human fellowship, imposes on personal independence impassable limits. Because this ideal of self-realisation has not come within the horizon of any of the ethnic religions, therefore in none of these has the founder received a place which can be compared with the significance of Christ. Even in the case of Zoroaster and of Moses, the ideal

1. By this is meant that the disciples of Jesus take the rank of sons of God (Matt. xvii. 26), and are received into the same relation to God in which Christ stands to His Father (John xvii. 21-23).

interests of their religions are so bound up with the natural consciousness of belonging to a particular nation, that the decision of the Parsees for Zoroaster, and of the Israelites for Moses, was the inevitable result of hostility toward the Hindus in the one case, and toward the Egyptians in the other.

There is yet another reason why the Person of Christ maintains its place in the Christian view of the world. Christ founds His religion with the claim that He brings the perfect revelation of God, so that beyond what He brings no further revelation is conceivable or is to be looked for. Whoever, therefore, has a part in the religion of Christ in the way Christ Himself intended, cannot do other than regard Christ as the Bearer of the final revelation of God. At the same time, this point of view is conclusive only in connection with what has already been set forth. For Islam also claims to be the perfect religion, and yet is content with a superficial recognition of its prophet, to whom, under this title, there is actually no place assigned in the Mohammedan view of the world. Thus the claim Christ makes to the perfect revelation of God in Himself is only defined as against the rival claim of Mohammed, by the fact that on the ground of His peculiar relation to God, Christ lived a life of mastery over the world, such as makes possible the community in which each Christian is to attain the similar destiny of the life eternal. Because this goal is not the reward of fulfilling a statutory law, Christ does not count, like Mohammed, merely as a lawgiver. On the contrary, since the aim of the Christian is to be attained under the form of personal freedom, therefore the twofold significance we are compelled to ascribe to Christ as being at once the perfect revealer of God and the manifest [offenbar] type of spiritual lordship over the world, finds expression in the single predicate of His Godhead.

This mutual relation between the *Godhead of Christ* and the raising of the members of His community to mastery over the world as their true destiny, is set forth with greatest clearness in that dogma of the Greek Church which affirms the consummation of the human race in Christ as the Word of God, Who is Himself God. The communication of ἀφθαρσία through the teaching—otherwise the incarnation—of the Divine Word, is regularly described also as θεοποίησις. Mastery over the world is the content of both these descriptions of the Christian, as well as the motive for defining clearly the idea of the Divine Word.

*   *   *

But if Christ by what He has done and suffered for my salvation is my Lord, and if, by trusting for my salvation to the power of what He has done for me, I honour Him as my God, then that is a value-judgment of a direct kind. It is not a judgment which belongs to the sphere of disinterested scientific knowledge, like the formula of Chalcedon. When, therefore, my opponents demand in this connection a judgment of the latter sort, they reveal their own inability to distinguish scientific from religious knowledge, which means that they are not really at home in the sphere of religion. Every cognition of a religious sort is a direct judgment of value. The nature of God and the Divine we can only know in its essence by determining its value for our salvation.[1] Let him who denies this see to it how he reconciles his position with the Larger Catechism, and with the fact that we know God only by revelation, and therefore also must understand the Godhead of Christ, if it is to be understood at all, as an attribute revealed to us in His saving influence upon ourselves. We must first be able to prove the Godhead that is revealed before we take account of the Godhead that is eternal. My opponents, however, being bent on getting first an acknowledgment of the latter, imagine that they can establish the Godhead of Christ upon the basis of a scientific idea, that

1. This is the attitude of Theremin in a sermon on the Divinity of Christ, of the year 1818, edited with a preface for 1881 by Kögel. The preacher's desire is to convince his contemporaries of the Divinity of Christ, if only they believe (1) that Christ is a good man, (2) that God is our Father, and (3) that there is a future life of blessedness. "This will suffice us to bring you to the avowal that Christ is the only-begotten Son of God." . . . Compare herewith the following sentences. . . : "The confession that Christ is true God lay already involved in your moral sense. . . . Beyond this, then, we will not go. . . . That we should be able to understand and explain in what way the Divine nature unites itself with the human—this God does not ask of us, He has not put it within the grasp of our understanding. But that holiness cannot lie—that we understand, and that may suffice us."

is, through an act of disinterested cognition, previous to all possible experience, and apart from all religious experience of the matter. And as representatives of a scientific conception of the Godhead of Christ, they pursue an impracticable method, inasmuch as their conception of the Word of God, eternally begotten by God before the world, rests only on tradition, detached from all the circumstances of its origin. Accordingly, they would have us make confession of the Godhead of Christ in this particular formula, before ever His Godhead has been proved to us in His saving influence upon ourselves, aye even although the said influence cannot possibly prove His Godhead in the aspects of it here concerned. These teachers must first of all be good enough to tell us what Christ's Godhead in its eternal essence is—what it is in its eternal relation to God; then it will be time enough to discuss whether and in what way this attribute is for us savingly effective and actually revealed. The method of cognition herein applied is false, and Luther's warning against teachers who would determine the things of God *a priori,* from above downwards, previous to all definite Divine revelation, holds good for this problem also.[1]

*　　*　　*

It is also a false assumption that a uniform *doctrine of the Godhead of Christ* can be exegetically constructed from the New Testament. Strictly speaking, the content of the New Testament books is not doctrine at all. Least of all can we discover in Christ's own words a doctrine of His Godhead. There, indeed, it is not to be expected. For the thought of Christ's Godhead is never other than the expression of that unique

1. Compare the remark of Luther on John xvii. 3 (Walch, viii. p. 697): "Observe how Christ in this word weaves into one web the knowledge of Himself and of the Father, so that only through Christ and in Him alone do we know the Father. I have often said this, and I keep on saying it, so that even when I am dead men may remember it, and may be on their guard against all teachers, as devil-driven and devil-led, who begin their teaching and preaching about God up in the heights, altogether separate and apart from Christ, in the way that hitherto in such schools they have speculated and played with His works in heaven above—what He is, thinks, and does in Himself."

acknowledgment and appreciation which the Christian community yields to its Founder. But there meet us in the New Testament two ways of conceiving Christ's Godhead which do not
directly correspond. On the one hand, the majority of the
apostles connect the name χύριος, which in Jewish usage is
equivalent to God, with the lordship over the world on which
Christ has entered by His exaltation to the right hand of God
(1 Pet. iii, 22; Jas. ii. 1; Phil. ii. 9-11; Heb. i. 3). The frequent
application of this attribute to Christ is to be understood in view
of the fact that faith has its necessary points of attachment always
in the present. Our faith in Christ is not faith in Him as One
Who was, but faith in Him as One Who continues to work,
namely, under the conditions corresponding to His present mode
of existence. This is the starting-point from which the apostles
recall even the circumstances of Christ's early life, and are confident, because of their faith in Him as Lord, that even His
death is an event fraught with blessing to the community. Paul
indicates a limit for the conjunction of the name χύριος with
the Person of Christ, in so far as he connects the bestowal of
this name by God with the exaltation, and puts the earthly
course of Jesus' life in the opposite category of an obedience
rendered in the form of a servant (Phil. ii. 6-11). With this,
however, must be compared the fact that in Rom. v. 15 Paul associates the specifically Divine attribute of grace with the contemplation of the man Christ, just as Christ in yielding His
obedience is at the same time a revelation of God. As Lord over
the world, Christ is also Lord over His community. But the latter
relation is the primary one, partly because the community acknowledges Him as God, and partly because, in definite statements, the community, of which Christ is head, is made to share
His position toward the world.

Whatever in the Epistles goes beyond this practical significance of the attribute χύριος as applied to Christ, and gives
to His relation toward the world a wider scope than His present
lordship over it, belongs to the sphere of special γνῶσις—that
is, of intellectual cognition, which creates problems rather than
solves them.

*   *   *

Jesus is the bearer of the perfect spiritual religion, which consists in mutual fellowship with God, the Author of the world and its final goal. In the idea of God as the final goal of all things lies the reason why Jesus recognizes as binding upon Himself for God's sake the widest conceivable aim of moral effort, namely, the union of mankind through love; while in the idea of God as the Author of the world lies the reason why Jesus for His own personal life repudiates every motive that is individual, worldly, and therefore less than Divine. But inasmuch as Jesus desired His own attitude to God to be shared by the rest of mankind, He laid upon His disciples, as their aim also, the union of mankind through love, or, in other words, the realisation of the Kingdom of God; and through His own personal freedom in relation to the world, He led His disciples, in accepting their view of the world from Him, to the assured conviction that human life is of more worth than all the world. By making the aim of His own life the aim of mankind, who are to be called into the fellowship of His community, He is before all else the Founder of a religion and the Redeemer of men from the dominion of the world. He is the author of a moral code only in so far as the raising of men above the world, and their fellowship in this relation, carries with it the ordering of their conduct towards each other in the Kingdom of God. But since this end is served by setting up the universal principle of brotherly love, it is not any defect in the moral code of Jesus as such that the ordering of the separate provinces of moral life is left to the free application of this supreme principle. Had Jesus directed His attention to the ethical regulation of the separate provinces of human life, the result would have been—since He meant to be the Founder of a community—that He would have drawn up definite legal enactments. Hence the objections of Strauss come in the end to this, that Jesus did not impose upon His disciples a system such as that of Islam. That he did not follow this path marks His unique and incomparable supremacy over all other founders of religions.

*　　*　　*

The problem here presented to theology is solved when we

have shown that there is no contradiction between the ethical and the religious apprehension of Christ, that the former finds its necessary complement in the latter, and that there is nothing here inconsistent either with the Christian idea of God, or with the complete conception of moral freedom. The origin of the Person of Christ—how His Person attained the form in which it presents itself to our ethical and religious apprehension—is not a subject for theological inquiry, because the problem transcends all inquiry. What ecclesiastical tradition offers us in this connection is obscure in itself, and therefore is not fitted to make anything clear. As Bearer of the perfect revelation, Christ is given us that we may believe on Him. When we do believe on Him, we find Him to be the Revealer of God. But the correlation of Christ with God His Father is not a scientific explanation. And as a theologian one ought to know that the fruitless clutching after such explanations only serves to obscure the recognition of Christ as the perfect revelation of God.

. . . On the other hand, we find our results verified in certain aspects of the life-work of Christ, which already incidentally have come more or less within our view. The Kingdom of God, the realisation of which forms the vocation of Christ, signifies not merely the correlate of the self-end of God, but also the goal that constitutes the highest destiny of man. Christ, therefore, would not have rightly or fully apprehended His vocation if He had not known that He was under obligation (Mark x. 42-45) to serve those whom, as the new religious community, He undertook to train for that destiny, and that this *obligatory service,* this obedience toward God, is the specific form of that *lordship* which He both acquires and exercises over men. Now in the idea of obligation the moral law is identical with the moral self-determination of the individual. For the sense of obligation—the subjective judgment that, in a particular and definitely limited case, it is necessary to act in accordance with the moral law, or some particular moral principle—is as much due to the moral disposition of the individual, as it is derived from the universal law. If, then, Christ was conscious that, in the exercise of His vocation, even in the resultant sufferings and voluntarily endured death, He was under obligation to serve men for their highest good, it follows, further, that here He obeyed love as His impelling motive. For love is the abiding disposition to further spiritual personalities in regard to their proper self-end, under the condition that in so doing we recognise and are seeking to attain our own self-end. This condition is evidently present in the case of Christ, since He could never have adopted as His vocation the founding of the Kingdom of God, if He had not regarded the loftiest possible destiny for mankind as the goal of His work, which He pursued for His own sake. And indeed the whole picture which has come down to us of the life of Christ reveals the loftiness of His love, and His lordship over friends and foes alike is made the more conspicuous by the fact that, even in the circle of those who stood nearest Him, He found no fitting help or support from any reliable or constant love toward Himself. In a certain quarter of theological speculation, we are met by the principle that perfect love requires the similar mutual relation of two personal wills. In so far as love is the principle of perfect fellowship between two personal beings, this may be true. But the perfect love, as motive power and guiding principle of the individual will, is independent of responsive love (Matt. v. 46); on the contrary, just there, where it meets with no answering love, perfect love proves in every possible case its peculiar sublimity. Such a case is the experience which befell Christ when those to whom He devoted His service, and whom He sought to save, on the one hand repelled Him in every possible manner, and on the other hand so imperfectly understood Him, that even the devotion of His most devoted disciples brought Him no return for the strain upon His own spirit. I do not need to complete in any further detail the picture of Christ's life to elicit the admission that the formula offered us by John—"grace and truth"—reflects most aptly the impression made by the personal conduct of Christ. For this is the type of love which reaches far beyond all possible return, and in the face of every rebuff persists unchanged. Inasmuch, then, as the love of Christ maintains its supremacy in all possible service, and even in the face of every hindrance, bent ever on the realisation of the Kingdom of God—that goal in which is attained, so far as God is love, God's own self-end—it follows that the "grace and truth" in Christ's whole activity is the specific and complete revelation of God. This result not only corresponds with the reflection of John, but also makes clear that the revelation of God in Christ, when referred to the technical notion of the Divine Word, surpasses those revelations which are given in creation, in the illumination of the nations, and in His presentation of Himself through the name Jahve. For in the characteristic activity of Christ in the discharge of His vocation, the essential will of God is revealed as love, since Christ's supreme aim, namely, the Kingdom of God, is identical with the supreme end of the Father. At the same time, however, we must understand John to mean that the exhaustive comprehension of Divine revelation in one human personality reckons on no other test than this "grace and truth," which, according to Old Testament standards, expresses the essential will of God. If these, then, are the criteria by which the conception of Christ's Godhead is framed, it follows that John does not mean us to seek in Christ for the Divine attributes of omnipotence, omnipresence, and omniscience, which, it is said, ought also, or even first of all, to occupy our regard. In so far as the Divine Revelation or Word of God is active in this personality, or is to be conceived as the form of its activity, the point at issue is clearly the definition of God's being. Since the being of God is spirit, and will, and above all love, it can therefore become effective in a human life, for human nature as such is laid on the lines of spirit, will, and love. On the other hand, the relation of God to the world, in so far as God creates and rules the world, could not be brought to direct manifestation in a human life, which is itself part of the world.

This remark, however, is confronted by the statement of Jesus that all things have been delivered unto Him of the Father (Matt. xi. 27), a statement which does not, it is true, denote an inborn omnipotence, but which does describe *power over the world* as something the possession of which Jesus claims for Himself, in virtue of Divine bestowal. This declaration cannot be got rid of by saying that it sounds too Johannine to be authentic. For on the whole it stands on no loftier level than when Jesus declares His intention to exercise that lordship of

God over the people of Israel which till then had been looked for in vain. With the appearance of the lordship of God there is bound up, in the prophetic vision of the future, the further prospect of a transformation of the natural world. As the expectations of the prophets were the norm by which Jesus formed His own conception of His vocation, it is a logical consequence that He should be convinced of a unique relation of His own Person to the world. The religion of the Old Testament represents the one spiritual God as the Creator and Ruler of the whole world; since the religious community of Israel obeys God and serves Him, it knows itself called not only to lordship over the other nations, but also to the unfettered enjoyment of natural good, which is protected through Divine appointment from the ordinary experiences of the opposite. This, however, betrays an inconsistency in Israel's view of the world, an imperfection in its very nature. For while the Divine purpose in the world is bound up with the naturally conditioned unity of the Israelitish nation, the position of this nation in the world is made dependent upon legal and political conditions and material advantages, which as such are of a mundane order, and do not correspond to the supramundane position of the one God. Thus there was forced upon Israel the necessity of always postponing to a future, which never became present, the reconciliation between its position in the world and God. Jesus rose above this standpoint, and introduced a new religion, by setting free the lordship of the supramundane God from national and political limitations, as well as from the expectation of material well-being, and by advancing its significance for mankind to a spiritual and ethical union, which at once corresponds to the spirituality of God, and denotes the supramundane end of spiritual creatures. But since Christ in this achievement of His life is at once the Revealer of God in the full sense, and also a man who according to His knowledge of God worships God and serves Him, it is a logical consequence that He asserts for Himself a position toward the world which corresponds to the idea of the one God and to the worth of God's spiritual Kingdom. If this latter, in the way Christ began to realise it, is the final aim of the whole world, it follows that the whole world is subject to Christ. The peculiar character of the religion founded, by Christ depends, therefore, of necessity upon the fact that He whom God knows, and Who has perfect knowledge of God, asserts supremacy over the world.

*   *   *

. . . *The lordship over the world possessed by believers,* which is the aim of reconciliation with God in the Christian sense, has its limits. For in so far as we are individually endowed with a corporeal nature, we are parts of the world and dependent on it as a system. But even "when the earthly house of this tabernacle is dissolved," the Christian hope of the survival of the spiritual life in an appropriate body is an evidence of what is an indispensable assumption, that as individual members of the race of spiritual beings we can never escape from the environment of the world. Lordship over the world, therefore, in the empirical sense, can be attributed neither to the individual nor to the human race as moulded by Christianity. No one can alter the mechanical conditions of sensible existence as such, no one can create new organic species; each, to secure his preservation within the system of the phenomenal world, must submit to the laws of mechanism and of organisms, laws which are valid once for all. Only within a limited range, and in harmony with the known laws of nature, can man use nature's forces, or artificially alter the given form of matter. . . . But man does make a comparison between himself and the whole system of nature when, in his spiritual feeling of self, he apprehends himself as a being who stands near to the supramundane God, and claims to live in despite of the experience of death. This religious estimate of self was not called into existence for the first time by Christianity; in every higher religion it breaks forth as an aspiration, or as a question addressed to the secret of existence. Christianity has only unfolded that view of the world in which this aspiration finds its confirmation, and the question about eternal life is answered. . . .

The lordship of the spirit over the world, in other words, over the system of the natural and particular motives of life, is connected in Christianity with the task of the Kingdom of God, as well as with that religious freedom in which evil in its many

forms is employed as a test and purifier of character. The task of
the Kingdom of God, however, includes likewise all labour in
which our lordship over nature is exercised for the maintenance,
ordering, and furtherance even of the bodily side of human
life. . . .

*   *   *

CHRISTIAN MYSTICISM

William Ralph Inge

(1860-1954)

WITHIN CONTEMPORARY Protestant ranks the point of view of "Christian Mysticism" is perhaps most strikingly exemplified in the thought of W. R. Inge, dean for more than a score of years at historic St. Paul's Cathedral in London. It is anomalous, indeed, that such a thorough type of mysticism should be revived in the midst of a noisy modern metropolitan center so close by the focus of the world traffic of business and especially by an ecclesiastic who so comfortably accepted the formal rituals and rules of the highly organized Anglican Church. And yet from here emanated mysticism-in-the-raw and a claim that it is of the essence in the Christian view of life.

Dean Inge was a philosopher of keenly analytic acumen in spite of his mysticism, well grounded in historical theology and the speculations of great critical thinkers. He is regarded to have been the leading recent interpreter of "the most divine" Plotinus (203-269), publishing the standard classic of that ancient mystic in a work called *The Philosophy of Plotinus* (1918).

In his Bampton Lectures entitled *Christian Mysticism* (1899), from which the excerpts in this volume are taken, he defends the compatibility of the mystics' approach with fundamental Christianity, both Catholic and Protestant. To him the world of reality is identical with the world of value; Christianity is a religion of spiritual redemption primarily; and philosophy and religion are indistinguishable as disciplines. He became widely known also for his *Outspoken Essays* in which he discoursed frankly upon touchy questions on the public mind, earning for himself the title of "the gloomy dean."

British born, he was educated at King's College, Cambridge. In 1888 he was ordained a deacon in the Anglican Church. His many publications were widely circulated, eagerly read, respected and discussed, even by those for whom mysticism is a strange and unfamiliar experience in this complex work-a-day world.

Editor

CHRISTIAN MYSTICISM

*   *   *

THE WORD mysticism had been almost always used in a slightly contemptuous sense in the nineteenth century. It was supposed to indicate something repugnant to the robust common sense and virile rationality of the British character. Subconsciously, the word suggested a foggy condition of the mind. These prejudices were enough to prevent Jowett, for example, in his great edition of Plato, from paying any attention to the interpreters of Plato under the Roman Empire. Were not Plotinus and Proclus "mystics," whose religion consisted in swooning into some sort of cataleptic trance? Moreover, has not a great German scholar declared that "mysticism is Catholic piety," and therefore a thing to be distrusted by good Protestants? So the subject was neglected, and even those who wrote about it, like R. A. Vaughan, whose *Hours with the Mystics* had a good sale, could not refrain from treating the poor mystics *de haut en bas*.

Continental philosophers knew better. They were aware that the essence of mysticism is the experience of coming into immediate relation with the higher Powers, whether these are called the One, as by the Neoplatonists, or by the names of Asiatic divinities, or, as in Christianity, are identified with the Divine Christ or the Holy Spirit. Thinkers so unlike each other as Hegel and Schopenhauer treated mystical philosophy respectfully. But the atmosphere of an age of rationalism was unfavourable to this type of religion. The Quakers, of course, were always mystics, and made valuable contributions to the literature of mysticism; but this sect, though its influence has been much greater than its numbers, was and is numerically very small.

In the Roman Church, the study of mysticism has always been encouraged. But the dualism of natural and supernatural, which in that Church is always insisted on, has led to an uncritical acceptance of what are called mystical phenomena, so that the older Catholic books on the subject are not very attractive to readers who belong to the Reformed Churches.

There have been, I think, two causes which have chiefly contributed to the revival of interest in this subject. The first is the growing conviction that in Christian apologetics the *testimonium Spiritus Sancti* has not been given its due weight as the primary ground of faith. The old argument from the appearance of design in nature has been somewhat weakened by the study of evolution. The time-honoured proofs from miracle and prophecy have lost their cogency, not only because our age demands a closer scrutiny of the evidence, but because, however well the abnormal facts may be established, they do not prove what the religious mind wishes to believe. And so the defenders of religion have been led to lay more stress on the inspiration of the individual, and I think we may say that this support of faith has proved strong enough to bear the weight. If some have objected that they themselves have had no such experiences, and that the alleged knowledge of the mystics is not transferable, they are answered by the reply that a genius for religious experience is like other exceptional endowments; that it can be acquired or perfected only by arduous discipline; and that in all other branches of human effort the average man is content to sit at the feet of the masters of an art or science. The great mystics are well aware that language was not made to describe these revelations, which are often formless and incapable of being reproduced; but that God has spoken to them they know, and in general their accounts of their journey up the hill of the Lord agree very closely. "Seek as we have sought, and you will see what we have seen." Such is their testimony, and it is not wise to disregard it.

The other cause which has led to careful study of mysticism is the new science of Psychology. In all the leading countries, but especially in America, many well-documented books have been written about "religious experience," which in theology is called the practice of the presence of God. One of the earliest of these, by William James, became famous. I do not think that this annexation of the subject by psychology has been altogether wholesome. Psychology is the study of states of consciousness as such. While it confines itself to its own domain it does not inquire whether there is any objective reality behind mystical experience. This abstract approach is proper for the psychologist; but too often there seems to be a latent assumption that the whole of mysticism is subjective. This is precisely not the view of the mystics themselves. They care nothing about states of consciousness; and if they thought that their revelations had no reality outside their own minds, they would conclude that they had been grievously deceived. Thus the psychological study of mysticism never penetrates to the heart of the subject; and it is not surprising that these writers collect mainly abnormal and even pathological cases, leaving the impression that they are dealing with a rare and probably unhealthy condition of the human mind. This defect is apparent in James' book and in many others; James, for example, has no study of Christ, who even among non-Christians holds a supreme place in the roll of religious genius.

Those who wish to understand mysticism need not trouble themselves about abnormal phenomena at all. Most of the famous mystics, at any rate in the Roman Church, lived in the cloister. Many of them suffered in physical and mental health from what in other fields would be called extreme specialization. Their absorption in what for them was the highest quest made them a little "queer," without actually destroying their sanity. But we cannot insist too strongly that the essence of mysticism —the mystical state in its purest form—is just *prayer*, "the elevation of the mind to God." Let anyone who has felt God near him when on his knees think what a perfect prayer would be like. It need not be vocal; it is probably not petitional; it is an act of worship, receptiveness, and self-surrender, to the Author of our being. This is the only proper way to approach the subject.

*   *   *

No word in our language—not even "Socialism"—has been

employed more loosely than "Mysticism." Sometimes it is used as an equivalent for symbolism or allegorism, sometimes for theosophy or occult science; and sometimes it merely suggests the mental state of a dreamer, or vague and fantastic opinions about God and the world. In Roman Catholic writers, "mystical phenomena" mean supernatural suspensions of physical law. Even those writers who have made a special study of the subject, show by their definitions of the word how uncertain is its connotation. It is therefore necessary that I should make clear at the outset what I understand by the term, and what aspects of religious life and thought I intend to deal with in these Lectures.

The history of the *word* begins in close connexion with the Greek mysteries. A mystic (μύστης) is one who has been, or is being, initiated into some esoteric knowledge of Divine things, about which he must keep his mouth shut (μύειν) ; or, possibly, he is one whose *eyes* are still shut, one who is not yet an ἐπόπτης. The word was taken over, with other technical terms of the mysteries, by the Neoplatonists, who found in the existing mysteriosophy a discipline, worship, and rule of life congenial to their speculative views. But as the tendency towards quietism and introspection increased among them, another derivation for "Mysticism" was found—it was explained to mean deliberately shutting the eyes to all external things. We shall see in the sequel how this later Neoplatonism passed almost entire into Christianity, and, while forming the basis of mediæval Mysticism, caused a false association to cling to the word even down to the Reformation.

The phase of thought or feeling which we call Mysticism has its origin in that which is the raw material of all religion, and perhaps of all philosophy and art as well, namely, that dim consciousness of the *beyond,* which is part of our nature as human beings. Men have given different names to these "obstinate questionings of sense and outward things." We may call them, if we will, a sort of higher instinct, perhaps an anticipation of the evolutionary process; or an extension of the frontier of consciousness; or, in religious language, the voice of God speaking to us. Mysticism arises when we try to bring this higher consciousness into relation with the other contents of our minds. Religious Mysticism may be defined as the attempt to realise the presence of the living God in the soul and in nature, or, more generally, as *the attempt to realise, in thought and feeling, the immanence of the temporal in the eternal, and of the eternal in the temporal.* Our consciousness of the beyond is, I say, the raw material of all religion. But, being itself formless, it cannot be brought directly into relation with the forms of our thought. Accordingly, it has to express itself by symbols, which are as it were the flesh and bones of ideas. It is the tendency of all symbols to petrify or evaporate, and either process is fatal to them. They soon repudiate their mystical origin, and forthwith lose their religious content. Then comes a return to the fresh springs of the inner life—a revival of spirituality in the midst of formalism or unbelief. This is the historical function of Mysticism —it appears as an independent active principle, the spirit of reformation and revivals. But since every active principle must find for itself appropriate instruments, Mysticism has developed a speculative and practical system of its own. As Goethe says, it is "the scholastic of the heart, the dialectic of the feelings." In this way it becomes possible to consider it as a type of religion, though it must always be remembered that in becoming such it has incorporated elements which do not belong to its inmost being. As a type of religion, then, Mysticism seems to rest on the following propositions or articles of faith:—

First, *the soul* (as well as the body) *can see and perceive—* ἔστι δὲψυχῆς αἴςθησίς τις, as Proclus says. We have an organ or faculty for the discernment of spiritual truth, which, in its proper sphere, is as much to be trusted as the organs of sensation in theirs.

The second proposition is that, since we can only know what is akin to ourselves, *man, in order to know God, must be a partaker of the Divine nature.* "What we are, that we behold; and what we behold, that we are," says Ruysbroek. The curious doctrine which we find in the mystics of the Middle Ages, that there is at "the apex of the mind" a spark which is consubstantial with the uncreated ground of the Deity, is thus accounted for. We could not even begin to work out our own salvation if God were not already working in us. It is always "in His light" that "we see light." The doctrine has been felt to be a necessary postulate by most philosophers who hold that knowledge of God is possible to man. For instance, Krause says, "From finite reason as finite we might possibly explain the thought of itself, but not the thought of something that is outside finite reasonable beings, far less the absolute idea, in its contents infinite, of God. To become aware of God in knowledge we require certainly to make a freer use of our finite power of thought, but the thought of God itself is primarily and essentially an eternal operation of the eternal revelation of God to the finite mind." But though we are made in the image of God, our *likeness* to Him only exists potentially. The Divine spark already shines within us, but it has to be searched for in the innermost depths of our personality, and its light diffused over our whole being.

This brings us to the third proposition—*"Without holiness no man may see the Lord";* or, as it is expressed positively in the Sermon on the Mount, "Blessed are the pure in heart: for they shall see God." Sensuality and selfishness are absolute disqualifications for knowing "the things of the Spirit of God."

These fundamental doctrines are very clearly laid down in the passage from St. John which I read as the text of this Lecture. [I John iii. 2, 3.] The filial relation to God is already claimed, but the vision is inseparable from *likeness* to Him, which is a hope, not a possession, and is only to be won by "purifying ourselves, even as He is pure."

There is one more fundamental doctrine which we must not omit. Purification removes the obstacles to our union with God, but our guide on the upward path, *the true hierophant of the mysteries of God, is love.* Love has been defined as "interest in its highest power"; while others have said that "it is of the essence of love to be disinterested." The contradiction is merely a verbal one. The two definitions mark different starting-points, but the two "ways of love" should bring us to the same goal. The possibility of disinterested love, in the ordinary sense, ought never to have been called in question. "Love is not love" when it asks for a reward. Nor is the love of man to God any exception. He who tries to be holy in order to be happy will assuredly be neither. In the words of the *Theologia Germanica,* "So long as a man seeketh his own highest good *because* it is his, he will never find it." The mystics here are unanimous, though some, like St. Bernard, doubt whether perfect love of God can ever be attained, pure and without alloy, while we are in this life. The controversy between Fénelon and Bossuet on this subject is well known, and few will deny that Fénelon was mainly in the right. Certainly he had an easy task in justifying his statements from the writings of the saints. But we need not trouble ourselves with the "mystic paradox," that it would be better to be with Christ in hell than without Him in heaven—a statement which Thomas à Kempis once wrote and then erased in his manuscript. For wherever Christ is, there is heaven: nor should we regard eternal happiness as anything distinct from "a true conjunction of the mind with God." "God is not without or above law: He *could* not make men either sinful or miserable." To believe otherwise is to suppose an irrational universe, the one thing which a rational man cannot believe in.

The mystic, as we have seen, makes it his life's aim to be transformed into the likeness of Him in whose image he was created. He loves to figure his path as a ladder reaching from earth to heaven, which must be climbed step by step. This *scala perfectionis* is generally divided into three stages. The first is called the purgative life, the second the illuminative, while the third, which is really the goal rather than a part of the journey, is called the unitive life, or state of perfect contemplation. We find, as we should expect, some differences in the classification, but this tripartite scheme is generally accepted.

The steps of the upward path constitute the ethical system, the rule of life, of the mystics. The first stage, the purgative life, we read in the *Theologia Germanica*, is brought about by contrition, by confession, by hearty amendment; and this is the usual language in treatises intended for monks. But it is really intended to include the civic and social virtues in this stage. They occupy the lowest place, it is true; but this only means that they must be acquired by all, though all are not called to the higher flights of contemplation. Their chief value, according to Plotinus, is to teach us the meaning of *order* and *limitation* (τάξις and πέρας), which are qualities belonging to the Divine nature. This is a very valuable thought, for it contradicts that aberration of Mysticism which calls God the Infinite, and thinks of Him as the Indefinite, dissolving all distinctions in the abyss of bare indetermination. When Ewald says, "the true mystic never withdraws himself wilfully from the business life, no, not even from the smallest business," he is, at any rate, saying nothing which conflicts with the principles of Mysticism.

The purgative life necessarily includes self-discipline: does it necessarily include what is commonly known as asceticism? It would be easy to answer that asceticism means nothing but *training*, as men train for a race, or more broadly still, that it means simply "the acquisition of some greater power by practice." But when people speak of "asceticism," they have in their minds such severe "buffeting" of the body as was practised by many ancient hermits and mediæval monks. Is this an integral part of the mystic's "upward path"? We shall find reason to conclude that, while a certain degree of austere simplicity characterises the outward life of nearly all the mystics, and while an almost morbid desire to suffer is found in many of them, there is nothing in the system itself to encourage men to maltreat their bodies. Mysticism enjoins a dying life, not a living death. Moreover, asceticism, when regarded as a virtue or duty in itself, tends to isolate us, and concentrates our attention on our separate individuality. This is contrary to the spirit of Mysticism, which aims at realising unity and solidarity everywhere. Monkish asceticism (so far as it goes beyond the struggle to live unstained under unnatural conditions) rests on a dualistic view of the world which does not belong to the essence of Mysticism. It infected all the religious life of the Middle Ages, not Mysticism only.

The second stage, the illuminative life, is the concentration of all the faculties, will, intellect, and feeling, upon God. It differs from the purgative life, not in having discarded good works, but in having come to perform them, as Fénelon says, "no longer as virtues," that is to say, willingly and almost spontaneously. The struggle is now transferred to the inner life.

The last stage of the journey, in which the soul presses towards the mark, and gains the prize of its high calling, is the unitive or contemplative life, in which man beholds God face to face, and is joined to Him. Complete union with God is the ideal limit of religion, the attainment of which would be at once its consummation and annihilation. It is in the continual but unending approximation to it that the life of religion subsists. We must therefore beware of regarding the union as anything more than an infinite process, though, as its end is part of the eternal counsel of God, there is a sense in which it is already a fact, and not merely a thing desired. But the word deification holds a very large place in the writings of the Fathers, and not only among those who have been called mystics. We find it in Irenæus as well as in Clement, in Athanasius as well as in Gregory of Nyssa. St. Augustine is no more afraid of "deificari" in Latin than Origen of Θεοποιεῖσθαι in Greek. The subject is one of primary importance to anyone who wishes to understand mystical theology; but it is difficult for us to enter into the minds of the ancients who used these expressions, both because Θεός was a very fluid concept in the early centuries, and because our notions of *personality* are very different from those which were prevalent in antiquity. On this latter point I shall have more to say presently; but the evidence for the belief in "deification," and its continuance through the Middle Ages, is too voluminous to be given in the body of these Lectures. Let it suffice to say here that though such bold phrases as "God became man, that we might become God," were commonplaces of doctrinal theology at least till after Augustine, even Clement and Origen protest strongly against the "very impious" heresy that man is "a part of God," or "consubstantial with God." The attribute of Divinity which was chiefly in the minds of the Greek Fathers when they made these statements, was that of *imperishableness*.

As to the means by which this union is manifested to the consciousness, there is no doubt that very many mystics believed in, and looked for, ecstatic revelations, trances, or visions. This, again, is one of the crucial questions of Mysticism.

Ecstasy or vision begins when thought ceases, *to our consciousness,* to proceed from ourselves. It differs from dreaming, because the subject is awake. It differs from hallucination, because there is no organic disturbance: it is, or claims to be, a temporary enhancement, not a partial disintegration, of the mental faculties. Lastly, it differs from poetical inspiration, because the imagination is passive.

That perfectly sane people often experience such visions there is no manner of doubt. St. Paul fell into a trance at his conversion, and again at a later period, when he seemed to be caught up into the third heaven. The most sober and practical of the mediæval mystics speak of them as common phenomena. And in modern times two of the sanest of our poets have recorded their experiences in words which may be worth quoting.

Wordsworth, in his well-known "Lines composed above Tintern Abbey," speaks of—

> "That serene and blessed mood,
> In which . . . the breath of this corporeal frame,
> And even the motion of our human blood,
> Almost suspended, we are laid asleep
> In body, and become a living soul:
> While with an eye made quiet by the power
> Of harmony, and the deep power of joy,
> We see into the life of things."

And Tennyson says, "A kind of waking trance I have often had, quite from boyhood, when I have been all alone. This has generally come upon me through repeating my own name two or three times to myself silently, till all at once, out of the intensity of the consciousness of individuality, the individual itself seemed to dissolve and fade away into boundless being: and this not a confused state, but the clearest of the clearest, and the surest of the surest, the weirdest of the weirdest, utterly beyond words, where death was an almost laughable impossibility, the loss of personality (if so it were) seeming no extinction, but the only true life."

Admitting, then, that these psychical phenomena actually occur, we have to consider whether ecstasy and kindred states are an integral part of Mysticism. In attempting to answer this question, we shall find it convenient to distinguish between the Neoplatonic vision of the super-essential One, the Absolute, which Plotinus enjoyed several times, and Porphyry only once, and the visions and "locutions" which are reported in all times and places, especially where people have not been trained in scientific habits of thought and observation. The former was held to be an exceedingly rare privilege, the culminating point of the contemplative life. I shall speak of it in my third Lecture; and shall there show that it belongs, not to the essence of Mysticism, and still less of Christianity, but to the Asiatic leaven which was mixed with Alexandrian thought, and thence passed into Catholicism. As regards visions in general, they were no invention of the mystics. They played a much more important part in the life of the early Church than many ecclesiastical historians are willing to admit. Tertullian, for instance, says calmly, "The majority, almost, of men learn God from visions." Such implicit reliance was placed on the Divine authority of visions, that on one occasion an ignorant peasant and a married man was made Patriarch of Alexandria against his will, because his dying predecessor had a vision that the man who should bring him a present of grapes on the next day should be his successor! In course of time visions became rarer among the laity, but continued frequent among the monks and clergy. And so the class which furnished most of the shining lights of Mysticism was that in which these experiences were most common.

But we do not find that the masters of the spiritual life attached very much importance to them, or often appealed to them as aids to faith. As a rule, visions were regarded as special rewards bestowed by the goodness of God on the struggling saint, and especially on the beginner, to refresh him and strengthen him in the hour of need. Very earnest cautions were issued that no efforts must be made to induce them artificially, and aspirants were exhorted neither to desire them, nor to feel pride in having seen them. The spiritual guides of the Middle Ages were well aware that such experiences often come of disordered nerves and weakened digestion; they believed also that they are sometimes delusions of Satan. Richard of St. Victor says, "As Christ attested His transfiguration by the presence of Moses and Elias, so visions should not be believed unless they have the authority of Scripture." Albertus Magnus tries to classify them, and says that those which contain a sensuous element are always dangerous. Eckhart is still more cautious, and Tauler attaches little value to them. Avila, the Spanish mystic, says that only those visions which minister to our spiritual necessities, and make us *more humble,* are genuine. Self-induced visions inflate us with pride, and do irreparable injury to health of mind and body.

It hardly falls within my task to attempt to determine what these visions really are. The subject is one upon which psychological and medical science may some day throw more light. But this much I must say, to make my own position clear: I regard these experiences as neither more nor less "supernatural" than other mental phenomena. Many of them are certainly pathological; about others we may feel doubts; but some have every right to be considered as real irradiations of the soul from the light that "for ever shines," real notes of the harmony that "is in immortal souls." In illustration of this, we may appeal to three places in the Bible where revelations of the profoundest truths concerning the nature and counsels of God are recorded to have been made during ecstatic visions. Moses at Mount Horeb heard, during the vision of the burning bush, a proclamation of God as the "I am"—the Eternal who is exalted above time. Isaiah, in the words "Holy, Holy, Holy," perceived dimly the mystery of the Trinity. And St. Peter, in the vision of the sheet, learned that God is no respecter of persons or of nationalities. In such cases the highest intuitions or revelations, which the soul can in its best moments just receive, but cannot yet grasp or account for, make a language for themselves, as it were, and claim the sanction of external authority, until the mind is elevated so far as to feel the authority not less Divine, but no longer external. We may find fairly close analogies in other forms of that "Divine madness," which Plato says is "the source of the chiefest blessings granted to men"—such as the rapture of the poet, or (as Plato adds) of the lover. And even the philosopher or man of science may be surprised into some such state by a sudden realisation of the sublimity of his subject. So at least Lacordaire believed when he wrote, "All at once, as if by chance, the hair stands up, the breath is caught, the skin contracts, and a cold sword pierces to the very soul. It is the sublime which has manifested itself!" Even in cases where there is evident hallucination, *e.g.* when the visionary sees an angel or devil sitting on his book, or feels an arrow thrust into his heart, there need be no insanity. In periods when it is commonly believed that such things may and do happen, the imagination, instead of being corrected by experience, is misled by it. Those who honestly expect to see miracles will generally see them, without detriment either to their truthfulness or sanity in other matters.

The mystic, then, is not, as such, a visionary; nor has he any interest in appealing to a faculty "above reason," if reason is used in its proper sense, as the logic of the whole personality. The desire to find for our highest intuitions an authority wholly external to reason and independent of it,—a "purely supernatural" revelation,—has, as Récéjac says, "been the cause of the longest and the most dangerous of the aberrations from which Mysticism has suffered." This kind of supernaturalism is destructive of *unity* in our ideas of God, the world, and ourselves; and it casts a slur on the faculties which are the appointed organs of communication between God and man. A revelation absolutely transcending reason is an absurdity: no such revelation could ever be made. In the striking phrase of Macarius, "the human mind is the throne of the Godhead." The supremacy of the reason is the favourite theme of the Cambridge Platonists, two of whom, Whichcote and Culverwel, are never tired of quoting the text, "The spirit of man is the candle of the Lord." "Sir, I oppose not rational to spiritual," writes Whichcote to Tuckney, "for spiritual is most rational." And again, "Reason is the Divine governor of man's life: it is the very voice of God." What we can and must transcend, if we would make any progress in Divine knowledge, is not reason, but that shallow rationalism which regards the data on which we can reason as a fixed quantity, known to all, and which bases itself on a formal logic, utterly unsuited to a spiritual view of things. Language can only furnish us with poor, misleading, and wholly inadequate images of spiritual facts; it supplies us with abstractions and metaphors, which do not really represent what we know or believe about God and human personality. St. Paul calls attention to this inadequacy by a series of formal contradictions: "I live, yet not I"; "dying, and behold we live"; "when I am weak, then I am strong," and so forth; and we find exactly the same expedient in Plotinus, who is very fond of thus showing his contempt for the logic of identity. When, therefore, Harnack says that "Mysticism is nothing else than rationalism applied to a sphere above reason," he would have done better to say that it is "reason applied to a sphere above rationalism."

For Reason is still "king." Religion must not be a matter of *feeling* only. St. John's command to "try every spirit" condemns all attempts to make emotion or inspiration independent of reason. Those who thus blindly follow the inner light find it no "candle of the Lord," but an *ignis fatuus;* and the great mystics are well aware of this. The fact is that the tendency to separate and half personify the different faculties—intellect, will, feeling—is a mischievous one. Our object should be so to *unify* our personality, that our eye may be single, and our whole body full of light.

We have considered briefly the three stages of the mystic's upward path. The scheme of life therein set forth was no doubt determined empirically, and there is nothing to prevent the simplest and most unlettered saint from framing his conduct on these principles. Many of the mediæval mystics had no taste for speculation or philosophy; they accepted on authority the entire body of Church dogma, and devoted their whole attention to the perfecting of the spiritual life in the knowledge and love of God. But this cannot be said of the leaders. Christian Mysticism appears in history largely as an intellectual movement, the foster-child of Platonic idealism; and if ever, for a time, it forgot its early history, men were soon found to bring it back to "its old loving nurse the Platonic philosophy."

* * *

The Gospel of St. John—the "spiritual Gospel," as Clement already calls it—is the charter of Christian Mysticism. Indeed, Christian Mysticism, as I understand it, might almost be called Johannine Christianity; if it were not better to say that a Johannine Christianity is the ideal which the Christian mystic sets before himself. For we cannot but feel that there are deeper truths in this wonderful Gospel than have yet become part of the religious consciousness of mankind. Perhaps, as Origen says, no one can fully understand it who has not, like its author, lain upon the breast of Jesus. We are on holy ground when we are dealing with St. John's Gospel, and must step in fear and reverence. But though the breadth and depth and height of those sublime discourses are for those only who can mount up with wings as eagles to the summits of the spiritual life, so simple is the language and so large its scope, that even the wayfaring men, though fools, can hardly altogether err therein.

Let us consider briefly, first, what we learn from this Gospel about the nature of God, and then its teaching upon human salvation.

There are three notable expressions about God the Father in the Gospel and First Epistle of St. John: "God is Love"; "God is Light"; and "God is Spirit." The form of the sentences teaches us that these three qualities belong so intimately to the nature of God that they usher us into His immediate presence. We need not try to get behind them, or to rise above them into some more nebulous region in our search for the Absolute. Love, Light, and Spirit are for us names of God Himself. And observe that St. John does not, in applying these semi-abstract words to God, attenuate in the slightest degree His personality. God *is* Love, but He also exercises love. "God so loved the world." And He is not only the "white radiance" that "for ever shines"; He can "draw" us to Himself, and "send" His Son to bring us back to Him.

The word "Logos" does not occur in any of the discourses. The identification of Christ with the "Word" or "Reason" of the philosophers is St. John's own. But the statements in the prologue are all confirmed by our Lord's own words as reported by the evangelist. These fall under two heads, those which deal with the relation of Christ to the Father, and those which deal with His relation to the world. The pre-existence of Christ in glory at the right hand of God is proved by several declarations: "What if ye shall see the Son of Man ascending where He was before?" "And now, O Father, glorify Me with Thine own self, with the glory which I had with Thee before the world was." His exaltation above time is shown by the solemn statement, "Before Abraham was, I am." And with regard to the world, we find in St. John the very important doctrine, which has never made its way into popular theology, that the Word is not merely the Instrument in the original creation,—"by (or through) Him all things were made,"—but the central Life, the Being in whom life existed and exists as an indestructible attribute, an underived prerogative, the Mind or Wisdom who upholds and animates the universe without being lost in it. This doctrine, which is implied in other parts of St. John, seems to be stated explicitly in the prologue, though the words have been otherwise interpreted. "That which has come into existence," says St. John, "was in Him life (ὃ γέγονεν, ἐν αὐτῷ ζωὴ ἦν). That is to say, the Word is the timeless Life, of which the temporal world is a manifestation. This doctrine was taught by many of the Greek Fathers, as well as by Scotus Erigena and other speculative mystics. Even if, with the school of Antioch and most of the later commentators, we transfer the words ὃ γέγονεν to the preceding sentence, the doctrine that Christ is the life as well as the light of the world can be proved from St. John. The world is the poem of the Word to the glory of the Father: in it, and by means of it, He displays in time all the riches which God has eternally put within Him.

In St. John, as in mystical theology generally, the Incarnation, rather than the Cross, is the central fact of Christianity. "The Word was made flesh, and tabernacled among us," is for him the supreme dogma. And it follows necessarily from the Logos doctrine, that the Incarnation, and all that followed it, is regarded primarily as a *revelation* of life and light and truth. "That eternal life, which was with the Father, has been *manifested* unto us," is part of the opening sentence of the first Epistle. "This is the message which we have heard of Him and announce unto you, that God is Light, and in Him is no darkness at all." In coming into the world, Christ "came unto His own." He had, in a sense, only to show to them what was there already. Esaias, long before, had "seen His glory, and spoken of Him." The mysterious estrangement, which had laid the world under the dominion of the Prince of darkness, had obscured but not quenched the light which lighteth *every* man—the inalienable prerogative of all who derive their being from the Sun of Righteousness. This central Light is Christ, and Christ only. He alone is the Way, the Truth, the Life, the Door, the Living

Bread, and the True Vine. He is at once the Revealer and the Revealed, the Guide and the Way, the Enlightener and the Light. No man cometh unto the Father but by Him.

The teaching of this Gospel on the office of the Holy Spirit claims special attention in our present inquiry. The revelation of God in Christ was complete: there can be no question that St. John claims for Christianity the position of the one eternally true revelation. But without the gradual illumination of the Spirit it is partly unintelligible and partly unobserved. The purpose of the Incarnaton was to reveal God *the Father:* "He that hath seen Me hath seen the Father." In these momentous words (it has been said) "the idea of God receives an abiding embodiment, and the Father is brought for ever within the reach of intelligent devotion." The purpose of the mission of the Comforter is to reveal *the Son.* He takes the place of the ascended Christ on earth as a living and active principle in the hearts of Christians. His office it is to bring to remembrance the teachings of Christ, and to help mankind gradually to understand them. There were also many things, our Lord said, which could not be said at the time to His disciples, who were unable to bear them. These were left to be communicated to future generations by the Holy Spirit. The doctrine of development had never before received so clear an expression; and few could venture to record it so clearly as St. John, who could not be suspected of contemplating a time when the teachings of the human Christ might be superseded.

Let us now turn to the human side of salvation, and trace the upward path of the Christian life as presented to us in this Gospel. First, then, we have the doctrine of the new birth: "Except a man be born anew (or from above), he cannot see the kingdom of God." This is further explained as a being born "of water and of the Spirit"—words which are probably meant to remind us of the birth of the world-order out of chaos as described in Genesis, and also to suggest the two ideas of purification and life. (Baptism, as a symbol of purification, was, of course, already familiar to those who first heard the words.) Then we have a doctrine of *faith* which is deeper than that of the Synoptists. The very expression πιστεύειν εἰς "to believe *on,*" common in St. John and rare elsewhere, shows that the word is taking a new meaning. Faith, in St. John, is no longer regarded chiefly as a condition of supernatural favours; or, rather, the mountains which it can remove are no material obstructions. It is an act of the whole personality, a self-dedication to Christ. It must precede knowledge: "If any man willeth to do His will, he shall know of the teaching," is the promise. It is the *"credo ut intelligam"* of later theology. The objection has been raised that St. John's teaching about faith moves in a vicious circle. His appeal is to the inward witness; and those who cannot hear this inward witness are informed that they must first believe, which is just what they can find no reason for doing. But this criticism misses altogether the drift of St. John's teaching. Faith, for him, is not the acceptance of a proposition upon evidence; still less is it the acceptance of a proposition in the teeth of evidence. It is, in the first instance, the resolution "to stand or fall by the noblest hypothesis"; that is (may we not say?), to follow Christ wherever He may lead us. Faith begins with an experiment, and ends with an experience. "He that believeth in Him hath the witness in himself"; that is the verification which follows the venture. That even the power to make the experiment is given from above; and that the experience is not merely subjective, but an universal law which has had its supreme vindication in history,—these are two facts which we learn afterwards. The converse process, which begins with a critical examination of documents, cannot establish what we really want to know, however strong the evidence may be. In this sense, and in this only, are Tennyson's words true, that "nothing worthy proving can be proven, nor yet disproven."

Faith, thus defined, is hardly distinguishable from that mixture of admiration, hope, and love by which Wordsworth says that we live. Love especially is intimately connected with faith. And as the Christian life is to be considered as, above all things, a state of union with Christ, and of His members with one another, love of the brethren is inseparable from love of God. So intimate is this union, that hatred towards any human being cannot exist in the same heart as love to God. The mystical union is indeed rather a bond between Christ and the Church, and between man and man as members of Christ, than between Christ and individual souls. Our Lord's prayer is "that they all may be one, even as Thou, Father, art in Me, and I in Thee, that they also may be one in us." The personal relation between the soul and Christ is not to be denied; but it can only be enjoyed when the person has "come to himself" as a member of a body. This involves an inward transit from the false isolated self to the larger life of sympathy and love which alone makes us persons. Those who are thus living according to their true nature are rewarded with an intense unshakeable conviction which makes them independent of external evidences. Like the blind man who was healed, they can say, "One thing I know, that whereas I was blind, now I see." The words "we know" are repeated again and again in the first Epistle, with an emphasis which leaves no room for doubt that the evangelist was willing to throw the main weight of his belief on this inner assurance, and to attribute it without hesitation to the promised presence of the Comforter. We must observe, however, that this knowledge or illumination is *progressive*. This is proved by the passages already quoted about the work of the Holy Spirit. It is also implied by the words, "This is life eternal, that they should know Thee, the only true God, and Jesus Christ whom Thou hast sent." Eternal life is not γνῶσις knowledge as a possession, but the state of acquiring knowledge ('ίνα γυγνώσκωσιν). It is significant, I think, that St. John, who is so fond of the verb "to know," never uses the substantive γνῶσις.

The state of progressive unification, in which we receive "grace upon grace," as we learn more and more of the "fulness" of Christ, is called by the evangelist, in the verse just quoted and elsewhere, *eternal life*. This life is generally spoken of as a present possession rather than a future hope. "He that believeth on the Son *hath* everlasting life"; "he *is passed* from death unto life"; "we *are* in Him that is true, even Jesus Christ. This *is* the true God, and eternal life." The evangelist is constantly trying to transport us into that timeless region in which one day is as a thousand years, and a thousand years as one day.

St. John's Mysticism is thus patent to all; it is stamped upon his very style, and pervades all his teaching.

*   *   *

St. Paul states in the clearest manner that Christ *appeared* to him, and that this revelation was the foundation of his Christianity and apostolic commission. "Neither did I receive the Gospel from man," he says, "nor was I taught it, but it came to me through revelation of Jesus Christ." It appears that he did not at first think it necessary to "confer with flesh and blood"—to collect evidence about our Lord's ministry, His death and resurrection; he had "seen" and felt Him, and that was enough. "It was the good pleasure of God to reveal His Son in me," he says simply, using the favourite mystical phraseology. The study of "evidences," in the usual sense of the term in apologetics, he rejects with distrust and contempt. External revelation cannot make a man religious. It can put nothing new into him. If there is nothing answering to it in his mind, it will profit him nothing. Nor can philosophy make a man religious. "Man's wisdom," "the wisdom of the world," is of no avail to find spiritual truth. "God chose the foolish things of the world, to put to shame them that are wise." "The word of the Cross is, to them that are perishing, foolishness." By this language he, of course, does not mean that Christianity is irrational, and therefore to be believed on authority. That would be to lay its foundation upon external evidences, and nothing could be further from the whole bent of his teaching. What he does mean, and say very clearly, is that the carnal mind is disqualified from understanding Divine truths; "it cannot know them, because they are spiritually discerned." He who has not raised himself above "the world," that is, the interests and ideals of human society as it organises itself apart from God, and above "the flesh," that is, the things which seem desirable to the "average sensual man," does not possess in himself that element which can be assimilated by Divine grace. The "mystery" of the wisdom of God is necessarily hidden from him. St. Paul uses the word "mystery" in very much the same sense which St. Chrysostom gives to it in the following careful definition: "A mystery is that which is everywhere proclaimed, but which is not understood by those who have not right judgment. It is revealed, not by cleverness, but by the Holy Ghost, as we are able to receive it. And so we may call a mystery a secret ἀπόρρητον for even to the faithful it is not committed in all its fulness and clearness." In St. Paul the word is nearly always found in connexion with words denoting revelation or publication. The preacher of the Gospel is a hierophant, but the Christian mysteries are freely communicated to all who can receive them. For many ages these truths were "hid in God," but now all men may be "illuminated," if they will fulfil the necessary conditions of initiation. These are to "cleanse ourselves from all defilement of flesh and spirit," and to have love, without which all else will be unavailing. But there are degrees of initiation. "We speak wisdom among the perfect," he says (the τέλειοι are the fully initiated); but the carnal must still be fed with milk. Growth in knowledge, growth in grace, and growth in love, are so frequently mentioned together, that we must understand the apostle to mean that they are almost inseparable. But this knowledge, grace, and love is itself the work of the indwelling God, who is thus in a sense the organ as well as the object of the spiritual life. "The Spirit searcheth all things," he says, "yea, the deep things of God." The man who has the Spirit dwelling in him "has the mind of Christ." "He that is spiritual judgeth all things," and is himself "judged of no man." It is, we must admit frankly, a dangerous claim, and one which may easily be subversive of all discipline. "Where the Spirit of the Lord is, there is liberty"; but such liberty may become a cloak of maliciousness. The fact is that St. Paul had himself trusted in "the Law," and it had led him into grievous error. As usually happens in such cases, his recoil from it was almost violent. He exalts the inner light into an absolute criterion of right and wrong, that no corner of the moral life may remain in bondage to Pharisaism. The crucifixion of the Lord Jesus and the stoning of Stephen were a crushing condemnation of legal and ceremonial righteousness; the law written in the heart of man, or rather spoken there by the living voice of the Holy Spirit, could never so mislead men as to make them think that they were doing God service by condemning and killing the just. Such memories might well lead St. Paul to use language capable of giving encouragement even to fanatical Anabaptists. But it is significant that the boldest claims on behalf of liberty all occur in the *earlier* Epistles.

*   *   *

The foregoing analysis of St. Paul's teaching has, I hope,

justified the statement that all the essentials of Mysticism are to be found in his Epistles. But there are also two points in which his authority has been claimed for false and mischievous developments of Mysticism. These two points it will be well to consider before leaving the subject.

The first is a contempt for the historical framework of Christianity. We have already seen how strongly St. John warns us against this perversion of spiritual religion. But those numerous sects and individual thinkers who have disregarded this warning, have often appealed to the authority of St. Paul, who in the Second Epistle to the Corinthians says, "Even though we have known Christ after the flesh, yet now we know Him so no more." Here, they say, is a distinct admission that the worship of the historical Christ, "the man Christ Jesus," is a stage to be passed through and then left behind. There is just this substratum of truth in a very mischievous error, that St. Paul *does* tell us that he *began* to teach the Corinthians by giving them in the simplest possible form the story of "Jesus Christ and Him crucified." The "mysteries" of the faith, the "wisdom" which only the "perfect" can understand, were deferred till the converts had learned their first lessons. But if we look at the passage in question, which has shocked and perplexed many good Christians, we shall find that St. Paul is not drawing a contrast between the earthly and the heavenly Christ, bidding us worship the Second Person of the Trinity, the same yesterday, to-day, and for ever, and to cease to contemplate the Cross on Calvary. He is distinguishing rather between the sensuous presentation of the facts of Christ's life, and a deeper realisation of their import. It should be our aim to "know no man after the flesh"; that is to say, we should try to think of human beings as what they are, immortal spirits, sharers with us of a common life and a common hope, not as what they appear to our eyes. And the same principle applies to our thoughts about Christ. To know Christ after the flesh is to know Him, not as man, but as *a* man. St. Paul in this verse condemns all religious materialism, whether it take the form of hysterical meditation upon the physical details of the passion, or of an over-curious interest in the manner of the resurrection. There is no trace whatever in St. Paul of any aspiration to rise above Christ to the contemplation of the Absolute—to treat Him as only a step in the ladder. This is an error of false Mysticism; the true mystic follows St. Paul in choosing as his ultimate goal the fulness of Christ, and not the emptiness of the undifferentiated Godhead.

The second point in which St. Paul has been supposed to sanction an exaggerated form of Mysticism, is his extreme disparagement of external religion—of forms and ceremonies and holy days and the like. "One man hath faith to eat all things; but he that is weak eateth herbs." "One man esteemeth one day above another, another esteemeth every day alike." "He that eateth, eateth unto the Lord, and giveth God thanks; and he that eateth not, to the Lord he eateth not, and giveth God thanks." "Why turn ye back to the weak and beggarly rudiments, whereunto ye desire to be in bondage again? Ye observe days, and months, and seasons, and years. I am afraid of you, lest I have bestowed labour upon you in vain." "Why do ye subject yourselves to ordinances, handle not, nor taste, nor touch, after the precepts and doctrines of men?" These are strongly-worded passages, and I have no wish to attenuate their significance. Any Christian priest who puts the observance of human ordinances—fast-days, for example—at all on the same level as such duties as charity, generosity, or purity, is teaching, not Christianity, but that debased Judaism against which St. Paul waged an unceasing polemic, and which is one of those dead religions which has to be killed again in almost every generation. But we must not forget that these vigorous denunciations *do* occur in a polemic against Judaism. They bear the stamp of the time at which they were written perhaps more than any other part of St. Paul's Epistles, except those thoughts which were connected with his belief in the approaching end of the world. St. Paul certainly did not intend his Christian converts to be anarchists in religious matters. There is evidence, in the First Epistle to the Corinthians, that his spiritual presentation of Christianity had already been made an excuse for disorderly licence. The usual symptoms of degenerate Mysticism had appeared at Corinth. There were men there who called themselves "spiritual persons" or prophets, and showed an arrogant independence; there were others who wished to start sects of their own; others who carried antinomianism into the sphere of morals; others who prided themselves on various "spiritual gifts." As regards the last class, we are rather surprised at the half-sanction which the apostle gives to what reads like primitive Irvingism; but he was evidently prepared to enforce discipline with a strong hand. Still, it may be fairly said that he trusts mainly to his personal ascendancy, and to his teaching about the organic unity of the Christian body, to preserve or restore due discipline and cohesion. There have been hardly any religious leaders, if we except George Fox, the founder of Quakerism, who have valued ceremonies so little. In this, again, he is a genuine mystic.

CHRISTIANITY AND THE SOCIAL CRISIS

WALTER RAUSCHENBUSCH

(1861-1918)

THE NAME of Walter Rauschenbusch is associated in American Protestant thought with the so-called "social gospel." Born of German Baptist immigrants he prepared for the ministry at Rochester Seminary in New York state. He served a small parish on the edge of Hell's Kitchen in New York City seeing at first hand the overcrowded and exploited slum area of the city and the misery of human beings. Such contacts could not help but reshape his thinking of religion as a self-centered matter to one of social significance, else it could matter very little. His growing passion for social reform is understandable and his dedication to a reconstruction of Christian theology in the direction of a social emphasis is but the corollary to the work of his ministry. The kingdom of God on this very earth he came to see as the central message of Christ. Nothing less than a redeemed society could be settled upon.

In 1897 he accepted an appointment at Rochester Seminary, a position which later developed in the field of church history. For twenty-one years he wielded a profound influence in his classrooms, by his passion for social reforms, by his recognized scholarship, by his stylistic books and public lectures.

He was not a radical in his social ideas; he was more a reconstructionist. Sin, for him, was as individualistic as in any orthodoxy. But it was more. Society itself needed redemption as much as individuals and was imbedded with accountable sins. Utopia was, for him, not just around the next corner. Optimism was tempered with conservative realism. Socialistic parties, he held, make their genuine contributions—but a party is not greater than the over-all reign of God.

His *Christianity and the Social Crisis* (here presented, in part) was published in 1907 and his *Theology for the Social Gospel* ten years later. Both works carry the stamp of his mind and the character of his dedicated ministry.

Editor

CHRISTIANITY AND THE SOCIAL CRISIS

INTRODUCTION

WESTERN CIVILIZATION is passing through a social revolution unparalleled in history for scope and power. Its coming was inevitable. The religious, political, and intellectual revolutions of the past five centuries, which together created the modern world, necessarily had to culminate in an economic and social revolution such as is now upon us.

By universal consent, this social crisis is the overshadowing problem of our generation. The industrial and commercial life of the advanced nations are in the throes of it. In politics all issues and methods are undergoing upheaval and re-alignment as the social movement advances. In the world of thought all the young and serious minds are absorbed in the solution of the social problems. Even literature and art point like compass-needles to this magnetic pole of all our thought.

The social revolution has been slow in reaching our country. We have been exempt, not because we had solved the problems, but because we had not yet confronted them. We have now arrived, and all the characteristic conditions of American life will henceforth combine to make the social struggle here more intense than anywhere else. The vastness and the free sweep of our concentrated wealth on the one side, the independence, intelligence, moral vigor, and political power of the common people on the other side, promise a long-drawn grapple of contesting forces which may well make the heart of every American patriot sink within him.

It is realized by friend and foe that religion can play, and must play, a momentous part in this irrepressible conflict.

The Church, the organized expression of the religious life of the past, is one of the most potent institutions and forces in Western civilization. Its favor and moral influence are wooed by all parties. It cannot help throwing its immense weight on one side or the other. If it tries not to act, it thereby acts; and in any case its choice will be decisive for its own future.

Apart from the organized Church, the religious spirit is a factor of incalculable power in the making of history. In the idealistic spirits that lead and in the masses that follow, the religious spirit always intensifies thought, enlarges hope, unfetters daring, evokes the willingness to sacrifice, and gives coherence in the fight. Under the warm breath of religious faith, all social institutions become plastic. The religious spirit removes mountains and tramples on impossibilities. Unless the economic and intellectual factors are strongly reënforced by religious enthusiasm, the whole social movement may prove abortive, and the New Era may die before it comes to birth.

It follows that the relation between Christianity and the social crisis is one of the most pressing questions for all intelligent men who realize the power of religion, and most of all for the religious leaders of the people who give direction to the forces of religion.

The question has, in fact, been discussed frequently and earnestly, but it is plain to any thoughtful observer that the common mind of the Christian Church in America has not begun to arrive at any solid convictions or any permanent basis of action. The conscience of Christendom is halting and groping, perplexed by contradicting voices, still poorly informed on essential questions, justly reluctant to part with the treasured maxims of the past, and yet conscious of the imperious call of the future.

*　　*　　*

In covering so vast a field of history and in touching on such a multitude of questions, error and incompleteness are certain, and the writer can claim only that he has tried to do honest work. Moreover, it is impossible to handle questions so vital to the economic, the social, and the moral standing of great and antagonistic classes of men, without jarring precious interests and convictions, and without giving men the choice between the bitterness of social repentance and the bitterness of moral resentment. I can frankly affirm that I have written with malice toward none and with charity for all. Even where I judge men to have done wrong, I find it easy to sympathize with them in the temptations which made the wrong almost inevitable, and in the points of view in which they intrench themselves to save their self-respect. I have tried—so far as erring human judgment permits—to lift the issues out of the plane of personal selfishness and hate, and to put them where the white light of the just and pitying spirit of Jesus can play upon them. If I have failed in that effort, it is my sin. If others in reading fail to respond in the same spirit, it is their sin. In a few years all our restless and angry hearts will be quiet in death, but those who come after us will live in the world which our sins have blighted or which our love of right has redeemed. Let us do our thinking on these great questions, not with our eyes fixed on our bank account, but with a wise outlook on the fields of the future and with the consciousness that the spirit of the Eternal is seeking to distil from our lives some essence of righteousness before they pass away.

*   *   *

THE HISTORICAL ROOTS OF CHRISTIANITY: THE HEBREW PROPHETS

It seems a long start to approach the most modern problems by talking of men who lived before Lycurgus and Solon gave laws to Sparta and Athens. What light can we get on the troubles of the great capitalistic republic of the West from men who tended sheep in Judea or meddled in the petty politics of the Semitic tribes?

History is never antiquated, because humanity is always fundamentally the same. It is always hungry for bread, sweaty with labor, struggling to wrest from nature and hostile men enough to feed its children. The welfare of the mass is always at odds with the selfish force of the strong. The exodus of the Roman plebeians and the Pennsylvania coal strike, the agrarian agitation of the Gracchi and the rising of the Russian peasants,— it is all the same tragic human life. And in all history it would be hard to find any chapter so profoundly instructive, and dignified by such sublime passion and ability, as that in which the prophets took the leading part.

Moreover, the life and thought of the Old Testament prophets are more to us than classical illustrations and sidelights. They are an integral part of the thought-life of Christianity. From the beginning the Christian Church appropriated the Bible of Israel as its own book and thereby made the history of Israel part of the history of Christendom. That history lives in the heart of the Christian nations with a very real spiritual force. The average American knows more about David than about King Arthur, and more about the exodus from Egypt than about the emigration of the Puritans. Throughout the Christian centuries the historical material embodied in the Old Testament has been regarded as not merely instructive, but as authoritative. The social ideas drawn from it have been powerful factors in all attempts of Christianity to influence social and political life. In so far as men have attempted to use the Old Testament as a code of model laws and institutions and have applied these to modern conditions, regardless of the historical connections, these attempts have left a trail of blunder and disaster. In so far as they have caught the spirit that burned in the hearts of the prophets and breathed in gentle humanity through the Mosaic Law, the influence of the Old Testament has been one of the great permanent forces making for democracy and social justice. However our views of the Bible may change, every religious man will continue to recognize that to the elect minds of the Jewish people God gave so vivid a consciousness of the divine will that, in its main tendencies at least, their life and thought carries a permanent authority for all who wish to know the higher right of God. Their writings are like channel-buoys anchored by God, and we shall do well to heed them now that the roar of an angry surf is in our ears.

We shall confine this brief study of the Old Testament to

the prophets, because they are the beating heart of the Old Testament. Modern study has shown that they were the real makers of the unique religious life of Israel. If all that proceeded from them, directly or indirectly, were eliminated from the Old Testament, there would be little left to appeal to the moral and religious judgment of the modern world. Moreover, a comprehension of the essential purpose and spirit of the prophets is necessary for a comprehension of the purpose and spirit of Jesus and of genuine Christianity. In Jesus and the primitive Church the prophetic spirit rose from the dead. To the ceremonial aspects of Jewish religion Jesus was either indifferent or hostile; the thought of the prophets was the spiritual food that he assimilated in his own process of growth. With them he linked his points of view, the convictions which he regarded as axiomatic. Their spirit was to him what the soil and climate of a country are to its flora. The real meaning of his life and the real direction of his purposes can be understood only in that historical connection.

Thus a study of the prophets is not only an interesting part in the history of social movements but it is indispensable for any full comprehension of the social influence exerted by historical Christianity, and for any true comprehension of the mind of Jesus Christ.

For the purposes of this book it is not necessary to follow the work of the prophets in their historical sequence. We shall simply try to lay bare those large and permanent characteristics which are common to that remarkable series of men and which bear on the question in hand.

The fundamental conviction of the prophets, which distinguished them from the ordinary religious life of their day, was the conviction that God demands righteousness and demands nothing but righteousness.

*   *   *

The prophets were public men and their interest was in public affairs. Some of them were statesmen of the highest type. All of them interpreted past history, shaped present history, and foretold future history on the basis of the conviction that God rules with righteousness in the affairs of nations, and that only what is just, and not what is expedient and profitable, shall endure. Samuel was the creator of two dynasties. Nathan and Gad were the political advisers of David. Nathan determined the succession of Solomon. The seed of revolutionary aspirations against the dynasty of David was dropped into the heart of Jeroboam by the prophet Ahijah of Shiloh. Some of the prophets would get short shrift in a European State as religious demagogues. The overthrow of the dynasty of Omri in the Northern Kingdom was the result of a conspiracy between the prophetic party under Elisha and General Jehu, and resulted in a massacre so fearful that it staggered even the Oriental political conscience. On the other hand the insight of Isaiah into the international situation of his day saved his people for a long time from being embroiled in the destructive upheavals that buried other peoples, and gave it thirty years of peace amid almost universal war. The sufferings of Jeremiah came upon him chiefly because he took the unpopular side in national politics. If he and others had confined themselves to "religion," they could have said what they liked.

Our modern religious horizon and our conception of the character of a religious leader and teacher are so different that it is not easy to understand men who saw the province of religion chiefly in the broad reaches of civic affairs and international relations. Our philosophical and economic individualism has affected our religious thought so deeply that we hardly comprehend the prophetic views of an organic national life and of national sin and salvation. We usually conceive of the community as a loose sand-heap of individuals and this difference in the fundamental point of view distorts the utterances of the prophets as soon as we handle them. For instance, one of our most beautiful revival texts is the invitation: "Though your sins be as scarlet, they shall be as white as snow; though they be red like crimson, they shall be as wool." The words are part of the first chapter of Isaiah, to which reference has been made. The prophet throughout the chapter deals with the national condition of the kingdom of Judah and its capital. He describes its devastation; he ridicules the attempts to appease the national God by redoubled sacrifices; he urges instead the abolition of social oppression and injustice as the only way of regaining God's favor for the nation. If they would vindicate the cause of the helpless and oppressed, then he would freely pardon; then their scarlet and crimson guilt would be washed away. The familiar text is followed by the very material promise of economic prosperity, and the threat of continued war: "If ye be willing and obedient, ye shall eat the good of the land; but if ye refuse and rebel, ye shall be devoured with the sword." Of course the text is nobly true when it is made to express God's willingness to pardon the repentant individual, but that was not the thought in the mind of the writer. He offered a new start to his nation on condition that it righted social wrongs. We offer free pardon to individuals and rarely mention social wrongs.

We have seen that the prophets demanded right moral conduct as the sole test and fruit of religion, and that the morality which they had in mind was not the private morality of detached pious souls but the social morality of the nation. This they preached, and they backed their preaching by active participation in public action and discussion.

*   *   *

The Hebrew prophets shared the fate of all leaders who are far ahead of their times. They did not themselves achieve the triumph of their ideas. It was achieved for them by men who did not share their spirit, and who insensibly debased their ideals in realizing them. The ethical monotheism of the prophets did not become common property in Judah till the priests and scribes enforced it. That is part of the Divine Comedy of history. The Tories carry out the Liberal programmes. The ideas preached by Socialists and Single Taxers are adopted by Populists, radical Democrats, and conservative Republicans successively, and in coming years the great parties will take credit for championing ideas which they did their best to stifle and then to betray. It is a beneficent scheme by which the joy of life is evened up. The "practical men" and conservatives have the pleasure of feeling that they are the only ones who can really make reforms work. The prophetic minds have the satisfaction of knowing that the world must come their way whether it will or not, because they are on the way to justice, and justice is on the way to God.

Here then we have a succession of men perhaps unique in religious history for their moral heroism and spiritual insight. They were the moving spirits in the religious progress of their nation; the creators, directly or indirectly, of its law, its historical and poetical literature, and its piety; the men to whose personality and teaching Jesus felt most kinship; the men who still kindle modern religious enthusiasm. Most of us believe that their insight was divinely given and that the course they steered was set for them by the Captain of history.

We have seen that these men were almost indifferent, if not contemptuous, about the ceremonial side of customary religion, but turned with passionate enthusiasm to moral righteousness as the true domain of religion. Where would their interest lie if they lived to-day?

We have seen that their religious concern was not restricted to private religion and morality, but dealt preëminently with the social and political life of their nation. Would they limit its range to-day?

We have seen that their sympathy was wholly and passionately with the poor and oppressed. If they lived to-day, would they place the chief blame for poverty on the poor and give their admiration to the strong?

We have seen that they gradually rose above the kindred prophets of other nations through their moral interest in national affairs, and that their spiritual progress and education were intimately connected with their open-eyed comprehension of the larger questions of contemporary history. Is it likely that the same attitude of mind which enlarged and purified the religion of the Hebrew leaders would deteriorate and endanger the religion of Chrisitan leaders?

We have seen that the religious concern in politics ceased only when politics ceased; that religious individualism was a triumph of faith under abnormal conditions and not a normal type of religious life; and that the enforced withdrawal of religion from the wider life was one cause for the later narrowness of Judaism. Does this warrant the assumption that religion is most normal when it is most the affair of the individual?

We have seen that the same political programme and the wise historical insight of the great prophets turned into apocalyptic dreams and bookish calculations when the nation lost its political self-government and training. How wise is it for the Christian leaders of a democratic nation to take their interpretation of God's purposes in history and their theories about the coming of the kingdom of God from the feeblest and most decadent age of Hebrew thought?

We have seen that the true prophets opposed the complacent optimism of the people and of their popular spokesmen, and gave warning of disaster as long as it was coming. If they lived among the present symptoms of social and moral decay, would they sing a lullaby or sound the reveille?

No true prophet will copy a prophet. Their garb, their mannerisms of language, the vehemence of their style, belong to their age and not to ours. But if we believe in their divine mission and in the divine origin of the religion in which they were the chief factors, we cannot repudiate what was fundamental in their lives. If any one holds that religion is essentially ritual and sacramental; or that it is purely personal; or that God is on the side of the rich; or that social interest is likely to lead preachers astray; he must prove his case with his eye on the Hebrew prophets, and the burden of proof is with him.

*   *   *

THE SOCIAL AIMS OF JESUS

*   *   *

The historical background which we have just sketched must ever be kept in mind in understanding the life and purpose of Jesus. He was not merely an initiator, but a consummator. Like all great minds that do not merely imagine Utopias, but actually advance humanity to a new epoch, he took the situation and material furnished to him by the past and moulded that into a fuller approximation to the divine conception within him. He embodied the prophetic stream of faith and hope. He linked his work to that of John the Baptist as the one contemporary fact to which he felt most inward affinity.

Jesus began his preaching with the call: "The time is fulfilled; the kingdom of God is now close at hand; repent and believe in the glad news."[1] The kingdom of God continued to be the centre of all his teaching as recorded by the synoptic gospels. His parables, his moral instructions, and his prophetic predictions all bear on that.

We have no definition of what he meant by the phrase. His audience needed no definition. It was then a familiar conception and phrase. The new thing was simply that this kingdom was at last on the point of coming.

We are not at all in that situation to-day. Anyone who has tried to grasp the idea will have realized how vague and elusive it seems. It stands to-day for quite a catalogue of ideas.[2] To the ordinary reader of the Bible, "inheriting the kingdom of heaven" simply means being saved and going to heaven. For others it means the millennium. For some the organized Church; for others "the invisible Church." For the mystic it means the hidden life with God. The truth is that the idea in the sense in which Jesus and his audiences understood it almost completely passed out of Christian thought as soon as Christianity passed from the Jewish people and found its spiritual home within the great Graeco-Roman world. The historical basis for the idea was wanting there. The phrase was taken along, just as an emigrant will carry a water-jar with him; but the water from the well of Bethlehem evaporated and it was now used to dip water from the wells of Ephesus or from the Nile and Tiber. The Greek world cherished no such national religious hope as the prophets had ingrained in Jewish thought; on the other hand it was intensely interested in the future life for the individual, and in the ascetic triumph over flesh and matter. Thus the idea which had been the centre of Christ's thought was not at all the centre of the Church's thought, and even the comprehension of his

1. Mark 1, 15.
2. See the list of definitions in Shailer Mathews, "The Social Teaching of Jesus," 53, note 1.

meaning was lost and overlaid. Only some remnants of it persisted in the millennial hope and in the organic conception of the Church.

The historical study of our own day has made the first thorough attempt to understand this fundamental thought of Jesus in the sense in which he used it, but the results of this investigation are not at all completed. There are a hundred critical difficulties in the way of a sure and consistent interpretation that would be acceptable to all investigators. The limits of space and the purpose of this book will not permit me to do justice to the conflicting views. I shall have to set down my own results with only an occasional reference to the difficulties that beset them.

*   *   *

When Jesus used the phrase "the kingdom of God," it inevitably evoked that whole sphere of thought in the minds of his hearers. If he did not mean by it the substance of what they meant by it, it was a mistake to use the term. If he did not mean the consummation of the theocratic hope, but merely an internal blessedness for individuals with the hope of getting to heaven, why did he use the words around which all the collective hopes clustered? In that case it was not only a misleading but a dangerous phrase. It unfettered the political hopes of the crowd; it drew down on him the suspicion of the government; it actually led to his death.

Unless we have clear proof to the contrary, we must assume that in the main the words meant the same thing to him and to his audiences. But it is very possible that he seriously modified and corrected the popular conception. That is in fact the process with every great, creative religious mind: the connection with the past is maintained and the old terms are used, but they are set in new connections and filled with new qualities. In the teaching of Jesus we find that he consciously opposed some features of the popular hope and sought to make it truer.

For one thing he would have nothing to do with bloodshed and violence. When the crowds that were on their way to the Passover gathered around him in the solitude on the Eastern shore of the lake and wanted to make him king and march on the capital, he eluded them by sending his inflammable disciples away in the boat, and himself going up among the rocks to pray till the darkness dispersed the crowd.[1] Alliance with the Messianic force-revolution was one of the temptations which he confronted at the outset and repudiated;[2] he would not set up God's kingdom by using the devil's means of hatred and blood. With the glorious idealism of faith and love Jesus threw away the sword and advanced on the intrenchments of wrong with hand outstretched, and heart exposed.

*   *   *

There was a revolutionary consciousness in Jesus; not, of course, in the common use of the word "revolutionary," which connects it with violence and bloodshed. But Jesus knew that he had come to kindle a fire on earth. Much as he loved peace, he knew that the actual result of his work would be not peace but the sword. His mother in her song had recognized in her own experience the settled custom of God to "put down the proud and exalt them of low degree," to "fill the hungry with good things and to send the rich empty away."[3] King Robert of Sicily recognized the revolutionary ring in those phrases, and thought it well that the Magnificat was sung only in Latin. The son of Mary expected a great reversal of values. The first would be last and the last would be first.[4] He saw that what was exalted among man was an abomination before God,[5] and therefore these exalted things had no glamour for his eye. This revolutionary note runs even through the beatitudes where we should least expect it. The point of them is that henceforth those were to be blessed whom the world had not blessed, for the kingdom of God would reverse their relative standing. Now the poor and the hungry and sad were to be satisfied and comforted; the meek who had been shouldered aside by the ruthless

1. Matthew 14. 22-23; John 6. 14-15.
2. Matthew 4. 8-10.
3. Luke 1: 52-53.
4. Mark 10. 31.
5. Luke 16. 15.

would get their chance to inherit the earth, and conflict and persecution would be inevitable in the process.[1]

We are apt to forget that his attack on the religious leaders and authorities of his day was of revolutionary boldness and thoroughness. He called the ecclesiastical leaders hypocrites, blind leaders who fumbled in their casuistry, and everywhere missed the decisive facts in teaching right and wrong. Their piety was no piety; their law was inadequate; they harmed the men whom they wanted to convert.[2] Even the publicans and harlots had a truer piety than theirs.[3] If we remember that religion was still the foundation of the Jewish State, and that the religious authorities were the pillars of existing society, much as in mediæval Catholic Europe, we shall realize how revolutionary were his invectives. It was like Luther anathematizing the Catholic hierarchy.

*   *   *

Jesus was not a child of this world. He did not revere the men it called great; he did not accept its customs and social usages as final; his moral conceptions did not run along the grooves marked out by it. He nourished within his soul the ideal of a common life so radically different from the present that it involved a reversal of values, a revolutionary displacement of existing relations. This ideal was not merely a beautiful dream to solace his soul. He lived it out in his own daily life. He urged others to live that way. He held that it was the only true life, and that the ordinary way was misery and folly. He dared to believe that it would triumph. When he saw that the people were turning from him, and that his nation had chosen the evil way and was drifting toward the rocks that would destroy it, unutterable sadness filled his soul, but he never abandoned his faith in the final triumph of that kingdom of God for which he had lived. For the present, the cross; but beyond the cross, the kingdom of God. If he was not to achieve it now, he would return and do it then.

1. Matthew 5. 1-12.
2. See the whole of Matthew 23.
3. Matthew 21. 23-32.

That was the faith of Jesus. Have his followers shared it? We shall see later what changes and limitations the original purpose and spirit of Christianity suffered in the course of history. But the Church has never been able to get entirely away from the revolutionary spirit of Jesus. It is an essential doctrine of Christianity that the world is fundamentally good and practically bad, for it was made by God, but is now controlled by sin. If a man wants to be a Christian, he must stand over against things as they are and condemn them in the name of that higher conception of life which Jesus revealed. If a man is satisfied with things as they are, he belongs to the other side. For many centuries the Church felt so deeply that the Christian conception of life and the actual social life are incompatible, that any one who wanted to live the genuine Christian life, had to leave the world and live in a monastic community. Protestantism has abandoned the monastic life and settled down to live in the world. If that implies that it accepts the present condition as good and final, it means a silencing of its Christian protest and its surrender to "the world." There is another alternative. Ascetic Christianity called the world evil and left it. Humanity is waiting for a revolutionary Christianity which will call the world evil and change it. We do not want "to blow all our existing institutions to atoms," but we do want to remould every one of them. A tank of gasolene can blow a car sky-high in a single explosion, or push it to the top of a hill in a perpetual succession of little explosions. We need a combination between the faith of Jesus in the need and the possibility of the kingdom of God, and the modern comprehension of the organic development of human society.

We saw at the outset of our discussion that Jesus was not a mere social reformer. Religion was the heart of his life, and all that he said on social relations was said from the religious point of view. He has been called the first socialist. He was more; he was the first real man, the inaugurator of a new humanity. But as such he bore within him the germs of a new social and political order. He was too great to be the Saviour of a fractional part of human life. His redemption extends to all human needs and powers and relations. Theologians have felt no hesitation in founding a system of speculative thought on the teachings of Jesus, and yet Jesus was never an inhabitant of the realm of speculative thought. He has been made the founder and organizer of a great ecclesiastical machine, which derives authority for its offices and institutions from him, and yet "hardly any problem of exegesis is more difficult than to discover in the gospels an administrative or organizing or ecclesiastical Christ."[1] There is at least as much justification in invoking his name to-day as the champion of a great movement for a more righteous social life. He was neither a theologian, nor an ecclesiastic, nor a socialist. But if we were forced to classify him either with the great theologians who elaborated the fine distinctions of scholasticism; or with the mighty popes and princes of the Church who built up their power in his name; or with the men who are giving their heart and life to the propaganda of a new social system—where should we place him?

* * *

THE STAKE OF THE CHURCH IN THE SOCIAL MOVEMENT

The demoralization of society which we have tried to bring before us in the preceding chapter ought to appeal most powerfully to the Church, for the Church is to be the incarnation of the Christ-spirit on earth, the organized conscience of Christendom. It should be swiftest to awaken to every undeserved suffering, bravest to speak against every wrong, and strongest to rally the moral forces of the community against everything that threatens the better life among men.

* * *

The gospel, to have full power over an age, must be the highest expression of the moral and religious truths held by that age. If it lags behind and deals in outgrown conceptions of life and duty, it will lose power over the ablest minds and the young men first, and gradually over all. In our thought to-day the social problems irresistibly take the lead. If the Church has no live and bold thought on this dominant question of modern

1. Peabody, "Jesus Christ and the Social Question," 89.

life, its teaching authority on all other questions will dwindle and be despised. It cannot afford to have young men sniff the air as in a stuffy room when they enter the sphere of religious thought. When the world is in travail with a higher ideal of justice, the Church dare not ignore it if it would retain its moral leadership. On the other hand, if the Church does incorporate the new social terms in its synthesis of truth, they are certain to throw new light on all the older elements of its teaching. The conception of race sin and race salvation become comprehensible once more to those who have made the idea of social solidarity in good and evil a part of their thought. The law of sacrifice loses its arbitrary and mechanical aspect when we understand the vital union of all humanity. Individualistic Christianity has almost lost sight of the great idea of the kingdom of God, which was the inspiration and centre of the thought of Jesus. Social Christianity would once more enable us to understand the purpose and thought of Jesus and take the veil from our eyes when we read the synoptic gospels.

The social crisis offers a great opportunity for the infusion of new life and power into the religious thought of the Church. It also offers the chance for progress in its life. When the broader social outlook widens the purpose of a Christian man beyond the increase of his church, he lifts up his eyes and sees that there are others who are at work for humanity besides his denomination. Common work for social welfare is the best common ground for the various religious bodies and the best training school for practical Christian unity. The strong movement for Christian union in our country has been largely prompted by the realization of social needs, and is led by men who have felt the attraction of the kingdom of God as something greater than any denomination and as the common object of all. Thus the divisions which were caused in the past by differences in dogma and church polity may perhaps be healed by unity of interest in social salvation.

As we have seen, the industrial and commercial life to-day is dominated by principles antagonistic to the fundamental principles of Christianity, and it is so difficult to live a Christian life in the midst of it that few men even try. If production could be organized on a basis of coöperative fraternity; if distribution could at least approximately be determined by justice; if all men could be conscious that their labor contributed to the welfare of all and that their personal well-being was dependent on the prosperity of the Commonwealth; if predatory business and parasitic wealth ceased and all men lived only by their labor; if the luxury of unearned wealth no longer made us all feverish with covetousness and a simpler life became the fashion; if our time and strength were not used up either in getting a bare living or in amassing unusable wealth and we had more leisure for the higher pursuits of the mind and the soul—then there might be a chance to live such a life of gentleness and brotherly kindness and tranquillity of heart as Jesus desired for men. It may be that the coöperative Commonwealth would give us the first chance in history to live a really Christian life without retiring from the world, and would make the Sermon on the Mount a philosophy of life feasible for all who care to try.

This is the stake of the Church in the social crisis. If society continues to disintegrate and decay, the Church will be carried down with it. If the Church can rally such moral forces that injustice will be overcome and fresh red blood will course in a sounder social organism, it will itself rise to higher liberty and life. Doing the will of God it will have new visions of God. With a new message will come a new authority. If the salt lose its saltiness, it will be trodden under foot. If the Church fulfils its prophetic functions, it may bear the prophet's reproach for a time, but it will have the prophet's vindication thereafter.

The conviction has always been embedded in the heart of the Church that "the world"—society as it is—is evil and some time is to make way for a true human society in which the spirit of Jesus Christ shall rule. For fifteen hundred years those who desired to live a truly Christian life withdrew from the evil world to live a life apart. But the principle of such an ascetic departure from the world is dead in modern life. There are only two other possibilities. The Church must either condemn the world and seek to change it, or tolerate the world and conform to it. In the latter case it surrenders its holiness and its mission. The other possibility has never yet been tried with full faith on a large scale. All the leadings of God in contemporary history and all the promptings of Christ's spirit in our hearts urge us to make the trial. On this choice is staked the future of the Church.

* * *

WHAT TO DO

We rest our case. We have seen that in the prophetic religion of the Old Testament and in the aims of Jesus Christ the reconstruction of the whole of human life in accordance with the will of God and under the motive power of religion was the ruling purpose. Primitive Christianity, while under the fresh impulse of Jesus, was filled with social forces. In its later history the reconstructive capacities of Christianity were paralyzed by alien influences, but through the evolution of the Christian spirit in the Church it has now arrived at a stage in its development where it is fit and free for its largest social mission. At the same time Christian civilization has arrived at the great crisis of its history and is in the most urgent need of all moral power to overcome the wrongs which have throttled other nations and civilizations. The Church, too, has its own power and future at stake in the issues of social development. Thus the will of God revealed in Christ and in the highest manifestations of the religious spirit, the call of human duty, and the motives of self-protection, alike summon Christian men singly and collectively to put their hands to the plough and not to look back till public morality shall be at least as much Christianized as private morality now is.

The question then immediately confronts us: What social changes would be involved in such a religious reorganization of life? What institutions and practices of our present life would have to cease? What new elements would have to be embodied? What social ideal should be the ultimate aim of Christian men, and what practical means and policies should they use for its attainment?

* * *

There are certain lines of endeavor which lead nowhere. Christian men have again and again attempted to find the way out of the maze in these directions, but experience has set up the sign, "No Thoroughfare."

One of these futile efforts is the attempt to make economic development revert to earlier stages. Christian men of conservative spirit recoil from the swift pace and impersonal hugeness of modern industry and look back to the simpler processes and more personal contact between master and men as a better and more Christian social life. The personal interest of the intelligent Christian middle class is likely to run in the same direction. Thus in our country we have the outcry of that class against the trusts and the department stores, and the insistence on returning to the simple competition of small concerns. But it is safe to say that no such return would be permanent. These great industrial undertakings extend the area within which coöperation and the correlation of forces rule, and competition is no match for coöperation. Our effort must rather be to preserve all the benefits which the elaboration of the productive machinery has worked out, but to make these benefits enrich the many instead of the few. Reform movements arising among the business class are often reactionary; they seek to revert to outgrown conditions and turn the shadow on the dial backward. Socialism is almost unique in accepting as inevitable and desirable the essential achievements of industrial organization, but only as halfway stages toward a vaster and a far juster social system.

For the same reasons it is futile to attempt to reform modern society on biblical models. The principle underlying the Mosaic land system is wholly right. The spirit pervading the Hebrew laws protecting the laborer and the poor is so tender and noble that it puts us to shame. But these legal prescriptions were adjusted to an agricultural and stationary population, organized under patriarchal and tribal coherence, and they would be wholly unworkable under modern conditions. It is rather our business to catch the bold and humane spirit of the prophetic tribunes of the people and do as well in our day as they did in theirs. Nothing could be more valuable than to understand the social contents of the Bible in their historical setting, and press home on the Christian Church the essential purpose and direction of its own inspired book. But here, too, it is true that "the letter killeth; it is the spirit that quickeneth."

One of the most persistent mistakes of Christian men has been to postpone social regeneration to a future era to be inaugurated by the return of Christ. In former chapters the origin of this hope and its original beauty and power have been discussed. It was at the outset a triumphant assertion of faith against apparent impossibilities. It still enshrines the social hope of Christianity and concedes that some time the social life of men is to pass through a radical change and be ruled by Christ. But the element of postponement in it to-day means a lack of faith in the present power of Christ and paralyzes the religious initiative. It ignores the revelation of God contained in nineteen centuries of continuous history. It is careful not to see the long succession of men and churches and movements that staked all their hopes and all their chances of social improvement on this expectation and were disappointed. It is true that any regeneration of society can come only through the act of God and the presence of Christ; but God is now acting, and Christ is now here. To assert that means not less faith, but more. It is true that any effort at social regeneration is dogged by perpetual relapses and doomed forever to fall short of its aim. But the same is true of our personal efforts to live a Christlike life; it is true, also, of every local church, and of the history of the Church at large. Whatever argument would demand the postponement of social regeneration to a future era will equally demand the postponement of personal holiness to a future life. We must have the faith of the apostolic Church in the triumph of Christ over the kingdoms of the world, *plus* the knowledge which nineteen centuries of history have given to us. Unless we add that knowledge, the faith of the apostles becomes our unbelief.

Another *cul-de-sac* of Christian endeavor is the organization of communistic colonies. There is no reason why a number of Christian people should not live in commons or organize for coöperative production if they can hope to make their life more comfortable, more free from care, and more moral in its relations. But past experience does not show that such colonies served to Christianize social life at large. The example is not widely contagious, even if the colony is successful. If the experiment fails through any of a hundred practical causes, its failure is heralded as a convincing demonstration that competition is the only orthodox and successful basis of society. Settlements with some communistic features are likely to increase in the future as the eyes of cultured people are opened to the wastefulness and unhappiness of ordinary life, and they may be exceedingly useful if they gather like-minded men and women in groups, and thus intensify and clarify their convictions by intercourse. But they will be influential on a large scale only if the ideas and experiences wrought out in these settlements find channels to run out freely into the general unregenerate life through books, newspapers, or lectures issuing from the settlement. In the main, the salt of the earth will do its work best if it is not stored in casks by itself, but rubbed in evenly and generously where it is most needed. The mass of society will ponderously move an inch where a select colony might spurt a mile toward the future; but the total gain in foot-pounds will be greater in the mass-movement. The coöperative stores in England and on the continent are a far more hopeful and influential education in the coöperative principle than the communistic colonies have been, because they are built into the mass of the general life.

If the Church should in the future really seek to Christianize social life, it will almost certainly be tempted to make itself the chief agent and beneficiary of the process. Attempts will be made to organize ecclesiastical duplicates of fraternal insurance societies, coöperative undertakings, labor bureaus, etc. There will be Christian socialist parties in politics. The Church will claim to be the only agency through which social salvation can come. It will seek to keep the social movement under clerical control. This effort will be prompted partly by the desire to put its organized power at the service of the poor; partly by the fear of non-Christian or anti-Christian influences which may dominate social radicalism; and partly by the instinct of self-assertion, self-protection, and self-aggrandizement which resides in every social organization. Just as the desire to save individuals is now frequently vitiated by the anxiety to increase church membership, so the desire to save social life may be vitiated by the anxiety to keep the Church to the front. Those ecclesiastical bodies which have the strongest church-consciousness are most likely to insist that this work shall be done through them or not at all. The history of the social movement in Europe has furnished most interesting and significant demonstrations of this tendency. But it is full of peril not only to the Church, but to the social movement itself. It beclouds the social issues by ecclesiastical interests and jealousies. It subtly and unconsciously changes the aim from the salvation of the people to the salvation of the Church. The social movement could have no more powerful ally than religious enthusiasm; it could have no more dangerous ally than ecclesiasticism. If the Church truly desires to save the social life of the people, it must be content with inspiring the social movement with religious faith and daring, and it must not attempt to control and monopolize it for its own organization. If a man wants to give honest help, he must fill himself with the spirit of Jesus and divest himself of the ecclesiastical point of view.

In personal religion the first requirement is to repent and believe in the gospel. As long as a man is self-righteous and complacently satisfied with his moral attainments, there is no hope that he will enter into the higher development, and unless he has faith that a higher level of spiritual life is attainable, he will be lethargic and stationary.

Social religion, too, demands repentance and faith: repentance for our social sins; faith in the possibility of a new social order. As long as a man sees in our present society only a few inevitable abuses and recognizes no sin and evil deep-seated in the very constitution of the present order, he is still in a state of moral blindness and without conviction of sin. Those who believe in a better social order are often told that they do not know the sinfulness of the human heart. They could justly retort the charge on the men of the evangelical school. When the latter deal with public wrongs, they often exhibit a curious unfamiliarity with the forms which sin assumes there, and sometimes reverently bow before one of the devil's spider-webs, praising it as one of the mighty works of God. Regeneration includes that a man must pass under the domination of the spirit of

Christ, so that he will judge of life as Christ would judge of it. That means a revaluation of social values. Things that are now "exalted among men" must become "an abomination" to him because they are built on wrong and misery. Unless a man finds his judgment at least on some fundamental questions in opposition to the current ideas of the age, he is still a child of this world and has not "tasted the powers of the coming age." He will have to repent and believe if he wants to be a Christian in the full sense of the word.

No man can help the people until he is himself free from the spell which the present order has cast over our moral judgment. We have repeatedly pointed out that every social institution weaves a protecting integument of glossy idealization about itself like a colony of tent-caterpillars in an apple tree. For instance, wherever militarism rules, war is idealized by monuments and paintings, poetry and song. The stench of the hospitals and the maggots of the battle-field are passed in silence, and the imagination of the people is filled with waving plumes and the shout of charging columns. A Russian general thought Verestchagin's pictures ought to be destroyed because they disenchanted the people. If war is ever to be relegated to the limbo of outgrown barbarism, we must shake off its magic. When we comprehend how few wars have ever been fought for the sake of justice or the people; how personal spite, the ambition of military professionals, and the protection of capitalistic ventures are the real moving powers; how the governing classes pour out the blood and wealth of nations for private ends and exude patriotic enthusiasm like a squid secreting ink to hide its retreat—then the mythology of war will no longer bring us to our knees, and we shall fail to get drunk with the rest when martial intoxication sweeps the people off their feet.

In the same way we shall have to see through the fictions of capitalism. We are assured that the poor are poor through their own fault; that rent and profits are the just dues of foresight and ability; that the immigrants are the cause of corruption in our city politics; that we cannot compete with foreign countries unless our working class will descend to the wages paid abroad. These are all very plausible assertions, but they are lies dressed up in truth. There is a great deal of conscious lying. Industrialism as a whole sends out deceptive prospectuses just like single corporations within it. But in the main these misleading theories are the complacent self-deception of those who profit by present conditions and are loath to believe that their life is working harm. It is very rare for a man to condemn the means by which he makes a living, and we must simply make allowance for the warping influence of self-interest when he justifies himself and not believe him entirely.[1] In the early part of the nineteenth century, when tiny children in England were driven to the looms with whips, and women lost even the physical appearance of womanhood in the coal mines, the owners insisted that English industry would be ruined by the proposed reform laws, and doubtless they thought so. If men holding stock in traction companies assert that municipal ownership is un-American; if the express companies say that parcels cannot be carried below their own amazing rate; if Mr. Baer in the midst of the coal strike assured a minister that "God in his infinite wisdom had given control of the property interests of the country" to him and his associates and they would do all things well—we must simply allow for the warping effect of self-interest and pass on to the order of the day. Macaulay said that the doctrine of gravitation would not yet be accepted if it had interfered with vested interests.

The greatest contribution which any man can make to the social movement is the contribution of a regenerated personality, of a will which sets justice above policy and profit, and of an intellect emancipated from falsehood. Such a man will in some measure incarnate the principles of a higher social order in his attitude to all questions and in all his relations to men, and will be a well-spring of regenerating influences. If he speaks, his judgment will be a corrective force. If he listens, he will encourage the truth-teller and discourage the pedler of adulterated facts and maxims. If others lose heart, he will stay them with his inspired patience. If any new principle is to gain power in human history, it must take shape and life in individuals who have faith in it. The men of faith are the living

1. John Graham Brooks, in the introductory chapter to "The Social Unrest," gives very interesting testimony to this fact.

spirits, the channels by which new truth and power from God enter humanity. To repent of our collective social sins, to have faith in the possibility and reality of a divine life in humanity, to submit the will to the purposes of the kingdom of God, to permit the divine inspiration to emancipate and clarify the moral insight—this is the most intimate duty of the religious man who would help to build the coming Messianic era of mankind.

*   *   *

It has always been recognized that the creation of regenerate personalities, pledged to righteousness, is one of the most important services which the Church can render to social progress. But regeneration merely creates the will to do the right; it does not define for a man what is right. That is defined for him in the main by the religious community whose ideas he accepts. If his church community demands total abstinence from liquor, he will consider that as part of the Christian life; if it sanctions slavery or polygamy, he will consider them good. While the Church was swayed by ascetic ideas, the dedication of the will to God meant surrender to the monastic life. In the past the Church has largely connected the idea of religious duty with the service of the Church. It has made itself the *summum bonum,* the embodiment of all religious aims. To that extent it has monopolized for itself the power of devotion begotten in regenerated hearts and has not directed that incalculable force toward social and political affairs. Now that the idea of social salvation is taking hold of us, the realm of duty spread before a mind dedicating itself to God's service is becoming more inclusive. The social work of the Y.M.C.A. and Y.W.C.A., of the Salvation Army and the Volunteers of America, of the social settlements and institutional churches, show what is coming. It is significant that several new religious sects have embodied the social ideal in their religious aims. If the Church in any measure will lay consecrating hands on those who undertake social redemption, it will hallow their work and give it religious dignity and joy. And when politicians and social exploiters have to deal with the stubborn courage of men who pray about their politics, they will have a new factor to reckon with.

The older conception of religion viewed as religious only what ministered to the souls of men or what served the Church. When a man attended the services of the Church, contributed money to its work, taught in Sunday-school, spoke to the unconverted, or visited the sick, he was doing religious work. The conscientiousness with which he did his daily work also had a religious quality. On the other hand, the daily work itself, the ploughing, building, cobbling, or selling were secular, and the main output of his life was not directly a contribution to the kingdom of God, but merely the necessary method of getting a living for himself and his family. The ministry alone and a few allied callings had the uplifting consciousness of serving God in the total of daily work. A few professions were marked off as holy, just as in past stages of religion certain groves and temples were marked out as holy ground where God could be sought and served.

If now we could have faith enough to believe that all human life can be filled with divine purpose; that God saves not only the soul, but the whole of human life; that anything which serves to make men healthy, intelligent, happy, and good is a service to the Father of men; that the kingdom of God is not bounded by the Church, but includes all human relations—then all professions would be hallowed and receive religious dignity. A man making a shoe or arguing a law case or planting potatoes or teaching school, could feel that this was itself a contribution to the welfare of mankind, and indeed his main contribution to it.

But such a view of our professional life would bring it under religious scrutiny. If a man's calling consisted in manufacturing or selling useless or harmful stuff, he would find himself unable to connect it with his religion. In so far as the energy of business life is expended in crowding out competitors, it would also be outside of the sanction of religion, and religious men would be compelled to consider how industry and commerce could be reorganized so that there would be a maximum of service to humanity and a minimum of antagonism between those who desire to serve it. As soon as religion will set the kingdom of God before it as the all-inclusive aim, and will define it so as to include all rightful relations among men, the awakened conscience will begin to turn its searchlight on the industrial and commercial life in detail, and will insist on eliminating all professions which harm instead of helping, and on coördinating all productive activities to secure a maximum of service. That in itself would produce a quiet industrial revolution.

Scatter through all classes and professions a large number of men and women whose eyes have had a vision of a true human society and who have faith in it and courage to stand against anything that contradicts it, and public opinion will have a new swiftness and tenacity in judging on right and wrong. The murder of the Armenians, the horrors of the Congo Free State, the ravages of the liquor traffic in Africa, the peace movement, the protest against child labor in America, the movement for early closing of retail stores—all these things arouse only a limited number of persons to active sympathy; the rest are lethargic. It takes so long to "work up public sentiment," and even then it stops boiling as fast as a kettle of water taken off the fire. There are so many Christian people and such feeble sentiment on public wrongs. It is not because people are not good enough, but because their goodness has not been directed and educated in this direction. The multiplication of socially enlightened Christians will serve the body of society much as a physical organism would be served if a complete and effective system of ganglia should be distributed where few of them existed. The social body needs moral innervation; and the spread of men who combine religious faith, moral enthusiasm, and economic information, and apply the combined result to public morality, promises to create a moral sensitiveness never yet known.

*   *   *

The fundamental contribution of every man is the change of his own personality. We must repent of the sins of existing society, cast off the spell of the lies protecting our social wrongs, have faith in a higher social order, and realize in ourselves a new type of Christian manhood which seeks to overcome the evil in the present world, not by withdrawing from the world, but by revolutionizing it.

If this new type of religious character multiplies among the young men and women, they will change the world when they come to hold the controlling positions of society in their maturer years. They will give a new force to righteous and enlightened public opinion, and will apply the religious sense of duty and service to the common daily life with a new motive and directness.

The ministry, in particular, must apply the teaching functions of the pulpit to the pressing questions of public morality. It must collectively learn not to speak without adequate information; not to charge individuals with guilt in which all society shares; not to be partial, and yet to be on the side of the lost; not to yield to political partisanship, but to deal with moral questions before they become political issues and with those questions of public welfare which never do become political issues. They must lift the social questions to a religious level by faith and spiritual insight. The larger the number of ministers who attempt these untrodden ways, the safer and saner will those be who follow. By interpreting one social class to the other, they can create a disposition to make concessions and help in securing a peaceful settlement of social issues.

The force of the religious spirit should be bent toward asserting the supremacy of life over property. Property exists to maintain and develop life. It is unchristian to regard human life as a mere instrument for the production of wealth.

The religious sentiment can protect good customs and institutions against the inroads of ruthless greed, and extend their scope. It can create humane customs which the law is impotent to create. It can create the convictions and customs which are later embodied in good legislation.

Our complex society rests largely on the stewardship of delegated powers. The opportunities to profit by the betrayal of trust increase with the wealth and complexity of civilization. The most fundamental evils in past history and present conditions were due to converting stewardship into ownership. The keener moral insight created by Christianity should lend its

help in scrutinizing all claims to property and power in order
to detect latent public rights and to recall the recreant stewards
to their duty.

Primitive society was communistic. The most valuable institutions in modern life—the family, the school and church—
are communistic. The State, too, is essentially communistic and
is becoming increasingly so. During the larger part of its history the Christian Church regarded communism as the only ideal
life. Christianity certainly has more affinity for coöperative and
fraternal institutions than for competitive disunion. It should
therefore strengthen the existing communistic institutions and
aid the evolution of society from the present temporary stage of
individualism to a higher form of communism.

The splendid ideal of a fraternal organization of society cannot be realized by idealists only. It must be supported by the
self-interest of a powerful class. The working class, which is
now engaged in its upward movement, is struggling to secure
better conditions of life, an assured status for its class organi-
zations, and ultimately the ownership of the means of production. Its success in the last great aim would mean the closing
of the gap which now divides industrial society and the establishment of industry on the principle of solidarity and the
method of coöperation. Christianity should enter into a working alliance with this rising class, and by its mediation secure
the victory of these principles by a gradual equalization of social
opportunity and power.

The first apostolate of Christianity was born from a deep
fellow-feeling for social misery and from the consciousness of
a great historical opportunity. Jesus saw the peasantry of Galilee
following him about with their poverty and their diseases, like
shepherdless sheep that have been scattered and harried by
beasts of prey, and his heart had compassion on them. He felt
that the harvest was ripe, but there were few to reap it. Past
history had come to its culmination, but there were few who
understood the situation and were prepared to cope with it.
He bade his disciples to pray for laborers for the harvest, and
then made them answer their own prayers by sending them out

two by two to proclaim the kingdom of God. That was the beginning of the world-wide mission of Christianity.[1]

The situation is repeated on a vaster scale to-day. If Jesus stood to-day amid our modern life, with that outlook on the condition of all humanity which observation and travel and the press would spread before him, and with the same heart of divine humanity beating in him, he would create a new apostolate to meet the new needs in a new harvest-time of history.

To any one who knows the sluggishness of humanity to good, the impregnable intrenchments of vested wrongs and the long reaches of time needed from one milestone of progress to the next, the task of setting up a Christian social order in this modern world of ours seems like a fair and futile dream. Yet in fact it is not one tithe as hopeless as when Jesus set out to do it. When he told his disciples, "Ye are the salt of the earth; ye are the light of the world," he expressed the consciousness of a great historic mission to the whole of humanity. Yet it was a Nazarene carpenter speaking to a group of Galilean peasants and fishermen. Under the circumstances at that time it was an utterance of the most daring faith,—faith in himself, faith in them, faith in what he was putting into them, faith in faith. Jesus failed and was crucified, first his body by his enemies, and then his spirit by his friends; but that failure was so amazing a success that to-day it takes an effort on our part to realize that it required any faith on his part to inaugurate the kingdom of God and to send out his apostolate.

To-day, as Jesus looks out upon humanity, his spirit must leap to see the souls responsive to his call. They are sown broadcast through humanity, legions of them. The harvest-field is no longer deserted. All about us we hear the clang of the whetstone and the rush of the blades through the grain and the shout of the reapers. With all our faults and our slothfulness we modern men in many ways are more on a level with the real mind of Jesus than any generation that has gone before. If that first apostolate was able to remove mountains by the power of faith, such an apostolate as Christ could now summon might change the face of the earth.

1. See Matthew 9. 32-10, 42.

The apostolate of a new age must do the work of the sower. When the sower goes forth to sow his seed, he goes with the certainty of partial failure and the knowledge that a long time of patience and of hazard will intervene before he can hope to see the result of his work and his venture. In sowing the truth a man may never see or trace the results. The more ideal his conceptions are, and the farther they move ahead of his time, the larger will be the percentage of apparent failure. But he can afford to wait. The powers of life are on his side. He is like a man who has scattered his seed and then goes off to sleep by night and work by day, and all the while the seed, by the inscrutable chemistry of life, lays hold of the ingredients of its environment and builds them up to its own growth. The mustard-seed becomes a tree. The leaven assimilates the meal by biological processes. The new life penetrates the old humanity and transforms it. Robert Owen was a sower. His coöperative communities failed. He was able to help only a small fraction of the workingmen of his day. But his moral enthusiasm and his ideas fertilized the finest and most self-sacrificing minds among the working classes. They cherished his ultimate hopes in private and worked for realizable ends in public. The Chartist movement was filled with his spirit. The most influential leaders of English unionism in its great period after the middle of the nineteenth century were Owenites. The Rochdale Pioneers were under his influence, and the great coöperative movement in England, an economic force of the first importance, grew in some measure out of the seed which Owen had scattered. Other men may own the present. The future belongs to the sower—provided he scatters seed and does not mistake the chaff for it which once was so essential to the seed and now is dead and useless.

It is inevitable that those who stand against conditions in which most men believe and by which the strongest profit, shall suffer for their stand. The little group of early Christian socialists in England, led by Maurice, Kingsley, and Hughes, now stand by common consent in the history of that generation as one of its finest products, but at that time they were bitterly assailed and misunderstood. Pastor Rudolf Todt, the first man in Germany who undertook to prove that the New Testament and the ethics of socialism have a close affinity, was almost unanimously attacked by the Church of Germany. But Jesus told his apostles at the outset that opposition would be part of their day's work. Christ equipped his Church with no legal rights to protect her; the only political right he gave his disciples was the right of being persecuted.[1] It is part of the doctrine of vicarious atonement, which is fundamental in Christianity, that the prophetic souls must vindicate by their sufferings the truth of the truth they preach.

* * *

Even for the social heretics there is a generous readiness to listen which was unknown in the past. In our country that openness of mind is a product of our free intellectual life, our ingrained democracy, the denominational manifoldness of our religious life, and the spread of the Christian spirit. It has become an accepted doctrine among us that all great movements have obscure beginnings, and that belief tends to make men respectful toward anything that comes from some despised Nazareth. Unless a man forfeits respect by bitterness or lack of tact, he is accorded a large degree of tolerance, though he will always be made to feel the difference between himself and those who say the things that please the great.

The certainty of opposition constitutes a special call to the strong. The ministry seems to have little attraction for the sons of rich men. It is not strange when one considers the enervating trials that beset a rich man in a pastorate. But here is a mission that ought to appeal to the rich young man if he has heroic stuff in him. His assured social standing would give him an influence with rich and poor alike which others attain but slowly if at all. The fear of being blacklisted for championing justice and mercy need have no terrors for him. To use his property as a coat of mail in fighting the battles of the weak would be the best way of obeying Christ's command to the rich young ruler to sell all and give it to the poor. When Mr. Roosevelt was still Police Commissioner in New York, he said to the young men of New York: "I would teach the young men that he who has

1. Nathusius, "Mitarbeit der Kirche," p. 476.

not wealth owes his first duty to his family, but he who has means owes his to the State. It is ignoble to go on heaping up money. I would preach the doctrine of work to all, and to the men of wealth the doctrine of unremunerative work."[1] The most "unremunerative work" is the work that draws opposition and animosity.

Mr. Roosevelt implies here that a man's duty to his family is the first and dominant duty, and that this exempts him in some measure from service to the larger public. It follows that the childless have a call to the dangerous work of the kingdom of God. A man and woman who are feeding and training young citizens are performing so immense and absorbing a service to the future that they might well be exempt from taxes to the State and from sacrificial service to the kingdom of God. If nevertheless so many of them assume these duties in addition, the childless man and woman will have to do heroic work in the trenches before they can rank on the same level. It is not fair to ask a man with children to give his time and strength as freely to public causes as if he had none. It is still more unfair to expect him to risk the bread and the prospects of his family in championing dangerous causes as freely as if he risked only himself. The childless people should adopt the whole coming generation of children and fight to make the world more habitable for them as for their own brood. The unmarried and the childless should enlist in the new apostolate and march on the forlorn hopes with Jesus Christ.

In asking for faith in the possibility of a new social order, we ask for no Utopian delusion. We know well that there is no perfection for man in this life: there is only growth toward perfection. In personal religion we look with seasoned suspicion at any one who claims to be holy and perfect, yet we always tell men to become holy and to seek perfection. We make it a duty to seek what is unattainable. We have the same paradox in the perfectibility of society. We shall never have a perfect social life, yet we must seek it with faith. We shall never abolish suffering. There will always be death and the empty chair and heart. There will always be the agony of love unreturned. Women will long for children and never press baby lips to their

1. Jacob A. Riis, "Theodore Roosevelt, the Citizen."

breast. Men will long for fame and miss it. Imperfect moral insight will work hurt in the best conceivable social order. The strong will always have the impulse to exert their strength, and no system can be devised which can keep them from crowding and jostling the weaker. Increased social refinement will bring increased sensitiveness to pain. An American may suffer as much distress through a social slight as a Russian peasant under the knout. At best there is always but an approximation to a perfect social order. The kingdom of God is always but coming.

But every approximation to it is worth while. Every step toward personal purity and peace, though it only makes the consciousness of imperfection more poignant, carries its own exceeding great reward, and everlasting pilgrimage toward the kingdom of God is better than contented stability in the tents of wickedness.

And sometimes the hot hope surges up that perhaps the long and slow climb may be ending. In the past the steps of our race toward progress have been short and feeble, and succeeded by long intervals of sloth and apathy. But is that necessarily to remain the rate of advance? In the intellectual life there has been an unprecedented leap forward during the last hundred years. Individually we are not more gifted than our grandfathers, but collectively we have wrought out more epoch-making discoveries and inventions in one century than the whole race in the untold centuries that have gone before. If the twentieth century could do for us in the control of social forces what the nineteenth did for us in the control of natural forces, our grandchildren would live in a society that would be justified in regarding our present social life as semi-barbarous. Since the Reformation began to free the mind and to direct the force of religion toward morality, there has been a perceptible increase of speed. Humanity is gaining in elasticity and capacity for change and every gain in general intelligence, in organizing capacity, in physical and moral soundness, and especially in responsiveness to ideal motives, again increases the ability to advance without disastrous reactions. The swiftness of evolution in our own country proves the immense latent perfectibility in human nature.

Last May a miracle happened. At the beginning of the week

the fruit trees bore brown and greenish buds. At the end of the week they were robed in bridal garments of blossom. But for weeks and months the sap had been rising and distending the cells and maturing the tissues which were half ready in the fall before. The swift unfolding was the culmination of a long process. Perhaps these nineteen centuries of Christian influence have been a long preliminary stage of growth, and now the flower and fruit are almost here. If at this juncture we can rally sufficient religious faith and moral strength to snap the bonds of evil and turn the present unparalleled economic and intellectual resources of humanity to the harmonious development of a true social life, the generations yet unborn will mark this as that great day of the Lord for which the ages waited, and count us blessed for sharing in the apostolate that proclaimed it.

DOGMATICS IN OUTLINE

Karl Barth

(1886-   )

KARL BARTH was born in Basel, Switzerland, the son of a university professor. He studied at several universities: Berne, Berlin, Tübingen and Marburg, at the latter place under his most influential theological teacher W. Herrmann.

He began his ministry in a small parish in Switzerland during which time he rethought his training as a young theologian in terms of the immediate job at hand, that of a parish minister serving a church. The two (the theological training and the preaching ministry) did not seem to him to complement each other. Why (he asked himself) should people listen to his opinions or the opinions of others on such grave matters as concern problems of their complex existence? Do they not come to church to find certainty for their religious questings, to hear, if possible, some Word from the Lord? The Bible (he answers) contains this Word and Christianity is a religion with a special revelation. Why, then, should interpretations (particularly philosophies) or experiences or personal feelings stand between worshipers and the Voice speaking out from that *other* World in the theophany of Christ and the Biblical Word?

He found Paul to be the instrument of that Word and he turned to a restudy of The Epistle to the Romans. In this adventure there came the joy of a new discovery. Beyond liberalism and fundamentalism, theological creeds, subjectivism, historical criticism and even beyond the historical Jesus, he found the Christ of Paul, the theology, soteriology and anthropology of Paul, to be the basic Christian Facts to be embraced, to be preached, and the matrix of a reconstructed theology. This was, he said, the old religion of the early church and particularly of the Reformers, Calvin and Luther. God is altogether God, man altogether man and the one not the other—such became his insight.

The Epistle to the Romans, published by Karl Barth in 1919 under the title *Der Römerbrief,* awakened mixed interests and reactions among academic theologians. Three years later a second rewritten edition was published with theological details filled in. In it appeared the "theology of crisis"—man's realization of his own bankruptcy in attaining the genuine knowledge of God as God. Apart from this crisis-experience (helplessness) man stands apart from the essence of the whole Biblical approach. God is wholly other. God is not a discovery but a disclosure. Faith is not belief in a God but an obedience to *the* God-as-God, an utter submission to this transcendent Other, an attitude set only in man's self-despair.

The Barthian Biblical theocentrism was hailed as a corrective to Protestant theology and Barth found himself the center of a new and widespread theological discussion. In 1921 he had become a professor of Reformed theology at the University of Göttingen where he began to develop what turned out to be a "Barthian theology." From Göttingen he moved to the University of Münster (Westphalia) and then on to Bonn (1930-1935).

Barth stands as a theologian squarely in the framework of the church which by tradition separates itself (in essence) from the world, claiming a unique order of authority and revelation and holding man to be utterly helpless and hopeless outside the circumference of the gospel which the church alone under Biblical inspiration can proclaim. In the English translation of this work (1932) * Barth prefaced the remark that he intended no new theology but desired only to direct attention to Scripture, particularly to Paul and that he was ready to amend his views insofar as his exegesis could be shown to move beyond Scriptural meaning.

In the summer of 1946 Barth gave a series of informal lectures based on the topics contained in the Apostles' Creed before University students in Bonn. Published in a first American edi-

* Not included in this Anthology, requested permission of the publishers of the English translation not being granted.

tion in 1949 the lectures carry the title *Dogmatics in Outline*. The material, he affirmed, is much the same as found in his larger work *Kirchliche Dogmatik,* thus giving the reader a briefer account of his general point of view, and, it may be added, in a more popular vein. Selections here are taken from this concise and warmly received Dogmatics.

Editor

DOGMATICS IN OUTLINE

* * *

2

FAITH AS TRUST

THE CONFESSION begins with the significant words, 'I believe'. This indicates that we link up all that is to be said as fundamental to our task with this simple introduction to the Confession. We start with three leading propositions, which describe the nature of faith.

> *Christian faith is the gift of the meeting in which men become free to hear the word of grace which God has spoken in Jesus Christ in such a way that, in spite of all that contradicts it, they may once for all, exclusively and entirely, hold to His promise and guidance.*

Christian faith, Church proclamation, which, as we stated, is the cause and basic reason for dogmatics, deals—well, what does it deal with? With the fact that Christians believe? And the way in which Christians believe? Actually, this fact, the subjective form of faith, the *fides qua creditur,* cannot possibly be quite excluded from proclamation. Where the gospel is proclaimed, there too of necessity the fact will be proclaimed along with it that there are men who have heard and accepted the gospel. But the fact that we believe can only be, *a priori,* a secondary matter, becoming small and unimportant in face of the outstanding and real thing involved in the Christian proclamation—*what* the Christian believes, that is, what must be confirmed as the content and object of his faith, and *what* we have to preach, that is, the object with which the Apostles' Creed deals: I believe in God, the Father, the Son and the Holy Spirit. More popularly the Confession is called the 'Belief'; and by this 'Belief' we are at the very least to realise the fact that we believe. In Christian faith we are concerned quite decisively with a meeting. 'I believe in'—so the Confession says; and everything depends on this 'in', this *eis,* this *in* (Latin). The Creed explains this 'in', this object of faith, by which our subjective faith lives. It is noteworthy that, apart from this first expression 'I believe', the Confession is silent upon the subjective fact of faith. Nor was it a good time when this relationship was reversed, when Christians grew eloquent over their action, over the uplift and emotion of the experience of this thing, which took place in man, and when they became speechless as to *what* we may believe. By the silence of the Confession on the subjective side, by its speaking only of the objective Creed, it also speaks at its best, deepest and completest about what happens to us men, about what we may be, do, and experience. Here too it is true that whoso would keep his life shall lose it; but whoso shall lose it for My sake shall gain his life. Whoso means to rescue and preserve the subjective element shall lose it; but whoso gives it up for the sake of the objective, shall save it. I believe—of course! It is my, it is a human, experience and action, that is, a human form of existence.

But this 'I believe' is consummated in a meeting with One who is not man, but God, the Father, Son, and Holy Spirit, and by my believing I see myself completely filled and determined by this object of my faith. And what interests me is not myself with my faith, but He in whom I believe. And then I learn that by thinking of Him and looking to Him, my interests are also best provided for. I believe in, *credo in,* means that I am not alone. In our glory and in our misery we men are not alone. God comes to meet us and as our Lord and Master He comes to our aid. We live and act and suffer, in good and in bad days, in our perversity and in our rightness, in this confrontation with God. I am not alone, but God meets me; one way or other, I am in all circumstances in company with Him. That is, I believe in God, the Father, the Son, and the Holy Spirit. This meeting with God is the meeting with the word of grace which

He has spoken in Jesus Christ. Faith speaks of God, the Father, the Son and the Holy Spirit, as Him who meets us, as the object of faith, and says of this God that He is one in Himself, has become single in Himself for us and has become single once more in the eternal decree, explicated in time, of His free, unowed, unconditional love for man, for all men, in the counsel of His grace. God is gracious to us—this is what the Confession of the Father, Son and Holy Spirit, says. This includes the fact that of ourselves we cannot achieve, have not achieved, and shall not achieve a togetherness with Him; that we have not deserved that He should be our God, have no power of disposal and no rights over Him, but that with unowed kindness, in the freedom of His majesty, He resolved of His own self to be man's God, our God. He *tells* us that this is so. God's telling us, 'I am gracious to you', is the Word of God, the central concept of all Christian thinking. The Word of God is the word of His grace. And if you ask me where we hear this Word of God, I can only point to Himself, who enables us to hear it, and reply with the mighty centre of the Confession, with the second article, that the Word of God's grace in which He meets us is called Jesus Christ, the Son of God and Son of man, true God and true Man, Immanuel, God with us in this One. Christian faith is the meeting with this 'Immanuel', the meeting with Jesus Christ and in Him with the living Word of God. In calling Holy Scripture the Word of God (and we so call it, because it is so), we mean by it Holy Scripture as the witness of the prophets and the apostles to this one Word of God, to Jesus, the man out of Israel, who is God's Christ, our Lord and King in eternity. And in confessing this, in venturing to call the Church's proclamation God's Word, we must be understood to mean the proclamation of Jesus Christ, of Him who is true God and true Man for our good. In Him God meets us. And when we say, I believe *in* God, the concrete meaning is that I believe in the Lord Jesus Christ.

*　　*　　*

This remarkable Word in which faith believes is the Word of God, Jesus Christ, in whom God has spoken His Word to man once for all. So faith means trust. Trust is the act in which a man may rely on the faithfulness of Another, that His promise holds and that what He demands He demands of necessity. 'I believe' means 'I trust'. No more must I dream of trusting in myself, I no longer require to justify myself, to excuse myself, to attempt to save and preserve myself. This most profound effort of man to trust to himself, to see himself as in the right, has become pointless. I believe—not in myself—I believe in God the Father, the Son and the Holy Ghost. So also trust in any sort of authorities, who might offer themselves to me as trustworthy, as an anchor which I ought to hold on to, has become frail and superfluous. Trust in any sort of gods has become frail and superfluous. These are the gods set up, honoured and worshipped by men in ancient and recent times: the authorities on whom man relies, no matter whether they have the form of ideas or of any sort of powers of destiny, no matter what they are called. Faith delivers us from trust in such gods, and therefore also from fear of them, from the disillusionments which they inevitably prepare for us again and again.

* * *

And faith is concerned with a decision *once for all*. Faith is not an opinion replaceable by another opinion. A temporary believer does not know what faith is. Faith means a final relationship. Faith is concerned with God, with what He has done for us once for all. That does not exclude the fact that there are fluctuations in faith. But seen with regard to its object, faith is a final thing. A man who believes once believes once for all. Don't be afraid; regard even that as an invitation. One may, of course, be confused and one may doubt; but whoever once believes has something like a *character indelibilis*. He may take comfort of the fact that he is being upheld. Everyone who has to contend with unbelief should be advised that he ought not to take his own unbelief too seriously. Only faith is to be taken seriously; and if we have faith as a grain of mustard seed, that suffices for the devil to have lost his game.

* * *

3

FAITH AS KNOWLEDGE

Christian faith is the illumination of the reason in which men become free to live in the truth of Jesus Christ and thereby to become sure also of the meaning of their own existence and of the ground and goal of all that happens.

POSSIBLY YOU may be struck by the emergence of the concept of *reason*. I use it deliberately. The saying, 'Despite only reason and science, man's supremest power of all', was uttered not by a prophet, but by Goethe's Mephisto. Christendom and the theological world were always ill-advised in thinking it their duty for some reason or other, either of enthusiasm or of theological conception, to betake themselves to the camp of an opposition to reason. Over the Christian Church, as the essence of revelation and of the work of God which constitutes its basis, stands the Word: 'The Word was made flesh.' The Logos became man. Church proclamation is language, and language not of an accidental, arbitrary, chaotic and incomprehensible kind, but language which comes forward with the claim to be true and to uphold itself as the truth against the lie. Do not let us be forced from the clarity of this position. In the Word which the Church has to proclaim the truth is involved, not in a provisional, secondary sense, but in the primary sense of the Word itself—the Logos is involved, and is demonstrated and revealed in the human reason, the human *nous,* as the Logos, that is, as meaning, as truth to be learned. In the word of Christian proclamation we are concerned with *ratio,* reason, in which human *ratio* may also be reflected and reproduced. Church proclamation, theology, is no talk or babbling; it is not propaganda unable to withstand the claim, Is it then true as well, this that is said? Is it really so? You have probably also suffered from a certain kind of preaching and edifying talk from which it becomes only too clear that there is talking going on, emphatic talk with a plenteous display of rhetoric, which does not however stand up to this simple question as to the truth of what is said. The Creed of Christian faith rests upon knowledge. And where the Creed is uttered and confessed knowledge should be, is meant to be, created. Christian faith is not irrational, not anti-rational, not supra-rational, but rational in the proper sense. The Church which utters the Creed, which comes forward with the tremendous claim to preach and to proclaim the glad tidings, derives from the fact that it has apprehended something—*Vernunft* comes from *vernehmen*—and it wishes to let what it has apprehended be apprehended again. These were always unpropitious periods in the Christian Church, when Christian histories of dogmatics and theology separated *gnosis* and *pistis*. *Pistis* rightly understood is *gnosis;* rightly understood the act of faith is also an act of knowledge. Faith means knowledge.

But once this is established, it must also be said that Christian faith is concerned with an illumination of the reason. Christian faith has to do with the object, with God the Father, the Son, and the Holy Spirit, of which the Creed speaks. Of course it is of the nature and being of this object, of God the Father, the Son, and the Holy Spirit, that He cannot be known by the powers of human knowledge, but is apprehensible and apprehended solely because of His own freedom, decision and action. What man can know by his own power according to the measure of his natural powers, his understanding, his feeling, will be at most something like a supreme being, an absolute nature, the idea of an utterly free power, of a being towering over everything. This absolute and supreme being, the ultimate and most profound, this 'thing in itself', has nothing to do with God. It is part of the intuitions and marginal possibilities of man's thinking, man's contrivance. Man is able to think this being; but he has not thereby thought God. God is thought and known when in His own freedom God makes Himself apprehensible. We shall have to speak later about God, His being and His nature, but we must now say that God is always the One who has made Himself known to man in His own revelation, and not the one man thinks out for himself and describes as God. There is a perfectly clear division there already, epistemologically, between the true God and the false gods. Knowledge of God is not a possibility which is open for discussion.

God is the essence of all reality, of that reality which reveals itself to us. Knowledge of God takes place where there is actual experience that God speaks, that He so represents Himself to man that he cannot fail to see and hear Him, where, in a situation which he has not brought about, in which he becomes incomprehensible to himself, man sees himself faced with the fact that he lives with God and God with him, because so it has pleased God. Knowledge of God takes place where divine revelation takes place, illumination of man by God, transmission of human knowledge, instruction of man by this incomparable Teacher.

We started from the point that Christian faith is a meeting. Christian faith and knowledge of Christian faith take place at the point where the divine reason, the divine Logos, sets up His law in the region of man's understanding, to which law human, creaturely reason must accommodate itself. When that happens, man comes to knowledge; for when God sets up His law in man's thought, in his seeing and hearing and feeling, the revelation of the truth is also reached about man and his reason, the revelation of man is reached, who cannot bring about of himself what is brought about simply by God Himself.

Can God be known? Yes, God can be known, since it is actually true and real that He is knowable through Himself. When that happens, man becomes free, he becomes empowered, he becomes capable—a mystery to himself—of knowing God. Knowledge of God is a knowledge completely effected and determined from the side of its object, from the side of God. But for that very reason it is genuine knowledge; for that very reason it is in the deepest sense free knowledge. Of course it remains a relative knowledge, a knowledge imprisoned within the limits of the creaturely. Of course it is especially true here that we are carrying heavenly treasures in earthen vessels. Our concepts are not adequate to grasp this treasure. Precisely where this genuine knowledge of God takes place it will also be clear that there is no occasion for any pride. There always remains powerless man, creaturely reason with its limitations. But in this area of the creaturely, of the inadequate, it has pleased God to reveal Himself. And since man is foolish in this respect too, He will be wise; since man is petty, He will be great; since man is inadequate, God is adequate. 'Let my grace suffice for thee. For my strength is mighty in the weak' holds good also for the question of knowledge.

In the opening statement we said that Christian faith has to do with the illumination of the reason, in which men become free to live in the truth of Jesus Christ. For the understanding of Christian knowledge of faith it is essential to understand that the truth of Jesus Christ is living truth and the knowledge of it living knowledge. This does not mean that we are to revert once more to the idea that here knowledge is not basically involved at all. It is not that Christian faith is a dim sensation, an a-logical feeling, experiencing and learning. Faith is knowledge; it is related to God's Logos, and is therefore a thoroughly logical matter. The truth of Jesus Christ is also in the simplest sense a truth of facts. Its starting-point, the Resurrection of Jesus Christ from the dead, is a fact which occurred in space and time, as the New Testament describes it. The apostles were not satisfied to hold on to an inward fact; they spoke of what they saw and heard and what they touched with their hands. And the truth of Jesus Christ is also a matter of thoroughly clear and, in itself, ordered human thinking; free, precisely in its being bound. But—and the things must not be separated— what is involved is living truth. The concept of knowledge, of *scientia,* is insufficient to describe what Christian knowledge is. We must rather go back to what in the Old Testament is called wisdom, what the Greeks called *sophia* and the Latins *sapientia,* in order to grasp the knowledge of theology in its fullness. *Sapientia* is distinguished from the narrower concept of *scientia,* wisdom is distinguished from knowing, in that it not only contains knowledge in itself, but also that this concept speaks of a knowledge which is practical knowledge, embracing the entire existence of man. Wisdom is the knowledge by which we may actually and practically live; it is empiricism and it is the theory which is powerful in being directly practical, in being the knowledge which dominates our life, which is really a light upon our path. Not a light to wonder at and to observe, not a light to kindle all manner of fireworks at—not even the profoundest philosophical speculations—but the light on our road which may stand above our action and above our talk, the light on our healthy and on our sick days, in our poverty and in our wealth, the light which does not only lighten when we suppose ourselves to have moments of insight, but which accompanies us even into our folly, which is not quenched when all is quenched, when the goal of our life becomes visible in death. To live by this light, by this truth, is the meaning of Christian knowledge. Christian knowledge means living in the truth of Jesus Christ. In this light we live and move and have our being (Acts 17.28) in order that we may be of Him, and through Him and unto Him, as it says in Romans 11.36. So Christian knowledge, at its deepest, is one with what we termed man's trust in God's Word. Never yield when they try to teach you divisions and separations in this matter. There is no genuine trust, no really tenable, victorious trust in God's Word which is not founded in His truth; and on the other hand no knowledge, no theology, no confessing, and no Scripture truth which does not at once possess the stamp of this living truth. The one must always be measured and tested and confirmed by the other.

* * *

4

FAITH AS CONFESSION

Christian faith is the decision in which men have the freedom to be publicly responsible for their trust in God's Word and for their knowledge of the truth of Jesus Christ, in the language of the Church, but also in worldly attitudes and above all in their corresponding actions and conduct.

CHRISTIAN FAITH is a decision. This is where we have to begin, and wish to begin. Christian faith, to be sure, is an event in the mystery between God and man; the event of the freedom in which God acts towards this man, and of the freedom which God gives this man. But this does not exclude, but actually includes the fact that where there is faith in the sense of the Christian Creed, *history* is taking place, that there something is being undertaken, completed and carried out in time by man.

Faith is God's mystery breaking forth; faith is God's freedom and man's freedom in action. Where nothing occurred—in time, of course, that is, occurred visibly and audibly—there would be no faith either. For Christian faith is faith in God, and when the Christian Confession names God the Father, the Son and the Holy Spirit, it is pointing to the fact that in His inner life and nature God is not dead, not passive, not inactive, but that God the Father, the Son and the Holy Spirit exist in an inner relationship and movement, which may very well be described as a story, as an event. God Himself is not suprahistorical, but historical. And this God has in Himself made a decree, an eternal decree, upon which everything rests of which the Confession of Faith speaks. Our fathers called it the decree of creation and of the covenant and of redemption. This decree of God was carried out in time, once for all, in the work and in the word of Jesus Christ, to which Article II of the Confession bears concrete testimony, 'who suffered under Pontius Pilate, was crucified, dead and buried. . . .' Faith is man's answer to this historical existence and nature and action of God. Faith has to do with the God who is in Himself historical and has fashioned a decree whose goal is history, and has set this history going and completed it. Christian faith which was not itself history would not be Christian faith, not faith in . . . Where there is Christian faith there arises and grows an historical form, there arises among men, among contemporaries and non-contemporaries, a *community*, a togetherness, a brotherhood. But by means of this community, we inevitably reach, at the point where faith is Christian, a human proclamation and message as well, to the *world* outside this communion and brotherhood. A light is kindled there, which lightens all them that are in the house. In other words, where Christian faith exists, there God's congregation arises and lives in the world for the world; there Israel gathers apart from the Gentiles of the world; and there the Church gathers on its own behalf, the communion of saints. Yet not for its own purposes, but as the manifestation of the Servant of God, whom God has set there for all men, as the Body of Christ. And this story happens—now we reach the human work which answers to God's work and nature in the election of His grace—in the answer of obedience. Faith is obedience, not just a passive accommodation of oneself. Where there is obedience, there is also choice on man's part; faith is chosen instead of its opposite, unbelief, trust instead of distrust, knowledge instead of ignorance. Faith means choosing between faith and unbelief, wrong belief and superstition. Faith is the act in which man relates himself to God as is appropriate to God. For this work takes places in a stepping out of neutrality towards God, out of any disavowal of obligation towards Him in our existence and attitude, out of the private sphere, into resoluteness, responsibility and public life. Faith without this tendency to public life, faith that avoids this difficulty, has become in itself unbelief, wrong belief, superstition. For faith that believes in God the Father, the Son and the Holy Spirit cannot refuse to become public.

*   *   *

5

GOD IN THE HIGHEST

God is He who according to Holy Scripture exists, lives, acts, makes Himself known to us in the work of His free love, resolved on and consummated in Jesus Christ: He, God alone.

*   *   *

WE MUST be clear that when we are speaking of God in the sense of Christian faith, He who is called God is not to be regarded as a continuation and enrichment of the concepts and ideas which usually constitute religious thought in general about God. In the sense of Christian faith, God is not to be found in the series of gods. He is not to be found in the pantheon of human piety and religious inventive skill. So it is not that there is in humanity something like a universal natural disposition, a general concept of the divine, which at some particular point involves the thing which we Christians call God and as such believe in and confess; so that Christian faith would be one among many, an instance within a general rule. A Christian Father once rightly said that *Deus non est in genere,* 'God is not a particular instance within a class'. When we Christians speak of 'God', we may and must be clear that this word signifies *a priori* the fundamentally Other, the fundamental deliverance from that whole world of man's seeking, conjecturing, illusion, imagining and speculating. It is not that on the long road of human seeking and longing for the divine a definite stopping-place has in the end been reached in the form of the Christian Confession. The God of the Christian Confession is, in distinction from all gods, not a found or invented God or one at last and at the end discovered by man; He is not a fulfilment, perhaps the last, supreme and best fulfilment, of what man was in course of seeking and finding. But we Christians speak of Him who completely takes the place of everything that elsewhere is usually called 'God', and therefore suppresses and excludes it all, and claims to be alone the truth. Where that is not realised, it is still not realised what is involved when the Christian Church confesses, 'I believe in God'. What is involved is man's meeting with the Reality which he has never of himself sought out or first of all discovered. 'What no eye hath seen nor ear heard, what hath not entered into the heart of any man, God hath given to those who love Him', is St. Paul's way of speaking of this matter. And there is no other way in which we can speak of it. God in the sense of the Christian Confession is and exists in a completely different way from that which is elsewhere called divine. And so His nature, His being is different from the nature and being of all alleged gods. We summarize all that is to be said of God, in the sense of the Christian Confession, in the words 'God in the Highest'. You all know where I take this idea from. It is in Luke 2. 14: 'Glory to God in the highest'; therefore our song is, 'Glory to God alone in the highest'. This 'in the highest', *in excelsis,* I shall now try to expound.

*　　*　　*

In the Christian Church there can be no speaking about God in any other way. God has not the slightest need for our proofs. He who is called God in Holy Scripture is unsearchable—that is, He has not been discovered by any man. But when our talk is of Him and we speak of Him as about a familiar entity, who is more familiar and real than any other reality and who is nearer us than we are to ourselves, it is not because there may have been particularly pious people who were successful in investigating this Being, but because He who was hidden from us has disclosed Himself.

And it is part of this, that God is not only unprovable and unsearchable, but also *inconceivable*. No attempt is made in the Bible to define God—that is, to grasp God in our concepts. In the Bible God's name is named, not as philosophers do it, as the name of a timeless Being, surpassing the world, alien and supreme, but as the name of the living, acting, working Subject who makes Himself known. The Bible tells the story of God; it narrates His deeds and the history of this God in the highest, as it takes place on earth in the human sphere. The Bible proclaims the significance and the importance of this working and acting, this story of God, and in this way it proves God's existence, describes His being and His nature. Knowledge of God in the sense of Holy Scripture and the Confession is knowledge of His existence, His life, His action, His revelation in His work. And so the Bible is not a philosophical book, but a history book, the book of God's mighty acts, in which God becomes knowable by us.

*   *   *

This work of creation, of the covenant and of redemption is the reality in which God exists, lives and acts and makes Himself known. From this work we must make no abstractions, if we would know God's nature and existence. Here, in this work, God is the Person who expounds Himself, and is thus the subject of this work. It is the work of God's free love. We may venture to describe the reality which the work expounds, the nature and the essence of God, by these two concepts of freedom and love. But we must be careful, lest we tumble back again out of the concrete into the abstract, out of history into the realm of ideas. I would not say that God is freedom or that God is love—even though the second pronouncement is a biblical one.

We do not know what love is and we do not know what freedom is; but *God* is love and *God* is freedom. What freedom is
and what love is, we have to learn from Him. As predicate to
this subject it may be said that He is the God of free love. In
His work of creation, covenant and redemption, He proves Himself to be this God. It is there that we experience what love is,
this desire of the other for his own sake, so that the one is no
longer alone, but completely together with the other. This is
love, this is God's *free* love. God is not lonely, not even without
the world. He does not need the other and nevertheless He loves.
This love cannot be understood apart from the majesty of His
freedom. It is God's love, that He, the Father, loves the Son, who
Himself is God. What in His work becomes visible is an uncovering of this mystery of His inner Being, where all is freedom
and all is love.

*　　*　　*

6

GOD THE FATHER

*The One God is by nature and in eternity the Father, the
source of His Son and, in union with Him, the source of the
Holy Spirit. In virtue of this way of being of His He is by
grace the Father of all men, whom He calls in time, in His
Son and through His Spirit, to be His children.*

*　　*　　*

SO ABOVE all we have to state that when God the 'Father' is
called 'our Father', we are thereby saying something about God
that is valid, that is true, and true, moreover, in the deepest
depths of His nature, true unto all eternity. He is the Father.
And exactly the same holds for the Son and for the Holy Spirit.
Thus God's name of Father is not merely a surname which we
men attach to God; so that the meaning would be that 'man
thinks he knows something like fatherhood, like man's relationship to his father in the flesh, and now he transfers this rela-

tionship to God; the presupposition being that His nature is ultimately something quite different and has nothing to do with what we term fatherhood. That God is the Father holds true in view of His revelation, in view of us. But in Himself, by nature and in eternity, we do not know what He is. But He issues forth from this mystery of His and is then, and in this way, the Father for us.' But that is inadequate to describe the content with which in fact we are concerned here. When Holy Scripture and along with it the Confession of the Church calls God the Father, its meaning is that God is first of all Father. He is Father in Himself, by nature and in eternity, and then, following on that, for us as well, His creatures. It is therefore not that there is first of all human fatherhood and then a so-called divine Fatherhood, but just the reverse: true and proper fatherhood resides in God, and from this Fatherhood of God what we know as fatherhood among us men is derived. The divine Fatherhood is the primal source of all natural fatherhood. As is said in Ephesians, every fatherhood in heaven and on earth is of Him. We are thinking the truth, the first and proper truth, when we see God the Father in the ultimate, when we recognise Him as the Father, and may be called His children.

God the Father—in these words we are speaking of God's way of being, as the source and origin of another divine way of being, of a second one which is distinct from the first and which is yet *His* way of being and so is identical with Him in His divinity. God is God in such a way that He is the Father, the Father of His Son, that he establishes Himself and through His own agency is God a second time. Established by Himself, not created by Himself—the Son is not created. But this relationship of Father and Son does not yet exhaust the reality, the nature of God. It is not that this establishing and being established of God threatens the unity of God. It is the Father and the Son *together,* who clinch the unity of God a third time in the Holy Spirit. God the Father and God the Son are together the origin of the Holy Spirit: *Spiritus, qui procedit a Patre Filioque.* It is this which the poor folk in the Eastern Church have never quite understood, that the Begetter and the Begotten are together the origin of the Holy Spirit, and so the origin of their unity. The Holy Spirit has been called the *vinculum caritatis.* Not *although* God is Father and Son, but *because* God is Father and Son, unity exists. So God, as He who establishes Himself, who exists through Himself, as God in His deity, is in Himself different and yet in Himself alike. And for that very reason He is not lonely in Himself. He does not need the world. All richness of life, all fullness of action and community exists in Himself, since He is the Triune. He is movement and He is rest. Hence it can be plain to us that all that He is on our behalf —that He is the Creator, that He has given us Himself in Jesus Christ and that He has united us to Himself in the Holy Spirit —is His free grace, the overflow of His fullness. Not owed to us, but overflowing mercy! It is His will that what He is for Himself should be not only for Himself; but He wills to be for us also the One He is in eternity. We have of ourselves no grip on this truth, that God in the power of His eternal Fatherhood —of free grace, not because it is His *métier*—wills to be also our Father. Because He is what He is, His work also can only be His Fatherly work. That God becomes the Creator of another, which in distinction from the Son is different from Him, that He wills to be present for this other, means nothing else than that He gives us a share in Himself. 'We become partakers of the divine nature' (2 Pet. 1. 4). We say no more and no less when we call God our Father. We may now call Him that which He names Himself in His Son. Man as such is not God's child, but God's creature, *factus* and not *genitus*. This creature man is, so far as the eye reaches, in rebellion against God, is godless and nevertheless God's child. It is God's free work, His condescension and mercy, that we may be His children. We are that, we are because He is the Father and because He makes us so. We are His children *in His Son and through the Holy Spirit,* not on the ground of a direct relationship between us and God, but on the ground of the fact that God of Himself lets us participate in His nature, in His life and essence.

*   *   *   **

7

GOD ALMIGHTY

God's power differs from powerlessness, is superior to the other powers, is victoriously opposed to 'power in itself', in being the power of law, i.e. *of His love activated and revealed in Jesus Christ and thus the content, the determination and the limit of everything possible, and the power over and in all that is real.*

BY THIS concept 'Almighty' the Confession names an attribute of God, a perfection of Him who was previously called God the Father. The Confession knows only this one attribute. When attempts were later made to speak systematically about God and to describe His nature, men became more talkative. They spoke of God's aseity. His being grounded in Himself; they spoke of God's infinity in space and time, and therefore of God's eternity. And men spoke on the other hand of God's holiness and righteousness, mercifulness and patience. We must be clear that whatever we say of God in such human concepts can never be more than an indication of Him; no such concept can really conceive the nature of God. God is inconceivable. What is called God's goodness and God's holiness cannot be determined by any view that we men have of goodness and holiness, but it is determined from what God is. He is the Lord, He is the truth. Only derivatively, only in a secondary sense can we venture to take His Word on our lips. In the Apostles' Creed there stands, in place of all possible descriptions of the nature of God, this one word, that He is Almighty, and significantly in connexion with the expression 'Father'. The one word explains the other; the Father is almightiness and almightiness is the Father.

'God is almighty' means in the first instance that He is might. And might means ability, possibility in view of a reality. Where reality is created, determined and preserved, there exists a possibility, lying at its basis. And now it is stated of God that He Himself has possibility, He has this ability which is the foundation of reality, its determinant and its support: he has almightiness, that is, He has *everything,* He is the basic measure of everything real and everything possible.

*   *   *

8

GOD THE CREATOR

In that God became man, it has also become manifest and worthy of belief that He does not wish to exist for Himself only and therefore to be alone. He does not grudge the world, distinct from Himself, its own reality, nature and freedom. His word is the power of its being as creation. He creates, sustains and rules it as the theatre of His glory— and in its midst, man also, as the witness of His glory.

*   *   *

IT IS of God the Creator we have to speak and therefore of His work as the *creation,* the making of heaven and earth. If we take this concept seriously, it must be at once clear that we are not confronted by a realm which in any sense may be accessible to human view or even to human thought. Natural science may be our occupation with its view of development; it may tell us the tale of the millions of years in which the cosmic process has gone on; but when could natural science have ever penetrated to the fact that there is one world which runs through this development? Continuation is quite a different thing from this sheer beginning, with which the concept of creation and the Creator has to do. It is assuredly a basic error to speak of creation myths. At best a myth may be a parallel to exact science; that is, a myth has to do with viewing what has always existed and will exist. A myth has to do with the mighty problem that at all times propounds itself to man and therefore is timeless, the problem of life and death, of sleep and wakening, of birth and dying, of morning and evening, of day and night, and so on. These are the themes of myth. Myth considers the world as it were from its frontier, but always the world which already exists. There is no creation myth because creation as such is simply not accessible to myth. Thus in the case of the Babylonian myth of creation, for example, it is quite clear that we are concerned with a myth of growth and decay which fundamentally cannot be brought into connexion with Genesis 1 and 2. At most we can say that certain mythical elements are to be found there. But what the Bible makes of that has no parallel in myth. If we are to give the biblical narrative a name, or put it in a category, then let it be that of saga. The Bible speaks in Genesis 1 and 2 of events which lie outside of our historical knowledge. But it speaks upon the basis of knowledge, which is related to history.

* * *

In the article on Creator and creation the decisive point is the recognition that God does not exist for Himself, but that there is a reality distinct from Him—namely, the world. Whence do we know that? Has not each of us put to himself the question whether this entire world around us might not really be a seeming and a dream? Has not this come over you too as a fundamental doubt—not of God; that is a stupid doubt! but—of yourself? Is the whole enchantment in which we exist real? Or is not that which we regard as reality only the 'veil of Maya' and thus unreal? Is the only thing left to us just to dream this 'dream' to the end as swiftly as possible, so as to enter the Nirvana from which we derive? The statement on creation is opposed to this horrible thought. Whence can we be told authoritatively that that is a perversion and that life is not a dream but reality, that I myself am, and that the world around me is? From the standpoint of the Christian Confession there can only be one answer: this Confession tells us in its centre, in the second article, that it pleased God to become man, that in Jesus Christ we have to do with God Himself, with God the Creator, who became a creature, who existed as a creature in time and space, here, there, at that time, just as we all exist. If this is true, and this is the presupposition everything starts with, that God was in Christ, then we have a place where creation stands before us in reality and becomes recognisable. For when the

Creator has Himself become a creature, God become man, if that is true (and that is the beginning of Christian knowledge), then the mystery of the Creator and His work and the mystery of His creation are open to us in Jesus Christ, and the content of the first article is plain to view. Because God has become man, the existence of creation can no longer be doubted. Gazing at Jesus Christ, with whom we live in the same space, there is told us—told as the Word of God—the Word of the Creator and the Word of His work and of the most astonishing bit of this work, of man.

The mystery of creation on the Christian interpretation is not primarily—as the fools think in their heart—the problem whether there is a God as the originator of the world; for in the Christian sense it cannot be that first of all we presuppose the reality of the world and then ask whether there is also a God. But the first thing, the thing we begin with, is God the Father and the Son and the Holy Spirit. And from that standpoint the great Christian problem is propounded, whether it can really be the case that God wishes to be not only for Himself, but that outside Him there is the world, that we exist alongside and outside Him? That is a riddle. If we make even a slight effort to look on God, to conceive Him as He reveals Himself to us, as God in mystery, God in the highest, God the Triune and Almighty, we must be astonished at the fact that there are ourselves and the world alongside and outside Him. God has no need of us, He has no need of the world and heaven and earth at all. He is rich in Himself. He has fullness of life; all glory, all beauty, all goodness and holiness reside in Him. He is sufficient unto Himself, He is God, blessed in Himself. To what end, then, the world? Here in fact there is *everything*, here in the living God. How can there be something alongside God, of which He has no need? This is the riddle of creation. And the doctrine of creation answers that God, who does not need us, created heaven and earth and myself, of 'sheer fatherly kindness and compassion, apart from any merit or worthiness of mine; for all of which I am bound to thank and praise Him, to serve Him and to be obedient, which is assuredly true'. Do you feel in these words Luther's amazement in face of creation, of the goodness of God, in which God does not will to be alone, but to have a reality beside Himself?

* * *

10

JESUS CHRIST

> *The heart of the object of Christian faith is the word of the act in which God from all eternity willed to become man in Jesus Christ for our good, did become man in time for our good, and will be and remain man in eternity for our good. This work of the Son of God includes in itself the work of the Father as its presupposition and the work of the Holy Spirit as its consequence.*

WITH THIS paragraph we pass into the heart of the Christian confession, whose text is indeed distinguished by particular explicitness and which is not only outwardly the heart of it all. Even in our introduction to these lectures, when we were speaking of faith, and in the first lecture, when we spoke of God the Father, the Almighty, Creator of heaven and earth, we could not avoid continually pointing to this centre. We could not possibly have given a genuine exposition of the first article without continually interpreting it by means of the second. Indeed, the second article does not just follow the first, nor does it just precede the third; but it is the fountain of light by which the other two are lit. It is also susceptible of historical proof, that the Christian Confession arose out of a shorter and indeed probably a quite short primitive form, which included only what we confess to-day in the second article. It is believed that the original Christian confession consisted of the three words, 'Jesus Christ (is) Lord', to which were only later added the first and third articles. This historical event was not arbitrary. It is also materially significant to know that historically the second article is the source of the whole. A Christian is one who makes con-

fession of Christ. And Christian confession is confession of Jesus
Christ the Lord.

Starting with this heart of the Christian Confession, all that
it expresses of God the Father and God the Holy Spirit is to be
regarded as an expanding statement. When Christian theologians wished to sketch a theology of God the Creator abstractly
and directly, they have always gone astray, even when in tremendous reverence they tried to think and speak of this high
God. And the same thing took place, when the theologians tried
to push through to a theology of the third article, to a theology
of the Spirit, to a theology of experience as opposed to the
theology of the high God in the first article. Then too they have
gone astray. Perhaps the whole of modern theology, as character-
istically found in Schleiermacher, could be, must be understood
as theology prepared by certain developments in the seventeenth
and eighteenth centuries. It became a one-sided theology of the
third article, which believed that it might venture with the
Holy Spirit alone, without reflecting that the third article is only
the explication of the second, the declaration of what Jesus Christ
our Lord means for us men. Starting with Jesus Christ and with
Him alone, we must see and understand what in the Christian
sense is involved by the mighty relationship, to which we can
only point again and again in sheer amazement, about which we
cannot help being in danger of great error, when we say, *God
and man*. What we mean by that can only be declared adequately, by our confessing that 'Jesus is Christ'. And as for
what is involved in the relationship between creation and the
reality of existence on the one hand, and on the other hand the
Church, redemption, God—that can never be understood from
any general truth about our existence, nor from the reality of
history of religion; this we can only learn from the relation between Jesus and Christ. Here we see clearly what is meant by
'God *above* man' (Article I) and 'God *with* man' (Article III).
That is why Article II, why Christology, is the touchstone of all
knowledge of God in the Christian sense, the touchstone of all
theology. 'Tell me how it stands with your Christology, and I
shall tell you who you are.' This is the point at which ways
diverge, and the point at which is fixed the relation between
theology and philosophy, and the relation between knowledge

of God and knowledge of men, the relation between revelation and reason, the relation between Gospel and Law, the relation between God's truth and man's truth, the relation between outer and inner, the relation between theology and politics. At this point everything becomes clear or unclear, bright or dark. For here we are standing at the centre. And however high and mysterious and difficult everything we want to know might seem to us, yet we may also say that this is just where everything becomes quite simple, quite straightforward, quite childlike. Right here in this centre, in which as a Professor of Systematic Theology I must call to you, 'Look! This is the point now! Either knowledge, or the greatest folly!'—here I am in front of you, like a teacher in Sunday school facing his kiddies, who has something to say which a mere four-year-old can really understand. 'The world was lost, but Christ was born, rejoice, O Christendom!'

This centre is the Word of the act or the act of the Word. I greatly desire to make it clear to you, that in this centre of Christian faith the whole contrast, so current among us, between word and work, between knowing and living, ceases to have any meaning. But the Word, the Logos, is actually the work, the *ergon*, as well; the *verbum* is also the *opus*. Where God and this centre of our faith are involved, those differences which seem so interesting and important to us, become not just superfluous but silly. It is the truth of the real or the reality of the true which here enters the field: God speaks, God acts, God is in the midst. The very Word with which we are here concerned is an act, this act, which as such is the Word, is Revelation.

When we pronounce the name of Jesus Christ, we are not speaking of an idea. The name Jesus Christ is not the transparent shell, through which we glimpse something higher—no room for Platonism here! What is involved is this actual name and this title; this person is involved. Not any chance person, not a 'chance reality in history' in Lessing's sense. The 'chance fact of history' is just the eternal truth of reason! Nor does this name Jesus Christ indicate a result of human history. It was invariably a human discovery, when the effort was made to show that the whole of human history was bound to have its culminating point in Jesus Christ. Not for one moment was it possible to say that of the history of Israel, not to mention world-history. Of course in retrospect we may and must say that here history is fulfilled. But fulfilled in a truth which, looked at from the standpoint of all historical results, is completely novel and offensive! To the Greeks foolishness, to the Jews a stumbling-block. So in the name of Jesus Christ we have not to do with the result of a postulate of man, with the product of a human need, with the figure of a redeemer and saviour to be explained and derived from man's guilt. Even the fact that he is a sinner cannot be known from man himself. It is rather the result of knowing Jesus Christ; in His light we see the light and in this light our own darkness. Everything that deserves to be called knowledge in the Christian sense lives from the knowledge of Jesus Christ.

* * *

At all times there have been combinations of these two concepts, God and man. The idea of incarnation is not alien to mythology. But the thing that distinguishes the Christian message from this idea is that all myths are basically just the exposition of an idea, of a general truth. A myth circles round the relation between day and night, winter and spring, death and life; it always implies a timeless reality. The message of Jesus Christ has nothing to do with this myth; it is formally distinguished from it by its possessing the unique historical conception that it is said of an historical human being that it happened in His existence that God was made man, that consequently His existence was identical with the existence of God. The Christian message is a historical message. And only by seeing eternity and time together, God and man, only then do we grasp what is expressed by the name Jesus Christ. Jesus Christ is the reality of the covenant between God and man. It is only when we look at Jesus Christ that we succeed, in the sense of the first article, in speaking about God in the highest; because it is here that we get to know man in the covenant with this God, in His concrete form as this man. And when in the third article of the Confession we may speak and hear of God in man, of God who acts with us and in us, it might be in itself an ideology, a description of human enthusiasm, an over-wrought idea of the meaning of man's inner life with its transports and its experiences, a projection of what takes place in us men into the height of an imaginary deity, which we call Holy Spirit. But if we look at the covenant which God has really concluded with us men, then we know that it is not so. God on high is really near to us men in the depths. God is present. We may make bold to speak of a reality of the Holy Spirit in view of this covenant between God and man, in which God became man, in this one who stands for all others.

* * *

11

THE SAVIOUR AND SERVANT OF GOD

The name Jesus and the title Christ express the election, the Person and the work of the Man in whom the prophetic, priestly and kingly mission of the nation Israel is revealed and set forth.

* * *

THE PERSONAL name Jesus really means in English 'Jehovah (the God of Israel) helps'. The official title of Christ or Messiah described in the Judaism of the time of Jesus a man expected by Israel, due to come in the last days, who was to reveal God's glory, God's hitherto hidden although promised glory. It described the man who was to free Israel, which for centuries was sunk in need and oppression, and, himself a man of Israel, to rule over the nations. When Jesus of Nazareth arose and preached and took His way out of the narrowness of Nazareth in the first instance into the spaciousness of the history of His own nation, which as in olden times was to find its fulfilment in Jerusalem, then the mystery of this figure, of this son of Joseph of Nazareth, was that He was the Messiah, this expected One in the last days, that He revealed Himself as such and was recognised as such. The name Jesus ('God helps', the Saviour) was a familiar name, and there were many of this name; and One of these many, because God so willed and disposed, was the unique person in whom the divine promise proceeded to fulfilment. And at the same time this fulfilment signifies the fulfilment of what was given to Israel, and the fulfilment and revelation of what this people was appointed to be for the history of the whole world, of all nations, in fact of the whole of humanity. He was not named Jesus Messiah by the first community, but Jesus Christ. Therein is revealed, therein is opened the door into the world. But there remains the Jewish name *Jesus*. His way into the spaciousness of the world leads out from the narrowness of Israel.

Perhaps you are surprised at my laying such stress on the name and title. We must be quite clear that in the whole of antiquity and also in Israel names and titles were not quite so external and incidental, as they are for us. This name and this title express something; and this must be understood in a quite concrete way: they are *revelation*. So they are not a mere designating or naming, an ornament which the person named might or might not wear. It was the angel who said to Mary, 'Thou shalt call thy Son Jesus, God helps, Saviour, *Soter!*' Nor is the title Christ to be regarded as the expression of some human deliberation, but it necessarily belongs to this man. This title is not to be separated from the Bearer of this name; the Bearer of this name is born in order to carry this title. There is no dualism between name and calling. At His very birth this title was so to speak lowered on to Him inevitably, like a crown, so that this person does not exist apart from this office, nor this office apart from this person. He is *the* Joshua, the 'God helps', because He is chosen for the work and office of the Christ, the prophetic, priestly and kingly Servant of God out of Israel.

We must pause a moment in face of the fact—for it is certainly important—that in this Jesus Christ we are dealing with the man in whom the mission of this one people, the people of Israel, the Jewish people, is set forth and revealed. Christ, the Servant of God who came from it, and the figure of God's Servant for all peoples, as well as this one people of Israel, are two realities inseparable from each other, not only at that time but for the whole of history, indeed for all eternity. Israel is nothing apart from Jesus Christ; but we also have to say that Jesus Christ would not be Jesus Christ apart from Israel.

*   *   *

What is the meaning of Israel's mission? When the Bible speaks of an election of Israel and of an unlikeness in this people to the other nations, when, that is, we apprehend in the Old Testament a special existence of Israel, what is thereby involved is a sending, a mission, an apostolate. What is involved in the existence of Israel is that a man appointed thereto by God is there in God's place on behalf of all other men. Such is Israel's reality, a man or a community, a people in God's service. Not for their own glory was this people picked out, not in the sense of a national claim, but for the other peoples and to that extent as the servant of all peoples. This people is God's commissioner. It has to proclaim His word; that is its prophetic mission. By its existence it has to be a witness that God not only speaks, but pledges Himself in person and surrenders Himself even unto death; that is its priestly mission. And, finally, in its political helplessness, it has as witness among the other nation to indicate the lordship of God over men; that is its kingly mission. Humanity needs this prophetic, priestly and kingly service. The Old Testament aims, in its complete reality, at making this mission of Israel visible, when again and again it expresses thankful praise of God for the miraculous succour and preservation of this tiny nation.

*   *   *

12

GOD'S ONLY SON

God's revelation in the man Christ Jesus is compelling and exclusive and God's work in Him is helpful and adequate, because this man is not a being different from God, but the only Son of the Father; that is, God Himself uniquely living through and of Himself; He is God's omnipotence, grace and truth in person and therefore the authentic Mediator between God and all other men.

WE COME to the question which is not a question because *a priori* the answer lies in the open—to the pronouncement of the true Deity of Jesus Christ. Let us try to make clear how we reach this pronouncement, or which is the question that leads to it.

Throughout our exposition we have come upon the concept of the revelation or the Word of God—that is, upon God's proclamation, the message that proceeds from Himself. There are all sorts of revelations and all sorts of words and messages, which have already reached men and are still reaching them, and which also raise the claim to be the Word and message of God. So the question arises—and we have to give our answer to it—how far what is here described as God's revelation is bound to be acknowledged and accepted as *the* revelation? There can be no doubt about it, that, by and large, in the history of humanity as a whole and in the life of every individual there are plenty of causes and opportunities, by which something or other becomes for us in a high degree illuminating, important and convincing, by which something 'overpowers' and imprisons us and draws us under its spell. Man's life alike in the microcosm as in the macrocosm is full of such experiences. There are 'revelations' of power and beauty and love in the life of men. Why then is just this, which is here termed God's revelation, the event that consists of the existence of Jesus Christ—why is it revelation in an emphatic, once-for-all way? The general answer to be given to this question (of the 'absoluteness' of Christianity, Troeltsch) is to this effect, that we admit that we are enveloped by other 'revelations', which carry a large degree of compulsion and rightly make large claims. But starting from Christian faith we must say of these revelations, that they are lacking in a final, simply binding *authority*. We may traverse this world of revelations, we may be illumined here and convinced there and over-powered somewhere else; but they do not have the power of a first and last thing which would hinder man from enjoying and being intoxicated by such revelations, and then going on further, like a man who beholds his face in a mirror and passes on and forgets what he has seen. All these revelations are notoriously devoid of any final, binding force. Not because they are not powerful, not because they are not fraught with meaning and fascination, but because they are all concerned, as we are bound to maintain from the standpoint of the Christian faith, merely with revelations of the greatness, the power, the goodness, the beauty of the earth created by God. The earth is full of miracles and glory. It could not be God's *creature* and the area of our existence appointed us by God, if it were not full of revelations. The philosophers and the poets, the musicians and the prophets of all times are aware of it. But these revelations of the earth and the earthly spirit lack the authority which might bind man conclusively. Man may pass through this world without being ultimately bound. But there could also be *heavenly* revelations, that is, revelations of that invisible and inconceivable reality of creation, with which we are girt about. This world, too, of the impalpable and invisible is conceived in continuous movement towards us. Truly there are occasions of wonder there too. What would man be without meeting with heaven and the heavenly world? But neither do these heavenly revelations have the character of an ultimate authority; they too are in fact creaturely revelations. They too give no final answer.

*   *   *

When we in the Christian Church speak of revelation, we are not thinking of such earthly or heavenly revelations, but of the Power which is above all powers; not of the revelation of a divine Above or Below, but of the *revelation of God Himself*.

That is why the Reality of which we are now speaking, God's revelation in Jesus Christ, is compelling and exclusive, helpful and adequate, because here we have not to do with a reality different from God, nor with one of those earthly or even heavenly realities, but with God Himself, with God in the highest, with the Creator of Heaven and earth, of whom we have heard in the first article. When in countless passages the New Testament speaks about Jesus of Nazareth as the Lord Jesus whom the Church recognises and confesses to be Jesus the Christ, it is using the same word which the Old Testament expresses by 'Jehovah'. This Jesus of Nazareth, who passes through the cities and villages of Galilee and wanders to Jerusalem, who is there accused and condemned and crucified, this man is the Jehovah of the Old Testament, is the Creator, is God Himself. A man like us in space and time, who has all the properties of God and yet does not cease to be a human being and a creature too. The Creator Himself, without encroaching upon His deity, becomes, not a demi-god, not an angel, but very soberly, very really a man. That is the meaning of the assertion of the Christian Confession about Jesus Christ, that He is God's only, or God's only-begotten Son. He is God's Son, and God in that sense of divine reality in which God is established by Himself. This God established by Himself, God's one Son, is *this man,* Jesus of Nazareth. Since God is not only the Father but also the Son, since in God's inner life this takes place continuously (He is God in the *act* of His Godness. He is Father *and* Son), He is capable of being the Creator, yet also the creature. This unheard-of 'yet also' has its inward analogy in the Father *and Son.* And since this work, this revelation of God, is the work of the eternal Son, it legitimately confronts the whole world of creatures, excellent beyond compare. Since here God Himself is involved, since this creature is His Son, the event in Jesus Christ is distinguished in truth as compelling and exclusive, as helpful and adequate above all else that happens round about us— though that too is by God's will and ordering. God's revelation and God's work in Jesus Christ is not any event on the basis of God's will, but is God Himself, who reaches utterance in the world of creatures.

*   *   *

13

OUR LORD

The existence of the man Jesus Christ is, in virtue of His divinity, the sovereign decision upon the existence of every man. It is based on the fact that by God's dispensation this One stands for all and so all are bound and obligated to this One. His community knows this. This is what it has to make known to the world.

* * *

I SHOULD like to try and indicate this basis of Christ's lordship quite shortly and concisely. The opening statement says that this sovereign decision is based on the fact, that this One by God's dispensation stands for all. The mystery of God, and thus also of Jesus Christ, is that He, this One, this man, by His being One—not an idea, but One who is quite concrete at that time and place, a man who bears a name and comes from a place, who like us all has a life-history in time—not only exists for Himself but is this One for All. You must try to read the New Testament from the standpoint of this 'for us'. For the entire existence of this man, who stands in the centre, is determined by the fact that it is a human existence, achieved and accomplished not only in its own framework and with its own meaning in itself, but for all others. In this one man God sees every man, all of us, as through a glass. Through this medium, through this *Mediator* we are known and seen by God. And we may, and should, understand ourselves as men seen by God in Him, in this man, as men made known to Him in this way. Before His eyes from eternity God keeps men, each man, in Him, in this One; and not only before His eyes but loved and elect and called and made His possession. In Him He has from eternity bound Himself to each, to all. Along the entire line it holds, from the creatureliness of man, through the misery of man, to the glory promised to man. Everything is decided about us in Him, in this one man. It is the likeness of this One, the likeness of God, after which man has been created man. This

One in His humiliation bears the sin, the wickedness and folly, and the misery and the death of all. And the glory of this One is the glory that is intended for us all. For us it is intended that we may serve Him in eternal righteousness, innocence and blessedness, even as He has risen from death, lives and rules in eternity. Such is God's wise dispensation, this cohesion of each man and all men with this One. And that is, seen so to speak from above, the basis of the lordship of Jesus Christ.

And now the same thing seen from man's side. Since this dispensation of God's exists, since we are set in this cohesion, since Jesus Christ is this one man and stands before God on our behalf, and we in Him are loved, upheld, led and borne by God, we are Jesus Christ's property, we are bound in duty to Him, this Proprietor. Note well that this appointment of us to be His property, this connexion from us to Him does not possess in the first instance anything like a moral or even a religious quality, but it rests upon a state of affairs, upon an objective order. The moral and religious element is a *cura posterior*. Of course the result will necessarily also include an element of morality and religion. But in the first instance the fact is simply that we belong to Him. In virtue of God's dispensation man is Christ's property, not in spite of but in his freedom. For what man knows and lives as his freedom, he lives in the freedom which is given him and created for him by the fact that Christ intercedes for him in the presence of God. That is the great good action of God, signified in this, that Jesus Christ is the Lord. It is the divineness of this good action, the divineness of the everlasting mercy which, before we existed or thought of Him, has sought and found us in Him. It is this divine mercy which is also for us the basis of Christ's lordship and which delivers us from all other lordships. It is this divine mercy which excludes the right of all other lords to speak and makes it impossible to set up another authority alongside this authority and another lord alongside this Lord and to hearken to him. And it is this eternal mercy, in which this dispensation over us is included, which makes it impossible to appeal past the Lord Jesus Christ to another lord and to reckon once more with fate or history or nature, as though these were what really dominated us. Once we have seen that Christ's *potestas* is based on God's mercy, goodness and love, only then do we abandon all reservations. Then the division into a religious sphere and other spheres falls out. Then we cease to separate between body and soul, between service of God and politics. All these separations cease, for man is one, and as such is subject to the lordship of Christ.

The community knows that Jesus Christ is our Lord, it is known in the Church. But the truth of 'our Lord' does not depend on our knowing or acknowledging it or on the existence of a congregation where it is discerned and expressed; it is because Jesus Christ is our Lord that He can be known and proclaimed as such. But no one knows as a matter of course that all men have their Lord in Him. This knowledge is a matter of our election and calling, a matter of the community gathered together by His word, a matter of the Church.

* * *

14

THE MYSTERY AND THE MIRACLE OF CHRISTMAS

The truth of the conception of Jesus Christ by the Holy Spirit and of His birth of the Virgin Mary points to the true Incarnation of the true God achieved in His historical manifestation, and recalls the special form through which this beginning of the divine act of grace and revelation, that occurred in Jesus Christ, was distinguished from other human events.

* * *

WE HAVE to do with the beginning of a whole series of pronouncements about Jesus Christ. What we have been hearing so far was the description of the subject. Now we listen to a number of definitions—conceived, born, suffered, crucified, buried, descended, rose again, seated on the right hand of God, from thence He shall come again . . . which describe an action or an event. We are concerned with the story of a life starting with generation and birth like any human life; and then a life-work remarkably compressed into the little word 'suffered', a passion-story, and finally the divine confirmation of this life in its Resurrection, its Ascension, and the still outstanding conclusion, that from thence He shall come to judge the quick and the dead. He who acts and lives is Jesus Christ, God's only Son, our Lord.

If we wish to understand the meaning of 'conceived by the Holy Ghost and born of the Virgin Mary', above all we must try to see that these two remarkable pronouncements assert that God of free grace became man, a real man. The eternal Word became flesh. This is the miracle of Jesus Christ's existence, this descent of God from above downwards—the Holy Ghost and the Virgin Mary. This is the mystery of Christmas, of the Incarnation. At this part of the Confession the Catholic Church makes the sign of the Cross. And in the most various settings composers have attempted to reproduce this *et incarnatus est*. This miracle we celebrate annually, when we celebrate Christmas.

> *If I to grasp this miracle should will,*
> *So stands my spirit reverently still.*

Such *in nuce* is God's revelation; we can only grasp it, only hear it as the beginning of all things.

But there is no question here of conception and birth in general, but of a quite definite conception and a quite definite birth. Why conception by the Holy Spirit and why birth of the Virgin Mary? Why this special miracle which is intended to be expressed in these two concepts, side by side with the great miracle of the Incarnation? Why does the miracle of Christmas run parallel to the mystery of the Incarnation? A noetic utterance is so to speak put alongside the ontic one. If in the Incarnation we have to do with the thing, here we have to do with the sign. The two should not be confused. The thing which is involved in Christmas is true in and for itself. But it is indicated, it is unveiled in the miracle of Christmas. But it would be wrong to conclude from that, that therefore 'only' a sign is involved, which therefore might even be deducted from the mystery. Let me warn you against this. It is rare in life to be able to separate form and content.

'Very God and very man.' If we consider this basic Christian truth first in the light of 'conceived by the Holy Spirit', the truth is clear that the man Jesus Christ has His origin simply in God, that is, He owes His beginning in history to the fact that God in person became man. That means that Jesus Christ is indeed man, true man, but He is not just a man, not just an extraordinarily gifted or specially guided man, let alone a super-man; but, while being a man, He is God Himself. God is one with Him. His existence begins with God's special action; as a man He is founded in God, He is true God. The subject of the story of Jesus Christ is therefore God Himself, as truly as a man lives and suffers and acts there. And as surely as human initiative is involved in this life, so surely this human initiative has its foundation in the fact that in Him and through Him God has taken the initiative. From this standpoint we cannot avoid saying that Jesus Christ's Incarnation is an analogue of creation. Once more God acts as the Creator, but now not as the Creator out of nothing; rather, God enters the field and creates within creation a new beginning, a new beginning in history and moreover in the history of Israel. In the continuity of human history a point becomes visible at which God Himself hastens to the creature's aid and becomes one with him. God becomes man. In this way this story begins.

And now we have to turn the page and come to the second thing expressed thereby, when we say, 'born of the Virgin Mary'. Now the fact is underlined that we are on earth. There is a human child, the Virgin Mary; and as well as coming from God, Jesus also comes from this human being. God gives Himself an earthly human origin, that is the meaning of 'born of Mary the Virgin'. Jesus Christ is not 'only' true God; that would not be real incarnation—but neither is He an intermediate being; He is a man like us all, a man without reservation. He not only resembles us men; He is the same as us. As God is the Subject in the life of Jesus Christ, so man is the object in this story, but in the sense not of an object to be acted upon, but of a man who is in action. Man does not turn into a marionette in this meeting with God, but if there is genuine humanity, here it is, where God Himself makes Himself a man.

That would constitute the one circle which is to be seen here; namely true divinity and true humanity in sheer unity. In the Council of Chalcedon, 451, the Church attempted to rail off this unity against all misunderstandings; against the Monophysite unification, which resulted in so-called Docetism, which is fundamentally unaware of any true humanity in Christ —God only apparently became man—and against the Nestorian attempt to widen the gap between God and man, which simply wanted to separate, and according to which the Deity of Christ can be thought of every minute as separated from His humanity. Moreover, this doctrine goes back to an older error, that of the so-called Ebionites. From these Ebionites the way led to the Arians, who wished to understand Christ merely as a specially exalted creature. The Council of Chalcedon formulated the thesis that the unity is 'without confusion, without change, without division, without separation'. Perhaps you are inclined to describe this as a 'theologians' foundling' or as a 'parsons' quarrel'. Yet in all such squabbles the concern has never been to set the mystery aside, as though we wanted by such formulae to solve the matter rationalistically; but the early Church's endeavour was—and that is why it is still worth while to listen to it—to lead the eyes of Christians in the proper way to this mystery. All other attempts were attempts to resolve the mystery into a human comprehensibility. God for Himself and a mysterious man, that can be grasped; and even the unique coincidence of this God and this man in the form of Jesus can be explained. But these theories, against which the Early Church turns, do not regard the mystery. But the early Orthodox were concerned to gather men about this centre, that the man who refuses to believe should leave it alone; but nothing must be watered down here; this salt must not lose its savour. Hence the great expenditure of effort by the early Councils and theologians. It is always a little plebeian of us nowadays, out of our on the whole somewhat barbaric intellectuality, to say that they went 'too far' in those days, instead of being grateful for the fundamental work that was done then. You need not, of course, mount the pulpit and recite these formulae; but you should take the matter as quite fundamental. Christendom has seen and fixed what is involved in the miracle of Christmas, namely, the *unio hypostatica,* the genuine unity of true God and true man in the one Jesus Christ. And we are challenged to hold on to it.

But now all of you certainly notice, that in these expressions 'conceived by the Holy Spirit' and 'born of the Virgin Mary' something special is still being expressed. The talk is of an unusual procreation and an unusual birth. This thing is called the *nativitas Jesu Christi.* A miracle points to the mystery of the true divinity and the true humanity, the miracle of this procreation and of this birth.

What is the meaning of 'conceived by the Holy Spirit'? It does not mean that the Holy Spirit is so to speak the Father of Jesus Christ; in the strict sense only the denial is thereby asserted, that the man Jesus Christ has no Father. At His procreation it was not as when a human existence starts, but this human existence starts in the freedom of God Himself, in the freedom in which the Father and Son are one in the bond of love, in the Holy Spirit. So when we look at the beginning of the existence of Jesus, we are meant to be looking into this ultimate depth of the Godhead, in which the Father and Son are one. This is the freedom of the inner life of God, and in this freedom the existence of this man begins in A.D. 1. By this taking place, by God Himself beginning quite concretely at this point with Himself, this man who of himself is neither capable of this nor willing, may not only proclaim the Word of God, but Himself be the Word of God. In the midst of the old the new humanity begins. This is the miracle of Christmas, the miracle of the procreation of Jesus Christ without a father. This has nothing to do with myths narrated elsewhere in the history of religion, myths of the procreation of men by gods. We have not to do with such a procreation here. God Himself takes the stage as the Creator and not as a partner to this Virgin. Christian art in earlier times attempted to reproduce this fact, that here there is no question of a sexual event. And it has been well said that this procreation was realised rather by way of the ear of Mary, which heard the Word of God.

'Born of the Virgin Mary.' Once again and now from the human standpoint the male is excluded here. The male has nothing to do with this birth. What is involved here is, if you like, a divine act of judgment. To what is to begin here man is to contribute nothing by his action and initiative. Man is not simply excluded, for the Virgin is there. But the male, as the specific agent of human action and history, with his responsibility for directing the human species, must now retire into the background, as the powerless figure of Joseph. That is the Christian reply to the question of woman: here the woman stands absolutely in the foreground, moreover the *virgo*, the Virgin Mary. God did not choose man in his pride and in his defiance, but man in his weakness and humility, not man in his historical rôle, but man in the weakness of his nature as represented by the woman, the human creature who can confront God only with the words, 'Behold, the handmaid of the Lord; be it unto me according as Thou hast said'. Such is human co-operation in this matter, that and only that! We must not think of making a merit of this handmaid existence, nor attempt once more to ascribe a potency to the creature. But God has regarded man in his weakness and in his humility, and Mary has expressed what creation alone can express in this encounter. That Mary does so and that thereby the creature says 'Yes' to God, is a part of the great acceptance which comes to man from God.

The miracle of Christmas is the actual form of the mystery of the personal union of God and man, the *unio hypostatica*. Again and again the Christian Church and its theology have insisted that we cannot postulate that the reality of the Incarnation, the mystery of Christmas, had by absolute necessity to take the form of this miracle. The true Godhead and the true humanity of Jesus Christ in their unity do not depend on the fact that Christ was conceived by the Holy Spirit and born of the Virgin Mary. All that we can say is that it pleased God to let the mystery be real and become manifest in this shape and form. But again that cannot mean that over against this factual form of the miracle we are as it were free to affirm it or not to affirm it, to make a deduction and say that we have listened, but make a reservation, that this matter could be also in another form for us. We perhaps best understand the relation of matter and form, which is presented here, by taking a look at the story, familiar to you all, of the healing of the paralytic

(Mark 2. 10) : 'That ye may know, that the Son of Man hath power to forgive sins. . . . Arise, take up thy bed and go thy way.' 'That ye may know . . .'; in this way the miracle of the Virgin Birth is also to be understood. What is involved is the mystery of the Incarnation as the visible form of which the miracle takes place. We should ill have understood Mark 2, if we wanted so to read the passage, that the chief miracle was the forgiveness of sins, and the bodily healing incidental. The one thing obviously belongs of necessity to the other. And so we should have to give a warning, too, against parenthesising the miracle of the *nativitas* and wanting to cling to the mystery as such. One thing may be definitely said, that every time people want to fly from this miracle, a theology is at work, which has ceased to understand and honour the mystery as well, and has rather essayed to conjure away the mystery of the unity of God and man in Jesus Christ, the mystery of God's free grace. And on the other hand, where this mystery has been understood and men have avoided any attempt at natural theology, because they had no need of it, the miracle came to be thankfully and joyously recognised. It became, we might say, an inward necessity at this point.

15

SUFFERED . . .

The life of Jesus Christ is not a triumph but a humiliation, not a success but a failure, not a joy but suffering. For that very reason it reveals man's rebellion against God and God's wrath against man which necessarily follows; but it also reveals the mercy in which God has made His own man's business and consequently his humiliation, failure and suffering, so that it need no longer be man's business.

IN CALVIN'S CATECHISM we may on this passage read the extraordinary conclusion that in the Confession the life of Jesus has been passed over up to the Passion, because what took place in this life up to the Passion does not belong to the 'substance of our redemption'. I take the liberty of saying that here Calvin is wrong. How can anyone say that the rest of Jesus' life is not substantially for our redemption? In that case what would be its significance? A mere superfluous narrative? I should think that there is involved in the *whole* of Jesus' life the thing that takes its beginning in the article 'He suffered'. In Calvin we have a delightful example before our eyes, of pupils of a great master often seeing better than he; for in the Heidelberg Catechism, composed by Calvin's pupils, Olevian and Ursin, Question 37 asks: 'What understandest thou by the little word "suffered"?' 'That He *all the time of His life on earth,* but especially at the end thereof, hath borne in body and soul the wrath of God against the sin of the whole human race.' For Calvin's view it might, of course, be adduced that Paul, and the Epistles of the New Testament in general, scarcely refer to this 'whole time' of Christ's life, and that the Apostles also, according to Acts, seem to have shown remarkably little interest in the matter. For them apparently only the one thing stands out, that, betrayed by the Jews, He was delivered to the Gentiles, was crucified and rose from the dead. But if the early Christian Church has so fully concentrated its gaze upon the Crucified and Risen One, that is not to be taken exclusively, but inclusively. The fact that Christ died and rose again is a reduction of the *whole* life of Jesus; but in that we must also see its development. The whole life of Jesus comes under the heading 'suffered'.

That is an extremely astonishing fact, for which we have not been straightway prepared by what has been said. Jesus Christ, God's only Son, our Lord, conceived by the Holy Spirit, born of the Virgin Mary, true Son of God and true son of man—what is the relation to that of the unfolding of His whole life under the sign of His having 'suffered'? We should expect something different, something resplendent, triumphant, successful, joyful. And as it is, we hear not a word of that, but, predominant for the entirety of this life, the assertion that 'He suffered.' Is that really the last word? We cannot overlook how this whole life ends: the third day He rose again from the dead. And the life of Jesus is not completely without sign of the coming joy and the coming victory. Not for nothing is there so much talk of glorification, and not for nothing is the picture of wedding joy so often mentioned. Although it is certainly not without amazement that we several times hear of Jesus weeping, but never that He laughed, it has still to be said that continuously through His suffering there was a kind of glint of joy in nature around Him, in children, and above all, of joy in His existence and in His mission. We hear once that it is said that He rejoiced over the fact that God had hidden it from the wise, but had revealed it unto the babes. And in the miracles of Jesus there is triumph and joy. Healing and help here break into the life of men. It seems to become visible who is in action. In the story of the Transfiguration, in which it is related that the disciples saw Jesus whiter than any white which is terrestrially possible, this other thing, the issue of this life—we might also say, its beginning and origin—becomes visible by anticipation. Bengel is undoubtedly right when he says of the Gospels before the Resurrection that we might say of all those stories of Jesus that they *spirant resurrectionem*. But more than that we cannot actually say. There is a fragrance of the beginning and of the end, a fragrance of the triumphant Deity who is in action there.

But the present time of His life is really suffering from the start. There is no doubt that for the Evangelists Luke and Matthew the childhood of Jesus, His Birth in the stable of Bethlehem, were already under the sign of suffering. This man is persecuted all His life, a stranger in His own family—what shocking statements He can make!—and in His nation; a stranger in the spheres of State and Church and civilisation. And what a road of manifest ill-success He treads! In what utter loneliness and temptation He stands among men, the leaders of His nation, even over against the masses of the people and in the very circle of His disciples! In this narrowest circle He is to find His betrayer; and in the man to whom He says, 'Thou art the Rock . . .', the man who denies Him thrice. And, finally, it is the disciples of whom it is said that 'they all forsook Him'. And the people cry in chorus, 'Away with him! Crucify him!' The entire life of Jesus is lived in this loneliness and thus already in the shadow of the Cross. And if the light of the Resurrection lights up here and there, that is the exception that proves the rule. The son of man *must* go up unto Jerusalem, must there be condemned, scourged and crucified—to rise again the third day. But first it is this dominant 'must' which leads him to the gallows.

*　　*　　*

But in it there is also disclosed the wrath of God against man. 'Suffered' is explained in the Heidelberg Catechism as that Jesus has borne the wrath of God His whole life. Being a man means being so placed before God as to have deserved this wrath. In this unity of God and man the man is bound to be this condemned and smitten person. The man Jesus in His unity with God is the figure of man smitten by God. Even this world's justice, which carries out this judgment, does so by God's will. God's Son became man in order to let man be seen under God's wrath. The Son of man *must* suffer and be delivered up and crucified, says the New Testament. In this Passion the connexion becomes visible between infinite guilt and the reconciliation that necessarily ensues upon this guilt. It becomes clear that where God's grace is rejected, man rushes into his own mischief. It is here, where God Himself has become man, that the deepest truth of human life is manifest: the total suffering which corresponds to total sin.

*　　*　　*

16

UNDER PONTIUS PILATE

In virtue of the name of Pontius Pilate being connected with Him, the life and passion of Jesus Christ is an event in the same world-history, in which our life also takes place. And by the co-operation of this politician it acquires outwardly the character of an action in which the divine appointment and righteousness, as well as human perversion and the unrighteousness of the State's ordering of what takes place in the world, become effective and manifest.

HOW DOES Pontius Pilate come into the Creed? Somewhat coarsely and bitingly, the answer might first of all be: like a dog into a nice room! In the way in which politics get into human life and then in one form or another into the Church also! Who is Pontius Pilate? Really an unpleasant and inconsiderable figure with a very unedifying character. Who is Pontius Pilate? That extremely subordinate functionary, a sort of commandant in the military government of an alien occupying power in Jerusalem. What is he doing there? The local Jewish community has passed a resolution, for the execution of which it had not sufficient authority. It has brought in a death sentence, and must now bring in the legalising and executive power of Pilate. And after some hesitation, he does what is required of him. A very insignificant man in a quite external rôle; for everything important, everything spiritual is played out between Israel and Christ in the Sanhedrin which accuses and rejects Him. Pilate stands by in his uniform and is used, and his rôle is not honourable; he acknowledges that the Man is innocent and yet he hands Him over to death. He was bound to act according to strict law, but does not do so and lets himself be determined by 'political considerations'. He does not venture to stand by the legal decision, but yields to the popular cry and gives Jesus up. He has the Crucifixion carried out by his cohorts. When in the midst of the Confession of the Christian Church, at the moment when we are on the point of stepping into the area of

God's deepest mystery, such things come into view, one might well ejaculate with Goethe, 'A foul business! Fie! A political trick!' But there it is, 'under Pontius Pilate . . .'; and so we must ask ourselves what this means.

*   *   *

This name in connexion with the Passion of Christ makes it unmistakably clear that this Passion of Jesus Christ, this unveiling of man's rebellion and of God's wrath, yet also of His mercy, did not take place in heaven or in some remote planet or even in some world of ideas; it took place in our time, in the center of the world-history in which our human life is played out. So we must not escape from this life. We must not take flight to a better land, or to some height or other unknown, nor to any spiritual Cloud-Cuckooland nor to a Christian fairyland. God has come into our life in its utter unloveliness and frightfulness. That the Word became flesh also means that it became temporal, historical. It assumed the form which belongs to the human creature, in which there are such folk as this very Pontius Pilate—the people we belong to and who are also ourselves at any time on a slightly larger scale! It is not necessary to close our eyes to this, for God has not closed His either! He has entered into it all. The Incarnation of the Word is an extremely concrete event, in which a human name may play a part. God's Word has the character of the *hic et nunc*. There is nothing in the opinion of Lessing that God's Word is an 'eternal truth of reason', and not an 'accidental truth of history'. God's history is indeed an accidental truth of history, like this petty commandant. God was not ashamed to exist in this accidental state. To the factors which deermined our human time and human history belong, in virtue of the name Pontius Pilate, the life and Passion of Jesus as well. We are not left alone in this frightful world. Into this alien land God has come to us.

To be sure, it is clear that this very fact that Jesus Christ under Pontius Pilate can only suffer and die, characterises this world-history as an extremely questionable one. Here it becomes obvious that we have to do with the passing world, the old era, the world whose typical representative, Pontius Pilate, confronts Jesus in complete powerlessness and helplessness. The Roman world-power is exposed, as Pilate the lieutenant of the great lord in Rome is exposed. This is how the whole political action appears in the light of the approaching Kingdom of God: everything making for a break-up and contradicted in advance. That is the one side: this world into which Christ has come, is illumined by Him in its complete frailty and folly.

But it would not be right to stop here. For the Pilate episode in all four Gospels has still too much importance, for us to be satisfied with stating that Pilate is just the man of this world in general. He is not only that, but he is the statesman and politician; so the meeting here between the world and God's kingdom is indeed a special one. It is not a matter of the meeting between God's Kingdom and human knowledge, human society, human work, but of the meeting between God's Kingdom and the *polis*. Pilate thus stands for the order which confronts the other order represented by Israel and the Church. He is the representative of the Emperor Tiberius. He represents world-history, so far as at all times it is ordered on State lines. That Jesus Christ suffered under Pontius Pilate therefore means also that He did subscribe to this State order. 'Thou hadst had no power over me, except it had been given thee from above.' Jesus Christ is completely serious when He says, 'Give unto Caesar what is Caesar's'. He gives him what is his; He does not attack the authority of Pilate. He suffers, but he does not protest against Pilate having to utter the judgment upon Him. In other words the State order, the *polis,* is the area in which His action too, the action of the eternal Word of God, takes place. It is the area in which, according to human insight, under the threat and application of physical force, the decision is taken as to right and wrong in the external life of men. That is the State, that is what we call politics. Everything that takes place in the realm of politics is somehow an application of this attempt. What takes place in the world is always ordered by the State as well, although fortunately not only by the State! In the midst of this State-ordered world Jesus Christ now appears. By suffering under Pontius Pilate He too participates in this order, and so it is worth while considering what this fact must signify, how the outward order looks, how the whole Pontius Pilate reality looks from the standpoint of the suffering Lord.

This is not the place to evolve the Christian doctrine of the State, which is not to be separated from the Christian doctrine of the Church. Still, a few words should be said here, for in this meeting of Jesus and Pilate everything is together *in nuce* that should be thought and said from the side of the Gospel regarding the realm of the *polis*.

State order, State power, as represented by Pontius Pilate *vis-à-vis* Jesus, is made visible in its negative form, in all its human perversion and unrighteousness. One may indeed say that if anywhere the State is visible as the State of wrong, it is here; and if anywhere the State has been exposed and politics has proved itself to be a monster, then once more it is here. What does Pilate do? He does what politicians have more or less always done and what has always belonged to the actual achievement of politics in all times: he attempts to rescue and maintain order in Jerusalem and thereby at the same time to preserve his own position of power, by surrendering the clear law, for the protection of which he was actually installed. Remarkable contradiction! His duty is to decide upon right and wrong; that is his *raison d'être*; and in order to be able to stay in his position he, 'from fear of the Jews', renounced doing really the very thing he was bound to do: he gives way. True, he does not condemn Jesus—he *cannot* condemn Him, he finds Him not guilty—and yet he surrenders Him. In surrendering Jesus, he is surrendering himself. By becoming the prototype of all persecutors of the Church and by Nero coming to view in him, by the unrighteous State, that is, entering into action there, it is the State as such that is disgraced. In the person of Pilate the State withdraws from the basis of its own existence and becomes a den of robbers, a gangster State, the ordering of an irresponsible clique. *That* is the *polis, that* is politics. What wonder that one prefers to cover one's face before it? And if the State has for years and decades long shown itself in this guise only, what wonder that one tires of the whole realm of politics? In fact the State so regarded, the State after the pattern of the Pilates, is the *polis* in its sheer opposition to the Church and to the kingdom of God. This is the State as it is described in the

New Testament, in Revelations 13, as the Beast from the abyss, with the other beast of the great muzzle which accompanies it, which the first Beast is continually glorifying and praising. The passion of Christ becomes the unmasking, the judging, the condemnation of this Beast, whose name is *polis*.

But that is not all and we cannot halt there. If Pilate, first of all, brings to view the deterioration of the State and so the unrighteous State, we must also not fail to recognise in this concave mirror the supreme good order of God which is here set up and remains and is effective, the *righteous* State, which is, indeed, disgraced by unrighteous human actions, but can as little as the right Church be completely set aside, because it rests upon divine institution and appointment. The power which Pilate has is no less given him from above because he misuses it. Jesus acknowledged it, exactly in the way in which later on Paul summoned the Roman Christians to acknowledge, even in Nero's state, the divine appointment and institution, to conform to this ordering and thus to renounce all non-political Christianity, and rather to recognise their responsibility for the maintenance of the State. That the order of the State is as such an order of God is indeed also clear in Pilate's case, in that— while as a *bad* statesman he gives Jesus over to death, he still cannot but, as a proper statesman, declare Him to be innocent. And also it becomes visible with uncanny force, that Pilate the bad statesman has power to will and to do the very opposite of what as a proper statesman he ought to have willed and done— to release Barabbas and put Jesus to death, and therefore (so differently from the way it is meant in 1 Peter 2. 14!) 'to reward the wicked, to punish the good'—but that in the result, (which does not excuse him, but which justifies the wisdom of God!) he must also fulfil the supreme law. That Jesus the righteous man should die in place of the unrighteous man, that accordingly this man—Barabbas!—should go free in Jesus' place, was indeed the will of God in the suffering of Jesus Christ. And in this way it is His suffering under Pontius Pilate, the bad statesman—righteous against his will. And that was the will of God in the suffering of Jesus Christ, that Jesus should be delivered by the Jews to the heathen, that the Word of God might come out of the narrow realm of the nation Israel into the Gentile world. The Gentile who accepts Jesus—from the filthy hands of Judas, of the high priests and the people of Jerusalem, he himself a man with filthy hands—this Gentile is the wicked statesman, Pontius Pilate—righteous against his will! He is also in this respect, as Hamann has called him, the executor of the New Testament, in a certain sense practically the founder of the Church of Jews and Gentiles. Thus Jesus triumphs over him, under whose wickedness He has to suffer. Thus Jesus triumphs over the world, in which by treading it He has to suffer. Thus He is the Lord also where He is rejected of men. Thus the political order itself, irrespective of its corruption through human guilt when Jesus was subjected to it, is bound to make it plain that it is in truth subjected to Him. That is why Christians pray for their governors. That is why they make themselves responsible for their maintenance. That is why it is a Christian's task to seek the best for the city, to honour the divine appointment and institution of the State, by choosing and desiring to the best of their knowledge not the wrong, but the right State, the State which makes of the fact that it has its power 'from above', not, like Pilate, a dishonour, but an honour.

* * *

17

WAS CRUCIFIED, DEAD, AND BURIED, HE DESCENDED INTO HELL

In the death of Jesus Christ God has humiliated Himself and rendered Himself up, in order to accomplish His law upon sinful man by taking his place and thus once for all removing from him to Himself the curse that affects him, the punishment he deserves, the past he is hurrying to meet, the abandonment into which he has fallen.

THE MYSTERY of the Incarnation unfolds into the mystery of Good Friday and of Easter. And once more it is as it has been so often in this whole mystery of faith, that we must always see two things together, we must always understand one by the other. In the history of the Christian faith it has, indeed, always been the case that the knowledge of Christians has gravitated more to the one side or to the other. We may take it that the Western Church, the Church of the Occident, has a decided inclination towards the *theologia crucis*—that is, towards bringing out and emphasising the fact that He was surrendered for our transgressions. Whereas the Eastern Church brings more into the foreground the fact that He was raised for our justification, and so inclines towards the *theologia gloriae*. In this matter there is no sense in wanting to play off one against the other. You know that from the beginning Luther strongly worked out the Western tendency—not *theologia gloriae* but *theologia crucis*. What Luther meant by that is right. But we ought not to erect and fix any opposition; for there is no *theologia crucis* which does not have its complement in the *theologia gloriae*. Of course, there is no Easter without Good Friday, but equally certainly there is no Good Friday without Easter! Too much tribulation and sullenness are too easily wrought into Christianity. But if the Cross is the Cross of Jesus Christ and not a speculation on the Cross, which fundamentally any heathen might also have, then it cannot for one second be forgotten or overlooked that the Crucified rose again from the dead the third day. We shall in that case celebrate Good Friday quite differently, and perhaps it would be well not to sing on Good Friday the doleful, sad Passion hymns, but to begin to sing Easter hymns. It is not a sad and miserable business that took place on Good Friday; for He rose again. I wanted to say this first, that you are not to take abstractly what we have to say about the death and the Passion of Christ, but already to look beyond it to the place where His glory is revealed.

This core of Christology has been described in the old theology under two main concepts of the *exinanitio* and the *exaltatio* of Christ. What is the meaning here of humiliation, and of exaltation?

The humiliation of Christ includes the whole, beginning with 'suffered under Pontius Pilate', and decisively visible in 'was crucified, dead, and buried, He descended into hell'. It is certainly first the humiliation of this man who suffers there and dies and passes into the outmost darkness. But what first gives its significance to the humiliation and abandonment of this man is the fact that this man is God's Son, and it is none other than God Himself who humbles and surrenders Himself in Him.

And so when this is countered by the exaltation of Jesus Christ as the mystery of Easter, this glorifying is certainly a self-glorifying of God; it is His honour that triumphs there: 'God goes up with a shout'. But the real mystery of Easter is not that God is glorified in it, but that man is exalted, raised to the right hand of God and permitted to triumph over sin, death and the devil.

When we hold these two things together, then the picture before us is that of an inconceivable exchange, of a *katalage*, that is, a substitution. Man's reconciliation with God takes place through God's putting Himself in man's place and man's being put in God's place, as a sheer act of grace. It is this inconceivable miracle which is our reconciliation.

*　　　*　　　*

What takes place in the Crucifixion of Christ is that God's Son takes to Himself that which must come to the creature existing in revolt, which wants to deliver itself from its creatureliness and itself be the Creator. He puts Himself into this creature's need and does not abandon it to itself. Moreover, He does not only help it from without and greet it only from afar off; He makes the misery of His creature His own. To what end? So that His creature may go out freely, so that the burden which it has laid upon itself may be borne, borne away. The creature itself must have gone to pieces, but God does not want that; He wants it to be saved. So great is the ruin of the creature that less than the self-surrender of God would not suffice for its rescue. But so great is God, that it is His will to render up Himself. Reconciliation means God taking man's place. Let me add that no doctrine of this central mystery can exhaustively and precisely grasp and express the extent to which God has intervened for us here. Do not confuse my theory of the reconciliation with the thing itself. All theories of reconciliation can be but pointers. But do also pay attention to this 'for us':

nothing must be deducted from it! Whatever a doctrine of reconciliation tries to express, it *must* say this.

In the death of Jesus Christ God has accomplished His law. In the death of Jesus Christ He has acted as Judge towards Man. Man has betaken himself to the point at which a verdict of God is pronounced upon him and has inevitably to be carried out. Man stands before God as a sinner, as a being who has sundered himself from God, who has rebelled against being what he may be. He rebels against grace; it is too little for him, he turns away from gratitude. Such is human life, this constant turning away, this coarse and subtle sinning. This sinning leads man into inconceivable need: he makes himself impossible before God. He puts himself where God cannot see him. He puts himself so to speak behind the back of God's grace. But the back of God's 'Yes' is the divine 'No': it is the judgment. As God's grace is irresistible, so His judgment is irresistible.

And now we have to understand what was declared of Christ, that He was 'crucified, dead and buried . . .', as the expression of that which is now actually accomplished upon man.

Crucified. When an Israelite was crucified, that meant that he was accursed, expelled, not only from the realm of the living but from the covenant with God, removed from the circle of the elect. Crucified means rejected, handed over to the death of the gallows inflicted on the heathen. Let us be clear what is involved in the judgment of God, in what the human creature has to suffer from God's side as a sinful creature; he is involved in rejection, in the curse. 'Cursed is he that dies on the cross.' What befalls Christ is what ought to befall us.

Dead. Death is the end of all present possibilities of life. Dying means exhausting the last of the possibilities given to us. However we wish to interpret dying physically and metaphysically, whatever may happen then, one thing is certain, that then there happens the last action that can happen in creaturely existence. Whatever may happen beyond death must at least be something different from the continuation of this life. Death really means the *end*. That is the judgment under which our life stands: it is waiting for death. To be born and grow up, to ripen and grow old, is to go towards the moment at which for each of us it will be the end, definitely the end. The matter looked at from this side is a matter which makes death into an element in our life, about which we prefer not to think.

Buried. It stands there so unobtrusively and simply superfluously. But it is not there for nothing. Some day we shall be buried. Some day a company of men will process out to a churchyard and lower a coffin and everyone will go home; but one will not come back, and that will be me. The seal of death will be that they will bury me as a thing that is superfluous and disturbing in the land of the living. 'Buried' gives to death the character of passing away and decay and to human existence the character of transitoriness and corruptibility. What then is the meaning of man's life? It means hurrying to the grave. Man is hurrying to meet his past. This past, in which there is no more future, will be the final thing: all that we are will have been and will have been corrupted. Perhaps a memory will remain, so long as there are men who like to remember us. But some day they too will die and then this memory too will pass away. There is no great name in human history which will not some day or other have become a forgotten name. That is the meaning of being 'buried'; and that is the judgment on man, that in the grave he drops into forgottenness. That is God's answer to sin: there is nothing else to be done with sinful man, except to bury him and forget him.

Descended into hell. In the Old and New Testaments the picture of hell is somewhat different from what developed out of it later on. Hell, the place of the *inferi,* Hades in the Old Testament sense, is certainly the place of torment, the place of complete separateness, where man continues to exist only as a non-being, as a shadow. The Israelites thought of this place as a place where men continue to hover around like flitting shaddows. And the bad thing about this being in hell in the Old Testament sense is that the dead can no longer praise God, they can no longer see His face, they can no longer take part in the Sabbath services of Israel. It is a state of exclusion from God, and that makes death so fearful, makes hell what it is. That man is separated from God means being in the place of torment. 'Wailing and gnashing of teeth'—our imagination is not adequate to this reality, this existence without God. The atheist is not aware of what Godlessness is. Godlessness is existence in hell. What else but this is left as the result of sin? Has not man separated himself from God by his own act? 'Descended into hell' is merely confirmation of it. God's judgment is righteous—that is, it gives man what he wanted. God would not be God, the Creator would not be the Creator, the creature would not be the creature, and man would not be man, if this verdict and its execution could be stayed.

But now the Confession tells us that the execution of this verdict is carried out by God in this way, that He, God Himself, in Jesus Christ His Son, at once true God and true man, takes the place of condemned man. God's judgment is executed, God's law takes its course, but in such a way that what man had to suffer is suffered by this One, who as God's Son stands for all others. Such is the lordship of Jesus Christ, who stands for us before God, by taking upon Himself what belongs to us. In Him God makes Himself liable, at the point at which we are accursed and guilty and lost. He it is in His Son, who in the person of this crucified man bears on Golgotha all that ought to be laid on us. And in this way He makes an end of the curse. It is not God's will that man should perish; it is not God's will that man should pay what he was bound to pay; in other words, God extirpates the sin. And God does this, not in spite of His righteousness, but it is God's very righteousness that He, the holy One, steps in for us the unholy, that He wills to save and does save us. Righteousness in the Old Testament sense is not the righteousness of the judge who makes the debtor pay, but the action of a judge who in the accused recognises the wretch whom he wishes to help by putting him to rights. That is what righteousness means. Righteousness means setting right. And that is what God does. Of course not without the punishment being borne and the whole distress breaking out, but through His putting Himself in the place of the guilty one. He who may and can do this is justified in the fact that He takes over the rôle of His creature. God's mercy and God's righteousness are not at variance with each other.

> *'His Son is not too dear to Him,*
> *He gives Him up; for He*
> *From fire eternal by His blood*
> *Would rescue me.'*

That is the mystery of Good Friday.

But actually we are looking away beyond Good Friday, when we say that God comes in our place and takes our punishment upon Himself. Thereby He actually takes it away from us. All pain, all temptation, as well as our dying, is just the shadow of the judgment which God has already executed in our favour. That which in truth was bound to affect us and ought to have affected us, has actually been turned aside from us already in Christ's death. That is attested by Christ's saying on the Cross, 'It is finished!' So then in view of Christ's Cross we are invited on the one hand to realise the magnitude and weight of our sin in what our forgiveness cost. In the strict sense there is no knowledge of sin except in the light of Christ's Cross. For he alone understands what sin is, who knows that his sin is forgiven him. And on the other hand we may realise that the price is paid on our behalf, so that we are acquitted of sin and its consequences. We are no longer addressed and regarded by God as sinners, who must pass under judgment for their guilt. We have nothing more to pay. We are acquitted gratis, *sola gratia*, by God's own entering in for us.

18

THE THIRD DAY HE ROSE AGAIN FROM THE DEAD

In the Resurrection of Jesus Christ man is once for all exalted, and appointed to discover with God his right against all his foes and thus set free to live a new life, in which he no longer has sin and therefore the curse too, death, the grave and hell, in front of him but behind him.

'THE THIRD day He rose again from the dead' is the Easter message. It asserts that not in vain did God humble Himself in His Son; by so doing He assuredly acted also for His own honour

and for the confirmation of His glory. By His mercy triumphing
in His very humiliation, the result is the exaltation of Jesus
Christ. And when we said earlier that in the humiliation God's
Son was involved and therefore God Himself, we must now
emphasise that what is involved in the exaltation is man. In
Jesus Christ man is exalted and appointed to the life for which
God has set him free in the death of Jesus Christ. God has so
to speak abandoned the sphere of His glory and man may now
take this place. That is the Easter message, the goal of reconciliation, man's redemption. It is the goal which was already visible
on Good Friday. By God interceding for man—the New Testament writers were not afraid to use the expression 'paying'—
man is a ransomed creature. Ἀπολύτρωσις is a legal concept
which described the ransoming of a slave. The goal is that man
is transferred to another status in law. He no longer belongs to
that which had a right over him, to that realm of curse, death
and hell; he is translated into the kingdom of God's dear Son.
That means that his position, his condition, his legal status as
a sinner is rejected in every form. Man is no longer seriously
regarded by God as a sinner. Whatever he may be, whatever
there is to be said of him, whatever he has to reproach himself
with, God no longer takes him seriously as a sinner. He has died
to sin; there on the Cross of Golgotha. He is no longer present
for sin. He is acknowledged before God and established as a
righteous man, as one who does right before God. As he now
stands, he has, of course, his existence in sin and so in its guilt;
but he has that behind him. The turn has been achieved, once
for all. But we cannot say, 'I have turned away once for all, I
have experienced'—no; 'once for all' is Jesus Christ's 'once for
all'. But if we believe in Him, then it holds for us. Man is in
Christ Jesus, who has died for him, in virtue of His Resurrection, God's dear child, who may live by and for the good pleasure of God.

If that is the message of Easter, then you realise that in the
Resurrection of Jesus Christ there is the revelation of the still
hidden fruit of Christ's death. It is this very turning-point which
is still hidden in the death of Christ, hidden under the aspect
in which man there appears consumed by the wrath of God.
And now the New Testament bears us witness, that this aspect

of man is not the meaning of the event upon Golgotha, but that behind this aspect the real meaning of this event is the one which is revealed on the third day. On this third day there begins a new story of man, so that we may even divide the life of Jesus into two great periods, the thirty-three years to His death, and the quite short and decisive period of the forty days between His death and the Ascension. The third day a new life of Jesus begins; but at the same time on the third day there begins a new *Aeon,* a new shape of the world, after the old world has been completely done away and settled in the death of Jesus Christ. Easter is the breaking in of a new time and world in the existence of the man Jesus, who now begins a new life as the conqueror, as the victorious bearer, as the destroyer of the burden of man's sin, which had been laid upon Him. In this altered existence of His the first community saw not only a supernatural continuation of His previous life, but an entirely new life, that of the exalted Jesus Christ, and simultaneously the beginning of a new *world.*

*　　*　　*

19

HE ASCENDED INTO HEAVEN, AND SITTETH ON THE RIGHT HAND OF GOD THE FATHER ALMIGHTY

The aim of the work of Jesus Christ, which happened once for all, is the foundation of His Church through the knowledge, entrusted to the witnesses of His resurrection, that the omnipotence of God and the grace of God that are active and apparent in Him are one and the same thing. And so the end of this work is also the beginning of the end-time, that is, of the time in which the Church has to proclaim to all the world the gracious omnipotence and the omnipotent grace of God in Jesus.

* * *

WHAT IS the meaning of the Ascension? According to what we have said about heaven and earth, it means at any rate that Jesus leaves earthly space, the space, that is, which is conceivable to us and which He has sought out for our sakes. He no longer belongs to it as we belong to it. That does not mean that it becomes alien to Him, that this space is not His space too. On the contrary, since He stands *above* this space, He fulfils it and He becomes present to it. But now, of course, no longer in the way at the time of His revelation and of His earthly activity. The Ascension does not mean that Christ has passed over into that other realm of the creaturely world, into the realm of what is inconceivable to us. 'On the right hand of God' means not only the transition from the conceivable to the inconceivable in the created world. Jesus is removed in the direction of the mystery of *divine* space, which is utterly concealed from man. It is not heaven that is His abode; He is with God. The Crucified and Risen One is where God is.

* * *

Whatever prosperity or defeat may occur in our space, what-

ever may become and pass away, there is one constant, one thing
that remains and continues, this sitting of His at the right
hand of God the Father. There is no historical turning-point
which approaches this. Here we have the mystery of what we
term world history, Church history, history of civilisation; here
we have the thing that underlies everything. This first of all
quite simply means the thing that is expressed again at the end
of St. Matthew's Gospel by the so-called missionary mandate:
'Go ye into all the world and make disciples of all the nations,
baptising them and teaching them to observe all things whatsoever I command you.' Consequently that knowledge, that 'God's
omnipotence is God's grace', is no idle knowledge. And the conclusion of revelation time is not the end of a spectacle, where
the curtain falls and the onlookers may go home, but it ends
with a challenge, with a command. The salvation event now
becomes a bit of world event. What now becomes visible to the
Apostles corresponds to the fact that here too on earth, as a
human history, as an action of the disciples, there is an earthly
place corresponding to the heavenly place, a life and action of
the witnesses of His Resurrection. With the departure of Jesus
Christ to the Father an establishment on earth is made. His
departure means not only an end but also a beginning, even
though not as the continuation of His advent. For it should
not be said that the work of Jesus Christ simply continues in
the life of Christians and the existence of the Church. The life
of the saints is not a prolongation of the revelation of Jesus
Christ upon earth. That would contradict His 'It is finished'.
What happened in Jesus Christ needs no continuation. But, of
course, what happened once for all possesses in what now happens upon earth a correspondence, a reflection; not a repetition
but a likeness. And all that Christian life is in faith in Christ,
all that is called the community, is this likeness, this shadowing
forth of the existence of Jesus Christ as the Head of His body.
Christ founds His Church by going to the Father, by making
Himself known to His Apostles. This knowledge means the call
to 'Go into all the world and proclaim the Gospel to every
creature'. Christ is the Lord. That is what all creation, what
all nations should know. The conclusion of Christ's work is

therefore not an opportunity given to the Apostles for idleness, but it is their being sent out into the world. Here there is no rest possible; here there is rather a running and racing; here is the start of the mission, the sending of the Church into the world and for the world.

* * *

20

THE COMING OF JESUS CHRIST THE JUDGE

The Church's recollection is also its expectation, and its message to the world is also the world's hope. For Jesus Christ, from whose word and work the Church knowingly, the world as yet unknowingly, derives, is the same who comes to meet the Church and the world, as the goal of the time that is coming to an end, in order to make visible, finally and for all people, the decision taken in Him—God's grace and kingdom as the measure by which the whole of humanity and every single human existence is measured.

'. . . FROM THENCE He shall come to judge the quick and the dead.' After many perfects and the present there now follows the future—'He shall come'. We might parse the whole of the second article in three tenses, that He *came,* that He *sitteth* on the right hand of God, and that He *shall come again.*

First let me say something about the Christian concept of time. We cannot but realise that here a quite strange light falls upon what in the genuine and proper sense is called real time—time in the light of God's time, eternity.

Jesus Christ's having come, all those past tenses, would answer to what we term the past. But how inappropriate it would be to say of that event that it was past. What Jesus suffered and did is certainly not past; it is rather the old that is past, the world of man, the world of disobedience and disorder, the world of misery, sin and death. Sin has been cancelled, death has been vanquished. Sin and death *did exist,* and the whole of world history, including that which ran its course *post Christum,* right down to our day, *existed.* All that is past in Christ; we can only think back on all that.

But Jesus Christ sitteth beside the Father, as He who has suffered and has risen from the dead. That is the present. Since He is present as God is present, it already admits of being said that He shall come again as the person He once was. He who is to-day just as He was yesterday, will also be the same to-morrow—Jesus Christ yesterday and to-day and the same to eternity. Since Jesus Christ exists as the person He was, obviously He is the beginning of a new, different time from that which we know, a time in which there is no fading away, but real time which has a yesterday, a to-day and a to-morrow. But Jesus Christ's yesterday is also His to-day and His to-morrow. It is not timelessness, not empty eternity that comes in place of His time. His time is not at an end; it continues in the movement from yesterday to to-day, into to-morrow. It has not the frightful fleetingness of our present. When Jesus Christ sitteth at the right hand of the Father, this existence of His with God, His existence as the possessor and representative of the divine grace and power towards us men, has nothing to do with what we are foolishly wont to conceive as eternity—namely, an existence without time. If this existence of Jesus Christ at the right hand of God is real existence and as such the measure of all existence, then it is also existence in time, although in another time than the one we know. If the lordship and rule of Jesus Christ at the Father's right hand is the meaning of what we see as the existence of our world history and our life-history, then this existence of Jesus Christ is not a timeless existence, and eternity is not a timeless eternity. Death is timeless, nothingness is timeless. So we men are timeless when we are without God and without Christ. Then we have no time. But this timelessness He has overcome. Christ has time, the fullness of time. He sitteth at the right hand of God as He who has come, who had acted and suffered and triumphed in death. His session at God's right hand is not just the extract of this history; it is the eternal within this history.

*   *   *

'. . . From thence He shall come.' In this 'from thence' is contained above all this fact, that He will issue out of the hiddenness in which He still remains for us to-day, where He is proclaimed and believed by the Church, where He is present to us only in His Word. The New Testament says of this future coming that 'He shall come on the clouds of heaven with great power and glory' and 'as the lightning goeth out from East to West, so shall be the coming of the Son of man'. These are metaphors, but metaphors of ultimate realities, which at least indicate that it takes place no longer in secrecy but is completely revealed. No one will any more be able to deceive himself about this being reality. So He will come. He will rend the heavens and stand before us as the person He is, sitting at the right hand of the Father. He comes in the possession and in the exercise of the divine omnipotence. He comes as the One in whose hands our entire existence is enclosed. Him we are expecting, He is coming and He will be manifest as the One whom we know already. It has all taken place; the only thing wanting is that the covering be removed and all may see it.

*　　*　　*

'. . . To judge the quick and the dead.' If we wish to understand aright here, we must from the start repress certain pictures of the world-judgment, as far as we can, and make an effort not to think of what they are describing. All those visions, as the great painters represent them, about the judging of the world (Michael Angelo in the Sistine Chapel), Christ advancing with clenched fist and dividing those on the right from those on the left, while one's glance remains fixed on those on the left! The painters have imagined to some extent with delight how these damned folk sink in the pool of hell. But that is certainly not the point. Question 52 of the Heidelberg Catechism asks: 'What comfort hast thou by the coming again of Christ to judge the quick and the dead?' Answer: 'That in all my miseries and persecutions I look with my head erect for the very same, who before yielded Himself unto the judgment of God for me and took away all malediction from me, to come Judge from heaven. . . .' A different note is struck here. Jesus Christ's return to judge the quick and the dead is tidings of joy. 'With head erect', the Christian, the Church may and ought to confront this future. For He that comes is the same who previously offered Himself to the judgment of God. It is His return we are looking for. Would it had been vouchsafed to Michael Angelo and the other artists to hear and see this!

Jesus Christ's coming again for judgment, His ultimate and universal manifestation is often described in the New Testament as *the* revelation. He will be revealed, not only to the Church but to everyone, as the Person He is. He will not only then be the judge, He is that already; but then for the first time it will become visible, that it is not a question of our Yes and No, our faith or lack of faith. In full clarity and publicity the 'it is finished' will come to light. For that the Church is waiting; and without knowing it the world is waiting too.

*   *   *

21

I BELIEVE IN THE HOLY GHOST

When men belong to Jesus Christ in such a way that they have freedom to recognise His word as addressed also to them, His work as done also for them, the message about Him as also their task; and then for their part, freedom to hope for the best for all other men, this happens, indeed, as their human experience and action, and yet not in virtue of their human capacity, determination and exertion, but solely on the basis of the free gift of God, in which all this is given to them. In this giving and gift God is the Holy Spirit.

*   *   *

THE UTTERANCES of the third article are directed towards man. While the first article speaks of God, the second of the God-man, so now the third speaks of man. Here we must, of course, not separate the three articles, we must understand them in their unity. We are concerned with man who participates in the act of God, and moreover participates actively. Man belongs to the Creed. This is the unheard-of mystery which we are now approaching. There is a faith in man, so far as this man freely and actively participates in the work of God. That this actually takes place, is the work of the Holy Spirit, the work of God on earth, which has its analogue in that hidden work of God, the outgoing of the Spirit from the Father and the Son.

What is the meaning of this participation of man in the work of God, of his free, active share? It would be comfortless if everything remained objective. There is also a subjective element; and we may regard the modern exuberance of this subjective element, which had already been introduced in the middle of the seventeenth century, and was brought by Schleiermacher into systematic order, as a strained attempt to bring the truth of the third article into force.

There is a general connexion of *all* men with Christ, and every man is His brother. He died for all man and rose for all men; so every man is the addressee of the work of Jesus Christ. That this is the case, is a promise for the whole of humanity. And it is the most important basis, and the only one which touches everything, for what we call humanity. He who has once realised the fact that God was made man cannot speak and act inhumanly.

But first of all, when we speak of the Holy Spirit, let us look not at all men, but at special men belonging in a special way to Jesus Christ. When we speak of the Holy Spirit, we have to do with the men who belong to Jesus Christ in the special way that they have the freedom to recognise His Word, His work, His message in a definite way and also to hope on their part the best for all men.

When we spoke of faith, we stressed the concept of freedom. Where the Spirit of the Lord is, there is freedom. If we wish to paraphrase the mystery of the Holy Spirit it is best to choose this concept. To receive the Spirit, to have the Spirit, to live in the Spirit means being set free and being permitted to live in freedom. Not all men are free. Freedom is not a matter of course and is not simply a predicate of human existence. All men are destined to freedom, but not all are in this freedom. Where the line of separation runs is hidden from us men.

The Spirit bloweth where He listeth. It is indeed not a natural condition of man for him to have the Spirit; it will always be a distinction, a gift of God. What matters here is, quite simply, belonging to Jesus Christ. We are not concerned in the Holy Spirit with something different from Him and new. It was always an erroneous conception of the Holy Spirit, that so understood Him. The Holy Spirit is the Spirit of Jesus Christ. 'Of mine He shall take and give to you.' The Holy Spirit is nothing else than a certain relation of the Word to man. In the outpouring of the Holy Spirit at Whitsun, there is a movement—*pneuma* means wind—from Christ to man. He breathed on them: 'Receive ye the Holy Ghost!' Christians are those breathed upon by Christ. Therefore we can never in one respect speak soberly enough of the Holy Spirit. What is involved is the participation of man in the word and work of Christ.

*　　*　　*

In the exposition of the first article of the Confession I said that creation is not a lesser miracle than the birth of Christ of the Virgin. And now thirdly I should like to say that the fact that there are Christians, men who have this freedom, is no lesser miracle than the birth of Jesus Christ of the Holy Spirit and the Virgin Mary, or than the creation of the world out of nothing. For if we remember what and who and how we are, we might well cry out, 'Lord, have mercy upon us'. For this miracle the disciples wait ten days after the Lord's Ascension into heaven. Not until after this pause does the outpouring of the Holy Spirit take place and with it the new community arises. There takes place a new act of God, which, like all God's acts, is a confirmation of the preceding ones. The Spirit cannot be separated from Jesus Christ. 'The Lord is the Spirit', says Paul.

Where men may receive and possess the Holy Spirit, it is of course a human experience and a human act. It is also a matter of the understanding and of the will and, I might indeed say, of the imagination. This too belongs to being a Christian. The *whole* man, right into the inmost regions of the so-called 'unconscious', is taken in claim. God's relation to man includes the whole of him. But there must be no misunderstanding: the Holy Spirit is not a form of the human spirit.

* * *

22

THE CHURCH, ITS UNITY, HOLINESS AND UNIVERSALITY

Since here and there through the Holy Spirit men meet with Jesus Christ and so also with one another, Christian community visibly arises and exists here and there. It is a form of the one, holy, universal people of God and a communion of holy men and works, in that it submits to sole rule by Jesus Christ, in whom it is founded, that it also aims to live solely in the fulfilment of its service as ambassador, that it recognises its goal solely in its hope, which is its limit.

* * *

IT WOULD be great gain, could Luther's urgent desire have been carried out and the word 'congregation' had taken the place of the word 'Church'. Of course we may find in the word 'Church' what is good and true, since Church means *Kyriake Oikia,* the Lord's House; or, derived from *circa,* a circularly enclosed space. Both explanations are possible, but *ekklesia* certainly means congregation, a *coming together,* arising out of the summons to the national assembly which meets at the call of the messenger or else at the sound of the herald's trumpet.

A congregation is the coming together of those who belong to Jesus Christ through the Holy Spirit. We heard that special men belong in a special way to Jesus Christ. This takes place when men are called by the Holy Spirit to participation in Christ's word and work. This special membership has its analogue on the horizontal level in a membership of those men with one another. The outpouring of the Holy Spirit directly effects the coming together of these men. We cannot speak of the Holy Spirit—and that is why at this point the congregation immediately appears—without continuing *credo ecclesiam,* I believe in the existence of the Church. And conversely, Woe to us, where we think we can speak of the Church without establishing it wholly on the work of the Holy Spirit. *Credo in Spiritum sanctum,* but not *Credo in ecclesiam.* I believe in the Holy Spirit, but not in the Church. Rather I believe in the Holy Spirit, and therefore also in the existence of the Church, of the congregation. So then we must eliminate all ideas of other human assemblies and societies which have come into being, partly by nature, partly by history, on the basis of agreements and arrangements. The Christian congregation arises and exists neither by nature nor by historical human decision, but as a divine *convocatio.* Those called together by the work of the Holy Spirit assemble at the summons of their King. Where the Church coincides with the natural living community, with, for example, that of the nation, the danger of a misunderstanding always threatens. It cannot be formed by men's hands; that is why the zealous, swift founding of Churches, such as took place in America and also sometimes in Holland, is a doubtful business. Calvin liked to apply to the Church a military conception, that of *la compagnie des fidèlis.* A company usually comes together on the basis of a command and not on that of a free agreement.

By men assembling here and there in the Holy Spirit there arises here and there a visible Christian congregation. It is best not to apply the idea of invisibility to the Church; we are all inclined to slip away with that in the direction of a *civitas platonica* or some sort of Cloud-cuckooland, in which the Christians are united inwardly and invisibly, while the visible Church is devalued. In the Apostles' Creed it is not an invisible structure which is intended but a quite visible coming together, which originates with the twelve Apostles. The first congregation was a visible group, which caused a visible public uproar. If the Church has not this visibility, then it is not the Church. When I say congregation, I am thinking primarily of the concrete form of the congregation in a particular place. Of course each of these congregations has its problems, such as the congregation of Rome, of Jerusalem, etc. The New Testament never presents

CLASSICS OF PROTESTANTISM

the Church apart from these problems. At once the problem of variations in the individual congregations crops up, which may lead to splits. All this belongs to the visibility of the Church, which is the subject matter of the second article. We believe the existence of the Church—which means that we believe each particular congregation to be a congregation of Christ. Take good note, that a parson who does not believe that in this congregation of his, including those men and women, old wives and children, Christ's congregation exists, does not believe at all in the existence of the Church. *Credo ecclesiam* means that I believe that here, at this place, in this visible assembly, the work of the Holy Spirit takes place. By that is not intended a deification of the creature; the Church is not the object of faith, we do not believe *in* the Church; but we do believe that in this congregation the work of the Holy Spirit becomes an event. The mystery of the Church is that for the Holy Spirit it is not too small a thing to have such forms. Consequently, there are in truth not many Churches but *one* Church in terms of this or that *concrete* one, which should recognise itself as the one Church and in all the others as well.

Credo unam ecclesiam: I believe one form of the one people of God which has heard the voice of the Lord. There are also parlous differences like those, for example, between our own and the Roman Catholic Church, in which it is not simple to recognise the one Church. But even there the Church is still more or less recognisable. But first of all, Christians are simply summoned to believe in God as the common origin, the common goal of the Church to which they are called. We are not placed upon a tower, from which we can survey all varieties of Churches; we simply stand on the earth at a definite place and *there* is the Church, the one Church. We believe in the unity of the Church, in the unity of the congregations, if we believe in the existence of our concrete Church. If we believe in the Holy Spirit in *this* Church, then even in the worst case we are not absolutely separated from the other congregations. The truly ecumenical Christians are not those who trivialise the differences and flutter over them; they are those who in their respective Churches are quite concretely the Church. 'Where two or three are gathered together in my name, there am I in their midst'—that is the Church. In Him, despite all varieties in the individual congregations, we shall somehow be bound up with one another.

'I believe one *holy* . . . Church.' What is the meaning of *sancta ecclesia?* According to biblical usage of the term, it means 'set apart'. And we think of the origin of the Church, of those called out of the world. 'Church' will always signify a separation. We heard that there are also natural and historical societies, but that only the Christian congregation is the *ecclesia sancta.* It is distinguished from all such societies because of its commission, its foundation and its goal.

'I believe one holy, *catholic* [universal] . . . Church'—the *ecclesia catholica.* The concept of Catholicity is tainted for us, because in this connexion we think of the Roman Catholics. But the Reformers undoubtedly made a claim upon this concept for themselves. What is involved is the one, holy and catholic people of God. Fundamentally the three concepts make the same assertion: *ecclesia catholica* means that through the whole of history the Church remains identical with itself. It cannot alter in its nature. Theer are, of course, different forms in the main Churches. There are also weaknesses, perversions, errors in all Churches. But there are not substantially different Churches. Their opposition could only be that of true and false Churches. We shall do well not to cast this opposition too swiftly and too often into the discussion.

The Church is the communion of the saints, *communio sanctorum.* Here there is a problem of exegesis: is the nominative *sancti* or *sancta?* I do not wish to decide the dispute, but just to ask whether there is not here intended a remarkable ambiguity in a deeper sense. For only when both interpretations are retained side by side, does the matter receive its full, good meaning. *Sancti* means not specially fine people, but, for example, people like the 'saints of Corinth', who were very queer saints. But these queer folk, to whom we too may belong, are *sancti,* that is, men set apart—for holy gifts and works, for *sancta.* The congregation is the place where God's word is proclaimed and the sacraments are solemnised and the fellowship of prayer takes place, not to mention the inward gifts and works, which are the meaning of these outward ones. So the *sancti* belong to the *sancta* and vice versa.

Let me recapitulate: *Credo ecclesiam* means that I believe that the congregation to which I belong, in which I have been called to faith and am responsible for my faith, in which I have my service, is the one, holy, universal Church. If I do not believe this here, I do not believe it at all. No lack of beauty, no 'wrinkles and spots' in this congregation may lead me astray. The thing involved here is an article of faith. There is no sense, when seeking after the 'true' congregation, in abandoning one's concrete congregation. Everywhere we are 'playing at man'. Of course, schism cannot be excluded; it may be objectively necessary. But no schism will ever lead to 'playing at man' being dropped completely in the newly separated congregation of the Holy Spirit. When the Reformers came and the Roman Church remained behind the Reformed Church and separated from it, there was in action in the evangelical Church no spotless Church, either, it too was and is full of 'spots and wrinkles' to this very day. In faith I attest that the concrete congregation to which I belong and for the life of which I am responsible, is appointed to the task of making in this place, in this form, the one, holy, universal Church visible. By saying Yes to it, as to one which belongs with the other congregations by the Holy Spirit, I hope and expect that the one Holy Spirit of Jesus Christ will in it and through it attest also to others and confirm that in it the one, universal holy nature of the Church will become visible.

* * *

1. Where the Christian Church is, we are obviously connected in some form or other with Jesus Christ. This name indicates the unity, holiness and universality of the Church. Whether this basis and appeal to it takes place *de jure* is the question that must be put to every congregation in every place. Where the Apostolic Church is, the Church which hears and transmits the Apostles' testimony, a definite sign will be living, a *nota ecclesiae*, that Jesus Christ, namely, is not only He from whom

the Church derives, but that Christ is He that rules the congregation. He, and He alone! At no time and in no place is the Church an authority which upholds itself out of itself, but —and here follows an important principle with regard to Church governments—fundamentally the Church can be governed neither monarchically nor democratically. Here Jesus Christ rules alone, and any ruling of man can only represent this government of His. It must let itself be measured by that government. But Jesus Christ rules in His Word by the Holy Spirit. Church government is thus identical with Holy Scripture, for it witnesses to Him. So the Church must continually be occupied with the exposition and application of Scripture.

*   *   *

2. The life of the one holy universal Church is determined by the fact that it is the fulfilment of the service as ambassador enjoined upon it. The Church lives as other communities live, but in its Church service its nature appears—proclamation of the Word of God, administration of the Sacraments, a more or less developed liturgy, the application of a Church law (the thesis of R. Sohm is a fantastic business, for even the first congregation had at least a Church-law order, namely Apostles and congregation), and lastly theology. The great problem, which the Church has again and again to answer, is this—what happens in and by all these functions? Is it a question of edification? Is the blessedness of individuals or of all involved? Is it the cultivation of religious living, or quite objectively an order (in accord with an ontological conception of the Church) which must simply be achieved as the *opus Dei*? Where the life of the Church is exhausted in self-serving, it smacks of death; the decisive thing has been forgotten, that this whole life is lived only in the exercise of what we called the Church's service as ambassador, proclamation, *kerygma*. A Church that recognises its commission will neither desire nor be able to petrify in any of its functions, to be the Church for its own sake. There is the 'Christ-believing group'; but this group is *sent out*: 'Go and preach the Gospel!' It does not say, 'Go and celebrate services!' 'Go and edify yourselves with the sermon!' 'Go and celebrate

the Sacraments!' 'Go and present yourselves in a liturgy, which perhaps repeats the heavenly liturgy!' 'Go and devise a theology which may gloriously unfold like the *Summa* of St Thomas!' Of course, there is nothing to forbid all this; there may exist very good cause to do it all; but nothing, nothing at all for its own sake! In it all the one thing must prevail: 'Proclaim the Gospel to every creature!'

* * *

3. And now the last point, that where the Church is, there it has an aim, the kingdom of God. This goal of the Church is bound to constitute a continuous restlessness for the men in the Church, whose action stands in no relation to the greatness of this goal. We must not allow Christian existence, that is the existence of the Church, and theological existence, to be spoiled by this. It may well happen that we might want to drop the hand that is put to the plough, when we compare the Church with its goal. We may often have a distaste for the whole of Church life. If you do not know this oppression, if you simply feel well inside the Church's walls, you have certainly not seen the real dynamic in this matter. In the Church we may be just like a bird in a cage which is always hitting against the bars. Something bigger is at stake than our bit of preaching and liturgy! But where the Apostolic Church is alive, one knows, indeed, this longing, we long for the mansion made ready for us, but we don't make off, we don't simply run away. We do not let ourselves be hindered, by the hope of the kingdom, from standing as a private soldier in the *compagnie de Dieu* and so making for the goal. The limit is set us by the goal. If we really hope for the kingdom of God, then we can also endure the Church in its pettiness. Then we shall not be ashamed to discover in the concrete congregation the one holy universal Church, and then every individual will not be ashamed of his particular confession.

* * *

23

THE FORGIVENESS OF SINS

The Christian man looks back and in spite of his sin receives the witness through the Holy Spirit and through holy baptism of the death of Jesus Christ and so of the justification of his own life. His faith in the latter is founded on the fact that God Himself, by taking man's place in Jesus Christ, has taken over the unconditional responsibility for his way.

*　　*　　*

I BELIEVE in the forgiveness of sins—this is the point at which the Christian man obviously looks *back* on the way from which he originates. Not just in the moment of his 'conversion', but it is always the case that when the Christian looks back, he is looking at the forgiveness of sins. That is the event that confronts him and sets him up, that and nothing else. There is nothing added to it, like forgiveness of sin *and* my experience or forgiveness of sins *and* my achievement! What in retrospect we know about ourselves, can always be only that we live by forgiveness. We are beggars, truly enough.

If forgiveness of sin means all that lies behind us, then a judgment is thereby passed upon our life. There is no merit at all, that of thankfulness, say, in which I have offered all sorts of things to the dear God. I have been a fighter! I have been a theologian! Have perhaps actually written books! No, that will not do. All that we were and achieved will be subject to the judgment that it was sin. And sin means transgression, deviation. And if there was something else, it was always the thing that came from above, of which we have no cause to boast, even though it be the mercy of God. Every day we ought to begin, we may begin with the confession: 'I believe in the forgiveness of sins.' In the brief hour of our death we shall still have nothing else to say. Perhaps we can best clarify the concept of forgiveness or *remissio,* as that something has been recorded in writing, namely, our life; and now a great stroke is drawn through the whole. It deserves to be stroked out and—thank God!—it will be stroked out. In spite of my sin, I may now accept a testimony that my sin is not reckoned to me. I cannot myself remove this from myself. Sin means man's eternal lostness. How should we manage to remove that ourselves? That I have sinned means that I am a sinner.

And against all this there goes forth the witness of the Holy Spirit, the witness of the heard Word of God and the witness of baptism. For the relevance of holy baptism is this, that we may our whole life long think upon the fact that we are baptised; just as Luther in temptation took a chalk and wrote on the table, *baptizatus sum*. Baptism concerns me completely, quite independently of whether I always perceive the witness of the Holy Spirit with the same liveliness. There is something wrong with our perception. There is a rise and fall in it; there are times when for me the word is not living, and that is where the fact may interpose, that I am baptised. Once in my life a sign has been established, which I may hold on to even at a time when the witness of the Holy Spirit does not reach me. Just as I was born, I was once baptised. As a baptised person I become a witness to myself. Baptism can attest nothing but what the Holy Spirit attests, but as a baptised person I may myself be the witness to the Holy Spirit and restore myself by this witness. Baptism recalls me to the service of witness, since it recalls me to daily repentance. It is a signal set up in our life. As the motions of swimming come again to one who has fallen into the water, so baptism recalls us to witness.

But this witness is the Word of God to us, saying: You, O man, with your sin belong utterly, as Jesus Christ's property, to the realm of the inconceivable mercy of God, who will not regard us as those who live as they live and act as they act, but says to us, 'You are justified'. For Me you are no longer the sinner, but where you are there stands Another.

*   *   *

24

THE RESURRECTION OF THE BODY AND THE LIFE EVERLASTING

A Christian looks forward and in spite of his death receives the witness of the Holy Spirit and of the Lord's Supper to the resurrection of Jesus Christ and thus to the completion of his own life. His faith in this is founded on the fact that since man is permitted to take in Jesus Christ God's place, there is bestowed upon him unconditional participation in the glory of God.

A CHRISTIAN looks back, we said in the preceding opening state-ment. A Christian looks forward, we now say. This looking back and looking forward constitute the life of a Christian, the *vita humana Christiana*, the life of a man who has received the Holy Spirit, who may live in the congregation and is called to be in it a light of the world.

A man looks forward. We take a turn, as it were, of 180 degrees: behind us lies our sin and before us death, dying, the coffin, the grave, the end. The man who does not take it seriously that we are looking to that end, the man who does not realise what dying means, who is not terrified at it, who has perhaps not enough joy in life and so does not know the fear of the end, who has not yet understood that this life is a gift of God, who has no trace of envy at the longevity of the patriarchs, who were not only one hundred but three hundred and four hun-dred and more years old, the man who, in other words, does not grasp the beauty of this life, cannot grasp the significance of 'resurrection'. For this word is the answer to death's terror, the terror that this life some day comes to an end, and that this end is the horizon of our existence.

*   *   *

And now the Christian man looks forward. What is the meaning of the Christian hope in this life? A life after death?

An event apart from death? A tiny soul which, like a butterfly, flutters away above the grave and is still preserved somewhere, in order to live on immortality? That was how the heathen looked on the life after death. But that is not the Christian hope. 'I believe in the resurrection of the body.' Body in the Bible is quite simply man, man, moreover, under the sign of sin, man laid low. And to this man it is said, Thou shalt rise again. Resurrection means not the continuation of this life, but life's completion. To this man a 'Yes' is spoken which the shadow of death cannot touch. In resurrection our life is involved, we men as we are and are situated. *We* rise again, no one else takes our place. 'We shall be changed' (I Cor. 15); which does not mean that a quite different life begins, but that '*this* corruptible must put on incorruption, and this mortal put on immortality.' Then it will be manifest that 'death is swallowed up in victory'. So the Christian hope affects our whole life: this life of ours will be completed. That which is sown in dishonour and weakness will rise again in glory and power. The Christian hope does not lead us away from this life; it is rather the uncovering of the truth in which God sees our life. It is the conquest of death, but not a flight into the Beyond. The reality of this life is involved. Eschatology, rightly understood, is the most practical thing that can be thought. In the eschaton the light falls from above into our life. We await this light.

* * *

The Lord's Supper ought to be more firmly regarded from the Easter standpoint, than is generally the case. It is not primarily a mourning or funeral meal, but the anticipation of the marriage feast of the Lamb. The Supper is a joyous meal: the eating of His, Jesus Christ's, flesh and the drinking of His blood is meat and drink unto life eternal in the midst of our life. We are guests at His table and so no longer separated from Himself. Thus in this sign the witness of His meal is united to the witness of the Holy Spirit. It tells us really, you shall not die but live, and proclaim the Lord's works! *You!*

* * *